Lucretia Spinning with her Maidens.

London, Arthur Hall, Virtue & Cº.

ROME,

REGAL AND REPUBLICAN.

A FAMILY HISTORY OF ROME.

BY

JANE MARGARET STRICKLAND.

EDITED BY

AGNES STRICKLAND,

Author of "Lives of the Queens of England," &c.

"The fourth kingdom shall be diverse from all kingdoms."—DANIEL, vii. 23.

"In every form and plan of government that man can invent some vice or corruption creeps in with the very institution which grows up along with it, and at last destroy it."—POLYBIUS.

First Published 1854

Republished 2023

PREFACE.

———◆———

A HISTORY OF ROME, upon a new plan, is now offered to the public, in a series of volumes expressly written for family use. This work will embrace ancient Rome in all its stages of conquest, civilisation, literature, and art, exhibiting its struggles for constitutionary liberty, its ages of national virtue—the gradual growth of luxury, its passage to absolute despotism, its revival with Christianity, and its decay and final fall.

The series, of which the first volume is now presented to the reader, will contain the early history of the Christian Church, and will faithfully delineate its trials, struggles, moral and civilising influence, charity, final triumphs, and unfortunate declension from its pristine purity of doctrine and simplicity of practice. In order to render the serial volumes more useful and interesting, the private biography of the most celebrated men of the successive periods, whether distinguished for their talents in war, legislature, patriotism, eloquence, literature, or piety, will be included therein. Thus the most eminent individuals in every age, whether they be heathen or Christian, will be exhibited just as they played their important part in the eventful drama of life.

The four eras being not only designed for the family library, but also for the mighty mass of the British people, to the unlearned portion of which the classic originals are utterly unknown, much care has been taken to render the study of Roman history a source of pure and profitable information, deprived of all those pernicious details that render heathen authors unfit for perusal.

In distinguishing between true liberty and its masked and false resemblance faction, some caution on the part of the reader is absolutely required; who, if he suffer eloquence to fix his standard in respect to public privileges will inevitably form erroneous views of civic rights. Facts are the only true criterion by which he can arrive at any just conclusion respecting the conduct of public men or measures, for no self-interested and ambitious person can ever deserve the name of a patriot. He will find that the rapacious idea of equalising property never was entertained by the ancient citizens of Rome at all; who, while contending, and that fiercely too, for their own rights, did not seek to violate the sacred ones of their own community.

Sensible that a History of Rome, including within it that of the Christian Church, was an actual want, the author has devoted a considerable portion of her life to supply it, and she trusts that the result of her labours will tend to fix this important fact upon the mind of the reader, that a minute research into the records of ancient Rome is but another method of investigating and elucidating scriptural truth, to which chain of evidence they afford many important links— links drawn from heathen writers themselves, who were not aware that their works would bear witness to the integrity of the sacred books of prophesy.

This volume, which forms the first of a series, will, if successful, be followed by others upon the same subject, and arranged upon the same plan.

-------◆-------

INTRODUCTION.

-------◆-------

THE History of Rome comprises four remarkable eras, or epochs, essentially different from each other in political government, and indeed in all features of national resemblance. These may be classed into the heads which form the title of this work. First in the order we have Rome regal, an era involved it is true in mythic fable and heroic tradition, indistinct and shadowy, yet not more so than the early records of any other state, with the solitary exception of the ecclesiastical history of the Jews, whose origin as a people for wise purposes was left distinct and clear, while that of the world in general was obscure and unknown. But however interwoven with superstition and romance the early history of Rome regal may be, she possessed a free constitution from her very dawn, not indeed one without defects, but a constitution admirably suited for the times in which it was framed, since its faults did not affect the present but the far-off future alone. The election of a sovereign was common to that age, when the votes of the senate and people were supposed to be given to the worthiest individual of the state, when the poverty of all necessarily precluded the corrupting influence of gold. Such an order of things, however, never has lasted and never can last, for the experience of history teaches us that in a free state monarchy must be hereditary to be secure, or in the struggle for power that takes place upon the demise of each sovereign civil wars ensue, the right of the strongest prevails, and public liberty is annihilated by a military despotism. Poland in our own times affords an example in her fall of the consequences contingent on such elective sovereignty; though freedom being confined to the aristocracy alone while the people remained in feudal slavery, led to foreign not to civic conquest. Rome regal enjoyed a constitution which conferred certain privileges upon the different orders of which the state was composed, but while she possessed an hereditary nobility she also contained a number of free citizens incapable of rising beyond their own degree, yet invested with certain legislative rights, which Servius Tullius enlarged, but of which their last king, Tarquin the Proud, entirely deprived them.

Some struggles for hereditary power took place even in the short space of time during which Rome was ruled by kings. For the idea of hereditary right being a natural and patriarchal one was not easily eradicated from the bosoms of those whose fathers had worn the elective diadem, or even from the people they had governed. The fate of Tarquin Priscus, slain by the sons of Ancus Marcius, and the murder of Servius Tullius by Tarquin the Proud, prove this, and show that monarchies, in order to be free from such disorders, ought to be hereditary, not elective.

In the revolution that displaced Servius Tullius the Romans lost their liberty entirely, for, by means of the mercenary army he raised, Tarquin tyrannised over the aristocracy who had elevated, and oppressed the commons who had permitted his elevation, and he made himself completely independent of the senate and people of Rome, till the tragic fate of Lucretia combined against his dynasty the moral indignation of a virtuous nation, and it fell.

Few records of the regal era remained in those ages when the Romans became sufficiently civilised to collect documents for their own history. The foundation of Rome, the life and actions of Romulus, the tragic story of Lucretia, the expulsion of Tarquin, and the change of government which then took place were preserved in the national lays of a simple people, who inconsistently worshipped their first king as a god, but who hated regality for the sake of the only bad sovereign they had found among their seven royal rulers. Many oral traditions, a few obsolete laws, some treaties painted on wooden shields, and those noble architectural works which have survived to be the wonder of our own times, were all the evidences left in the time of Livy of the first Roman Era.

The second Roman Era, or epoch, commenced with the name of a republican form of government, which was less advantageous to the commons, or free citizens who composed the middle class of Rome, than the regal constitution it had displaced. The reason is obvious, it had not originated with them but with the aristocracy themselves, who, in revenging the insult done to their own order, had no intention of restoring to the people those privileges granted to them by Servius Tullius, in whose time little was wanting to perfect the monarchical form but a legal hereditary head bound by certain restrictions to observe and maintain the constitutionary laws, and a people rendered capable by those laws of attaining under him to those honours and privileges which are the essential rights of subjects in a free state. Montesquieu, in his "Spirit of the Laws," a work full of profound research and close reasoning, considers the early monarchical government of Rome infinitely better than that which succeeded it, because under the first the power was divided between the king, the nobility, and the people.

Servius Tullius, by inclining the balance towards the popular side, prepared for a democracy, since what he took from the nobility he gave to the people— but under the consular government the commons certainly did not regain what Servius had given and Tarquin had taken away. In the natural order of things, the banishment of Tarquin ought to have been followed either by a democracy or an hereditary monarchy, under which the people would have been admitted to the same privileges now enjoyed by every British subject, in which case Rome would have been happier, freer, and more full of internal prosperity than with the consular government with which her second stage of political power commenced. The aristocracy, however, dreading to find another Tarquin, devised a constitution which afforded every member of it in turn an opportunity of exercising for a time the regal functions, this limitation apparently securing them

5

from the people and from themselves. If the Romans had then conceived the idea of conquering the world they could not have chosen a better school for training up statesmen and generals, than the consular government, which naturally inspired each person while in office with a laudable ambition to surpass his predecessor. Several states of Italy were under this form, which seems to have been peculiar to that country. The Volscians and Samnites, both warlike races, were governed by consuls.

The Roman people ought to have secured their own liberty before they engaged in a long and arduous struggle with the exiled dynasty, but the patrician grant of seven jugers of land to the impoverished plebeians, from the royal demesnes, was so acceptable to them that they overlooked all other advantages for the sake of that benefit. The policy of the inter-reges had foreseen that this bribe would bind the commons fast to their party, since the restoration of Tarquin would, as a matter of course, involve that of the crown lands, a serious consequence to these poor citizens. The struggle with the banished family becoming, therefore, the individual interest of the whole mass, ensured its success, and it was gallantly maintained and gloriously won; but the commons had afterwards a far more difficult task to achieve, that of winning back their own liberty, of which the consular government had left them only the shadow. In order to understand the cause of the civic contests between the patrician and plebeian orders, we must consider the actual wants of the Roman people, and what means they possessed of satisfying them. Rome was even then a great city, with an increasing population and a territory too small to find her citizens with bread, the plebeians were all compelled to serve in war without pay and to find themselves in provisions during their period of service. Surrounded by warlike enemies at her very gates, Rome must win the lands of her neighbours, or her people must starve. She had no resources in commerce, her situation was disadvantageous for trade, and she had no convenient port, every craft or calling was engrossed by foreigners and libertini, who were the members of the nine Roman guilds, in whose privileges the plebeian citizens were not permitted to share. They were small landholders or agriculturists, either possessing allotments of their own or hiring others of the state, the cultivation of these lands and the care of their flocks occupying all their time not spent in war. The increase of their families decreased their means of support, and when they served in the army, if they received any share at all of the lands they won, it was a very inadequate one, by no means proportioned to the danger and toils they had incurred. To obtain a remedy for this increasing evil was the more difficult, because all the magistracies were engrossed by the patrician order, who enriched themselves at the expense of the middle class, which they were determined to keep down, but this important class never can be kept down, for it forms the life, the heart, the vital energy of every free state; it must eventually achieve its liberty, and the Roman middle class did achieve its emancipation and maintained it during many centuries. Some attempts had been made to redress the wrongs of the plebs by persons belonging to the privileged orders, but these disinterested persons had been accused of aspiring to the sovereignty of Rome, and this charge had made the people abandon them to a fate from which they could and ought to have delivered them. The tyranny of the decemviri was a tyranny the people had imposed upon themselves, a yoke which the immolation of Virginia broke, but it was not till after the dissensions of both orders and the banishment of Camillus, the sack of the city by the Gauls, its resuscitation from its ashes, and the destruction of one of its best champions in the person of Manlius Capitolinus, that the people made good their claim to a share in the consulate. The attempt made by them to destroy their second founder originated in his arbitrary measures, but it was the glory of Camillus to give a fine example in the closing days of his career by throwing his weight into the popular side, and redeeming the pride which had sullied his character by according to the commons their long-contested rights. He died in full possession of the affections of the Roman people, who had more than once forgotten in the arbitrary magistrate their great and patriotic deliverer.

Several ages of public virtue followed the admission of the plebeians into the participation of the high offices of the Roman state. In these ages pure examples of exalted patriotism were given by both orders, which have never been surpassed by any nation in the world. The isolated and necessitous condition of the republic first taught her to conquer, and Pyrrhus and Hannibal were her masters in that destructive science, in which she afterwards excelled every nation upon earth. Never, indeed, did Rome appear greater than in her contest with these distinguished warriors. When the Epirot prince found his dear-bought victories were scarcely less ruinous than defeats would have been, he tried the effect of crafty diplomacy, on which occasion one blind and aged senator ordered himself to be borne into the senate-house to protest against any treaty made with an invading power. That senator was Appius Claudius, whose middle life had been passed in the construction of those magnificent roads and public works which form his imperishable monument, and whose closing hours were spent in convincing his countrymen of their folly and short-sightedness. They looked upon the blind and bed-ridden censor as upon one risen from the grave, and listened to his powerful and patriotic eloquence as to the voice of inspiration and prophecy. The treaty was broken off, and Pyrrhus was not permitted to establish himself upon the Italian shore. Here we admire the Roman spirit of the censor, who had been formerly distinguished for unbending hatred to the people, and that arrogant pride which had ever been the characteristic of his tyrannical house; but he loved his country; his energies, his affections, his ambition were for Rome; he curbed the democracy, nay he would have crushed it beneath his feet, but only his last breath could divorce his soul from its patriotic devotion to his country. This feeling was not confined to the blind old censor who by his iron determination then laid the foundation of his country's glory; it was the spirit of the middle ages of the republic implanted by virtuous Roman matrons in the sons they reared—it was a nobler species of idolatry of which Rome was the object. In the contest with Hannibal, at a later period, we find this grand principle continually developed—defeated in almost every battle, her colonies destroyed, her allies subdued or fallen from her, little was left to Rome but the invincible nationality of her indomitable people. The war had found the Romans at strife among themselves, and the plebeians had chosen Terentius Varro to head the army for no other reason than the meanness of his birth, unless that demagogue really had persuaded them that he possessed military talents equal to the emergency in which he was placed. This mistake or wilfulness of the commons lost the battle of Cannæ, and gave to the slaughtering Carthaginian host the flower of the republic, but it did not crush the spirit of resistance in the Roman people, who never for a single moment entertained the idea of submission. The women sacrificed their jewels, the men gave their substance, loans were negotiated, and in order to repel the foreign invader from her sacred soil, Rome burdened herself with a national debt; a debt, however, which her conquests enabled her afterwards to pay off. The maintenance of this war cost Rome some of her greatest and noblest sons, but it was not only a school for military tactics but a school for public virtue, in which Scipio grew up to be the avenger of his country.

The evacuation of Italy by Hannibal sealed the downfall of that ungrateful and avaricious senate, whose vices and intrigues had retarded her noblest son in his career of conquest, and had denounced his bold invasion of Italy—the very measure which, if followed up by their co-operation, would have saved them— as an act of foolish hardihood. Hannibal, compelled to defend his own country from the invasive war in which his youthful antagonist had only copied him, reluctantly consented to stake the fate of Carthage on a battle-field, and then not without a personal attempt at negotiation. The victory of Zama opened to Rome at once that vast extent of foreign conquest which identified her with the mighty fourth monarchy of Daniel and made her the mistress of the civilised world. It is a remarkable fact that Polybius, the historian, a man admirably skilled in the military tactics of that period, upon reviewing the dispositions of both armies, and the talents of the generals who led them, gives his opinion that Hannibal did not lose the battle through any error of his own, nor through any want of courage in his soldiers; nor, on the contrary, does he adjudge the victory to any superiority upon the part of Scipio. He ascribes it "to a Divine Power which had decreed that the Romans should rule over all the nations of the earth," and indeed if Polybius had actually seen the scriptural prophecies respecting the future domination of Rome, he could not have arrived at a more certain conclusion. The Romans, from this precise point of their history, went onward conquering and to conquer, and the fall of Carthage and the subversion of the Macedonian dynasty proved the truth of the remark already cited from Polybius; but foreign conquests of any great extent always prove fatal to the freedom of that republic which has made them. Riches are not favourable to the growth and continuance of public virtue, and Rome, full of luxury and gold, underwent a corrupting change, and the fall of the democracy was only delayed by two remarkable men, who united in themselves the blood of the Semproniuses and Scipios. These were two distinguished brothers, whose bright names, though stolen by venal orators to adorn and gild the cause of faction, ought never to have been mixed up with the unholy ones of anarchy and rebellion. Tiberius Gracchus first, and Caius afterwards, stood forth as champions of their own order, and took the leading part in that political struggle between the rival parties by which each sought to gain the ascendancy in the state. We must not suppose that equality of degree, still less of property, was the object the democracy had in view; such a state of things was never contemplated for a single moment by the Romans. We find such principles advocated by the factious citizens of Florence, and fearfully exemplified in republican France of the eighteenth and nineteenth centuries, but the Romans were wiser because they were more virtuous; and that democracy of which the patriotic brothers were the advocates was recognised as the constitutional order of the government, which, however, was not its original one, but that which successive contests had won from the aristocracy. The Gracchi therefore only sought the restitution of certain privileges, and the administration of laws which, though passed in favour of the commons, had fallen into disuse. Nothing indeed could be worse than the situation of the poor citizens of Rome at this time, who were tied to one calling, that of agriculture, and forestalled in the free-labour market by foreign slaves. Can we wonder then that free men who could obtain no employment from the rich were urgent in claiming their share of those conquered lands which they had won by their valour, and were willing to cultivate by their individual industry.

In their patriotic and disinterested attempt to maintain the rights of the poor against the rich and noble, both Tiberius, and afterwards his greater brother Caius Gracchus, found themselves opposed by the wealthy and corrupt among their own order as well as by their own near relations, who were the leaders of the aristocracy. They were deserted too by the very people whose cause they had espoused, a result which might not have occurred if they had started into public life together. They fell within ten years of each other, and public virtue and public spirit perished with them. The inviduous praises of factious writers and the censures of the historians who flourished under the rule of imperial despotism have left a stain on their bright and glorious names which only a candid examination into facts can remove; but when the Gracchi are tried by this criterion we shall find them the champions of the laws and constitutionary freedom of their country. The results of the contest which both brothers had separately maintained were equally unfortunate, and almost for the first time we find Rome guilty of the blood of her citizens, of which till then she had been remarkably tender. In fact the conquests of Rome were gradually undermining her republican constitution, for foreign intercourse and the introduction of foreign luxury corrupted her manners, while the necessity of keeping regular standing armies to protect the frontiers of provinces torn by force from other states, was subversive of national freedom. The close of this era of the republic left Rome in her full career of military glory, but deprived of her boasted public liberty.

CONTENTS

OF

THE FIRST VOLUME.

———◆———

HISTORY OF ROME.

==========

CHAPTER I.

A.U.C. 1-244. B.C. 753-510.

Foundation of Rome, B.C. 753. (*Varro*.)—Roman constitution.—Rape of the Sabine Virgins.—Latin war.—Victory of Romulus—*Spolia opima* borne by him at his first triumph.—Sabine war.—Treachery of Tarpeia—her reward.—Affecting appeal of the Sabine daughters.—Union of Rome and Sabinia.—Death of Tatius.—Roman tribes named and divided into curies and decuries.—Comitia.—The calling of the Plebeians— Tyranny of Romulus—his disappearance and pretended message. Accession of Numa Pompilius.—His benevolence—wise laws.—Poetical fable of the Nymph Egeria—her cave.—Temple of Janus.—Numa's nine guilds.—His priesthoods.—Institution of the Vestal Order.—Numa's calendar—his lunar year.—His death and burial.—Election of Tullus Hostilius.—His gift of the Crown lands.—His quarrel with Alba.—National combat.—Horatii and Curiatii.—Stratagem of Horatius—his barbarity to his sister.— Expiates the murder.—Combination against Rome.—Doubtful conduct of Fuffetius— his execution.—Alba demolished.—The Albans become Roman citizens.—Shower of stones on the Alban mount.—Mysterious death of Tullus Hostilius.—Election of Ancus Martius.—Manner of proclaiming war.—Victories over the Latins.—Latin colonists.— His public works.—His port at Ostia.—His prison and bridge.—Admits Lucius Tarquinius into the Senate.—Death of Ancus Marcius.—Accession of Tarquinius Priscus.—His idolatry.—His Latin and Sabine wars.—His conquests in Etruria.— Capitoline temple.—His mighty works.—His games.—His quarrel with Nœvius.— Accused of his death.—Assassinated by the Marcii.—Accession of Servius Tullius.—His origin.—His constitution.—Census.—Lustrum.—Manumission of slaves when well-conducted.—His *pagi*.—Coinage.—Commentaries.—Marries his daughters to the Tarquins.—Conspiracy of the younger Tullia and Tarquinius.—Murder of Servius Tullius.—Unnatural conduct of Tullia.—Accession of Tarquinius Superbus.—His tyranny—unpopularity—military talents.—Wars.—Takes Gabii by storm.—Advice to his son.—Great public works.—Capitoline Temple.—Sibylline books.—Murders Marcus Brutus.—Visit of his sons to Delphi.—Siege of Ardea.—The passion of Sextus Tarquinius for Lucretia.—His violence.—Domestic tribunal.—Death of Lucretia.— Oration of Junius Brutus.—Expulsion of the Tarquins.—End of Rome Regal.

FROM her very foundation, Rome, according to her mystical description in the Book of Daniel, "was diverse from all nations;"[1] even the singularly romantic history of her founder being a part of that distinctive difference by which the mighty Fourth Monarchy was to be distinguished from every other people upon the face of the earth.

Rome was founded by Romulus, a chief of unknown parentage, to whom, in later times, tradition assigned a regal origin, superstition—a divine one[2]—the supposed royal ancestry of the Latin foundling being as difficult to establish upon the solid basis of historic truth, as his mythic descent from a vestal priestess and the god Mars, or his nurture by a wolf.

The early history of Romulus appears to have been a national lay[3]—the popular legend being perpetuated afterwards by sculpture; for art seized upon the poetical idea and transmitted it to posterity, though perhaps in ruder forms than the celebrated bronze group still in existence at Rome.[4]

In the place of fact we are reduced to take the most probable part of the tradition, and presume, that for some services performed for Numitor, King of Alba, by Romulus and Remus, foundlings reared by Faustulus, a shepherd, that sovereign bestowed upon the brothers some waste lands lying about the Tiber for the site of a city and colony.[5] Each brother being equally desirous of giving his name to the new settlement which both were to rule in concert, the dispute was referred to the King of Alba, who recommended them to decide it by augury. The augurs determining that he who should first discover a flight of vultures should become the founder of the new city, Remus watched from Mount Aventine, Romulus from Mount Palatine. The younger brother, however, soon despatched a messenger to inform the elder that he had seen six vultures, claiming, in consequence, the benefit of his good fortune. Romulus, who had not then discovered a single bird, sent word that he had seen twelve before his brother's message had been received. At that moment he really saw that number,[6] and confidently pronounced B.C. 753-717. the auspices to be in his favour,[7] and instantly commenced the foundation of the city, by fixing a copper share on a plough, and yoking to it a bullock and a heifer, drawing a furrow round the Palatine Hill, which he enclosed a considerable way below, taking care, according to the custom on such occasions, that all the clods should fall inwards, being followed by others, who were to leave none turned the other way.[8] The Comitium enclosed a vault built under ground, filled with the firstlings of all the natural productions of the earth, to which was added by each foreign settler a portion of his own native soil. To this spot was given the name of Mundus; it represented the door of the world below, and was opened thrice a year for the spirits of the departed.[9] "A line drawn between one to two hundred paces to the south, and parallel with one running from Santa Maria Liberatrice to the Temple of Concord, now supposed to be the Basilica of the Cæsars, would pass through the Comitium."[10]

By the custom of the age, the violation of the consecrated bounds by any person would be followed by his instant death, as an atonement to the deities to whom it had been dedicated. A wall and a ditch enclosed the site of the city on the line of the Pomœrium, which had been thus consecrated by heathen superstition. Remus, who had watched with scorn the progress of his brother's work, leaped the sacred boundary, upon which he was immediately slain by Romulus, or Celer, in revenge for the act of sacrilege he had rashly and impiously committed, Faustulus and his brother being killed in a vain attempt to part the rival brothers.[11]

Romulus lamented the fratricidal act, rejecting food and consolation, till persuaded by his foster-mother to attempt the propitiation of the manes by the institution of a festival called the Lemuria, in commemoration of Remus. A vacant throne, adorned with the insignia of royalty, and placed by the side of Romulus, was supposed a sufficient atonement to the injured spirit.[12]

The quarrel between the brothers presents no difficulty; it agrees but too well with the lawless customs and uncivilised manners of barbarous times, which rarely are influenced and softened by natural affection. Such is the outline of one of the old heroic lays which were proudly transmitted from sire to son from the mythic ages of Rome to the period of her meridian glory and splendour. It is difficult, and perhaps impossible, to reduce to anything resembling fact the legendary and mythic history of the founder of Rome.[13]

Rome was not advantageously situated for trade, having no port and possessing no facilities for commerce. Nor indeed was it fitted for the habitation of an agricultural population; for the soil was poor and the water bad, but the locality was suited well to the predatory habits of a people at the period when they were about to pass from the pastoral to the warrior state. Such changes are natural to every nation in the world, and always precede civilisation; the shepherd becoming a hunter from necessity, and a warrior by choice. The gradation is easily traced—the mighty empires of Asia in ancient and the European kingdoms of modern times having passed through the same nomadic and pastoral stages.

The site of the city destined to become the future mistress of the world occupied the hollow of an extinct volcano—a conclusion at which the survey of the ground has enabled modern geologists to arrive;[14] the appearance of the hills, and the immense deposit of pozzolana still underlying the foundations of ancient Rome, sufficiently establishing a fact which throws some light upon one of the picturesque traditions of the old Republic.[15]

The foundation day of Rome was kept upon the 21st of April, at the same time as the festival of Pales, which was B.C. 753-717. held by the country people to propitiate the goddess, to whose care they confided the preservation and increase of their flocks.[16]

The extent of Roma or Rome, the city destined in future ages to rule the civilised world, was confined to Mount Palatine at first, and consisted of a thousand huts, lying square, and being about a mile in compass;[17] the whole extent of the infant colony not exceeding eight miles.

The colony was composed of a mixed multitude of Tuscans, Italians, Latins, Greeks, Trojans, slaves, criminals, besides the inhabitants of Pallantium and Saturnia, who united with Romulus in an enterprise, whose success in after ages not only became instrumental in civilising the world, but aided in bringing to pass events connected with its redemption.

Two peculiar features distinguished Rome from every other city or state. It possessed a temple before its foundations were laid, and it boasted a free constitution, not indeed without many imperfections, but as perfect as that age and the rude state of society would admit. The temple, however, reared to the Asylean Jupiter, owed its origin more to policy than piety. It was opened as an asylum to runaway slaves, criminals, and debtors, who might here be safe from the claims of their masters, judges, and creditors, and form a part of the new colony.[18] "In regard to the constitution, it is absurd to impute that to Romulus, which must have been the work of those leading persons who joined him in his new settlement and formed his senate."[19] The Roman constitution, of which Romulus was the elected head, was the security of free persons against the possibility of tyranny or oppression, on the part of their prince or chief, who combined in his own person the offices of Sovereign and Prime-minister in times of peace, and of General in those of war. Some of its distinguishing features must have had a later origin than others, springing out of circumstances which afterwards occurred.

In its first infancy, the Roman state was most probably composed of two classes only—freemen, who afterwards represented the patrician order, and slaves; but of the first Romulus selected a hundred persons to form the Senate, called Patres Conscripti, or Conscript Fathers, whose privileges were inviolable. The proper business of the Senate was to debate and resolve upon any public affairs proposed by the King or chief, as well as to inspect all matters he referred to their examination. The people or freemen had the power of creating magistrates, making laws, and determining upon any war proposed by their regal head.

To the King was left the direction of all religious rites; the guardianship of the laws and customs, the decision of all private causes between man and man, as their judge. He possessed the privilege of summoning the Senate, and calling the assembly of the people to consider his propositions, and afterwards to ratify them by a majority of voices.[20]

In the field, the King possessed absolute power, similar to that of the Dictator in a later age.[21] The division of the people into tribes probably did not take place till the plebeian order was formed. To each of his followers he assigned two jugers of land[22] as inheritable property. The privilege of feeding their cattle within the enclosure of the Pomœrium appears to have been common to them all.

The constitution, or code of legislative laws, for the government of the infant state having been settled, the B.C. 753-717. increase of the colony by marriage was the next thing that engaged the attention of Romulus. The founder himself and most of his followers being unmarried men, whose unsettled habits made the women of Italy unwilling to form alliances with them,[23] the enterprising spirit of Romulus soon found a remedy for this evil by seizing upon the persons of the young Latin and Sabine virgins who came with their parents to the games given by him in honour of the Equestrian Neptune. Only one married woman was carried off by the Roman ravishers upon this occasion.[24] This was Hersilia, whose maternal anxiety for her young daughter occasioned her own detention.[25] Romulus married himself to this lady with the formula used afterwards in the Roman marriages, "Take thou of thy husband's fire and water." He officiated as priest to his robber-followers, whom he united to their stolen brides with the same sentence. In memory of their descent from these forced nuptials, newly-wedded Roman wives were lifted over the threshold of their husbands' houses. Their hair was also parted with a spear to denote that their female ancestors were won by force of arms by their forefathers. No part of Roman history rests on stronger foundations than this incident, which is inseparably blended with the laws and institutions of Rome.

In the attempt to avenge the insult offered to them in the abduction of their young women, the Latins were foremost. Three cities, Antemnæ, Cænina, and

Crustumerium took up arms singly against the Romans, while the Sabines lingered until all three had fallen singly before Romulus, and he had won the royal spoils of Acron, king of Cænina, whom he slew in single combat, instituting upon that occasion a sort of pageant or triumph, in which the armour and garments of the vanquished monarch formed the most interesting part of the show. The *spolia opima* of Acron were fastened to a trophy, fashioned in the shape of an armed man. This effigy was fixed to the trunk of a young oak and borne on the right shoulder of Romulus, who entered Rome on foot, having his head crowned with laurel, and being preceded and followed by his victorious army. He marched to the Hill Saturnius—the eminence afterwards called the Capitoline Mount, where, in pursuance of a vow made by him to Jupiter Feretrius, he dedicated the spoils of Acron, depositing them in a miniature temple erected for the occasion. This fane, we are told, was only ten feet in length and about five in width.[26]

With humane and enlightened policy, the conqueror not only spared the inhabitants of the vanquished cities, but rendered them free colonists and citizens of Rome. "Thus he made those fellow-citizens at night," remarks the Emperor Claudius, "whom in the morning he had encountered as enemies in the field."[27]

These captives, it is supposed, afterwards formed the plebeian order. The Sabines, after the fall of Acron, king of Cænina, advanced on Rome with an army of five-and-twenty thousand men, headed by their king, Tatius. Romulus, unable to maintain the field against such a body of men, retired into his city, whose capability of defence rested upon the maintenance of the citadel, which stood on Mount Saturnius, and commanded Rome.

Before commencing hostilities, the Sabines despatched a herald to the gates of Rome, demanding the restoration of their young women. This was peremptorily refused by Romulus, and the war commenced in form. At that remote period, the space between the hills—afterwards occupied by the Forum Romanum—was a swampy valley. Tatius encamped between the Saturnian and Quirinal Mounts, which he found too strongly guarded to carry by assault.

Romulus had entrusted the important fortress that crowned the Saturnian Hill[28] to Tarpeius, a brave man, who, unfortunately for himself and the Romans, had a daughter named Tarpeia; who, dazzled by the sight of the B.C. 753-717. golden bracelets worn by the Sabines on their left arms, offered to admit these foes into the citadel, provided the ornaments she coveted were given to her.[29] Tatius agreed to the propositions, whereupon Tarpeia opened a private door to the Sabines, who, with the bracelets she had purchased by her treason, flung down upon her the bucklers they likewise carried upon their left arms,[30] and crushed the traitress to death.

The treason of the covetous Tarpeia and the possession of the citadel would have been followed soon after by the capture of Rome and the recovery of the Sabine daughters, if Hersilia and the captured females, now become Roman mothers as well as Roman matrons, had not interposed between their husbands and fathers. For Romulus and his followers, when on the point of being vanquished, were succoured by their Sabine wives, who, rushing forth with their infants in their arms, their hair hanging loose upon their shoulders, and their eyes filled with tears, interposed their persons between their incensed parents' vengeance and their beloved consorts, whom they sought to defend in the unequal contest.

Moved by the grief of their daughters, and touched with the sight of their grandchildren, the Sabines relented, and peace was made upon certain conditions very advantageous to the Romans. The union of the two nations under the joint sway of Romulus and Tatius was proposed and accepted, the city retaining still the name of Rome from its founder, while the inhabitants took that of Quirites from Cures, the native town of Tatius, the Sabines becoming free citizens of Rome.[31]

Romulus chose from their nobility a hundred senators, and added a thousand men to that select part of his army, to which he had given the name of Legionaries.

The union between Rome and Sabinia gave rise to the festivals of the Matronalia, Carmentalia, and many others, founded to commemorate the peace mediated by the Sabine women.[32]

The Roman tribes at this time received the name of Ramnenses, Tatienses, and Luceres. The two first were called after the two sovereigns, or chiefs; the third was derived from Lucus, or grove, in which the temple of the Asylum stood.[33] The subdivision of the tribes, or wards, into ten curiæ—an arrangement not unlike the modern English parishes—probably[34] took place after this union with Sabinia. Each curia had its temple and officiating priest, though no image of the presiding deity occupied the fane. A high priest called Curio Maximus was the supreme director of these heathen ministers. Each curia was subdivided into ten decuriæ, governed by civil officers appointed for that purpose. The curiæ had votes in all important public matters. Their resolutions were carried by a majority of voices, each individual being entitled to a vote. Their assembly was called Comitia Curiata.[35] Some analogy will be found between the early Roman constitution and our own, with this essential difference, that the Commons could not acquire the privileges of the patrician order, a defect afterwards productive of much mischief in the state.

The plebeians were either the inhabitants of towns, who surrendered upon certain conditions, by which they retained their freedom and civic rights, or were those fugitives who took refuge in the asylum opened by Romulus. They were agriculturists on a small scale; a body of landowners, or farmers, who were not permitted the exercise of any other calling or trade, the ancients considering that of agriculture to be the proper business of the free citizen, as well as the best school for soldiers. Besides the two jugers of land assigned to each Roman citizen by Romulus, these men hired certain proportions of the public lands, much in the same manner as persons now rent the corporation lands of towns or cities at this day in England. Many of the plebeians had patrons among the patricians appointed by Romulus to take care of their interests, and to defend them from aggression; to assist them on all occasions in which the poor and weak might need the help of the rich and strong.[36] The plebeians receiving this patronage were called clients; but as the whole body did not either claim or receive this assistance, there is some reason for believing that it had been accorded to persons not always possessed B.C. 753-717. of the Roman franchise.[37] The lands were divided into as many parts as there were curiæ, which were thirty in number, with a reservation of two allotments for public exigencies, and the maintenance and support of religion. The patrician order engrossed the whole of the magisterial, and, with one exception, all the sacerdotal offices; no share in the government of the country being permitted by the ancient constitution to the plebeians.

The celeres or body guard of Romulus were a band of young men furnished by the curiæ, ten from each curia, whose proper office was to defend the king's person in battle with their spears. The celeres fought on horseback or on foot, and usually began the attack on the day of battle. They were three hundred in number, and obtained their name from the swiftness of their motions.[38]

The equestrian order was not founded according to Livy till after the union of the two nations. The equites or knights were all men of noble birth, and formed the Roman cavalry. They were possessed of remarkable privileges, and wore a gold ring as a symbol of their rank. Besides the celeres who attended him in war, Romulus was always followed by twelve lictors or serjeants, bearing bundles of rods, with axes in the centre of the rods. These bundles were called fasces. These fasces represented the power of Romulus to punish offenders according to their degrees of guilt.[39]

Romulus and Tatius took the city of Cameria, transferring the inhabitants to Rome, and replacing them with a Roman colony. Soon after this exploit, Tatius was slain by the Lavinians, in return for the protection he had afforded some persons who had plundered their territories, and his murder of the ambassadors they had sent to remonstrate with him on the subject. Romulus made no attempt to revenge his colleague, but he gave him a sumptuous funeral. The Camerians took the opportunity afforded them by a famine to assert their ancient freedom, but the revolt was soon put down by Romulus. He obtained a triumph for the conquest of Fidenæ, a city which had seized upon a convoy of corn on its way to Rome during the famine. The Crustumarians were severely punished for their slaughter of his colonists, and for this successful enterprise he claimed a third triumph. Upon the Veientines resenting his conduct to the Fidenatans, Romulus made war upon them, and after defeating them in two battles, granted them peace for the term of one hundred years.[40] The Veientines purchased the pacification by the sacrifice of their salt-pits near the river, and the evacuation of the seventh part of their territories. They also gave Romulus fifty hostages of noble birth. The king of Rome did not incorporate the captives taken in these wars with his own people according to his usual custom, but sold them for slaves.[41]

These wars terminate the records of Romulus, whose attempts to render his government despotic and independent of the senate ended with his unaccountable disappearance, which the superstition of after ages regarded as a translation to heaven. According to the general testimony afforded by the ancient Latin authorities, Romulus was holding a religious festival in the meadow called Capræ, when the sun became totally eclipsed, attended by a thunder storm, which dispersed the people, who left the king alone with the senate on the spot. From that day the founder of Rome was seen no more.[42]

Valerius Maximus, though he has not given a more probable account of the disappearance of the first king of Rome, has afforded a clue for the elucidation of the mystery by stating, "that he had convoked the senate to the temple of Vulcan for the arrangement of the public business, when he suddenly vanished from among them."[43] He was no doubt murdered by the disaffected senators, and buried upon the spot. Nor is the fact more unlikely than the assassination of Julius Cæsar, whose body perhaps might have been disposed of secretly, if he had not had friends as well as enemies near his person.

The loss of Romulus was afflicting to the people at large, who charged the patricians with murder and falsehood.[44] Julius Proculus, an old friend and companion of the missing sovereign, took upon himself the task of pacifying the plebeians, by assuring them in full comitia B.C. 753-717. "that Romulus had appeared to him, and accounted for his own disappearance by informing him that the gods from whom he originally came had recalled him to heaven, and that he was to assure the Romans, that by the exercise of temperance and fortitude the city he had founded should become the mightiest upon earth."[45] This mythic fable was doubtless the invention of later times, and it is not unlikely that a breach in the Roman annals has been filled up in this manner by some imaginative hand, and that Romulus died a natural death. If he founded Rome some centuries earlier than history assigns for that event, oral tradition may have heaped upon fact a mass of fable. It seems indeed almost incredible that at the end of his reign the city of Rome should possess a standing army of forty-five thousand men, and a thousand cavalry soldiers. Romulus is said to have reigned thirty-seven years. He was surnamed Quirinus, one of the appellations of the god Mars, either from his skill in war, or from his fabulous relation to that heathen deity. He afterwards received divine honours under that name, and a temple was erected to him, in which, in after ages, his statue was placed.

Although the history of Romulus, as related by Livy, is evidently a sort of rude poem, one too of which a fragment alone has been preserved, yet the supposition that an uncivilised people is capable of composing a tale in verse purely imaginative is quite as improbable as the fable itself. Truth has been the groundwork upon which the ideality of the poet has worked, just as we find in our own early chronicles real history mixed up with fiction, and recorded in rugged verse. Romulus left a daughter by Hersilia, but the city he founded has continued his name to posterity. He was addicted to magic, and many virtues were afterwards ascribed to his staff. The religious rites he instituted were of Tuscan origin, derived from Cœlius, a Tuscan chief, one of the early colonists of Rome, who built upon the Cœlian hill. To attempt to give the chronology of Rome during the regal period, beyond stating the extent of each reign, would be useless.[46]

NUMA POMPILIUS.

It is uncertain how many months or years elapsed between the disappearance of Romulus and the accession of Numa. The senators ruled by turns under the titles of *Inter-reges*, till the people by whom their late sovereign had been beloved insisted upon having once more a regal head. Their choice fell upon Numa Pompilius.[47] The new king was the son-in-law of Tatius, the Sabine, colleague of Romulus. This prince united in his own person the character of high-priest and legislator. To civilise the people and encourage the arts of peace appeared to him more worthy of a sovereign than the devastating art of war. To improve the morals of the Romans—to render them humane, industrious, and pious, was his chief aim. All his institutions were designed to make them wiser and better. He softened the severity of the paternal law, by which fathers could sell or otherwise dispose of their unmarried daughters. He divided the lands Romulus had acquired from the neighbouring states by right of conquest among the most indigent of the Roman people.[48] To defend the weak from the robbery of the strong and covetous, he deified the stones which marked the boundaries under the name of the god Terminus. This consecration of the boundary stones[49] he imagined would secure the land to its possessors, since the violation would add the crime of sacrilege to that of theft.[50] As the lands thus divided had been left open before for general occupancy, the violation of the lines marking the divisions was very likely to B.C. 753-717. occur; but the wisdom of Numa should have prevented the aggression by inculcating a principle of honour and honesty, not by introducing the grossness of idolatry.

There is reason to believe that he possessed a juster notion of the Supreme Being than he thought proper to impart to the people he governed;[51] he saw the advantage of religion as a great political agent in civilising and reforming men, but preferred enslaving them by superstition to enlightening their minds with the truth.

"If Romulus founded a city and colony, Numa became its supreme legislator." His laws he ascribed to "divine agency," in order to make them received and obeyed by the people. "They were dictated to him," he said, "by the nymph Egeria, by whom he gave out he was beloved."[52] The cave and fountain of his imaginary love are still shown to travellers, who find the lovely spot well suited to the elegant poetical allegory under which Numa veiled his policy. The austerely virtuous life of the prince—his reputation for sanctity and frequent retirement to the place where he stated he held converse with Egeria—impressed his subjects with veneration for his person and reverence for his laws. The temple of Janus was built by Numa in the first year of his reign. Janus was supposed by some to personify Time. He was represented with two faces, one looking forward, the other backward, as if to observe the past and future. His temple had two brazen gates, which were shut in time of peace, but remained open during war.[53] These gates were shut during the peaceful reign of Numa, but through the long centuries that succeeded it they were only closed thrice, so fiercely warlike grew the Roman people.

Numa was the founder of the nine guilds into which the corporations of the city were divided. Pipers, goldsmiths, carpenters, dyers, curriers, tanners, copper-smiths, potters, and a ninth, common to the other trades,[54] completed the number of these guilds. The trades were chiefly exercised by the *libertini*, (slaves, who had been made free by their masters,) or fugitives from neighbouring states who had fled from slavery to exercise some craft or calling in Rome. Poor colonists, free but unable to maintain themselves at home, were glad to exercise their craft under the protection of these companies or guilds.[55] The guilds or companies yet exist in our own civic corporations. Much of Rome may still be found in our regulations respecting the exercise of trades and crafts—in our jurisprudence and in our free and noble constitution. Rome, in fact, can hardly be said to be extinct while her language, laws, and many of her customs linger thus among us.

Numa instituted various orders of priesthood, as the Salii[56] and Feciales: it is not very clear what was the proper office of the Salii, but their dances were of a warlike character, calculated to please a martial people. The Feciales were the arbitrators of peace or war, and the Roman state was not allowed to take up arms against another till they had decided upon the justice of the quarrel.[57]

The augural and pontifical colleges were founded by him, and he regulated the time of mourning. He also revived the worship of Vesta, and consecrated Gegania and Verania, the first female priestesses of this order at Rome.[58] The vestals were chosen from the patrician and plebeian orders, from the ages of six to ten years: their persons must be without blemish, and their birth derived from virtuous and honourable families. If a sufficient number were not voluntarily offered by their parents for this priesthood twenty young virgins were selected, and those upon whom the lot fell became vestals. To console the Roman maiden for the loss of the endearing conjugal and maternal ties she was almost deified by the people, who believed their glory and national existence depended upon B.C. 715-673. her personal chastity as much as on her vigilance in watching the sacred fire. The privileges of the vestals were exceedingly great. They had the fasces borne before them whenever they went abroad, and when they pleased rode in a chariot drawn by white horses, followed by their numerous attendants, clad like themselves in white. Whosoever pressed upon their chariot, chair, or litter was immediately punished by their attendant lictor with death. They might snatch from punishment the condemned criminal on his way to execution, provided they declared that the meeting was accidental, for the affirmation of a vestal was considered equivalent to an oath, and was equally binding in a court of justice.[59] This unbounded privilege of mercy must have been very precious to females, whose tender feelings of compassion lead them naturally to be more merciful than just. The vestals were sedulously guarded from every insult painful to the modesty of women; the slightest infraction of which was punished with death. Their vow of chastity was binding upon them for thirty years, after which they might quit their college and marry. The vestals, however, seldom or never claimed their exemption from the vow of celibacy made in their childhood, since with it they must have also given up the honours accorded them by the Roman people.[60] They were assigned at all games and festivals the chief place, they arbitrated the disputes respecting wills, and every man they met made way for them. Nor in the Republican age were they treated with less reverence, for the consuls observed the same rule, causing the lictors to lower the fasces reverently before them. In the latter days of the Commonwealth, and throughout the rule of the heathen emperors, they took charge of the wills of distinguished persons, and that of the Emperor Augustus was left in their keeping.[61] The privileges of the vestals remained till the reign of Theodosius the Great, when their sacred fire was extinguished and their order suppressed. The dress of these sacerdotal females consisted of a white vest with purple borders, a white linen surplice, a large purple mantle, whose ample folds descended to the ground, and a close fitting head-dress, decorated with ribbons, hanging from it like the modern cap. They lived in a sumptuous style, being maintained at the public charge in a luxurious manner. If a vestal were sick she was given into the charge of two noble Roman matrons, who nursed her alternately in their own houses. Even death added to their privileges, for the vestal virgin was allowed the rare one of intramural interment.[62] But if these honours were lavished upon the vestals the penalties to which she was exposed were equally proportioned to them. Her negligence in the case of the sacred fire exposed her to severe scourgings, and its extinction to death. "If she broke her vow by the law of Rome she was stoned; but in the reign of Tarquin this punishment was altered to living interment, attended with circumstances of peculiar horror."[63]

So many mythic stories are related of Numa, that his formation of the Roman Calendar alone separates his reign from the world of fable. The year of Numa was not a solar but a lunar one, and therefore his useful work was still imperfect.[64]

In the eighth year of Numa a great plague devastated Italy. The legend of a sacred shield falling down from heaven, and of his intrusting it to the care of the Salian priesthood, is related in connexion with this pestilence,[65] which was the only calamity that occurred in his long and peaceful reign.

Numa gave names to the months, some of which are still retained. He built temples and altars, instituted festivals, and turned all his attention to the civilisation of his people. He did not, however, provide for their education. Great resemblance was discovered by Plutarch B.C. 672-641. between the philosophy of Numa and that taught by Pythagoras.

Numa built himself a palace near the temple of Vesta, which was long called Regium, where he passed his time in giving the priests instruction and in regulating the services proper to religion.[66]

Numa dismissed the guards of Romulus, trusting to the affection and veneration of the people more than to their swords, deeming their love the only safeguards of the prince.[67]

This king lived eighty years, and died of natural decay after a long peaceful reign of nine-and-thirty years. He left one daughter, by his wife Julia, named Pompilia, who was the mother of Ancus Marcius, the fourth King of Rome.[68] He was buried by his own desire under the hill Janiculum, in a stone coffin, and by his side was placed another containing his writings.

The records of this ancient king and legislator are so mystified by superstition that but for his code of laws and his calendar we might suppose the lover of Egeria to be, like the nymph who loved him, the creation of a vivid poetical fancy. His lunar year is, however, solid ground upon which we may safely rest our faith in Numa's personal identity, though much of his history is involved in mythic gloom. An interregnum occurred between this and the succeeding one.

TULLUS HOSTILIUS.

The regal government of Rome still remained purely elective, a state of things frequently found when a people are just emerging from a savage state, whose choice naturally falls upon the man best calculated to govern them in peace and lead them in war. Tired of the wars and fatigued with the conquests of Romulus, the Romans selected a legislator and pontiff in Numa; "and if they had been destined to remain in obscurity such kings would have been best suited to their condition, but in order to become powerful they needed sovereigns like Tullus Hostilius."[69] Numa was distinguished for piety, and Tullus for arms, "religion and war being the characteristics of their reigns."[70] Both these attributes grew out of necessity. Numa could not control a number of uncivilised men without a code of sacred laws, and Tullus could not feed an increasing population without adding to the territorial possessions of Rome. He gave up the lands held by the late sovereigns[71] to meet this exigency, remarking "that his own patrimony was sufficient for his personal expenses." The promised gift of these lands most likely placed Hostilius on the vacant throne, for we are assured he owed his elevation to the Roman people.[72] The grandfather of Tullus was a citizen of Medullia, who had fought against the Sabines under the command of Romulus.[73] Tullus despised alike the superstition inculcated by Numa and his pacific temper. He commenced exercising the youth of Rome in arms in preparation for the wars he was meditating. These exercises provoked Cluilius, the dictator or governor of Alba, to make a predatory incursion on the Roman territory, which being revenged by Tullus Hostilius, led to a war between these neighbouring states,[74] a fact that is alone sufficient to prove that the descent of Romulus from the royal line of Alba was a fable,[75] Alba, after the death of Numitor, having changed from the regal to the popular form of government.

The war with Alba being determined upon, both armies took the field and encamped within five miles of Rome.[76] The sudden death or murder of Cluilius in his tent, and B.C. 672-641. the intelligence that the Veientines and Fidenatans were about to fall upon the belligerent parties as soon as they had weakened themselves by a battle, compelled them to give over the contest.[77] The Albans elected Metius Fuffetius for their dictator, and proposed a union between their rival states as the best means of defending themselves against their common enemies.[78] The proposal appeared advantageous to the Romans, who spoke the same language and were closely allied by the ties of blood to the Alban people. Instead of arranging the union of the two states peaceably, the contracting parties mutually agreed to refer it to what would have been styled in the nomenclature of modern chivalry a passage of arms. A beautiful but romantic poetical episode narrates the contest between three Roman and three Alban champions, by whose valour the momentous question of national superiority was to be decided. To pass over the legend, which sufficiently boasts celebrated ancient authorities to justify its insertion here, would be unwise; but the reader must not attach too much importance to it, though we are assured by Livy that the form of the treaty was extant at the time he quoted it, and that he took it from an existing document which had been attested by Tullus Hostilius and Metius Fuffetius, and confirmed by sacrifices.[79] The senate and people of Rome chose for their champions the three Horatii, who had been born by an Alban mother at one birth to Valerius Horatius. The Albans selected the three Curiatii, who boasted the same natal distinction, being also the offspring of a single birth, and the sons of the maternal aunt of the Horatii. We are told that Sequinius, an illustrious Alban, was the grandfather of the six champions.[80] Till the war occurred between Rome and Alba the combatants had been as closely allied in friendship as by relationship, and Horatia, the daughter of Valerius Horatius, was actually betrothed to one of the sons of Curiatius.[81] Before the commencement of the combat the champions embraced each other with tears and lively demonstrations of attachment, and the people, moved by their mutual affection, lamented that the choice of their rulers should change the tender ties of friendship into blows and hatred. The champions, nevertheless, fought valiantly and well, and two of the Horatii fell beneath the swords of the Curiatii.[82] Publius Horatius, after the fall of his brothers, fled, to the horror and consternation of the Romans, but his flight was the result of a well-planned stratagem, for when pursued by the Curiatii, he successively killed them all. While hailed as the deliverer of his country on every side, and loaded with the praises of his Sovereign, his sister Horatia rushed forth to meet the slayer of her lover, and passionately reproached and upbraided him. The victorious brother, moved with indignation, plunged his sword into her bosom, and tarnished, by the death of an unfortunate and distracted female, the laurels he had won for his country.[83] Valerius Horatius, far from blaming his son, refused his daughter the rites of burial in the family sepulchre, because she had valued her lover more than her country.[84] The homicide remained unpunished, though by the laws of Rome he ought to have been hanged on a tree near the pomœrium; but his father and the people of Rome delivered their fratricidal champion, with the permission of the Sovereign, who allowed the murder to be expiated.[85] That the victorious Roman champion slew his sister seems not unlikely, for the ties of natural affection are not usually held sacred in semi-barbarous states. Poetry has, however, adorned the tale with some romantic touches which have thrown discredit upon the whole. The tragic muse, in later ages, loved to paint the conflicting feelings of the unfortunate Roman daughter, and the stern patriotism of her father. Hostilius, for this victory over the Albans, demanded and obtained a triumph—a circumstance not very likely to promote the union between the Romans and the vanquished people.[86] B.C. 672-641. Fuffetius, dissatisfied with the result of the national combat, privately invited the Veientines and Fidenatans against Rome, though Rome and Alba, by the terms of the treaty, were become nominally one people.[87] In the battle fought between the Veientines, Fidenatans, and the Romans he took no part, remaining, with the Albans under his command, a mere spectator of the hostile scene. The Romans, discouraged and fearful of treachery, were unwilling to continue the engagement till assured by Tullus Hostilius that the separation of the Albans was a manœuvre of his own planning. This ruse saved the Roman army, nor were the allied troops better satisfied with the conduct of Fuffetius, whom they imagined to be laying a snare to entrap them.[88] As soon as the Romans had gained the victory, Fuffetius joined them, when Tullus Hostilius, enraged at his treachery, obliged the Albans to give up their dictator to his vengeance. Fuffetius was torn to pieces by horses, while Alba was razed to the ground, and its inhabitants transplanted to Rome,[89] where they were admitted to the Roman franchise. The Alban nobility were enrolled in the Senate. Particular mention is made of the Tullii, Servilii, Quintii, Geganii, Curiatii, and Clœlii in the list. Ten troops of horse were selected from the Alban cavalry,[90] and the incorporation became complete. Mount Cœlius was the spot appointed to receive the Albans, and the desolation of Alba conduced greatly to the aggrandisement of Rome.[91] Tullus Hostilius gained a second triumph for the success of his arms against the Veientines and Fidenatans,[92] and also gained a victory over the Sabines, for which he obtained his third triumph.[93] He maintained a war with the Latins, in the course of which he stormed and plundered Medullia, which had received formerly a Roman colony, and had revolted from its allegiance. The Sabine war, still carried on by the brave and ambitious Hostilius, was discontinued from the superstitious dread inspired by the fall of a shower of stones on the Alban Mount, for which the volcanic nature of the adjacent country sufficiently accounted without the necessity of seeking for a supernatural cause. This eruption of stones was succeeded by the plague—a calamity frequently following, and supposed to originate from, such subterranean agency. Both were referred to the decay of piety. "The King, whose failing health rendered him more open to this superstitious idea, sought to obtain from the offended deities themselves an answer respecting the manner in which the atonement of their displeasure was to be made. Tullus Hostilius, while invoking the offended powers at the altar of Jupiter Elicius, was slain by a thunderbolt through some mistake in the performance of the mysterious rites of Numa, the King and his whole house becoming the victims of the lightning. He is said to have reigned thirty-two years."[94]

The warlike character of this prince has gained him the admiration of the Roman historians and poets, for he gave the first impetus to that career of conquest which afterwards rendered the city he ruled the mistress of the world. His reign was not, however, free from the calamities of pestilence and famine. In fact, the territorial acquisitions of Rome did not increase in proportion to her population; and if the plague affected the cattle, want immediately ensued, for the lands under B.C. 672-641. cultivation were not sufficient to provide food for her citizens. The wars of Tullus Hostilius began to open with the sword a way into the harvest-fields of her neighbours—the only method by which the Romans could hope to obtain food for their increasing numbers.

ANCUS MARCIUS.

The successor, and perhaps murderer, of Tullus Hostilius, Ancus Marcius, was a Sabine by birth, and the grandson of Numa. He was elected by the Senate and people of Rome to fill the vacant throne. If the commencement of his reign was marked by treason and regicide, its general character was peaceful and prosperous. The warlike neighbours of the Romans, conceiving a mean idea of his military talents, gave him an opportunity for displaying them to advantage. He despatched an ambassador, wearing the woollen sash and peculiar costume proper to his office, to the Latins, complaining of their aggressions on the Roman territory. This functionary remained three-and-thirty days endeavouring to arrange the differences between the two nations. His negotiations failing to effect the object, the feciales, or sacred heralds, followed the embassy arrayed in their proper habits, carrying javelins headed with iron, but burnt and stained with blood at the ends; when in the presence of three young men, as the Roman custom required, they threw their javelins into the borders of the inimical country after making a solemn declaration of war against it in the name of the gods and the people of Rome.[95]

Ancus Marcius commenced the Latin war by the storm of Politorium, sparing the inhabitants whom he carried off to Rome, not as slaves but colonists. The Aventine Mount was the place assigned by him to these men, to whom he immediately granted the Roman franchise.[96] This town lay fifteen miles south-east of Rome. The expatriated Latins were, of course, only admitted into the plebeian order; but this traditional fact confirms the opinion "that that order originally rose out of a body of freemen thus incorporated with the state; the Aventine Mount being the peculiar focus of the plebeian city in a later age."[97] Each of the hills then included in the growing city was peopled by a distinct colony. The Romans occupied their first station on Mount Palatine; the Sabines remained in possession of the Capitoline, or Saturnian, as it was then called, which they had won in their war with the husbands of their daughters. The Tuscans and Albans dwelt on the Cœlian, and the Latin colony occupied the Aventine. Ancus captured Tellene, Ficania, and Medullia, transplanting the people to the other Latin colony on the Aventine, retaking and demolishing Politorium.[98] The second campaign he made against the Latins was equally fortunate, for he forced them to sue for peace, obtaining a triumph for his successful conclusion of the war.[99] He also subdued the Veientines, Fidenatans, and Volscians; for which victories and the advantages he gained over the Sabines, he was allowed a second triumph.[100]

Ancus Marcius having established peace by the sword, maintained it by his wisdom; the internal improvement of the Roman state henceforth becoming his peculiar care. In the old historic lays he is styled "the good," because he distributed the conquered lands in shares to the people.[101] He had in the course of his wars extended the Roman frontier to Veii, won the forests upon the sea-coast and the salt-marshes, besides opening the mouth of the Tiber to the Romans. He founded the town of Ostia, which he peopled with a colony, depriving the revolted colonies of Fidenæ, Crustumerium, and Medullia of their privileges, as a punishment due to their rebellion.[102] "Ostia became the harbour of Rome; indeed ships of considerable size could in those days run into the Tiber, which has since, partly from neglect, and partly from ill-judged erections, become more inaccessible than any other river discharging its waters into the Mediterranean."[103]

The oldest monument of Rome, the prison formed out B.C. 640-617. of a quarry opened in the Capitoline Hill, is the work of Ancus. He likewise built the first bridge over the Tiber, and a fort before it upon the Janiculum, as a bulwark against Etruria. On the other side, he protected the newly-settled district, the valley of the Temple of Murcia, by a ditch called Fossa Quiritium.[104]

Ancus Marcius, mindful of the ritual taught by Numa, transcribed the ceremonial law upon tables, and fixed them up in the market-place; for at that time the whole mystery of the national religion was not engrossed by the Pontifical College.[105] He rebuilt the Temple of Jupiter Feretrius, and enlarged the pomœrium of the city, whose frontiers he had considerably extended by his conquests. He gave great encouragement to foreigners, and particularly to the remarkable man who succeeded him on the throne, whose surprising works have survived by centuries the city they adorned. Lucius Tarquinius, so called from Tarquinii in Etruria, where his father Damaratus, a Corinthian exile, had settled,[106] came to Rome with Tanaquil, his wife,[107] bringing with him a considerable patrimony. This stranger was a person of taste and talent, combining with general knowledge much skill in architecture and the fine arts, in which Rome—a vast collection of wooden huts—was yet deficient. Tarquinius became a favourite with Ancus Marcius, who not only admitted him into the Senate but committed to him the guardianship of his sons; and it is to him that Rome was mainly indebted for her rise in civilisation and importance.[108]

Ancus Marcius reigned twenty-four years,[109] and the manner of his death is uncertain, some imputing it to the treachery of his friend and Prime Minister, Tarquinius. He is described by Livy as being "great alike in peace and war," and is commended for his justice, wisdom, piety, and foresight. He was much beloved by his subjects, who regretted his death. He had added to the Roman state a considerable part of Etruria and Latium through his success in wars, not undertaken for the sake of conquest, but to ensure peace.

L. TARQUINIUS PRISCUS.

An interregnum again occurred in the government of Rome; during which Tarquin employed his influence with the Senate and people to procure his own election. A foolish story is related about his sending the young sons of Ancus Marcius to the chase while he assembled the people, and by an eloquent and insinuating oration, induced them to confer the regal dignity upon him, as the fittest person for the office.[110] But in an elective monarchy, in which nothing like hereditary descent had been either claimed or accorded, such a mean subterfuge would neither have been required nor adopted, the descendants of Ancus Marcius having no legal right, even if their childish years had not formed a sufficient bar of exclusion. Tarquinius Priscus was a sovereign reigning by the joint concurrence of the Senate and people of Rome. He made an important

27

concession to the Commons, by admitting a hundred persons from the plebeians into the Senate. Had the succeeding sovereigns and the patrician rulers of the Commonwealth adopted the same wise and enlightened policy, the fierce contests between the two orders would never have distracted and torn the state.

Tarquinius Priscus is supposed by modern authors to have been the conqueror of Rome, not her adopted citizen, as the ancient Roman historians have affirmed.[111] His honourable reception at Rome has already been recorded, and it is worthy of remark, that Florus and other Latin writers give the same account of his origin.[112] His title of Lucumo, or lord, was changed into the prenomen of Lucius, and he assumed the surname of Tarquinius, from the place of his nativity.[113]

Tarquinius having gained the good will of the plebeians B.C. 616-579.by granting the senatorial dignity to many of them, proceeded to ingratiate himself with the people at large by his care for religion, which till his time retained its ancient simplicity. He added four to the number of the Vestal College. He was the first who offered victims to the gods, and placed their statues in the temples, where, under a human form, they received the worship of the Roman people.[114] The reverence with which the Romans regarded the gods to whom they had erected temples had not yet become gross idolatry.[115] Even this was rendering undue honour to deceased heroes rather than idol worship. Tarquinius, however, naturally adopted the faith of his father, Damaratus, and adored with him the deified forms of Greece, where false piety ennobled sculpture while it debased the man; for the superiority we still accord to Grecian art undoubtedly emanated from the ideal beauty with which the sculptor's imagination had clothed his gods.

Tarquinius made war with the Latins, from whom he took Collatia, a town lying five miles north-east of Rome. He gave the government of the conquered place to his nephew, Egerius, who assumed the surname of Collatinus from that office.[116] This war with the Latins was a territorial one; in which Tarquinius took several towns, and forced the Latins, notwithstanding the assistance they received from their Etruscan allies, to sue for peace.[117] He next turned his arms against the Sabines, over whom, by means of a stratagem, he gained a complete victory. This he effected by throwing a quantity of brushwood into the Anio, and setting it on fire, which being driven against the bridge, ignited it. The Sabines, seeing themselves cut off by this ruse from all hope of retreat, could not maintain the contest. Many perished in attempting to cross the river, and more were slain. The floating corses of their foes being carried forward by the current to Rome, proclaimed the victory gained by the king before the tidings reached the citizens.[118] A second victory concluded Tarquinius' Sabine campaign, and obtained for him his first triumph.[119] He built the Circus Maximus out of the spoils acquired in these successful wars.[120]

The Etruscans, alarmed at his rapid conquests, combined their tribes against him. They took Fidenæ, and ravaged the Roman territories. As soon as Tarquinius could raise an army, he defeated them in several battles, forcing them to resign Fidenæ, and other conquests.[121] After his victory at Eretum—a place about ten miles' distance from Rome,—the Etruscan nations submitted to him, and sent him very costly regalia, consisting of an ivory chair, an embroidered tunic wrought with golden flowers and palm-leaves, royal purple robes, and a sceptre adorned with an eagle.[122] For this wonderful people, who have left enduring monuments in architecture, sculpture, and painting in Italy, were far advanced in civilisation when the Romans were yet ignorant and barbarous, their works still surviving their states and the empire of their conquerors.[123] Tarquinius consulted the senate respecting the propriety of his acceptance of the regalia. By the advice of the Conscript Fathers they were accepted; and we are told, "that the Etruscans became his tributaries and vassals."[124] We may, however, if we follow the old customs of Rome, suppose, that Tarquinius was not the lord but the vassal of Etruria, of whom he was content to hold the crown. The royal robes resembled those of the Lydian and Persian kings, the purple gown being pinked in a similar manner, though in shape it differed; these being cut four-square, while the outer one of B.C. 616-579. Tarquinius was of a semi-circular form. The Etruscan fashions were, after this period, copied for the robes and coats of the augurs and heralds."[125]

Rome, if she possessed little territorial advantages, had that within herself which always obtains them—men, courage, necessity. Her sovereigns hitherto had been furnished by semi-barbaric nations. In Tarquinius Priscus she had chosen a man comprising in his own person the civilisation proper to Greece and Etruria—a man of talent, capable of turning the martial temper of the Romans into a channel by which he could obtain gold to execute those works necessary for the improvement and ornament of his capital. The state that possesses steel will win gold, was the remark of a Grecian sage. Tarquinius was, of course, well acquainted with this aphorism: his wars gave him wealth; but he borrowed from Etruria her customs, her civilisation, and her worship, to enrich the state that had adopted him for her citizen, and chosen him for her king. Whenever Niebuhr traces the footsteps of the Roman kings through the misty shadows of the mighty past, he fixes the attention of the reader by bringing before his eyes the very antiquities he describes. He speaks thus of the fifth king of Rome:—"What has made the name of Tarquinius Priscus ever memorable is, that with him begins the greatness and the splendour of the city. Often the legend fluctuates in ascribing a work or an exploit to him or to his son; but the vaulted sewers by which the Velabrum, the forums, the country down to the lower Subura, and the valley of the Circus, till then swamps and lakes or bays in the bed of the river, were drained,—are most of them called the work of the elder king; and coupled with this undertaking must have been the embanking of the Tiber."[126] The Cloaca, the most useful and enduring of his works, is still in existence.[127] Much of the interest with which we regard these mighty monuments of the past is diminished upon reflection. They rarely were the fruits of free-hired labour; but were constructed by a sacrifice of human happiness and human life. The captive mingled his bread with tears, and gave out his strength beneath the lash of the taskmaster. Even the Roman citizen might have found his portion of labour a heavy burden; though, in order to lighten its weight, Tarquin commenced those public amusements which formed the delight of the Roman people to the latest moment of their national existence.[128] Niebuhr comments upon this fact in that lucid and animated manner which occasionally lightens the weight of his learned history. He says: "Works that rival the greatest of the Etruscan cannot have been accomplished without oppressive taskwork any more than those of the Pharaohs. The king cheered his people during their hard service with games, which from his time forward were celebrated annually in September, under the name of the Roman or great games. Among the contests which drew the Greeks to Olympia, only the chariot-race and boxing were practised by the Etruscans. The spectacle was a source of delight to the people of Italy; but the contests were the business of hirelings or slaves." Indeed, no Roman citizen would ever have degraded himself so low as to exhibit his skill or talents for the public amusement; for, however admired the Roman games might be, the freeman who engaged in them, instead of being immortalised by sculpture or song, and becoming the pride of his family, forfeited his honour and his civic rights. The charioteer and the player were in no higher estimation than the gladiator. Not that the Romans clung to their spectacles of all kinds with less vehemence than the Greeks; but if, like the Greeks, they B.C. 616-579. could have honoured the object that excited their passions, they would not have lost themselves in that extravagant fury which, even in early times, maddened the factions of the Circus in behalf of their despicable favourites.[129] "But the chariot-race was not the only enjoyment of the Circensia; there were also processions, the images of the gods borne along, robed in kingly garments, the armed boys, the war dances, and the ludicrous imitations of them."[130] In these national entertainments, in a delightful climate whose bright blue sky and brilliant sunshine afforded a cheering influence alike to the free citizen and the slave, the captive might, for a few brief hours, forget his chain, and the plebeian labourer his taskwork, while the body reposed from its fatigues and the mind was diverted from its cares. In providing rest and diversion for his people, Tarquinius proved himself an able governor, who knew how to ensure the loyalty and affection of those he governed. Not that the amusements he provided for a heathen people will bear the scrutiny of the Christian reader; for they were such as delighted pagan men in a dark, remote, and idolatrous age. The morality of Rome was never apparent in her holydays and recreations.[131]

Tarquinius, in the heat of the Sabine war, had vowed a temple to Jupiter, Juno, and Minerva, in pursuance of which he levelled the rugged crest of the Capitoline rock for the foundation of the building.[132] The temple, however, was the work of Tarquinius Superbus, his son or grandson. This last design he did not live to complete, but he justly deserved the title, accorded him by his people, of the Second Founder of Rome.

We have now described those architectural works which made this king remark, "that he found Rome built of wood, but left it of marble." War and works of architecture seemingly engrossed the attention of Tarquin; for we know nothing of his laws and revenues, and are ignorant in what manner he regulated his finance; but we are assured that, when Attius Navius, the chief augur, opposed the innovations of his sovereign, and would not allow him to make three new centuries of celeres, as contrary to the Constitution granted by Romulus, Tarquinius effected his object by doubling the old ones. In this incident we see the despotic innovation of the king frustrated by a man supposed to excel in divination.

The disappearance of the obnoxious augur soon after his sovereign had carried the point by an equivocation which despotism alone could have conceived, occasioned a quarrel between him and the Marcii, the sons of the last king, who accused him of having caused the death of Navius. From this charge Servius Tullius, the popular son-in-law of Tarquinius, cleared his character. But the hatred of the Marcii was not confined to calumny; they conspired against the life of this great prince. To effect his assassination, they sent a number of their fellow conspirators, disguised as shepherds, to his tribunal, as if to obtain his decision respecting some matter of dispute among themselves. This pretext affording them the opportunity they sought, they slew the king as soon as they were permitted to approach his person.[133]

Thus perished Tarquinius Priscus, after a long and prosperous life of eighty, and a glorious reign of thirty-eight years. His stupendous works remain his best and most enduring monument. It is uncertain whether Tarquinius Superbus was his son or grandson; but his own advanced age makes the supposition more probable that he was his grandson.[134]

SERVIUS TULLIUS.

The accession of Servius Tullius formed a remarkable B.C. 578-535.era in Roman history, for a new feature was given to the Constitution, by the admission of the plebeians to those privileges, which were lost in the following reign, and not recovered without many civic tumults and long-continued scenes of strife. Rome looked back for ages upon the king of the people with regretful affection as her best and wisest ruler; nor did the conquering ages of the Republic ever efface the memory of Servius Tullius the Good.[135]

If we follow the Latin and Greek historians of Rome, it appears conclusive enough that the sixth king of Rome was the son of Ocrisia, a captive,[136] whose husband had been slain in the storm of Corniculum, from which town Tarquinius brought and presented her to Tanaquil, his consort. The delicate situation of the newly-made widow interested Tanaquil; and though the son of Ocrisia was born in slavery, he was tenderly cherished and liberally educated by Tarquinius and his queen. Poetry adorned the cradle of Servius with a crown of flame, which played round his head without injuring him, at once attracting the attention of Tarquinius and Tanaquil to the infant captive, whom they imagined to be destined for great things.[137] "The legend which assigned to Servius Tullius a captive mother has been quoted by Juvenal, and was then currently believed at Rome; but a different origin was assigned this sovereign by the Emperor Claudius, on the admission of two Lugdunese Gauls into the Senate, which has been preserved on two tables discovered at Lyons in the nineteenth century; which tables, since Lipsius, have been often printed with the works of Tacitus."[138] "In this document the Emperor Claudius, after recounting from the first origin of Rome how often the royal dignity had been bestowed upon strangers, makes this comment upon the early history of Servius Tullius: 'According to our annals he was the son of the captive Ocrisia; but if we follow those of the Tuscans, he was the most faithful follower of Cæles Vibenna, and shared all his fortunes. At last, being overpowered by a variety of mischances, he quitted Etruria with the remains of the army which had served under Cæles, went to Rome, and occupied the Cælian hill, which he so named after his former commander. He exchanged his Tuscan name, Mastarna, for the Roman, obtained the kingly power, and wielded it to the great good of the state.' "[139] It is curious that the opinion of the Emperor Claudius on this point of ancient history should have survived all his voluminous works. It proves at least that other annals beside those of Rome had treated of Servius Tullius, though they had assigned him a different origin. There is, however, no reason why we should adopt the Tuscan authority in preference to the Latin, since the learning of the Emperor Claudius, though considerable, never gave any weight to his opinions, he being regarded as a prince of no judgment. Servius Tullius, whether a Tuscan chief or captive, obtained the friendship of his sovereign, who promoted him to honour, and gave him the hand of his daughter in marriage as a reward for his faithful services.[140]

Servius, in the declining years of his father-in-law, had assisted him in the government of Rome, and likewise aided him in carrying out the great designs of that prince. He had succeeded in gaining the good will of the people, but not without alienating those of the patrician order. It is said he was indebted for the regal dignity to Tanaquil, who carefully concealed the death of her husband till after Servius had secured his own election, assuring the citizens that the king was recovering from his wounds.[141]

Servius, who had made himself inter-rex on the spot, appealed in person to the people, whom he persuaded to banish the Marcii, and choose him for their sovereign. He was elected in the Comitia Curiata, but the senate refused to ratify the choice of the people till compelled B.C. 578-535. by circumstances to do so. His promised division of the public lands among the poor plebeians overpowered all attempts to invalidate his election on the part of the aristocracy.[142]

The peculiar situation of Servius Tullius had made him early acquainted with the different grades into which Rome was divided. Born, or at least brought up in slavery—at first an enfranchised slave, then admitted into a body which represented the middle class, and finally, exalted to the second place in the kingdom—his wise and enlightened mind had profited by an extensive experience not often known to sovereigns. He had discerned in the plebeians a counterbalance to an oligarchical aristocracy, and beheld in them a band of freemen full of vital energy and power, to whom the Roman franchise had only restored that freedom which had been their ancestral birthright. Distinguished from the populace by their education, perhaps haunted by the remembrance of their noble birth, yet shut out by a strong bar of constitutional exclusion from rising in the state, or even from defending themselves from the encroachments of the privileged order, and debarred from trade, this body of landholders really formed the vital heart of the state; it might fall into a miserable state of poverty, and still retain its freedom, but the hope of becoming rich by application to any business but agriculture was forbidden by the loss of freedom. Such a state of things could not continue; and Servius Tullius not only discovered this truth, but wisely turned it to his own advantage. He did therefore in Rome "what Henry

32

VII. afterwards did in England—increased the power of the Commons in order to lower that of the aristocracy; for, in increasing the privileges of the people, he diminished that of the senate."[143] By the word "people," we must not suppose the populace of Rome signified—a mistake wilfully made by inflaming popular orators, who speak of the Romans as if every class not absolutely servile, that is, in slavery, formed a part of it, while in reality the plebeians were a body of citizens possessed of the franchise, and certain privileges never extended to the more numerous class immediately beneath them. Rights shared with the populace would have been scorned by the free, impoverished plebeian, who held very different views respecting liberty and equality from those imputed to him by the leaders of the French revolutions in this and the last century.

The reader must bear this definition continually in mind, never confounding the mass of libertini, or even foreign tradesmen or craftsmen, with the plebeians or commons who formed what was styled the people. We may find in the freeholder of England a parallel to this order, if the practice of any calling but agriculture were held to disfranchise him, or if he were denied the power to rise in the state.[144] The first change Servius Tullius effected was the assignment of seven jugers or hides per man of the conquered lands to the plebeians, thereby fulfilling his promise to the body of freemen who had placed him on the throne.[145] Hitherto the poorer portion of this order had borne the chief burden of the levies, but the king resolved to give them relief by fixing a certain standard by which each tribe in the kingdom should contribute to the exigencies of the state according to its capabilities. To effect this, and to procure levies of troops in the same ratio, Servius established the census.[146] The supplies for the exigencies of the government had previously been raised by a poll-tax, which exacted as much from the poor as the rich. It is pretty certain, however, that the patrician class paid no tax at all. The division relieved the poorer plebeian by assigning the sum to be paid by him according to his means. To effect this, the king caused a census to be made of all the tribes; including the descent, names, ages, and occupations of every family in Rome. These he divided into six classes, each of which was to furnish so many centuries or companies of foot in time of war, according to their estates or effects. Thus the first class, which was valued at one hundred and ten thousand asses, contained ninety-eight centuries, inclusive of the equites or knights; the second, valued at seventy-five thousand asses, containing twenty-two centuries, taking in artificers; the third, which also contained twenty-two centuries, was valued at fifty thousand; the fourth, of twenty centuries, B.C. 578-535. was valued at twenty-five thousand asses; the fifth, of thirty centuries, was rated at twenty-five thousand; the sixth, of the poorest citizens, was reckoned at one century.[147]

The quotas of foot soldiers were furnished in due proportion to this assessment. The knights were provided with horses by a tax being levied upon the Roman widows for that purpose, who were exempted from all imposts but this.[148] As there was a body of plebeian knights, this crown service was probably performed by them.

The first lustrum was celebrated by Servius Tullius immediately after the census or tax had been raised.[149] According to his appointment, all the citizens, completely armed and ranked in their proper classes and centuries, met in the Campus Martius, when the city was expiated or lustrated by the sacrifice of a hog, a sheep, and an ox. This ceremony took place every five years, when the census was taken again, and a fresh valuation made of the property of the Roman rate-payers.

At this first lustrum, the free citizens of Rome amounted to eighty-four thousand seven hundred.[150] Servius, in order to encourage good conduct, and increase the number of free men, bestowed the Roman franchise upon a number of slaves; some receiving this gift as the reward of virtue, while others were permitted to purchase their freedom. These he distributed among the four civic tribes. To some prisoners of war he gave the choice of settling at Rome, or returning to their own countries. Many availed themselves of his permission, but more remained with their wise and merciful master.[151] But while Servius manumitted slaves, and conferred solid benefits upon the plebeians, he certainly deprived them of the power they possessed, by taking away from them the right of voting in the Comitia Curiata, where their numbers gave them the majorities in the election of magistrates, making or abrogating laws, or decreeing peace or war.[152] He effected this change by assembling the whole Roman people by centuries, called Comitia Centuriata, and taking their votes in this manner—a measure that afterwards left them in a minority;[153]—so difficult is it for even an excellent prince to set bounds to his own privileges, or to fence in those of other persons when he holds the supreme power in his hands, a power which he had certainly obtained from the Roman Commons. If the other regal heads of Rome had acted in concert with the senate without due regard to the people, this king deprived the senate of their privileges by reigning without that body altogether—an illegal method for which he afterwards paid very dear. In fact, he was not justified in sacrificing the interests of the aristocracy entirely; his safest and justest policy would have been to keep each order in exact equilibrium, himself holding the balance of power between them.

Servius Tullius did not limit his legislative care to the city alone; he divided the Roman territorial possessions into twenty-six parts, called by the name of tribes, semi-dividing them into pagi, or fortified villages. It is uncertain whether these pagi were defended by a castle, or were merely surrounded by a mound and a ditch. In either case the pagi were designed for safeguards to the country people upon any invasion of the Roman territory.[154] He enlarged the bounds of Rome, taking within the city the Quirinal, Viminal, and Esquiline Hills,[155] which he united by raising a vast mound of earth, which served for their defence in war.[156]

The Latin and Etruscan nations occupied Servius for twenty years in continual war. We find the triumphs of this prince enumerated on the Capitoline marbles—an ancient monument dug up in the sixteenth century, supposed to have been compiled by a Roman knight in the Augustan age.[157] These triumphs are dated A.U.C. 182, 186. [The computation in these tables is different from the Varronian.] His treaty with the Latins was extant as a document in the time of the Empire,[158] from which it appears he made peace with them upon the same terms as his predecessor, Tarquin. Three out of the twelve Latin nations were, however, excluded from its benefits. These were the Veientines, Cærites, and

Tarquinians, who had B.C. 578-535. been the ringleaders in the revolt.[159] At the conclusion of his wars, Servius built two temples, which he dedicated to Fortuna Bona and Fortuna Virilis. The Temple of the Moon, afterwards destroyed in the conflagration of the city in Nero's reign, was the work of this prince.

The festival of the Saturnalia was founded by him as a holiday for the unfortunate servile class, to which he had once himself belonged—a touching proof that the monarch did not disdain his former origin; for though the Latin authorities assure us that the captive of Corniculum was of a noble family, that circumstance did not render slavery less bitter. Juvenal alone speaks of him as the son of a poor maid-servant.[160] In after ages, indeed, every benevolent institution, every just law, was, by the gratitude or fond partiality of the Roman people, ascribed to this admirable prince.[161] A coinage, bearing the image of a sheep, and called *pecunia*, was numbered among the useful works of Servius;[162] but this is by no means certain. He fixed the weight of the *as* of brass at twelve ounces. It was long supposed that an *as* of this remote period was in existence till it was ascertained that the lump only weighed eight ounces, which, being below the fixed standard assigned by Servius Tullius, proved that the piece of money was either spurious, or of a later age.[163] The commentaries of Servius Tullius are cited by Verrius Flaccus, which are supposed to contain the substance of his constitutional laws.[164] "The Roman documentary records of the regal period of her history were scanty, nor was much care taken to secure them. The laws of Rome for a considerable period were either engraved on oaken tables, or painted on such tables after they had been plastered."[165] Tradition, however, transmitted the memorial of the regal heads of Rome, sometimes linking the true history with some heroic lay. The fate of the good Servius, it has been thought, may be thus mixed up in its transmission to us. We are told that he had only two daughters, who both were named Tullia; the elder, a mild and gentle princess, he married to Lucius Tarquinius, her cousin, the eldest grandson of the late king; while his youngest, who was fierce, implacable, and ambitious, he bestowed upon Aruns Tarquinius, whom she despised for his meek temper.[166] Servius is said to have crossed the inclinations of the contracting parties, hoping to soften the dispositions of the fierce Lucius and younger Tullia by giving them amiable partners. The untimely deaths of the younger Tarquinius and elder Tullia, not without suspicious circumstances, was followed by the union of the widow and widower.[167] The ambitious couple from this time aspired to the throne, of which Tullia considered her husband had been deprived. Lucius Tarquinius joined the aristocratic party, and took advantage of the increasing years and infirmities of his father-in-law to attempt his deposition.[168] Beloved by the people,[169] but not by the senate, it was to them that Servius Tullius made his appeal when charged with usurpation by his son-in-law in the Forum. He alleged that the monarchy was elective, and that even if it had been otherwise, the sons of Ancus Marcius had more right than the grandson of Tarquinius Priscus. The people answered his defence with loud cries—"Let Servius reign, but let Tarquinius die." At these ominous sounds the rebel prince fled affrighted to his house, where he was met and reproached by his ambitious wife for his cowardice.[170] Tarquinius assumed some appearance of contrition, and was forgiven by the parents of his wife. Soon after this, he tampered with the disaffected senate, and arraying himself in royal robes, repaired to the temple, where the national assembly was held, and placing himself upon the throne, asserted his claim to it in a long and violent oration. He chose the harvest-time for this attempt, when the commons, who loved the king, were employed in the fields.[171] Servius Tullius arrived while he was in the act of declaiming, and indignantly attempted to pull the usurper from his seat. The struggle was momentary; for the youth and strength of Tarquinius prevailed against the age and feebleness of his opponent, whom he hurled B.C. 578-535. violently down the steps to the Forum, none of the assembly making the slightest attempt to defend the king, or put an end to the unnatural contest. Three only of the senators less cruel than the rest raised the wounded monarch, and were leading him slowly to his own palace, when they were overtaken by assassins despatched by Tarquinius, who immediately concluded the murderous and parricidal act of the usurper, by putting the aged monarch to death after a long and glorious reign of forty-four years.[172] History and local tradition accuse the inhuman daughter of Servius Tullius as the instigator of her husband's crime; she alleging to him that while her aged parent lived, he could not hope to reign. As soon as the parricide was accomplished and the revolution of the nobles, headed by Tarquinius, completed, Tullia, we are told, mounted her chariot, and paraded the streets with all the pomp and pride of a newly-made queen. In the street, which ever after this tragic occurrence was denominated Vicus Sceleratus, the charioteer attempted to prevent the chariot of the unnatural daughter from passing over the body of the murdered parent. She, however, would not permit him to turn back. The charioteer urged forward his frightened steeds, when the carriage wheels and even the garments of Tullia were dyed with the blood of her father and sovereign, while hurrying to welcome her husband[173] as the seventh king of Rome; for the furies of her wickedness were upon her. The Latin annalists perhaps might have considered this horrid incident fabulous, if the scene of the tragedy had not been pointed out from age to age as an ill-omened place. A curious remark is made by the ancient historians, that Tullia was not ashamed of being seen by a multitude of men. As this is related of her before she saw the body of her father, it applies to her want of delicacy,[174] and proves how closely retired women were kept in that age.

The mother of Tullia died that night, and the freedom of the commons perished with Servius Tullius. In the Republican era it was erroneously supposed that the sixth king of Rome was about to establish a Republic when he was cut off by Tarquinius—a very improbable and unfounded statement. Nor can we imagine why this king should substitute the popular for the regal government, which, even in the elective form, was infinitely superior to that which finally replaced it. The tragical fate of the fifth and sixth kings of Rome affords, however, a painful illustration of the personal insecurity of regal heads when unprotected by hereditary descent; nor is the liberty of the subject under such a monarchy more secure than the life of the sovereign. Both are continually menaced by the domination of party.

Tarquinius Superbus, or the Proud, ascended the throne of the good and great Servius Tullius under a cloud, through which it is difficult, even at this day, to discover the eminent qualities he really possessed; for his wickedness and tyranny were too trying to the impartiality of the historians of the Republic for them to mention him without prejudice; and, indeed, to the despot and murderer none felt inclined to accord even the merit of the general and architect. As he owed his elevation to the patrician order, he resolved to bind the dominant faction to him by the sacrifice of the party which had supported the murdered king. He, therefore, abrogated the law which had given to the plebeian order allotments of land from the ager publicus, a part of the conquered lands which were the property of the state. No real claim, unless conferred by the law, could be made by either order on the public domain, which was usually let on lease, or sold to the highest bidder for the exigencies of the state.[175] Occasional grants were made in the preceding reign to the plebeian order, therefore the munificence of Servius was not without precedent.

A large proportion of waste or unproductive lands, like the commons of England in former times, were left for the general occupation, or perhaps for the benefit of the poorer citizens, upon the payment of the tenth part of the fruit and corn to the crown—an easy rent, which being raised in B.C. 534-510. proportion to the produce, did not hurt the cultivator in the worst of seasons.[176] Hitherto the grants from the conquered lands to the plebeians had been considered in the light of hereditary property, and could be willed, or sold, at the pleasure of the possessor. The resumption of the grant made by Servius Tullius was therefore an unprecedented wrong to the rising middle class of Rome. Injuries done to this class always find avengers. Tarquinius knew this, and therefore resorted to an expedient calculated to render him, as he thought, secure from its resentment. He raised a great mercenary army, which made him completely independent of the patrician order which had raised him, and the plebeian which he had given abundant cause to hate him. Henceforth he ruled by his own despotic power, without any regard to the senate or people of Rome.[177] The memory of the good Servius Tullius became more endeared by the contrast afforded by his successor; and in the children of the parricidal Tarquinius and Tullia the Romans only saw a rising race of tyrants. A whole people cannot be kept down, even by a foreign military force, for any length of time, particularly in a state where every citizen is a soldier. A reaction must eventually take place, and, however slow the progress of the revolutionary movement may be, it is nevertheless sure and certain.

In his wars Tarquin displayed considerable military talents. He defeated the Sabines and the Volscians, and took Suessa Pometia, a city twenty-six miles south-east of Rome, in which he found great wealth. He obtained a triumph for these exploits.[178] His treaty with the Sabines was long extant. The manner in which he is said to have made himself master of Gabii appears improbable:—

This city, which stood eleven miles from Rome, had taken part with Suessa Pometia, Tarquinius invested; but finding it capable of making a long resistance, employed his eldest son, Sextus, as an agent in his crafty plan to gain possession of the place. The prince deserted to the Gabians, assigning some alleged injuries received from his father as the cause of his revolt. He was warmly welcomed by the besieged, who made him the governor of the city.[179] Having obtained the command, he sent a message to his father, asking his advice as to the disposal of the principal citizens, who immediately took the messenger into his garden where he cut off the heads of the tallest poppies, imitating in this mute method of conveying political counsel, Thrasybulus, the Milesian, and dismissed the messenger without a word.[180] Sextus understood the apologue, and beheaded the principal citizens of Gabii, which he governed afterwards in the name of his father. Tarquinius, by granting to the people the franchise of Rome, and to the Romans the civic privileges of Gabii, left them no great cause of discontent.[181] His treaty with the Gabians, painted upon a wooden shield, was one of the few existing documents of regal Rome in the latter days of the Republic.[182]

From war Tarquinius turned his attention to architecture, for which, like his grandfather, Tarquinius Priscus, he possessed considerable talents. Taste in the fine arts is always a proof of civilisation and education in the prince; but the manner in which the great public works of the Tarquins were carried on could not but displease the people, for whose benefit nevertheless they were designed, for they were not remunerated for their labours; and while Tarquinius, with the pride of laudable ambition, was building for posterity, the poor Romans wanted means to purchase bread. It is to be feared that most of the magnificent works of antiquity were executed at the expense of unpaid workmen, much in the same manner as the great works of Mahomet Ali in our own day, at a vast expenditure of human life and suffering. Where mighty architectural designs are carried on by free states, through the agency of hired workmen, the benefit is not confined to futurity, but is a blessing to the present time, extending to the distant age. To the magnificent Capitoline Temple might be applied the Scriptural allegory, "Woe to him who ceileth his house with cedar and keepeth back the wages of the workmen, for the beam of the chamber shall cry out against him, B.C. 534-510. and the mortar in the wall shall answer him." This denunciation proves how common the oppressive method of embellishing cities and palaces at the expense of the poor workman had become, even in a free country, possessing the finest code of moral laws in the universe. The Capitoline Temple,[183] the work of Tarquinius, formed the pride and glory of Rome in those ages when the oppressive measures by which it was raised had sunk into oblivion. Ancient tradition derived the name of the Capitoline Temple from the following circumstance:—While digging the foundations, the head of a man named Tolus was found fresh and bleeding, though long buried; from whence the building was called Capitoline, or the head of Tolus—superstition inferring from the preservation of that ghastly relic, that Rome, crowned by this temple, would become the greatest city in the world, and the head of all other nations.[184] Tarquinius and his architectural works are thus quaintly noticed:—"Tarquinius was a great and mighty king, but he grievously oppressed the poor, and he took away all the good laws of King Servius, and let the rich oppress the poor as they had done before the days of Servius. He made the people labour at his great works; he made them build his temple and dig and construct his drains; and he laid such burdens on them, that many slew themselves for very misery; for in the days of Tarquin, the tyrant, it was happier to die than live."[185] This is an affecting picture of the distress of the Roman people under their tyrannical and despotic sovereign; while the liberal manner in which he remunerated his foreign architects and labourers added to the intense hatred they bore their sovereign.[186]

A curious incident made Tarquinius the possessor of that collection of ancient literature, afterwards known by the name of the Sibylline Books. Livy relates, "that an aged female brought twelve books of prophetic verses for sale to the palace gate, and, requesting to see the king, offered them to him at a very exorbitant price; which he refusing to give, she departed home, and burnt three, but soon afterwards returned, and offered the remaining nine at the same rate she had demanded for the complete set. This being declined, she went away, and again destroyed three; once more appearing at the palace gate with her merchandise, telling Tarquinius as before what she had done,"[187] but still demanding of him the original price for the remaining volumes. The king, astonished at her conduct, bought them at the sum she had first named, and placed them in the Capitol, under the care of two officers, or duumvirs, of noble birth. This story may be easily reduced from its romantic mysteriousness to an every-day occurrence common to any age. A valuable collection of ancient literature falls into the hands of an ignorant woman, who has some traditional notion that the books are worth a large sum of money; she brings them to her sovereign, who refuses to purchase them, returns home, supposing herself mistaken as to their value, and kindles her fire with the leaves of which they were composed. Her sovereign, in the meantime, has consulted some learned person, who advises him to give the price she had demanded. He finally purchases the remnant of the volumes at the original sum she had named. But, in stripping the circumstance of its romance, we need not deprive the books of their value, which were undoubtedly a collection of all the wisdom the heathen world[188] possessed in their oracles, interspersed with many of the sublime prophecies of Holy Writ. That such was the case, a quotation made by Josephus from the Sibylline volumes sufficiently proves,[189] since the dark ignorance of heathenism could not have forged the passage. It is gratifying to think that the Divine Being B.C. 534-510. had permitted some rays of light to shine through the gloom of an idolatrous land. The mysterious contents of these books naturally excited public curiosity; but the punishment of one of the guardian duumvirs, who incautiously repeated them, effectually put an end to such indiscretion on the part of the duumviri for the future; the guilty duumvir having undergone, we are assured, the ignominious doom of the parricide.[190]

Tarquinius, like most despots, was jealous of his own relations, and he put to death his brother-in-law, Marcus Brutus, the husband of his sister, Tarquinia;[191] but he spared his nephew Lucius Junius Brutus, either from pity to his youth or contempt for his talents, not beholding anything in the young man that could excite his suspicions, or point him out as the future avenger of his murdered family.[192] Brutus appears to have been brought up with his cousins, to whom his feigned or occasional fits of insanity afforded amusement and excited contempt. Fear lest Tarquinius should destroy him, as he had destroyed his father and elder brother, for the sake of his great inheritance, are the reasons assigned for his conduct in those ancient lays which formed the groundwork of the early Roman history.[193] "He was not really dull, but very subtle," is the remark of the historian; and of this subtilty he gives the following example:—A pestilence in Rome, and the evil omen of a serpent creeping forth from a crevice and devouring the offering laid upon the altar in the court of his palace, alarmed the king, who resolved to consult the Delphic oracle respecting the plague and the portent.[194] He sent his sons, Titus and Aruns, to Delphi, and with them his nephew Junius Brutus. The princes carried costly gifts, according to the general custom on such occasions, but their kinsman a hollow cane, apparently of no value, as a votive offering to the shrine. This present amused his cousins, who were not aware that the interior was filled with gold.[195] Beside the legitimate object upon which Tarquin had despatched them, the princes had a more private one in view; they wished to consult the oracle respecting the succession,[196] from which both desired to exclude their elder brother, Sextus, who might be supposed to derive from his father and great grandfather a shadow of hereditary right. Junius Brutus presented his staff, apparently with the same wish of learning which of the company would be the future sovereign of Rome. To the question, the priestess gave this curious response—"He who shall first kiss his mother." While the princes were making arrangements for deciding, by lot, who should first, upon their return to Rome, kiss Tullia, their kinsman descended the steps of the temple, and, pretending to stumble, threw himself on his face to the ground, which he kissed, saying to the priestess, "The earth is the real mother of us all."[197] A length of years must be supposed to intervene between this fact or fable before Brutus re-appears; for the next time we meet with him he is the parent of grown-up sons, and himself holds the important post of Tribune of the celeres, or body-guard, of his uncle, Tarquinius,[198] whom he is assisting in the siege of Ardea, formerly a tributary city, acknowledging the paramount and dominant power of Rome, but which had revolted, as Medullia had frequently done. The defence of the Ardeans was obstinate, so that, to continue the siege, Tarquinius was compelled to load the commons with additional taxes, and even to lay his hand upon the wealth of the nobility. The citizens, to whom his government had long been odious, resented these new imposts, and began to meet in secret to discuss and find a remedy for these grievances; when an incident of a strange and tragical character occasioned that revolt which terminated in the change of the Roman government from the Regal to the Republican form, under which Rome became the warlike mistress of the civilised world. If we follow the ancient heroic legend B.C. 534-510. recorded by Livy, and attested by the Latin historians, we shall believe that a convivial entertainment, given by Sextus Tarquinius, in the camp before Ardea, to his brothers, Aruns and Titus, and his cousins, Brutus and Collatinus, ushered in that deep tragedy with which the royal dynasty of Tarquinius and the Regal state of Rome closed.[199] At supper the kinsmen discoursed together respecting the comparative beauty and merit of their wives, when Collatinus was the loudest in praise of the fair Lucretia, to whom he had not long been married, and whose merit, he declared, surpassed that of all other women. It was at length agreed that the disputing parties should ride in company and visit their consorts, assigning the palm of superiority to her whom they should find the best employed.[200] As the Roman supper answered in time to a three o'clock dinner, and Ardea was not more than twenty miles from Rome, the distance presented no obstacles to high-spirited men, well-mounted, and determined upon a harmless frolic. Arrived at Rome, the princes found their wives engaged in amusement, and apparently contented and happy in their absence. Collatinus repeated the praises of his wife to the disappointed husbands, whom he assured they would find very differently employed. It was night when they entered his house at Collatia, where they found the fair Lucretia spinning with her maidens, to whom she was speaking of her absent husband. The beauty and domestic virtues of the young matron, her cordial reception of her midnight guests, and her conjugal affection, compelled the royal kinsmen of Collatinus to assign the palm of superior merit to her without a dissenting voice.[201]

Although Sextus Tarquinius must have often seen the fair Lucretia before, as Collatinus was his relation, he had never perhaps regarded her with admiration till he beheld her in her own home, adorned with those domestic virtues which form the peculiar charm of an amiable woman. He conceived a violent passion for his beautiful hostess, whose modest manners and conjugal affection deprived him of all hope of seducing her from her duty and allegiance to her husband. He therefore resolved to effect her dishonour by fraud and force. A few days after his first visit, he paid a second and more private one to Collatia, under the pretence of bringing a message to the fair Lucretia from her absent husband.[202] He was received with the same frank hospitality by the wife of his kinsman, whose matronly carriage effectually deterred him from daring to avow the guilty passion with which she had inspired him. In the dead hour of night he violated the privacy of her apartment, threatening her with death, and, what was worse to a proud and pure woman, with a false accusation of adultery with a slave. The dread of posthumous shame prevailed with the unfortunate Lucretia, who nevertheless determined not to survive her dishonour. She sent messengers to her husband and father, requesting them to call a family council to consult with her upon matters of deep importance. This was doubtless done that they might sit in judgment upon her, and decide the question of her innocence or guilt. In after ages we shall find this custom of family trial, which was a very ancient one, often resorted to.[203] That it was to the domestic tribunal Lucretia appealed, seems apparent by her pathetic declaration, after relating to her astonished auditors the history of the outrage she had suffered—"I am not guilty;" as if to claim from their justice a verdict favourable to her innocence. She then concluded her recital by these emphatic words: "If ye be men, revenge my wrong."[204] Her male relations solemnly swore to avenge her injuries. They pronounced her guiltless, and endeavoured to console and soothe her irritated feelings.[205]

"I am not guilty," she replied; "I am innocent, yet must I be punished for this deed, lest my example should be pleaded by some immodest woman as an excuse for surviving her dishonour." With these words, she drew a B.C. 534-510. dagger from beneath the folds of her robe, and stabbed herself to the heart.[206] For, acquitted by her jurors, the chaste Lucretia could not acquit herself; so lofty in that age was the standard of purity of the Roman matron. The cries of horror uttered by the husband and father of the heroine were not reiterated by Junius Brutus. While they lamented, he determined to avenge her.[207] Drawing from the bleeding bosom of the dead Lucretia the fatal dagger, he called upon her kinsmen to revenge her,[208] in a burst of eloquence that shook the hateful dynasty of Tarquinius from the throne of Rome. In that work of vengeance his position as tribune of the celeres, or body-guard, of Tarquinius[209] would materially aid him; nothing was wanting but the co-operation of those thus cruelly wronged, to achieve a revolution upon which the public mind had been long brooding. For twenty years, Lucius Junius Brutus had concealed the stern energies of a mighty mind beneath the veil of assumed madness and imbecility, which he shook off that day for ever.[210] His own family had been deceived, and the head of that family was Tarquinius; for the injury done by Sextus Tarquinius was to his own house, Collatinus being his near kinsman. The revolution was to be accomplished, therefore, by the kindred of the dynasty then occupying the throne. The agent of Divine Providence was Brutus, in that change of government to which the rise of the mighty Fourth Monarchy may be attributed. Brutus nerved the softer natures of the father and husband of Lucretia, who listened to him with amazement,[211] and obeyed him with awe not untinctured with superstition; for, till this dreadful day, they too had considered him insane. By his advice Lucretius, who was governor of Rome during the absence of Tarquinius, closed the gates of the city, and denied egress to its inhabitants.

Publius Valerius, a young patrician who had formed a part of this family council, and who was also related to the victim, joined Brutus in denouncing vengeance against Sextus Tarquinius, and in taking measures for exciting the popular feeling by the exhibition of the corse of the fair Lucretia in the Forum.[212] The absence of Tarquinius and his sons, who were then in the camp before Ardea, gave the insurgent Romans time to accomplish their mighty object, while the distance of their tyrants inspired the citizens with hope; so that, stirred alike by the eloquence of Junius Brutus, and the sight of Lucretia's bleeding body,[213] they demanded to be led against Tarquinius, that they might revenge her injuries upon him and his iniquitous family. The Senate was then appealed to in the same manner, and with the like success, and united with the people in a decree for the perpetual banishment of Tarquinius and his posterity.[214] This revolution at Rome took place 510 years before the Christian era.[215] Tullia, apprised of the revolt, fled precipitately from her house, followed by the curses of the people, who wished "the furies of her father's blood" (to use the singular expression of Livy) "might visit her with vengeance."[216]

It was fortunate at this crisis that Spurius Lucretius and Junius Brutus held the civil and military government of Rome, which was, in fact, legally vested in their hands; so that without even the concurrence of the people they could have barred Tarquinius out of his capital. To effect a permanent change in the state, it was requisite to gain the army without and the people within. The first object had been accomplished by the sight of the dead body of Lucretia, and the story of her wrongs. "Such an outrage made the people feel their slavery—to feel a yoke is virtually to shake it off. They had been individually wronged, and had borne taxation, oppressive taskwork, and infringement B.C. 534-510. on their civic rights; but the injury done to Lucretia was a public insult which these Roman husbands, fathers, and brothers could not forgive; so high was the moral standard in regard to the purity of women."[217] Lucretius as inter-rex called the people together in their comitia, where the crier summoned them to the tribune of the celeres, Lucius Junius Brutus, whose eloquent and affecting appeal to their feelings, and indignant recapitulation of the tyranny of Tarquin and his house, procured a decree of banishment against the despot, whose yoke they had sworn to shake off.[218] The men of Collatia had been previously excited by Brutus and Lucius Tarquinius Collatinus, the husband of Lucretia, whom they had followed to Rome, after setting a watch about the closed gates of their city, in order to prevent any traitor from carrying tidings of the insurrectionary movement to Tarquinius.[219] The escape of the wicked Tullia, however, soon made the events of that day known to the king, who was on his way to Rome, while Brutus was taking a bye-path to his camp before Ardea. His nephew was equally successful in his appeal to the army, whom he won by the same arguments as he had employed in rousing the disaffected citizens of Rome.[220] Tarquinius heard his sentence of banishment pronounced from the walls of Rome, while he found her gates barred and manned against him. The news of the revolt of the army made him yield to a storm against which he found himself unable to contend. He withdrew with his wife and sons to Cære,[221] not to remain there in exile and inactivity, but to turn all the energies of his mind towards one point—the recovery of his kingdom and capital city. The deposed monarch had carried despotism to an extreme height, rarely exhibited by the sovereign of a free state. "He chose to reign by his own power, in virtue of what he considered hereditary right, and treated Servius Tullius, from whom he took the crown, as an usurper." He was not chosen by the people, and if he was aided by the Senate, he reigned without that body. In fact, "he destroyed many senators, and consulted none. The three powers of the state were united in his own person; but the people at a critical minute remembered that they were legislators, and the reign of Tarquinius came to an end."[222]

Lucius Junius Brutus and Lucius Tarquinius Collatinus were chosen as inter-reges, to exercise the regal functions till the Senate and people had decided upon the form of government under which the Roman state was to exist.

There is no reason to believe that the exiled sovereign had any knowledge of the event that had awakened the resentment, the inexpiable wrath of the Roman people. Lucretia had become by her marriage a part of his own family, her father at the time held the highest office in the state, and the man who accomplished the revolution was his own nephew, yet he was considered responsible for his son's crime. "Behold the deeds of the wicked family of Tarquinius!" had been the general cry of the Roman people when they saw the pale victim of Sextus' unbridled passion; and Brutus, forgetting that he shared their blood, had solemnly sworn to visit that deed upon Tarquinius and all his accursed race, declaring that "Rome should be kingless, lest any other man should do the like wickedness."[223]

The mainspring that sometimes upholds despotic power is the good feeling that exists between the absolute monarch and the people; but Tarquinius treated the commons as arrogantly as if he had conquered them, relying upon his mercenary troops for the maintenance of his authority. His own family or their connections held every post of trust in the state, and his hand was against all the rest; hence it came that, hated and detested as he was and deserved to be by the people at large, the revolution originated in members of his own family, and really emanated from the aristocracy themselves. Tarquinius, with great talents, courage, and energy, sank under a weight of popular hatred which clave to his memory even when men like Tiberius, Caligula, and Nero filled the throne. These emperors, however, took care to leave the great mass untouched; their tyranny victimised the great and rich, and never burdened the poor citizens; B.C. 534-510. for the history of the expulsion of the seventh king of Rome had given them an important and useful lesson, which they did not forget.

The first era of Roman power closed with Tarquinius the Proud; regality became odious to the people, who overlooked the virtues of their former regal rulers while indulging their intense hatred towards one despotic and wicked prince. When we consider the elective form of the early Roman government, we must feel surprised that Rome had not been harassed with continual civil wars. Montesquieu attributes the freedom from internal strife "to the equal distribution of power among the three orders of the state, which was broken when Servius Tullius, who owed his throne to the commons, elevated the class that raised him, and thus prepared the way for a democracy, which ought naturally to have followed the expulsion of the Tarquins and Monarchy."[224] The revolution, however, was not the work of the people, but of the aristocracy; therefore the new government was not democratical. Far from diminishing the privileges of the patrician order, it added to them.[225] This class had more cause to dread regal despotism than the plebeians; thus it was their interest to destroy the Monarchy and found a Republic, which they intended to rule in turn. In order to reconcile the people to the change, they restored many of the laws and institutions of Servius Tullius, and spread abroad "that the new form of government was the same as that he had planned himself for their benefit." In no other way can we account for such an assertion, unless we suppose it originated in that motive. For to imagine that King Servius really designed the republican constitution of Rome, seems very far-fetched and improbable. The gift of seven jugers of land to each poor citizen, and their late experience of kingly oppression, made them consent to the proposed change, although they did not regain by it that liberty they had possessed under Servius Tullius, or even that which they had enjoyed under their earlier kings. They lost the favourable moment for claiming their old and demanding new privileges; and all those struggles between the patrician and plebeian orders which afterwards convulsed the state, were the result of the rash precipitancy with which the Roman people acceded to the constitution, without securing themselves from the tyranny of the great, or increasing their civic rights. In fact, they had followed the impulse of their feelings, not the dictates of their reason; for an excited populace have no other guide, and seldom, if left to that, commit a moral error, but very commonly fall into a political one, when directed

44

by the self-interests of others: and thus it happened here. In their indignation against Sextus Tarquinius they resolved to expel his dynasty, and consented to abolish regality without considering whether they themselves would be eventually benefited by becoming republicans.

Few records of the regal state existed in Rome at the time when Livy wrote the history of the greatest power that ever swayed the destinies of mankind, the only original documents cited as belonging to that period being the treaty of Servius Tullius with the Latins,[226] that of Tarquinius Superbus with the Gabians, and another with the Sabines.

The jurist Papirius, by the direction of Tarquinius the Proud, made a collection of the laws of the kings, "the antiquity of which," remarks Niebuhr,[227] "is unquestionable." Some part of this code, which long bore the name of the Papirian, is very barbarous, but throws some light upon the manners of those early times. "Men were permitted by Romulus to expose their younger daughters; but no child of either sex could be abandoned in this manner after it had attained the age of three years, however poor or overburdened with offspring the father might be." In these cases the female parent appears to have possessed no power, for the strong feeling of maternity would always have made her the protector of her infant.

"To Romulus is also referred the domestic tribunal, by which the wife was tried by her husband's relations and her own for three faults, for any one of which she could be divorced, upon her conviction before these jurors—adultery, counterfeiting his keys in order to drink wine, or poisoning."[228] The male parent had the right of putting his children to death, or selling them; he could B.C. 534-510. also take his daughter from the husband he had given her, and marry her to another man. But though this law, so barbarous, immoral and unjust, was ancient, there is no example of the kind cited till towards the close of the Commonwealth, when the practice became dreadfully frequent, and occasioned that general corruption of female morals which disgraced the last age of the Republic and the first of the Empire. The domestic tribunal, which dated from the earliest regal period, was conducive to that purity of manners which for centuries was the glory of Roman matrons. The father could put his daughter to death for any breach of the family code of honour, nor would he suffer himself, perhaps, to be disgraced by her divorce, when he could prevent the public trial which would have permitted the injured husband to repudiate her, by putting her to death himself.[229] Over the person of his son the Roman father possessed the same absolute rights; he might sell or slay him, and could also make him over to his own creditors as part payment of his debts;[230] yet notwithstanding this severe parental yoke, no country in the world ever produced more splendid examples of filial piety than heathen Rome.

Such was the state of Rome when her regal era closed, two hundred and forty-five years after its foundation by Romulus. Such are the evidences of her political existence, drawn from the sources already carefully collated and enumerated. The truth of her whole regal history, from first to last, has been doubted, but to receive it, with some modifications, appears to involve less difficulties than its entire rejection, since we cannot replace the contested points with anything more veracious. If we strip the old Roman traditions of their mythic colouring, and divest them of some poetical allegory, we shall find them authentic pictures of those remote heroic times.

<hr size=2 width="10%" align=center>

[1] Daniel, vii. 23.

[2] Livy, Plutarch, Florus.

[3] The early traditions of regal and republican Rome were adopted by Virgil and Ovid, who, struck by their dramatic beauty, polished the rude lays of the people; while Livy honoured these ancient legends by giving them a place in History.

[4] Niebuhr, Rome, vol. i. p. 175.

[5] Appendix. (p.2)

[6] Plutarch, in Romulus.

[7] In the time of Augustus, Vettius considered that the twelve vultures seen by Romulus denoted twelve ages of power. His explanation actually coincided with the duration of the Roman state. Niebuhr, in his learned History of Rome, notices this singular fact, which happened as the augur had predicted.

[8] Niebuhr, 190.

[9] Plutarch, in Romulus. Festus, v. Mundus.

[10] Niebuhr, History of Rome, vol. i. p. 190, footnote 73.

[11] Plutarch, in Romulus. Hooke. Echard.

[12] Niebuhr, History of Rome, p. 190.

[13] Appendix. (p. 4)

[14] Lyell, Elements of Geology.

[15] Curtius and the gulf.

[16] Romulus was supposed to have commenced building his city in the fourth year of the sixth Olympiad, according to Varro, which is parallel to the years B.C. 753, and A.M. 3252; and in Usher's *Annales* agrees with the seventh year of Jotham, king of Judah, the eighth of Pekah, king of Israel. Echard's Rome, vol. i. p. 7. Plutarch has given several other traditional versions of the foundation of Rome, but the one adopted here has been selected as the most

ancient extant, having been taken by Livy from Fabius, the oldest Latin, and Diocles the Peparethian, the earliest Greek authority.

[17] The plough had been lifted up four times in tracing the boundary line. These vacant spaces were left for the gates,—the Latin word *porta*, a gate, being derived from the custom of carrying the plough. All within the line thus included was denominated *Pomœrium*, from *Post Murum*. These enclosures were never to become less, at least such was the design of the founder of the town or city. It was consecrated to the gods, and its profanation was an act of unpardonable sacrilege.

[18] Plutarch, in Romulus.

[19] Niebuhr, History of Rome.

[20] Echard, Rome Regal, vol. i. p. 10.

[21] *Ibid.*

[22] Niebuhr, History of Rome, vol. iii. p. 13.

[23] Livy, lib. i. cap. 9; Plutarch, in Romulus; Dion. Hal., lib. ii. p. 99.

[24] In the Book of Judges, chap. xxi. 19-25, we find the remnant of the tribe of Benjamin obtaining wives after the same method. Many of the tribes of India destroy all their female children, and carry off women from other septs for wives for the community.

[25] Livy, lib. i. cap. 9; Plutarch, in Romulus; Dion. Hal., lib. ii. p. 99.

[26] Florus; Plutarch, in Romulus.

[27] Livy; Tacitus, Annal. xi. § 24, speech of Claudius on foreign claims to civic rights.

[28] Afterwards called the Capitoline Hill.

[29] Plutarch; Florus, i.

[30] Appendix. (p. 9)

[31] Plutarch, in Romulus; Dion. Hal., lib. ii. p. 109; Echard.

[32] Appendix. (p. 9)

[33] Echard, vol. i. p. 15.

[34] *Ibid.*

[35] Echard, Rome, vol. i. p. 9.

[36] Echard; Hooke.

[37] Appendix. (p. 11)

[38] Echard, vol. i. p. 11.

[39] *Ibid.*

[40] Plutarch, in Romulus; Dion. Hal., ii. p. 14.

[41] Echard.

[42] Plutarch, in Romulus; Livy; Florus, i. 15.

[43] Val. Max. v. 3, 1, 2; Ovid Fast.

[44] Plutarch, in Romulus.

[45] Livy; Florus; Plutarch, in Romulus; Suetonius, in Augustus. Florus is elegantly brief in relating the fabulous message of Romulus: "It had pleased the Gods to recall Quirinus to heaven, and to decree that the people of Rome shall reign."

[46] Appendix. (p. 14)

[47] Livy; Florus, i. 2; Plutarch, in Numa; Hooke; Echard.

[48] Plutarch, in Numa.

[49] Plutarch, in Numa; Niebuhr.

[50] "This was the first worship of an actual sensible terrestrial object on record among the inhabitants of the new city. All ancient legislators, and, above all, Moses, rested the result of their ordinances for virtue, civil order, and good manners, on landed property; or, at least, on the secured hereditary possession of land for the greatest possible number of citizens. Not till then did Numa legislate for religion." Niebuhr, History of Rome, vol. i. p. 202.

[51] Plutarch, in Numa.

[52] Plutarch; Florus, i. 2; Livy, i.

[53] Plutarch, in Numa.

[54] Plutarch, in Numa; Niebuhr, History of Rome, vol. i, p. 526.

[55] Niebuhr.

[56] Plutarch, in Numa; Florus, 2.

[57] They were heralds, uniting the sanctity of the priestly character to that office. The Romans were accustomed to send the Feciales to complain of any public injury and to demand satisfaction for the wrong. If the negociations of the Feciales did not procure redress, they called upon the gods to witness against the offending people and their country, and so denounced war; but not, however, till every attempt at reconciliation and peace had been tried in vain. Plutarch, in Numa. This was a beautiful and benevolent institution, calculated to lessen the amount of human misery by referring public aggressions to peaceful negociation rather than to the cruel decision of the sword.

[58] Appendix. (p. 16)

[59] Plutarch, in Numa.

[60] *Ibid.*

[61] Suetonius, in Augustus; Tacitus, Annal.

[62] Plutarch, in Numa.

[63] <u>Appendix. (p. 18)</u>

[64] "The year of Romulus consisted of ten months, according to the description given of it by Macrobius and Censorinus. Their lunar year was, according to Scaliger, brought into harmony with the solar, by intercalating a month alternately of twenty-two and twenty-three days every other year, or during periods of twenty-two years, in each of which periods such an intercalary month was inserted ten times, the last biennium being passed over. As five years made a lustre, so five of these periods made a secle of one hundred and ten years. Much of the difficulty in reconciling the events recorded in Roman history with its chronology originates in this calendar, which was greatly inferior to that in use by the Mexicans at the time the Spaniards effected the conquest of their country." Niebuhr, History of Rome, i. p. 335.

[65] Florus; Plutarch, in Numa.

[66] Plutarch.

[67] Plutarch, in Numa.

[68] *Ibid.*

[69] Montesquieu, Décadence de l'Empire Romain.

[70] Seneca, Epit. 40.

[71] Echard.

[72] Minellio, Notes to Florus; Echard.

[73] Dion. Hal., iii. 1. It is very probable that between the reigns of Numa and Tullus Hostilius a great number of years may intervene. "His reign apparently belongs to a period when the character of historical events, though blended still with the mythical, were of a less poetical character. Between the completely poetical age, which stands in a relation to history altogether irrational, and the purely historical age, there intervenes in all nations a mixed age, which may be called the mythic-historical. It has no precise limits, but it reaches to the point where contemporary history begins, and its character is the more strongly marked the richer the nation has been in heroic lays. The later writers, neglecting those songs, without calling up in their minds any distinct image of the past, have filled up the void in its history from monuments and authentic documents. To this era may be referred the reign of Tullus Hostilius, the third king of Rome." [Niebuhr.] The fact that he was the grandson of Hersilia, the wife of Romulus, seems to allow some grounds for a considerable lapse of time between each reign.

[74] Florus; Echard; Hooke.

[75] Niebuhr.

[76] Livy, i. 22.

[77] Dion. Hal., iii. 150.

[78] *Ibid.*; Florus; Livy; Echard; Hooke.

[79] Livy.

[80] Niebuhr supposes that these champions really represent the three tribes into which the people of Rome and Alba were divided, [Niebuhr, History of Rome, 298,] a far more probable conclusion than that the rival cities each possessed three individuals so distinguished. Nor indeed would they have entrusted to persons of feebler growth and mould a combat that required not only personal prowess, but personal strength.

[81] Livy; Dion. Hal.; Florus.

[82] Livy, i. 25.

[83] *Ibid.*, i. 24.

[84] *Ibid.*; Florus; Dion. Hal.; Hooke; Echard.

[85] Livy, i.; Echard; Florus; Hooke.

[86] Capitoline Marbles; Echard.

[87] Livy, i. 27.

[88] *Ibid.*; Florus; Echard; Hooke.

[89] Livy, i. 30; Florus, i. 3.

[90] Livy.

[91] Livy; Florus. This part of Roman history has been considered doubtful by modern writers, and Niebuhr has made strong objections to the struggle, the combat, and the fall of Alba Longa; yet the spot affords proof that this city had a geographical existence; and, since we have no other account of its destruction, it seems more prudent to adopt that given us by the Roman annals. The only thing in the narrative which may be questioned is the treachery of Fuffetius, since that part of the history rests solely upon the authority of his enemies; still, his conduct agrees very well with the character of the age, for such actions as are imputed to him were only considered base when they were unsuccessful.

[92] Livy; Capitoline Marbles; Echard; Hooke.

[93] Livy, i. 31; Echard; Capitoline Marbles.

[94] Livy; Dion. Hal.; Echard; Niebuhr, History of Rome, vol. i. p. 301. Modern science may afford some clue to this extraordinary story, and pronounce that the result of the mysterious rites in which Tullus made such a fatal mistake, was no other than what has occurred several times in the last

century—that in drawing the electric fluid from the cloud, he had not guarded his own person or those of his own family, who probably surrounded the altar, from the flash. This, however, is not the only account left us of the fate of Tullus Hostilius, some authors affirming that he was slain at the altar at which he was sacrificing, by his successor, Ancus Marcius; others, that Ancus destroyed his sovereign by setting fire to his house, and that the family of Hostilius perished in the same conflagration. [Pliny.] Dionysius of Halicarnassus imputes the death of this king to a thunderbolt, which, falling upon his palace, consumed him and his whole family. [Dion. Hal.]

[95] Echard.

[96] Cicero De Republicâ, ii. 18; Livy, i. 33; Echard.

[97] Niebuhr, vol. i. p. 355.

[98] Echard.

[99] *Ibid.*

[100] Echard.

[101] Livy, i. 33; Cicero, De Republicâ, ii. 18.

[102] Niebuhr; Echard; Hooke; Florus; Cicero.

[103] Niebuhr, History of Rome, vol. i. p. 303.

[104] *Ibid.*: Livy, i. 33; Echard; Florus.

[105] Lucretius; Ennius; Zonaras; Niebuhr, History of Rome, i. p. 301; Livy, i. 32; Dion. Hal., iii. 36.

[106] Cicero, De Republicâ, i. 19; Livy, i. 34; Dion. Hal., iii. 44-48.

[107] Livy, i. 34.

[108] Livy; Cicero; Dion. Hal.

[109] Florus; Livy.

[110] Echard.

[111] Appendix. (p. 28)

[112] Florus, i. 5; Seneca; Livy.

[113] There appears nothing incredible in the account given of the origin of Tarquinius Priscus; and Polybius, a learned Greek, would undoubtedly have started some objections to the Corinthian ancestry of this prince, if he had deemed the exile of Damaratus irreconcilable with the annals of Corinth. Niebuhr is inclined to believe that an Etrurian sovereign conquered Rome, and gave Tuscan names to the tribes, Tuscan rites to religion, and Tuscan civilisation to the city he made the capital of his dominions. [Niebuhr, History of Rome.] This is conjecture; nor need we assign a better reason than that the

son of an Etrurian mother might adopt the customs of her country, even if Tarquinii were indeed a Latin town.

[114] Niebuhr.

[115] St. Paul, in his noblest Epistle, censures the Romans more than any other people for their departure into idolatry; which evidently alludes to this time of comparative light.

[116] Livy, i. 35-38; Hooke; Echard; Dion. Hal. iii. p. 187.

[117] Florus, i. 5.

[118] Livy, Epit.; Echard.

[119] Capitoline Marbles.

[120] The Sabine wars make it apparent that the former union between Rome and Sabinia only related to the tribes from which the virgins had been stolen.

[121] Dion. Hal., iii. p. 187.

[122] *Ibid.*, p. 195.; Florus; Sallust, in Cat.

[123] Florus; Livy; Echard; Hooke.

[124] His conquests over Sabinia, Etruria, and Latium, are recorded by Florus; "but," observes Niebuhr, "his absolute sovereignty over these countries is not mentioned by any other historian. To the Sabine War, the vow of the Capitol, and the introduction of the ornaments afterwards proper to boys of noble birth, are referred. The king's son, a youth of fourteen, received from his father a golden ball and a purple-bordered robe, as a reward for having killed a foe." The wars waged by Tarquinius Priscus with Sabinia and Latium are mentioned in the Epitome of Livy, in which he is said to have conquered the Latins.

[125] Livy, iii. 8-35; Dionysius, iii. 47, 48.

[126] "In the valley thus gained between the ancient town of Rome and the Tarpeian Hill, he allotted a space for a market, and for the meetings of the people, built porticoes around it, and gave ground to such as wished to set up booths and shops there. Between the Palatine and the Aventine the meadow redeemed from the water was levelled, and converted into a race-course; every curia had a place here assigned for it, where the senators and knights erected scaffolds to view the games from, and where they will also have made room for their clients. He surrounded the city with a wall of hewn stone, after the Etruscan manner, or at least made preparations for it." [Niebuhr, History of Rome, i. 308, 9.]

[127] Appendix. (p. 32)

[128] Livy; Dion. Hal.

[129] Niebuhr, History of Rome, i. 309-10.

[1130] *Ibid.*; Dion, Hal., vii. 72.

[1131] Niebuhr, History of Rome, i. 309-10.

[1132] Livy; Echard; Florus.

[1133] Echard, History of Rome, i. 38; Livy.

[1134] Whether the son of this king was the husband of that Caia Cecilia whose amiable temper, domestic virtues, and skill in spinning, made her afterwards recommended as a model to the Roman brides, is uncertain; but to wish the young spouse the good fortune in wedlock of this lady, and to charge her to practise the same skill in that useful and industrial art, became a part of the Roman marriage ritual. Tanaquil, the wife of Tarquin, survived her husband, whom she had accompanied from Tarquinii to Rome, and therefore must not be confounded with this Caia Cecilia, who most likely was his daughter-in-law. Nor does the fact that she lived fifty years with her own husband, Tarquinius, at all render the supposition unlikely, as her father-in-law was eighty years of age when he was slain by the Marcii, and the Roman ladies were married very early. Echard, and some other historians, have stated that Tarquinius Priscus left only grandsons, his son having died before him.

[1135] Dion. Hal., iv. 13.

[1136] Cicero, De Republicâ, ii. p. 1; Juvenal; Livy.

[1137] Livy, Epit.; Florus.

[1138] Niebuhr, History of Rome, vol i. p. 327; Gruter, DII.

[1139] Gruter, DII.; Niebuhr, History of Rome, i. p. 327.

[1140] Livy; Florus.

[1141] Livy, i. 40.

[1142] Dion. Hal., xiii. 14, 15.

[1143] Montesquieu, Décadence, cap. i. p. 4.

[1144] Appendix. (p. 38)

[1145] Dionysius; Livy.

[1146] *Ibid.*; *Ibid.*

[1147] Livy; Florus; Echard; Hooke.

[1148] Appendix. (p. 39)

[1149] Echard; Sallust; Livy.

[1150] Sallust; Livy.

[1151] Hooke; Echard; Dion. Hal., iv. 206.

[1152] Appendix. (p. 39)

[153] Echard.

[154] Niebuhr, History of Rome, ii. p. 249.

[155] Livy, i. 43.

[156] *Ibid.*

[157] Echard.

[158] Tacitus, Annal.

[159] Livy; Sallust; Florus.

[160] Juvenal, Satir.

[161] Niebuhr.

[162] Niebuhr, History of Rome, i. 211.; Festus, v. Procrum and pro Censor.

[163] Niebuhr, History of Rome; Dion. Hal., iii. 36.

[164] Livy, i. 44.

[165] Hooke; Echard; Livy, i. 46; Florus; Dion. Hal., iv. 38.

[166] Dion. Hal., p. 240.

[167] *Ibid.*, 241.

[168] *Ibid.*, iv., 38; Livy, i. 47 and 48.

[169] Dion. Hal., iv. 38.

[170] Livy; Florus; Dion. Hal.; Echard.

[171] Livy, i. 48.

[172] Livy; Dion. Hal.; Florus.

[173] Livy; Dion. Hal.; Florus.

[174] Livy.

[175] Livy, i. 48.

[176] Niebuhr; Nonius on Plebites; Cassius Hemina.

[177] Livy; Florus; Sallust.

[178] Capitoline Marbles; Florus; Livy; Echard; Dion. Hal., iv. 49.

[179] Echard; Arnold; Livy, i. 53-4.

[180] Echard; Livy, i.

[181] Dion., iv.

[182] Niebuhr, History of Rome.

[183] Appendix. (p. 47)

[184] Echard; Florus; Hooke; Justin, xviii. 5.

[185] Cassius Hemina, from Servius, lib. xii. 403; Arnold, History of Rome, vol. i. p. 48.

[186] Echard.

[187] Livy.

[188] "The Sibylline Books, from the custom of their guardian duumvirs, having two Greek interpreters, or servi publici, attached to their office, for the purpose of explaining the meaning of any difficult passages, amounts, it is thought, to a direct testimony that these oracles were written in Greek; and," Niebuhr supposes, "that every Greek city had its collection of such prophecies; and it certainly was in Greece that Rome sought to obtain the restoration of these mysterious books, by collecting what was extant in that country. They are supposed to have been written in Greek hexameters, upon palm leaves, partly in verses, partly in hieroglyphs. Such is the account of these mystic books, given by the learned Varro, after their destruction in the wars of Sylla, when their guardians were no longer forbidden to communicate their form to the public." [Niebuhr, History of Rome.]

[189] Josephus, Antiquities of the Jews.

[190] Niebuhr, History of Rome; Dion. Hal., iv. 42; Val. Maximus, i. 13.

[191] Echard.

[192] The name of Brutus in Oscan signified a "runaway slave," and this surname Niebuhr considers may have originated the idea that he feigned madness, or idiotcy; but a different signification has been given it in Latin. There certainly is something in his character which resembles that of persons occasionally subject to mental malady, and we know that several of the greatest men of ancient and modern times have been thus afflicted.

[193] Arnold; Livy.

[194] Livy, i. 56.

[195] Livy.

[196] Livy; Arnold; Hooke.

[197] Livy, i. 57; Niebuhr, History of Rome, i. 452.

[198] Livy, i. 57.

[199] Livy, book i. 56.

[200] *Ibid.*, i. 58.

[201] *Ibid.*

[202] Livy, i. 58.

[203] Livilla was thus given up to her mother-in-law, Antonia, by Tiberius, and Pomponia Graecina was resigned to the judgment of her husband respecting her departure from the idolatrous ritual of Rome, who called a family council, composed of the relatives of both, by whom the lady was acquitted.

[204] Livy, i. 58.

[205] *Ibid.*

[206] Livy, i. 59; Florus; Dion. Hal., 265.

[207] *Ibid.*; *Ibid.*; *Ibid.*

[208] Niebuhr, History of Rome, vol. i. p. 452.; Pomponius, i. 2; De Origine Juris.

[209] *Ibid.*

[210] Livy, i. 59.

[211] *Ibid.*

[212] Livy, i. 59; Plutarch.

[213] Livy.

[214] *Ibid.*

[215] The self-destruction of Lucretia, which produced the change in the government, rather deserves our pity than demands our praise. It had its origin in a false love of glory, and was more the offspring of weakness than strength of mind. Suicide is always an act of cowardice, even when exemplified by a Lucretia or a Cato. To endure injury, and meet adversity with firmness, denotes true heroism; to fly from them is weakness and timidity. The love of glory was the leading principle that had been inculcated in the Roman lady; this was the basis of the virtue of heathenism, and the unfortunate Lucretia knew no higher standard; yet her tragical and affecting story has claimed and won the sympathy of every reader from age to age, though it ought not to be considered as a justifiable precedent for suicide.

[216] Livy; Arnold's Rome.

[217] Montesquieu, La Décadence de l'Empire Romain.

[218] Livy, i. 60.

[219] Arnold; Livy.

[220] Livy.

[221] *Ibid.*, i. 60.

[222] Dion. Hal. v. Spirit of the Laws, book xi. cap. 13.

[223] Arnold; Livy, i. 59.

[224] Montesquieu, Spirit of the Laws.

[225] *Ibid.*

[226] Montesquieu, Spirit of the Laws.

[227] Festus, v. Procrum and Pro Censor.

[228] Tertullian, in Apology.

[229] Montesquieu, Spirit of the Laws.

[230] *Ibid.*

CHAPTER II.

SECOND ERA—ROME REPUBLICAN.

A.U.C. 245-295. B.C. 509-459.

Embassy from Tarquinius.—Conspiracy to restore him discovered.—Judgment of Brutus on his sons.—Expulsion of Collatinus.—War with Veii and Tarquinii.—Death of Brutus.—Publius Valerius displeases the people.—His surname.—Dedication of the Capitol.—Siege of Rome.—Caius Mucius Scævola attempts the life of Porsenna.—Generous behaviour of Porsenna.—Roman hostages.—Story of Clœlia.—Historical mistakes.—Rome subject to Porsenna.—Kindness of the Romans to his vanquished army.—Restoration of the hostages.—League formed against Rome.—Attus Clausus becomes a Roman citizen.—Death of Poplicola.—Spurius Cassius defeats the Sabines.—Conspiracy to restore Tarquinius.—Distress of the Plebeians.—Law of debt and credit.—First dictatorship.—Roman and Latin wives.—Postumius made dictator.—Battle of Regillus.—Death of Sextus Tarquinius.—Resumption of the grant made to the Plebeians.—Servilius induces them to march.—His victory.—Military revolt.—Ingenious apologue.—Tribunes of the people.—Coriolanus.—Treaty between Rome and the Latin towns.—Famine.—Agrarian law of Spurius Cassius.—Cruelty of his father.—Cassius hurled from the Tarpeian rock.—Concession to the people.—The Fabian family.—Cæso Fabius.—Departure from Rome and slaughter of the Fabii.—Bold reply of Servilius.—Coriolanus and the Commons.—His exile.—Takes refuge with a foreign enemy.—Impeachment of the Consuls.—Sudden death of Genucius their accuser.—Volero Publilius.—Injustice of the Consuls.—Volero a tribune.—Appius Claudius opposes the Agrarian law.—His suicide.—Filial piety of his son.—Drawn battle.—Terentius Arsa.—His law.—Oration made by a cow.—Cæso Quinctius forfeits his bail.—Integrity of his father.—Seizure of the Capitol by Appius Herdonius.—Generous aid of the Tusculans.—Publius Valerius recovers the Capitol.—His heroic death.—Great games.—Coriolanus.—His success.—Meditated revenge.—Marches to Rome.—Obduracy.—Valeria and the Roman ladies.—Interview between Coriolanus and his mother.—Affecting speech.—Coriolanus makes a truce with the Romans.—His death.—Victory of the Romans over the Æqui and Volsci.

THE Roman Republic rushed into political existence without any safeguard for its internal freedom. The people, in expelling one tyrannical dynasty from the throne, had left themselves at the mercy of an aristocracy more powerful than the hated house of Tarquinius. An aristocracy, which is the natural support of a free monarchical government, is an anomaly in a popular one; but the Roman Commons, who had acted from the impulse of feeling, did not discern the chains with which their rash precipitation had left them still burdened. The second era of Rome dawned therefore with less political advantages than those her citizens had enjoyed during the continuance of her regal state. B.C. 509. Instead of a king, Rome had now at its head two Consuls[1] or chief magistrates, annually chosen. The restoration of some of the laws of Servius satisfied the people, who were again allowed the privilege of choosing their own judges for the decision of all private causes unconnected with the state. They also enjoyed the right of convoking meetings in the town or country, and of offering their sacrifices in their own tribes and districts.[2] Some show of regard to the public liberty was displayed in the limitation annexed to the exercise of the consular authority, which was not to be in the hands of both the consuls at the same time, lest the Romans should see themselves governed by two sovereigns at once. These elective magistrates were to rule alternately from month to month, the lictors with their rods and axes being attendant alone upon the person of that consul who then held the supreme power.[3] This regulation, however, was rather the offspring of patrician jealousy than the emanation of a purely patriotic principle. It concerned the plebeians very little, since the nobles had engrossed to themselves all power, sacred, political, civil, and military.[4] They might fear each other, but had no reason then to dread the people, whom they had deceived. A reaction would come indeed, but that reaction they neither foresaw nor feared. Livy has given the outlines of a counter-revolution; but that abortive attempt, closed by a tragedy, did not originate from the people, but with the families of the consuls themselves. The account transmitted by the Roman historian has been doubted, because it has come down to our times in a poetical form; but if the Romans were sufficiently civilised to write heroic ballads, it is by no means certain they were capable of inventing the subjects to which they gave a metrical arrangement. The conspiracy now about to be related has always been considered a part of Roman history, and the only question that seems to demand discussion relates to the guilt or innocence of the accused parties, not to their accusation or execution. It appears that Tarquinius made some attempt to conciliate his former subjects by means of an Etruscan embassy, his envoys making use of great promises of amendment on his part if the people would permit him to resume his regal functions.[5] This proposal meeting with no encouragement, he limited his next demand to the restitution of his family possessions.[6] The consul Collatinus was inclined to grant the request of his former sovereign;[7] he even opposed his colleague, Junius Brutus, and obtained a decree for their restoration in the senate, and also by one vote in the Comitia of the people.[8] This promised restitution was probably designed to conciliate the Etruscan states, whose protection of the exiled king naturally alarmed the new-born republic; but the prolonged stay of the ambassadors gave some cause of suspicion, that the recovery of his goods was not the particular object of Tarquinius in sending the embassy to Rome.[9] While the regal effects were packing, for their removal from Rome, a slave named Vindicius, belonging to the household of the Aquillii, a powerful family of Rome, related to both consuls and also to the exiled sovereign himself, gave notice of a conspiracy among the young nobility to restore Tarquinius. In making known this plot, Vindicius denounced to Publius Valerius the sons of his master Aquillius, and those of the consul Junius Brutus.[10] This accusation, whether true or false, caused a domestic tragedy in the houses of the two consular magistrates who governed Rome; for the Aquillii were the children of the sister of Collatinus, while the Vitellii, who were likewise implicated in the conspiracy, stood in the same degree of relationship to Brutus, their mother Vitellia being his own sister.[11]

According to the statement of Vindicius, the young conspirators had bound themselves by fearful oaths to kill the consuls and restore Tarquinius, having touched the entrails and drunk the blood of a murdered man to ratify their unlawful compact. The meetings held for this treasonable object, he said, took place at the house of the Aquillii, adding "that, happening to be in the room where B.C. 509. the last was held, he had concealed himself upon hearing the approaching footsteps of the traitors, and had thus become accidentally privy to their design."[12] Valerius immediately shut up the slave Vindicius in his own house, a necessary precaution, since the vengeance of his master would have occasioned his instant destruction should he fall into his hands.[13] He then invested the house of the Aquillii, from whence he took all the conspirators, and with them the treasonable correspondence with Tarquinius and the ambassadors, upon which he rested the proof of their guilt. Some tumult was made in the Forum before the arrival of the consuls, who, ascending their tribunals in haste, proceeded to examine a matter that so intimately concerned the dignity of their station and the honour of their families.[14] The young sons of Brutus were then arraigned before their own father's tribunal, and the slave Vindicius was brought as a witness against them. The letters they had written to Tarquin were also produced, and they were ordered to make their defence. They only answered the accusation by their tears.[15] "Titus and Tiberius," demanded the stern consul, "what have you to offer in your defence?" The tears and agitation of the accused, the natural results alike of conscious guilt, or of the terrible circumstances in which they were placed, were still, as before, their only reply. Thrice were they called upon to plead, and thrice their silence left them without defence.[16] Collatinus wept—even the people were touched with pity, and a distinct murmur reached the tribunal of the unhappy father, as if to soften the dreaded sentence. "Banish them, banish them,"[17] was the suggestion of all. The people, awed and trembling, awaited the decision of the consul. Valerius, too, was silent, and made no attempt to steel the public mind against the compassion they felt for the young criminals. The judge—the father, then rose up, and with a firm voice pronounced the sentence of death upon his sons in these words: "Lictors, I deliver them over to you, the rest is your part."[18] A cry of horror burst from the lips of the assembled multitude, but neither this public demonstration of feeling nor the passionate entreaties of the youthful criminals, who called upon their father to save them, could change the iron determination of the inflexible judge. From his lofty station he beheld his sons' bodies torn by the torturing and dishonouring scourge; he saw their heads stricken off, and exposed by the lictors to the gaze of the people, without a tear or even the least change of countenance;[19] and only descended from the tribunal when his severe trial was over, and his sons were no more. The people, nevertheless, discovered beneath that stern exterior the suppressed grief of the parent, and regarded with wonder and admiration the consul who had loved justice more than his children, not sparing his own blood when it had rebelled against his country.[20]

Collatinus, less rigid in principle, or less credulous than his colleague, would not pronounce sentence upon his own nephews and those of Brutus. He gave the accused a day to prepare for their defence, and he ordered the slave to be restored to his master.[21] Whether this determination arose from any doubt of the sole witness of the young men's guilt, or from a desire to save them, does not appear, but it was opposed by Publius Valerius, who refused to deliver him up. The ambassadors, on account of their office, were dismissed unpunished. The slave Vindicius was given his liberty, and was rewarded[22] for his patriotism, or, possibly, his treachery. For a question may arise in these remoter times whether the accused were actually guilty of the crime for which they suffered. During the period of great popular excitement that preceded their execution, doubts did not arise in the public mind that may naturally suggest themselves to the impartial reader now. Did the slave invent the story of the conspiracy—were the letters forgeries, and Publius Valerius the instigator of a plot against the lives of these young patricians? Had any person been missing in Rome whose blood had sealed the vows of the conspirators? What interest had a slave in B.C. 509. the freedom or subjection of Rome—a slave who has no free-will, no people, no country? Nor should the tears and silence of the sons of Brutus be taken as a direct acknowledgment of guilt. The nature of the evidence against them, and the fact of their standing before the tribunal of their own father, might affect their feelings and deny them utterance. If they were of a timid temperament, the dreadful circumstances in which they were placed might have this effect. While we admire the impartial justice of the magistrate, we must condemn the pride that led the father to be present at the execution of the sentence upon his sons, to behold the agonies of those to whom he had given life. Even patriotism did not demand such a violation of the tender feelings of paternity. To weep over his children in prison, and mourn over them when dead, could not violate the ties that bound the Roman consul to his country.

If his sons were guiltless, the stern sacrifice of Brutus was made in vain, and Collatinus was wiser in his merciful intentions than the Roman father in his tremendous judgment. The example itself is without a parallel—it stands alone in its fearful grandeur. The delay of Collatinus displeased Brutus and the Roman people. The stern consul who had expected from his colleague the same inflexibility of purpose as he had displayed himself, deposed him from his office. Valerius Poplicola succeeded him in the consulate, and sentenced the Aquillii and Vitellii to death. The condemnation of his nephews was followed by the exile of Collatinus to Lavinium, where he ended his days in privacy and retirement.[23]

The possessions of Tarquinius were divided among the people, and the Campus Martius was restored to them. This celebrated field formed no part of the royal demesnes; it was the gift of the Vestal Tarratia to her fellow-citizens. The Horatian law conferred honours upon the lady for her generous grant of this plain to the public.[24] In this field the citizens found green corn growing, which they flung into the Tiber, which is said to have given rise to the island afterwards called Insula Sacra.[25]

Among much that is incredible, or at least improbable, relating to the first years of the republic, we find one authentic document copied by the historian Polybius from the brazen tablets then in existence among the archives of the Ædiles. This Greek author saw it in the obsolete language of the period, and translated a muniment that had become almost unintelligible to the Romans themselves. This document was the first treaty concluded between the republics of Rome and Carthage, and is dated the year following the expulsion of the Tarquins. From this record we are able to determine the extent of the Roman territory in the second year of the consular government.[26] "The new Roman republic actually contained the undivided possessions and acquisitions of the monarchy; Ardea, Antium, Aricia, Circeii, and Terracina, are in this treaty enumerated as subject cities included therein. The whole coast is styled Latin, the land Latium, and the range is even more extensive than from Ostia to Terracina. Even in the part not dependent upon the Romans, the Carthaginians were prohibited from making conquests or erecting forts. The Romans and their allies were inhibited from sailing into any of the harbours south of the beautiful or Hermecan Cape, which bounds on the east the Gulf of Carthage. The Carthaginians secured to the Roman merchants the same privileges as to their own. At Carthage and the Libyan coast west of the Gulf, or in Sardinia, the Romans might land for the purposes of traffic, but the sale of their goods must be made by public auction, in which case the state made itself responsible to the Roman merchant for his payment. The table contained the names of Brutus and Horatius, as the consuls by whom the treaty was concluded."[27] Although the name of one of the consuls does not coincide with that given by Livy, who assigns Valerius as the colleague of Horatius Pulvillus, there appears to be better reason for trusting the evidence of the treaty than the traditionary tables of the ancient Roman annalists.

To the first consulship of Brutus we must ascribe the assignment of farms to the plebeians, in lots containing B.C. 508. seven jugers of arable land. This is conjectured to have been the royal demesnes, which alone could have been sufficiently extensive for such a distribution, whereby "all who received an allotment were united against the old order of things."[28] Nothing was more likely to secure the fidelity of the commons of Rome to the republican government than this grant, which made the restoration of Tarquinius a measure opposed to the individual interest of every plebeian.

Tarquinius, finding all attempts to recover Rome by negotiation or treachery useless, persuaded the cities of Veii and Tarquinii to espouse his quarrel.[29] The battle between the Romans and their former king and his allies took place within the frontiers of the new republic. During the contest the consul Brutus and Aruns Tarquinius fought hand to hand, and were mutually slain. It appears that the Romans beat the Veientines, but were themselves defeated by the Tarquinians. This battle was a drawn one, the loss being nearly equal, but the Romans, having slain one man more than their enemies, claimed the victory, which they declared had been ascribed to them by a supernatural voice[30]—a political ruse, no doubt, of their leaders, to deceive the soldiers, who might have considered this sanguinary engagement a bad beginning of the war. Brutus was buried with suitable honours, Valerius himself speaking his funeral oration, this being the first occasion of the kind known in Rome.[31] The Roman matrons did honour to the avenger of Lucretia, by the long period of their mourning, which they wore for a whole year.[32] The Romans did not adopt black for this purpose, but a very dark blue.[33] Lucius Junius Brutus is generally supposed to have left no descendants;

for though the celebrated Marcus Brutus, who conspired against Cæsar, claimed his descent from this hero, it was believed that he derived his family name from Brutus, a plebeian demagogue who had thought proper to conceal his mean origin under that illustrious appellation.[34]

Publius Valerius reigned like a king after he had buried his colleague, whose vacant place he made no attempt to fill up.[35] He built a house which united the strength of a fortress to the appearance of a palace upon the Velian Hill, for so the rising ground under the Palatine Hill was then called. The situation of this mansion, which completely overlooked the Forum, displeased the Roman people, who said to one another, "Publius wishes to become a king, and is building a citadel in which he may dwell with his guards, and oppress us."[36] These words being duly reported to Valerius occasioned him to pull down his house—a measure which satisfied the citizens, who gave him permission to build one on the same scale, but at the bottom of the Velia, in which the doors opened back into the street. The sacrifice of private property made by Publius Valerius to public opinion gained him the surname of Poplicola, by which he was ever after distinguished.

Poplicola chose for his colleague in the consulship Lucretius, the father of the unfortunate wife of Collatinus, and at his death, which happened soon after his elevation, procured the election of Horatius Pulvillus. The temple of Jupiter Capitolinus was dedicated this year, for though finished by Tarquinius, it had not yet been consecrated. Poplicola was desirous of this honour. Some jealousy on the part of the senate made them nominate his colleague, Horatius Pulvillus;[37] upon which Marcus Valerius, the brother of Poplicola, disturbed the ceremony, by crying in a loud voice, "O consul, thy son lies dead in the camp." With an unmoved countenance, Horatius replied, "Then cast the body where you please, I admit not of mourning," and concluded his religious rite without noticing the evil tidings.[38] The assertion was false, and probably Horatius was assured in his own mind that it was so. Marcus Valerius, though a brave man, at least wanted the soul of honour—truth. It was during the second consulship of Poplicola that the quæstorship was instituted; two officers, called quæstors, being appointed by his advice to take care of the public money, which was laid up in the temple of Saturn. P. Veturius and M. Minucius were the first persons upon whom this important office devolved. Like all other posts of trust, the quæstorship was engrossed by the senatorial body.[39] Poplicola is said to have filled up the vacancies in the senate.[40] He made it unlawful to take any office in the state without the consent of the people, and granted to them the right of appeal from the consular power—a concession, however, rendered nugatory by several heavy fines imposed upon those who should disobey the commands of the consul.[41] Another law, which in the course of this history we shall find frequently in force, gave to any man the power of slaying, unheard and untried, that individual who should presume to arrogate to himself the supreme sovereignty of the state.[42]

B.C. 508.

The alliance between the exiled king and Porsenna, the sovereign of the Clusians, a people of Etruria, obliged Poplicola to take measures for the defence of Rome, against which that monarch immediately led a powerful and well-appointed army.[43] Poplicola was still in office, Titus Lucretius, the brother of

Lucretia, being his colleague at the time of the Clusian invasion. We again meet with a commemorative series of interesting historical ballads in Livy, derived from Fabius and other early annalists, which they took from old traditions, transmitted from the nænia sung at funerals, or the poems recited at the suppers of great men.[44] There is some reason to question the truth of many incidents recorded as fact by the Romans, but we must be careful how we reject the whole mass of evidence contained in these poetical chronicles; for though the reader must be familiar with them, it seems better to give them their usual place in history, than entirely to exclude them. According to the narrative of Livy, Clusium was one of the Etruscan states, and its king or chief, Lars Porsenna, having espoused the cause of Tarquinius, drove from Mount Janiculum the inhabitants of the Roman villages to whom that fortress had been assigned by the consuls as a place of refuge.[45] The fugitives being hotly pursued to the wooden bridge over the Tiber, the Etruscans endeavoured to win the city at that point, but were opposed by the consuls, who, in defending that important post, were both dangerously wounded and carried into the city. Horatius Cocles, Lartius, and Herminius then singly maintained this entrance to Rome by their own efforts,[46] and when two of these gallant men were disabled, Horatius faced the enemy alone, calling to his countrymen "to cut the bridge down." Nor did he quit his post till the last prop was sundered, and the bridge fell. His prayer to the river Tiber has been preserved by Livy, though, doubtless, a poetical interpolation. He is said to have gained the shore after his leap from the bridge, though not without losing an arm and an eye, besides receiving many other dangerous wounds, from the mangling swords of the disappointed Clusians.[47] The Roman champion was received with much honour by the people, who granted him a sufficient maintenance from the public demesnes to place him above want, and erected a statue of brass, in commemoration of his valour, in the Forum. Polybius declares Horatius Cocles was killed, in which he differs from the Latin legend.[48] The enraged and disappointed Etruscans changed the siege of Rome into a blockade, and Porsenna, aware that famine was wasting the beleaguered citizens,[49] offered them bread and their old sovereign, but they replied with indignation, "that starvation was less dreadful than slavery." The multitude, who suffered more than their rulers, began to waver, when, at a critical moment for the liberty of Rome, a young patrician named Caius Mucius offered to enter the hostile camp and slay Porsenna.[50] The consuls joyfully accepted a proposal deemed heroic in those unscrupulous times; and Mucius, assuming the habit of a Tuscan slave, departed on an enterprise requiring courage, presence of mind, and address.[51] The disguise adopted by the adventurer made the approach to the camp and tribunal of Porsenna no difficult matter, but the person then occupying the seat was not the king himself but his secretary, who wearing, like the master he represented, a purple robe, received in B.C. 507. his bosom the dagger designed by the Roman assassin for Porsenna. He was made prisoner at the same moment in which he discovered his mistake, and was brought before the king to answer for his crime.[52] "Execrable villain, who art thou, whence hast thou come, where are thy accomplices?" demanded the monarch.

"Caius Mucius, and a Roman," was the proud reply. "One whom Roman bravery has made capable of daring all that man can dare, and of suffering all that man can endure." So saying, with fortitude worthy of a better cause, Mucius thrust his right hand into a pan of burning coals, and held it in the flame with unshrinking firmness.

Porsenna hastily asked the reason of this strange action of the singular assassin.

"It is because I have slain another instead of thee," replied Mucius.

Porsenna was moved; he pronounced the pardon of the criminal, and extending to him the dagger with which Mucius had designed his death, "bade him depart in peace."[53]

Mucius received the weapon with his left hand (from which circumstance, it is related, he was afterwards called Scævola), and said, "I can overcome the terror of Porsenna, but not his generosity. Gratitude, O king! compels me to declare a secret that no tortures should have forced me to betray—more than three hundred valiant young men have bound themselves by oath to kill a monarch who deserves rather to be the friend of the Roman people than their foe."[54]

The great soul of Porsenna was touched; he declared himself willing to treat with the Roman senate. He sent ambassadors, confining his demands in Tarquinius's favour to the restitution of the family property of his ally, and seven small towns which had been taken by him from the Veientines.[55] The senate were inclined to accept these terms, but the commons would not listen to them. We must remember that the estates of Tarquinius had been confiscated to the public use, which accounts for their determination. At length it was agreed to refer to the decision of Porsenna, the dispute between Tarquinius and the Roman people.[56] A truce was concluded, and ten virgins of patrician families, with a like number of youths of the same rank and age, were given by the Romans as hostages to the king of Clusium.[57]

The well-known story which has found a place in the Roman annals respecting the bold achievement of Clœlia and her female companions, who, we are assured, asked permission to bathe in the Tiber, and actually swam the stream and returned to their homes, but were brought back by the consuls to the king of Clusium's camp, who laughed at the adventure, and rewarded Clœlia for her intrepidity,[58] not only involves a question respecting the possibility of the enterprise, which the strongest swimmer in our own degenerate days cannot now accomplish, but also contradicts the statement of Pliny, from whose account it appears that the Tarquins, determining to break the truce between the Romans and Clusians, set upon the hostages the moment they entered the king of Clusium's camp, and murdered them all with the exception of Valeria, who, being well mounted, fled from the general massacre to Rome.[59] If Clœlia really swam the Tiber, and regained the city, the feat was never performed before nor since. We are compelled to give up the pretty incident, and conclude that she perished in the attempt, and that Valeria remained the sole survivor of the Roman hostages. Porsenna soothed the irritated feelings of the consul by causing a statue of Valeria to be erected to her honour, which he presented to the Roman people.

This effigy, we are told, stood for many years in the Via Sacra, a monument of the courage of the consul's daughter, and the generosity of the king.

According to the account given by the Roman and Greek historians,[60] Porsenna renounced his alliance with the exiled king of Rome, and granted peace to the Romans upon honourable terms. We find, however, from Tacitus, that Rome opened her gates to him, preferring to receive B.C. 507. him as her lord paramount to admitting Tarquin as her king.[61]

Porsenna, when he broke up his camp, generously left his stores for the relief of the famishing city he had reduced to such extremity, in return for which the Romans placed his statue in the Comitium. The costly regalia he sent the republic denoted his having taken it under his protection. The gift of an ivory curule chair, a golden sceptre, a jewelled crown, and a triumphal robe, was the symbol of his power; and by the reception of them Rome virtually acknowledged his sovereignty.[62] In the after-days of the king-making republic, her tributary princes delivered up and received again at her hands the insignia of regality, as a mark of their holding their power from her.[63]

The defeat of Porsenna by the Latins and Cumæans at Aricia,[64] enabled the Romans to recover from a state of foreign subjection so humiliating to their national pride—a degradation they did not choose to perpetuate in their annals, otherwise than in a cursory manner.[65] The Romans had lost all their dominions formerly won from the Etruscans and Latins, and the number of their tribes was reduced from thirty to twenty, though the census had given the amount of men capable of bearing arms at one hundred and thirty thousand, comprehending the male population between sixty and sixteen.[66] If a false return was made, and the same expedient once more resorted to, showing a farther increase of many thousands, we may suppose that the deception was a political expedient to increase the confidence of the Roman people in their own strength. The defeated Etruscans found an asylum with the Romans, who healed the wounded and succoured the weary; which conduct pleased King Porsenna so well, that he sent back the hostages he had taken with him to Clusium.

Tarquinius finding himself at a discount at his court, retired to Tusculum, to his son-in-law, Mamilius Octavius, who ruled that small city. His sojourn at this place was followed by a combination of the thirty Latin towns in his favour. The Sabines, too, revolted, but were defeated with great loss near the Anio by the consuls, who were both honoured with a triumph. This was the first victory ever gained by the republic—the herald of the future conquest of the world.[67] Poplicola was made consul for the fourth time, Titus Lucretius being associated with him again in that office. The Sabines, caballing with Tarquinius, and conceiving a dislike to Appius or Attus Clausus, a person of high rank and great wealth, on account of his aversion to the league against Rome, resolved upon his banishment.[68] To this noble, who brought with him to Rome so many followers as to form a distinct tribe, called from him the Claudian, was granted the honours of the Roman franchise, and lands beyond the Anio, between Fidenæ and Ficulea, were given to him, he receiving twenty-five acres for his own estate.[69] The defeat of the revolted Sabines was the last public action of Poplicola's life, who expired soon B.C. 505. after his triumph. His remains were honoured with intramural interment, and his funeral expenses were paid by a grateful people.[70]

Emboldened by the death of Poplicola, the Sabines marched to Rome, and defeated the consul Postumius.[71] The consular army soon after gained a victory over the Sabines at Eretum, on which occasion the lesser triumph of an ovation[72] was only granted to Postumius, on account of his late defeat.[73] The consuls Spurius Cassius and Opiter Virginius concluded the Sabine war. Camerium, in Latium, was razed to the ground. This instance of severity did not prevent the Latin nations from combining to restore Tarquinius. A conspiracy among the slaves to seize the Capitol and burn the city, was discovered, and the conspirators were crucified. Yet who can blame the slaves, whose state was at once a blot and an anomaly in a free republic? This was a mine of mischief in Rome always ready to explode.

Tarquinius, aided by the Latins, who had reduced Fidenæ to extremity, endeavoured to effect a counter-revolution in his favour, by his promises to the slaves, debtors, and poor citizens.[74] Publius and Marcus Tarquinius, though active conspirators, were men of weak minds. They had bad dreams, and resolved to ask a soothsayer, "if the affair they had in hand would prosper." He probably suspected the reason of the inquiry, by giving them this startling reply—"Your project will end in your ruin. Disburden yourselves of a heavy load." Upon which they ran to the house of the consul, Sulpicius, and confessed the plot.[75] The consul prudently shut up his informers, and placing a guard over them, made the Senate acquainted with the conspiracy. The senate quietly dismissed the Latin ambassadors, assuring them that the Romans would neither receive back the Tarquins, nor recall their army from Fidenæ. As for the necessary steps to be taken with the foe within their gates, the senate left all to the vigilant and active Sulpicius. The consul, thus invested with full discretionary powers, sent a trusty messenger to his colleague, Mænius, to desire him to leave Fidenæ for Rome with a chosen body of soldiers, whom he was to post near the ramparts. Then he ordered the informers to gather the conspirators together in the Forum at midnight, having taken care to garrison the houses near it with the Roman knights, while the patricians and their clients secured the posts of danger. The consul Mænius arrived from Fidenæ that same night, and took up a position in the Campus Martius. When the conspirators intended to disperse at dawn, they found themselves blockaded on every side. In this hopeless situation they were tried and condemned to death by the comitia and the senate. After the sentence was given the people withdrew, and the conspirators were put to death by the soldiers. These executions were followed by expiations for having shed Roman blood, thanksgivings, and festivities. The consul Mænius was killed by a fall from his chariot, in the midst of these public rejoicings. Sulpicius quitted the consulate with a brilliant reputation. Titus Lartius took Fidenæ two years after the conspiracy.

It was during his consulship with Q. Clœlius that the contests between the patricians and plebeians first commenced;[76] contests often to be renewed, till the rival names were finally lost in the despotic sovereignty. The condition of the plebeian was extremely hard, particularly when called upon to serve as a soldier, for at that time the Roman military had no pay. In order to provide for his wants when on duty in the army, the impoverished plebeian must sell his little patrimony, or raise money, for which he paid usurious interest. Then the debtor could be sold by the creditor for several years,[77] and if several creditors claimed him, he could be disposed of for their general benefit, or even be cut in pieces, and his body divided among them. Each soldier must find his own arms, and thus the poorest were only armed with slings. No wonder Tarquinius worked upon a class who might be bettered by any change, B.C. 500. since nothing could be worse than their present condition. To have allowed them pay when on duty would have remedied the evil partly; but the senate only forbade any creditor to enforce his claim upon a debtor during the war. The people resolved upon creating a new magistrate called a Dictator, whose power, for a limited time, was to be superior to that of the consuls, who nominated him.[78] Clœlius named his colleague for this new office, and then descending from the tribunal, resigned the fasces.[79] The dictator named Cassius his general of horse. He caused a census to be taken, when it was found that Rome contained 150,700 men capable of bearing arms, out of which number he formed four armies. Titus Lartius gave a beautiful instance of generosity, when, having intercepted a body of Latin troops who were on their way to ravage the Roman lands, he succoured the sick and wounded, and dismissed the prisoners, unransomed, to their own country. A truce between Rome and the Latins followed this noble action, and Lartius, when he laid down his office at the close of the year, had the singular merit of having fulfilled its important duties without abusing its great power.

In the next consulship an agreement was made between Latium and Rome to permit the married women of either nation to return to their own countries, with their girls, before the beginning of the war.[80] All the daughters of Rome availed themselves of the privilege, and left their sons with their husbands, but only two Latin females quitted Rome for Latium. For the Roman ladies loved their country more than their husbands, and the Latins their husbands more than their country. When the truce expired, the Latins, in conjunction with the Tarquins, made preparations for war; when a second dictatorship was resolved upon, and Postumius the consul was elevated to that dignity. He named Æbutius Elva for his general of horse. The battle of Regillus silenced the claims of the Tarquins for ever.[81] In the ardour of a contest for the liberty of Rome on the one hand, and for its sovereignty on the other, the generals fought hand to hand as if in an individual quarrel. Victory, a dear and hard-bought victory, at length crowned the army of the republic,[82] and the sons of Tarquinius were slain. Sextus, the cause of the revolution, when he found the day was lost, threw himself in the midst of a squadron of Roman knights, and, fighting like a lion to the last, perished there. The claims of his family expired with Sextus Tarquinius. The Romans numbered among their dead the brave Marcus Valerius, the brother of Poplicola, and the two young sons of that illustrious Roman. The Valerii had died in their attempt to recover their uncle's body, and their fate excited great sympathy as well as admiration. Titus Herminius also fell in the defence of the republic. The dictator, Postumius, and his valiant general of horse, Æbutius, greatly distinguished themselves upon this day. Postumius took the surname of

Regillensis, from the scene of his victory.[83] The Volscians and Hernicians, two turbulent nations who were upon their way to join the Latins, offered their services to the victors. The dictator, aware of their intentions, displayed their own despatches by way of reply, upon which they broke up their camp in the night, and hastily departed. Tarquinius, throneless and sonless, wandered from city to city, till Aristodemus, tyrant of Cumæ, gave shelter to his restless head. He died at the court of this prince, after having lived upwards of ninety years.[84] Thus gloriously closed the struggle of Rome with the exiled house of Tarquinius.[85]

After the contest had been decided in the favour of the Roman republic, her patrician rulers no longer conciliated the plebeian order. They even resumed their grant of the public lands, of which they took exclusive possession.[86] The ager publicus, as we have before stated, really belonged to neither party, being in fact the property of the state, a reserve according to the constitutional laws of Rome, not to be appropriated, but let on lease, or in B.C. 496. some cases sold, for the public benefit; actual occupation in any other way being illegal, for this portion was not that from which the allotments were taken. The distress occasioned by the resumption of the grant, and the prohibition which forbade the poor plebeian to better his fortunes by trade, occasioned those intestine divisions, of which, in the consulship of Appius Claudius and P. Servilius, the Volscians took advantage to march to the gates of Rome before its divided inhabitants were aware of their approach. Both the consuls armed themselves in haste, but found, upon their mustering their troops, the call disregarded by the plebeians, who declared they might as well become slaves to a foreign enemy, as to their creditors at home. In this emergency Servilius engaged in the name of the senate that their debts should be paid. Upon the faith of this promise the plebeians joined him, the Volscians were defeated, and the insult they had offered to Rome was avenged by the capture of their own capital.[87] As the senate refused to ratify the engagement Servilius had made, he fell into disgrace with that body, who were also displeased with his having bestowed the plunder of the Volscian capital upon his soldiers without reserving any part to recruit the public treasury. For this cause he was refused the triumph his valour had merited, his own colleague, Appius Claudius, moving for his exclusion from that honour. In the comitia of the people full justice was done to Servilius, who enjoyed through their favour the triumphal entry denied him by the jealous patrician assembly. He however lost his popularity after his return from Latium, from which country he had, in conjunction with Postumius Regillensis, driven the Aruncians with great slaughter; for upon coming home he found that Appius Claudius had caused those poor debtors to be imprisoned to whom he had granted liberty upon the occasion of the Volscian invasion. Servilius, unable to redress their grievances, joined the patricians, losing thereby the esteem of one party and gaining the contempt of the other.[88]

A remarkable revolution was effected, attended by a train of singular circumstances which led to the appointment of officers whose proper business was to protect the rights of the people against the all powerful aristocracy. This struggle commenced with the sixteenth consulship; the office being then held by A. Virginius and T. Veturius—men by no means fitted for that important position at such a crisis. For the Sabines were then in open revolt, and had engaged a Roman colony at Medullia in a league with them and the Æquians; and the Volscians had sent an embassy to Rome to demand the restitution of their lands. As the danger to the State seemed pressing, the consuls were ordered to make the usual enrolments, but the people would not enlist without their debts were first paid, so the Forum was filled with noise and confusion. The senate in this emergency created a dictatorship, and though the law had provided that one of the consuls should always fill this office, the exigency of the times, in the present instance, seemed to warrant a deviation[89]—and they named Manius Valerius, a brother of the great Poplicola, a measure likely to please the people, as he was friendly to the popular party. Before his departure he induced the senate to promise some relief to the poor debtors; and upon the credit of the public faith, led his army against the Sabines, displaying in this campaign, at seventy years old, all the fire and vivacity of youth. His victory over the Sabines, and those gained by the consuls over the Æquians and Volscians, made the senate resolve to break their word to the plebeians now that the threatened danger had been removed by their efforts, and they wrote to the dictator to that effect. Scorning their double-dealing, Manius immediately created four hundred knights from those plebeians who had best deserved the honour. After which he disbanded his army and returned to Rome to induce the senate to keep their word with the people. That body treated his remonstrances with derision, upon which Manius Valerius threw up the dictatorship in disgust, and informed the soldiers why he did so.[90] The victorious soldiery immediately quitted the two consuls, and marching in good order towards Rome, took up their quarters upon Mount Sacer, a hill about three miles distance from Rome. A military revolt was a new feature B.C. 495. in the records of the Republic, and it filled the citizens with fear and apprehension. The senate sent a deputation from their own body to treat with them, but the soldiers would not receive them. This conduct was the natural consequence arising from the frequent breaches of the national faith—a faith that should never falter, that should be as fixed as the laws of Heaven itself. As the plebeians were foot soldiers they were the most important part of the Roman army; for as a military author of transcendant talent has justly observed, "whenever the world has been won—it has been won by infantry."[91] Properly speaking the Roman soldier of this period resembled the militia of modern times—his business being to defend the frontier not to attempt conquests, but he found his own provision and received no pay; his little allotment of land being the price of his services in the field. This small grant was not increased when his family became numerous; therefore we need not wonder at his debts and difficulties multiplying with his campaigns. No persons appeared as candidates at the approaching election, so serious were the apprehensions entertained by the patricians of a civil war. The senate, therefore, named Postumus Cominius and Spurius Cassius for the consulate—two men esteemed by the Roman people, and likely to conciliate them at this crisis. It will be impossible to enter into the particulars of the revolt, or relate those debates in the senate where the unbending pride of Appius Claudius was opposed by a good and great man, Titus Lartius, who strove to give redress to the poor debtors without ruining their creditors,—because the limits of this History will not admit of it, though well worthy the attention of the reader. The deliberations ended in a new deputation from the senate, composed of Valerius (the late dictator), Menenius Agrippa, and Titus Lartius, to the camp.

They found Licinius, the leader of the revolt, ably supported by a plebeian orator, called Lucius Junius, who had assumed the name of Brutus to give his harangues more weight with the people. He was averse to any compromise, but his bold speech was answered very wisely by Menenius Agrippa in the following apologue which, though well known, must find its natural place here.[92]

"The members of the body once mutinied," said he, "against the belly, and accused it of lying idle and useless while they were all labouring and toiling to satisfy its appetites, but the belly only laughed at their simplicity, who knew not that though it received all the nourishment into itself, it prepared and distributed it again to all parts of the body. Just so, my fellow-citizens, stands the case between the senate and you. For necessary counsels and acts of government are productive of advantage to you all, and distribute their salutary influence amongst the whole people." The wisdom of Menenius Agrippa made a deeper impression upon the mutinous soldiery than the fiery oration of Brutus. It has since had the honour of being quoted by St. Paul in the 12th chapter of 1st of Corinthians, who has enlarged upon it for the benefit of his early converts to Christianity.

The senate agreed to make some concessions to the distressed plebeians, who, if insolvent, were neither to be enslaved nor imprisoned. The prudent and virtuous among them were to have their debts paid by the State, if they had been incurred in the service of the country. This privilege was not to be extended to the idle and improvident. Two magistrates, called tribunes of the people, were to be chosen from among the plebeians, to examine their affairs and redress their wrongs.[93] These magistrates were to be considered sacred both in their persons and goods; and no person was to strike or wound them under penalty of loss of life and confiscation of goods. They were to be assisted by two officers, also taken from the plebeians, called ædiles of the people. The soldiers were satisfied with these concessions: they laid down their arms, and erected a temple upon the spot, which they dedicated to Jupiter the Terrible; and, having offered their sacrifices to this divinity, entered Rome in peace. This was the first concession wrung from the aristocracy by the rising democracy of Rome, and there is reason to believe that any refusal on the part of the senate would have led to the abandonment of the city by the oppressed class. The demand of payment of debts may seem startling to modern ears, but the reader must consider that the private debts of the plebeians B.C. 493. originated in their public service for the State, and that the wars constantly maintained by the Republic made the impoverished citizen a ruined man; therefore such a precedent cannot be quoted in modern times with any propriety, unless the same state of things that led to it exists. The proper business of the tribunes was to protect the tribes from the aggression of the dominant aristocracy, and to annul any unjust sentence against the people though pronounced by the consuls themselves.[94] Niebuhr declares "that their office, upon its first institution, principally related to the regulation of landed property."[95] They were called tribuni or tribe-masters, and were chosen annually by the centuries; their power extended over the whole commonwealth,[96] and was as vast as the necessity in which it had originated. If the tribunitial office had never been used by factious and ambitious men for evil purposes, it would have been a noble and efficacious remedy for the defects existing in the Roman Constitution. Menenius Agrippa died this year very poor, and was buried at the expense of the senate. The plebeians, who had collected a sum for his funeral, gave it to the children of the impoverished patrician, that they might learn to be virtuous.[97]

The Roman histories place the taking of Corioli in the next year.[98] In the war maintained by the Romans against the Volscians and Antiatans, the consul Cominius was materially assisted by a young patrician named Caius Marcius. This war is said to have immediately followed the revolt of the Roman army, which led to the institution of the tribunitial magistracy.[99] The storming of Corioli, which gained Marcius the name of Coriolanus, was succeeded by a second exploit which secured to his commander the victory over the Antiatans. The grateful consul gave his lieutenant a fine horse and offered him the tenth part of the spoil. The booty was declined by the hero, who asked for the freedom of a captive Volscian, in whom he recognised an old friend of his family.[100] Corioli was probably ceded to the Latins, from whom, perhaps, the Volscians had taken it. In the league made in this year, it is numbered among the Latin towns that made peace with Rome, the record of which was still extant on a brazen pillar in the time of Cicero, with the name of Spurius Cassius the consul.[101]

In the next year a famine in Rome happened, and that memorable quarrel between Coriolanus and the people which led to his exile, is said to have taken place by the ancient historians; but Rome was often visited with the calamity of death, and we may readily imagine, that in the course of thirty years a city which, at the census this year, displayed on its list one hundred and ten thousand men, might often experience a repetition of that misfortune. Indeed, the amount of the population had decreased since the last estimate, by disease and want—unless we suppose that a false return was formerly made. Rome, environed by hostile nations, without commerce or lands sufficient to feed her population, often endured great privation. The unpopularity of Coriolanus might here commence, but the events themselves that led to his exile will be given in their proper place.

In his third consulship, Spurius Cassius concluded a league with the cities of the Hernicans, upon the same plan as his celebrated treaty with the Latins.[102] His proposal of the agrarian law,[103] and the fatal consequences to which that act of pure and disinterested patriotism conduced, have immortalised the memory of a great man who better deserved to be held in reverence by his countrymen than the assassin of Julius Cæsar, who bore the same family name. It seems that the encroachments of the patricians upon the public land, from which they chiefly derived their estates, increased so much that Cassius, in order to put a stop to the evil, proposed the division of a part among the poor, letting the remainder at the easy rate of paying the tenth of the produce into the public treasury, the sums to be applied to the B.C. 486. payment of the plebeians while serving in the field as soldiers. His colleague Proculus Virginius, who furiously opposed these measures, though founded on justice and humanity, placed himself at the head of a party, who saw limits put to their robbery by a noble-minded individual of their own order. His character stood too high for any charge founded on truth to reach, but no man can be above false accusation and envy. His treaties with cities once subject to Rome were styled disgraceful by the patricians who, unaccustomed to peace, considered no advantage valuable that was not won by the sword. His enemies did not make any attempt against the life of the obnoxious consul till he was out of office, and they could hunt him down without danger to themselves, upon an accusation which subjected any Roman convicted of aspiring to the throne of Rome to the punishment awarded to the parricide. The consuls Quintus Fabius and Servius Cornelius scarcely entered upon their office before articles of impeachment were exhibited against their predecessor by the quæstors Cæso Fabius and Lucius Valerius. The charge alienated from Cassius the affections of the popular party: that it had such an effect must be referred to some vague idea of the resumption by the sovereign of the seven jugers of land per man, formerly distributed among the commons by Brutus, for they had been long enough under the consular government to have discovered that the aristocracy were worse masters than Tarquinius. The prosecutors of Cassius dared not mention to the commons the agrarian law—the true cause of their hatred to the idol of the people. In accusing him of taking bribes from the Latin and Hernican nations to raise them to the privileges of Roman citizens, they offended the pride of the commons, while in charging him with aspiring to the sovereignty, they enlisted their self-interest against him. So cruel and unnatural is party-spirit, that the aged father of Spurius Cassius is said to have been the man who fixed the charge of treason upon his son.[104] The accounts respecting his death vary. According to some authors, he was hurled from the Tarpeian rock by the plebeians by whom he had been once adored, while others say he was, like the sons of Brutus, scourged and beheaded, after which his house was razed to the ground.[105] This illustrious patriot had been three times consul, but neither his dignity of station, former estimation, nor the tears and entreaties of his sons, could soften the severity of a sentence that rendered the popular idol a popular victim. Livy, who wrote in a period when liberty was no more, speaks of him as of a criminal justly condemned,[106] but posterity has done him justice, and ranked his bright name among the purest patriots of antiquity.[107] Cæso Fabius, stained with the murder of Cassius, succeeded to the fasces; his colleague, Lucius Æmilius, was defeated in battle by the Volscians; but his ill-success being imputed to the misconduct of Opimia, a vestal, that unfortunate priestess was buried alive.[108] The plebeian party soon regretted their champion Spurius Cassius. They refused to serve in the wars of the republic, whereupon the consuls caused their cottages to be destroyed, and their fruit-trees to be cut down.[109] These oppressive measures led to a reaction. The following year Caius Mænius interposed his power as tribune of the people, to protect the estates and persons of those who refused to enlist. He was baffled, by the consuls forming their musters without the gates, beyond which the tribunitial power did not extend. Condemned to struggle for their actual existence, the commons insisted upon choosing in their centuries one of the consular magistrates—a privilege granted them, though their choice was limited, of course, to a man of the patrician order.

This adjustment between the two parties did not take place without fierce contentions, and an inter-rex was called in to quiet the dissensions. A. Sempronius Atratinus was the person who held that dignity till the consular dispute was decided. The commons chose C. Julius Julus, but a Fabius was elected by the aristocracy, for one or other of that powerful family was always in office at this peculiar period of Roman history. The plebeian party were greatly elated with the small advantage they had gained; they wished to put in force the agrarian law which Cassius had carried, to his own destruction, and they determined to elect no patrician who was unfavourable B.C. 479. to a measure of such vital importance to them. The following year Spurius Furius was the choice of the people: Cæso Fabius again of the patrician party. The plebeians cheerfully followed the general they had elected, and their co-operation enabled him to make a successful campaign against the Æquians, while Fabius, being detested by his own soldiers, effected nothing against the Veientines. Marcus Fabius, the brother of the last patrician consul, was chosen by the same party, but his high spirit preserved him from the like disgrace. He, jointly with his colleague Cneius Manlius, addressed the army when about to engage the Etruscans. "You have deceived my brother," said the indignant consul, "but you cannot deceive the gods. I will not therefore give the signal for battle unless you swear to conquer or to die on the field." In reply, a valiant plebeian, raising his sword, swore by his faith that he and his fellow-soldiers would engage to do so.[110] In the hard-fought day Quintus Fabius and Manlius were killed, upon which the consul Marcus, being grieved for his brother's death, refused the triumph decreed him by the senate. Cæso Fabius who had displayed great courage in the last battle, took care also of the wounded, he and the consul Marcus receiving more invalided soldiers than any other persons in Rome. This distinguished race suddenly became extremely popular with the plebeian order, who, forgetting the murder of Cassius, united to choose Cæso for their consul. His first public act was an endeavour to put the agrarian law in operation—a measure that disgusted the party he had virtually deserted.[111] The remembrance of the dreary tragedy, in which nine patricians had perished was then recent, and might perhaps have its influence upon Cæso's mind, when he took the resolution of quitting Rome with his whole family, amounting to three hundred persons, all bearing the same patronymic and boasting the like illustrious descent. A large band of clients attended the consul, who determined to found a colony on the Cremera, a station very suitable for the defence of the frontier. On the ides of February, after sacrificing on the Quirinal Hill, the consul Cæso Fabius led forth his kindred, and, preceded by the fasces being still in office, departed through the Carmental Gate never to return.[112] "This gate is described as having two arches, one for persons quitting the city, the other for those returning to it, each party keeping to that on his right hand. For five centuries after the departure of the Fabian family no Roman would leave the city by the Carmental Gate; the day on which they quitted Rome, as well as that on which they fell at Cremera, being marked in the Roman Calendar as for ever accursed."[113] A solitary Fabius alone remained behind to perpetuate one of the noblest families of the Republic; this was the progenitor of the great Rullianus, so celebrated afterwards in the annals of Rome. Why the consul was permitted to depart we are not informed, but as he certainly built the fortress on the Cremera, the new colony might be considered beneficial by securing the border. On the eighteenth of Quinctilis (July) the fall of the Fabii took place, of which two different accounts are given. One states that the whole family were on their way to Rome unarmed, to offer up their sacrifices in the chapel of their house, when they were suddenly set upon by an Etruscan army, and treacherously slain by the darts of men who dared not encounter them hand to hand. That of Livy charges the Fabii with following some herds of cattle belonging to the Etruscans too far, and falling into the snare laid for them by a wily enemy. The catastrophe was the same in effect, though the cause might be different, and whether as guardians of the frontier, or the founders of a new military colony, the whole race with the exception of one person perished near Cremera. Suspicion was busy with the name of T. Menenius the consul, who, being encamped within four miles of the place, it was thought might have prevented or at least avenged this calamity. Niebuhr supposes that the Fabii fell by the hands of Romans.[114] We must remember, however, that Menenius lost his camp and a battle, and that being routed, he and his army fled to Rome in great disorder, followed by the Veientines, who pursued him to the very gates, taking possession of Mount Janiculum to the consternation of the citizens. This defeat seems to justify him from a charge so dark and B.C. 476. treasonable, since the same want of military skill that led to such a disaster might also prevent him from succouring the Fabii. The consul Horatius returned from his Volscian campaign in time to defeat the enemy at the gate Collina; but the honour of giving these intruders on their native soil a complete overthrow was reserved for the new consuls, A. Virginius and Spurius Servilius, who assured the people who were threatened with famine that they must fight or perish by dearth. A glorious victory was the result of this necessity; but the Romans had bought it with such a loss of human life, that the senate refused to grant the consuls a triumph. During this consulship Menenius was fined for his imputed desertion of the Fabian family: the sum, though little more than six pounds of British money, involved him in difficulties, and he died of grief some days after the fine had been inflicted.[115] "He had inherited," it was said, "nothing but his father's poverty."

Spurius Servilius was cited by two of the tribunes in the consulship of P. Valerius and C. Nautius, for having gained the late victory over the Etruscans at a great sacrifice of life. He had also been guilty of storming the intrenchments of the enemy's camp with a rash temerity that had led to the slaughter of many soldiers.[116] The reader will remember that Rome was exposed to the double peril of war and famine from the Etruscan army, from which this brave consul, in conjunction with Virginius, had delivered them.

To this accusation Spurius Servilius nobly replied, "If I am summoned, Romans, to give an account of the late war, I am ready to do so; but if I am already sentenced and condemned, here is my body; do with it what you please." The people, won by the fearless courage of the accused, bade him speak boldly, and certainly Servilius fully availed himself of this permission, for he not only justified his rash bravery in the defence of his country (his colleague Virginius bearing witness to its necessity, as well as imputing the victory to it,) but accused the tribunes of having hunted Menenius to death, although the very office they held was the fruit of the patriotism of Menenius Agrippa his father. He was triumphantly cleared, and the part he took in the great victory won by the consul Valerius added fresh laurels to his military renown.[117]

We find Rome visited by a grievous and devastating famine,[118] which at that time the indigent classes considered a conspiracy of the rich to starve them—a mistake common to the uneducated in every country and age during such visitations, as it seldom occurs to the mind of the populace that an affluent man does not actually consume more bread than a poor one. The tribunes of the people inflamed them by following up the erroneous idea by their seditious orations. The senate therefore called an assembly of the Commons to convince them that it was a scarcity of corn, not the machinations of the patrician order, that caused their miserable distress.

The senate also sent commissioners to Sicily to furnish the discontented and starving population with food.[119] These agents soon returned with a seasonable supply, half of which had been purchased on commission, the rest being the generous gift of the king of Syracuse, who, compassionating the state of the Roman people, sent them a quantity of wheat from his own granaries.[120] Livy does not mention the name or city of this merciful monarch; he calls him "the king of the Greeks," without any other designation.[121] The debates respecting this corn led to that breach between Coriolanus and the commons which occasioned his exile, and afterwards threatened the destruction of Rome. If we suppose this hero was above twenty when he took Corioli from the Volscians,[122] we shall find him to be about the requisite age for legally holding the fasces when he experienced that slight from the commons which, at a time of life when the judgment is generally mature, he endeavoured to revenge, on this occasion. Coriolanus who had offered himself as a candidate for the last consulship, for which he canvassed B.C. 475. before the vacancy occurred, had obtained the promises of the plebeian votes, his fine person and the exhibition of his scars, which it was then the fashion to display on such occasions, having favourably impressed the popular mind. He had just before this made an expedition against Antium with great success, and had bestowed the corn and plunder upon those who had volunteered with him, keeping nothing for himself. This probably had induced the plebeians to promise him their votes, though when the time came, they had changed their views, and he found himself deserted by all his fickle friends. This insult was fresh in his memory when the supplies of corn were brought into the city, and when it was proposed in the senate to sell the purchased grain at a low price, but to distribute the King of Syracuse's generous gift gratuitously, he made in the very hearing of the tribunes of the people an intemperate and unfeeling speech, in which he demanded great concessions from the poor citizens in return for the corn, and among other things, insisted that the tribuneship should be given up, concluding with the emphatic remark to the senate "that the seditious being now in their power, they might make their own conditions with them."[123] Before Coriolanus quitted the senate he received a summons from the tribunes to answer before the people for his insulting speech.

He returned a haughty refusal. Then the tribunes and a strong body of plebeians, attended by the ædiles, made an attempt to seize upon the person of the obnoxious patrician. They were driven back by those young senators who admired the valour of Coriolanus, and copied his faults. The Tribunes immediately sentenced the rash speaker to be hurled from the Tarpeian rock. The consul vainly endeavouring to mitigate the penalty by calling the offensive oration "a few hasty words rashly and inconsiderately spoken." Coriolanus did not choose to avail himself of the friendly offices of the consular magistrate: far from softening in his defence the meaning of his speech, he stood to his words with the daring integrity and firmness which marked his unbending character,— avowing them openly in the hearing of an offended and infuriated people.[124] An attempt was then made to carry the sentence into immediate execution, upon which the young patricians gathered round their leader and successfully defended his person, and Coriolanus with his friends withdrew in safety.

Brutus, a more politic, but not less vindictive, enemy than Licinius to Coriolanus, assured that tribune "that he had gone too far, for he had seen many among that crowd start at the idea of putting a brave man to such a disgraceful death." He therefore advised Licinius to cite Coriolanus to take his trial before the people, "but to collect their votes by tribes and not by centuries—a measure which would defeat any attempt on the part of the patricians to pervert justice." By the advice of the consul, Valerius, Coriolanus agreed to submit to this course, and a decree was obtained from the senate for that purpose.[125] When the day came the charges at first exhibited against him only included tyranny and hatred to the people.[126] Coriolanus rose with dignity to repel this sweeping charge. He recited his services at large, and opening his bosom displayed his scars, "many of which," he said, "had been gained by his endeavours to save his fellow-citizens from the swords of their foes." He called upon some of these by name to attest the truth of his assertions. The men thus cited came eagerly forward, and besought the people not to destroy their preserver, since they would rather die in his stead than aid his condemnation. These were plebeians, and the fickle crowd were moved even to tears by their appeal in Coriolanus' favour.[127] The accused took advantage of this revulsion of feeling, and once more drawing aside the folds of his robe, remarked that it was to save those worthy citizens he had risked his life; adding, "Can you, my countrymen, believe or be persuaded that an enemy of the people in a period of peace, would expose his own life to save them in a time of war." Many of the plebeians cried out in answer to this defence, "That they ought to acquit such a good citizen;" and the tribunes, fearful of this reaction, instantly exhibited another charge. Decius, one of them, undertaking to change once more the popular feeling against the accused.[128] B.C. 475. He spoke of the affair of Antium—of Coriolanus having reserved no part of the money and spoil for the public use, and of having given to the friends, who followed him, the people's due. He, Decius, called this tyranny, "People of Rome you know that by our laws this booty ought to have been sold and the money put into the hands of a quæstor, and paid into the public treasury. I call this a proof of tyranny. What was his dividing the spoil among his friends, but making himself creatures and providing himself guards at the public expense? In disposing of this booty he violated the laws: let him answer to this charge alone." To this unexpected accusation Coriolanus could not reply. His silence turned once more the current of popular feeling against him; and twelve of the twenty-one tribes, voted for his perpetual banishment. He withdrew to his house, a legally expatriated man.[129] Like many other men of stern character, the unpopular Roman, disliked and traduced abroad, was tenderly beloved at home. He had been brought up solely by his mother, Volumnia, a noble Roman matron, who had devoted her youth to the careful education of her orphan child, whose heroic qualities had excited her maternal pride as well as her affection—she lived but for her son. His filial piety for her rose to veneration. His wife, Veturia, regarded him with feelings that almost amounted to idolatry. To these domestic ties—to that beloved hearth the reported fiat of the people had carried the deepest affliction. Even the powerful mind of Volumnia sank beneath the astounding intelligence; and when Coriolanus returned to his house, he found his mother and his wife bathed in tears; he took a brief leave of his family, exhorting them to moderate their affliction, and to bear their reverses with constancy. The patricians and many of the senators attended him to the gates of the city, but he took no leave of them, considering himself deserted by his own order. Without breaking his ominous silence, he passed through the gates of Rome. It was the stillness preceding the storm.[130]

The following night the servants of Attius Tullius, while preparing the evening meal, were startled by the entrance of a man of noble presence, who, approaching the hearth, veiled his face with his mantle and seated himself upon that sacred place, silently, claiming the protection of the household-gods.[131] Tullius, summoned by his slaves, entered his house and requested his mysterious guest to unveil his face and declare the cause of his coming. The suppliant instantly displayed his features to the Volscian enemy whom he had often defeated in battle. "I am Caius Marcius," he replied, "a Roman driven into exile by my ungrateful countrymen, and I come to thy household-gods not as a suppliant for life, but for vengeance. If thy republic needs my service, it lies in their power to accept my sword and employ it against our common enemy the Romans. If not, it is at least in thine, to slay an old enemy of thy people." "Rise up, Marcius," replied Tullius, extending his right hand to the Roman exile; "you have made an inestimable gift to the republic in your person."[132] Livy adds to this reply, that Attius Tullius said to himself, "Caius who used to fight against us, is now on our side; we will make war again with the Romans;" but the Volscians were afraid. This dread on the part of the warlike people with whom the banished Coriolanus had taken refuge was the cause of the long interval that really occurred between his exile from Rome and his revengeful infraction of the frontier, which did not occur till B.C. 459, seventeen years after this period.[133]

The blockade of Veii by the consuls Manlius and Furius the following year occasioned a truce with that people for forty years. They were impeached[134] as soon as they gave up the fasces to L. Æmilius and Vopiscus Julius, for not dividing the conquered lands, such being the method adopted by the tribunes of the people, in order to carry into effect the agrarian law of Spurius Cassius. The consuls advised the aspirants to the consulship to decline an B.C. 478. honour always followed by a vexatious prosecution, and cited the banishment of Coriolanus, and the broken heart of Menenius as a warning to all ambitious patricians. Their counsel made a profound impression upon the young men of that order. Upon the day of trial Genucius, the accusing tribune, did not appear against the accused, and upon being cited, it was discovered that he had himself been summoned to a higher tribunal.[135] His sudden death—for Genucius had been found dead in his bed—alarmed his fellow tribunes, for, however sacred the privileges might be which secured their persons from public outrage, the fact showed that they might yet become victims to private revenge.[136] The warning example was not lost upon them; they became more guarded in their attacks upon the patrician body,[137] and the prosecution of Manlius and Furius was entirely dropped. Although the tribunes abandoned for a time the agrarian law, a great disturbance happened upon making the new enrolments, when a young centurion named Publilius Volero refusing to serve as a common soldier, was rescued by the people from the scourging the consuls had ordered him. A tumult followed Volero's appeal to the people, in which the consuls took refuge in the senate-house from the popular fury. As the attempt of the magistrates to flog a free citizen of Rome was an infringement of the Lex Valeria, they were unable legally to justify their attack upon Volero. He, from that moment, became a great favourite with the plebeians.[138] He did not prosecute his persecutors when he became a popular tribune and they were out of office, for he aimed at their power, not at their persons, and struck a decisive blow to that, by proposing that at the election of tribunes, the votes should be taken by tribes and not by curiæ (but in the comitia tributa, not in the comitia curiata). This occasioned great divisions in the following consulship, the people resolving to continue Volero in the tribuneship another year, to carry a measure likely to promote their interest. The senate immediately resolved to counteract Volero's measures, by nominating Appius Claudius to the new consulship, in conjunction with T. Quinctius.[139] Rome then became the theatre of a contest that threatened to end in a civil war. Volero proposed his new law respecting tribunitial election, with the amendment, that the ædiles should also be chosen by the votes of the tribes. To stop the violent opposition made by Appius Claudius, Laetorius, another tribune, ordered his viator to turn out some young patricians who supported the obnoxious consul. Claudius declared that the plebeian magistrate had no legal right to do this; that the formula "Depart, Romans, if you please," was the customary way of dismissing an assembly, and gave no power to any magistracy to expel a free Roman citizen.[140] The tribune Laetorius made no other reply than sending his viator to arrest Claudius. The proud consul ordered his lictor to arrest him, and the scene that followed would have ended in bloodshed if Quinctius, the other consul, had not pacified the people, while the friends of Claudius appeased him. The law was passed in the senate,[141] but not till the plebeians had taken possession of the Capitol, and were in open revolt. Volero, who was no match in eloquence or learning to his patrician adversary, had said the day before this contest took place, "Romans, I am not so ready at speaking as doing; come to-morrow, and I will get the law passed, or die upon the spot before you."[142] This speech was in the very best style of oratory.

The invasion of the Æquians and the Volscians called the consuls into the field. To Appius Claudius was entrusted the charge of defeating the warlike Volscians, but he was deserted in the field by his own men, and had the mortification of being forced by the pressure of the fugitives to join in the general flight. He took a fearful vengeance upon the instigators of this act of national disgrace, by scourging and beheading the guilty officers, and decimating the private soldiers; but his mind was deeply wounded; for when he was compelled to appear before his citizens as a defeated general, the defection of his troops had given him a severer punishment than that he had inflicted. Quinctius, dearly beloved by his soldiers, had driven out the Æquians without striking a blow. He brought home with him more B.C. 475. spoil than had ever before been won, and had the satisfaction of hearing his soldiers say, "That the senate had given them a father in Quinctius, but a despot to the troops of Appius."

The agrarian law and its train of disputes was again brought forward in the consulate of L. Valerius and Tib. Æmilius. It must have passed, as both the consuls favoured it, but for the vehement opposition of Appius Claudius— "Æmilius, declaring for it from revenge, because the senate had formerly refused him a triumph, and Valerius, to atone for having caused the death of Cassius, who first proposed the law."[143] Appius Claudius had braved the storm, and the popular tempest now fell upon him. He was accused of injuring the interests of the people in the senate, which was true, and of having been defeated with great slaughter in the field, which was not his own fault; his offering violence to the sacred person of a tribune forming also a part of his indictment. "At the bar of the people he maintained the same undaunted and courageous demeanour that had ever distinguished his character."[144] The plebeians astonished, and even dismayed by his intrepidity, deferred his trial to another day. Appius Claudius destroyed himself before the morning, either because he anticipated his sentence, or in reality wanted moral courage to face the people once more. His son, instead of attending his father on his trial, brought his remains into the forum, and commenced speaking his funeral oration. The tribunes interrupted him, but the people interfered, and, strange to say, heard his praises with pleasure. Perhaps the filial piety of the son found its way to the hearts of a class always more influenced by appeals addressed to its feelings than to its judgment. Appius Claudius had been premature in his act of self-destruction; it is probable that some admiration was mingled by the people even in the hatred they bore him. They attended his obsequies in crowds, but his suicidal act was concealed by his relations, because the Roman law condemned suicide, and forbade the rites of sepulture to those who committed it.

The consulate of Tiberius Æmilius and Q. Fabius threatened to revive the agrarian law dispute. However, Fabius proposed placing a Roman colony in Antium, which had been depopulated by war. The poorest Romans were unwilling to gain lands at a distance from Rome, and the commissioners were obliged to call in foreigners to carry out the measure. The former inhabitants made a vain attempt to recover their lands. A calamity more awful than war devastated the city during the consulate of P. Servilius Priscus and L. Æbutius, when the plague raged with a degree of violence hitherto unknown at Rome.

Both the consuls became its victims, and the living were unable to bury the dead.[145] At this time of national distress, the Æquians and Volscians combined to besiege Rome. The ædiles, the only public magistrates left to care for the republic, took the proper steps for defending the death-stricken metropolis.[146] All that were capable of bearing arms assumed them, and even the senators stood as sentinels upon the thinly-guarded walls. The enemy, alarmed at the pestilence, broke up the siege in haste, and retreated to Tusculum, for the conquest of Rome seemed to threaten them with certain death. Rome having lost her consuls, was governed by inter-reges till the year was out. The new consular magistrates gave the Æquians and Volscians a dreadful overthrow, and delivered the republic from their continual encroachments upon her territories.

During the absence of the consuls, Terentius Arsa endeavoured to bring about the establishment of fixed laws for the better administration of justice, from which no magistrate could deviate.[147] This wise proposition was opposed very violently in the senate by Q. Fabius. We must remember that he was nephew to those brothers who had borne the consular purple for several years in succession, and who enjoyed an absolute power from the closeness of their family union. They had all perished in war, but their love of unrestricted government had survived in this last scion of their ambitious house, who set himself against a wise and beneficial regulation that would have tended to quiet the minds of the people.

P. Volumnius and S. Sulpicius came into office when Terentius' law was again to be proposed, which he had withdrawn, through fear of ill consequences, soon after he B.C. 475. had brought it before the senate. Many portents alarmed the superstitious Romans at this period of public discord. A cow made an oration,[148] though nobody attended to it sufficiently to record whether she spoke for the new law, but as the patricians were the persons who heard her, her eloquence probably was exerted against it. The law proposed in the comitia was to this effect: "That the people should, in lawful comitia, depute ten individuals, venerable for age and prudence, whose sole ambition was true glory, to form a body of laws for the regulation of public and private affairs. That these laws, when compiled, should be proposed in an assembly of the people, and when approved and enacted by them, should be fixed up in the forum, that every man might know what were his own rights, and what the rights of the annual magistrates."[149] There is certainly only one fault in the wording of this celebrated bill, if it be proper to call it so, the omission of the senate to whose final fiat it ought to have been referred, for all men are equally interested in the administration of justice; therefore the national council was most improperly left out. S. Quinctius Cæso, one of the bravest young patrician senators, the son of that Quinctius Cincinnatus afterwards so renowned in the annals of the republic, opposed the bill with such violence, that he was marked out for a victim by the plebeian party. At their instigation, one Volscius stood forth and accused the patrician with having murdered a brother of his in a drunken frolic. He justified himself for not having brought this charge before, because it was in the time of the plague, when both the consuls lay dead. Although no witnesses were produced to speak to the fact, the populace would have slain Cæso upon the spot if the consuls had not interfered. By the intercession of Cincinnatus, the father, and Titus Quinctius, the uncle of the accused, bail was taken for the appearance of the young man at his trial on a future day.[150]

Cæso, however, considering himself prejudged, fled into Etruria, and thus forfeited his recognisances. Unfortunately for his honour, this was the first instance in which bail was offered and accepted in the annals of the republic. Quinctius Cincinnatus would not permit the sureties who had aided his son to suffer loss for him. He sold his patrimony to redeem the family honour, and retired to a poor cottage on the other side of the Tiber, cultivating for his subsistence, with his own hands, the only farm his son's breach of faith had left him.[151]

The young nobility during the consulate of C. Claudius and P. Valerius behaved very condescendingly to the plebeians, who were greatly conciliated by their obliging behaviour. The tribunes beheld this friendly feeling between the commons and nobles with great displeasure. They took some unwarrantable steps to break the amicable terms existing between them by pretending to discover a plot against the liberty of the people, of which they made Quinctius Cæso the hero; forging a letter as a proof that their assertions were based on truth. The consul Claudius by the plain questions of "Who wrote it? Where did it come from?" refuted the story, which was then treated with the contempt it deserved. But though no conspiracy at this time existed within the walls of the city, a daring plan to surprise Rome was laid by a Sabine chief named Appius Herdonius,[152] who, arming his clients and dependents, and being joined by a body of outlaws and slaves came down the Tiber in a fleet of boats and seized upon the Capitol, putting to death all within its walls, with the exception of two or three who escaped into the Forum, where they cried out "Arm! arm! the enemy are within our gates." The fact that four thousand men were in Rome, was not discovered till the day dawned, for the patricians believed that the slaves were the authors of all the confusion, tumult, and bloodshed of the night. From the height of the Capitol, Herdonius uttered these words, "Liberty to the slaves; I come to help the miserable and the oppressed, and to restore the exiles to their country. If the people of Rome will not aid me, I will call in the Æquians and Volscians to my aid."[153] The tribunes treated the threatened danger as some device to prevent the celebrated Terentilian bill from passing; they assembled the people, not for the defence of the city, but B.C. 475. for legislation. The authority of the consul, Valerius, had no weight with them, nor did the gallantry of his behaviour inspire them with any ardour. His threats of punishing them as traitors to their country if they were disobedient to his commands, and refused to arm and follow him, alone preventing them from taking advantage of the present crisis. Night found Herdonius still master of the Capitol, and at dawn the sentinels announced that a large body of men were approaching the city. The prospect of war without and within the walls increased the alarm of the patricians; a nearer approach showed the army to be friends come to aid the Romans.[154] Mamilius, the chief magistrate, and the citizens of Tusculum, hearing of the distressed situation of the Romans, had resolved to aid their ally without being summoned. They marched into the Forum, and joined Valerius, who having at length prevailed upon the plebeians to enlist, was marshalling them in order of battle when the auxiliaries arrived. He led them up to the very portico in gallant style, when he received a mortal wound and fell. His nephews died in defending him, covering with their own bodies the fallen consul, and receiving their death wounds in endeavouring to rescue him.[155] Upon Volumnius devolved the honourable task of commanding the army and recovering the remains of the consul. The Capitol was not regained till night, when the deaths of the Roman consul and that of Herdonius became known. The invaders were slaughtered without mercy, and the temple-fortress was solemnly purified. A public funeral was voted to Publius Valerius, the fund being increased by private contributions. The poor plebeians threw farthings into his house to augment the sum—a touching proof of their poverty and respect for the memory of a hero who had fallen in defending his country.[156] The generous Tusculans received the thanks of the senate and people of Rome for their valuable assistance. The late consul, Valerius, had promised the plebeians that the Terentilian bill should be passed before his consulate was over. Death had prevented him from performing his promise or breaking his word. The people called upon Claudius to clear the memory of his colleague from reproach by fulfilling the vow he had made. This the consul would not do, but he nominated L. Quinctius Cincinnatus to the vacant office, well knowing that the tribunes would scarcely gain their point with the father of the exiled Cæso. The new magistrate carried matters with a high hand, both with the senate and people. He alarmed the tribunes and commons by talking of a winter campaign; a measure that effectually kept them quiet till the end of his consulship. The senate wished to nominate him again for the office, a measure he sternly forbade as being unlawful, remarking, "That if the senate did not respect their own decrees, they need not be surprised at the disregard of the plebeians."[157] The Romans did not forget the assistance so generously afforded them by the Tusculans, for they compelled the Æquians to break up the siege of their city, who had invested it some months after the deliverance of the Capitol. The Æquians who had won the citadel were compelled to pass under the yoke, and were annihilated on their march home by the consul Fabius. The Æquians and Volscians after the invasion of their territories by two consular armies were glad to obtain from their victorious enemies a truce of ten years. We have now arrived at that part of the Roman history when the long-delayed revenge of Coriolanus visited the people who had exiled him.[158] B.C. 475. It appears that after the former expedition of Coriolanus against the Antiatans, which was of a private nature, Antium itself fell into the hands of the Romans, who carried off the inhabitants and proposed to replace them by a colony from Rome; but the poor citizens refusing to profit by the occasion, a Latin one was formed there. This year the Volscians dispersed the colony and won Antium, and hence we may date the employment of Coriolanus by that active and warlike nation, and the capture of some of those thirty Latin towns which, in B.C. 493, had made a league with the Romans. The reverses suffered by the Volscians in the following year compelled them to sue for peace, and if the accounts of the re-celebration of the great games be true, they must have occurred immediately after this new league between the Romans and the Volscians, and not in the year after the consulate of Sulpicius and Lartius, when the incident occurred which occasioned them to take place again; this was the scourging of a slave during the solemnity, which was supposed to have been displeasing to Jupiter.[159]

The great games were celebrated with much pomp, and it was during this second celebration that the machinations of Attius Tullius occasioned the new league to be broken between the Romans and his countrymen. This chief and his followers were present at the games; but before their commencement, he privately recommended the consul to dismiss his Volscian retinue before sunset, alleging, as his reason for the request, some fear on his part lest his people should fall out with the Romans as the Sabines had formerly done. The consul sent the crier round to give due notice of this unusual regulation; but the measure gave great displeasure to the Volscians, who considered it as a personal affront. Their departure in a rage was anticipated by their wily leader, who met them, on their way home over the Alban Hills, by the well-head of the water of Ferentina, a place in which the Latins had been anciently accustomed to assemble for council. He asked the reason of their sudden departure from Rome, and upon being informed, led them from the road to the grassy margin of the stream, where he inflamed their minds by an artful oration, in which he pronounced their exclusion from the city at that early hour to be equivalent to a declaration of hostility. "They have made war upon us; see to it if ye be men that they may rue their deed." The Volscians eagerly listened to his words, and all their tribes combined together to raise an army, and to choose Attius Tullius and Caius Marcius the Roman, for their leaders.[160] Such is in substance the account given by Livy of the campaign, in which Coriolanus was about to lead a hostile host against his country, no longer confining his arms to attacking her allies, from whom he had already taken Circeum, Satricum, Longulum, Polusca, and Corioli.[161] The present campaign was opened by the conquest of Lavinium; then followed the capture of Corbio, Vitellium, Trebia, Lavici, and Pedum, which last-named place closed the career of conquest ascribed to the united chiefs, and brought them in the vicinity of Rome.[162] The spot selected for their encampment was the Cluilian dyke, about four miles from the city, which having expelled one of her bravest sons many years before, beheld him return with his victorious arms and a heart filled with the burning hatred which those years of exile had only served to embitter and aggravate. While he wreaked his vengeance upon the plebeian order, to whom he ascribed his wrongs, Attius Tullius ravaged in his turn the lands of the patricians;[163] thus the whole Roman people felt the dreadful effect of the combination between the ambition of the Volscian leader and the revenge of Coriolanus. They had been visited with repeated famines and plagues; but these direful evils, and others induced by continual strife among themselves, were aggravated by the presence of an army in their territory led by a man whose courage and talents for war were employed against his native land. If he had been wronged by the Commons, we must acknowledge that his sins against them had been of a more cruel and aggravated nature; for he had tried to impose hard and illegal conditions upon them with the corn, which was a free and generous gift to the Romans from a foreign B.C. 475. power. The terror of the poor citizens, however, induced them to clamour for peace, and their cries compelled the senate to send five eminent men of their own order to propose terms to Coriolanus.

Two personal friends of Coriolanus, Minucius and Cominius, formed a part of the deputation despatched to the Volscian general.[164] They entreated him to return to Rome, where the arms of the republic should be opened to receive him as her son and citizen once more. This he haughtily declined, reciting his wrongs with terrible minuteness. On the part of the Volscians, he proposed confining Rome entirely to her ancient limits, and demanded for his adopted country the same rights and privileges the Romans had granted to the Latins: they were also required to withdraw their colonies. He gave them thirty days to consider these proposals. To his former friends his tone was less haughty. They had afforded protection to his family, and he thanked them with warmth and emotion for that proof of generous regard. It was for their sakes alone he granted a truce. The answer of the senate was dignified and concise: "Rome was not accustomed to receive laws from an enemy sword in hand. When the Volscian army was withdrawn from the vicinity of Rome, they would treat with its leader."[165] Coriolanus sternly gave them three days longer for consideration. It is probable that in granting this time, he entertained some fears for his family, or perhaps he still hesitated respecting the performance of his threatened vengeance.

No consular army ventured to meet him in the field—for his terrible renown had left him without an opponent—the consuls made active preparations for the defence of the city; the men were engaged on the ramparts; the women were at prayer in the temples. A deputation of priests was sent by the senate to Coriolanus: he received its members with respect, but gave the same reply he had already returned the senate. At this momentous crisis, while a number of noble Roman ladies were engaged in a solemn act of devotion in the temple of Jupiter Capitolinus, the idea of softening the anger of Coriolanus through the influence of his own family occurred to Valeria, a descendant of the great Poplicola. Inspired with the hope of inducing Volumnia, the mother, and Veturia, the wife of Coriolanus, to become suppliants to their son and husband, Valeria imparted her design to her companions, and proceeded with them to Volumnia's house, which was emphatically styled by its aged mistress "a house of sorrow."[166] "It is not by the sword or strength of arm that we are to prevail, for these do not belong to our sex," was the remark with which Valeria had silenced the objections raised by her friends; "let us rather engage the venerable mother of Coriolanus to intercede for our country; stern as he is, he will relent when he sees her who gave him birth a weeping suppliant at his feet." Nothing can be more beautifully and touchingly feminine than this speech, though the courage of a Roman—the lofty moral courage that marked the female character of that period was fully displayed in the noble resolution of Valeria.[167] Volumnia received the female deputation courteously, but she did not give Valeria much hope of success. No intercourse, she said, had taken place between the exile and his family since their separation. The parting words of Coriolanus seemed to have renounced them with Rome. "Mother, you have no longer a son. Your country has deprived you of the prop which should have supported your old age. Nor to you, Veturia, can Caius Marcius henceforth be a husband. Mayst thou be more fortunate with another man. My children, you have lost your father."[168] It seems strange that the wife and mother of the expatriated hero did not share his exile, but the tie which bound the Roman matron to her country was stronger than those affecting relations—a fact often attested in the annals of Rome. Volumnia, after reciting the last words of her son, assured Valeria "that he seemed to include his own family in the same vindictive hatred he felt for Rome," but she finally consented to intercede with him for her country. The Consuls accepted the offered mediation of the ladies with joy, and Volumnia and Veturia, attended by the B.C. 475. children of Coriolanus, were accompanied to his camp by the vestal virgins, and the noblest women of Rome, headed by the high-spirited Valeria, the author of the female mission.[169]

Coriolanus, from his lofty tribunal, discerned the long procession of his country-women, and rightly conjectured that his wife and mother were included in it. He armed himself to meet this unexpected trial, by concealing his emotion under the appearance of inflexibility of purpose, and resolved to receive them with indifference. He knew not his own heart; Valeria had fathomed the depth of its undying tenderness when she once more surrounded him with these holy domestic ties, and brought his noble but erring mind within their sacred influence.[170] Before his family could reach his tribunal, the stern Roman, forgetful of his iron resolution, had descended from his seat to press them in his arms with the affection due to his mother, wife, and children.[171] Volumnia repulsed his offered embrace, by asking him "whether she beheld in him an enemy or a son, and if he regarded her as his captive or his mother?" His silence emboldened her to plead for his country, she reminding him "that if she had never given him birth, Rome would have remained free from the disgrace and danger he had brought upon his native city. She was too old to bear his shame and her misery, but besought him to look upon his wife and children, whom he was dooming to death or bondage by his rash enterprise." He listened silently to these reproaches, but related what had befallen him since they parted, and the generous reception he had received from the Volscians, finally "entreating his family to remain with him." Volumnia indignantly rejected the proposition, and, falling at his feet, "bade him march forward to Rome over her prostrate form, and to consummate his fierce, ungenerous revenge by the destruction of his mother as well as his native city."[172] The tears and cries of the noble ladies, upon hearing the intrepid address of Volumnia, the caresses of his wife and children, and the suppliant posture of his revered parent, softened the soul of the apostate Roman, who suddenly uttered these pathetic words: "O mother! what hast thou done to me?" but vehemently wringing her hand as he raised her up, he said, "Mother, thine is the victory, a happy victory for Rome and thee, but shame and ruin for thy son."[173] Then falling on her neck and once more embracing her and his family, he sent them back to Rome with certain conditions, upon the performance of which he engaged to grant a truce.[174] The peace made on the part of the Volscians by Coriolanus with his own countrymen, probably confirmed them in the possession of the Latin towns, and if the Volscian chiefs stood round the tribunal and were witnesses of the affecting scene between the expatriated Roman and his family, we may suppose this truce of a year must have offered advantageous terms for them, or they would not have consented to the measure.[175] His distribution among the Volscians of the plunder gained in the expedition, was followed by his disbanding the army and returning to Antium. It appears that Attius Tullius, and the soldiers under his command, made a second inroad into Latium, but that it proved unfortunate, for the Æquians, who were in alliance with the Volscians, did not choose to obey him. A battle was the result of the dispute, in which these two predatory nations turned their arms upon each other, to the great joy of the Romans.[176] The death of Coriolanus has been variously related. Livy relates, "that he lived and died among the Volscians, and that when very old, and deprived by his banishment of the society of his wife and children, he was accustomed to say, 'that in old age, he knew the full bitterness of exile.' "[177] This account may be perfectly true, if we suppose with Niebuhr, that his murder, as described by Plutarch and Dionysius,[178] did not take place till some years after his celebrated expedition B.C. 475. against Rome.[179] His trial for an act in which filial affection had influenced him more than the interests of his adopted country, might not be instituted against the strong warrior but the feeble and aged man. The jealousy of Attius Tullius, or Tullius Aufidius, for Plutarch calls him by the latter name, might not have been able to effect the destruction of his rival at so early a period, nor is the assertion of Cicero,[180] that he killed himself, at all incompatible with that generally received, since men of rank in heathen nations considered death from their own hand, as less disgraceful than the axe of the executioner. The poetical character of this interesting portion of early Roman history has caused it to be doubted. But there is no better reason for excluding the touching history of Coriolanus than its forming a most beautiful episode in an epic poem: "The state of Latin literature does not warrant such a conclusion, for the wars of the republic, upon which their existence as a people actually depended, fixed the popular idea upon one subject—the maintenance of the state by arms—an idea not favourable to flights of imagination. If a rude epic of the kind existed at all, it was founded upon a fact. The composition of a tale at such a period involves far more difficulties than belief in a portion of history quoted by the Roman historians, the chronology of which has been misplaced."[181] The grateful senate and people of Rome commemorated the deliverance of Rome from the Volscian army by the dedication of a temple "to the Fortune of Women," of which Valeria became the priestess.[182] Tullius, according to some historians, perished in a battle fought the following year, between the Volscians, Æquians, and the Romans.[183] If this is mis-dated, either the death of Coriolanus happened in the order in which Plutarch and Dionysius placed it, immediately after his return from his expedition against Rome,[184] or some other person bearing the same name was guilty of his murder. Plutarch ascribes the death of Coriolanus to a tumult raised in the Volscian senate by Tullius Aufidius, to whom, perhaps, he ascribed, in the early part of the biography, the acts of a person whose surname resembled his prenomen.[185] National pride may, however, have given a victory to the Romans, which they did not win, that they might appear to posterity as the avenger of a man "whose worst fault had left him Roman still."

<hr size=2 width="10%" align=center>

[1] Prætors were the earliest titles of these magistrates: they were not called consuls till long afterwards.—[Echard, Rome, i. 59.]

[2] Dion. Hal., v. 2; Arnold, i. 107.

[3] *Ibid.*

[4] Montesquieu, Spirit of the Laws.

[5] Plutarch, in Poplicola.

[6] Livy, ii. 3, 4.

[7] Plutarch, in Poplicola.

[8] Livy; *Ibid.*

[9] Plutarch, in Poplicola.

[10] *Ibid.*

[11] *Ibid.*

[12] Plutarch, in Poplicola.

[13] *Ibid.*

[14] *Ibid.*

[15] Plutarch, in Poplicola; Livy, ii. 5; Juvenal.

[16] *Ibid.*

[17] Plutarch, in Poplicola.

[18] *Ibid.*

[19] Plutarch, Life of Poplicola.

[20] Livy, ii. 5.

[21] Plutarch, in Poplicola.

[22] *Ibid.*; Juvenal.

[23] Plutarch; Dion. Hal.; Livy.

[24] Niebuhr, Rome, vol. i. p. 464; Gellius, vi. 7.

[25] Plutarch; Echard.

[26] Niebuhr, Hist. Rome, vol. i. pp. 469-70; Polybius.

[27] Polybius; Niebuhr, Hist. Rome, vol. i. pp. 469-470.

[28] Pliny, xviii. 4; Columella, de Re Rust. I. iii. 10; Niebuhr, Hist. Rome, i. 464.

[29] Plutarch, in Poplicola.

[30] Livy; Val. Max.; Plutarch.

[31] Plutarch, in Poplicola.

[32] Livy; Arnold.

[33] Niebuhr.

[34] Hooke.

[35] Plutarch, in Poplicola; Livy, ii. 7.

[36] *Ibid.*; *Ibid.*

[37] Plutarch, in Poplicola; Livy, ii. 8.

[38] *Ibid.*

[39] Hooke.

[40] Plutarch, in Poplicola.

[41] Plutarch, *Ibid.*

[42] *Ibid.*; Echard, Rome, i. 65.

[43] Livy, ii. 7; Hooke; Echard.

[44] Niebuhr.

[45] Livy, ii. 10.

[46] Plutarch, in Poplicola; *Ibid.*

[47] Plutarch, in Poplicola; Dion. Hal.; Livy, ii. 10.

[48] Polybius, vi. 55.

[49] Plutarch, in Poplicola.

[50] Livy, ii. 12.

[51] Plutarch, in Poplicola.

[52] Livy; Dion. Hal.; Hooke; Plutarch, in Poplicola.

[53] *Ibid.*; *Ibid.*

[54] Plutarch, in Poplicola; Livy; Dion. Hal.

[55] *Ibid.*; Livy, ii. 13.

[56] Plutarch, in Poplicola.

[57] *Ibid.*

[58] Livy; Dion. Hal.; Plutarch, in Poplicola.

[59] Pliny, xxxiv. 13; Niebuhr, Rome, vol. i. p. 483.

[60] Plutarch, in Poplicola.

[61] Tacitus, Hist., iii. § 72.

[62] Dionysius, v.; Niebuhr, i. 482.

[63] Tacitus, in speaking of the destruction of the Capitol in the civil war that hurled Vitellius from his throne, mentions "that Porsenna, when Rome surrendered to his arms, dared not violate a temple built in ancient times, with solemn rites and religious auspices,"[A] and we find, in his Annals, the Emperor Claudius referring to the fact that this prince compelled the Romans to give him hostages.[B] Of the subjection of his countrymen Pliny gives a decided proof, when he allows "that they gave up their arms, and only used iron for their agricultural instruments."[C] If the plough-shares of the Romans were made of copper,[D] the passage may be disputed; or, at least, the word metal ought to have been substituted. The fact that the Romans ceded what they had formerly won from the Etruscans, and that, upon their compliance, Porsenna restored to them Mount Janiculum,[E] affords a strong presumption that Tacitus and Pliny were more correct in admitting that he conquered Rome, than Livy, Dionysius, and others, in making him so romantically generous; while it really appears that he pursued his private interest, instead of furthering the views of Tarquin. We need not disbelieve, however, his courtesy to the Romans, to whom he might prove a liberal lord, since his memory was always held by them in respect and reverence.

[A] Arnold, i. 127; Tacitus, Hist., iii. § 72.

[B] Annals.

[C] Pliny, xxxiv. 14.

[D] Niebuhr.

[E] Arnold, i. 127, note 3.

[64] Plutarch, in Poplicola.

[65] See Appendix. (p. 73)

[66] Arnold, Rome, i. 131.

[67] Echard; Plutarch, in Poplicola; Hooke.

[68] Livy, ii. 19; Plutarch, in Poplicola.

[69] He is styled a citizen of Regillus,[F] and by some authors his exile is stated to have been voluntary, not compulsory, originating in dislike to the enterprise in which his fellow citizens were about to engage.[G] The foreign name of this new patrician and senator was soon lost in that of Appius Claudius. This Sabine chief was the general ancestor of that great family, which, before Tiberius mounted the throne, had given fifty-five consuls to Rome.

[F] Livy, ii. 16; Dion. Hal., v. 40.

[G] Plutarch, in Poplicola.

[70] Plutarch, in Poplicola; Hooke. And see Appendix (p. 75).

[71] Dion. Hal., book v. p. 311.

[72] So called from ovis, a sheep, that animal being sacrificed instead of an ox.

[73] Pliny, xv. c. 29.

[74] Dion. Hal., v. 319.

[75] Dion. Hal., v. 321.

[76] Tacitus, Annal.

[77] Such slaves were called Nexi, in contradistinction to Servi, or perpetual slaves.

[78] Livy, ii. 18; Dion. Hal., v.

[79] Hooke styles the dictator "an absolute monarch, who possessed the power of life and death over any citizen, without appeal. He might raise or disband armies at pleasure, and could appoint a general of horse, who served under his orders, and in time of war he had no occasion to consult the senate or comitia, nor was he obliged to give any account of his administration to either of these national assemblies. He was attended by twenty-four lictors, in the same manner as the kings of Rome had formerly been."

[80] Dion. Hal., vi.

[81] Livy, ii. 20.

[82] Dion. Hal., vi.

[83] *Ibid.*

[84] Livy, ii. 21; Dion. Hal.

[85] See Appendix. (p.78)

[86] Niebuhr; Nonius, on Plebitas; Cassius Hemina.

[87] Dion. Hal., vi.

[88] Hooke.

[89] Livy, ii. 30.

[90] Dion. Hal.

[91] Napier, in Peninsular War.

[92] Plutarch, in Coriolanus; Livy, ii. 32.

[93] Dion. Hal.

[94] Arnold, Hist. Rome, i. 149.

[95] Niebuhr.

[96] Arnold.

[97] Dion. Hal., vi.

[98] See Appendix. (p. 83)

[99] Livy; Plutarch, in Coriolanus.

[100] Hooke.

[101] See Appendix. (p. 84)

[102] Arnold, Hist. Rome, i. 161.

[103] Niebuhr, ii. 188. The merit of first proposing this law has been ascribed to Sempronius Atratinus by Dionysius of Halicarnassus, who relates that the proposition met with the approbation of the Senate;[H] but Livy imputes it to Cassius (with far more probability), who certainly carried it in that assembly.[I]

[H] Dion. Hal., viii.

[I] Livy, ii, 41.

[104] Dion. Hal., viii.

[105] Dion. Hal.

[106] Livy, Epit., ii.

[107] See Appendix. (p. 85)

[108] Livy, ii. 42.

[109] Dion. Hal., viii.

[110] Dion. Hal., ix.

[111] Livy, ii. 47.

[112] Dion. Hal., ix.; Livy, ii. 48, 49.

[113] Niebuhr, Hist. Rome, ii. 195.

[114] Niebuhr, Hist. Rome, ii. 202.

[115] Livy, ii. 52.

[116] Dion. Hal., ix.

[117] Hooke.

[118] See Appendix. (p. 90)

[119] Plutarch, in Coriolanus.

[120] Dion. Hal., vii.; Hooke.

[121] Arnold.

[122] Corioli had probably been taken by the Volscians from the Latins, and upon its being won by Coriolanus, might be restored to its own people, who

were included in the Latin league concluded by Spurius Cassius, B.C. 493. Those who have objected to the manner in which ancient historians have accounted for the distinctive appellation by which Caius or Cneius Marcius is known in history, have forgotten how frequently such cessions of places are made in diplomatic arrangements.

[1123] Dion. Hal., vii.; Livy.

[1124] Plutarch, in Coriolanus; Dion. Hal., vii.

[1125] Plutarch, in Coriolanus.

[1126] Dion. Hal., vii.

[1127] *Ibid.*

[1128] Dion. Hal., vii.

[1129] Plutarch, in Coriolanus.

[1130] Dion. Hal., vii. Plutarch in Coriolanus.

[1131] Plutarch; Livy, ii.; Dion. Hal., viii.; Val. Max.

[1132] Plutarch, in Coriolanus.; Livy, ii. 18.

[1133] Niebuhr, Rome, ii. pp. 98, 99. If the computation made by Niebuhr be correct, seventeen years elapsed before the approach of Coriolanus to the gates of Rome. Between his Roman campaign and his exile many events happened of vital moment to the Commonwealth.

[1134] Livy, ii. 54.

[1135] Livy, ii. 54.

[1136] Livy.

[1137] See Appendix. (p.95)

[1138] Livy, ii. 55; Dion. Hal., ix.

[1139] Dion. Hal., ix.

[1140] Dion. Hal.

[1141] *Ibid.*

[1142] Livy, ii. 56.

[1143] Livy, ii. 61; Dion. Hal., ix.

[1144] Livy, ii. 61; Dion. Hal., ix.

[1145] Dion. Hal.; Livy.

[1146] *Ibid.*

[1147] Livy, iii. 9.

[1148] Livy, iii. 10; Dion. Hal., x.

[149] Dion. Hal., x.

[150] Livy, iii. 13; Dion. Hal., x.

[151] Livy, iii. 13; Dion. Hal., x.

[152] Livy, iii. 15.

[153] Livy, iii. 16, 17.

[154] Livy, iii. 18.

[155] This gallant defence of the dying Roman consul, P. Valerius, by his nephews, has been much admired. It has been paralleled in our own times, during the late war in the Punjab, and on the field of Jhelum. The following affecting fact appeared in the "Times," March, 1849, and by that mighty and influential organ was spread over the civilised world, to the honour of British valour and filial piety. "The 24th Regiment marched, on the 13th of January, against the Sikh army. It was unsupported, exposed to the full sweep of the Sikh batteries and to the deadly play of their destructive musketry. More than one-half the regiment went down in ten minutes; the remainder, assailed by many thousands of infantry, exposed to the batteries, and menaced by the cavalry, could no longer keep their ground. Brigadier Pennycuik had fallen, and was being carried off by two of our soldiers, who were pressed so closely by the Sikhs, that they dropped their honourable burden, and drew back. The gallant boy, the son of the noble dead, a youth of seventeen, now first aware of his misfortune, sprang forward, sword in hand, bestrode his father's still breathing body, and then fell across it a corpse." Such is the simple record of Brigadier Pennycuik and his son, given by a veteran who knew them both. May the memorial of the valour and filial piety of a British youth, cut off in his glorious early promise, find a place in our annals, as the gallantry of the two Valerii have in those of ancient Rome.

[156] Plutarch.

[157] Livy, iii. 21.

[158] See Appendix. (p. 102)

[159] See Appendix. (p. 103)

[160] Livy; Arnold's Rome.

[161] *Ibid.*

[162] Arnold; Plutarch; Vertot, Roman Republic.

[163] Dion. Hal., viii.

[164] Dion. Hal.; Plutarch.

[165] Dion. Hal., viii.; Plutarch, in Coriolanus.

[166] Plutarch, in Coriolanus.

[167] Plutarch, in Coriolanus; Dion. Hal., viii.

[168] Plutarch; Dion. Hal., viii.

[169] Plutarch, in Coriolanus.

[170] *Ibid.*

[171] *Ibid.*

[172] Dion. Hal., viii.

[173] Plutarch, in Coriolanus.

[174] *Ibid.*

[175] Arnold suggests that possibly the army of the Volscians comprised many Roman citizens; and if it were indeed so, that would give Coriolanus the power to spare Rome, and withdraw the troops from the vicinity of the place. Arnold, Rome, i. 190.

[176] Niebuhr, ii. 103; Livy.

[177] Fabius; Livy, ii. 40.

[178] Dionysius relates that the Volscians raised a tomb to the memory of their victim. Dion. Hal., viii.

[179] Plutarch, in Coriolanus; Dion. Hal.

[180] Cicero, in Lælius.

[181] See Appendix. (p. 109)

[182] Livy, ii. 40; Dion. Hal., viii.

[183] Echard's Rome, i. 95.

[184] Plutarch, in Coriolanus; Dionysius, viii.

[185] Plutarch, in Coriolanus; Dionysius, viii.

CHAPTER III.

SECOND ERA—ROME REPUBLICAN.

A.U.C. 358-400. B.C. 457-498.

Civil discord.—Insolence of Gracchus the Æquian.—Cincinnatus found at the plough.—His dictatorship.—Concessions made to the people.—Fire additional Tribunes.—The Aventine Mount granted to the Commons.—Agrarian law.—Exploits of Dentatus.— The Romans wish for laws.—Commissioners sent to Greece.—First Decemvirate.— Popularity of the Decemvirs.—Second Decemvirate.—Decemviral incapacity for war.— Murder of Dentatus.—Third Decemvirate.—Decemviri detested by the Romans.— Affecting story of Virginia.—Appeal of her father to the people.—Counter-revolution.— New laws.—Punishment of the Decemviri.—Deaths of Appius Claudius and Oppius.— Duilius and the tribunitial college.—Trebonius reforms it.—Abolition of the law forbidding the intermarriage of patricians and plebeians.—Profound peace.—Renewal of disputes.—Gallant speech of the consul Quinctius.—His victory.—Military tribuneships replace consulships.—Dishonesty of Roman arbitrators.—Censors.—Cincinnatus dictator.—Conspiracy of Mælius.—Ahala kills him.—Commended for the deed.— Cornelius Cossus kills king Tolumnius in battle.—Æmilius Mamercus fined by the censors.—Speech of Mamercus to the soldiers.—Imprudence of the consul Sempronius.—Noble speech of a captain.—Prosecution of Sempronius.—Generosity of Hortensius to the accused.—The agrarian law discussed.—Two new quæstors.— Discovery of a plot to burn Rome.—Murder of Postumius Regillensis.—Veientine war.—Pay issued to the soldiers serving in the field.—First solar eclipse recorded by the Romans.—Camillus given the conduct of the siege of Veii.—Old prediction.—Delphic oracle.—The Alban lake drained.—Marks of the work discovered.—Camillus dictator.— Takes Veii.—His prayer.—Triumphal entry with white horses and painted face.—His vow to Apollo.—His unpopularity.—Question respecting Veii.—Noble courage of the senators.—Its effect on the people.

INTERNAL dissensions always followed peace in the divided commonwealth. An invasive war seldom failed to rouse the intense nationality of the Roman people, but when the danger was past, the struggle was once more renewed between the patrician and plebeian orders, never to subside till the rising middle class had wrung its civic freedom from the aristocratic oligarchy.

The tribune Virginius again brought forward the Terentilian law, which he made a vigorous attempt to put in operation, giving, however, some weeks to the magistrates to reconsider the question.[1] While this measure was in deliberation, the Æquians and Sabines invaded the lands of the people of Lavici and Tusculum, which they plundered, finally encamping on Mount Algidus, to the great annoyance of the Romans, with whom the Lavicans and Tusculans were in alliance.[2] Here again we meet with one of the beautiful poetic lays in which ancient Rome was wont to commemorate wise counsels and heroic deeds. Of this episode of Fabius or Ennius, Livy availed himself, and the virtuous poverty of Cincinnatus has become "familiar to us as household words." The Roman deputation to the Æquians found their leader, Gracchus Clœlius,[3] encamped under the shade of an evergreen oak. To the remonstrances of the complainants he returned this insulting answer: "I am engaged with important business, and cannot hear you. Tell your message to yonder oak." To this rude speech one of the deputies made a reply full of dignified rebuke: "Yea, let this sacred tree hearken, and let the gods also incline their ears, and listen to your treacherous infraction of the peace. They will hear, and also avenge the wrong, for ye have defied alike the laws of gods and men."[4] The report of the deputies made the senate resolve upon sending a consular army into the field against the Æquians, under the command of Lucius Minucius, while Caius Nautius marched against the Sabines. Gracchus was an accomplished warrior,[5] full of stratagem and courage, quite an overmatch for his consular opponent, upon whose approach he broke up his camp on Mount Algidus, and retreated before them, followed by the Romans in pursuit, till they reached a nameless valley between lofty and precipitous hills, whose heights were immediately occupied by the Æquian army. The gorge was bare and barren, affording no grass for the support of the horses, nor corn nor edible roots for the soldiers. Five horsemen succeeded in extricating themselves from this gloomy prison, who hastened home with the disastrous tidings of the blockade of the army.[6] The report of its dangerous situation occasioned Quintus Fabius, the governor of Rome, to send for Nautius from Sabinia, and when that consul was come, the matter was laid before the senate, who with one voice declared, "We must make Lucius Quinctius Cincinnatus master of the people." Caius Nautius immediately named him dictator, hastening back to his own army before sunrise.[7] B.C. 457. A curious fact regarding costume has been transmitted to us respecting the dictator chosen by the senate upon this occasion, who "wore his hair long and curled, and bestowed so much care upon his ringlets, that he had acquired the appellation of Cincinnatus, or the Crisp-haired."[8] This description does not assimilate with the stern plainness of manner and frugality of Cincinnatus in mature years, he probably acquired, in early youth, that foppish soubriquet which he retained and rendered illustrious in age. The deputation from the senate, upon crossing the Tiber to acquaint the impoverished patrician with the dignity imposed upon him, found him employed in tilling his field of four jugers, the only patrimony his redemption of his son's sureties had left him.[9] This grant was no doubt unalienable, or "all but honour" would have been lost to the noble-minded man to whom his country looked for her deliverance. His visitors bade him resume his cloak that he might pay fitting respect to the senatorial message, whereupon Cincinnatus quitted the plough, and calling to his wife Racilia, bade her bring the garment. Upon his inquiring "whether any evil had befallen the state," he received notice of his dignity, and the danger of the consular army, and, entering the boat, prepared to exchange his rustic employment for the highest office his country could bestow.[10] At Rome the dictator was met by his three sons, and a numerous body of kinsmen and senators, being conducted to his former residence by four-and-twenty lictors—a state exceeding that anciently accorded by the people to their kings. He chose Lucius Tarquitius, an impoverished patrician, who had not even a steed, for his master of horse,[11] after which he ordered all the shops and booths to be closed, considering the danger of the consular army as more important than any matter of private interest. Every man who was of age to defend his country was summoned to the Campus Martius, before the sun went down, for the energetic citizen to whom Rome had committed the dictatorial power, had said, "Let us come up to the enemy this night."[12] Twelve stakes and five days' provisions were furnished by each soldier, and the hastily raised army only halted before midnight from their forced march upon perceiving the camp of the Æquians. Cincinnatus rode forward to examine the manner in which the foe was posted,[13] and upon his return issued his orders for surrounding the encampment of the invaders, whereupon each soldier commenced digging the trench and setting in the stakes he had brought with him. Upon the completion of their work the dictatorial army raised a loud shout, which alarmed their slumbering enemies, but gave courage to their blockaded countrymen, who rushed forth to assault the Æquian camp, calling to each other, "Rescue is at hand, for that is the shout of the Romans," and they defended the line drawn by their countrymen which the Æquians vainly endeavoured to force. Morning found the invaders encamped between two armies, and wholly at the mercy of the Romans—a mercy which they only obtained by giving up their leaders, and passing under the yoke. The Æquian army unarmed and despoiled of their upper garments marched home, having purchased their lives at the expense of their national honour. The chiefs were put to death after the triumph of Cincinnatus, who refused, in the division of the spoil, a share to the consular army he had delivered.[14] No offence was taken by the consul or his soldiers, who gave a golden crown to their deliverer as a mark of their gratitude and esteem.[15] In the treaty Cincinnatus made with the Æquians Corbio was ceded to the Romans. Upon his return to Rome the old man gave up the dictatorship, which he had held with great glory for sixteen days.[16] This expedition was commemorated by the national lays, and was thus orally transmitted from generation to generation. The advantages gained were of a temporary nature, for the Æquians kept advancing, no treaty ever binding that brave, restless, and predatory people. Corbio was soon lost, and the measures taken by the consuls Q. Minucius and C. Horatius, to recover the place were delayed by the struggle between the two orders respecting the agrarian and Terentilian laws, the tribunes not suffering the people to enlist unless they came into B.C. 457. operation.[17] The approach of the Sabines to the very walls occasioned a compromise between the disputing parties, when the addition of five tribunes to the college, by doubling the number of the popular magistrates, seemed to ensure to the people the privileges for which they were contending.[18] But however just the demands of the commons might be, they ought not to have taken advantage of a crisis which called upon every man to stand forth as the defender of his native land—a duty paramount to all others in a citizen. The tribune Icilius during the public distress carried the claims of the plebeian order to the Aventine Mount.[19] The commons, in receiving back their rights, acted with moderation; they compensated those who had built upon the ground, fairly attained by purchase or permission, while they ejected those who had become its unlawful possessors.[20] The first received the value of the edifices raised, which was fixed by arbitration; the others were treated like interlopers and robbers. The patrician body hoped that the restoration of the Aventine Mount would content the commons, while the measure showed the middle class its power by demonstrating that its energies and talents only required time and union to wring from the dominant party those privileges to which it was really entitled. "The increase of the plebeian order did not allow each individual head of a family sufficient ground plot whereon to build his house; therefore several united in the work, occupying the different stories thus raised.[21] This labour conduced to the maintenance of the public tranquillity though the rainy season proved inimical to the harvest."[22] In the two following consulates the question of the agrarian and Terentilian laws was revived with the utmost fury, the tribunes even citing the consuls before the people to give an account of their conduct, threatening at the same time to inflict a fine upon those supreme magistrates. In the midst of these scenes of civic discord, the tribune Icilius once more proposed the agrarian law, on which occasion Sicinius Dentatus, a valiant plebeian, related his exploits, and displayed the military rewards he had received for those public services which had failed to obtain for him a single juger of the conquered lands. Dentatus, then fifty-six years of age, had borne a part in one hundred and twenty engagements, and was now past the period when his services could legally be demanded for the defence of his country. He had received forty-five wounds during the wars in which Rome had been striving for her political existence, and the approach of age made him naturally press for a law that promised to provide for his future wants.[23] The veteran, though past the years at which he could be required to serve, volunteered against the Æquians, being joined by eight hundred veterans as patriotic as himself. The consuls, hoping to rid themselves of the man, ordered him to ascend the hill on which the enemy were entrenched, and storm their camp. Dentatus achieved the difficult enterprise, afterwards joining the consuls who were engaged on the plain with surprising celerity.[24] The night after the victory he deprived the consuls of their triumph by burning the spoil, and killing the prisoners which, in concert with his band, he effected without discovery. In the consulship of A. Aternius and Spurius Tarpeius, the long-contested Terentilian bill passed, and the senate sent deputies to Athens and the states of Greece, to collect the laws of those countries, which were destined to form a code for the Roman republic.

To Spurius Postumius, A. Manlius, and S. Sulpitius, were given this honourable office.[25] It is to be lamented that they did not carry their researches to Judea, where the only perfect code of moral laws was to be found. The Jews, though returned from their captivity, had not yet recovered their distinctness as a people. The Romans would not have looked among the emancipated slaves of the Persian monarch for a jurisprudence as faultless as the nature of the times would allow. Let any impartial reader compare the moral law of Moses with that of the Twelve Tables, and convince himself of the truth of this assertion. The Romans, in discovering their need of laws, gave a proof of their advance in civilisation, and it is remarkable that this want was generally felt by every B.C. 454. order of men in the state. It was the cry of a great people seeking for national wisdom.[26] They had not yet arrived at that period when the human intellect is sufficiently educated to produce good laws; but they resolved to avail themselves of the wisdom of the Greeks, from whom they obtained that celebrated but defective code which bears the name of the Twelve Tables.[27] Christianity alone in after ages presented a system of laws capable of restraining by moral engagements men from injuring each other; and if barbarous penal codes and the cruel question by torture continued to exist in states that had embraced Christianity, those codes and that mode of examination had their origin in the retention of heathenish laws and customs by Christian countries. This practice did not belong to Christianity, but originated in the deviation of half-converted men from the true and perfect standard presented to them in the gospel code. Yet how often are the crimes of men professedly Christian charged upon Christianity itself, which always remains pure, perfect, and unchangeable as when its precepts first issued from the lips of its Divine Founder, and were sealed with his blood. In the consulship of T. Menenius and P. Sestius, the three deputies returned with the code of which only a fragment now remains.[28] The Roman people, becoming impatient for its appearance, nominated Appius Claudius and T. Genucius to the consulship, under the impression that they would expedite the digest which was not then begun. Appius Claudius, a bold, artful, and ambitious man, considered this time a fitting opportunity to possess himself of the supreme authority; and under the specious pretext of governing by the law, to place himself and his colleagues above all law. He therefore proposed a decemvirate, or government of ten persons, each decemvir ruling the state in turn, for one year only, while the new code was preparing, the consular and tribunitial magistracies being wholly suppressed during the period of their office.[29] It is surprising that the senate and people consented to such a measure, or that a Roman citizen could dare to propose an oligarchy to a free state. The willingness of the new consuls to resign their power seemed to give a pledge of disinterestedness and patriotism which not only ensured the proposed change, but occasioned their being placed at the head of the decemviral list, which contained the names of Appius Claudius, T. Genucius, P. Sestius, Spurius Postumius, S. Sulpitius, A. Manlius, T. Romilius, C. Julius, Sp. Veturius, and P. Curatius. Each of these new magistrates exercised the supreme authority for a day in regular rotation, sitting on a tribunal in the forum to dispense justice. The pride that had marked the proud Claudian family, and for which Appius Claudius was formerly remarkable, seemed to have died away. He courteously saluted every citizen by name—a condescension which made him the idol of the populace—till from the man of the people he became an absolute sovereign, to whom the name of king alone was wanting. Appius was content to reign without the name. How many sovereigns of the people have lost their lives and empires in aiming at a legal title to the authority they actually possessed! Not so the bold head of the decemvirs, the artful popular favourite, who knew that courteous words and smiles, were more likely to deprive a people of their liberty than the stern bearing and unbending oppression hitherto exercised by his family. In making the digest of the new laws, the decemvirs were aided by the Ionian sophist, Hermodorus, whom they brought with them from Athens for that purpose.[30] The year of the decemvirate expired, and a portion of the laws were read, approved, and fixed up in the forum.[31] The people had been so quietly governed that they did not wish for change; indeed, as Appius Claudius had only completed ten tables, the digest of the other two being still in preparation, he required another year for the conclusion of the important code. A second decemvirate was decreed, and Appius not only named himself as the chief of the oligarchs, but carefully excluded all persons whom he thought likely to oppose his designs. The nine introduced in the list by his influence were Fabius Vibulanus, M. Cornelius, L. Sergius, L. Minucius, T. Antonius, M. Rabuleius. He also nominated three B.C. 451. plebeians—Q. Pœtilius, Cæso Duilius, and Spurius Oppius; men devoted to his interest. The whole body of decemvirs cemented in private their union by solemn oaths, each agreeing to support his colleagues in office with his whole influence and authority.[32] The decemvirs having secured the government, suddenly shook off the gentle winning manners they had hitherto assumed. They surrounded their tribunals with one hundred and twenty lictors, and were attended by a body of dependants ready to arm in their defence.[33] The laws were now completed, and the last upon the twelfth table contained a clause forbidding intermarriages between plebeians and patricians, in order to destroy any chance of the two bodies gradually blending into one. To divide that he might rule the Roman people, was the motive imputed to Appius Claudius for this new law, though perhaps it originated in pride rather than policy. The second year of the decemvirate was out, but the decemvirs chose to reign by their own authority, and kept possession of their power without any reference to the people. The approach of the Æquians and Sabines to Rome obliged the decemvirs to appear in new characters, as military commanders. There being no precedent for any officers but consuls and dictators raising the levies, they were obliged to convene the senate to consider the manner in which this should be done. The people, greatly disgusted by the absolute and tyrannical government of the decemvirs, saw the senate resume its functions with pleasure.[34] Valerius and Horatius, though interrupted by the oligarchy, dared to reproach them with having subverted the liberty of their country, and their orations made a deep impression upon the people. It was finally determined, after a stormy debate, that the decemvirs should raise the levies, and lead the Roman armies, Appius Claudius and Spurius Oppius being left at Rome to protect the city, and defend it, if necessary, from assault without or tumult within.[35] The decemvirs soon gave proof of their inability to command. Those sent against the Sabines met with a reverse at a place called Eretrum, yet by no means sufficient to justify them for a hasty and disgraceful retreat.[36]

The other army was defeated, leaving both camp and baggage in the hands of the invaders.[37] These disasters filled the people with sullen resentment; and they spoke with contempt of their cowardly tyrants. Sicinius Dentatus indignantly pointed out to the multitude the military faults committed by the decemvirs, and loudly lamented the national dishonour.[38] His complaints reached the ears of Appius Claudius, who resolved to destroy the brave old veteran. He sent for him, asked his advice, and despatched him to Crustumerium, in the sacred character of a legate, to assist, as he pretended, the generals at a period so critical and momentous. The colleagues of the decemvir followed his secret instructions, and Dentatus was murdered while choosing the ground for the camp. The decemvirs ordered the remains of the murdered veteran to be conveyed to Rome, and honoured with a public funeral.[39] The Roman people, groaning under the heavy yoke of the decemvirate, regarded their rulers with contempt and horror, and they were ripe for revolt when an event more tragical than the fate of Lucretia roused them to break their chains. The charms of an innocent young maiden, whom the decemvir, Appius Claudius, beheld reading in one of the public schools in the forum, kindled the unlawful passions of a man possessed of unbounded power, whose principles opposed no obstacle between his passion and its pure object.[40] The virgin, whose ill-fortune had made her so attractive in the eyes of Appius, was the motherless daughter of a brave plebeian centurion, named Virginius, from whom she took the patronymic of Virginia.[41] Appius would gladly have made Virginia his wife, but he was himself a married man, and though the Roman law permitted divorce in case of the barrenness, infidelity, or drunkenness of the wife, no distinct precedent existed, at that time, for intermarriage with another woman during the life of even a misconducted consort. The plebeian birth of Virginia, or at least the poverty which had caused her family to lose its patrician privilege, it having formerly been noble,[42] would also have B.C. 450. formed a bar to his union with her, even if he had been free to choose, since he had lately placed that law on the Twelve Tables, prohibiting the intermarriages of patricians with plebeians.[43] Virginia, moreover, was betrothed to Icilius, the very man who had secured to the commons the possession or restitution of the Aventine Mount. To extricate himself or her from their marital ties must involve him in difficulty and danger; therefore the seduction of the fair maiden appeared to him the easiest expedient. The wicked decemvir commenced his evil designs by attempting to corrupt the fidelity of her nurse, but the woman proving faithful to her trust, he resolved to conspire against her honour under the cover of law and justice; a client of his own, named Marcus Claudius, consenting to become his agent.[44] This man was to seize upon the person of Virginia by force, as the child of one of his female slaves, whom he was to pretend had been *sold* by her mother, and imposed upon Virginius by Numitoria his wife, as his own daughter.[45] Marcus Claudius asserted his false claim by entering the playground where the fair Virginia was sporting with her young companions, when seizing her rudely by the arm, he bade her follow him to his own house. The cries and tears of a terrified girl, hardly out of childhood, while dragged through the forum, naturally attracted public attention, and gathered a concourse of people together, who, taking pity upon her distress, obliged the ruffian to release her, but the villain, by immediately citing her to appear before the decemviral tribunal, compelled Virginia to follow him. He there began to open his claim, but this the populace opposed by loud clamours, insisting that the young virgin had a right to be supported by her own relations before her accuser was heard. Appius Claudius was obliged to consent to the demand of the people, and Numitorius, the uncle of Virginia, and some of her paternal relations, soon appeared to afford the trembling girl that protection her tender age and timidity required.[46] Claudius related the preconcerted story respecting the barrenness of Numitoria, the wife of Virginius, and the birth of the child in slavery, her pretended death and sale to her reputed mother, whom, he said, imposed the infant upon her husband, as his own free-born and legitimate offspring. He concluded his iniquitous narrative by offering to produce witnesses who could attest to the fact that Virginia had been born in his house, pledging himself to call before the decemviral tribunal the slave herself, whom he styled her lawful mother. He therefore demanded the custody of Virginia's person till the return of her father to Rome.[47] Numitorius easily discerned the motive that had induced the client of Appius Claudius to make this false claim to his free-born niece, and was certain that it originated with the powerful patron himself. He proceeded, however, with great caution, pleading that the absence of the young maiden's father from Rome, in the service of his country, made it expedient that she should remain with her own friends till her trial, which need not be delayed beyond two or three days after the return of Virginius. In the mean time, he entreated the decemvir not to imperil the fair fame of a Roman virgin, by leaving her in the hands of a stranger, in defiance of a law expressly stating, "that every person shall be considered free until his servile condition be proved." Appius declared the statute to be good, and one of his own enacting, but in regard to the maiden pronounced it wholly inapplicable; "for she cannot," he said, "in any case be free; she must belong either to her father or her master. Now, her father being absent, who but her master can have any right to her? wherefore let Marcus Claudius keep her, after giving sureties for her re-appearance before my judgment-seat, when the cause shall be tried between them."[48] The extreme state of subjection in which the Roman female was kept all her life proves that in this decision Appius Claudius acted with more law than justice. But the angry remonstrances of Numitorius and Icilius were answered by a sympathising and indignant multitude, and the cries of Virginia drew about her person a number of women, who, comprehending better than the unfortunate young girl the nature of the danger that threatened her, came to give her their matronly counsel and countenance B.C. 450. in her hour of peril. The populace too, openly took part with the affianced lover, whom they aided in his attack upon the base client of the crafty decemvir.[49] Appius reluctantly gave way to this popular commotion in Virginia's favour. He cited her, however, to appear with her father before his tribunal upon the following day, concluding with the menace, "that in case of Virginius's non-appearance, he should award her to his client, and that neither he nor his colleague wanted the means of enforcing justice or putting down sedition."[50] Claudius, the claimant of Virginia, insisted that Icilius should find security for her appearance upon the morrow; upon which every man present but the creatures of the decemvir held up his hand in token of his willingness to become his bondsman. Icilius, touched with this proof of affection and respect, shed tears, as he returned thanks to his generous sureties. "To-morrow," said he, "I may require your help; to-day Numitorius, myself, and the other relations of Virginia, are sufficient security for her appearance." Virginia was then conducted to her uncle's house.[51] Appius Claudius immediately sent letters to his colleagues, who were with the army about eleven miles from Rome, requesting them to imprison Virginius for three days, till the trial and the excitement attending it should be over. He also desired them to prevent the prisoner from receiving any intelligence of what was passing at Rome.[52] But prompt as he had been in his iniquitous machinations against the liberty of

Virginius, the friends of Virginia had been more so, for the son of Numitorius and the brother of Icilius had already reached the camp, and informed the astonished father of the danger that threatened the liberty and honour of his innocent child. Virginius asked leave of the generals to attend the funeral of a near relation at Rome, and his stratagem was so successful, that he passed upon the road the messengers of Appius, and even eluded the vigilance of the soldiers sent by the other decemviri to apprehend him. The following morning he entered the forum[53] leading his young daughter, who, like himself, was attired in the deepest mourning. They were attended by their own relations and friends, and Virginia was not only surrounded by the generous females who had protected her the preceding day, but also by a train of patrician matrons, whose compassionate feelings led them to afford her their support upon this trying occasion.[54] Appius Claudius, though surprised at the appearance of Virginius, did not yield up his ill designs upon the daughter to whom her father's presence seemed to give sufficient protection from his dishonourable attempts. His tribunal was strongly guarded by his own lictors and those of his colleagues, and he had a numerous band of clients at his command.[55] He was a crafty man, and was aware of the fact that mobs rarely prevent unjust public actions; he, however, had yet to learn that if multitudes are too timid to oppose the perpetration of crimes, they are always brave enough to revenge them.

Claudius boldly produced his false witnesses, including among them the pretended servile mother of Virginia; but he opened his case by beseeching the judge not to permit a false compassion to overweigh the evidence of truth.[56] Virginius called upon his own relations to disprove the base system of imposture contrived by Claudius—persons who could speak to his early marriage to Numitoria, her frequent pregnancies, the deaths of the children she had borne, and the birth of her daughter, which several matrons who had been present upon that occasion could attest. He added that Numitoria had nourished her infant at her own bosom—a fact known to many of her friends. He reasoned upon the improbability of the story, since, if his wife had been disposed to impose the spurious offspring of a slave upon him, she would naturally have preferred a male to a female infant. "For fifteen years," he said, "the pretended claim had slept, and was only made when Virginia was marriageable, and adorned with that great beauty which all behold in her this day."[57]

Beauty, however, in her case, was an unfortunate gift, and in later ages Juvenal considered "that the fair Virginia might have envied even Rutilia her hump-back;"[58] for she stood at that time before the tribunal of her unjust B.C. 450. judge, doomed by that very beauty to the worst evils of slavery, or only fated to escape them by an unheard-of sacrifice.

Appius Claudius assured the agitated centurion that his client had often urged his rights to Virginia to him, but that public business had hitherto compelled him to withhold his attention from his cause; yet justice now obliged him to award the custody of Virginia to Claudius till she could be proved to be free-born.[59] This open violation of a law enacted by himself excited the feelings of the multitude, who saw a free-born person treated like a slave, although not proved to belong to that servile condition, and given into the hands of a man known to be the creature of the decemvir,[60] there to remain exposed to his seductive arts or open violence till some distant day of trial. But what were their feelings to those that agitated the bosom of the Roman father, who, raising his hand to the tribunal, menaced the vile magistrate in words that pointed him out as the secret conspirator against the honour of a pure Roman maiden. "Appius, I reared my daughter for Icilius in honourable marriage, and not for shame and thee. I know not how the citizens may bear these wrongs, but I at least will not endure them."[61] To this burst of paternal indignation, and to the loud imprecations of the crowd, Appius Claudius opposed the instruments of his absolute power, bidding his lictors drive back the multitude, that Claudius might take possession of Virginia—a declaration which, while it consigned the innocent Virginia to the keeping of his base pander, affected her honour more than her future liberty; for that question had still to be determined by a legal trial, which might award the dishonoured daughter of the centurion to his parental guardianship again; this decision not really settling the claim, but merely, though unjustly, that of the wardship, which against all right was thus assigned by the decemvir to his client.[62] The crowd gave way, as in almost every case the populace always does give way, unless taught by bolder spirits the secret hidden in concentrated strength to redress or perpetrate wrong. That neither Icilius, the affianced husband of the injured Virginia, nor her indignant and stern father, made this attempt, must always be a matter of regret and wonder. The people retreated, and the unfortunate maiden was left alone before the judgment-seat. Some authors declare that a band of armed patricians surrounded the tribunal; but this would have been such an open violation of the Roman law, that their assertions seem improbable. Virginius, who had formed in his own mind a terrible resolution, suddenly changed his angry tone to one of supplication, and humbly besought permission of the decemvir to speak one word to the nurse in his daughter's hearing, that he might be satisfied whether Virginia were his child or that of an alien. "If I am not indeed her father, I shall better bear the loss of her society,"[63] were his concluding words. The decemvir did not refuse the petition of the centurion, who drew his daughter to a place afterwards called the new booths, but rendered memorable and interesting by the tradition that marked it as the scene of the tragedy. The unhappy father then for one moment embraced his daughter, who clung to his bosom in feminine helplessness and sorrow. Snatching a knife from the butchers' shambles, Virginius addressed her thus: "My child, there is but one way to keep thee in freedom and honour," and with these words plunged the weapon in the unresisting Virginia's heart; but quickly withdrawing it from the wound, held it up to the guilty and horror-stricken decemvir, whom he addressed by name. "Appius Claudius, by this innocent blood I devote thy head to the infernal gods—on thee be the curse,"[64] his voice alone breaking the deep silence into which that deed had hushed the mighty Roman people. Recovering from his astonishment and horror, Appius called upon his lictors to seize Virginius, but in vain, for he had forced his way among the throng, still holding the knife wet with his daughter's blood, and, passing through the forum, hastened out of the city, mounted a horse, and gained the camp by Tusculum.[65]

It was to no timid, unarmed multitude that the outraged centurion addressed himself, but to bold men, fellow-citizens, and warriors of his own order; to fathers, B.C. 450. husbands, and brothers, who beheld in Virginia another victim immolated by Roman honour at the shrine of chastity. His blood-stained garments and intense agitation drew at once a martial throng about him, and Virginius told his dreadful story to auditors who swore to revenge him. They plucked their standards from the ground, calling upon their officers to lead them to Rome. Their demand was granted, and the decemvirate was virtually no more. The army then elected ten military tribunes, and took their way to the Aventine Mount.[66] In the mean while, the sight of Virginia's bleeding remains had inflamed the people, to whom 'the dead maiden was held up by her uncle Numitorius, and affianced husband Icilius.[67] The eloquence, the passionate appeals that might have saved the Roman virgin from her dreadful fate, were then exerted to revenge her. The multitude elected leaders, and discovered their own power. Appius Claudius found it impossible to resist the popular storm, to quell which defied the force of his lictors and numerous clients. Nor were the male relatives of the victim, or the commons of Rome her only revengers. L. Valerius and M. Horatius, men of noble birth, engaged in the defence of her remains, of which the decemviral party vainly endeavoured to obtain possession.[68] From a strife, become as dangerous as useless, the decemvir, Appius Claudius, fled, covering his head with his robe, either to show his friends that his life was in peril, or to defend it from the missiles flung at him by the crowd; for the Romans of that period, and indeed for several centuries later, wore no covering upon the head but the lappet of the mantle, unless in time of battle. Oppius, the plebeian colleague of the fugitive decemvir, came into the forum to support him; but finding that he had taken shelter in a neighbouring house, dared not interpose between the people and their victory.[69] He called the senate together, but that body were too timid to support the decemvirs, and too cautious to trust the plebeian party, whose ascendancy they saw when once attained would diminish their own power. Icilius and Numitorius hastened to Fidenæ to induce the army there encamped to co-operate with them in their work of vengeance, and to strike for the restoration of the Roman constitution. Their appeal was successful; this army also elected ten military tribunes, and marched for the Aventine Mount, answering all remonstrances on the part of the decemvir with these brief words, "We are men, and have swords in our hands."[70]

The remains of the martyr of Roman honour were placed upon a litter, and paraded through the Forum, and principal streets of Rome, exposed to the eager gaze of the curious or sympathising. The women who had dared to support her cause while living with their generous championship, bewailed her dead. They flung garlands and fillets of ribbon upon the lifeless form of the youthful victim, and even cut from their own hair long ringlets, scattering them upon the bier.[71] Never did the Roman citizens follow their eagle standards with such stern determination in battle as while gathering round the funeral procession of the Roman daughter. The demands of the army and commons of Rome were not immediately answered by the senate. Nothing less than the deposition of the decemvirs and the re-establishment of the tribunitial magistracy would content the insurgents—measures to which the senate refused consent. Upon which, the patriotic party, acting upon the advice of M. Duilius, quitted the Aventine Mount, and marching through the city with their families, passed through the Colline gate, and encamped on the Sacred Mount,[72] apparently bent on abandoning Rome rather than their just rights. In this mighty movement the senate recognised the stern resolution of a free people. They consented to the deposition of the decemvirs, and the abolition of the decemvirate.[73] In the whole struggle, Oppius, the plebeian colleague of the guilty Appius Claudius, alone had striven against the people: remorse, fear, and horror, appear to have paralysed the man whose crimes had brought the impending revolution to a climax.

The senate despatched Valerius and Horatius to the Sacred Mount to hear the demands made by the Roman people. The restoration of the tribunitial magistracies, B.C. 450. they expected as the necessary consequence of the deposition of the decemvirs and the abolition of the oligarchy; they also demanded a general amnesty for the insurgents, and the execution of the decemvirs. The outraged feelings of Icilius prompted this condemnation of the tyrants to a cruel death, who were proclaimed in the name of the commons to be public enemies, and therefore worthy to die. "Give them up to us," said the betrothed husband of the dead Virginia, "that we may burn them with fire."[74] But this dreadful sentence was not carried into effect. Valerius and Horatius induced the commons to be contented with the agreement of the senate to the terms proposed, and to withdraw that clause from the treaty. Valerius then announced the accomplishment of the revolution in these words, "Return, soldiers, to your country, to your household gods, to your wives and children, and may this return prove fortunate to you and the commonwealth." The soldiers answered this animating charge with exulting plaudits, and taking up their ensigns re-entered Rome, where they were received with joyful congratulations.[75] They posted themselves upon the Aventine, and invested the Capitol[76] till such time as the arrival of the Pontifex Maximus should allow them to hold the comitia for the election of the tribunes of the people. This assembly was held on the Aventine Mount, where ten tribunitial magistrates were elected. Among the list we find the names of Virginius, Numitorius, Icilius, and Duilius. It is remarkable that the consent of the commons was necessary in order to render their own amnesty and indemnification from the senate legal. A parallel to this curious circumstance may be found in English history, upon the accession of Henry VII., whose first parliament was chiefly composed of members formerly attainted by one or other of the rival sovereigns who had occupied the throne; the king himself, being of the number, occasioned an objection to its meeting, which the prerogative of the Crown was afterwards deemed sufficient to cover, though the judges to whom the question respecting the attainted members of both houses was referred, advised their being withdrawn, till they were cleared by the reversal of the attainder. This not being complied with,[77] placed them when they took their seats, much in the same circumstances as the Roman commons in the comitia summoned for the indemnification of the insurgents. As far as regarded the fate of Virginia, the law gave her father the absolute power of life and death over the person of his child, but until this amnesty was passed he, his friends and partizans, were legally deemed the enemies of the country they had redeemed from slavery, for the insurrection of which that dreadful act had been the cause. They cleared themselves by consenting to the ratification of this instrument.[78] Icilius proposed the indemnity to the Roman people in the Flaminian Meadows outside the Carmental Gate, just below the Capitol, which was still occupied by the commons.[79] Duilius recommended the restoration of the consular magistrates. For the first time in Roman history the name of consul is used, that of prætor, or captain-general, being till then the one in use.[80] The commons, even in electing Valerius and Horatius, took care to secure the right of appeal from the judgment of their disinterested champions, for they were jealous of their newly-acquired liberty, and resolved to guard it with sedulous care. The laws with which they fenced their recovered freedom will be mentioned after the punishment of the decemvirs has been discussed.

Virginius, clothed with the sacred authority of a tribune of the plebs, cited Appius Claudius before the people, impeaching the fallen decemvir, but still powerful patrician, for his unjust judgment respecting the wardship of Virginia.[81] How strange it appears that so foul a conspiracy could only be legally punished as an infraction of the law which held Virginia to be free, till proved otherwise by a sentence to that effect on her trial. By this statute the father of the maiden, while in Rome, was still deemed B.C. 447. her natural guardian, which though violated by Appius, could not involve the penalty of death. The haughty patrician knew this, and appeared in the Forum surrounded by his clients and young patrician friends. His sons probably swelled the number, for Appius had children who had attained their majority. Whether his crime were bailable or not, Virginius would not receive bail for his person,[82] and the criminal dared not have the question of his judgment submitted to a judge to be appointed for that purpose. He appealed to the tribunes to prevent his imprisonment. They would not interfere: he then made his protest to the people to prevent his being imprisoned, being aware that that prison would prove his grave.

Virginius, as Appius declined his trial before a judge, could legally treat him as a criminal; he was therefore thrown into prison[83] previously to pleading his cause before the people. The entreaties and tears of Caius Claudius, the uncle of the accused, moved the assembly so much, that but for the recapitulation of his wrongs by Virginius, the family of the Claudii would have been saved that indignity. He reminded the people "that Appius had shown no contrition for the terrible necessity which had made him the executioner of an only and beloved daughter to save her honour, but that the decemvir had disturbed the dying agonies of his child by endeavouring to tear her from the arms of her affianced husband." He concluded his sad narrative by the words, "Remember Virginia," and those words consigned Appius Claudius to a prison and a tomb.

Eight of the decemvirs went into banishment as a voluntary expiation of their public offences, but the pretended master of Virginia was suffered to escape. Appius Claudius either destroyed himself in prison,[84] or perished by the hands of the father and lover of Virginia.[85] His plebeian colleague Oppius shared his fate, whatever that fate may have been. The law considered Appius as a suicide, and made no minute inquiries respecting him; but he has been confounded with the consul of the same name, who had destroyed himself in prison more than twenty years before, and that too, by the framer of the celebrated Fasti Capitolini.[86] This is the second instance of a revolution in Rome, occasioned by dishonourable attempts upon feminine chastity[87]—a proof how highly female honour was prized, which cost Lucretia and Virginia their lives, and Tarquinius and Appius Claudius their power; so pure in morals, so lofty in reputation were the women of the ancient Roman republic. These women were the mothers of the men by whom the world was subdued and ruled. The tragic history of Virginia has been doubted by the scepticism of modern times; but what is such incredulity when weighed against the testimonies of the Greek and Latin historians who attest its truth? Cicero quotes it,[88] and tradition pointed out from age to age the scene of the parental sacrifice.

The constitution was not only restored but improved. The old Valerian law of Poplicola was revived, which gave the right of appeal from the sentence of the consul to the people when that sentence endangered the life of a citizen. "A plebiscitum[89] or decree of the commons, was to be binding upon the whole people." In what manner this privilege was restrained is not known.[90] The commons of Rome were acknowledged to be the Roman people, being allowed to elect their own magistrates. In our own corporations something resembling the Roman constitution is still to be found. It is certain that various concessions to the people were included in the laws of the Twelve Tables, but they probably had not been put in force. The tribune, Duilius, in order to compel the yearly magistrates to resign their several offices, enacted a very barbarous law enforcing their vacation, under the penalty of the offending parties being burned alive.[91] This was doubtless the revival of that under which several illustrious men had been put to that horrid death in the preceding century. The last laws of this eventful consulship related to the national decrees of the senate, which Valerius and his B.C. 448-47-46. colleague caused to be preserved in the Temple of Ceres on the Aventine Mount, thus calling in the aid of religion to guard the records of the Roman state.[92] The part taken by the consuls in remodelling the constitution displeased their own order, who refused them, in the August of that year, the reward due to their exploits against the Æquians and Sabines. They appealed to the Roman people, and obtained their triumph, notwithstanding the denial of the senate. Icilius was the tribune through whose influence the consuls carried their point.[93] Some dispute occurred respecting the tribunitial magistracies, which the commons wished to fill with the same persons the ensuing year. This measure was opposed by Duilius, one of the re-elected tribunes, who disinterestedly opposed his own advancement,[94] nor would he permit his colleagues to take office. This led to only five persons being elected. He finally dissolved the assembly, declaring the election complete, but decided that each tribune should choose his own colleague, thus making up their number of ten. Two patricians were included in the number[95]—a measure that of necessity must neutralise the politics of the whole body, since the unity of the entire college was absolutely required in order to legalise its decrees. Patrician consuls, as usual, were chosen, and in fact there is no evidence of any concession on the part of the senate in regard to preferring a plebeian to this office. Trebonius, one of the popular tribunes, abolished the innovation in the tribuneship by proposing a law that obliged the canvass to be continued till the legal number of ten were duly elected.[96] The law that forbade the intermarriages of the rival orders had been virtually expunged from the code of the Twelve Tables by the blood of the innocent Virginia, but it was not formally repealed till some years after that tragic event,[97] when its abolition began to prepare the way for that era of public virtue which adorned the middle ages of the republic.

A year of profound tranquillity followed that eventful one which had restored liberty to the commonwealth, Lartius Herminius and T. Virginius being men of no party, their consulship conduced to the internal repose of the state. The succeeding one was also marked by the same pacific character, and was memorable for its absence from civic and foreign broils. But the old dissensions revived when the fasces were transferred to T. Quinctius Capitolinus and Agrippa Furius, for neither party would forbear from offering provocations to the other.[98] Of these internal divisions the restless nations of the Æquians and Volscians took advantage, as they always did when Rome was convulsed with civic discord. The slaves within the walls were probably the channel through which their countrymen derived their information, and those domestic spies knowing that their only chance of liberty depended upon the predatory incursions of their friends, doubtless took care to give them notice of these feuds. The cattle feeding before the Esquiline Gate became the prey of the invaders. The herd most likely belonged to the patricians, for the plebeians, encouraged by their tribunes, refused to arm in the defence of the city, and made no attempt to recover the booty. The passionate appeal of the consul Quinctius, however, overcame the selfish determination of the people, whom he reminded of "his three former consulships, in which he had served his country with glory, though for his fourth was reserved a period of infamy which must stand on record to all posterity, that an enemy was at the gates of Rome, and her citizens refused to arm in her defence." "What, Rome taken and I her consul! Of honours I have had sufficient—of life enough—three consulships. I should have died then." The veteran concluded, by telling them that their own factious spirit was the cause of their beholding an enemy at their gate.[99] His reproaches awoke in them the old Roman spirit, and they never listened to the speeches of their tribunes with more attention than to this reproof. The people armed, and the consuls gained a glorious victory. Agrippa greatly distinguished himself in the battle against the Æquians, by flinging an ensign into the midst of the enemies' battalions, and rushing forward to recover it—which action, it was thought, insured the victory to the Roman army. The consuls B.C. 446. demanded no triumph;[100] they were satisfied with having done their duty.[101]

A dispute happened in this consulship respecting some lands, to which the people of Ardea and Aricia lay claim, but which they mutually agreed to submit to the arbitration of Rome. The Romans dishonestly decided the matter by keeping the lands for themselves, P. Scaptius, an aged plebeian, having declared that they belonged to Corioli before her conquest by the Romans, and therefore had become the property of the commonwealth. The consuls Quinctius and Agrippa opposed a measure so dishonourable to the Roman people, but in vain.[102] After the republic became a mighty power, she constantly acted in this manner. In a small state such conduct is considered robbery; in a great one it is termed policy. Caius Curtius and M. Genucius, the consuls for the following year, wished to prepare for the war which the open revolt of the Veientines and the discontent of the Ardeatanes appeared to render necessary. The tribune Canuleius considered some reformation in the laws more necessary than fighting. That forbidding the intermarriages of the two orders, though abolished, had never been removed from the Twelve Tables, and therefore the restriction still remained in force, which limited the rank of the children to that of the plebeian mother, nor were such children capable of inheriting from the father, not being even under his guardianship. These regulations, in fact, placed them on the same footing as if they had been the illegitimate offspring of guilt, and not the issue of virtuous wedlock. For this hardship the tribune proposed a legal remedy. The dispute respecting it was carried to such a height on Mount Janiculum, whither the people had withdrawn, that the senate allowed the restriction to be removed.[103] According to Dionysius of Halicarnassus, the storm was not raised respecting this question, but originated in the demand of Canuleius, who asked "what prevented the admission of the plebeian order to the consulship." To which one of the consuls imprudently replied: "that no plebeian could hold an office which required the auspices, since they could only be taken by men of pure and unmixed blood." This answer was received by the commons with such a burst of indignation, that in order to allay the popular feeling, the law respecting the intermarriage of the rival orders was instantly repealed.[104] From the union between the noble and plebeian classes sprang the glorious men who became the ornament and pride of the Republic of Rome.

The admission of the plebeians to the consulship was violently opposed by many of the patricians. The Horatian and Valerian families took no part in the discussion which was maintained by Caius Claudius with great heat against the commons, but which was finally adjusted by the moderation of the Quinctian family,[105] who proposed a change in the supreme magistrates, substituting six military tribunes, invested with consular power, to be taken indiscriminately from the two orders. All parties were satisfied with this arrangement, which was warmly seconded by the consul Genucius; but when the people assembled in comitia to elect the new magistrates, they chose only three, and those from the patrician body,[106] though their old favourites, the tribunes, were present dressed in the white robes of candidates to solicit their votes. The tribuneship only lasted three months, for some informality was discovered in taking the auspices. An inter-rex was named, and two consuls were chosen. Nothing remarkable occurred during the short time of their consulate. The sixty-sixth consulship was rendered memorable by the institution of two officers called censores or censors, who were instituted to relieve the consuls of a troublesome part of their duty— that of taking the census—which occurred every fifth year, by which the persons of the Roman people were enumerated, and their goods assessed.[107] Titus Quinctius and Geganius were chief magistrates when the censorial office was exercised, for the first time, by Papirius Mugillanus and Sempronius Atratinus, the consuls of the preceding B.C. 443-42-39. year. The consuls who had replaced

111

the military tribunes were men who had the interest of their country at heart. Titus Quinctius gained the good-will of the people, while Geganius defeated the Volscians, who were besieging Ardea, and put an end to the civil war within that place. In the consulship of M. Fabius and Posthumius Æbutius, the lands of which the Ardeans had been defrauded by the Roman people were restored, and a colony was planted there. The commissioners employed in this business were prosecuted, because they had not received their commission from the people, upon which T. Clœlius, Agrippa Menenius, and M. Æbutius, the accused parties, withdrew to Ardea, of which city they declared themselves citizens. After three years of peace Rome was visited with a grievous famine, rendered memorable by the conspiracy of Spurius Mælius, a wealthy knight. The Roman historians have all united to brand this member of the equestrian order with a stigma which he most probably did not deserve. Minucius, the purveyor-general, had been sent by the consuls to buy corn; but obtaining very little, not only discovered that Mælius overbid him in the market, but heard that he was conspiring against the government. Arms, he was told, were carried into his house, where he held midnight meetings, the object of which was his usurpation of the regal dignity.[108] Minucius did not bring this intelligence to Rome till Titus Quinctius Capitolinus was in his sixth consulship in conjunction with Agrippa Menenius.[109] Of the conspiracy itself there was no proof beyond the assertion of the purveyor-general, and the fact that Mælius was purchasing corn to feed his starving countrymen at his own expense, who in return loved and venerated their benefactor. In the jealousy of his own order alone any traces of the treason of Mælius are to be found. As soon as Quinctius learned the danger of the state he named his brother Cincinnatus dictator, with the entire approbation of the senate. The old man, who was at the advanced age of eighty, endeavoured to excuse himself from the arduous office, and when about to accept it, piously prayed that his country might not suffer for his infirmities. He created Servilius Ahala his general of horse, and having invested the city with troops, sent him to summons the conspiring knight before his tribunal. Mælius refused to obey, caught up a butcher's knife,[110] and took refuge among the people, who drove away the lictor who had taken him into custody, upon which the newly-appointed general of horse drew his sword and slew the suspected knight, after which he re-entered the Forum, and addressed the dictator in these words, "Mælius refused to obey your summons, and endeavoured to raise a rebellion; he has by this hand received his due punishment." "It was greatly done," replied the dictator, "and you have saved the liberty of the commonwealth."[111] The tribunes and the people were justly incensed at the punishment of a man, without the formality of a trial,[112] who had fed, in this period of dearth, the starving population. They forced Ahala to leave Rome,[113] and chose military tribunes instead of consuls, as magistrates for the ensuing year, but elected three patricians to this office. L. Minucius, the master of the markets, whose representations, whether true or false, had caused the death of Mælius, dexterously got rid of the odium he had incurred with the commons by selling grain at so low a rate to them, that he acquired an immense share of popularity. It was the sale of the corn Mælius had bought up, which, becoming the property of the state, so reduced the price that at the end of three market-days the poorest citizen was able to become a purchaser. An ox with gilded horns was presented to Minucius by the plebeians as a sacrifice,[114] while a statue was raised to his honour at their expense without the Porta Trigemina, formed out of the coins which each contributed, at the rate of an ounce, or twelfth part of an *as*, per man.[115] The story of his becoming an eleventh tribune, and passing from his own order into that of the commons, does not appear probable, unless we suppose B.C. 437-36-35. that he was either degraded by the censors for some alleged crime, or evaded the prosecution of which he might have become the subject for his accusation against Spurius Mælius, by the renunciation of his patrician privileges. We are assured that no Minucii were found in the order of nobility after him.[116] This story, if true, proves how fleeting and uncertain is popular opinion, since the people not only forgot their benefactor, but heaped honours upon the man whose accusation had occasioned his death.

The revolt of Fidenæ to Tolumnius, king of the Veientines, was followed by the murder of four Roman ambassadors, to which atrocity the Fidenatans were excited by their new ally.[117] As this colony had been Roman ever since the time of Romulus, its defection was considered very criminal. The consulship was once more restored, and L. Sergius and M. Geganius were elected. It fell to the lot of the latter to conduct the war. He was successful, but lost so many soldiers, that it was judged proper to choose a dictator who, with equal bravery, would be less prodigal of human life. Æmilius Mamercus was named by the consuls, and he carried on the war with great success. Tolumnius, the king of the Veientines, was slain in single combat by Cornelius Cossus, one of the dictator's legionary tribunes, who carried the royal robes and armour he had won from him on his shoulders, at the triumph of Mamercus. He deposited these *spolia opima* in the Temple of Jupiter Feretrius, where Romulus had formerly placed those of King Acron. As this was only the second occurrence of the kind in Rome it excited great attention.[118]

In the following consulship Servilius Ahala was prosecuted for the murder of the Roman knight Mælius by another Sp. Mælius, a tribune.[119] The ground of his accusation was, "that he had put a Roman citizen to death untried and uncondemned." It is uncertain whether he was acquitted or punished.

The plague raged with great fury in the consulships of Julius Iulus and L. Virginius, upon which the Veientines and Fidenatans marched up to the gate of Rome called Collina, and encamped thereby, to the consternation of the sick citizens. Upon this emergency the consuls named Quintus Servilius Priscus as dictator, who marched out to attack the enemy, upon which they retreated to Nomentum, where he totally defeated them, and afterwards took Fidenæ. The victor assumed the surname of Fidenas in memory of his victories, but was allowed no triumph, as the war was considered civic.[120]

Æmilius Mamercus, on a false report of an Etruscan war, was appointed dictator a second time.[121] His services were not required in the field, and his attempt to shorten the period of the censorship from five years to eighteen months led to the infliction of an enormous fine upon him by Furius and Geganius who then held the office. The people, who loved Æmilius, would have torn the censors to pieces if the generous dictator had not saved them. He paid the money exacted from him, though eight times more in amount than it ought to have been.

The fourth military tribuneship, being composed of patricians, was so displeasing to the influential plebeians, who imagined that they owed this preference to the politeness of their behaviour at elections, that they passed a law to prevent those who aimed at the chief offices in the state from wearing robes of superior whiteness (from whence they were called candidates), and soliciting votes thus attired. The Roman consuls next year were defeated at Algidus, this disaster being attributed to the dissensions between them. The senate proposed a dictator, whereupon the rival consuls declared there should be none, but at length were compelled to nominate one by lot. Quinctius, who gained it, named his father-in-law, Postumius Tubertus, who chose L. Julius Iulus for his general of horse. The dictator was a man of military talent and great resolution. He soon drove the enemy out of the field, though not before he had gained a hard-fought battle, for which he was granted a triumph. Postumius Tubertus, in the course of the war, publicly executed his son for a breach of military discipline in engaging the enemy without orders.[122]

The fifth military tribuneship did not increase the B.C. 426. reputation of the republic, for the tribunes were defeated in battle by the Veientines, and Æmilius Mamercus was made dictator to repair their blunders. The revolt of the Fidenatans added to the difficulties of Æmilius; these people united with those of Veii, and encamping near their own city, gave battle to Æmilius, and during the fight exhibited a new feature in military tactics. A band of soldiers dressed like furies, armed with flaming torches, which they brandished on every side, suddenly rushed out of the gates of Fidenæ. The Romans recoiled at this unexpected sight. "What," cried the brave dictator, "are you a swarm of bees, that you are thus terrified at smoke? Beat down those torches with your swords, and then fire the city with them."[123] His orders were obeyed, the allies were defeated, and Fidenæ was taken. Æmilius laid down the dictatorship, which he had only held sixteen days.

Three years after this victory, Sempronius, a brave soldier, but inexperienced general, engaged the Volscians with more valour than prudence; but the bravery and skill of Tempanius, a veteran captain of horse, saved the Roman army from destruction. Leaping from his horse, he rallied the legions, crying out, "Follow my lance as your standard, and let us show the enemy that on foot or horseback nothing can withstand it!" This gallant speech was followed up by gallant deeds, and though surrounded by the enemy, Tempanius firmly maintained his ground till the Volscians retreated on one side, and the consul Sempronius with the infantry on the other, both being ignorant that Tempanius and the cavalry were fighting on foot between the main body of the Volscians. Great was the surprise of the old veteran when he could discover neither friends nor enemies in the field. Both camps were deserted, and not knowing what had become of their Roman and Volscian tenants, he returned to Rome, where a false report of the destruction of the consular army had already preceded him. The tribunes of the people immediately summoned Tempanius, to inform them what had really happened; but he could tell them nothing beside his own exploits, and those of his new infantry. Of the fate of the Roman army with that of the Volscian he was equally ignorant; though he knew that Sempronius had fought bravely. Upon the question of the military skill of the general, he generously refused to give an opinion; but he praised his valour, and, as if to put an end to more minute inquiry, asked leave to retire, in order to have his wounds looked to. The discovery that the consular army was safe, restored the public tranquillity.[124] In the eighth military tribuneship, L. Hortensius, a tribune of the people, cited Sempronius, the late consul, to answer for his misconduct during the war; but Tempanius and three others, who had lately been chosen tribunes of the people, stood generously forth in defence of the unfortunate general, to whose bravery they bore witness, finally declaring that they could not condemn one whom they and the whole army loved and honoured as their father; that they did not presume to deprive the Roman people of the authority to punish a magistrate, but that they would assume the same mournful attire as the accused to prove their sympathy, not with his faults, but with his misfortunes. "Not so," replied Hortensius; "Rome shall not see her tribunes in mourning; I drop the prosecution altogether. I will advance no accusation against a commander thus tenderly beloved by his soldiers."[125]

The acquisition of lands won from the Volscians and Veientines occasioned the question of the agrarian law to be agitated again. These lands were either occupied by the patricians, or let out to them, no portion of the money coming into the treasury.[126] When we remember that the services of the plebeians were without pay, being performed on military tenure, and that the great increase of this order demanded an increase of such grants, we must consider their demand based on the just grounds of absolute necessity. Nor can we consider men who asked for a share of what they had won, factious, for they only asked for a plot of ground whereon to raise bread for their families.

Two additional quæstors were added to the number of those magistrates during the consulship of T. Quinctius Capitolinus and Fabius Vibulanus. The commons claimed B.C. 416-14-13. a right to choose half from their own order— a privilege which was granted them. They did not, however, avail themselves of this concession, for both the quæstors and military tribunes were elected from the patricians.[127] A design of the slaves in Rome to fire the city and seize the Capitol, was discovered by some of the servile conspirators themselves in time to prevent its execution.[128]

An agrarian law was made in the thirteenth military tribuneship, by which fifteen hundred plebeians received allotments of two jugera per man out of the lands lately won from the Lavicans.[129] To weaken the growing influence of the commons by gaining the tribunes was the astute policy of Appius Claudius, the grandson of the decemvir. His advice was agreeable to the senate, and six of the popular tribunes were won over to the patrician party, not, however, by the base influence of gold, but by that of courtesy, to the great mortification of Mæcileus and Metileus, the head tribunes, who found themselves opposed by their colleagues and outvoted; consequently the agrarian law was dropped again. It was the distinguishing attribute of the whole Claudian family to oppose fraud or force against the plebeian party. To half measures in the pursuit of ambition and pleasure they never submitted, and we shall find them hereafter on the throne, still displaying the same individuality of crime.

The fifteenth military tribuneship presented the extraordinary feature of the assassination of a general by his soldiery. P. Postumius Regillensis, one of the military tribunes, had retaken Volæ from the Æquians, the plunder of which place he had promised his soldiers previously to the capture; but broke his word with them after the town was won, because they were chiefly plebeians. A mutiny instantly broke out in the camp,[130] and a stone was thrown at Sestius, a military quæstor, who was attempting to quell the storm. Such was the state of things when Postumius returned from Rome with the resolution of severely punishing the ringleaders of the revolt. His measures provoked retaliation instead of reducing mutiny, and the military tribune was stoned to death. This disaster had never occurred to a Roman general in the camp before.[131] In the punishment of the late mutiny, the consuls acted mercifully, condemning few, and allowing these the choice of failing by their own hands, untortured by those of the lictor; the severity of Postumius having, they considered, provoked the military mutiny.[132] The consul Furius took Ferentinum from the Volscians this year, and bestowed it upon the Hernicans, whose lands that people had ravaged. The three following years were marked by plague, famine, and civic disputes, and the consuls were compelled to buy corn for the relief of the starving population. To relieve the plebeians the tribune, Icilius, again brought forward the agrarian law, and Mænius, another tribune, would not suffer the consular levies to be raised, though the Volscians were ravaging the lands of the Hernicans, by which proceeding Carventum, a town of Latium, fell into the enemy's hands. The other members of the tribunate were so disgusted with the conduct of Mænius, that they instantly ordered the levies to be made, punishing those who refused to enlist. Valerius, one of the consuls, recovered the citadel, in which he found a rich booty, which he paid into the quæstor's hands for the use of the state. This proceeding displeased his soldiers, who chose to remember it at the ovation granted by the senate to their general, upon which occasion they divided themselves into two bands—one of which recited the praises of the tribune Mænius, while the other sang verses in depreciation of their commander. This was a precedent frequently followed from that time forward, the rude lyrics of the soldiers often converting the triumph of their general into a day of humiliation and shame.[133] The truce between Rome and Veii having expired, the republic made some additional demands upon this state before they would engage to renew it. The people of Veii entreated them not to enforce them till their internal divisions were allayed.[134] The Volscians took Verrugo from the Romans, and slew the garrison, but it was retaken by the military tribunes, and reprisals made upon the slayers.

The conduct of Fabius Ambustus, and his colleagues, opened the way to the conquest of Italy and the world B.C. 404. by a new regulation, for after they took Anxur (Terracina), these military tribunes divided the spoils among their armies, a measure which led to the Roman soldier receiving a stated sum for his services in the field. This arrangement displeased the tribunes of the people, but the patricians were so desirous that it should take place that they valued their own estates, in order to furnish the quota. Whether in this they paid the vectigal, or tithes as occupiers of the public land, is not certain, but it is probable they did. The plebeians saw the vectigal they paid to the state applied to this purpose with great pleasure, and even the prospect of a tax or tribute levied upon the whole people to make up any deficiency did not alter their opinion. They greeted the senators with the endearing name of fathers, and the poorest among them paid the tax with cheerfulness and alacrity. We must remember that the body of the army was composed of plebeians, commanded by patrician officers. The tax they paid would, therefore, return to them in the shape of pay. The first eclipse, recorded in the "Annales Maximi," fell on the nones of June B.C. 402.[135]

Veii was a strong Etruscan city, five miles in circumference, strongly entrenched, and very wealthy, and its siege, which commenced in the nineteenth military tribuneship, was as tedious as the real or fabulous one of Troy. The second year found the Romans before it, and the Etruscan states as its defenders, policy compelling them to unite against the growing power of the Romans. In the third year of the siege the Etruscans withdrew their aid under the pretence that the Veientines had elected a king—a measure displeasing to these republicans, but the real cause of their departure was the invasion of the Gauls. The besieged, soon after this, made a successful sally upon the Romans, whom they defeated, destroying also their war engines. The Roman people were not discouraged by this misfortune. The equestrian order offered to furnish their own horses, and to serve without pay. Their example was followed by the commons; for the senate had scarcely expressed their thanks, and accepted the gratuitous services of the knights, before the commons crowded round the Comitium to volunteer their services in the same disinterested manner. The senate, touched by their generosity, exclaimed, as they quitted the Comitium to thank the people in person, "Oh glorious day! Happy, eternal, and unconquerable is Rome made by this concord,"[136]—words prophetic of the future greatness of the republic, and which, if not entirely fulfilled to the letter, must have been so if the public feeling of unanimity had continued that gave them birth. The senators and people wept together with joy, yet the republic had suffered a reverse, two of the military tribunes being defeated by the Faliscans and Capenatans, and one of these generals was slain.[137] It is uncertain whether Furius Camillus was elected at this crisis military tribune or dictator, but his great talents were for the first time brought into notice during the last year of the siege of Veii.

Furius Camillus had been censor some years before, and during his office had passed a law which had rendered him obnoxious at the time, and contributed to his future unpopularity. This edict compelled the second marriages of the widows who had lost their husbands at the siege of Veii. The women of Rome, who considered such connections infamous, murmured at what they thought a conspiracy against their honour; nor were the bachelors, young and old, much better pleased with the censorial regulation, not supposing their domestic peace would be insured by these constrained political unions.[138] He also laid a tax upon orphans who had hitherto been exempted from bearing any part in the public charges. Though of a patrician family, this illustrious Roman was the first of his

117

name who graced the annals of his country. He is more generally known by his appellation of Camillus than by the patronymic of his family, which was Furius,[139] and his descendants were always styled Camilli.

In the next but one military tribuneship, which was chiefly composed of plebeian names, a victory was won over the Fidenatans and Capenatans, the allies of the Veientines; but the public joy on that occasion was damped by the excessive mortality occasioned by the plague, which B.C. 401-396. followed the unusual heat and drought. This unhealthy summer had been preceded by a terrible winter, and the national calamities demanded a remedy. The duumvirs sought for one in the Sibylline books, which were solemnly opened in order to discover in what way the wrath of the gods might be expiated. Their search occasioned the celebration of the first lectisternium ever held in Rome.[140]

The history of a natural phenomenon, followed by a great national work, has been so mixed up with superstition, and adorned by the poetical legend, that the introduction of the following tale would be impertinent and ridiculous but for the existence of the works that released the pent-up waters of the swollen Alban lake, and sent them to fertilise the plains they threatened to inundate and destroy:—It appears that the lake of Alba suddenly rose to the height of the rocks that surrounded it,[141] whereupon an old Veientine, who had made acquaintance with a Roman sentinel, told him that Veii would never be taken till all the water ran out of the lake of Alba. The sentinel, instead of treating the matter as a boast, captured the old man and brought him to the generals, who, finding he had quoted an ancient prophecy, sent him to Rome, the senate despatching three patricians to Delphi to consult the oracle upon the prediction.[142] The answer brought by the deputation from Delphi confirmed the Romans in the notion of draining the Alban lake.[143] This was immediately done, a noble work, whose remains may still be traced in the present day;[144] the tradition that linked the draining of the Alban lake with the fate of Veii rather proves that the work was carried forward during the last years of the siege, which was finally brought to a close during the dictatorship of Camillus. Some reverses sustained by the army reminded the people that this commander had never been defeated, a conclusion which led to his nomination; the complete victory he gained over the allies of the unfortunate Veientines at Nepete, justified the opinion of the Romans respecting the personal valour and military skill of the great dictator. Camillus, aided by a fine army, augmented by a band of volunteers, and by the Latins and Hernicans, then in alliance with the republic, prosecuted the siege with such vigour that the Veientines sent an embassy to Rome to implore for peace,[145] which was harshly refused by the senate. The peremptory answer to the prayer of the distressed people, excited this indignant rejoinder from one of the deputies: "A goodly answer indeed you have made us, for though we humble ourselves before you, ye will have no mercy, but ungenerously threaten utterly to destroy us. Ye neither care for the anger of the gods nor for the revenge of men, but the gods shall punish your pride and lay waste your country, as you are destroying ours."[146] The military skill of Camillus was fast bringing the protracted siege of Veii to a close, and being certain of the capture of the city, when he had undermined the citadel, and bored a passage to the temple of Juno, the tutelar deity of Veii, he sent to Rome to inquire the pleasure of the senate respecting its spoil. After a long debate, it was determined that every man should possess the plunder won by his own hand at the storm of the city, a measure that greatly increased the army of the dictator.

The Veientine general was in the very act of sacrificing in the temple of Juno, when Camillus suddenly appeared before him, followed by a chosen band of soldiers, and concluded the sacrifice, actually fulfilling the words of the diviner who had just pronounced, "That the gods had declared that he should be the victor who finished that sacrifice."[147] The presence of the armed conqueror within the city, and the assault given by his legions without, sealed the fate of Veii, which Camillus considered rather as the fruit of his vow of the tenth part of the spoil to Apollo than of his sword. His good fortune alarmed him by its excess, and he prayed "that if any ill were about to fall upon Rome or him, on account of this prosperity, it might be upon his own head, and not upon his country." As Camillus concluded the patriotic prayer before the shrine of Juno, he stumbled and fell in the very act of turning to depart,[148] the veil which covered his B.C. 396. head by confusing his sight, naturally occasioning the accident, which he interpreted as a favourable response to his petition. It was a beautiful heathen custom for the votaries of the gods to veil themselves in token of their unworthiness to approach their presence. The protecting deity of the Veientines, Juno, was removed to Rome, with her own consent, "which was humbly," the legend assures us, "solicited by the victors," for upon their asking her if she would go with them to Rome, she graciously replied, "I will." A stately temple was raised to the honour of this courteous deity, upon the Aventine Mount, by Camillus, in accordance with his vow.[149] The tutelar goddess left Veii to the mercy of the Romans, "which, after its ten years' siege, was at once despoiled of its wealth, its inhabitants, and its gods."[150] The return of Camillus to Rome was the signal of universal joy. Four days were set apart for a general thanksgiving to the gods, the triumph of the victor being the most splendid that had yet been seen in Rome. The heroic dictator appeared in a chariot drawn by white horses, crowned with laurel, and with his face painted with vermilion.[151] Superstition regarded the colour of the steeds of the victor, and the paint on his countenance, with horror. The gods had hitherto engrossed the use of both to themselves. The vermilion was not simply a proof of personal vanity; it was not merely a mark of bad taste in Camillus; it was impiety and presumption in a superlative degree. He became unpopular with the people and senate; and, a year after his triumph, with his own soldiers also. He had forgotten his vow to Apollo respecting the tenth part of the spoil, and his remembrance of it after the whole had been appropriated, irritated the army.[152] They refunded the dedicated portion with reluctance,[153] and but for fear of falling under the wrath of Apollo, would have kept it back, but their superstition did not prevent them from hating their general.

The question respecting the colonisation of Veii was fiercely discussed in the senate and comitia. Licinius, one of the tribunes of the people, even proposed sending half the senate and inhabitants of Rome to that fine city. This was negatived by the nobles, upon the plea, "that a people so prone to dissensions while under one government, would certainly become more factious when divided into two." The measure was, however, a popular one; and the people, who favoured it, would have come to blows, if some of the senators had not interposed their persons to the rioters, with the words,[154] "Strike, kill, and destroy us." When was boldness and decision ever lost upon this extraordinary people! The tumult ceased, and the project was abandoned.

<hr size=2 width="10%" align=center>

[1] Livy, iii. 24.

[2] Livy, iii., 25.

[3] Hooke; Arnold, i. 202; Livy, iii., 25.

[4] *Ibid.*

[5] Arnold; Dion. Hal., x. 23.

[6] Dion. Hal., x. 23; See Appendix. (p. 112)

[7] Dion. Hal., x. 23.

[8] Arnold, i. 204; Zonaras, vii. 344.

[9] Livy, iii. 26.

[10] Livy; Florus; Hooke.

[11] Livy, iii. 27.

[12] *Ibid.*, 28.

[13] Livy, iii. 27.

[14] *Ibid.*, 29.

[15] *Ibid.*

[16] *Ibid.*

[17] Livy, iii. 29.

[18] *Ibid.*

[19] See Appendix. (p. 115)

[20] Dion. Hal., x. 31.

[21] Arnold; Dion. Hal., x. 32.

[22] Livy, iii. 31.

[23] Livy, iii. 31.

[24] See Appendix. (p. 116)

[25] Dion. Hal., x.

[26] See Appendix. (p. 117)

[27] See Appendix. (p. 117)

[28] See Appendix. (p. 117)

[29] Livy; Dion. Hal.

[30] Dion. Hal.; Livy, iii. 33.

[31] Arnold; Pomponius, De Origine Juris, 4; Strabo, xiv. 1 § 25.

[32] Livy, iii. 34; Dion. Hal., x.

[33] Livy; Dion. Hal.

[34] *Ibid.*; *Ibid.*

[35] Livy, book iii. c. 39.

[36] *Ibid.*, 41.

[37] *Ibid.*, 42.

[38] Dion. Hal., xxi.

[39] Livy, iii. 43; Dion. Hal., ii. 78.

[40] See Appendix. (p. 120)

[41] Livy, iii. 44.

[42] If a patrician were unable to furnish his quota to the rapport of the state, or committed any glaring political offence, he lost the privileges of his nobility, and became a plebeian. If a plebeian were struck off the censorial roll, he lost his franchise, and sank into an ærarian.—Niebuhr's Rome.

[43] Cicero, De Republicâ, ii., 37.

[44] Livy; Hooke.

[45] Livy, Dion. Hal., xi.; Suetonius, in Tiberius.

[46] Livy.

[47] Livy.

[48] *Ibid.*, iii. 45.

[49] Livy, iii. 45.

[50] *Ibid.*

[51] *Ibid.*, iii. 44; Dion. Hal., xi.

[52] Livy, iii. 46.

[53] *Ibid.*

[54] Livy, iii. 47.

[55] *Ibid.*

[56] Dion. Hal., xi. 15, 16.

[57] *Ibid.*

[58] Satires.

[59] Livy, iii. 47.

[60] *Ibid.*

[61] *Ibid.*

[62] Montesquieu, Spirit of the Laws.

[63] Livy, iii.

[64] Dion. Hal., iii. 11; Livy, iii. 47.

[65] Livy, iii. 50.

[66] Livy, iii. 50.

[67] *Ibid.*, iii. 43, 49.

[68] *Ibid.*

[69] *Ibid.*

[70] Livy, iii. 51.

[71] Livy, 33; Dion. Hal., xi.

[72] Livy, iii. 25.

[73] Livy, iii. 28.

[74] Here an allusion seems to be made to some precedent in which that dreadful punishment had been inflicted on men whose crime had been their desertion of their own order to befriend the commons. This mysterious infliction is, however attested by local tradition, and recorded by a fragment. Livy, iii, 54. See Niebuhr's comment and restoration of the mutilated passage. Hist Rome.

[75] Livy.

[76] Cicero, Pro Cornelio, i. Fragment.

[77] Rapin.

[78] Livy, iii. 64.

[79] Arnold's Rome, i. 314.

[80] Arnold's Rome, i. 314; Zonaras, vii. 19.

[81] Livy, iii. 56; Montesquieu, Spirit of the Laws.

[82] Livy, iii. 56.

[83] *Ibid.*

[84] *Ibid.* 58.

[85] Dion. Hal., xi.

[86] Arnold's Rome, i. 284; and See Appendix. (p. 132)

[87] The final fall of Rome originated in the same proud sense of virtue; for after the regenerating influence of Christianity had revived this feeling, an outrage offered to the Empress Eudoxia induced her to call the Vandals to revenge her wrongs—a revenge which proved fatal to her country.

[88] De Finibus.

[89] See Appendix. (p. 132)

[90] Arnold's Rome, i. 218.

[91] Diodorus, xii. 25; Livy, iii. 55.

[92] Livy, iii. 55.

[93] Arnold.

[94] Livy, iii. 64.

[95] Livy, iii. 65; Cicero, De Republicâ, ii. 35; Arnold's Rome.

[96] Livy, iii. 27.

[97] *Ibid.*

[98] Livy, iii. 66.

[99] *Ibid.*

[100] From no allusion having been made to this victory in the Fasti, it is supposed that the Quinctian family furnished from their own records the panegyric of Quinctius, and this exploit, so honourable to their ancestor.J But why such records should be considered invalid by any historian must appear singular.

J Arnold's Rome, i. 335.

[101] Livy, iii. 66.

[102] Livy, iii. 71, 72.

[103] Zonaras; Arnold; Florus, i. 25.

[104] Hooke; Dion. Hal., xi.

[105] Arnold's Rome, i. 338.

[106] Livy, iii. 6; Dion. Hal.

[107] See Appendix. (p. 136)

[108] Hooke; Arnold; Zonaras.

[109] Livy, iv. 12, 13; Zonaras, vii.

[110] Arnold; Dion. Hal. xii. 1. Fragment. Mai.

[111] Livy, iv. 15.

[112] Hooke considers that there was no proof of Mælius's guilt, but his extreme popularity and the accusation of Minucius, an accusation most likely false.[K] This victim of the envy of the purveyor-general and the senate belonged to the plebeian section of knights. It seems fair to consider any man innocent who is slaughtered unarmed and without trial; although the dictatorial office conferred the right of putting any individual to death accused of treason untried.

K Hooke, Roman Republic.

[113] Arnold; Val. Max., v. 3 § 2.

[114] Arnold; Livy.

[115] Arnold; Pliny, xviii. 4.

[116] Arnold, Rome, i. 341.

[117] Livy, iv. 17.

[118] Livy, iv. 18, 19, 20.

[119] Livy says that he remained unpunished; Cicero, that he was banished and afterwards recalled. Cicero; Val. Max.

[120] Hooke.

[121] Livy, iv. 29; Diodorus, xii. 64; Aulus Gellius, xvii. 21.

[122] Livy, iv. 24.

[123] Livy, iv. 33; Florus, i. 12.

[124] Hooke.

[125] Livy, iv. 42.

[126] Arnold, Rome, i. 365.

[127] Livy, iv. 43.

[128] Hooke.

[129] Arnold; Livy, iv. 47.

[130] Livy, iv. 50.

[131] Livy, iv. 50; Florus.

[132] Hooke, Roman Republic.

[133] Hooke, Roman Republic.

[134] *Ibid.*; Livy. iv. 58.

[135] Cicero; Niebuhr.

[136] Livy, v. 7.

[137] Livy, v. 18.

[138] Plutarch, in Camillus.

[139] *Ibid.*

[140] See Appendix. (p. 147)

[141] Dion. Hal., xii. Fragment.

[142] *Ibid.*; Livy, v. 15; Plutarch.

[143] Livy, v. 16.

[144] Hooke, Roman Republic; and see Appendix. (p. 147)

[145] Dion. Hal., xii.

[146] Arnold; Livy, v. 16.

[147] Plutarch, in Vita Camilli; Livy, v. 22.

[148] Livy; Dion. Hal., xii.; Plutarch, in Camillus.

[149] Livy, v. 22.

[150] Hooke, Roman Republic.

[151] Plutarch, in Camillus; Livy, v. 23; Pliny, xxxiii.

[152] Plutarch, in Camillus; Livy, v. 23.

[153] The offering vowed by Camillus to Apollo being gold, and the currency of Rome being in copper, rendered the performance of his vow very inconvenient to the public. The matrons of Rome, to assist their countrymen in this difficulty, brought their golden trinkets to the Treasury. The senate would not accept these ornaments as a gift; but paid the value of them in copper; and, in order to reward these patriotic females, granted them the use of two kinds of carriages, one for every-day use, and the other, of a better construction, for attendance at the games or sacrifices. Livy, v. 25.

[154] Hooke, Roman Republic, iii.

CHAPTER IV.

A.U.C. 359-387. B.C. 395-367.

Magnanimous conduct of Camillus at Falerii.—Flight of the Romans to Verrugo.—Victory of Postumius.—Camillus accused of embezzlement, and cited for his Trial.—His prayer.—Retires to Ardea.—The Gauls in Italy.—Embassy of the Clusians.—Reply of Brennus to the Roman Ambassadors.—Their misconduct.—March of Brennus to Rome.—Battle of the Allia.—Self-devotion of Roman consulars.—Marcus Papirius and his friends put to death.—Sack of Rome.—Blockade of the Capitol.—Camillus delivers the Ardeatans.—Camillus made Dictator.—Adventure of Pontius Cominius.—Midnight attack of the Gauls.—Gallantry of Marcus Manlius.—His reward.—Honours paid to Geese.—Famine in Rome and the Capitol.—Brennus makes a bargain with the Romans.—His false weights and insolence.—Appearance of Camillus.—His victories and triumphant return.—The Romans wish to abandon Rome.—Good omen given by a centurion.—The muniments and records of Rome collected.—Rome rebuilt in a mean manner.—Combination against Rome.—Gallantry of Camillus.—New Roman tribes.— Trial and condemnation of Marcus Manlius.—Insolence of Furius to Camillus.—The Tusculans made Roman citizens.—Jupiter Imperator carried to Rome.—Volscian War.—Poverty of the Plebeians.—Pride of Fabia the younger.—Licinian law.—Licinius Stolo a tribune for five years.—Camillus defeats the Gauls.—Cited before the people.— Attempt to pull him from the tribunal.—His vow.—Camillus induces the senate to accede to the demands of the people.—His son first prætor of Rome.—New ædiles.— Popularity of Camillus.—His death, and character.

THE capture of Capena brought Camillus before Falerii, the capital city of the Faliscans. While he was engaged in the siege of this place, the public schoolmaster delivered up to him all the boys intrusted to him for education with this remark—"that with them he had brought the keys that would open the city.[1]"

Camillus, who was himself a tender father, turned from the traitorous preceptor with disgust, and addressing some of his own friends, uttered this fine remark—"What a calamity is war, which is so often begun and ended with injustice; but to good men there are certain laws in war itself. Victory, however desirable, ought not to be purchased by the help of the wicked. A great general must rely upon his own valour, not upon the deceit and treachery of the base." He ordered his soldiers to strip and bind the vile schoolmaster, and to put scourges into the hands of his pupils, to whom he left the punishment of their betrayer.[2] The parents, who from the walls of their city had beheld their children led into the Roman camp with an agony of solicitude, saw the magnanimous conduct of the general with astonishment and admiration. They sent a deputation to the Roman camp to thank Camillus, and to assure him "that they considered themselves twice conquered by him: once in the field, and again by his generosity; and that they would now yield to his virtue what they had refused to his arms."[3] An honourable peace was the fruit of this negotiation. The soldiers murmured at the loss of the plunder of Falerii; but the triumphal entry of Camillus was greeted by admiring groups of citizens, who felt that the real glory of Rome had been advanced by a virtuous action more than by an additional laurel in her blood-stained wreath. The Faliscans, some years after the surrender of their city, were admitted into the four new Roman tribes.[4] The magnanimity of Camillus was remembered from age to age in the heroic lays of the people, and being grafted into the records of Rome, was immortalised by the history of Livy and the biography of Plutarch. While Camillus had been engaged in the war with the Faliscans, Æmilius and Postumius were fighting with the Æquians. The personal bravery of Postumius changed a defeat into a victory. His army were flying panic-stricken to Verrugo, where Æmilius was in garrison. The reproaches of the deserted general made the troops ashamed of their conduct, and they suffered him to lead them back into the field, where he gained a complete B.C. 393-91. victory by moonlight. The garrison ran away from Verrugo, believing that Postumius had lost his camp, and brought the tidings of the supposed misfortune to Rome. The laurel-crowned letter of Postumius undeceived the senate, and the general consternation was changed into joy.[5]

Consuls were elected again the year following these conquests; L. Lucretius Flavus and Servius Sulpicius Camerinus, holding this dignity, which for some time had been laid aside. Licinius, a tribune of the people, once more proposed retiring to Veii; he even fined those tribunes who had opposed it the preceding year. The senators went in a body to the Forum, where they dissuaded the people from a course that would have ruined the republic. They obtained a majority against the measure, and immediately assigned seven acres to each free citizen of the lands won from the Veientines, to enable them to bring up their families.

Rome was devastated with plague and famine, and one of the censors, Caius Julius, was carried off by this malady. He was succeeded by M. Cornelius. The sickness of both consuls led to the election of military tribunes. Thus Rome was governed by two distinct magistracies this year.[6]

Two years later, the prosecution of the great Camillus[7] led to more memorable events than the victories of Lucretius and Æmilius over the Vulsinians.

Camillus is supposed to have compelled the consuls of the preceding year to resign, and it is certain that M. Manlius—to whom he afterwards showed deadly enmity—was one of those persons; but if their neglect of the defence of Pyrgi which was taken by Dionysius of Syracuse from the Cærites—a people in alliance with Rome—was the ground of their deposition,[8] no blame attached to Camillus. But his politically opposing the grant lately made to the people, rendered him unpopular with the citizens; nor had his reclaiming the tenth part of the spoil conciliated the army. Apuleius, a tribune of the commons, was the person who accused Camillus, whom he charged with having appropriated the spoils of Veii to his own use, in proof of which he declared that the brazen gates of that city were still in his house, and he cited him in form to take his trial before the people.[9] Camillus was employed in closing the eyes of a promising son when the summons came, and he would not leave the newly-dead, but called his friends to the house of mourning to consult with them upon the propriety of making his defence:[10] they assured him that his sentence was already pre-determined, and that they could only promise him assistance towards the fine, but would not engage to do more.[11] This answer convinced Camillus that private friendship would be no shield against public insult and injury. He bade his family farewell, and walked in silence to the gate of the ungrateful city,[12] giving no utterance to his indignant feelings till he had passed through the barrier, and stood without the gates of Rome an expatriated and impoverished man, cast forth from the country he had enriched and served. He then knelt down, and invoking Nemesis, stretched forth his hands towards the Capitol, and prayed "that if he were driven out without any fault of his own, and merely by the violence or envy of the Roman people, they might quickly repent it, and express to all the world their want of Camillus, and their regret for his absence."[13]

Camillus retired to Ardea, where he was received with the respect due to his merits and misfortunes. He had scarcely taken refuge in that city before he was fined fifteen thousand asses of brass by the tribunes of the people. This fine amounted to about forty-eight pounds of our currency, although it was accounted a considerable sum in Rome at that time.

A few days after Camillus had gone into exile, an embassy arrived in Rome from Clusium in Etruria,[14] praying the republic to grant them aid against the Gauls who had entered Italy and were then besieging their city.[15] This embassy was said to be the cause of the misfortunes that afterwards befel the Romans, by drawing B.C. 390. upon Rome the resentment of a revengeful and incensed people.[16] The Senonians, a people located near the present site of Paris, were the nation whose attack had given the Clusians so much alarm, and had occasioned them to send an embassy to Rome.[17] The Romans, though not in alliance with the Clusians, sent ambassadors to Brennus, the Gallic chief, requiring him to break up the siege of Clusium, upon the grounds that the people with whom he was at war had done no previous injury to him.[18] The ambassadors, who were the sons of Fabius Ambustus, were interrupted by the scornful laugh of the king, or leader, of the Gauls. "No injury!" replied Brennus. "They have done us a great wrong, for they have more land than they can cultivate, and have refused to give a part of it to us who are strangers, numerous, and very poor.[19] The most ancient of all laws ordains that the weak must yield to the strong, and the brave be lords of the world." Brennus added to this blunt speech, "that he had never before heard of the Roman name."[20] His answer deeply offended the haughty Fabii, who showed their resentment by taking part in the defence of Clusium, for Quintus Fabius actually headed a sally made by the besieged, and slew a general of the Gauls, whose magnificent person and distinguished bravery had attracted his attention. While in the act of despoiling the slain of his armour, the Roman ambassador was seen and recognised by Brennus, who immediately sent a herald to Rome to complain of this violation of the laws of nations on the part of the Romans, and to demand that the offenders should be given up to him. If this justice were refused him, the herald was instructed to declare war against the Republic on the part of the chief.[21]

The senate, the college of feciales, or heralds, and the priests, considered the conduct of the ambassadors highly culpable, and the demand of Brennus perfectly just. Nothing, in fact, but the birth and influence of the offenders prevented them from delivering up the Fabii to the Gauls. The assembly of the people, however, decided against the measure. Fabius Ambustus not only successfully carried the point in favour of his sons, but got them nominated to the military tribuneship for the new year, in concert with Q. Sulpicius, Q. Servilius, and Sergius Cornelius.[22] The return of the Gallic herald was the signal for the march of Brennus; that barbarian, we are told, calmed the fears of the terrified country-people belonging to the villages through which he passed, by declaring with savage magnanimity that "he was at war with the Romans only." In the general consternation prevailing at Rome when the tidings reached the doomed city that Brennus with seventy thousand men was at hand, the necessary preparations for its defence were neglected,[23] no dictator was named; even the usual religious ceremonies were omitted. The military tribunes, who were young and inexperienced commanders, put themselves at the head of the hastily raised levies, and marched out to meet the enemy, whom they found near the Allia, upon the bank of the Tiber. The situation of this stream is not distinctly known; but in a country subject to commotions of the earth alterations are not uncommon, and the precise site may be lost. This battle was fought on a day considered unfortunate in the annals of the republic, being the same on which three hundred Fabii had perished by the swords of the Etruscans. It is probable that the Roman soldiers who were led to the contest by three of this name and family, were even then impressed by the evil omen. The position taken up by the six leaders was disadvantageous, and Brennus seizing the hill upon which they had placed a body of troops to guard their right flank, dispersed them with such celerity, that the greater part of the legions of the right wing fled without striking a blow to Rome, and without even shutting the gates upon the enemy took shelter in the citadel. The left were driven into the river by the charge of the Gauls.[24] Many were drowned, but the greater part escaped to Veii, and shutting themselves within its gates, abandoned the city of Romulus to its fate. This memorable defeat happened upon the sixteenth of July, B.C. 390. The rush of the panic-stricken soldiery towards the Capitol told the shameful history of the day to the B.C. 390. affrighted inhabitants of Rome.[25] The venerable patricians, who had formerly fought her battles, could not resolve to leave her. Incapable of defending her, they determined to perish with her. They advised the women and children to fly, and exhorted the garrison within the Capitol to maintain that temple fortress to the last "as the remains of a state that, for more than three hundred and sixty years, in all its wars, had been victorious." After giving this counsel, they withdrew to the Forum followed by the tears and lamentations of the distracted populace.

Over the Sublician bridge poured the mighty multitude, unknowing whither to fly, without a leader or a home. The vestal virgins, bereft of their state, and encumbered with their sacred relics, followed the throng on foot;[26] but even in that moment of general despair the Roman people did not forget their veneration for the priestesses of Vesta. Albinus, a plebeian, perceiving them encumbered with the weight of their burdens, made his family descend from the cart in which he was conveying them to a place of safety, to make way for the sacred order, who were still holy in his eyes as in the proud days of their prosperity.[27] The small city of Cære in Etruria received the vestals and the symbols of their religion, and its rites from being duly performed there, took the name of cerimoniæ,[28] from the place of asylum, from whence our English word "ceremony" is derived. To this spot of refuge the priests also repaired, having first buried the sacred objects of their misplaced veneration in the earth.[29] The aged citizens, with whom the name of Rome was associated with the strength and glory of their vanished youth, alone remained within the walls of the deserted city, with the exception of the soldiers who guarded the Capitol, and those who were sick or unable to fly. These venerable men, by their generous self-devotion, hoped to avert the wrath of the gods from the survivors, and to fix it upon the victorious enemy. It was the superstitious notion of that age, that those who, by a voluntary sacrifice, devoted themselves to the infernal gods, purchased for their country every blessing, and secured the annihilation of her foes; it was perhaps some vague tradition of the great atonement that had lingered among the Gentile nations, and had been corrupted from its original purity. Before his departure, Fabius, the Pontifex Maximus, had hastily pronounced over the victims' heads the oath of consecration, who, attiring themselves in their robes of state, and seated in the Forum on curule chairs,[30] awaited the hour of their sacrifice.[31] Towards sunset the scouts of Brennus informed their chief that the gates of Rome stood open, but that the city appeared deserted by its inhabitants. Brennus would not believe that a warlike people like the Romans could have yielded up their capital without a blow, till the death-like silence that reigned in the deserted streets convinced him that this was indeed the case. He entered with the Gauls at the Collina gate, and found that the same stillness prevailed everywhere.[32] Upon the fortified heights of the Capitol, armed men alone were seen, for the population was gone. Yet the wary leader of the barbarian army still dreaded some stratagem, for he carefully invested every street and avenue leading to the Capitol before he advanced into the Forum, attended by a band selected from the flower of his army, where the sight of the aged and self-devoted Roman consulars[33] attracted his attention, and filled his mind with superstitious awe. The bold barbarian looked long and fixedly upon their venerable faces; to him they appeared the tutelar gods, the protecting deities of the forsaken city,[34] as arrayed in their magnificent purple habits, they sat in silent majesty unmoved by the presence of the foreign soldiers or their kingly leader. The Gauls, as superstitious as their chief, kept in the background, nor attempted to offer violence to the devoted Romans, whose mortality they evidently doubted. One soldier at length ventured to draw near to Marcus Papirius, determined to convince himself if he were really flesh and blood or only a visionary being, so, stretching forth his hand, he gently touched the long white beard of the old man.[35] Marcus Papirius, who disapproved of the experiment, B.C. 390. convinced the curious soldier of his actual existence by striking him smartly with his ivory staff. The revengeful Gaul instantly slew the high-spirited veteran, and his example was followed by his companions in arms, who massacred these ancient patriots, amounting to the number of eighty; after which, they dispersed themselves through the city in search of plunder, putting to the sword all those whom age, feebleness or sickness had confined within the houses. Not content with this impotent revenge, they fired Rome in many places, and reduced it to a heap of mouldering ashes.[36] Brennus upon the following day invested the Capitol, which he hoped to carry by assault, but finding it bravely and obstinately defended by the garrison, whom he proved to be more courageous than when he met them near the Allia, he changed the siege into a blockade, confidently expecting to starve the Romans into submission.[37] Of water he could not deprive them, for the well of the Capitol remains a curious and undoubted monument of that remote time.[38] To all human appearance, Rome had fallen to rise no more. Her people were dispersed, her walls cast down, and a powerful barbarian nation was encamped within her scorched and blackened ruins. But she must rise again, for the mighty destiny, foretold of her by the prophet Daniel,[39] was to be accomplished, and how could this be if she were never to be rebuilt? Therefore she was to arise from her ashes, for the sword of the great fourth monarchy was to cleave the way for the seed of the Gospel to be shed abroad, and under the shadow of her eagle wings was Judea to repose during the period when the Prince of Peace was to be born, his wondrous mission unfolded, and atonement made for the sins of the whole world.

Brennus and his army soon experienced the ill consequences of their savage destructiveness, for they were in want of provisions, and the Capitol still held out. They were not men, however, likely to starve while food could be had for blows. They dispersed themselves in all directions to obtain forage, and levied contributions on every side from the affrighted towns and villages. A large body of Gauls encamped before Ardea, the city that had afforded an asylum to the exiled Camillus, and demanded supplies. That illustrious Roman, willing to repay the debt of gratitude he owed the generous Ardeatans, counselled them to refuse the demand of the Gauls. He offered to train their youth to arms, and lead them against the barbarians. The Ardeatans recalled to mind his great military prowess, accepted his offer with acclamations, and resolved to follow his directions. They accordingly shut their gates against Brennus, and commenced their military education under the greatest captain of that age.[40] The Gauls, who spent their days in ravaging the fruitful plains of Italy, and their nights in feasting, entertained no dread of the besieged Ardeatans, or their Roman leader.[41] Camillus took advantage of their security to storm their camp, and the sleepers only started from their stupor of intoxication, at the sound of the Ardeatan trumpets, to fall by the sword. Camillus, who resolved to wage a war of utter extermination against the destroyers of his native city, posted a strong body of troops in the neighbouring fields to cut off the stragglers. Few escaped to tell the tidings to their brother barbarians in the ruined city.[42] The news of the victory reaching Veii filled the fugitive Roman legions who had shut themselves up there with shame and regret. They remembered the prayer of Camillus which, they thought, had been answered by the offended gods. They blushed for their past conduct, and resolved to entreat the exile to lead them against the Gauls. Rome that had cast him forth into exile was no more; and they hoped his resentment had perished with her. They sent a deputation to Ardea to this effect, and Camillus, more noble and forgiving than Coriolanus, gave them a favourable answer,[43] contingent however upon the consent of the senate to his acceptance of the dictatorship, which the army offered to confer upon him. As the senate was blockaded in the Capitol, their assent was not easy to obtain, but the patriotic Roman declared "that while that citadel remained, and contained her senators, Rome had still a political existence. The ruined walls of the city marked the bounds of his country; to him, Rome in the dust was yet Rome; therefore, B.C. 389-388. from the Romans in the Capitol he must derive his commission."

Pontius Cominius[44] undertook to obtain the consent of the senate, yet the task might have deterred any one less patriotic, or less ambitious of glory, than the young Roman. The temple-fortress was invested on every side but one by Brennus and his Gauls, and that unguarded point was considered inaccessible. As the bridge was held by the invaders, Pontius must swim across the Tiber in the darkness of night, at a part of the stream where the current was strongest, and the danger most imminent, and when this difficult object was accomplished, there was still the craggy and hitherto untrodden heights of that part of the rock to be attained. Before the resolution of the patriotic youth these difficulties quickly vanished. With the aid of bladders (for it is doubtful whether he could swim the Tiber without such aid) he floated with the current down the stream, and landing near the Carmental Gate, climbed the steep precipice, and conveyed his tidings to those within the walls. That Camillus was in arms, and at the head of an army of Romans and foreigners of forty thousand strong, and awaiting their consent to lead his legions to Rome, appeared almost incredible good fortune to the besieged, and Pontius returned with letters from the senate confirming the appointment of Camillus.[45] While the dictator was preparing to relieve the Capitol, that important fortress was nearly lost by the very means used by the adventurous Pontius for its preservation. Some Gauls wandering near the Carmental Gate observed the print of the daring Roman's footsteps, and plainly perceived that communication had been lately held by some person with the garrison in the citadel. They immediately hastened to their chief, to whom they communicated their important discovery.[46] Brennus, who knew that what man had done man might do again, determined to turn this discovery to his own advantage. He resolved to storm the Capitol by following the path scaled by the unknown enemy; selecting from his army a band of mountaineers, to whom such adventures were familiar, he directed them to ascend the precipice at night, two abreast, in the direction of the steps of the stranger. In silence and darkness the Gauls climbed the eminence, not even arousing the vigilance of the sentinels nor the fury of the watch-dogs;[47] but, fortunately for the Romans, though these were sleeping, more wakeful creatures were stirring at the moment when the Capitol was scaled. The sacred geese, kept in the court of the temple in honour of Juno, heard the approach of the Gauls, and commenced a noisy cackling.[48] A patrician named Manlius, struck with their clamour, roused his fellow-soldiers from their sleep, and seizing his sword, hurried to the rampart, where he found two Gauls awaiting the arrival of their comrades below. Possessed of extraordinary strength and invincible courage, Manlius struck off the right hand of one of his opponents with his sword, while he dashed his buckler full in the face of the other, hurling him down the rock upon his ascending countrymen. The gallant defender was then joined by the rest of the soldiers; the Gauls were slain or driven back, and the besieged delivered from their perilous position. One of the negligent sentinels, as a warning to the rest, was condemned, by the military tribune Sulpicius, to be hurled from the ramparts; while the addition of Capitolinus to his name, and the gift of so much wheat and wine from every soldier, comprised the rewards and honours that were bestowed upon Manlius; but in a time of scarcity the corn was more valuable than gold, and the family of Manlius continued to be distinguished by the surname in the most glorious eras of the Republic.[49] Upon Roman geese was conferred the substantial and unwonted distinction of being fattened, but never eaten—a privilege not extended to those of other countries.[50] In Italy, even at this remote period, a goose is never brought to table. A golden image of one of these watchful B.C. 389. birds was made to commemorate their vigilance, and upon a certain day in every year one was placed in a sumptuous litter, and carried in state about the city, while a dog was impaled upon an elder-stake, that act of barbarity being a manifestation of the national hatred and contempt for the animal.

At the end of seven months[51] both the besieged in the Capitol and the besiegers were in a starving condition, for Camillus had invested all the roads leading to the ruined city, so that Brennus himself was in a state of blockade. The plague was making terrible ravages in his army; it was the consequence of his victory, for the slain Romans had been left unburied, and the great heat had generated this formidable disease. The Roman garrison, who had heard nothing from the dictator, and were ignorant of his intention to raise the blockade, began to listen to offers of accommodation, which commenced by dialogues carried on between the sentinels of the two nations.[52] The result of their negotiations was quickly communicated to their commanders, when Brennus demanded ten thousand pounds weight of gold as the price of his departure.[53] The tribune Sulpicius, with the consent of the senate, agreed to the terms, and, on the appointed day, brought the gold, amounting to forty thousand pounds sterling of English currency, to the appointed place, whither Brennus with his scales and weights came[54] "to receive the ransom of the people destined to conquer the world."[55] The leader of the barbarian army, who did not possess a very nice sense of honour, produced false weights to get more gold from the Romans than was his due. Sulpicius detected his enemy's unfair dealing, and remonstrated with him upon his want of faith. Brennus immediately flung his sword and buckler into the scale Sulpicius had considered too heavy, accompanying the action with a gesture indicative of defiance and contempt. The Roman, deeply offended, demanded the meaning of his conduct. *Væ victis* (woe to the conquered) was the insolent reply of the rapacious Gaul, whose bad Latin was perfectly comprehensible to his incensed auditors. Sulpicius was about to carry back his gold into the Capitol against the entreaties of his companions, some of whom were less scrupulous, when Camillus himself appeared upon the scene, who, confronting Brennus with a boldness worthy of the bravest of the Romans, cried out, "By steel and not by gold are the Romans accustomed to deliver their country." The dictator then flung the gold from the scale with contempt, and commanded it to be carried back into the citadel.[56] Brennus upbraided the Romans with their non-fulfilment of their agreement with him, and from words the Gauls and the troops of Camillus came to blows.[57] The contest was not decisive, for the streets were crowded with rubbish, and presented no arena for the combatants. Brennus retreated to his camp, which he broke up on the following morning, and commenced his retreat from Rome, encamping, however, on the Gabinian way, about eight miles from the ruined city. Here he was overtaken by Camillus, who offered him battle, and having gained a great victory, stormed his camp and put to the sword all whom he found there.[58] The story of the return of Camillus just in time to prevent the payment of the Roman ransom has been disputed by some modern historians, and is differently related by several ancient ones.[59] Upon the thirteenth of February Camillus entered the ruined city in triumph.[60] The returning population of Rome met the besieged in the Capitol. The soldiers and people crowded round the chariot of the conqueror, whom they hailed in their songs as "Romulus father of his country and second founder of Rome."[61] As soon as he had purified the city he rebuilt the temples, and erected a new one upon the spot where Marcus Cædicius heard the mysterious warning of the approach of the Gauls. This fane was dedicated to "Aius Locutius."[62] While Camillus was taking care for the restoration of the religion of the Romans, such as it was, the first enthusiasm of the public had faded away. They were discouraged at the laborious task of rebuilding their houses, and turning their thoughts to the noble city of Veii, which would contain them all, wished to transfer themselves and the government of Rome to that place. This project was B.C. 389-388. strenuously opposed by the senate and the dictator. The tribunes of the people, who wished for the measure, ungratefully charged Camillus with the ambitious design of being styled the second founder of Rome, to which they imputed his aversion to make the flourishing and prosperous Veii the capital of the Republic. The important matter was decided by a singular incident.[63]

The senate, being assembled to debate the question, called upon Lucius Lucretius to give his vote for Rome or Veii. As he was rising to speak, he and the whole assembly heard the centurion who came with his company to relieve the guard say, "Ensign, plant the standard here; this is the place to stay in." Struck with the singular coincidence these random words bore to the subject before them, Lucretius and the senators ran out of the temple where the assembly was held, crying out, "A happy omen. The gods have spoken, and we obey."

The superstitious people were convinced, and abandoned the idea of removing to Veii for ever. The augural staff of Romulus was found among the ruins of Rome, buried among its ashes, yet unconsumed.

The thirty-second military tribuneship, which had proved such an unfortunate era for Rome, lasted nearly two years, as the magistrates were supposed to be too unlucky to preside at the election of new ones. Camillus and Cornelius Scipio were alternately inter-reges, and the former held the election for the magistrates for the ensuing year. Notwithstanding the national calamity that had attended the last tribuneship, six military tribunes were chosen instead of consuls. Their employment was wholly confined to re-collecting the regal and decemviral laws, and transferring what could be found of the latter to tables of brass set up in the Forum.[64] The priests claimed the right of preserving and keeping the laws and records relative to religion, and expounding them to the people. A list of lucky and unlucky days was made, in which the 18th day of July as the day of the slaughter of the Fabii, and of the defeat at Allia, held a pre-eminent place among those marked as inauspicious to the republic. The rebuilding of Rome proceeded with more rapidity than attention to architectural beauty. The streets were irregularly planned, and the houses mean and inconvenient, being built from the old material, the government furnishing money for the roofs from the public treasury. Rome, the destined queen of the universe, rose out of her ashes with an appearance by no means suited to the lofty and unrivalled fortunes awaiting her. Her fall and her ransom by the sword, and not by gold, were celebrated in the heroic legends of the land; and to draw the line accurately where truth ends and fictitious ornament begins, appears impossible. It may be that Camillus merely reduced the ransom to its original standard of weight, or that he actually drove Brennus from Rome; but in either case he was hailed by his country as her deliverer and second founder, and the Gauls were chased from the land they had invaded by an incensed and indignant people. To ancient or modern Rome, a French army has always been fatal. Neither her strong walls nor valiant sons have ever successfully contended with France, and the events of her last siege only attest a fact often recurring in her annals, that one people at least have never found her invincible.

The annals of the world exhibit to the eyes of the historian continual phases of national progression and retrogradation. In that mirror he beholds the rise, the advance, and the fall of nations, each displaying a sort of resting-point in which the work of civilisation is effected, and the symptoms of decay are yet unfelt. The people of Italy had gained this climax before the infancy of Rome had passed away, and Etruria, with her beautiful works of art, her tombs, and her luxury, was awaiting the time when "that people who possessed more steel should win her gold." If we were asked at what precise period of her history a country begins to retrograde, the answer given by experience would be, "when wealth becomes her standard of merit, and is considered the sole requisite in those who compose her government, instead of talent and moral worth." Such a people abandon themselves to luxury, patriotism becomes extinct, and they fall into ruin to rise no more, the moral degradation always preceding the political death. Thus was it with the ancient empires of Assyria, Babylon, Persia, Macedonia, with the mighty republic of Carthage, and finally with Rome herself; B.C. 388-387. but Rome at this period was struggling for her existence, while the possessors of the fair garden of Europe, Italy, had reached their culminating point; their star was about to decline before the Romans, who had raised from her ashes a city mean in architecture, and despoiled of her records and her wealth.[65] The immediate neighbours of Rome—the Etruscans, Æquians, and Volscians—beheld her rise from those ashes, which they hoped had annihilated her political existence, with jealousy and hatred. Even the Latins and Hernicans, those ancient allies of the republic, united with her enemies in the attempt to crush her. In this era of danger the eyes of the Roman people were fixed upon Camillus, who was chosen dictator for the third time.[66] He left a strong body of troops under Manlius to guard the city, despatching another under Æmilius to keep the Etruscans in check, while he stormed and fired the camp of the confederates. The total destruction of the

135

combined army led to the reduction of the Volscians, who had been the formidable opponents of the republic for more than a century. Marching into the country of the Æquians, the dictator took their camp, and stormed Bola, their principal city. He next turned his victorious arms against the Etruscans, who were besieging Sutrium, a city belonging to the allies of Rome. He came too late to prevent the capitulation of Sutrium, but not to revenge her; for, upon meeting the dispossessed, homeless people, he assured them that their sorrow should soon be turned to joy. He fulfilled his promise by retaking the city that same day, and restoring it to its rightful owners in the evening.[67] "Camillus returned to Rome in triumph, having concluded three wars with glory in the short space of three years." His entry was very magnificent, and the sale of the Etruscan captives was applied to repay the Roman ladies for the jewels they had patriotically lent the state on some former occasion of public distress. Three vases of gold, inscribed with the name of the great dictator, were placed by order of the senate at the feet of the statue of Juno, in the temple of Jupiter, for that goddess was the tutelar deity of the valiant Roman.[68] War, however, was not the sole employment of the Romans; for they faced the Capitol with stone, and so improved and adorned it, that even in the Augustan age the work was greatly admired for its architectural beauty.[69] The restoration of the temple fortress was unfortunately undertaken at a time when the increase of the tributum, or taxes, pressed upon men whose means the destruction and rebuilding of Rome had greatly reduced. Four new tribes were added to the number this year, to which the names of Stellatina, Fromentina, Sabitina, and Anniensis were given.

The invasion of the Antiatans, or Volscians of Antium, again placed Camillus at the head of an army. Near Satricum he met the invaders, when, perceiving that his soldiers were discouraged by their numbers, he rode through their ranks to reassure them, and alighting from his horse, took a standard-bearer by the arm, whom he led towards the hostile ranks, with the words, "Soldiers, advance!" The Romans followed their heroic leader, and the battle was won.[70] He raised the siege of Sutrium,[71] which was again on the point of falling into the hands of the Etruscans, and retook Nepete, which had surrendered voluntarily to the Etruscans, putting the revolted garrison to the sword. An invasion of the Pomptine territory by the united forces of the Latins, Volscians, and Hernicans, was one of the leading features of the following military tribuneship, the Volsci claiming these lands by right of inheritance, which the Romans held by that of conquest. The event that stained the annals of the next tribuneship but one was the impeachment and condemnation of Marcus Manlius Capitolinus, the very man who had saved the temple fortress, the pride and ornament of the city, from the possession of the Gauls. To avert the real or pretended danger originating from the popularity of this eminent person, as well as to head the armies of the republic, a dictator was named in the person of Cornelius Cossus. This new magistrate appointed T. Quinctius Capitolinus for his master of horse, the title by which the republican cavalry general was generally distinguished.[72] It is difficult and perhaps impossible to decide from the B.C. 381. scanty evidence before us whether we are to consider Manlius as a patriot or a victim, as the jealous rival of Camillus, or a noble-minded man, who stood forth to support and succour the distressed, or the guilty and ambitious aspirant aiming at absolute power through the favour of the people. Under each of these aspects we might view the patrician, who was tried and executed with the concurrence of the commons, on the accusation of the dictator Cossus. If we follow the narrative, the supreme magistrate was recalled from his victories over the Volscians to protect Rome from the daring ambition of Manlius[73].

If Manlius were really a traitor, his treason took the shape of charity; for on every occasion in which the payment of debt was enforced on the aged and impoverished debtor, he satisfied the rapacious creditor, not without expressing his indignation against the exactor of usurious interest.[74] The sight of a centurion who had served with him dragged through the Forum, on his way to the creditor's house as his bondsman, gave publicity to these compassionate deeds; and the lofty patrician, who stooped from his position to redeem upon the spot the veteran who had served with him in the field, was recognised at once as the glory of his own order, and the hope and champion of the plebeian.[75] After this he sold the principal part of his landed estates to alleviate the distresses of four hundred debtors,[76] probably being conscious that the lands of the rich had been stolen out of the ager communis of the poor; for it was by such encroachments that the patrician order had become rich. Acts like these had obtained for the generous benefactor of the commons the endearing appellation of "Father." His house in the Capitol was the resort of the poor and oppressed, in whose hearing he uttered invectives against the senate, accusing that body of having appropriated the gold that had been offered as a bribe to Brennus to their own use.[77] This large sum he proposed compelling them to restore for the general benefit of poor plebeian debtors, whose obligations he calculated it would discharge. Such was the state of the republic when Cornelius Cossus, the dictator, was called from fighting her battles, to prevent or wage a civil war at home. Ascending his tribunal in the Forum, he sent a lictor to summon the popular Roman leader before him.[78] Manlius obeyed, but entered the place accompanied by an army of retainers or clients, looking more like a general about to engage an enemy than a factious citizen called upon by the chief magistrate to answer for his sedition.[79] The dictator's chief object was to clear the senate from the charge of having stolen the treasure, and to express his willingness to appropriate it to the purposes proposed by Manlius if it could be found. He therefore called upon him to name the parties who had taken possession of it, under the penalty of imprisonment as a slanderer of the senatorial body.[80] The proposition was a fair one; but if the accounts be not garbled, it was not met as candidly by Manlius. "Am I to reveal the place where your thefts are concealed?" haughtily retorted Manlius. "Ought not you rather to be compelled to reveal it?" The dictator immediately committed him to prison, whereupon Manlius passionately invoked all the celestial deities, and Juno in particular, whom he addressed as the queen of heaven, to deliver him from his enemies. "Will you suffer your defender to be thus treated by his enemies? Shall this right hand be locked in chains with which I drove the Gauls from your sanctuaries?"[81] was the indignant prayer of her votary. The people saw their champion conducted to prison with tears, but they made no attempt to save him from that indignity. They confined their impotent pity to lamenting his misfortunes beneath the walls of his prison, neglecting their hair and beards, and assuming mourning habits.[82] The committal of Manlius was followed by the dictatorial triumph. This show did not calm the irritated minds of the plebeians, who said openly, "that Manlius in his chains was wanting to swell the arrogance of the victor." They affected to marvel at his absence, nor did the assignment of the territories of Satricum, as a colony, with the gift of two acres and a half of arable land to B.C. 381. each man who would repair thither, at all allay the public discontent. The senate, not willing that Manlius should owe his liberty to the people, who threatened to take him out of prison by force, released him by an act of their own power. The thirty-eighth military tribuneship was remarkable for the termination of the contest between the plebeian party with its illustrious patrician leader and the aristocracy, headed by Camillus, who was this year chosen military tribune[83] for the fifth time. But the enmity of the aristocracy was not the sole cause in action to crush the leader of the people, the destructive force emanated from the democracy itself. The tribunes of the people hated him, and M. Manius and Q. Petilius, two of that college, boldly said, "Why do we make that to be a strife between the senate and commons, which ought to be a war of the state against one pestilent citizen? We will cite him to take his trial before the people. Nothing is more odious to the people than royalty, and when they are made judges in the cause, they will unquestionably show that there is nothing they regard so dearly as their liberty."[84] Too well had the tribunes of the people read the disposition of the Roman multitude. Manlius was cited to appear on his trial before the commons, in an assembly of centuries; and the man, who had saved the Capitol, exhibited in his mourning dress and deserted state what little reliance can be placed in the attachment of an interested and uneducated crowd. Yet the popular leader did not fall without a struggle on his part to awaken chords that might yet respond to his call in the bosoms of his fellow citizens. He cited forty persons whose necessities had been relieved and debts paid by his money, for the use of which he had received no interest. He exhibited two golden crowns, won for being the first man who entered towns taken by assault, and eight civic crowns of oak leaves, the simple yet honourable reward of him who had saved the life of a citizen in battle, of whom C. Servilius, a former general of horse, was one. He produced the spoils of thirty enemies, slain by his hand in single combat, and opening his bosom displayed the scars he had received there in the service of his country. His last appeal was to the Capitol, which he had saved, and the deities whose images it contained. He invoked its gods, and bade the people turn their faces towards that sanctuary, and think of those divine beings who resided there when about to pronounce judgment upon him.[85]

The Campus Martius, in which the assembly was held, presented to the eyes of the people that temple citadel which was the object of their deep though misplaced veneration, and they could not resolve to condemn him who had saved it while it remained in their view. The military tribunes perceiving the bent of their feelings,—for such impulses are the actuating principles of an uneducated multitude—adjourned the conclusion of the trial to another day, and place.[86] The trial of Manlius, thus adjourned, did not re-commence under the same form. His enemies, or the friends of the republic, for the prosecutors may be ranked under either head, saw at once that if they continued to defer the sentence of the accused, his acquittal would be certain. We are told that an assembly was summoned the following morning in the Pœtelinian wood without the gate Nomentana, where the Capitol was no longer visible, and that in that place Manlius was condemned by the voice of the people to be hurled from the height of the Tarpeian rock, the very stronghold his gallantry and personal prowess had saved.[87] Such, remarks Livy, "being the end of a man who if he had not been born in a free state would have deserved to be remembered with honour by posterity."[88] By a public decree, the house of Manlius was razed, and no patrician was permitted from that time to dwell in the Capitol. A temple to the goddess Moneta was built upon the hearth of the state victim, while his family determined that none of their race should ever bear the fatal name of Marcus, thus in a measure justifying the sentence that condemned him. His own brother, Aulus Manlius, a usurious patrician, was one of his bitterest enemies. His crime, with his own order, appears to have been seeking popularity from the people, and with the tribunes of the commons for belonging to the patrician rank. He was the victim of an ill constituted government in times of universal ignorance. A warning example that B.C. 379. the popular idol of the hour may in the next become the victim of his worshippers.

Camillus, burdened with years, thought the plea of age might have excused him from forming a part of the military tribuneship, but neither the senate nor the people would permit the exemption he claimed; he therefore served in the forty-first, the conduct of the Volscian war being committed to his charge. His prudence displeased the younger tribune serving with him; who, upon the refusal of his veteran coadjutor to fight, told him, "age had cooled his blood, and that he ought to comply with the general wish of the army, and engage the enemy." Camillus calmly replied, That the Roman republic had appeared perfectly satisfied with his method of conducting the war; that he wished the army success, since he could not restrain it from fighting, but that he should remain with the reserve body on account of his age and infirmities.

Having wrung this reluctant consent from the veteran general, Furius and his troops made a vigorous charge upon the Volscians; but being carried away by their ardour, were exposed to the disgrace of a defeat, but for the aid of Camillus, who joined them with the reserve in time to gain the victory. Among the prisoners, he found some Tusculans; and as that city had been the constant ally and friend of Rome, he dreaded lest its near vicinity might render it a new and dangerous enemy. He thought the matter of sufficient consequence to require the counsel of the senate, and therefore quitted the camp for the metropolis. Furius and his officers were alarmed at the departure of the commander-in-chief; and even the senate, who had heard of the disaster of the rash tribune, expected to receive a complaint instead of a recommendation, for Camillus named his brave adversary as his colleague in the war they had decided against the Tusculans, who were reported to be in open revolt. His conduct gained him the gratitude of Furius, and the esteem of the army.[89]

Camillus found the inhabitants of Tusculum employed in the arts of peace, and not engaged in preparation for war. He advised the people to send a deputation to the senate to ask pardon for the rashness committed by some of the citizens. His wise and merciful counsel was followed; and this small city that had often assisted Rome in her time of need or danger, easily obtained the clemency she implored at the hands of her mightier neighbour. The privilege of Roman citizenship was conferred upon the Tusculans. The Prænestines took this crisis to invade the Roman territories, marching to the very gates of Rome; but finally encamping on the banks of the Allia, a spot they considered fatal to the Roman people. Titus Quinctius, who was made dictator, defeated them on that memorable spot, took all their towns, and forced them to surrender Præneste, their capital city, from whence he bore away the statue of Jupiter Imperator, which he placed in the Capitol.[90] The idols of Rome were always won from the nations they conquered.

The Volscian war, conducted by the two Manlii, was unfortunate, those tribunes being drawn into an ambuscade by a Latin soldier in Roman military attire, who bade them hasten to save their foraging party then engaged with the Volscians. Nothing but the consummate personal bravery of the commanders saved themselves and their legions from being cut to pieces.[91] This misfortune arose from the Latins speaking the same language as the Romans; such nations should never be foes.

The predatory incursions of the Volscians increased the distress of the poor debtors, of whose grievances no notice could be taken by the censors during the war. The tribunes of the people would not allow the levies to be made until the senate agreed to suspend the payment of public and private debts during the contest.[92] The Volscians were then driven out with loss, and public tranquillity was restored. A stone wall, built by the censors, occasioned much displeasure, as the poorer classes were forced to contribute to its erection, a measure they considered oppressive.[93] The Romans were engaged in a series of petty wars with the Latins and Volscians, but had the good fortune to retake Tusculum from them, which they restored to its inhabitants. A quarrel between these predatory nations occasioned them to abandon the contest with the republic. The restoration of peace did not calm the discontented citizens of Rome. The poor B.C. 379. plebeian landholder endured hardships and privations unknown to the ærarian class below him. He possessed, indeed, greater civic privileges, but then he wanted bread, or was reduced to the state of a bond-slave to a creditor, who often used him hardly. This law was, however, the amelioration of an ancient or more horrible one, by which the bankrupt debtor, after proclamation by the public crier upon three successive market days, could be killed, and his person divided among his creditors, unless redeemed by the payment of his debts. No instance of this law having been put in force is extant, but it must have been made when the people of Italy, from whom the Romans took it,[94] were cannibals. The plebeians, thus oppressed and humbled, could hope for no relief while their order was prevented from exercising the supreme magistracy. They wished for the restoration of the consulship, and the nomination of a commoner to that dignity, as the best means of defending their interests, and recovering the privileges anciently granted them by King Servius. This privilege, which ought to have been revived when the regal gave place to the republican form of government, was finally accorded them, not as a matter of right, but to dry the tears of a weak, vain woman. It happened in the beginning of this military tribuneship[95] that the younger daughter of Fabius Ambustus, who was married to a rich plebeian named Licinius Stolo, paid a visit to her elder sister, who was the wife of the military tribune Sulpicius. The lictor, who preceded the magistrate, made such an ostentatious knocking at the door, that Fabia, alarmed at the noise, asked her sister "what it meant." Her sister, laughing at her fears, informed her "that it was caused by the lictor's staff, who announced in this manner the return of her husband to his home." "A very small matter," remarks Livy, "will disturb the quiet of a woman's mind." He might have added when weak as Fabia; whose uneasiness was increased by the throng of visitors who came to pay their court to the wife of Sulpicius, and to request her good offices. The envious sister was so unhappy, that her father noticed her trouble, and kindly asked the cause. At first she was silent, being unwilling to confess that she was jealous of her sister, or dissatisfied with her own condition. Fabius Ambustus was of a family renowned for parental affection, and his tenderness drew from his weak daughter the fact that she was unsuitably married, and the manner in which she had made this mortifying discovery.[96] The warrior and statesman laughed heartily at her confession, bade her dry her tears, and have patience, promising that in the course of a few years her ears should ring with the noise at home, which had become the object of her foolish ambition. Fabia was forced to be content with this promise, which her fond father soon performed, aided by Licinius Stolo and Sextius, a talented young patrician. His coadjutors stood for the tribuneship of the people, and no sooner entered upon their office, than they proposed the entire abolition of the military tribuneship, and the revival of the consular magistrates, who were to be chosen by the people, one always being a plebeian. They also proposed two new laws. The first related to the payment of debts, and provided that the interest already paid should be deducted from the amount of the principal, which was to be refunded in three equal payments in three years. The second is known in history by the name of the Licinian law; it was an agrarian law apparently instituted to remedy the evils suffered by the plebeian order.[97] Licinius Stolo, the actual framer of the agrarian law, designed it as a stepping-stone to his own elevation to power. If we could merely regard this powerful and influential person through the medium of the measures he proposed, he would be justly entitled to our admiration; but Licinius was no real patriot, but an able and dishonest demagogue—a lawgiver who never intended to be restricted by the statutes he made. Oratory was a gift in the Licinian family, who were fine speakers, and had the art of gaining popularity and amassing wealth. Notwithstanding his want of public integrity, the law proposed by Licinius was founded in justice and reason.[98] This tribune wanted the noble qualities of the popular victim, Spurius Cassius, who had been not only deserted by the commons, but immolated by them.

The struggle to prevent the agrarian law passing in this form was not limited to the aristocracy; the rich B.C. 377-371. plebeians, who had become possessed of the ager publicus while serving in those offices of state to which their order had been admitted, or as recipients of grants from their patrician relatives, dreaded a statute which would not only put a stop to such acquisitions in future, but would enforce and compel their restitution by the limitations it proposed. The tribunes of the people, whose peculiar office it was to regulate the possession of the public domain, saw themselves through their illegal occupation of it exposed by the new agrarian law, and therefore united in giving their veto against the offensive measures of their two colleagues.[99] Licinius and Sextius chose to adopt the same word when the time came for the election of the new military magistrates; and it is the generally received opinion, grounded upon the Roman Fasti, that these two popular tribunes with the plebeian ædiles were the only magistrates remaining in office for the space of five years. The truth is not easily discovered; but whether the reign of Licinius Stolo and his colleague, L. Sextius, lasted five months or five years, the Latin war with the people of Tusculum compelled them to withdraw their veto, and permit the comitia to be held for the election of six military magistrates,[100] of patrician houses, but well-disposed to the people. Two of these were near relations of Licinius Stolo, whose hardest battle was with the wealthy plebeians of his own order. The relief of Tusculum was effected, and the siege of Velitræ formed when the election for military tribunes placed the father-in-law of Licinius Stolo at the head of those magistrates[101]—a circumstance which considerably strengthened the influence of his plebeian son-in-law, whose long continuance in the tribuneship of the people had lessened the opposition in his own college from eight to three.[102] Velitræ still held out, and Sextius and Stolo proposed another law, by which the office of keeping the Sybilline books should be shared by the plebeians by the change of duumvirs into decemvirs, five of whom were to be taken from the commons.

Licinius Stolo and Sextius retained their seats in the tribunitial college, though illegally, through the favour of the people, and their continuance in an office limited in its utmost extension to fifteen months, must have convinced the clear-sighted of their ultimate triumph. In fact, they were resolved to carry their views in despite of all opposition, and this important crisis led to the revival of the dictatorial office. Camillus, notwithstanding his great age, was the man upon whom his country fixed their choice. He accepted the dignity for the fourth time with visible reluctance; for it placed him in the front of the battle, not against the enemy, but against the commons, by whom he had never been beloved. Seated in his tribunal, the veteran confronted the storm, "declaring that he came to protect the commons, and that he would never suffer one part of its tribunes to deprive the other of its right of opposition." The two men of the people laughed at the speech, and proceeded to take the votes of the tribes without acknowledging the supreme power vested in the person of the dictator.[103]

Camillus obliged the people to quit the Forum by means of his lictors threatening at the same time to enlist and lead them into the field. Stolo and Sextius, in return, brought in a bill to fine the dictator. Camillus either abdicated to avoid the fine, or discovered some defect in the auspices at his inauguration. P. Manlius was elected to succeed him in his short-lived office.[104] Manlius chose C. Licinius, a plebeian, for his general of horse—an unprecedented measure, which excited as much surprise and indignation as if he had actually named

Licinius Stolo, the factious tribune of the people, to that honourable office. He pleaded that Licinius was his relation, and had been a military tribune. In this case the ties of blood and private friendship were neither forgotten nor forsaken in the war of party. The leaders of the opposing faction threatened to give up the laws relating to usury and the conquered lands, unless the people stood by them in that of the consulate. They even offered to resign the contest for the tribuneship. The people re-elected them, and the senate conceded to them the law relative to the keeping of the Sybilline books, of which patricians and plebeians were now constituted the mutual guardians.[105]

B.C. 367. Pleased with their victory, no opposition was made by the tribunes to the government being lodged in the hands of six military tribunes.

The forty-ninth military tribuneship was hardly formed, when the old war-cry, "The Gauls! the Gauls!" was raised, and Camillus was called by the voices of patrician and plebeian, people and senate, to repel the barbaric inundation flowing from the coasts of the Adriatic towards the city of Rome.[106] Camillus accepted the dignity for the fifth time.[107] He caused great alterations and improvements to be made in the armour and weapons of the Roman soldiery, which had hitherto been of an inferior construction to those of the Gauls. The Roman arms were crowned with victory. On the banks of the Arno the camp of the Gauls was taken and plundered, and the greater part of their host destroyed. It was nearly twenty-three years since the loss of the battle of the Allia had occasioned the desolation of Rome by these barbarians; but the Romans had no longer cause to dread defeat or invasion from these formidable foes. Camillus closed his military career by marching to Velitræ, which immediately surrendered to him.[108] A triumph was granted to him for the successful campaign. He wished to conclude his public life by laying down the dictatorship, but the senate would not allow him to resign; for a political convulsion was at hand, and the venerable octogenarian who had so long wielded the sceptre of military glory, was exposed once more to greater danger than he had ever confronted in the field, for he was compelled to face the fury of an ungrateful and infuriated mob. The dictator was seated on his tribunal in the Forum, dispensing justice according to established custom, when an officer was despatched by the tribunes of the people to arrest and bring him before them. The patricians sprang forward to defend his person, while the infuriated people seconded the attempt of the officer, calling to one another, "Pull him down! pull him down!" Surrounded by an enraged and exasperated mob, the aged dictator displayed the courage that had always marked his eventful course, and retained his seat, regardless of their threats and imprecations, till a gallant band of patricians delivered him from his imminent peril, and guarded him in safety to the senate-house.[109] Before entering that privileged place, he turned his face towards the Capitol, vowing to erect a temple to Concord if the gods would grant to the divided Roman people the blessings of peace.[110] The senate, after this popular outbreak, permitted the agrarian law of Licinius to pass, and also that relating to debt. The concessions made by the Senate did not satisfy the tribunes, who resolved to ensure the participation of the consulship to their own order. This demand was wise and just, leading not only to the vast political importance of Rome, but to her moral ascendancy and internal greatness. The people, headed by their most influential tribunes, Caius Licinius Stolo and Lucius Sextius, decreed the abolition of the military tribuneship, nominating Æmilius Mamercinus a patrician, and Sextius then tribune, the successful plebeian candidates for the consulship. The senate pronounced the election to be invalid. But the dictator Camillus, from whom such a decision was least expected, over-ruled their objections, and recommended them to yield to the wish of the people.[111]

To a patrician officer, called a prætor, was assigned the authority of supreme judge, an office hitherto attached to the consular dignity. To this magistrate was granted a curule chair, a purple robe, and attendant lictors. Spurius Camillus the son of the dictator, was the first man who held the office, being elected to it by the commons, as a mark of respect to his father. The announcement of these concessions to the people by the dictator, raised him to a height of popularity he had never known before. The commons were satisfied with their victory, and nothing was manifested by them but joy.[112] Camillus raised his temple to Concord, on the same spot formerly occupied by his tribunal when he was attacked by the mob. A fourth day in memory of the reconciliation of the senate B.C. 366. and people was added to the great games, which were celebrated with unusual splendour. The ædiles refused to preside on this occasion for some unknown reason, or perhaps because the additional day was to mark the position assumed by the commons, who took their place by the side of the three old patrician tribes, Ramnenses, Titienses, and Luceres.[113] Two new ædiles were appointed to be taken every other year from the two orders. These magistrates exercised the functions of the quæstores parricidii,[114] trying criminals for various offences, and if any accused person appealed from their sentence, they prosecuted the party in the comitia of the centuries. But the functions of the curule ædiles were not limited to jurisprudence alone, but were multifarious and embraced a variety of objects. These magistrates, who were allowed curule chairs, held jurisdiction over all meetings, assemblies, theatres, or places of public resort for business or pleasure; overlooked the repairs of theatres and temples and the city walls; suppressed all novelties in religion; and when the Romans became a literary people, examined all books, particularly those pieces written for the stage.

The great Camillus, with the halo of popular favour round his venerable brow, expired soon after the civic disputes had been decided in the people's favour, "more deeply regretted by his country than the whole multitude who died of the plague, the disease that carried him off."[115] Rome never boasted a prouder name than that of Furius Camillus. This great dictator lived fourscore years, of which he had passed more than sixty in the service of his country. Greece may rival his fame, but she never surpassed it. The reader has seen the public fault that dimmed the glory of this great patriot and soldier, if great attachment to his own order deserves so harsh a name, melt away like clouds before the setting sun. There is no actual foundation for the supposition that he occasioned the death of Manlius; but the hatred between them made it so generally believed, that it is not easy to clear the character of Camillus from the stain tradition has affixed to his name. But if we must not pronounce this mighty Roman a perfect man, we may admire and venerate him as the second father of his country. His military fame, great as it was, being exceeded by that undying attachment to Rome which her ingratitude could not annihilate. He did not, like Coriolanus, lead a foreign army against his country, but sought and succoured her in her ashes and degradation, giving to her citizens a noble example of public virtue. He saved the people who had cast him forth into exile, and finally consented to a measure of political justice in the senate which the furious attack of a mob could not wring from him. In the last days of his long life, he received the reward of his public services in the love of the people—a love he had always merited, but which was not fully accorded to his worth till then.[116]

<hr size=2 width="10%" align=center>

[1] Plutarch, in Camillus; Livy, v. 27. The dates assigned to the exploits of Camillus are confused and uncertain, and the actions themselves bear a poetical character, being taken from the lays in which Rome recorded the heroic deeds of her great men. To give any chronological list of the military campaigns of the conqueror of Veii appears impossible; but Livy records that he was a military tribune this year, and Falerii being won by him during one of his tribuneships, makes it probable that it was acquired at the same period. The manner in which he gained it has been considered romantic and improbable; but the incident connected with the surrender of Falerii is not of a character likely to have been the fruit of an imaginative mind. The conquest of Veii had extended the Roman territories along the right bank of the Tiber, from its embouchure to the length of thirteen miles above Rome.[L] "Northward of the Tiber, it stretched as far as the Lago di Bracciano, Lacus Sabatinus, and the edge of the Campagna at Monterosi, passing thence in a line including the remarkable eminence of Monte Musino to the Tiber, opposite the Ager Crustumerinus."[M]

[L] Arnold; Pliny, Hist. Nat., iii. 9.

[M] Arnold, Hist Rome, i. 402, 3.

[2] Plutarch, in Camillus; Livy, v. 27.

[3] Plutarch; Livy.

[4] Arnold; Livy, vi. 4.

[5] Hooke.

[6] Hooke, Roman Republic.

[7] The supernatural voice that proclaimed the future march of the Gauls, was said to have preceded the accusation of Camillus, but the mean birth of Marcus Cædicius prevented the magistrates to whom he was charged to deliver the message from paying any attention to the revelation. That the presence of

the Gauls in Italy suggested the message to Cædicius is the only probable solution of the enigma.

[8] Niebuhr, History of Rome.

[9] Livy, v. 32; Plutarch, in Camillus.

[10] Livy, v. 32.

[11] *Ibid.*

[12] Plutarch, in Camillus.

[13] See Appendix. (p. 154)

[14] Chiusi, in Tuscany.

[15] Livy, v. 33.

[16] See Appendix. (p. 155)

[17] The tract of country possessed by the Senonians, comprised Sens, Auxerre, and Troyes, as far up as Paris.—Langhorne.

[18] Diodorus, xiv. 113.

[19] Plutarch, in Camillus.

[20] Livy, v. 36.

[21] *Ibid.*

[22] See Appendix. (p. 156)

[23] Diodorus Siculus.

[24] *Ibid.*, xiv. 114, 115; Livy, v. 38; Plutarch, in Camillus.

[25] Plutarch.

[26] Livy, v. 40.

[27] *Ibid.*

[28] Hooke. *Cære*, and *manere* to remain. Valerius Maximus.

[29] Livy, v. 41.

[30] Plutarch, in Camillus; Livy, v. 41.

[31] Before their own houses, according to Livy.

[32] Plutarch, in Camillus.

[33] Livy.

[34] Auctor Vir. illustr. in Camillo.

[35] Livy.

[36] Plutarch; and see Appendix. (p. 159)

[37] Livy.

[38] See Appendix. (p. 159)

[39] Daniel, xi. 40.

[40] Plutarch, in Camillus.

[41] *Ibid.*

[42] *Ibid.*

[43] *Ibid.*

[44] Diodorus, xiv. 116; Plutarch, in Camillus.

[45] Plutarch. In relating this incident,[N] Livy considers that the scruple respecting the dictatorship arose not from Camillus, but the Romans themselves. We have followed Plutarch's narrative, as more consistent with the character of his hero, who, having been driven into exile by the commons and his own discontented soldiers, might not choose to hold his commission upon their authority alone.

[N] Livy, v. 46.

[46] Plutarch, in Camillus.

[47] Plutarch, in Camillus; Diodorus, xiv. 116; Livy, 47.

[48] Plutarch, in Camillus.

[49] Livy, v. 57; Plutarch.

[50] Pliny.

[51] Polybius, ii. 22; Plutarch, in Camillus.

[52] See Appendix. (p. 163)

[53] Polybius, ii. 18.

[54] Plutarch, in Camillus; Livy, v. 48.

[55] Rollin.

[56] Rollin.

[57] Plutarch, in Camillus.

[58] *Ibid.*

[59] See Appendix. (p. 164)

[60] Plutarch, in Camillus.

[61] *Ibid.*

[62] *Ibid.*

[63] Plutarch, in Camillus; Livy.

[64] Livy, vi. 1.

[65] See Appendix. (p. 167)

[66] Plutarch, in Camillus.

[67] Livy, vi. 3; Plutarch.

[68] Livy, vi. 4; Hooke's Rome.

[69] Pliny.

[70] Livy, vi. 7.

[71] *Ibid.*, c. 10.

[72] Hooke; Plutarch, in Camillus.

[73] Livy, vi. 11.

[74] *Ibid.*

[75] *Ibid.*, vi. 14.

[76] *Ibid.*

[77] Livy, vi. 16. We have seen that some historical objections exist as to the fact of the gold having been recovered from Brennus, and that Polybius, nearer the time than Livy or Plutarch, considered that the departure of Brennus was purchased. If M. Manlius Capitolinus knew this, and accused the senators of this defraud, he was guilty of falsehood; but is not the charge rather a confirmation of the story that it was not paid?

[78] Livy, vi. 16.

[79] *Ibid.*, 20.

[80] *Ibid.*

[81] *Ibid.*

[82] *Ibid.*

[83] Livy, vi. 18; See Appendix. (p. 171)

[84] Livy, vi. 20.

[85] Livy, vi. 20.

[86] Plutarch.

[87] Plutarch, in Camillus; Livy.

[88] *Ibid.*

[89] Livy, vi. 25; Plutarch.

[90] Livy, vi. 29.

[91] *Ibid.*, vi. 30.

[92] *Ibid.*, vi. 32.

[93] *Ibid.*

[94] See Appendix. (p. 175)

[95] Livy, vi. 34.

[96] Livy.

[97] Appian, Bell. Civ., book i.

[98] See Appendix. (p. 176)

[99] Livy, vi. 35.

[100] Hooke; Livy, vi. 36.

[101] Livy, vi. 36.

[102] Arnold; Livy; Hooke.

[103] Plutarch, in Camillus; Livy, vi. 38.

[104] Fasti Capitolini.

[105] Livy, vi. 42.

[106] Plutarch, in Camillus.

[107] Livy, vi. 42.

[108] Plutarch, in Camillus.

[109] Hooke; Plutarch, in Camillus. In this furious outbreak upon the greatest military commander of Rome in that age, we mentally recur to the attack of a British mob upon the venerable person of Wellington, the Camillus of our own day, regretting that the British capital should have furnished a parallel by an outrage offered to her noblest citizen.

[110] Plutarch, in Camillus; Livy, vi. 42; Fasti Capitolini.

[111] Plutarch, in Camillus.

[112] Arnold, Rome, xi. 60.

[113] Livy, vi. 42.

[114] Niebuhr, Hist. Rome.

[115] Plutarch, in Camillus.

[116] In their military renown and political career Camillus and Wellington greatly resemble each other. Both these illustrious men delivered their country from impending danger, and afterwards experienced ingratitude in return for their services; the hardest battles ever fought by Camillus and Wellington being with lawless mobs. Each were defended by a band of gentlemen who armed to defend lives so dear to all good citizens. Both Camillus and Wellington lived to recover their popularity, which indeed they never deserved

to lose, and were lamented by every order in the state, receiving public funeral honours, and descending to the tomb mourned by the heartfelt tears of their countrymen.

CHAPTER V.

A.U.C. 390-454. B.C. 364-300.

Licinius Stolo made Consul.—The Plague.—Ludi Scenici.—Manlius and his son.—Filial Piety of Titus Manlius.—Curtius and the Fiery Gulf.—Combat between Manlius and a Gaul.— Victory of Sulpicius.—Licinius Stolo fined.—Latin leagues and combinations.—Aid afforded to poor Debtors by the State.—Greek Pirates driven away by the Gauls.—The son of Camillus Dictator.—His victory over the Gauls.—Valerius Corvus.—Camillus compels the Greeks to put to sea.—Rome and Samnium.—Gallantry of Decius Mus.— Roman victory.—Embassy from Carthage.—Military Revolt.—Latin war.—Manlius puts his son to death for breach of discipline.—Self-devotion of Decius.—Conquest of Latium.—Concessions of the Senate to the Roman People.—Conspiracy of Roman Ladies.—Privernum declared free.—Samnite war.—Papirius Cursor's quarrel with his Cavalry General.—The People obtain his Pardon.—Victories of Papirius.—Caudine forks.—Self-devotion of the Consuls.—Repentance of Pontius.—Siege of Luceria.— Pontius passes under the yoke.—Conclusion of the War.—New Roman Tribes.— Quintus Fabius Dictator.—His speech.—Political changes.—Censorship of Appius Claudius.—Importance of the Libertini.—Appius makes a road.—Builds an Aqueduct.—Exhausts the Treasury.—Victory of the Consul Brutus.—Slaughter of the Samnites.—Refusal of Appius Claudius to resign the Censorship.—Flavius Libertinus his clerk.—Consulship of Quintus Fabius.—Brilliant Etruscan Campaign.—Required to name his enemy Dictator.—Victory of Papirius.—Appius Claudius Consul.—Divorce of Antonius.—Fabius Pictor paints the Temple of Health.—Battle of Allifæ.—Battle of Bovianum.—Calendar of Flavius.—His curule ædileship.—Amusing Anecdote.— Censorship of Fabius and Decius.—Insolence of the Pontifex Maximus.—Temple of Concord.—Descent of Cleonymus.—Ogulnian Law.—Speech of Decius in its favour.— Privileges obtained by the Commons.—Valerian Law.—Dawn of the Fine Arts.— Message of Demetrius Poliorcetes to the Roman Senate.—Mistakes Rome for a Grecian city.

TEN years had elapsed since Fabius Ambustus had dried the tears of his youngest daughter, by the promise that her husband should be first magistrate. Licinius Stolo was chosen for the ninety-first consulship, in conjunction with C. Sulpicius, and the vow of Fabius was performed.[1] The plague still continued its ravages, and the Romans, hoping to avert the scourge, introduced some new rites, in order to propitiate the offended gods. Shows, called Ludi Scenici, a sort of low comedies, were performed near the banks of the Tiber, in honour of them. This was the first dawn of the dramatic art in Rome; and though the pestilence did not decrease, the people were pleased with an amusement hitherto unknown to them. The performers were all Etruscans.[2] In the following consulship, L. Manlius Imperiosus was made dictator, for the express purpose of driving a nail into the wall of the temple of Minerva.[3] The dictator did not mean to pass his dictatorship in the construction of calendars; he refused to resign his authority, determining in his own mind to lead the Roman army against the Hernicans, but the consuls compelled him to resign. His going out of office was followed by his citation by Pomponius, a tribune of the people, to answer before them for his late conduct. Among other charges against Manlius, he enumerated the ill-treatment of his own son, who, on account of an impediment in his speech, was considered weak-minded by his haughty father, by whom he was kept to hard labour at his country house, having no companions but slaves. It is probable that the stern Roman made this toil a part of his son's education; for the tribune Pomponius had scarcely sent the citation before he was startled by the appearance of the young client (of whom he had become the self-appointed patron) in his bed-chamber, who, drawing a poignard from under his garments, bade him swear to withdraw his accusation against his father, or die upon the spot.[4] Pomponius, either convinced by the rough reasoning of young Titus Manlius, or alarmed at the alternative, promised to clear the accused of this charge.[5] He kept his word, and gave the people the history of the courageous filial piety of the youth, as the cause of his withdrawing his accusation against the father. They extolled the conduct of young Titus, and gave a proof of their regard by placing him the second on the list of six legionary tribunes they were allowed the privilege of electing.[6] The preceding year had been marked by alarming inundations, the Tiber overflowing the Circus Maximus at the time when the games for the propitiation of the gods were being performed in order to remove the plague. But this year an earthquake opened a great chasm in the Forum, B.C. 363. which continued to increase in depth and width to the terror and consternation of the Roman people, who laboured in vain to fill it up by casting in earth and stones.[7] When we consider the volcanic nature of the site occupied by Rome, the opening of a gulf, from which flames frequently issued, will no longer be considered fabulous, but appear the natural result of such a situation. The augurs, when consulted upon the danger that threatened the city, declared it could not be averted until that in which the power and strength of the Roman people consisted was cast into the chasm, when it would not only close upon the sacrifice, but the offering would procure from the gods the eternal duration of the Roman state.[8] The ambiguous meaning of the augurs, so evidently pointing at the immolation of the worthiest Roman citizen, escaped the penetration of the multitude. Each individual cast in what he deemed most valuable of his worldly possessions, but the chasm remained unclosed till Marcus Curtius, a noble Roman youth, declared "that Rome had nothing more precious to offer than arms and valour." Arming himself as for the field, and mounting his battle charger, the generous young man entered the Forum at full speed, when, turning towards the Capitol, he invoked at the chasm, the celestial and infernal deities, declaring that he offered himself as a sacrifice for the welfare of his country; then spurring his horse, plunged headlong into the flaming gulf, burying in that living grave his youth and heroic qualities, to become the victim of a wild and cruel superstition. The people flung down upon him many precious moveables, and with these, it was said, the gulf was speedily filled up.[9] It was most likely closed by another shock of earthquake—a phenomenon of not unfrequent occurrence in the natural history of Italy. This beautiful legend is said to have given to the marshy spot the name of the hero, but it was certainly called the Curtian Lake before this date.

The republic was employed in a continual series of wars with the Latin, Etruscan, and Gaulish nations, from the time when the great Camillus closed his military career. In the commencement of the contest with the Hernicans, the first plebeian consul who ever led a Roman army into the field lost a battle and his life. The dictator, Appius Claudius, soon after retrieved the honour of the republic, but his victory was attended with such an immense loss of life, that he was allowed no triumph. The Cis-alpine Gauls put themselves on the march for Rome, when the bridge of the Anio, which was between them and the Roman army, became the scene of a remarkable duel. A gigantic warrior, the Goliath of the Gauls, repeatedly challenged the Romans, when young Titus Manlius asked permission of the dictator, Quinctius Pennus, to encounter the boastful foe, the strictness of military discipline not permitting him to leave the ranks. "Go, Manlius, and be as valiant for Rome as thou wert for thy father," was the reply of a commander who remembered the noble filial piety of the youth. Manlius slew his huge adversary, and took from his neck a rich collar, from which circumstance he afterwards bore the surname of Torquatus.[10] The Gauls, alarmed at the fall of their champion, hastily broke up their camp. They returned the following year, while the consuls were employed in the Latin war, but were defeated by Servilius Ahala under the walls of Rome. The victor refused a triumph for his public service.[11] In the following year, the plebeian consul Popillius was offering up a sacrifice to the goddess Carmenta, when the populace suddenly rose against the senate, upon which he hurried in his linen robe to the scene of contest, and, by his prompt appearance, put an end to the sedition. He was ever after distinguished by the name of Lænas.[12] The appearance of the Boian Gauls in the plains of Præneste, caused C. Sulpicius to be created dictator, to repel the threatened danger.[13] The Latins, who had reason to dread the coming of these barbarian hordes, at this critical juncture renewed their alliance with Rome, and furnished their usual quota of men and arms. This seasonable supply enabled the dictator Sulpicius to raise a considerable force for the war. Though within sight of the enemy, he did not think it prudent to engage with an army far more numerous than his own. His soldiers, upon his refusal to fight, mutinied, and, headed by an old centurion, Sextius, rushed tumultuously B.C. 361. into his presence. The dictator, who greatly esteemed the veteran for his worth and wisdom, took him aside, and expressed his surprise at finding him at the head of a mutiny. Sextius ingenuously replied, "That he consented to be leader to prevent a worse man from being chosen;" adding, "that the soldiers were determined to fight without the dictator, unless he yielded to their demands." Sulpicius then consented to head them, and sending his muleteers into a neighbouring wood, covered by a stratagem the thinness of his army. The enemy seeing them advance from a distance, while the Romans were charging them in front, were deceived by the notion that a body of a thousand horsemen were approaching; for the mules, being covered with war furniture, presented a formidable appearance. At the sight of this new sort of cavalry, they fled in disorder, and Sulpicius put the greater part of them to the sword. For this victory Sulpicius obtained a triumph.[14] A new law was passed to prevent the sale of votes. The following year one was enacted which fixed the rate of interest at one

153

per cent. per month. High as this rate appears to us, it was better than remaining at the pleasure of the lender.[15] Licinius Stolo was fined for having a thousand acres of land in his possession, being double the quantity his own law allowed. He had made a pretended gift of five hundred to his son—a subterfuge that exposed him to general contempt.[16] As the limitation only regarded the public lands unlawfully taken possession of without purchase, the robbery perpetrated by this plebeian patriot upon the property of the state was particularly rapacious.[17]

A fresh confederacy was formed against the Romans by the Faliscans and Etruscans, when the plebeian consul, Popillius, named C. Plautius Proculus magister equitum, who gained a complete victory over the combined armies, and took eight thousand prisoners. He was not, however, allowed to preside in the comitia for the election of the consuls for the ensuing year, as the auspices could only be taken by a magistrate of unmixed blood. The objection made by the patricians was considered valid. Two years later the consulship was held by patricians, M. Fabius Ambustus and T. Quinctius Pennus. The campaigns of these experienced commanders were equally successful. Fabius Ambustus reduced the Tibertines, while his colleague defeated the Tarquinians in a pitched battle. After the victory he put all the prisoners to death with the exception of those who were reserved for severer punishments, in return for the murder of three hundred and fifty Romans by the Tarquinians. By a decree of the senate, these victims were cruelly scourged with rods and then beheaded.[18] The victories and executions of Quinctius Pennus reached the ears of the Samnites, who sent an embassy to desire the friendship of the warlike Romans, upon the same terms as the Latins. An alliance was then formed, which the haughty character of the contracting parties soon changed into a lasting quarrel. Sulpicius Peticus and M. Valerius Poplicola had scarcely taken the fasces before the Etruscans, Volscians, Faliscans and Tarquinians were in arms against Rome. As the consuls were obliged to march in different directions, and the Cærites were also in this offensive league, Titus Manlius Torquatus was named dictator to command the third army. Manlius had never been consul, but this point, a necessary qualification for a dictator, was ceded to his great merit. Cære submitted to his authority, and her citizens pleaded, in extenuation of their faults, the hospitality formerly accorded to the vestal virgins and priesthood of Rome. The claim was a second time allowed, and the dictator made a truce with them for a hundred years.[19] No enemy appeared in the field against Manlius, who ravaged the lands of the Faliscans and returned to Rome.

C. Marcius Rutilus and Valerius Poplicola united together in the patriotic act of easing the distressed debtors. Five men of worth and probity were employed to pay their debts out of the public treasury. They were called bankers,[20] and made a strict investigation into the manner B.C. 354. in which debt had been incurred. To those whose improvidence had brought them into bad circumstances, they lent money upon interest, taking security for the public property, and by this means eased their burdens without injuring the state.[21]

The Gauls again appeared in arms, but were defeated by the plebeian consul Popillius, his patrician colleague Scipio being sick.[22] Camillus, the son of the great Camillus, was chosen dictator. He nominated himself and Appius Claudius Crassus to the consulship, and, leading an army into the field, proved himself worthy of his father's name and reputation. The Gauls, who had taken refuge among the hills of Alba, again invaded the Latin territory, at the very time when a body of Greek pirates appeared on the sea-coast, and took possession of that part of the country. The Gauls drove the robbers back to their ships, not wishing them to share their spoils. Camillus, after sending Pinarius, the prætor of Rome, to guard the sea-shore from the Greeks, encamped among the Pomptine Marshes, intending to starve his enemies, not to fight with them. The prudence of the general was overcome by a fortunate accident. As the armies were in sight of each other—a gigantic Gaul challenged Marcus Valerius, a tribune, to single combat, which being accepted, brought on a general engagement.[23] The Roman champion, we are gravely assured by Livy, received great assistance from a raven, who incessantly annoyed his adversary by buffeting him during the combat. Valerius slew his enemy, and gained the name of Corvus. The Romans were completely victorious, slaying all those who did not fly to the shores of the Adriatic. Camillus rewarded Valerius with a crown of gold and ten oxen. The dictator hoped to conclude the campaign before he was out of office, but he was still in the field when Valerius Corvus, though very young, was chosen in conjunction with Popillius Lænas, for the one hundred and seventh consulship. Camillus succeeded in driving the pirate Greeks to sea, and left Rome once more in possession of profound peace. The most memorable event of the next year was the alliance between the republic and Carthage,[24] which the African state sent an embassy to Rome to propose. No taxes or levies were raised in the next consulship, and the amount of interest was reduced one-half per cent.—a sure proof of the internal prosperity of Rome. The debtors also obtained three years time for the payment of their debts.

While the consuls Manlius Imperiosus and C. Marcius Rutilus were consecrating the temple of Juno, the foundations of which were laid upon the spot where the house of the unfortunate Marcus Manlius had formerly stood, a shower of stones fell accompanied with sudden darkness.[25] This was upon the 1st of June, and was probably occasioned by some distant volcanic eruption. This temple was afterwards used for the public mint.

The Sidicines, a people of Ausonia, were attacked by the Samnites, and being unable to repel the invasion, applied to the Campanians, a rich commercial people, for assistance, who willingly undertook their defence. The Samnites, who were well acquainted with the unwarlike dispositions of the Campanians, cast their eyes upon their wealth, and abandoning the conquest of the inconsiderable Sidicines, turned their arms against their rich and imprudent allies. The Campanians, who knew nothing of war, sent an embassy to Rome, entreating the aid of the republic, and offering to present Capua and all their lands to the senate, if the Romans would secure them from the ravages of the Samnites.[26] As the republic was in strict alliance with Samnium, they comforted the Campanian deputies, who were in tears, with the promise of using their influence with the Samnites, to withdraw their arms from their territories. Nevertheless, they accepted the investiture, and sent an embassy to Samnium, to entreat them to spare a people in alliance with Rome. The Samnites, displeased with the interference of their allies, of whose double dealing they were doubtless aware, gave the deputies no answer. They even ordered their general to ravage Campania in their presence. This insult was a declaration of war. Valerius Corvus marched with an army to defend Campania, while his colleague, Cornelius Cossus, invaded Samnium. Near Mount B.C. 344. Gaurus, Valerius gained a victory over the Samnites, in whom, notwithstanding their defeat, he found determined bravery.[27] Cossus, less fortunate, was surrounded at Saticula, a place upon the borders of Samnium, and must have perished there with his legions, but for the boldness and bravery of Decius Mus. This valiant plebeian requested his general to give him the command of half a legion, and permission to post himself with these troops upon an eminence, in order to cover the retreat of the Roman army. His request was granted, and aided by the darts of this body of devoted men, the army cleared the dangerous defile.[28] No escape was left to Decius and his band but through the camp of the enemy. They effected this hazardous enterprise in the night, by sliding down the hill, and passing through the sleeping host, yet not without discovery, for one of the legionaries struck his foot against the buckler of a foe, which accident roused the camp. The darkness favoured the Romans, who joined the army by break of day, without loss or injury.[29] Cossus commenced an oration in praise of Decius, but the brave soldier bluntly interrupted him to point out a part of the Samnite camp which he thought assailable, advising the consul to attack it without delay.[30] Cossus immediately surprised the Samnites, who lost thirty thousand men.[31] The consul placed upon the bold brow of the brave plebeian, Decius, the golden, the obsidional, and oaken crowns in succession. He gave him a hundred oxen, and one milk-white bull with gilded horns. With the generosity that marked his character, Decius refused the oxen, but accepted the bull as a sacrifice to the god of war. His followers were rewarded by the gift of military habits, and a double allowance of corn for life.[32] Valerius Corvus prosecuted the war in Campania with vigour and success. He made himself master of the Samnite camp, and took one hundred and seventy standards from them. This splendid campaign closed with the triumphs decreed by the Roman senate and people to the victorious consuls, whose triumphal entries were soon followed by the appearance of the ambassadors from Carthage, bringing presents and congratulations to the Roman republic upon the success of her arms.[33] It is a curious fact that the wily African state offered a crown of gold to Jupiter Capitolinus, in gratitude for the Roman victories won under his auspices. The following year the valiant plebeian consul, Rutilus, marched to join the Roman forces in Campania, who discovered that the Roman soldiers left in Capua by Valerius Corvus had forgotten their love and allegiance to their country, having formed the wicked design of expelling the inhabitants of this fine city to found a state for themselves.[34] Under various pretences, Rutilus despatched the most disaffected in the direction of Rome; but when he sent away whole companies, the rest of the army took the idea that their comrades had been tried and executed. They deserted the consul, and marched to Anxur, in Lautulæ, where they encamped in a strong position between a ridge of mountains and the sea. In this dangerous state of affairs, Valerius Corvus, a man much beloved by the Roman soldiery, was chosen dictator.[35] He met the rebels about eight miles from Rome, on the Appian way. Although at the head of an army, Valerius did not wish to slaughter the revolted, who were not only his own countrymen, but the troops he had led to victory the preceding year. He addressed them in an able oration, in which he endeavoured to bring them back to their duty. Observing that T. Quinctius, a very valiant soldier, was their leader, he bade him "retire to the rear when the battle commenced, as a less shameful act than leading Romans against Romans." Quinctius,[36] whom the rebels had compelled to be their leader, burst into tears, and advised his legions to throw themselves upon the mercy of the dictator, who had always treated them with fatherly kindness. The revolted, moved at the tears of their general, and touched by the conduct of their former revered commander, Valerius, laid down their arms, upon which the dictator obtained for them a general amnesty from the senate and comitia of the people.

The revolt of Privernum and the invasion of the Volscians of Antium obliged the consuls for the new year, C. Plautius Hypsæus and A. Æmilius Mamercinus, to take the field. The former took Privernum, and fought with the Antiatans. The battle was a drawn one, but the B.C. 342. enemy, discouraged by the loss they had sustained, retreated to Antium in the night. Æmilius Mamercinus, at the same time, ravaged Samnium, when that brave people were forced to sue to him for peace. He granted it upon their giving the Romans a year's pay for the army and three months' provisions. To this treaty a strange clause was attached by the Samnites: they asked and obtained permission from the Roman senate to make war upon the Sidicines.[37] This small people applied to the Romans for help, which was refused, because they had not asked for it before. The Campanians and Latins combined, however, with the Sidicines against Samnium, which country they laid waste, to the great indignation of the Samnites, who vainly applied to Rome for redress. The senate told the ambassadors that they would order the Campanians to withdraw from their country, but they had no power over the Latins. In fact, they were well aware that the Latin and Campanian nations were combining at that very time against Rome. For the Latins, on the strength of their late achievements in Samnium, were resolved to establish their complete independence, unless the Romans would admit them into the senate, and select one of the consuls from their nation.[38] This demand was made in the consulship of Manlius Torquatus and Decius Mus by the two Latin prætors, L. Annius and L. Numicius, in the temple of Jupiter Capitolinus, where the senate and comitia were met to deliberate upon the answer to be given to the Latin embassy. Manlius spoke with great heat, and was answered with equal warmth by the Latin prætor, Annius, who insulted the idol, to whom the Romans accorded peculiar honours in his own fane. In turning to depart in a rage, Annius stumbled and fell from the top of the stairs to the bottom, which accident the proud patrician consul interpreted into a mark of divine wrath from the Capitoline Jupiter himself.[39] War was instantly declared, and the two consuls marched into the countries of the Marsians and Pelignians, where the Samnites, their late enemies, appeared in the quality of allies. In the camp near Capua both the consuls had, or pretended to have, a remarkable dream. A man of majestic stature

157

appeared to each leader in the night, and proclaimed victory to that army whose general should devote himself to the Dii Manes, or infernal gods. The haruspices, upon being consulted, predicted the same thing, upon which the consuls determined that he whose soldiers gave way should offer himself up for the good of his country. As the Latins were a well-disciplined and brave nation, it became necessary for the consuls to re-establish the ancient discipline if they hoped to conquer the Latins. They issued an order forbidding any Roman soldier to quit his ranks, whatsoever his degree might be, or however high his quality, without leave being first obtained from his general.[40] "Nor was the precaution unnecessary, as the Latins spoke the same language with their enemies, with whom they had lately been united in friendship, as well as relationship." Young Manlius, brave and rash like the proud family from whence he sprang, accepted the challenge of a Latin, whom he chanced to meet while heading a squadron of horse. The Latin, who commanded a troop, knew him well; and the gallant Roman, not choosing to be outbraved by him before his band, paid no regard to the new military order, but fought and conquered. Perhaps the remembrance of a similar deed performed by his own parent made him engage in this combat. Having stripped his enemy of his rich armour, he hurried to the tent of his father, and in animated language related his victory, and displayed the spoils he had won from the Latin chief.[41] The consul regarded him sternly—ascended his tribunal, summoned his army, and condemned his son to die by the hands of the lictors for this avowed breach of military discipline.[42] Yet there was something of paternal pride displayed in his manner when he crowned his son as a victor, and not without a touch of parental tenderness bewailed the sad necessity that obliged him to sacrifice his offspring to his stern sense of military justice.[43] He bade him remember the spirit of his family in this dreadful hour, and submit with courage and dignity to his inevitable doom. The youth, whose veins were filled with the proud blood of the Manlii, bent his head in silent acquiescence to his fathers sentence, and died by the axe of the lictor on the spot.[44] Loud murmurs and deep execrations from B.C. 340. the army were levelled at the general, whose lofty integrity could not stoop to save a son full of hopeful promise for a fault he would not have overlooked in a private soldier. They murmured as unreflecting minds will murmur, but they made no attempt to save the victim. Even the stern consul would doubtless have pardoned the general rebellious movement that preserved his son. The incident will remind the reader of a passage in Holy Writ,[45] but the Hebrew soldiery rescued Jonathan from the severe sentence of his father; the Romans, less noble, left their young champion to die by the decree of his parent and general. Remarkable funeral honours were paid to the gallant youth who had been sacrificed to military etiquette in the morning of his days; nor was the terrible example lost upon the army, for the obedience of the Roman soldier to his commander became a link that could only be severed by death.

Near Mount Vesuvius the Roman consuls gave the Latin army battle. The combat was fiercely and furiously maintained on both sides with obstinate and determined valour. "Upon the left wing of the Roman army where Decius commanded, the front line fell back, whereupon the plebeian consul, following the Pontifex Maximus, Marcus Valerius, in the form of prayer proper to the occasion, and standing on a spear with his head veiled, uttered the dedicatory words of his own self-immolation for the victory he hoped to procure by his death for his country." "Thou Janus, thou Jupiter, thou Mars, our father; thou father Quirinus, thou Bellona; ye Lares, ye the nine gods (dii Novensiles, Etruscan deities supposed to hurl lightning); ye the gods of my ancestors; ye the gods who rule over us and our enemies; ye the gods of the dead. To you I pray, you I beseech that ye would bless and prosper the Roman people and Quirites with might and victory, and send upon their enemies terror, dismay, and death. Thus do I on behalf of the Roman people and of the Quirites, on behalf of the army, both the legions and the allies of the Roman people and the Quirites, devote the legions and the allies of the enemy, together with myself, to the gods of the dead and to mother earth."[46] From the moment the self-devoted consul appeared on horseback, he was beheld with superstitious awe by the enemy. He rushed upon death in the midst of the Latin legions, and from that instant throughout the hardly-contested day the Romans fought with the assurance of victory, which Manlius and his triarians finally won. The body of Decius was not found till the following morning, under a heap of enemies: it was buried with great splendour. In this sanguinary engagement the Latins lost the fourth part of their troops, and their camp fell into the hands of the Romans.[47] Manlius had received the intelligence of his colleague's death with tears of admiration; though Cicero, in a more enlightened age, condemned the action of Decius as barbarous and unbecoming in a general; but in that heroic one of which we write, his self-devotion was considered an act of sublime virtue. The Latin war cost Decius his life, and Manlius his son. The triumphs of this brilliant campaign were certainly dearly purchased by the Romans at such sacrifices.

Near Capua, Manlius again defeated the Latins and their allies. After this victory, he entered Latium, laying that country waste on every side.[48] The Latin towns made no resistance; Privernum, in the country of the Volscians, surrendering to him, as well as those of Campania. Their lands were distributed among the plebeians of Rome.[49] The report of his campaign of victories brought forth all the old men to greet the consul's return to Rome. The young Romans, however, remained at home to mark their displeasure at the decree that had consigned the son of Manlius to an untimely tomb. They absented themselves from his triumph, and execrated his severity.[50] They forgot that Manlius in his youth had endured from his father cruelty and degradation far bitterer than death, when they added to his affliction by this public manifestation of their feelings. The dangerous illness of the stern consul was doubtless caused by grief for his son. Upon this occasion L. Papirius Crassus was created dictator, who named Papirius Cursor as his general of horse.

The revolt of the Latins was partially put down by the plebeian consul, Publilius, who obtained a triumph. B.C. 339. This honour was denied his colleague, Tiberius Æmilius, who demanded it upon insufficient grounds. He became from that time an enemy to his own order, and having named the plebeian consul dictator out of opposition to the senate, caused some alteration in the constitution of Rome; for Brutus Scaeva, the general of horse named by Publius, procured the commons several important privileges. "That their decrees should be observed by all the Romans; that the laws passed by the centuries should be authorised by the senate before they were put to the vote in the comitia; that one of the censors should always be a plebeian."[51]

Camillus, the grandson of the great dictator, defeated the combined Latin army, and took Pedum the same day. This brilliant success was followed by the reduction of Latium. The consuls were granted not only a splendid triumph, but equestrian statues, which were erected to their honour in the Forum. Camillus, in his oration to the senate, said, "It depends upon your pleasure, conscript fathers, whether the Latins exist as a people; yet it beseems the Romans to show mercy to the conquered." A noble sentiment worthy of a brave man.[52] Some of the Latin towns were made municipal, while others were razed. From Antium its galleys were taken and destroyed. The beaks of brass with which these vessels were adorned, called rostra, afterwards ornamented the pulpit in the Forum, from whence that celebrated place obtained its name. The inhabitants of Præneste and Tibur lost their lands, as well as the cities of Campania. Thus a successful war added two fine countries to the Roman republic, "that republic destined to bear rule over all nations upon earth."[53]

Rome was at peace at home and abroad. The public magistracies being equally divided between the two orders was conducive to public virtue, as well as public harmony. No state is ever truly great until the formation of a middle class, and this was now effected by the talent and ability of the educated among the plebeians, for poverty did not prevent good citizens from the exercise of any office of trust in the republic. The unhealthy and degrading influence of wealth was little felt in this age of Roman virtue.[54] The office of prætor was for the first time held by a plebeian the following year. The consulship of Atilius Regulus and Valerius Corvus, was remarkable for the invention of new machines, moveable towers with covered galleries, by Valerius. They were employed by him in the siege of Cales, which he took by assault, and it was made a Roman colony the following year.

The warlike preparations made by the Samnites disturbed the public mind, till it was found they were only raising troops to drive Alexander, king of Epirus, from Pæstum, upon which he had made a descent. Two new tribes were added to those already established at Rome, which received the names of Mæcia and Scaptia.

It has long been a question among the learned, whether about this time the Romans sent an embassy to Alexander the Great to request his alliance. That mighty victor seated on his throne at Babylon, received ambassadors from all parts of the world, Italy included. The Roman annalists are silent upon the subject.[55]

The year of Rome 423, was remarkable for an alleged conspiracy of a number of Roman ladies to poison their husbands. As the accusation rested solely upon the evidence of their female slaves, who probably intended to fill their places, these matrons may have been innocent of the crime with which they were charged. It is pretended that more than a hundred patrician ladies poisoned themselves at the instigation of Cornelia and Sergia, the B.C. 331. leaders of the plot, who set them the example in this sweeping act of self-destruction.

The rebellion of Privernum, headed by Vitruvius, a Latin, to whom the privileges of Roman citizenship had been accorded, found employment for both the consuls. One reduced Fundi into submission, while the other besieged Privernum, which was not taken till the following year. Vitruvius the leader of the rebellion was scourged with rods and beheaded, and the Privernatans were brought up for judgment by the consuls to the senate-house.[56] A senator asked one of the captive Privernatans, "What punishment he thought they deserved." "That due to men who think themselves worthy of liberty," was his bold, brief reply to the puerile question. The consul Plautius, willing to soften the rejoinder added, "But suppose we should pardon you, how will you conduct yourselves for the future?" "If you grant us an honourable peace, very faithfully, but if the terms be hard, not long." This manly avowal displeased some of the senators, but others who possessed more liberal minds, thought it rather deserved commendation than reproof. The brave and generous consul Plautius, who appeared as the advocate of the captives, declared, "that the people whose only ambition was freedom, and their only dread a fear to lose it, were deserving of liberty." This magnanimous sentiment was responded to by the Roman senate, and Privernum was declared free.[57] The consul Æmilius took the surname of Privernas, but the name of Plautius must have been written in the hearts of the captive people for whom he had so generously pleaded. Both consuls obtained a triumph.

The Romans gave umbrage to the Samnites,[58] by rebuilding and colonising Fregellæ, a city formerly razed by that people in their war with the Sidicinians, to whom it then belonged. The Palaeopolitans, before the rupture took place, invaded the territories of the Roman republic during the time when the elections for the consulship were about to be held, but the new consuls, L. Cornelius Lentulus and Q. Publius Philo, marched with their armies into the field, the first taking up a strong position between Palaeopolis and Neapolis (Naples), cut off the communication between the sister cities, whilst his colleague watched the movements of the Samnites, being stationed near Capua for that purpose. He reported to the senate that they were tampering with the fidelity of the Roman colonies, and had strongly garrisoned the two cities with which the Romans were at war. The Samnites denied the charge altogether.[59] The garrisons of Palaeopolis and Neapolis, they said, were reinforced by a band of independent volunteers. If this explanation did not satisfy the Roman ambassadors, the Samnites were equally discontented respecting the colonisation of Fregellæ, and replied with great excitement to the arbitration proposed by the Romans: "Arbitrators we will have none, but the gods and our swords. Let our armies face each other between Capua and Suessula, and try there the question whether the Samnites or the Romans shall be lords of Italy."[60] "Our legions," replied the Roman plenipotentiaries, "take their orders from their own generals, and not from their enemies." The quarrel was taken up by the Roman Fecialis,[61] who, stepping forward, referred it immediately to the martial deities, by raising his hands to heaven, and uttering a prayer, which appealed to the gods for the decision of the approaching contest between Rome and Samnium.

The campaign was not opened till the following consulship, when C. Pætelius Libo and L. Papirius Mugillanus, being aided by the people of Apulia and Lucania, took from the enemy three towns. For the first time in Roman history, we hear of the pro-consular magistracy, which originated in the sound policy of retaining the services of an eminent commander in the field, longer than the lawful period of his consulship. Publilius had been left before Palaeopolis, with the title of pro-consul, to conclude the military operations he had so skilfully commenced. As the besieged were not only straigtened for provisions, but greatly oppressed by the Samnite garrison and other foreign auxiliaries, the chief magistrates Nymphius and Charilaus, with the consent of the inhabitants, devised a plan for putting the city into B.C. 326. the hands of the pro-consul, as the least evil of the two.[62] Charilaus escaped to the Roman camp, and led the consular army to that part of the town which was defended by the Samnites. Nymphius persuaded the Samnite garrison to equip the fleet against the Romans. The Samnites fell into the snare, leaving the walls weakly defended, upon which the Romans made themselves masters of the city, to the joy of the inhabitants and great mortification of the Samnites.[63] The pro-consul was honoured with a triumph for this important acquisition to the dominions of the republic. The Samnites, not to be outdone by the Romans in wiles, contrived to withdraw the Lucanians from their newly-formed alliance with that people, by bribing some young Lucanians to endure a hearty scourging, which they pretended had been done in the Roman camp by the consul's order. War between the Lucanians, who were deceived by the tale, and the Romans, who resented it, was the immediate consequence of this falsehood.[64]

An affecting incident changed the custom of seizing the person of the debtor for his liabilities, or accepting a substitute in the person of his son, on the part of the creditor. Publilius, a young plebeian, through a sense of filial duty, became a *nexus* or bond-slave, in the place of his father, to a man of base mind, named Papirius, from whom he received such injurious treatment that he claimed the protection of the Roman people.[65] A law was passed restricting the claims of the creditor to the goods, but not allowing him to seize the person, of the debtor.

Camillus, who had the important charge of the Samnite war, fell sick, and was obliged to nominate Papirius Cursor dictator, who selected the brave young Fabius Rullianus for his general of horse. The dictator, though a great man, was a very superstitious one. He fancied that something had been omitted in the auspices at his inauguration, and departed for Rome to have the ceremonies renewed. He left the command of the army to Fabius, forbidding him to engage the enemy in his absence. The aspiring general of horse was young, brave, and less superstitious than his commander. He hazarded a battle on his own responsibility, and gained a great victory, twenty thousand Samnites being left dead on the sanguinary field. Once, indeed, Fabius was in danger of losing the honour of the day, which was only redeemed by his own impetuous charge with the Roman cavalry, which nothing could withstand.[66] The young victor added to this breach of military discipline the graver fault of burning the spoil taken from the enemy, instead of placing it in the quæstor's hands. This he did to prevent its adorning the triumph of Papirius. Moreover, he wrote to the senate an account of his victory, instead of communicating it first to the dictator, according to the customary rules of military etiquette.[67] The news of his successful disobedience enraged his commanding officer so much, that he quitted Rome to punish him in an exemplary manner. The occasion of his hasty return was made known to Fabius by some friends in the city, who reminded him of the fate of Titus Manlius, and warned him to provide for his personal safety. He assembled his victorious army, and obtained a promise from them that they would stand forth in his defence in case Papirius was inclined to keep his severe resolution. He had scarcely gained their suffrages before he was cited by the public crier to appear before the stern dictator's tribunal.[68] The sight of the rods and axes of the lictors presented a more formidable appearance to the brave young man than the front of the hottest battle. Yet he boldly entered upon his defence, and that too in terms that increased the displeasure of the incensed dictator, who immediately passed sentence of death upon him, which was to be preceded by the accustomed scourging. Upon the lictors endeavouring to disrobe Fabius, he called upon the soldiers to deliver him; and breaking from the executioners, took shelter with the triarians, who opened their ranks to allow him to pass through, the only means they thought proper to use in his behalf. Fabius was at Rome the following day, where his affectionate father, justly proud of his gallant son, had already disposed the senate in his favour, when young Fabius came to plead his cause in person before that august assembly. In the B.C. 325. midst of his defence, the dictator entered with his lictors, and regardless of the sanctity of the place, or the dignity of the assembly, claimed the criminal, whose life was forfeited to military law.[69] The fond father of the daring cavalry general was no Manlius Torquatus; he appealed to the tribunes and the people in comitia, a power that Papirius himself dared not defy, although the appeal was without a precedent. The cause in dispute was transferred to the Forum, whither the senate, the stern military judge, and the multitude, hurried to decide the fate of the unfortunate master of the horse.[70] Both the Fabii ascended the rostra, meaning to harangue the people, but Papirius, whose rightful place it was in quality of dictator, ordered six lictors to dislodge them from that vantage ground; but the father would be heard. He complained of the cruelty and jealousy of Papirius. He extolled the bravery of his rash son. He called upon the gods for help; he appealed to the people; and, overcome by his paternal feelings, threw himself upon the neck of young Fabius, bathing him with tears,[71] holding him locked in his arms, as if to defend his person from assault at the peril of his own life. The Fabii were fond fathers; in that illustrious line—and Rome never boasted a nobler—the best affections of the heart were as deeply venerated and cherished as valour. The senate and people, greatly moved, regarded the father and son with interest and compassion. The stern eloquence of the Roman dictator was then heard. He reminded his auditors of Titus Manlius, condemned by his own father for the crime for which his guilty officer then stood amenable. He pronounced the military code and the glory of Rome to be inseparable, and reproached the Romans with having lost that heroic love of country which formerly had been the supreme object of their affections.[72] That proud feeling of patriotism was not appealed to in vain. The Roman people, and even the Fabii themselves, with a sudden revulsion of feeling, avowed the justice of the dictator's sentence; and, falling simultaneously at his feet, besought his clemency; Papirius Cursor immediately granted the general prayer, declaring "that the strictness of military discipline was equally maintained whether he took or gave the life of Fabius, since he pardoned the condemned at the intercession of the Roman people."[73] This concession did him honour; and well, in after years, did the young warrior whose life they had saved, deserve the affection of the Romans, who, from the moment in which they became his preservers, regarded him as their adopted son. Papirius returned to Samnium, where he found his severe behaviour had done much mischief. His own relation and master of horse, Papirius Crassus, had been braved in his camp by the Samnites, without daring to resent their insults.[74] The army was disaffected to him, and in the next engagement made no effort to ensure him a triumph. Papirius did not punish his refractory soldiers, but took the wiser course of regaining their affection. He effected this by visiting them when sick, and conversing with them familiarly at other times. His soldiers formed a strong attachment to his person, and from that time the Samnites found him invincible. The dictator, by a series of brilliant victories, obliged the Samnites to sue for peace, which was granted them upon condition that they clothed his army and gave them one year's pay. As the treaty was only to be in force for that period, the return of Papirius Cursor to Rome was the signal of its cessation on the part of the Samnites.

Although the name of Roman citizens had been long accorded to the people of Privernum, and more recently to those of Tusculum, neither had received the privilege of voting for the different magistracies, their civic rights being extended to them as private individuals, not incorporating them with a great political body of freemen. These discontented Roman citizens took an opportunity to revolt during the absence of the consuls Sulpicius Longus and Q. Aulius Cerretanus from Rome, the first leading an army into Samnium, while his colleague posted himself in Apulia. The insurgents elected a consul in the person of L. Fulvius Curvus, a Tusculan chief, and at midnight were at the gates of Rome. The citizens hurried to the walls to defend the city from this unexpected attack, and compelled the enemy to retreat. The danger alarmed the senate and people of Rome so much, B.C. 323. that some arrangement was made by negotiation, by which the Tusculans received their full rights, and their leader was chosen for the Roman consulate the following year. These concessions arose from the idea that the whole Latin people would have united with the Tusculans and Privernatans, and passed over to the Samnites.[75] The knowledge that the inhabitants of Velitræ had been incited by them to join the revolt, formed however the ground of the accusation afterwards made by Flavius, a tribune of the people.[76] This small republic, which had been often useful to that of Rome, implored the clemency of the Romans, which every tribe but the Pollian was willing to grant, the dissentient voting for beheading the men and enslaving the women and children. The Tusculans, who were incorporated with the Papirian tribe, never forgot this insult, for, even in the time of Livy, it would not give a vote to enable any man belonging to the Pollian to fill a public office.

Quintus Fabius and L. Fulvius Curvus, the consuls for the year, united their armies and marched into Samnium, where they gave the Samnites a dreadful overthrow, but not before their brave opponents had contested the victory with the Roman legions from nine in the morning till two in the afternoon. Alarmed by the progress of the consuls, they considered this defeat as the vengeance of the gods upon their broken faith.[77] Accordingly they despatched an embassy to Rome to sue for peace, taking with them for punishment the man who had advised them to break the truce. Brutulus Papius, the national victim, was a person of distinguished birth and factious spirit. He died by his own hands on the way to Rome; but the corpse of the self-murderer was presented in due form by the ambassadors to the senate, who did not choose to grant the peace they demanded.[78] This impolitic conduct led to results very different from what the Roman legislators expected, and left a blot upon the annals of the republic which could never be effaced.

The choice of the Roman people for the 133rd consulship fell upon T. Veturius and Spurius Postumius, who were to conduct the Samnite war. That valiant people elected a brave and able general in the person of Pontius Herennius to meet the coming danger. The Samnite commander was well acquainted with the nature of the country he was called upon to defend. This knowledge enabled him to lay a successful snare for the Roman army. When the two consuls were approaching Caudium, near which place he was encamped, he spread a false report that the Samnite army was besieging Luceria. In order to make this rumour appear more credible, he disguised some of his own soldiers as herdsmen, and ordered them to put themselves in the way of the Romans to repeat the same story. The Romans, as Pontius expected, immediately marched to the relief of Luceria, forsaking the highway, which was broad and open, for a shorter route through a narrow defile between impending rocks. The road was marshy leading to a passage through a hollow rock, which was narrow, deep, and difficult.[79] Not at all aware of the danger that surrounded them, the Romans fell into the trap laid for them, till upon reaching the valley just described, they found their egress barred by fragments of rock and trunks of trees. Struck with consternation, they turned back in the vain hope of escaping by the entrance, which had been secured in like manner. The rocks above them were manned by the Samnites, who scornfully looked down from the heights upon their imprisoned enemies. The soldiers silently formed their camp about the consuls' tent, and passed the long night without sleep and without hope. "The gods themselves," remarks Livy, "could hardly have given them any assistance." The fate of the armed multitude within their power required some deliberation on the part of the Samnites. They sent to consult Herennius, the father of their general, respecting the best method of dealing with the Roman legions. "Do them no injury, but open a passage for them home," was the wise and merciful reply of the prudent old man.[80] The Samnites did not like the advice, and sent to him a second time, upon which a council of war was formed, in which Herennius gave a different B.C. 321. opinion. "Slay them all," was the laconic and puzzling sentence he now uttered upon the important subject in debate.[81] This apparent contradiction in a man of well-known wisdom excited great surprise, and Pontius was entreated to send for his father, that he might explain his own reasons for such differing counsel. "If you dismiss your enemies with kind treatment," replied Herennius, "you make them friends, and this seems to me the wisest and best means you can adopt. If you slay them you diminish their strength; but there appears to me to be no middle way between mercy and severity." Pontius and the council thought differently, and they resolved to fix a stain upon the military honour of the Roman people. They dictated hard terms to the captive warriors, who were to pass, man by man, unarmed and half naked under the yoke. The consular armies were not only to evacuate Samnium, but to restore the lands and towns the Romans had taken from them in the course of all their wars.[82] The consuls remained silent; human valour could not now deliver them from a choice of evils which human foresight might have prevented. "Starvation and massacre alone awaited them in that gloomy valley. The destruction of the Roman army at this critical period would be the ruin of Rome; but the proposed disgrace might be obliterated by future deeds of glory." Thus argued Lentulus, a distinguished officer, and his counsel prevailed. The consuls signified to Pontius their acceptance of the part of the treaty relative to the army; that which regarded Samnium could only be made with the senate. They could but promise and leave hostages for the performance of those conditions.[83] Six hundred Roman knights were chosen for this purpose, whose heads were to answer for the non-ratification of the treaty by the senate. A yoke, or gallows, was then set up, under which the hostages, man by man, passed on their way to the Samnite camp, divested of their arms and upper garments. In this manner the consuls, chief officers and the whole army, marched out of the defile. If any one resisted, or refused compliance with the degrading ceremony, he was slaughtered without mercy.[84] The disgraced Roman army halted in the fields near Capua rather than enter the city in such woeful plight. The report of their misfortunes had, however, preceded them, and the magistrates of Capua, as soon as they heard of their arrival, sent them food, arms, horses, tents and clothing. Even the delicate attention of lictors and fasces were not forgotten, as the consuls had lost theirs. The following morning the magistrates and Campanian nobility conducted the Romans to the frontier;[85] but these tokens of respect could not dispel the general dejection. Some of the Campanians in the senate the next day declared that the Roman spirit had for ever deserted these soldiers. An old man replied, "This dejection will prove fatal to the Samnites, for the Romans will have this shameful treaty before their eyes whenever they encounter a Samnite army, nor will these everywhere find Caudine defiles."[86] The army entered Rome, each soldier regaining his home in the silence and secresy of night. Postumius, when he appeared before the senate to report the treaty he had made with the Samnites, declared that the Roman people were not bound by it, expressing the willingness of himself and his colleague Veturius to give themselves up to that people, to atone for the infraction of the treaty. The self-devotion of Postumius was extolled and accepted. A new army was raised, and the Caudine legions were once more enrolled.[87] Cornelius Arvina being appointed fecialis to conduct the devoted consuls and their officers to Samnium. The fecialis took the way to the Samnite camp, bringing with him his unhappy countrymen, whom he delivered up to Pontius in the name of the senate and people of Rome, who had, he said, refused to ratify the treaty. Postumius then struck the fecialis with his knee, for his hands and feet were fettered, saying, "Thou art a Roman ambassador, and I am now one of the Samnite people; with this blow I compel you to war with us." Pontius indignantly reproved the artifice, and dismissed the prisoners,[88] but he repented of his severity to the Roman army, and wished he had followed the counsel of his wiser father. The Romans, resolving to deliver the knights, chose Publilius and Papirius Cursor B.C. 321. for their consular generals. As the hostages were in Luceria, Papirius marched towards that place, while the dictator Cornelius Lentulus, gave battle to Pontius; and so eager were the Romans to engage with the Samnites, that they would not listen to the speech of the dictator, but clashing their arms cried out, "To battle! to battle!" The Samnites were defeated with great loss, and their camp was stormed and taken. The dictator, after his victory, marched to the assistance of Papirius, who was lying before Luceria, and in want of provisions. Lentulus not only supplied his colleague's wants, but cut off the supplies of the Samnite army, who were encamped at Luceria. Papirius knowing that the besieged were suffering the horrors of famine, resolved to bring the Samnite army to a battle, but the enemy would not engage with him. He was obliged to attack them in their entrenchments, where he gave them a dreadful overthrow. Every Samnite would have perished by the hands of the Romans, but Papirius reminded them that six hundred of their countrymen were prisoners in Luceria, who would be put to death if they totally exterminated their enemies.[89] The famine-stricken inhabitants of Luceria offered to give up the hostages, but Papirius would not receive them, nor agree to any capitulation, unless the garrison and all the inhabitants passed under the yoke. Pontius and seven thousand men went through this ceremony. The hostages were delivered, and the degradation of the Roman name effaced in the eyes of her enemies, but the Romans themselves never forgot the Caudine forks.[90] Their remembrance of the national disgrace outlasted the existence of Samnium. The second year after these events, the Roman senate, made some objection to prolonging the truce with Samnium, nor would they extend the term for more than two years. The Falerina and Ufentina tribes were added at this time to the Roman people, making the number thirty-one. A census was also taken, by which it appeared that the free citizens of Rome, capable of carrying arms, amounted to two hundred and fifty thousand. The acquisition of Apulia was made by the consul, Junius Brutus, who rendered illustrious once more, by that conquest, names so dear to Roman liberty. In the following consulship the war with Samnium commenced with the siege of Saticula, in Campania, which was conducted by L. Æmilius, who was named dictator for that purpose. It is uncertain whether this town in Campania belonged to the Samnites, or had been drawn into an alliance with that people. Papirius Cursor and Publilius Philo received the fasces, and forced Saticula to surrender. The revolt of Sora, by obliging one of the consular armies to march thither, while the other remained in Apulia, left Campania exposed to the irruption of the brave and restless people with whom the Romans were at war. The Samnites raised quickly a third army for the occupation of Campania, without withdrawing their armies from Apulia, and the vicinity of

Sora.[91] Papirius Cursor and his colleague named Quintus Fabius Rullianus for dictator. The impetuosity of Aulius Cerretanus, whom Fabius had chosen for his master of horse, led to his destruction. He slew with his own hands the Samnite general, but was himself slain by the brother of the fallen leader in the very moment of victory.[92] He had charged without orders, following the example formerly given by the dictator himself. An obstinate fight was maintained by the cavalry on both sides, for Roman knight and Samnite equestrian warrior, dismounting from their steeds, fought hand to hand on foot. This battle took place at the pass of Lautulæ, between Anxur and Fundi; but though the victory was claimed by the Romans, it must have been a defeat, since every town in the vicinity revolted from the republic to the Samnites,[93] Campania, and even Capua becoming disaffected to the Roman interest.[94] The extension of the Roman franchise to the Volscians and Latins had secured their fidelity at this critical juncture. Plistia had been won by the Samnites immediately after the fight at Lautulæ. The victory at Sora, gained by the dictator, was followed by the siege of that place. Sulpicius Longus won a great battle over the Samnites, near Caudium, and encamped before Bovianum, a large city B.C. 314. in Samnium, where he took up his winter quarters.[95] Luceria, Sora, and some other towns were taken, but all the inhabitants were put to the sword.

Several Roman colonies were planted at Luceria, lately desolated by war; one at Suessa Aurunca, and another in the volcanic island of Pontia (now Ponza); while two were ordered to be formed at Interamna on the Liris, and at Casinum, one of its tributary streams. This measure not only relieved Rome of her growing population, but provided the republic with a line of defence wherever she planted her colonies. In this branch of political economy Rome has never been surpassed, for if she destroyed towns and cities, she founded new ones on their ruins.[96] One of the leading events of this year was the trial of A. Atilius Calatinus, on the charge of betraying the garrison of Sora, of which he had been governor at the time that city was surprised. His escape, or ransom from an enemy who had reduced his whole garrison to slavery, irritated the minds of the Roman people. His defence was undertaken in the comitia by his illustrious father-in-law, Quintus Fabius, whose mild policy and great public services had endeared him to that people to whose generous prayer he owed his life. "This charge," he said, "is groundless; for were it true, I should not have allowed my daughter to remain the wife of a traitor."[97] The manly declaration of the patriotic Roman occasioned the acquittal of the unfortunate officer.[98]

We have now arrived at a celebrated period of Roman history, the censorship of Appius Claudius, who applied the resources lately gained in the Samnite war, to those noble works which still exist, as enduring public blessings in our own day.[99] In the beginning of his censorship, Appius Claudius made some important changes in the state, which gave immense offence not only to the plebeian, but also to that patrician order of which he was a distinguished member. War and pestilence having created many vacancies in the senate, and the increased power of the republic making it necessary to fill them up, this censor, passing by those members of the aristocracy who expected it as a right, and those plebeians who naturally made their admission to the senate a laudable point of ambition, placed on his list a class of men called libertini, the sons of manumitted slaves—a race combining the intelligence of advanced civilisation, with the industrial habits of craftsmen, mechanics, and scribes. Forbidden the pursuits of war and agriculture, the libertini became rich by the arts of peace, and cultivated sciences unknown to the poor oppressed plebeian citizen of Rome, whose civic privileges, while they maintained his political freedom, did not find him sufficient land to furnish his family in bread. Appius Claudius, a man of learning and genius, able, scientific, and astute as his race, was not slow in discovering the political importance of this hitherto despised class. He recognised in the libertini some of the ablest persons of the commonwealth, in which till then they had enjoyed such slender privileges. They were the notaries of the republic. The pen in the early ages was seldom used in literary compositions, but an immense deal of public business was committed to writing by this class.[100] That part of his office which gave Appius Claudius the power of excluding his countrymen from their senatorial and civic privileges, was exercised by him in a very arbitrary and unjust manner. In order to lessen the political importance of the Roman people, and to destroy the ascendancy of his personal opponents in the patrician order, he actually deprived them of their seats in the senate, filling the vacancies with the sons of freedmen, who probably were his own clients.[101] The innovation made by Appius Claudius on the senatorial customs was not the only one he introduced. He gained the consent of the Potitii for the transfer of the priesthood of Hercules, which their traditionary records declared had been instituted by Evander, and given to their ancestor. The altar belonging to this priesthood B.C. 310. was called Ara Maxima, which he assigned to the slaves employed upon his vast public works. This measure gave general dissatisfaction to the Romans,[102] though founded upon sound political wisdom, and perhaps even upon benevolent principles. Some of the labours of Hercules had been performed in slavery, and in associating piety and industry together, Appius Claudius lessened the physical degradation of the labourers, by the example presented to them in the god they worshipped. He also sought to raise this large body of servile workmen, by giving them an altar, priests, and sacrifices; and however low the standard of religion might be in the Roman republic, it was certainly better than atheism, into which slavery is so apt to fall. His public works commenced in the first year of his censorship, but took some years to bring them to a close.[103]

The great Appian way lasted entire for more than eight hundred years. It led from Rome to Capua, and was afterwards continued from that place to Brundusium, on the Adriatic coast.[104] In the construction of his famous aqueduct, the censor considered the wants of the poor, whose health had suffered from their being hitherto compelled to drink the unwholesome and turbid water of the Tiber. To the impoverished citizens the science of the great censor at least brought health and comfort. Employment it did not give them, for the pride of the Roman citizen would have classed the laborious industry of forming his road, digging his canals, or boring his water course, with the bitter toils of slavery.[105] The costly public works of this celebrated censorship exhausted the whole revenue of Rome, and it is conjectured that in order to prosecute his grand designs, Appius Claudius must have sold a great part of the domain land of the republic.[106] Though the supposition has no historic basis, it is by no means unlikely; and how could the resources and treasures of the state have been better employed than in works of such grandeur and utility? The resignation and death of C. Plautius, his colleague, before his year was out, left the remaining censor more funds to prosecute his designs. It is said that Plautius, finding himself overborne by Appius, and his censorial list disregarded, abdicated.[107] His death enabled the survivor to pursue his plans unopposed—a state of independence suited to his governing mind and arbitrary will. His changes in the state being unpopular, the first act of the new consuls, Junius Brutus and Q. Æmilius Barbula, was to annul the privileges lately granted to the libertini by Appius Claudius. In this consulship two officers, called naval duumvirs, were instituted to take charge of the nautical affairs of the republic. This looks as if the Romans had a navy, though we know not of what it consisted. To the people was accorded the power of choosing sixteen out of the twenty-four legionary tribunes. The consul Brutus carried on the war in Samnium with such success, that Cluvia and Bovianum were both carried by assault. Near the lake Avernus the Samnites laid an ambush for the consular army, which was discovered in time to permit the Romans to form in order of battle. Twenty thousand Samnites were slain on this occasion. The consul Æmilius was equally successful in Etruria, where he gained a victory for which he was decreed a triumph.[108]

The time had arrived for Appius Claudius to resign his office, his eighteen months being completed; but he refused to give up his censorial authority, not choosing to leave his immortal works unfinished to adorn the name of another censor. The tribune, Sempronius Sophus, threatened to fine and imprison him; but Appius, who had secured to his interest three voices out of the ten composing the tribunitial college, set his veto and those of his six colleagues at defiance, and continued to exercise his functions in defiance of the laws and customs of Rome—functions which the most despotic sovereign of regal Rome had never exercised—resolutely carrying on his great public works, which made even his disobedience glorious. The libertini whom he had raised, and the poor plebeians, for whom he was constructing his aqueduct, must have stood by the censor through his long reign of five years. In all his intrigues to retain his power, Appius was materially assisted by a libertinus named Cneius Flavius, his clerk, a man of worth and talent.[109]

The first consulship of Quintus Fabius Rullianus took B.C. 310.place this year. He had already opened a splendid military career by the victory that had made him amenable to military law, from the penalty of which the general intercession of the Roman people alone had saved him. Fourteen years had now elapsed since their prayer had prolonged his glorious existence, and his elevation to the consular dignity was now an additional proof of their love for their favourite patrician. He opened the Etruscan campaign by the victory of Sutrium, passing through the recesses of the Ciminian forest, which no Roman army had ever till then penetrated.[110] In the dead of night Fabius attacked the Etruscans, destroyed their camp, and slew sixty thousand men.[111] The fruits of this brilliant consular campaign were the delivery of Sutrium, and a truce concluded for thirty years with the three principal Etruscan cities—Perusia, Arretium, and Cortona.

The consul Marcius was less fortunate in the Samnite campaign, and the first Roman navy that ever put to sea was robbed of the plunder it had won in its victorious descent on Pompeii, by the Campanians, who overtook the expedition on the return, and having despoiled them, drove them back empty-handed to their ships[112]—a glorious exploit, though very mortifying to the Romans. This was most likely the mischance which occasioned a deputation to be sent to the victorious Fabius, entreating him to nominate a dictator, in the person of his old general, Papirius Cursor, to conduct the Samnite war. The consul heard the senatorial decree read, and listened in deep silence to the eloquent appeal of the senators who composed the deputation. The sacrifice required by his country was severe to a man who had never forgiven Papirius, and we cannot wonder that he was loth to make it. He withdrew without uttering a word. In the dead of night, he nominated his old commander to the dignity, but when the deputation thanked and praised him for his magnanimity, he abruptly quitted, and dismissed them without breaking his indignant silence.[113] At Viterbo, Fabius gained a third victory over the Etruscans, though the battle was obstinately contested, and the consul wounded; but the desperate valour of the Roman knights finally retrieved the day.[114] This engagement must have been hazarded by those Etruscan cities who had not made the late treaty with Rome.

Papirius Cursor did not lose his old reputation in this his last Samnite campaign. The enemy made a splendid appearance, some wearing white garments, others the gay parti-coloured plaid, the national costume of the Celts; for the Samnites had settled in Oscan or Celtic cities. The silver shields borne by numbers[115] marked them as members of a sacred band, devoted to conquer or die for their country. They had been admitted previously into a white tent, in secresy, darkness, and silence, where they had been pledged by fearful oaths to stand by each other; any hesitation on the part of the person to be initiated occasioning him to be immediately slain by an invisible foe.[116] The report of the solemnity had found its way into the Roman camp, and alarmed the superstitious, who looked with uneasiness upon the silver or gilded shields of the devoted, upon whose helms lofty plumes were fixed, to add to their magnificent appearance the advantage of height.[117] Papirius removed the prevalent feeling of awe from the minds of his army by drily remarking, "that the Samnite finery would not look very well when stained with dust and blood, but that the shields would make a rich prize for valiant soldiers."[118] He faced the plaided warriors, but Junius Brutus Bubulcus, his master of horse, who was posted directly opposite the white bands, effaced the impression their sight made on the cavalry by crying aloud, "I devote those men in white to Pluto," as he gallantly headed the charge, before which the white cohorts gave way. "What! with the dictator at your head, shall the victory of this day begin on the left?" was the remark of Papirius to his infantry, when he beheld the daring bravery of his master of horse. His own lieutenants, Valerius and Decius, nobly seconded their general, and the last great victory of Papirius Cursor ended with the destruction of the Samnite camp. It was B.C. 309. during this battle that Junius Brutus Bubulcus vowed a temple to health, if the victory fell to the Romans. A very splendid triumph was granted to the dictator, who made his public entry on the fifteenth of October,[119] the silver shields and gay garments won from the Samnites making the pageant remarkable for its magnificence. The shields were divided among the silversmiths whose shops lined the Via Sacra, to adorn the square pillars looking towards the Forum.[120] But it was not upon the gorgeous spectacle afforded them by the campaign of Papirius Cursor, that the Roman people looked with sole interest that year; for the dictatorial triumph was soon followed in November by that of the consul, Quintus Fabius Rullianus, which gratified them more because the popular conqueror of Etruria was, though a patrician of the highest rank, the friend and idol of the commons. Papirius Cursor retired from the dictatorship to the repose of private life, and left to Fabius the charge of sustaining in the next campaign the glory of the Roman arms against Etruria and Samnium. The third consulship of Fabius, in conjunction with Decius, was marked by great success. Decius forced the Etruscans to sue for peace, but would not grant a treaty for more than one year, for nothing less than the complete reduction of Etruria could now satisfy the growing greatness and ambition of the Roman people. He was continued in the field as pro-consul—an honour that had been accorded to him once before.

The long censorship of Appius Claudius was drawing to a close; the tribunes, whose influence had supported his power, had successively gone out of office, and not one in the whole college was inclined to favour its retention. His canvass for the consulship was certain to be a successful one; but he aspired to something beyond it, wishing to unite in his own person the censorial and consular magistracies—honours destined several centuries later, with the additional one of the perpetual tribuneship, to meet in the persons of his direct descendants, Tiberius, Caligula, Claudius, Nero, and Galba.[121] This year, Appius Claudius received the fasces, with L. Volumnius for his colleague. He insisted upon retaining his censorship, which he had already held five years, but such an innovation upon the Roman constitution was not suffered to become a precedent, for the tribunitial college would no longer support his ambitious measures, to which L. Furius opposed his veto, forbidding the comitia to proceed with any business relative to the elections till the aspirant to a second consulship had resigned the censorship. His election immediately followed his abdication.[122] The new censors, Junius Bubulcus Brutus, and M. Valerius Maximus, excluded from the senate L. Antonius, for divorcing his wife without having assembled his friends to pass judgment upon her. This divorce took place before that of Spurius Carvilius Ruga, which is erroneously supposed to be the first instance of the kind.[123] In the same year, C. Fabius painted the Temple of Health for the censor Junius Bubulcus Brutus, from which he acquired the name of Pictor,[124] and the subject is conjectured to have been the battle against the Samnites which had occasioned the vow of the founder. Dionysius praised this painting, which, according to him, was very correctly drawn and finely coloured.[125] Marcus Valerius afterwards placed in this temple a picture of his battle against Hiero.[126] Rome in the ages of her military glory was, however, never celebrated for her works of art; for war is no nursery of those refinements which are the offspring of peace. To Rome the peaceful and the Christian, belonged, in after centuries, the re-creation of sculpture and painting. The censors, in imitation of their able predecessor in office, made several roads, and that from Rome to Tibur was ever after distinguished by the name of the Valerian Way, B.C. 308. although only the first twenty miles was the work of Valerius.[127]

Literature was beginning to dawn, and its first gleams emanated from the same genius that had given Rome in the fifth century roads and aqueducts. There existed in the days of Cicero a poem of Appius Claudius the Blind, of which some fragments have been discovered.[128] This composition bore a strong resemblance to a poetical piece written by Pythagoras—a likeness supposed to have originated in the censor's knowledge of Greek.[129] Oratory seems to have been an hereditary gift in the family. The Claudii were all good speakers, but were more distinguished for eloquence than principle. Of the Claudian race, Appius Claudius was undoubtedly the best, if not the greatest son. That he was well-intentioned, the conduct of the patricians towards him during his long usurpation of the censorship appears to afford a proof; for their forbearance can hardly have originated in a fear of driving him to extremities, but rather in their conviction that the completion of his vast and patriotic designs was his sole object. During the consulship of Appius Claudius and Volumnius Flamma, Fabius was continued in the command of an army, with the title of pro-consul. He defeated the Samnites at Allifæ, and took many prisoners. The Samnites he disarmed and sent away unhurt, for what reason we are not informed, but doubtless they had surrendered upon those express conditions. The troops of various nations he sold for slaves,[130] those of the Hernicans were sent to Rome; the senate committed them to the wardship of the Latin allies of the republic. L. Volumnius Flamma, the plebeian colleague of Appius Claudius, was placed at the head of an army; he subdued the Salentines, while his associate in the chief magistracy was employed in finishing his great public works. Volumnius though much beloved by the soldiers, had not yet attained the splendid military renown for which he was afterwards distinguished. It is uncertain what treatment the Hernican prisoners received in consequence of the consuls, Marcius Tremulus and P. Cornelius Arvina, bringing their case before the senate.[131]

The third treaty between Rome and Carthage was ratified this year, for as yet no rivalry subsisted between these warlike states. The victory of the consuls Postumius and Minucius at Bovianum over the Samnites was very decisive, though the latter was slain in storming their camp. In these battles Postumius took the Samnite general prisoner, and forty-six ensigns. Bovianum was taken by Fulvius Curvus, the brave successor of the slain consul, for which exploit he was decreed a triumph. The commencement of the consulship of Sempronius Sophus and Sulpicius Saverrio was remarkable for the peace concluded with the Samnites, and for the war with the Hernicans and Æquians, which terminated so disastrously for these nations,[132] who lost forty-one towns in the course of fifty days, of which the chief part were destroyed. In the remains of their massy walls, the desolating hand of the conquering Roman "may still be distinctly traced in the pastoral upland valley of the Himella or Salto, from Alba to the vicinity of Reate,"[133] to attest to the truth of the ancient records that relate their fall. The remains of the Æquian nation submitted to the consuls, receiving the name of Roman citizens without those political rights which rendered the civic franchise so valuable; but we find them only five years later admitted to this enviable privilege, and enrolled among the tribes.[134] The greater portion of their territory was, however, appropriated by the victorious commonwealth. Many colonies were planted in the conquered country. C. Flavius made a calendar for the use of the Roman people, which he effected by fixing up boards, painted white, upon which the days and weeks were marked in every month. This useful work enabled the people to find out the days upon which law business might be transacted, without applying to the pontifices, who had hitherto preserved a secret which gave them power over the commons. Few even of the B.C. 305. patricians understood the mysteries of the pontifical rules, therefore the painted calendar of the learned scribe, which noted the holidays, was very acceptable to them; and was remembered at a time when their gratitude could be really serviceable to the man who had conferred such a lasting benefit upon them.[135] The beneficial labours of the scientific libertinus deeply offended the patrician pontifices, from whom the plebeians had hitherto received the necessary information of times and seasons, days and years. From a fragment of Cato the Censor we find that the computation of the eclipses of the sun and moon belonged exclusively to the pontiffs, and were duly registered in their annals.[136] But the regulation of time and the revolutions of the great heavenly bodies, were not the sole employment of the pontifical college, for Rome was indebted to this priesthood for its earliest records, known by the name of the Pontifical Annals, which, though styled by a great historian lately deceased,[137] "a dry and meagre skeleton of history," was still very useful and valuable, as giving some stability to facts adorned by poetry, and commemorated in the songs of an ancient people.[138]

Some curious particulars are related of Cneius Flavius's ædileship. When the first votes were given to this libertinus, the presiding ædile insolently refused to receive them, accompanying his harsh refusal with this sarcastic remark—"It is not a proper thing for a clerk to hold a curule magistracy." The observation was particularly cutting, because the ambitious aspirant to that dignity was attending upon the curule ædile with his tablets and style in his hand, ready to register the votes as a humble notary.[139] He was, however, determined that his lowly calling should not stand in the way of his rising fortunes, so putting down his tablets, he declared upon oath, that from that hour he gave up his clerkly profession for ever. The haughty ædile reluctantly received the votes for the *ci-devant* scribe, and pronounced Cneius Flavius duly elected for the curule magistracy. His colleague was a native of Præneste, but the opposing candidates were men of high birth.[140] The blow the affection of the commoners gave to the patricians by the election of Flavius, was shown by a deep and general mourning; the senators laid aside their gold rings, while the younger members of their families put off their gold chains, and the knights the silver curbs of their horses, in proof of their sorrow for the curule magistracy being represented by the grandson of a slave.[141] His colleague did not stand so low in their estimation, for when he was indisposed, some young noblemen paid him a visit of condolence, treating him with the respectful attention due to his official dignity. While conversing with the sick ædile, they were interrupted by the entrance of C. Flavius, whom they did not choose to recognise by any courteous salutation, much less to quit their seats, as

174

the customary etiquette required them to do. Like most risen men, the curule ædile, Cneius Flavius attached much importance to the homage and prestige of his situation. He therefore resolved to compel these haughty youths to render that respect to his office which they churlishly denied to his person. He directed one of his attendants to bring in his curule chair and place it directly in the doorway of the apartment. Cneius Flavius seated himself in great state, reducing the patrician visitors of his colleague to the necessity of waiting his pleasure to go home. Their rising to do so looked like respect to his person and as for pushing the curule chair on one side—the contempt they had displayed for the libertinus they dared not extend to the insignia of his office.[142] We are not informed which party yielded up the point, but it is certain that the curule ædile must have either departed himself when he had mortified them sufficiently, or have ordered his chair to be removed, that they might leave the apartment. The lesson obliged these patricians to treat him for the future with more respect. The intrigues and dissensions his election had caused to both orders—for the rich plebeians were as angry with the choice of the people as the nobility—made Flavius vow a temple to Concord whenever the internal state of Rome should become pacific and united. He laid by the sums he had acquired in his ædileship, arising from the B.C. 304. penalties enforced upon those wealthy money-lenders who had exacted usurious interest from their creditors, for this purpose—a noble proof of disinterestedness. Rarely indeed was this precedent imitated by future ædiles, whose fines helped to fill the pockets which they had emptied in giving costly shows to the people. "This fane was of bronze, and stood within the precincts of one dedicated to Vulcan, near the northern side of the Comitium."[143] Flavius made no attempt to pursue any further the thorny and ambitious path he had chosen; the wealthy and learned libertinus having discovered that political power had been dearly purchased by the grandson of the slave.

The censorship of Fabius Rullianus and his colleague Decius was memorable for the changes they made in the constitution. To his eminent civil services, and not to his military talents, the noble patrician censor is said to have derived the name of Maximus. In order to destroy the independence of the commons, he removed the freedmen and citizens[144] who had been engrafted in the Roman tribes by Appius Claudius, from the main body, among which they had been divided, and placed them in the four old civic tribes; thus remedying the evil their inclusion had occasioned without depriving them of the political and civic rights they had acquired; for these ancient tribes were less likely to be influenced by these new citizens than any other of the thirty-one into which the Roman people were divided. At the dedication of the Temple of Concord vowed by Cneius Flavius, which was finished during this censorship, the Pontifex Maximus, L. Cornelius Scipio, haughtily refused to pronounce the necessary formula the libertinus was to repeat after him, but the people in comitia compelled the reluctant patrician to complete the consecration;[145] though if Flavius had not won their favour by his obliging conduct and public services, they would probably have regarded his temple, the fabric vowed by the grandson of a slave, with as much contempt as the exclusive pontiff himself.

The descent on Italy made by Cleonymus, the youngest son of Cleomenes, king of Sparta, and grandson of that Cleombrotus who fell at Leuctra, was the next remarkable event in Italian history. This expedition was undertaken at the entreaty of the Tarentines, who were jealous of the Lucanians[146] securing their own independence by the aid of the Romans, who had compelled the Samnites to withdraw their garrisons from all the Lucanian towns. Areus, the nephew of the enterprising chief, being then on the throne of Sparta, aided his design with all his influence with the state, so that, with five thousand Greek mercenaries, Cleonymus was enabled to land near Thurii, with the evident intention of forming a colony on the sea coast, which doubtless was the true object of his coming to Italy, rather than to assist the Tarentines against the Lucanians. The Romans dislodged this prince from Thurii,[147] but the piracies committed by Cleonymus after he was driven from his first station, occasioned the Grecian cities to combine against their general enemy. He made a second descent near the spot where the city of Venice now stands, but was compelled to abandon that position, and return to Sparta with great loss.[148]

Intestine divisions in Arretium brought about the Etruscan war. The high aristocratic party implored the aid of the Romans, which was granted, for even in this early part of their history, we find them actuated by the crafty policy which afterwards led to the subjugation of Greece. Some Etruscan noblemen, disguised as shepherds, endeavoured to lead the Roman army into a snare, but Valerius detected their quality by the superiority of their language and manners, which did not suit the class to which they pretended to belong. He dismissed them uninjured, with the observation, "that their countrymen would find it as hard to deceive as to overcome the Romans."[149] The Etruscans attacked Fulvius, his lieutenant, and besieged him in his fort near the Roman camp, upon which Valerius marched to his relief and defeated them with great loss, when the Etruscans sued for peace, but obtained a cessation of hostilities for two years only.

During the consulship of Valerius a bill was proposed by the tribunes Quintus and Cneius Ogulnius, to increase B.C. 301. the pontifical and augural colleges, by the admission of the commons of Rome. Appius Claudius opposed the law with great vehemence,[150] which was finally passed through the manly eloquence of the Censor Decius, who reminded them of the self-immolation of his father, who, devoting himself to death to render the Roman people victorious, had himself become a sacrifice. "If my father were as eligible as his patrician colleague, to become an expiatory victim to the deities, he could not have been unfit to preside and direct their worship." This allusion to the patriotism of Decius Mus caused a majority for the measure, the bill was allowed to pass, and the pontifices received four commoners, which completed the number of nine. Five plebeian augurs were at the same time added to the four patrician members, to sanctify the three original tribes of Rome by a religious ministration.[151] The consul Valerius, in reviving a law of his ancestor Poplicola, which had been once before restored by a scarcely less famous man in that Valerius who had expelled the decemvirs, conferred a greater public benefit. This law was the Valerian, which permitted the accused, in capital cases, to make his appeal to the people—

a statute that rendered the execution of a citizen of Rome an event of rare occurrence in that and the two next centuries, unless by the illegal method of military law under the pretext of the republic being in danger.

"About this time the arts began to flourish, and the celebrated group still extant of the she-wolf nurturing the twin founders of Rome was set up in the Capitol. Let no one suppose that the Romans, before they adopted the civilisation of the Greeks, were barbarous. That people, which under its kings, constructed such gigantic sewers, and which at this time possessed a painter like Fabius Pictor, and a sculptor able to produce a work like the Capitoline she-wolf, cannot," remarks Niebuhr, "have been without some kind of literature."[152] To this era the sarcophagus of Lucius Cornelius Scipio belongs, the oldest sepulchral monument yet discovered in Rome, an existing proof of the excellency of statuary and design in the fifth century of the Roman age. Papirius Cursor dedicated a sun-dial in the temple of Quirinus, taken from the spoils of Samnium.[153] Rome was adorned at this time with many fine buildings and new streets; the buildings were of peperino, but the statues were of brass or bronze.[154]

In this period King Demetrius Poliorcetes, or the Besieger, sent the prisoners he had taken in Roman privateers to the senate with a complaint, that a Greek people, which thought itself entitled to the dominion of Italy, and had erected a temple in its market-place to the Dioscuri, the tutelar gods of navigation, should allow pirates to sail out.[155] These acts of piracy on the Greek sea were committed by some of the maritime towns subject to Rome. The circumstance is curious, because it shows that this prince ascribed to the Romans a Greek descent.

<hr size=2 width="10%" align=center>

[1] Livy.

[2] Val. Max., ii. 1; Livy, vii. 2.

[3] See Appendix. (p. 184)

[4] Cicero De Off.; Livy, vii. 5.

[5] Roman parents possessed the power of killing their children, but not of debasing them to the level of their own field slaves, though they could sell them in payment of their debts; but their children were entitled to the privileges of education, and at this period the company of the slaves was forbidden to the young Roman: therefore the neglect and abandonment of a noble youth very properly formed a subject of inquiry from the Roman people by one of their tribunes.

[6] Livy, vii. 5; Val. Max., v. 4.

[7] Livy, vii. 6; Val. Max., v.; St Augustine, De Civit. Dei, v.

[8] *Ibid.*; *Ibid.*; *Ibid.*

[9] *Ibid.*

[10] Aulus Gellius, ix. 13; Livy, vii. 10.

[11] Livy, vii. 11.

[12] Cicero, in Brut.; Livy, iii.

[13] Appian, in Celtic.

[14] Appian, in Celtic.

[15] Livy, iv. 35.

[16] Livy, vii. 16.

[17] In many corporations in England, we shall find public lands similarly situated, and appropriated by degrees or sold, to the injury of the inhabitants; exhibiting on a less scale the wrong complained of by the Roman commons. Small, feeble bodies murmur, but are unable to protest, on account of the ruinous expense of advocating their rights in a court of law. A mighty one, like the Roman commons, made itself heard, and sought and obtained redress.

[18] Livy, vii. 19.

[19] Hooke.

[20] From the benches upon which they sat to investigate the claims of the debtors.

[21] Hooke's Rome, vol. iii. p. 194.

[22] Livy, vii. 34; Polybius, xi. 18.

[23] Livy; Gellius, ix. 11.

[24] Livy, vii. 27.

[25] *Ibid.*, c. 28.

[26] Livy, 30.

[27] Livy, c. 32.

[28] *Ibid.*, 34.

[29] *Ibid.*, vii. 36.

[30] *Ibid.*

[31] *Ibid.*

[32] Aul. Gel., v.

[33] Livy, vii. 38.

[34] *Ibid.*, 39.

[35] *Ibid.*

[36] *Ibid.*, 41.

[37] Livy, viii. 2.

[38] *Ibid.*, 3, 4.

[39] *Ibid.*, 6.

[40] Livy, viii. 7.

[41] *Ibid.*

[42] *Ibid.*

[43] Zonaras.

[44] Livy; Zonaras.

[45] 1 Samuel, xiv. 44, 45.

[46] Arnold.

[47] Livy.

[48] Niebuhr, History of Rome, iii. 137.

[49] Livy, viii. 11.

[50] Fasti Capit.

[51] Livy, viii. 12.

[52] *Ibid.*, 13.

[53] *Ibid.*

[54] Hooke.

[55] The Greek writers Aristobulus and Ptolemæus are supposed to allude to the Romans in this brief notice. "The Tyrrhenians sent an embassy to the king to congratulate him on his conquests." Strabo states that the Italian piracies upon the Greek trading vessels having been reported to Alexander the Great, he sent remonstrances to the Romans upon these acts of aggression. As the Romans were in alliance with the kinsman of the royal Macedonian, Alexander of Epirus, their distinctness as a people from the Tyrrhenians would have been known to these authors. Arnold, however (Rome, ii. 173), leans to the assertion of Arrian, that a Roman embassy did appear before Alexander of Macedon, to claim the friendship of the relation of their ally, the king of Epirus, and to justify themselves from the injuries done to Grecian commerce. Whether such was the case, and that the victor monarch praised the noble bearing of the men whose descendants were destined to subvert Macedon, see ma conjectural and uncertain. Yet the policy of the Roman Republic, which was as remarkable as her achievements, might have led her to such an act of conciliation, without any degradation from her distinguishing national pride.

[56] Livy, viii. 18; Val. Max., ii. 5.

[57] *Ibid.* 21; *Ibid.* vi. 2.

[58] See Appendix. (p. 199)

[59] Arnold; Livy, viii. 23.

[60] Hooke; Livy, viii. 23, 25.

[61] Arnold; Dion. Hal., xv. 13. Fragment. Mai.

[62] Livy, viii. 23, 25.

[63] *Ibid.*

[64] Hooke.

[65] Livy, book viii. c. 28.

[66] Aurel. Victor, De Viris Illustr. 31.

[67] Livy, v. 30.

[68] Val. Max., ii. 7.

[69] Val. Max.

[70] Eutrop., ii. 8; Livy, viii. 33.

[71] *Ibid.*

[72] Livy, viii. 34.

[73] Livy, viii. 34.

[74] *Ibid.*, 36.

[75] Arnold.

[76] Livy, vii. 37.

[77] Livy, viii. 39; Dion. Cassius, Fragm. Ursin. xiv. 3.

[78] Appian, iii. Fragm. 4.

[79] Livy, ix. 3; Eutropius; Florus; Zonaras; Orosius; Hooke's Rome.

[80] Livy, ix. 3.

[81] Livy, ix. 3.

[82] *Ibid.*, 4.

[83] *Ibid.*, 5.

[84] *Ibid.* See Appendix. (p. 207)

[85] Livy, ix. 7.

[86] *Ibid.*

[87] *Ibid.*, 8.

[88] *Ibid.*, 11.

[89] *Ibid.*, 15.

[90] Orosius, iii. 15.

[91] Diodorus, xix. 7.

[92] Hooke, Roman Republic.

[93] Livy, ix. 23.

[94] *Ibid.*, 25, 26.

[95] Livy, ix. 25.

[96] See Appendix. (p. 211)

[97] See Appendix. (p. 211)

[98] Arnold.

[99] It has been an opinion—if opinion unsupported by facts be worth quoting (however learned the author)—that the early victories of Rome were mostly the unreal fables of national pride; but the power that gave rise to the works we are about to describe must have been founded by actual conquests; for even if we admit that free labourers assisted in forming the Appian Way, as overseers, the toil was undoubtedly performed by slaves, who must have been captured in this and the preceding Samnite war.

[100] See Appendix. (p. 212)

[101] See Appendix. (p. 212)

[102] Hooke.

[103] See Appendix. (p. 213)

[104] Hooke; see Appendix (p. 213).

[105] Arnold, Rome, ii. 290. See Appendix (p. 213).

[106] Diodorus; Arnold; Niebuhr.

[107] *Ibid.*

[108] Hooke.

[109] See Appendix. (p. 214)

[110] Livy, ix. 35, 36.

[111] Diodorus. See Appendix. (p. 215)

[112] Livy, ix. 38.

[113] Arnold; Hooke; Livy, ix. 38.

[114] Hooke.

[115] Livy, ix. 40.

[116] This ceremony will remind the reader of the admission to the lodges of the Illuminati, or even of the manner in which persons are initiated into the Freemasons' and Trade-unions of the present day. See Disraeli.

[117] Livy, ix. 40.

[118] *Ibid.*, 38.

[119] Fasti Capitolini.

[120] Arnold, Rome, ii. 256, footnote, 110.

[121] Suetonius.

[122] Livy, ix. 10.

[123] "In the case of a marriage solemnised with the religions sanction of the confarreatio, divorce was so difficult as to be scarcely possible. The husband, however, might put the guilty wife to death. The marriage of Antonius had doubtless been thus solemnised, and his wife was either innocent of the crime of adultery, and the divorce a matter of caprice, or he was too merciful to enforce the law. The censure passed upon him by the magistrate is a strong proof that the lady was injured and innocent. In the case of an unsolemnised union, the separation was entirely left to the pleasure of the parties."—Law of Divorce, Niebuhr, Hist. Rome, iii. 355.

[124] Val. Max., viii. 15; Pliny, N. H. xxxv. 7; Livy, x. 2.

[125] Niebuhr, History of Rome, iii. 356.

[126] *Ibid.*

[127] Arnold, Rome, ii.

[128] Niebuhr, § iv. 23; Cicero, Tuscul., iv. 2.

[129] Niebuhr, Rome, iii.

[130] Arnold; Livy, ix. 42.

[131] Arnold conjectures, from the indignation that made every city excepting three unite in a declaration of war against Rome, that these captives were scourged and beheaded. The revolt was soon put down, and the people subjected to Rome.

[132] Fasti Capitolini.

[133] Arnold, ii. 312.

[134] *Ibid.*; Cicero De Officiis., i. 11.

[135] See Appendix. (p. 221)

[136] Niebuhr, Rome, i. 213.

[137] Niebuhr. See Introduction to Lectures on Roman History, i. 12.

[138] See Appendix. (p. 221)

[139] L. Piso, Annal., from Gellius, vi. 9.

[140] Pliny, Nat. Hist., xxxiii. 6.

[141] Hooke.

[142] Niebuhr, Rome, iii. 317; Piso, apud Gell., vi. 9; Livy, ix. 46.

[143] Arnold, Rome, ii. 300.

[144] Livy, ix. 46.

[145] Livy, ix. 46.

[146] Arnold; Diodorus, xx. 104.

[147] Hooke.

[148] Hooke.

[149] Livy, xvi. 4.

[150] Arnold; Livy, x. 7.

[151] *Ibid.*; *Ibid.*

[152] Niebuhr, § iv. 23.

[153] *Ibid.*; Pliny, Nat. Hist., vii. 60.

[154] *Ibid.*

[155] Strabo, v. 232; Niebuhr, Hist. Rome, iii. 423.

CHAPTER VI.

A.U.C. 455-513. B.C. 299-241.

Samnite war.—Ædileship of Fabius Maximus.—Cornelius Scipio.—His epitaph.—Victory of Appius Claudius and Volumnius Flamma.—Gellius Egnatius in Campania.—Roman ladies at prayer.—Patrician devotees and Aula Virginia.—Victory of Volumnius.—Destruction of a legion.—Fabius and Decius reconciled.—Battle of Sentinum and self-devotion of Decius.—Roman victories.—National spirit of the Samnites.—Midnight attack.—Campaign of Papirius Cursor.—Fate of the Augur.—Consulship of Fabius Gurges.—Intercession of his father.—Roman victory.—Pontius Herennius a prisoner.—The plague.—Serpent of Epidaurus.—Fabian Triumph.—Campaign of Curius Dentatus.—Samnite embassy and offered bribe.—Reply of Dentatus.—He is accused of embezzlement.—His vindication.—Unknown leader.—Insulting conduct of the Tarentines.—Their summons to king Pyrrhus.—His embarkation for Italy.—Dialogue between the king and his minister.—Young Tarentines.—Pyrrhus offers to arbitrate between Rome and Tarentum.—Bold answer of Lævinus.—The Romans not barbarians.—Pyrrhus' belief in destiny.—His disguise.—His elephants.—Kindness to his captives.—Roman embassy.—The consul Fabricius.—His introduction to an elephant.—Cineas at Rome.—Favourable progress of the negociation.—Appius Claudius.—His blindness.—His speech in the Senate.—Terms offered by Pyrrhus rejected, Cineas leaves Rome.—His opinion of Rome and the Romans.—Battle of Asculum.—The Carthaginians offer their services to the Romans.—The Carthaginian fleet defeats King Pyrrhus.—His victory over the Mamertines.—Curius Dentatus defeats Pyrrhus.—His return to Epirus.—Rewards bestowed upon Dentatus.—Ptolemy Philadelphus.—Integrity of the Roman ambassadors.—Death of King Pyrrhus.—Punishment of a rebel legion at Rhegium.—Samnite robber chief.—First silver coinage.—Justice of the Roman people.—Battle in Picenum.—Roman colonies.—Roman finance.—Fabius Gurges slain before Volsinii.—Punishment of the freedmen.—First Punic war.—Victories of Appius Claudius.—Siege of Agrigentum.—Roman navy.—Naval tactics.—Capture of the Consul Cornelius.—Victory of Duilius.—Self-devotion of a legionary tribune.—Roman defeat at Lipara.—Naval victory at Tyndarus.—Expedition of Marcus Regulus to Carthage.—His poverty.—His passage disputed at Bagrada by a serpent.—His victories.—His hard terms rejected.—Xanthippus offers his assistance to the Carthaginians.—He defeats and takes Regulus prisoner.—Cruelty of the Carthaginians to Regulus.—His long captivity.—Clypea besieged.—The naval victory of the Romans saves the garrison.—Shipwreck of the victorious fleet.—Panormus taken by the Romans.—Battle of Panormus.—Return of Regulus to Rome.—Cruel policy of the Senate.—Regulus goes back to Carthage.—His death.—Siege of Lilybæum.—Exploit of Hannibal.—Battle of Drepanum.—Claudius Pulcher recalled.—His choice of a Dictator.—Expedition of the Consul Junius.—His fleet destroyed by tempest.—He plunders a temple and takes Eryx.—His suicide.—Hamilcar Barca regains Eryx and keeps it for years.—Claudia fined for her insolent remark.—First prætor Peregrinus.—The Consul Lutatius wishes to have his fortune told.—Forbidden by the Senate.—His wound and naval victory.—Treaty of Peace between Rome and Carthage.—Prudence of Gisco.—End of the first Punic war.—Splendid triumph of Lutatius and Valerius.—The Romans send a Prætor and Quæstor to Sicily.

THE Roman consul, M. Fulvius Paetinus, besieged for a long time the strong Umbrian town of Nequinum on the Nar, the resistance of the inhabitants being aided, it is thought, by a Samnite garrison.[1] The Roman war in Etruria afforded that people an opportunity of breaking the treaty with Rome, while the irruption of the Gauls enabled them to form a powerful combination against the general enemy. The name of the Gauls sounded ominously in Roman ears, and several nations of this warlike and predatory people were already seated in Italy, which circumstance favoured their march across the Alps.[2] The Sabines joined the confederacy against Rome, but the Lucanians gave hostages to their Roman allies, dreading much the rule of the Samnites, who had already made themselves masters of a great part of their territories. The Roman people wished to elect Fabius Maximus to the consulship, but he declined the honour, accepting the curule ædileship, an office of great importance at a time when Rome was threatened with famine. He took care to purchase corn from distant countries, and provided so bountifully for the wants of the people, that dearth and its attendant horrors were averted from Rome. He really rendered greater service to his country by his careful ædileship, than by his ever-victorious consulships. The death of the consul Manlius, who was killed by a fall from his horse, occasioned Valerius Corvus to be chosen in his place. The old man fought throughout the campaign with all the fire and energy of youth, everywhere compelling the Etruscans to fly before him.[3]

Cornelius Scipio and the consul Fulvius Centumalus marched into Lucania, where the presence of a Samnite army had banished the loyalty lately demonstrated by that people for the Romans. Of the conquests of Cornelius Scipio, nothing is known but the ancient eulogistic verses on his tomb, which may or may not have a foundation in fact. In his epitaph he is said to have subdued the whole of Lucania.[4]

The people insisted this year on re-electing Fabius Maximus to the consulship, and they carried their point, notwithstanding the opposition their favourite made to the illegality of the proceeding by reading the law they B.C. 298. chose to break, in order to advance him to that dignity. Decius, his old plebeian colleague, was chosen with him. Fabius named Cornelius Scipio for his lieutenant and Valerius and Fulvius served under him as military tribunes.[5] The consuls made their campaigns in Samnium; Fabius directing the military operations by Sora and the upper Liris, while Decius occupied the country of the Sidicines and the Vulturnus. Both these great commanders devastated the country round them with fire and sword, the legions under them encamping in one hundred and thirty-one places.[6] The loss of a pitched battle on the part of the Samnites led to this destructive warfare on the part of the Roman invaders. "The nature of the country, which in its lofty vales and cliffs afforded refuge to the people and pasture for their flocks, enabled them to retreat from the deserts created by their enemies."[7]

When Fabius returned to Rome to hold the comitia for the new consulship, he found Appius Claudius intriguing with the popular party to procure the patrician hero of the day for his colleague. He was sure of his own election, but he did not approve of Volumnius Flamma for his coadjutor in the office. He had served ten years before the same office with that valiant plebeian, but not in the field; for Appius, being employed in concluding his great public works, had prevented their coming into collision with each other. Appius Claudius, though brave, did not possess the brilliant military talents and reputation of his plebeian colleague, L. Volumnius Flamma, with whom he scorned to co-operate. His pride and jealousy deeply offended that consul, who would have left him in Etruria, and made the campaign in Samnium, but for the entreaties of his rival's officers, who assured him the measure would be productive of much injury to the republic at this critical crisis.[8] The approach of the Samnite army compelled Appius Claudius to forget his pride and jealousy, and Volumnius his resentment, and a great victory was the result of their harmony.[9] Volumnius arrived in Samnium in time to assist the Campanians, upon whom the Samnites had made a descent, headed by Gellius Egnatius, their talented and valiant general, who had averted the war from his own country by carrying it into the Roman possessions. The danger was met at Rome by a great enrolment for the service of the republic; even citizens above the age of five-and-forty were called upon by the prætor, P. Sempronius Sophus to enlist, and for the first time the freedmen of the four city tribes were mustered to swell the legionary force of Rome. All legal business was suspended,[10] and Fabius and Decius entered upon the consulship,[11] to allay the storm which the return of Volumnius to hold the comitia for the consular election had caused. At this period of the war the Roman patrician and plebeian ladies passed a great part of their time in prayer in the temples of Rome; but even these united acts of devotion did not extinguish the prejudices which still existed between the rival orders. The patrician ladies chose to exclude from the temple of the ox-market Aula Virginia, a nobly descended female, the wife of the plebeian consul, Volumnius, on the grounds that the fane was dedicated to patrician chastity. "Is my birth mean, or my virtue suspected? Have I had two husbands?" the indignant Roman lady replied, to the exclusives of that day,[12] second marriages being considered dishonourable by the Roman matrons in that age. Aula Virginia justly considered her alliance with the good and great consul, Volumnius, formed no real ground for her exclusion. She immediately founded a temple to plebeian chastity, beseeching the votaries of this altar to emulate the proud patrician ladies in their purity, without imitating their insolence.[13] The march of Volumnius was so rapid, that he compelled the Samnites to retreat from Campania, overtaking and despoiling their army of the plunder lately won from the Campanians.[14] The success of the consul B.C. 296. obtained for him the honour of a day of thanksgiving. These acts of grateful piety to the gods were usually called supplications, and being offered up in the name of the victorious consul, were considered very honourable. We have seen the eyes of the Roman people fixed upon Fabius and Decius at this crisis, when the renewed league between the Gauls, Umbrians, and Samnites threatened such danger to the state. These fast friends fell out about their respective provinces, Fabius claiming that of Etruria as his peculiar right, on account of the exploit he had performed in his early career by passing the trackless Ciminian forest. The people assigned it to him, to the great displeasure of Decius Mus. These military comrades were reconciled before Fabius marched with his army for Etruria, by his making a request to the senate that Decius might be associated with him in the Etruscan campaign. Volumnius was retained in command as pro-consul; Appius Claudius was still stationed in Etruria as prætor; while to Cneius Fulvius and Posthumius Megellus were assigned honourable posts in the army with the rank of pro-prætors—a dignity we first hear of in this war. Appius Claudius displayed more caution than enterprise in Etruria, in which country he had taken up his winter quarters. He had before this been reproached by Volumnius with understanding the art of speaking well much better than fighting;[15] but his rival being stationed in Samnium, he was left to his own discretionary powers. Encompassed with enemies, the Roman prætor employed his architectural talents in fortifying his camp, preferring defensive measures to the heedless valour which generally renders a commander popular with his soldiers. As his situation was considered dangerous, this prudence, which dispirited his army, might nevertheless be good generalship. Fabius undertook not only to deliver him from his perilous position, but to give him some lessons in war. This patriotic and enterprising commander found no difficulty in raising a small army of volunteers, at the head of which he marched into Etruria, levelled the fortifications upon which Appius had employed his soldiers, sent the prætor to Rome, and placed a division under Cornelius Scipio, in the country of the Camertine Umbrians, to intercept the passage of the Gauls across the Apennines.[16] The dispositions made by the renowned consuls, Fabius and Decius, were able and effective, and the presence of the consular armies, with a large additional number of allies—the Campanian cavalry, and the troops under the pro-consul, Volumnius—and the pro-prætors offered a fine defence on every point from which the territorial possessions of the republic expected invasion.[17] Volumnius, according to the plan of the campaign sketched by the consuls, was to invade Samnium with two legions; while Fulvius, the pro-prætor, defended the passage of the Tiber, keeping the communication free between Rome and her armies, while covering her from attack on the Faliscan side.[18] The legion stationed in Camerinum under Cornelius Scipio to defend the passage of the Apennines was attacked by the Gauls and Samnites, and completely defeated, being mostly cut to pieces, near old Clusium.[19] The Gaulish cavalry, elated with their victory, fixed the heads of the unfortunate legionaries to their long lances, or suspended them round the necks of their horses. This sight informed the consular armies of the misfortune that had befallen their countrymen; for they encountered the victors on the march, and recognised the ghastly trophies they bore. On the plains of Sentinum the Romans revenged the slain, but the battle between the league and the forces of the republic was very sharply contested. This Umbrian town, on the northern side of the Apennines, probably occupied the site of the Sassoferrato.[20] The combined forces of the Gauls and Samnites amounted to one hundred and forty thousand foot and forty thousand horse; that of the Romans must have reached sixty or seventy thousand men. The Gauls had armed war chariots, and kept a strong body of reserve to surprise Rome—a manœuvre that Fabius prevented by despatching the two pro-prætors, Postumius and Fulvius, to ravage Etruria. This was one of those master-strokes that mark an able general.[21] The Umbrians and Etruscans who formed this corps de reserve abandoned their post to defend

Umbria and Etruria.[22] B.C. 295. The consul Fabius, who commanded the right wing of the Roman army, was opposed to the Samnites, headed by Egnatius; but Decius faced the Gauls, whose recent victory and armed chariots made them at first an overmatch for his legions.[23] The charge of the Roman and Campanian cavalry was brilliant and effective, as long as they encountered those of the Gauls; but the armed war-chariots, when brought down upon them, terrified the horses and intimidated their riders. To stop the fight of the cavalry defied even the military skill and personal prowess of the consul Decius; who, on this momentous occasion, invoked superstition to his aid, and calling upon M. Livius, one of the pontifices, bade him receive his command,[24] and dictate his awful vow. Covering his head, while standing on a spear, he solemnly devoted himself to death,[25] as his father had formerly done at the battle of Vesuvius, and rode into a squadron of Gauls just at the moment when Fabius, perceiving the danger of his colleague and ancient friend, sent Scipio and Marcus, his lieutenants, to his assistance. But the self-devotion of the plebeian consul, had already transfixed him on the hostile spears of the Gauls. His fall gave an assurance of success to his army, while the reinforcement from the right wing enabled it to sustain an obstinate fight with the enemy. The victory won by Fabius over the Samnites[26] decided the fate of the Gauls; for when the vanquished fled to their camp, they left their allies' flank undefended. Fabius despatched the principes of the third legion and the Campanian horsemen to attack them in the rear, while he followed the Samnites, vowing aloud in the hearing of friend and foe a temple to Jupiter the victorious, if he won the desperately-contested day.[27] Beneath the bulwarks of their camp the Samnites rallied, and once more renewed the fight, till the death of their gallant leader, Gellius Egnatius, forced his army to retreat in good order to their own country. The combined forces lost twenty-five thousand men in the battle of Sentinum; the Romans, eight thousand; the prisoners amounted to eight thousand. The loss on the part of Fabius was comparatively small; on that of Decius it was great.[28] The body of Decius was found under heaps of slain.[29] Fabius himself performed the obsequies of the self-devoted hero, and pronounced the funeral oration of his old friend and comrade, the beloved associate of his youth, and the sharer of his glory. In consequence of a vow made in the course of this hard-fought battle, Fabius Maximus burned all the spoil on the field in honour of Jupiter the Conqueror. But neither his victories nor those won by the pro-prætors, Fulvius and Postumius, in Etruria,[30] nor the successful day gained at Mount Tifernus, in Samnium,[31] by Volumnius, could quench the love of freedom in the Samnite and Etruscan. Fabius returned to Rome after this fortunate campaign; but his magnificent triumphal entry was interrupted by funeral processions, for the plague raged at Rome, and the public joy was chequered by deeper public woe.[32]

Illness detained the consul Postumius in Rome, and his colleague Atilius Regulus departed without him to open the Samnite campaign. On the confines of Campania the Samnites made a midnight attack upon the consular camp, aided by a thick fog, and had actually reached the quæstor's tent, when the consul, awakening, put himself at the head of some manipuli, and drove them back with loss. Atilius was, in a manner, shut up in the camp by the Samnites till the arrival of his colleague, when two sanguinary drawn battles were fought between the armies of Rome and Samnium, which so dispirited the enemy, that the general found it difficult to bring his soldiers into the field. Regulus gained a victory near Apulia, but obtained a triumph with difficulty on account of the great loss of Roman life, and because he had allowed the prisoners to depart after having made them pass under the yoke.[33] Postumius, finding nothing left for him to do in Samnium, marched his army into Etruria, where he took so many towns that the Etruscans sued for peace, which they obtained upon the payment of five hundred thousand pounds of brass.[34]

A census was taken this year, by which it appeared that the number of Roman citizens capable of bearing arms amounted to 262,322, an immense force when compared B.C. 294. with the small means Rome then possessed for the maintenance of her inhabitants; but this warlike people could not exist without violence and rapine, their very subsistence depended upon arms. Peace would have brought them only famine.

At Samnium solemn preparations were made for war. A fearful oath, attended by terrific ceremonies, was exacted from every soldier by the priests, and a law was passed, by which any Samnite refusing to take arms was devoted to the sword, and might be slain wherever he was met. Sixteen thousand of the bravest men, arrayed in white, were dedicated to the service of their country, being sworn under a tent to stand or fall together.[35]

Lucius Papirius Cursor, son of the famous dictator, was chosen to head the Roman armies in the Samnite war.[36] Some dissimulation was used by the general about the feeding of the chickens, whose behaviour was thought extremely promising, because they fed very speedily, probably because they had been kept purposely without food. The young nephew of Papirius penetrated into this ruse, having heard some dispute about it between the augurs.[37] The consul, however, declared that the chickens fed well enough for him, and that if the augur had made a false report the gods would punish him. Notwithstanding the doubt, the stern Roman warriors conquered, but the augur was slain in the battle, having been placed in a dangerous post by Papirius as a test of his truth.[38]

This campaign against Samnium was eminently successful. The towns of Aquilonia, Cominium, and many others were taken, and with them an immense booty.[39] Upon the consul's return, he obtained a triumph, and paid into the treasury the whole amount of the money taken in the war. This act alienated the affections of his soldiers which had been gained by his cheerful and amiable manners. The citizens were also displeased at being taxed to pay his army.[40] Papirius dedicated a temple to Quirinus or Romulus, to which the first sun-dial ever seen at Rome was affixed—a public benefit, as the people till then reckoned the hours by chance.[41] This year Atilius brought in a law for the benefit of orphan children, of whose unfortunate condition the state for the first time took cognizance, by appointing them guardians.[42]

The new consul, Fabius Gurges, the son of Fabius Maximus, possessed no talents for war, and was a young man of effeminate pursuits and immoral habits. His election was opposed by his father; but as Gurges had filled several public offices with credit, and amended his past life, the people stood by their choice, viewing him with favour for the sake of his family.[43] The conduct of the consul justified his father's opposition to his election, for preferring a rash display of courage to the circumspection of a general, he was defeated by the Samnites. In fact, he threw himself into the midst of the enemy's squadrons instead of marshalling his troops for battle.[44] The senate and the people would have displaced the patrician consul, but his father reminded them "that his son had been placed in a responsible situation for which his youth and headlong valour unfitted him; that he had committed an error, but no crime that could justify such a harsh measure." He concluded his apology for Gurges, by offering to serve under him as his lieutenant.[45] His proposal was joyfully accepted, and old Fabius Maximus departed to redeem the military mischances of his son. In a battle, doubtless planned by the wisdom of his experienced father, Gurges again forgot the consular dignity, by displaying his usual heedless valour, and was surrounded by the enemy. From this hopeless situation the gallantry of old Fabius delivered him,[46] though not without encountering the greatest peril in the undertaking.[47] Such an exploit in a man of his years astonished the whole Roman army. Twenty thousand Samnites were left dead upon the field, and four thousand prisoners were taken. Among these was Pontius Herennius, the man who had made the Romans pass under the yoke at Caudium.[48] The Fabian triumph was rendered remarkable by the illustrious father of the young pro-consul following his son on horseback; for the B.C. 292. exploits of Gurges in the latter part of the campaign had obliterated the remembrance of his former faults, and the paternal pride of Fabius Maximus was now fully gratified by the fame of his son.[49] Nor was this the most memorable circumstance; for the aged Samnite general, the hero of the Caudine Forks, followed the chariot of the conqueror. Pontius Herennius was put to death as its wheels were turned towards the Capitol,[50] forming a precedent for slaying the captives at future triumphs in succeeding ages. This barbarous custom affixed a stain to the Roman name as lasting as the victories of the republic, and dimmed the glory of Fabius Maximus.

While the Roman arms were thus victorious abroad, the Sibylline Books were opened, in order to discover some remedy for the plague-smitten city at home. The oracles directed the Romans to send to Epidaurus in Greece for the tame serpent, into whose reptile form the god Æsculapius was said to have transmigrated.[51] The republic despatched an embassy, whose object was to purchase this creature, to stay the pestilence.[52]

The succeeding consul, Curius Dentatus, proved a masterly general; he stormed the towns of Samnium, and laid waste the country, till that brave people, who had lost their great general Pontius Herennius, sent an embassy to Rome to sue for peace. It was granted, but the terms were left to the wisdom of Dentatus. The Samnite ambassadors found the man, who was to prescribe the conditions of peace cooking for himself a dinner of herbs.[53] The meanness of his diet and employment deceived them. They saw in it a depth of poverty rather than excessive stoical pride, and offered a large sum of money to the stern Roman warrior. Curius Dentatus rejected the bribe with philosophical contempt. "My indigence," he said, "has inspired you with the hope of corrupting me, but you are mistaken. Indeed I prefer commanding rich men, to being rich myself. Take away that metal which men only use for their own destruction, and go tell your nation that they will find it as difficult to conquer as to bribe me."[54] The abashed Samnite ambassadors knew this to their cost, and admiring the grandeur and disinterestedness of the Roman consul's mind acceded to his conditions. The peace gave great joy to the belligerent nations, for the war had lasted forty-nine years, and both Rome and Samnium were weary of its length.[55]

In the division of the conquered lands the conduct of Dentatus was marked by the same lofty integrity; he allotted to himself only seven acres, the same share granted to every other man.[56] Envy accused him of appropriating a great part of the spoil to his own use; but the production of a solitary wooden oil vessel, which he had taken to offer libations to the gods with more decorum, covered his accusers with shame. He was granted a splendid triumph for his victories. The conquest of Sabinia afforded him another before his year expired.[57] Postumius, in this consulate, was fined for the task he had compelled the Roman army to undertake for his B.C. 290. benefit; the heavy fine inflicted on this occasion made him pay dearly for having cleared his wood at the public expense.[58] Curius Dentatus, when his year was out, was left in Lucania to finish the war. This great soldier fully established the Roman dominion throughout the tract of country extending from the Adriatic to the Tyrrhenian and Sicilian seas. The consuls employed their time in founding a great many colonies; that in the city of Hadria gave its name to the sea and coast, which were called by the general appellation of Adriatic.[59]

The consulship of M. Claudius Marcellus and C. Nautius Rutilus was a period of civil strife, in consequence of which Q. Hortensius was made dictator, for the labourers and artificers had withdrawn from Rome on account of various abuses in the jurisprudence of the country. The dictator dying in office, Q. Fabius Rullianus Maximus was chosen by the general voice of the senate and people to succeed him. He adjusted the disputes, and revived the law that forbad Roman citizens to become nexi or bondmen. At this time he was president, or prince, of the senate.[60] Under his able hands the new laws were framed that reconciled the differences between the Roman people. He died as soon as he had accomplished this work, honoured to the last by that people who had loved and saved him in his youth, and venerated him in his age.[61] The rich and poor vied with each other to contribute to the expenses of his funeral obsequies, so that his son, with the victims offered on that occasion, gave a public feast to the whole city. The Roman republic never boasted a better or greater man than Quintus Fabius Rullianus Maximus.

In the consulate of C. Servilius Tucca and Cæcilius Metellus the Senonian Gauls laid siege to Aretrium, a city of Etruria, in alliance with Rome. The Senonian Gauls murdered the ambassadors sent from Rome, and continued the siege. This was the signal for war, and the pro-consul Cæcilius Metellus was sent to defend Aretrium. Here he was met by the confederated Gauls, and slain, together with thirteen thousand soldiers, many officers, and seven legionary tribunes.[62] Curius Dentatus revenged his countrymen by ravaging the territories of these Gauls with fire and sword, upon which they put themselves on the march for Rome, to retaliate upon the Roman capital the injuries they had sustained from the invasive war of Dentatus.[63] The Boians, Etruscans, and Samnites, incited by the republic of Tarentum, at once declared war with the Romans while the Senonian Gauls were upon their road to Rome. Domitius marched to meet the Senonians in Etruria, and almost exterminated them.[64] Cornelius Dolabella defeated the Boians and Etruscans, and obliged them to sue for peace.[65] Notwithstanding these reverses, all Italy was in arms against the Romans, who had acquired the general name of robbers. Etruria fell to the lot of the consul Æmilius. Lucania to that of Fabricius, who encountered the confederate army and defeated it. Following up his victory, he resolved to storm the enemy's camp, which was very strongly fortified. Here an unknown warrior headed a legion, calling upon the soldiers to follow him for the honour of their country, then planting a ladder, led them to the attack himself.[66] The soldiers obeyed their new general, whose person was unknown to them, though distinguished from the rest of the combatants by the feathers that adorned his helmet. Under him they succeeded in their bold enterprise. The camp was taken, and twenty-five thousand of the enemy, with their general Statilius, were put to the sword. In the tumult the brave stranger disappeared. Search was made for him by the command of the consul but in vain, and it was believed that Mars himself had led the Roman armies in person that day.[67] Some historians have considered this incident as a device framed by the consul, who wished to insure the hearty co-operation of his soldiers in a difficult and dangerous enterprise.

Hitherto the Tarentines had disguised their hatred against the Romans, or at least, had not proceeded to an open rupture with them, till the arrival of Valerius, the admiral of the Roman fleet, who entered their port during B.C. 284. a time of public festivity, when they attacked the fleet, of which they captured and destroyed a part, selling for slaves all those who had escaped falling by their swords in the fight. The republic sent an ambassador to Tarentum to complain of the outrage, and demand a suitable compensation for the loss of the fleet. Postumius Megellus, an honourable person, who had three times filled the office of consul, was at the head of the deputation. The Tarentines, far from coming to an accommodation with Postumius, treated his representations with irony and contempt, and one low person actually defiled his garments. Postumius held up his robe in the view of this licentious and thoughtless people, accompanying the action with these words, "Laugh on, Tarentines, laugh while you may, for the time is coming when your mirth will be changed into tears; for it is not a little blood that will purify this garment."[68] The Tarentines, who had pushed matters to extremities, resolved to engage Pyrrhus, the warlike king of Epirus, upon their side. Accordingly they sent an embassy to his court, inviting him to head the confederate armies of Italy. Pyrrhus, who was one of the greatest generals of the age, accepted the offer of the Tarentines, which appeared to open to him a new field of ambition in the fruitful fields of Italy. If this enterprising and ambitious prince expected to find Italy an easy conquest, he was singularly mistaken. The Roman middle class had, by working out its own independence, given to the state new life and vigour. The age was one of public virtue. The highest offices lay open to brave and wise men, though poor and upright like Curius Dentatus and

Fabricius, whose brightest heritages were integrity and honour. In a free state, all ranks naturally vied with each other in serving their country well. Rome owed her greatness to civic privileges wrung from the senate by the plebeian order.

The embassy of the Tarentines found Pyrrhus[69] employed in adorning his capital, Ambracia, with the best works of ancient art his fine taste could select or money procure. He awoke from his six years' repose from war at the call of the Tarentines, to the surprise of his friend and minister, Cineas, to whom the enterprising and ambitious sovereign unfolded his plans. This trusted servant listened with attention to his master's projected campaign for the conquest of Italy, when he expressed himself in a style calculated to damp the king's ambition.[70]

"The Romans," remarked Cineas, "are said to be great warriors and lawgivers, ruling over many nations. Say that the gods permit us to conquer them, what use shall we make of our victory?"

"What a question!" replied the prince. "When we have once conquered the Romans, no city in Italy will be able to resist us. The whole country will be at our disposal, and no one knows better than yourself the value of the acquisition."

"And when we have conquered Italy?" continued the philosophic minister.

"Then is not Sicily quite at our command; for, since the death of Agathocles, every city in that beautiful island is in a state of anarchy and confusion."

"Will the conquest of Sicily terminate our acquisitions?"

"No," replied the monarch; "that is only the beginning of our conquests. We should pass into Africa, and take Carthage, which would be but a step. Then we would recover Macedon, and make ourselves masters of Greece."

"And when we have done all this, what are we to do next?"

Pyrrhus smiled at his friend's question. "Oh, then we will live at our ease—eat, drink, and be merry, and pass our time in agreeable conversation."

"What prevents your enjoying that happiness now which you propose to yourself as the reward of so many toils and dangers?" was the able rejoinder of his wiser friend; but king Pyrrhus only heard the voice of his own ambition.[71]

The Roman consuls, Q. Marcius Philippus and Æmilius Barbula,[72] were sent to the relief of Thurii; but that place had fallen before they arrived before it. Marcius was ordered to attack the Etruscans, while Æmilius quitted Samnium to form the siege of Tarentum. As Agis, the B.C. 280. commander of the garrison, was of that party which considered an alliance with Rome offered more lasting advantage than the friendship of Pyrrhus, Æmilius hoped to conclude a treaty with him before the arrival of the king and his allies. To conciliate the Tarentines, he restored all the prisoners he had taken in the course of the siege.[73] Cineas, the friend of Pyrrhus, frustrated these hopes by obtaining the dismissal of Agis, and taking the important command of the citadel himself. Æmilius, who was on the march for his winter quarters in Apulia, narrowly escaped destruction; for the Epirots and Tarentines met him in the defiles near the sea, and assailed him with their balistæ from their ships. Æmilius covered his troops from the attack by placing some Tarentine prisoners in front, and thus secured himself from the attacks of their countrymen.[74]

Valerius Lævinus and Tiberius Coruncanius were chosen for consuls at this important period; the latter was by birth a Latin, his distinguished merit obtaining for him an honour seldom bestowed upon a foreigner.

Pyrrhus embarked for Italy with a great fleet, which narrowly escaped shipwreck upon the coast of Messapia. The vessel in which this ambitious prince had trusted his fortunes was in such danger, that he plunged into the sea, and swam boldly to shore, notwithstanding the darkness of the night and the raging of the water. The Messapians showed him great kindness, rendering also assistance to that part of the fleet which neared their coast. Pyrrhus marched for Tarentum with two thousand foot, two elephants, and some cavalry, leaving his great army and the rest of his elephants to follow him.[75] He was received with general joy, but this feeling only lasted a short time; for when the king wished to restore the ancient discipline of the Lacedæmonians, for the Tarentines derived their origin from the Spartans, they openly murmured, for they were fond of pleasure, and detested the restraint their new ally chose to place upon their corrupt inclinations. The discourse of some young libertines was overheard in the streets respecting these measures, and their imprudent remarks were repeated to Pyrrhus, upon which that prince ordered them into his presence, and asked them "if the report of their behaviour was true?" One of them replied, "Yes, quite true; and we should have said much more if our wine had not failed us." Pyrrhus admired the ingenuity of the answer, and dismissed the case.[76]

Before proceeding to open hostilities with the Romans, the Epirot prince tried the efficacy of diplomacy, and endeavoured to persuade Lævinus to name him arbitrator between Tarentum and Rome, hinting that he knew how to enforce his decision. To this implied threat the consul boldly answered, "that the Romans would neither admit him as a judge, nor fear him as an enemy"[77]—a reply that convinced Pyrrhus that he would have to encounter bold and valiant enemies in the Romans. He marched with this persuasion to meet the consul Lævinus, whom he found encamped on the banks of the Siris, in Lucania. The scientific eye of the king took in at a glance the disposition of his opponent's camp. His admiration was singularly expressed to his friend—"Megacles, this order of barbarians are not barbarian. We shall see hereafter of what they are capable in battle."[78]

Lævinus began the attack by crossing the river, in the hope of surrounding the army of Pyrrhus, but that prince met him with his usual intrepidity, displaying the coolness of the general and the bravery of the soldier. The splendour of his arms and dress made his person conspicuous to the whole field, and he was singled out by an Italian horseman who seemed resolved to attack him. On a friendly warning given by Leonatus the Macedonian, Pyrrhus uttered these memorable words, "No man, Leonatus, can avoid his destiny; be assured, however, that neither that Italian nor any other man shall have reason to boast of an encounter with me this day." Most great generals have held the same notions as Pyrrhus upon this point, whatever in other respects their creeds might be. Scarcely had the king spoken in this manner when the Italian rode up to him and aimed a blow at his person which fell upon his horse; Leonatus in defending the king wounded that upon which the Italian rode. Both riders fell to the ground, but Pyrrhus B.C. 280. was rescued by his people while the Italian was slain.[79]

The danger the king had encountered obliged him to be more careful of his person, and before heading his infantry he exchanged his mantle and arms for those of Megacles. This exchange nearly cost Megacles his life and Pyrrhus the victory, for the former was wounded and unhorsed by a Roman knight who bore off the regal mantle and helmet to Lævinus, crying out, "That he had slain Pyrrhus." This report was re-echoed by the Romans with shouts of victory, which struck the Greeks with dismay. Pyrrhus upon this rode bare-headed along the line, calling to his soldiers "to recognise their king." Then ordering his elephants to be brought to assist his wings he changed the doubtful combat into a victory.[80] Unused to such assailants the Romans fled from the field leaving their camp undefended, and fifteen thousand soldiers upon the field of battle. This victory cost Pyrrhus thirteen thousand men.[81] The king of Epirus treated the Roman prisoners kindly even after they had declined entering his service, for their refusal raised them still higher in his estimation. The possession of the Roman camp and the honours of the hard-fought day did not console Pyrrhus for the heavy loss he had sustained, and he felt more inclined to have the vanquished for friends than foes. He possessed as much skill in politics as war, and hoped to overcome a frank and open-minded people by negotiating a peace with them which would be more advantageous to himself than his late dear-bought victory. He expected however that the overture for a treaty would come from his Roman enemies. As Lævinus had behaved with great bravery the senate did not displace or recall him home. He was desirous of redeeming his credit by bringing Pyrrhus to another battle in Campania, for he had been reinforced with fresh troops, and was anxious to refute the patriotic though severe remark of Fabricius, "that Pyrrhus had vanquished Lævinus, not the Romans." Conscious that he owed his dear-bought victory to his elephants Pyrrhus commanded these beasts to be brought forward and to be made to roar in a frightful manner. These discordant sounds were answered by loud shouts from the Roman legions, upon which Pyrrhus, knowing that he had no reliance but in the bravery of his own troops, thought proper to decline the combat and retreat to Tarentum.[82] The senate after this sent an embassy to Pyrrhus, not to solicit for peace and alliance with him, as he hoped, but merely to ransom the Roman prisoners. Upon which the monarch despatched Cineas to Rome offering terms of pacification, and proposing to release the prisoners without ransom. While these negotiations were pending the King of Epirus requested and obtained a private interview with Fabricius whose fine qualities had attracted his notice. He lamented[83] the poverty of the noble-minded Roman and offered to enrich him from his own treasury. He told him "that he had need of a friend and counsellor like himself whose wisdom would direct his affairs of state while his bravery aided him in the field, and that when the peace was happily established he should delight to take him to Greece, where his merits would be appreciated, and a wide field be opened for the display of his talents." Perhaps Pyrrhus was sincere in this, though these offers at such a juncture looked like bribery. Fabricius in reply said that, "The report of his poverty was correct, as a small house and an inconsiderable spot of ground comprised his sole wealth. This poverty, however, did not prevent him from serving his country in honourable offices, nor did it render her less dear to him, virtue and ability being the only qualifications she required in her sons. What value," added he, "can I set upon gold or silver, who have a mind free from self-reproach, and an honest name?"[84] The king honoured the magnanimity of the answer, and pressed Fabricius on this point no more, but being desirous of making a trial of his courage, ordered, at their next interview, his largest elephant to be placed behind some hangings. During their conference, at a sign from the king, the curtain was withdrawn, and the huge creature stretched out his trunk directly over the head of the ambassador, accompanying the action with a terrible noise.[85] Fabricius calmly looked up and smiled; then turning to the king remarked, "that neither his gold yesterday, nor his great beast to-day, could excite the least emotion in his B.C. 278. mind." Pyrrhus admired the boldness and simplicity of the man, and again urged him to become his friend and subject. Finding Fabricius inflexible, he sought to do him honour by permitting the Roman prisoners to revisit their own country to celebrate the feast of the Saturnalia upon the ambassador giving him his own word for their return.[86] He sent at the same time his friend Cineas with terms of peace to Rome, trusting to his graceful manners and profound policy for the accomplishment of his designs. Cineas carried to Rome terms that appeared to the senate highly advantageous. The friendship of the Roman people and peace with the Tarentines comprised all the demands of Pyrrhus, who promised upon their acceptance to aid his new allies in the conquest of Italy. The conditions pleased the senate, the objection of one senator alone preventing a unanimous national agreement to such liberal and flattering proposals. Indeed the brilliant and insinuating eloquence of Cineas would have obtained the peace it was exerted to gain but for the opposition of one member, whose blindness and infirmities had long left his seat vacant. This was Appius Claudius, who to the title of Censor, which he never lost, had gained the appellation of Cæcus, or the blind. The infirmities which had paralysed his frame and deprived his eyes of the light of day had not shattered the intellect of the proud patrician, nor extinguished his love for his country, since he preserved to the latest hour of his long existence the patriotism that formed the real religion of the Roman of that period. He heard with indignant sorrow the resolution the senate was about to take, and was carried across the forum in a litter and borne up the steps of the senate-house, where his sons and sons-in-law received their venerable relative, and holding him in an upright position supported him to his long vacant seat. He commenced his speech with the ancient formula still in use then and for some time afterwards; that form was one of prayer: "I first pray to Jupiter the Best and Greatest, and to the other gods under whose protection are this city and the Roman people and the Quirites, that they will allow my words to be of advantage to the state." Affecting words when considered with the infirmities and blindness of the aged speaker. "Many things," said he, "have frequently increased the sorrow I feel on account of my blindness, since the more my years elapse the less does my memory make amends for it. A generation is growing up in my own house whose faces I have never seen, and of those who are dearest to me, I only know that they are no longer the same as I remember them. The magnificent buildings and statues which now adorn Rome are unknown to me, and it is not permitted to my old age to behold the triumphal pomps go up to the Capitol with that increased grandeur to which we have contributed to raise our country, a grandeur wanting to our days of vigour. I however no longer regret my loss of sight.[87] But I thank the gods that the light of these eyes are now extinct, that they have not seen in the forum, and within these walls, the ambassador of a king who has conquered us, that they have not seen you exchange greetings with your future friend and ally, nor will be obliged to see the Greek king and the Tarentines present, in concert with you on the Capitol, offerings and donations on account of their victory over you." Appius Claudius continued in the same indignant strain; he wished himself deaf as well as blind, and he reproached them for their credulity. "How is it," said he, "how is it, that your souls have bent thus, which formerly stood firm against every storm? You are speaking of peace, but is there one among you that honestly deceives himself that it is not submission?" The enmity the speaker had ever borne to the commons of Rome he carried with him to the grave; for he adverted to the admission of the plebeians into the high offices of the state as the occasion of the present wish to purchase a dishonourable peace. "By such a peace," he said, "Rome would give up in one day the conquests of five and forty years."

Pyrrhus had threatened them with the fate of the prisoners: upon this subject broke forth from the bosom of the stern old man a sentence that proved that to the Romans of that day he considered the aggrandisement of Rome ought to be everything and kindred nothing. "I am of opinion," said he, "that prisoners, in case their ransom is not settled, are always to be regarded as dead," an B.C. 278. opinion on which we shall often see the Republic acting in after times. "Every one is the architect of his own fortune," continued the venerable monitor; "you stand at the point where the road divides to destruction, or leads to all those hopes which the arrival of Pyrrhus alone banished from us. I trust that it is only ourselves who can destroy ourselves. I cannot, it is true, divine, but I tell you once more that what you are about to determine upon is ruin. My counsel is that you inform Cineas that we too shall willingly accept the friendship of his king if he return across the upper sea, and will sue for it without interfering in the affairs of Italy; but that so long as he remains there we will listen to none of his messages. Order the insinuating ambassador to quit our city before the next sun dawns upon us. What we have provided hitherto let us continue to provide, and make if possible still more vigorous preparations. To the Etruscans let us grant voluntarily such an alliance as may bind them for ever to us. They are hostile to the Greeks and strangers to the Italians, but connected with us by the ties of religion and friendship. Let your subjects feel that you are kind to the obedient but implacable to the rebellious."[88]

The senate listened to that blind and aged man as if they had received an oracle from the invisible world. Loaded with years and infirmities, his sightless eyes saw in the perspective the future glory of his country, which their timidity or credulity was about to blast for ever. His lofty spirit influenced them more than in those days when he had been bold, insolent, and defying—now he was dead to everything but his love to Rome and his exclusive attachment to his own order.

This oration of Appius Claudius the Blind, to dissuade his deceived countrymen from the league with Pyrrhus, Cicero criticised as an "unpleasant speech."[89] He looked upon it as a composition, but not as a cause productive of a great result, as it really was. The best and truest criticism on that oration of a blind and bed-ridden man in the extremity of old age, was its success. What greater praise could be given to Demosthenes and Cicero than to say that their brilliant periods and artificial eloquence accomplished the objects the orators wished to gain? If Appius Claudius had not made his appeal, Rome would never have been mistress of the world. Like many other ancient orations, its genuineness has been doubted; but it possesses a marked individuality which ought to have secured it from suspicion. "Every man," remarks the former builder of temples and aqueducts, "is the architect of his own fortunes." A professional figure borrowed from the occupations in which the blind orator had taken such delight in former years, but which would hardly have suggested itself to the imagination of an author.

The senate dismissed Cineas with the answer, dictated by the glorious octogenarian, "that they could enter into no pacific treaty with the king of Epirus while his armies remained in Italy."[90] Cineas, who had in vain endeavoured to gain by presents and conciliatory words the good offices of the Roman ladies during his embassy, quitted Rome that day, and returning to his master observed to him, "that Rome was a temple, and the senate an assembly of kings."[91] Pyrrhus, thus foiled in his hopes of making an alliance with the Romans, prepared for the renewal of war with the greatest celerity. The determination upon the part of the Romans to drive Pyrrhus out of Italy was met by equal resolution on his side to remain there. The Romans chose Decius Mus for commander in this war. This Roman consul was the son and grandson of those superstitious but devoted men who had sacrificed themselves for the supposed good of their country; Sulpicius Saverrio was his colleague. The soldiers of Pyrrhus dreaded the coming of the new consul, whose very death they thought would ensure victory to his army. Pyrrhus, aware of the superstitious notion entertained by his army, sent a warning message to the consul to this effect, "That his act of self-devotion to the infernal gods would prove terrible to himself, but useless to his country, as the Epirots were charged to take him alive in order to inflict upon him a lingering and cruel death."[92] Decius calmly replied, "Pyrrhus is not formidable enough to force us to devotements. To show him how little we fear him we will give him the choice of passing B.C. 278. the river unmolested, or of permitting us to do so." The king of Epirus suffered the Romans to have the free passage of the river that parted the hostile armies.[93] This was agreeable to the chivalric disposition of a brave prince, who was generous even while pursuing his ambitious and unwarrantable enterprises. The battle of Asculum, if a victory, was dearly purchased by the Epirots; the loss of life on their side being great. Pyrrhus was dangerously wounded, but the consul Decius was killed. The king fell back upon Tarentum, and the remaining consul took up his winter quarters in Apulia. It was after this battle that Pyrrhus, upon being congratulated on the success of his arms by his friends, replied, "Such another victory and we are undone."[94]

The Carthaginians sent their fleet, consisting of 150 sail, under the command of Mago, to the assistance of the Romans, for the promise Pyrrhus had made to the Syracusans of assisting them against Carthage as soon as he had brought the Romans to terms, had alarmed them. The Romans declined their services, but proffered their aid to the Carthaginians in case Pyrrhus should attack them, which offer was gratefully accepted.[95] The consuls while encamped near Tarentum, within sight of Pyrrhus, received a communication from Nicias, his chief physician, who offered to poison his master.[96] Far from profiting by this iniquitous proposal, they sent the letter back to Pyrrhus accompanied by another, which has been preserved by the Latin and Greek historians: "Caius Fabricius and Quintus Æmilius to king Pyrrhus health,—You have made an unhappy choice both of your friends and enemies. When you have read the letter sent us by one of your own people, you will see that you make war upon good and honest men, while you trust and promote villains. We give you this notice of your danger, not for your sake or to pay court to you, but to avoid the scandal which might be brought upon us by your death, as if for want of strength or courage to overcome you we had recourse to treachery."

Pyrrhus, astonished at the magnanimity of the Roman consuls, cried out, "This is the doing of that Fabricius, whom it is harder to turn aside from the paths of justice and honour than to divert the sun from its course." He did not, however, confine his gratitude to these words, for he immediately sent back, without ransom, all the Roman prisoners he had taken in the war; and despatched Cineas again to Rome with conditions of peace.[97] These terms were rejected by the senate, and the consuls were too proud to receive a reward for what they considered a duty; therefore they set free an equal number of Tarentines and Samnites in return for the courtesy of king Pyrrhus. The death of Ptolemy Ceraunus king of Macedon, and the invasion of that country by the barbarians, obliged Pyrrhus to leave Italy. He chose, however, to land in Sicily, lured by the hope of effecting the conquest of Africa, which appeared more glorious in his eyes than the reduction of the Macedonian kingdom. Fabricius fell upon the general enemies of Rome in his absence, driving the Bruttians, Lucanians, Tarentines, and Samnites before him and ravaging their territories with fire and sword.[98] Both consuls triumphed for their exploits in this war.

The consulate of Rufinus and Junius Brutus was memorable for the shameful defeat these generals received from the Samnites, whom they rashly attacked among the fastnesses of their native mountains, from which their troops were driven with great loss.[99] Rufinus, who imputed the mischance to Brutus, took the towns of Croton and Locri, besides defeating Nicomachus in battle.

A vestal priestess was buried alive about this time, whose misconduct was foolishly suspected to be the cause of a plague,[100] which proved fatal to pregnant women—a superstitious and unjust conclusion.

Pyrrhus, who had despoiled Carthage of nearly all her possessions in Sicily, proclaimed his son by the daughter of Agathocles, king of that island. He so disgusted the Sicilians by his haughty conduct and perpetual extortions, that they combined with the Carthaginians to drive him out. At this critical time, the nations lately vanquished by the Romans solicited his return to Italy, which he accepted. He was desirous of making another son king B.C. 275. of Italy, forgetting that if he made conquests he never was able to retain them.[101] As he was departing he looked back upon the land he was quitting, and said to those persons who enjoyed his friendship, "What a noble field are we leaving for the Romans and Carthaginians to fight in."[102] Prophetic words which were destined to be fulfilled in due season. The Carthaginian fleet met that of Pyrrhus and defeated it with great loss; and the Mamertines sent ten thousand men to oppose his landing at Rhegium.[103] Here Pyrrhus was wounded in the head, but this wound though severe did not prevent his cleaving to the waist a Mamertine who had challenged him. The enemy, struck with consternation at the terrible personal prowess of the king of Epirus, did not follow up the advantage they had gained, but permitted him to retreat to Tarentum. On his way he punished the Locrians very severely who had killed the garrison he left at Locri. He plundered the temple of Proserpine to recruit his finances, which were at a low ebb. The treasure thus obtained he sent by sea to Tarentum, but upon the ships being wrecked with their treasure he repented of the sacrilege he had committed, and ordered that which had been cast upon the shore to be collected and restored to the plundered temple.

At Rome some difficulty was experienced in raising levies for the war[104] against king Pyrrhus, till the consul sold both the persons and goods of those who refused to enlist. This consul was Curius Dentatus, so celebrated for his victories over the Samnites, who was appointed for the express purpose of carrying on the war against Samnium, while his colleague entered Lucania.

The king of Epirus, who was fully aware of the great military talents of Dentatus, marched to meet him near Beneventum, intending to attack him in his camp. The Roman general, who had chosen his ground in a place whose inequalities would not permit the full action of the celebrated Grecian phalanx, repulsed the Epirot prince with great loss and took some of his finest elephants from him. Encouraged by success Dentatus quitted his camp, and descending into the plain drew out his army for battle. One of his wings was broken by the elephants and put in disorder, but this being perceived by some troops whom the Roman general had left to guard the camp, they charged the animals with lighted torches, who fled back to the Epirot army trampling and destroying their own ranks.[105] This accident turned the fortune of the day, for Pyrrhus lost three and twenty thousand men as well as his camp, which last excited the admiration of the conquerors, to whom it served as a model.[106] Perhaps this was the greatest advantage derived from the victory. After this dreadful defeat, Pyrrhus abandoned all hope of the conquest of Italy; he sailed for Epirus with eight thousand foot and three hundred horse, the small remains of his noble army.[107] The triumph of Dentatus, into whose hands the spoils of the Epirot camp had fallen, was magnificent beyond any that Rome had yet seen. Painting and statuary, then little known in the warlike capital of the republic, attracted the admiration of many; while gold and gems and plate glittered on every side. Nor were the elephants overlooked by the multitude, who considered these creatures, with their war accoutrements and towers, as the rarest part of the show.[108] To the victor was voted fifty acres of the lands he had won, a small reward for his great merit, yet too large in his estimation, for he only accepted seven, a rare instance of moderation even in that age of public virtue. To Lentulus a triumph was decreed for the conquest of Caudium, which he had taken from the Samnites. A census and lustrum closed the consulship of these fortunate generals. The censors Caius Fabricius and Æmilius Pappus who held this office, paid so little respect to persons in its exercise, that they effaced the name of Rufinus from the senatorial roll because he had a silver service for his table of ten pounds weight. The number of Roman citizens capable of serving their country in the field amounted to 271,224.

Ptolemy Philadelphus, the best and most enlightened monarch of the age, sent an embassy to Rome to request the alliance of the republic. This honour was very gratifying to the nation in general. The senate despatched Fabius Gurges and three curule ædiles to Egypt to B.C. 274. express the pleasure the friendship of Philadelphus had given to the state. Ptolemy gave them a magnificent reception, and presented the ambassadors with crowns of gold. True to the integrity and simplicity of manners enjoined upon the citizens of Rome in that day, they placed these crowns upon the head of the king's statue, paying into the Roman treasury on their return the value of the rich presents the generous monarch had made them.[109]

The return of Pyrrhus being now expected, Papirius Cursor and Spurius Carvilius were elected consuls for the year. But Pyrrhus never returned into Italy[110]—he died in battle, and—

"Left his name at which the world grew pale
To point a moral, or adorn a tale."

Papirius Cursor undertook the punishment of the Samnites. That brave people no sooner learned the fate of Pyrrhus than they risked a battle, which they lost, and with it almost the traces of their country and capital. "The ruins of their cities were so ruined," remarks Florus, "that Samnium might vainly be sought for in Samnium." This struggle had lasted seventy-two years, and the Romans had gained during its long course thirty-one triumphs. While Papirius Cursor was completing this exterminating war, Curius Dentatus in his censorship was constructing aqueducts with the spoils he had won in the battle of Beneventum.[111] He also drained the Lake Velinus,[112] a work of immense utility, which act created the beautiful cascade of Terni, which is a far more enduring monument of Curius than his martial exploits. Man's destructiveness is seldom useful beyond his own era, and rarely benefits his country long, but his beneficence may remain a blessing for many centuries to come. What now to Italy are the conquests of Curius over the Samnites? yet in the fruitful land he rescued from the water, in this magnificent cascade, we see his noblest exploits and read his proudest epitaph. What indeed, in comparison with Terni, is the boast of Curius Dentatus after the conclusion of the Samnite war?—"I have conquered such an extent of country that it must have become a wilderness had the men whom I have left our subjects been fewer. I have subjected such a multitude of men that they must have been starved if the territory conquered with them had been smaller." The misery caused by his victories over the Samnites and Sabines survive in the ancient records of Rome, but the works of his peaceful censorship were a reclaimed morass, and the second aqueduct seen in republican Rome. The falls of Terni remain an ornament and blessing to Italy in our own remote day.

The advance of the Roman arms, the growing power of the republic and the bravery of her people, rendered her an overmatch for her enemies. No league could prosper against her, and the combined nations of Italy yielded up the contest. Tarentum, which was guarded by Milo's Epirot garrison, preferred making terms with the Romans to admitting the Carthaginians whose fleet lay before the town.[113]

The senate, as soon as the consuls chosen for the year came into office, resolved to punish a legion composed of Campanians who had seized upon Rhegium, a city they had been sent to garrison. This had happened ten years before, but no opportunity had occurred till now for the punishment of the rebels. Lucius Genucius Clepsina and Quinctius Claudius received the command of the consular armies for the express purpose of punishing the revolted legion. The siege was long, and attended with great loss of life, for the consuls had to contend not only with soldiers accustomed to Roman discipline, but with men in despair. Being distressed for provisions they must have given up the enterprise if Hiero, king of Syracuse, had not sent them corn and a reinforcement of troops.[114] Rhegium was at length taken, and the garrison, once four thousand strong but now reduced to three hundred, were sent to Rome for judgment. The civic rights were not allowed these unhappy men, who were scourged and beheaded. The winter which followed these events was remarkably severe; the snow lying forty days in the Forum, in a country where it is seldom seen at all.

C. Fabius Pictor and Q. Ogulnius Gallus were sent against B.C. 272. a famous Samnite hostage, named Lollius, who, escaping from Rome, had made himself master of Caricinium, which served him for a storehouse in which he placed his hoards, for he had been a robber by profession. The consuls recovered the place, but obtained no triumph for their victory, for the war was considered a civil one, Samnium being then a province of Rome.[115] No silver money was coined at Rome till the consuls, who had found a quantity of silver bars among the hoards of Lollius, issued them in the form of denarii, quinarii, and sestertii;[116] copper coins, bearing the figure of some animal, being the usual currency. The silver denarii and quinarii were marked with the Roman numerals X and V, the sestertii H S. These devices have excited much curiosity, and occasioned great labour to the learned men of modern times. The mint was in the temple of Juno Moneta, and this circumstance occasioned the origin of our word money.[117]

The consulship of Sempronius Sophus and Appius Crassus Claudius was distinguished less by the triumph of the republic than by its justice. Claudius the consul took Camerinum, a strong town near the Apennines that divide Picenum from Umbria; and granted the inhabitants honourable terms; but broke his word and sold them all for slaves; he also disposed of their lands, paying the purchase money into the public treasury. The senate nobly redressed the wrongs of the conquered people, restored them to liberty, gave them the privilege of Roman citizens, and indemnified them for their losses, by assigning them new lands in the environs of Rome and dwellings in the Aventine Mount.[118] This act of national justice reflects great honour upon the Roman name, and is a proof of the high pitch of morality and virtue which then existed at Rome. The integrity of a Fabricius or a Curius Dentatus originated from that of the country itself, whose service was at once their glory and their reward. Sempronius Sophus, the other consul, carried on the war in Picenum with great success. He took Asculum the capital, and wholly subjugated the country. The first pitched battle was fought in the midst of an earthquake, but the consul dispelled the dread of his soldiers by declaring "that the earth only shook for fear of changing its masters."[119] This speech satisfied the Romans, and the strife of man and the struggle of the element at his feet were acted together; and never had any victory been purchased more dearly, since Sophus nearly lost his army though he gained the day.[120] Rome, with admirable policy, established colonies throughout the lately conquered countries; while to the Sabines she granted the rights of citizenship, an act that made them from that time essentially Roman.

In the war carried on against the Sallentines, by Lucius Julius Libo and Marcus Atilius Regulus, the consuls for the following year, the Romans found themselves opposed by a brave people, who defended their country with great energy and skill. Atilius took Brundusium, but the campaign was concluded by Fabius and D. Junius Pera, who having previously subdued the Sassinatians in Umbria, entirely conquered the brave Sallentines. They severally obtained triumphs at Rome for these exploits, (a thing unprecedented before their consulate,) which added to the republic a great accession of men, arms, and territory. Mistress of the greater part of Italy, Rome desired to incorporate her conquests with herself.[121] To those brave men who had withstood her ambitious designs, she offered a field for honourable exertion in her legions; others were permitted to retain their own laws and customs, while to some were granted rights of suffrage in the centuries, or were, like the Sabines, fully invested with the privileges of Roman citizens. Many of these nations were treated like free allies, while others remained in a state of vassalage, retaining their lands upon the tenure of furnishing provisions, arms, or men for the Roman armies. The terms upon which these different towns or cities had capitulated generally regulated the privileges enjoyed by the vanquished, which were gradually increased, according to their services or fidelity to the republic. These wise and humane regulations preserved her acquisitions, and there is little doubt that the conquered nations really enjoyed more internal prosperity under a government like Rome than when exposed by their B.C. 267. independence to continual war without, and strife within. In these arrangements the senate seems to have followed the advice of the blind old censor Appius Claudius.

The city of Apollonia, situated in Macedonia, nearly opposite Brundusium, sent an embassy to Rome to solicit the friendship and protection of the republic. The ambassadors were received by the senate with respect, but were molested in the streets by two young men of high rank, named Fabricius and Apronius, at that time holding the office of Ædiles.[122] Upon complaint being made of the insult, the senate delivered up the culprits to the injured strangers, who carried them to Apollonia. The Apollonians treated them with kindness, and set them at liberty. A new law, in consequence of the insult offered to the Apollonians, was enacted at Rome, that from henceforward if any citizen insulted an ambassador he should be given up to the nation whose representatives had been affronted;[123] a measure that must have acted as a useful check upon those insolent and ill-behaved persons who were inclined to persecute foreigners.

The consuls Fabius Gurges and L. Mamilius Vitulus, in the interval of peace left to the republic, found leisure to regulate her financial affairs, and adjust the revenues arising from her new possessions in eastern Italy. These were derived from the rents of lands reserved by the state from those distributed among the citizens, from the tribute of the tenth part of the produce of those countries which were dependent upon her, and from the imposts upon all foreign merchandise.[124] Hitherto four officers, called quæstors, had received and paid away the public money, but the recent conquests, and consequent increase of revenues, had made this office so difficult and laborious that four provincial quæstors were appointed to preside in the conquered countries, which were then divided into provinces, called the Ostian, Campanian, Gallic, and Apulian, where these officers were stationed.

The plague again making its appearance in Rome, caused an examination of the Sybilline books. This oracle declared that the pestilence was a punishment sent by the gods for a great crime. A victim was soon found in Caparonia, a vestal, whose guilt, real or imputed, was supposed to have drawn down this national calamity upon her country. She was condemned by the pontifices to be buried alive, but the vestal avoided a cruel death by destroying herself in prison.[125] This act of despair did not prevent her interment taking place with the solemn rites prescribed on such occasions, though the senseless clay was no longer conscious of shame or suffering. This terrible expiation had been resorted to before. Nothing is more blindly cruel than a barbarous superstition.

The republic did not long enjoy the blessings of peace. The freedmen of Volsinii, a city of Etruria, which had been suffered to retain its ancient constitution, being more numerous than their former masters, filled the city with violence and licentiousness, oppressing so cruelly the class whose slaves they had lately been that the Volsinians called in the Romans[126] to quell their new lords. Fabius Gurges received a mortal wound when about to win this city.[127] The consul had lived long enough to efface the faults and follies of his youth, and he died with the reputation of an able soldier and wise legislator. His fall prevented that of Volsinii, though his lieutenant, Decius Mus, carried on the siege, but the place was not won till the consulship of Appius Claudius Caudex and Fulvius Flaccus, when it was stormed by the consul Flaccus, who put the freedmen to death and removed the inhabitants to another city.[128] This history of Volsinii affords a painful commentary upon the evils produced by slavery. After a lapse of time the slaves subdue and rule their masters, these masters are compelled to call in a powerful state who rid them of their foes within, but remove them from their own city, their costly statues and works of art becoming the property of their new friends. The Romans settled them in another spot, "on the site now occupied by the modern town of Bolsena, but their city was totally destroyed."[129]

One of those trivial circumstances which sometimes convert the hollow peace between rival states into open B.C. 264. war, broke the friendly relations between Rome and Carthage, these mighty republics having been brought into too close proximity by their mutual conquests. Pyrrhus, while looking back upon the beautiful island of Sicily, then for the most part possessed by the great mercantile republic of Carthage, had foreseen the coming rupture. If the king of Epirus had not fallen prematurely in battle he might have seen, in the First Punic War, the accomplishment of his parting prediction. The cause of the rupture between Rome and Carthage took its rise in this manner.[130] Some years before it occurred a band of Mamertines quitted Campania, their native country, and entered the service of Agathocles, tyrant of Syracuse. Under that able and enterprising prince, these adventurers improved in military science, adding to the roving habits of their former piratical calling, the profession and military science of the soldier. Upon the death of Agathocles they marched for Messina, and, being in want of food, persuaded the hospitable inhabitants to open their gates to them. Once admitted within the walls, the treacherous guests seized upon the city, massacred the principal citizens, and remained masters of the place, from the inability of the new king of Syracuse to punish them. The revolt of the Campanian legion, sent to garrison Rhegium, which took place during the first invasion of Pyrrhus, greatly strengthened the power of the usurpers of Messina, as these rebels immediately made a close alliance with each other, which, from the situation of the towns they occupied, became very annoying to merchant-vessels sailing up the straits, as they were directly opposite, and, in avoiding one nest of robbers, they were likely to become a prey to that in league with them on the other side. The fall of Rhegium, and the severe punishment of the remnant of the rebel legion there, left the Mamertines defenceless and without hope, since Hiero, king of Syracuse, who had lent money and troops to the Roman consul to carry that place, would naturally require the assistance of Rome to reduce them. In this emergency nothing could save the treacherous Mamertines but the protection of some mightier state than that which was preparing to punish them.[131] In the expediency of this plan all were unanimous, but not in the choice of the protecting power; the men who occupied the citadel declaring for Carthage, while those in the city were equally decided in naming Rome. As neither party would yield up the disputed point, both acted according to their own determination;[132] those in the fortress sent to solicit the aid of the republic of Carthage, while the others despatched ambassadors to Rome, offering to bestow Messina upon them if they would defend them from the Syracusans. The matter was long debated in the senate, for some of the senators reminded the assembly of the good offices they had received from Hiero at the siege of Rhegium on a similar occasion, and that it would be contrary to good faith and honour were they now to assist the Mamertines against him. Though negatived in the senate[133] the measure was carried by the consuls in the comitia by the argument, "that anything was better than to bring the Carthaginians nearer to the coasts of Italy, as this great maritime power already possessed Sardinia, a large part of Sicily, and the whole of the Italian isles; and that if they established themselves in Messina, they would soon cross the strait and make themselves masters of Rhegium." These considerations gained the people, and the senate were finally induced to accept the offer of the Mamertines and send the consul Appius Claudius to take possession of Messina.[134] When Appius Claudius arrived at Rhegium, he found the citadel of Messina in the possession of the Carthaginians. It is not generally known what induced him to cross the strait in an open boat to confer with the garrison,[135] but he must have received some private intimation from the commanding officer, since that person afterwards evacuated the fortress with all his troops, leaving the city free for the entrance of those of the consul when they could effect their landing. Appius Claudius from this daring adventure obtained the name of Caudex. The republic of Carthage learned the misconduct of their officer with indignation, and immediately put him to death,[136] which he certainly deserved. B.C. 264. The Carthaginians immediately equipped a fleet and army, and inviting Hiero to join them in the enterprise against Messina, invested it by land and sea. Appius Claudius did not know how to effect the landing of his army, for though he had borrowed a fleet from some neighbouring nations, he could not hope that boats and small vessels could cope with a naval power like the Carthaginian. What however he could not effect by force he accomplished by stratagem, for having taken his troops on board he steered his course as if about to depart for Rome with the intention of leaving the Mamertines to their fate. Upon which the Carthaginian fleet, making themselves too sure of getting rid of the Romans, did not keep a proper look out upon their movements; and the able consul availing himself of the first dark night tacked about and landed at Messina.[137] Still the prospect of being starved in the city was not at all agreeable to a man of Appius' boldness and forecast, and he endeavoured to make terms on behalf of the Mamertines with the besiegers, but the ambition of the Carthaginians and the wrongs of king Hiero would not allow of any other alternative than that of the Romans abandoning their new allies and returning home.[138] Nothing then remained for Appius but war. He risked an attack and was repulsed,[139] but as he imputed his failure to the strong position of the enemy, he accepted their offer of a battle on open ground which he won. Some authors suppose by the great loss sustained by the troops of king Hiero, that Claudius only engaged with the allies of the Carthaginians.[140] The consequences of the Roman victory were so disastrous to this prince, that he broke up his camp that very night and retired to Syracuse.[141] Appius Claudius, animated by his late success, attacked the Carthaginians the next morning and defeated them with great slaughter. The siege of Messina was broken up, and the Roman consul following his advantage encamped with his army before Syracuse; but as his term of office was nearly out he left the war to the new consuls, Manius Valerius and Manius Otacilius, who were despatched into Sicily with four legions to reduce the towns that had yielded to the Carthaginians and Syracusans. These places instantly admitted the Romans. After the loss of sixty-seven towns,[142] Hiero, perceiving that his small state was likely to be annexed to Rome or Carthage, prudently came to terms with the Romans, whose friendship he purchased upon this occasion with a thousand talents of silver.[143] From that time the Romans possessed a firm and faithful friend in this prince, although they certainly were very far from deserving the friendship of a sovereign they had treated so ill. Enraged at the loss of the Sicilian towns, the Carthaginians hired a great body of mercenary troops and occupied Agrigentum, which served them for a general depôt for their troops and magazines, being aware that, if they wished to retain their possessions in Sicily, they must lose no time in stopping the progress of the Romans. The recovery of many of the captured towns followed these energetic measures.[144] The consuls, who saw the importance of Agrigentum to the Carthaginians, immediately blockaded the place, but as their foragers had been cut off by the enemy who had followed them to their encampment, they caused a deep trench to be dug between their camp and the walls of the town to prevent any similar attempt.[145] The siege of Agrigentum had continued full five months, and both the besieged and besiegers were in great distress for provisions. Hannibal, the Carthaginian admiral, who was confined within the walls with fifty thousand men, sent to Carthage in this emergency for help. The republic immediately despatched troops and elephants to Hanno, their general in Sicily, commanding him to relieve the garrison at Agrigentum. Hanno marched from Heraclea to Herbessus, a town of great importance to the Romans. The inhabitants, who were disaffected to them, put Hanno in possession of their town. Hanno next encamped about ten furlongs from[146] the Roman army, which was besieged by him while prosecuting the siege of Agrigentum. Disease made great havoc among the troops, and but for some provisions conveyed to them by Hiero they must have given up their attempt upon Agrigentum.[147] But the distress of the B.C. 262. Romans was trifling compared to the famine in the town, and Hannibal by signs informed Hanno that if he could not bring the Romans to an engagement, he must capitulate. The battle was fought between the Roman and Carthaginian camps, and was long and obstinately contested. The misbehaviour of fifty elephants belonging to the Carthaginians decided the fortunes of the day against them. These unruly animals alarmed by the flight of their own vanguard became unmanageable, and entirely disordered Hanno's army. The Romans defeated him with great loss, taking a number of elephants and all his baggage.[148] Hannibal resolved to evacuate Agrigentum in the night. With the natural address of a Carthaginian he filled up the deep trench that surrounded the enemy's camp with faggots, and over this strange bridge marched with his army unperceived and unimpeded.[149] The consuls entered the undefended town the following morning, which was treated with severity. The Romans then turned their eyes upon Carthage itself, instead of prosecuting the war in Sicily, for the Carthaginians being a great naval power could throw troops into any part of that island, while, if they were attacked in Africa, the superiority of the Roman power by land might lead to the subjection of this rival state. The Romans were however not only unskilled in nautical affairs, but they had no fleet, nor even a single galley that could serve them for a model. An accident enabled them to put their design into execution. A Carthaginian galley was stranded upon the coast of Italy, and being uninjured served as a pattern to the Romans, and one hundred vessels upon this construction were built and fitted for service.[150] While the vessels were building, the men destined to navigate them were instructed in the art of rowing on dry land by means of rows of benches placed upon the beach. Between these benches stood proper officers, who showed them how to handle their oars, by dipping and recovering them in concert.[151] After they became expert on shore, they practised rowing in the water, coasting about Italy till they fully understood their business.[152] This incident, though apparently accidental, originated in that Divine Wisdom which rules and governs the affairs of the universe. The dominion of Rome was destined to extend over the principal kingdoms of the earth, to prepare the way for the gospel. Every rival power was doomed to fall before her; but human, not miraculous means, were to be the agency employed for this purpose, and Carthage could not be reduced without her rival possessed a fleet. It is probable that the conquests of England, as well as her colonies, are extended for the same end, and that the blessings of Christianity and civilisation will follow the ravages and horrors of war. For it is the prerogative of the Lord alone to bring good out of evil, while man is striving continually to turn good into evil.

As soon as the consuls Cornelius Scipio and C. Duilius entered into office, it was determined to make the former commander of the fleet, a post for which he was by no means qualified. Not being at all aware of his own incapacity, he made an attack upon Lipara, an island held by the Carthaginians. Hannibal, the admiral of the rival republic, was at sea, and taking advantage of the inexperience of his opponent, blockaded him in the harbour during the night. Day revealed his unfortunate situation to the Roman commander, who, abandoned by his mariners, was obliged to yield himself and seventeen vessels composing his fleet to the skilful and wily Carthaginians.[153] The other consul possessed an intuitive genius for naval warfare, and his talent soon recovered the advantages his colleague had lost. Confident in his own skill, and having his vessels furnished with the grappling machines called corvi, then newly invented by the Romans for this occasion, he resolved to go in search of Hannibal, and give him battle.[154] Hannibal, however, had committed the imprudence of reconnoitring the main fleet of the Romans with a very inadequate force, and fell in with it, drawn up in order of battle, when being unprepared he lost fifty vessels, escaping with difficulty, after losing in slain and prisoners ten thousand men.[155] The victorious fleet carried to Duilius the news of Cornelius's disaster, and its own success in the same moment. The Roman consul immediately left the command of B.C. 260. the land forces to his tribunes and put to sea. The Carthaginians, notwithstanding their late disasters, were too full of self-confidence to consider the expediency of taking the same precautions against the Romans that they would have done against a more experienced naval power, but found their mistake directly Duilius threw out his grappling irons and linked their ships to his own. This manœuvre enabled his soldiers to leap upon the decks of the Carthaginian vessels, where their skill in the use of their swords and superior bravery made them an overmatch for their enemies. Victory declared for the Romans, upon which the Carthaginians sheered off after losing eight of their galleys.[156] Following up his victory Duilius relieved the town of Segesta, stormed Macella, and after these successes by land and sea returned home to claim his well-earned triumph; a splendid one was unanimously accorded to him,[157] and a rostrate pillar was set up in the forum in commemoration of his victory. This monument was discovered in the last century and is adorned with six Roman galleys, the sculpture of which though mutilated is still discernible. A long inscription, injured, and partly defaced, yet relates to posterity the first victory ever gained at sea by the Romans over the rival republic, the great naval power of that remote day.[158] Duilius, not content with this time-enduring trophy, devised a sort of continual triumph for himself. Whenever he supped abroad he chose to be attended home by torch-bearers and music, thus departing from the severe simplicity that marked the manners of Rome at that virtuous era.[159] Many medals were also issued to record his victory. He built a temple to Janus in his censorship, which was restored in the reign of Tiberius.

The consulship of Lucius Cornelius Scipio[160] and C. Aquillius Florus had scarcely commenced before four thousand Samnites, employed as rowers in the Roman galleys, engaged three thousand captives in a conspiracy to regain their liberty. Their own elected leader betrayed them to the Romans, by whom the mutiny was quickly put down.[161] The consul Aquillius found Sicily torn by dissensions, and the Roman affairs in confusion. Hamilcar, the Carthaginian general, took advantage of these divisions to slay four thousand Sicilians and capture several towns.[162] Aquillius did all that lay in his power to calm these internal commotions, and when his consulate was out retained his command on the island with the title of pro-consul. The war was carried on against the Carthaginians both by land and sea by the new consuls, A. Atilius Calatinus and C. Sulpicius Paterculus. Mytistratum surrendered to Calatinus, who commanded the land forces, as soon as he arrived in Sicily, but this success was the means of bringing him into great danger, for in marching to Camerina he led his army into a deep valley which was surrounded by the troops of Hamilcar. From this perilous situation the bravery and self-devotion of the legionary tribune, Calpurnius Flamma, extricated him, for seizing an eminence he sustained the attack of the Carthaginian army while the consul and the Roman troops marched through. Of three hundred devoted men one only was found still breathing, and that person was their heroic leader.[163] He was drawn from under a heap of dead and dying Carthaginians sorely wounded, but by care was recovered. A crown of grass was the simple but honourable reward bestowed by the consul upon Calpurnius, for, as we have already noticed, the men of the fifth century of Rome considered the glory of having served their country their best recompence.[164] Calatinus took a great many Sicilian towns, but lost the renown he had gained by the ill-success of his attack upon Lipara, which he hoped to find unguarded by the Carthaginians. Hamilcar, who was within the walls, repulsed him with B.C. 258. great loss. The disgrace of this defeat obliterated his rapid conquests and concluded the campaign. Sulpicius his colleague gained some successes in Sardinia and Corsica, but having more skill in nautical affairs he resolved to draw the Carthaginian fleet into an engagement, when finding them averse to put to sea he spread abroad a report of his intention of burning their vessels in harbour. To avoid this supposed evil the Carthaginian admiral came to attack Sulpicius, but a storm drove them asunder, and Hannibal was glad to shelter himself in a harbour of Sardinia, where he was surprised by Sulpicius, who took many of his galleys. This misfortune was productive of dreadful consequences to the Carthaginian commander, for the crew mutinied and crucified him.[165] Another naval victory during the consulship of C. Atilius Regulus and Cn. Cornelius Blasio at Tyndaris, showed the Carthaginians that they must no longer hope to maintain the empire of the sea. In this action Regulus took the command of the fleet and defeated the enemy, who at first appeared likely to carry off the honour of the day, as the consul had imprudently attacked them with only ten ships. The fleet came up in time to retrieve his rashness, and the Carthaginians fled to Lipara, having sustained great loss.[166]

It was to another celebrated consul of the same name that the memorable expedition against Carthage was entrusted, which had been long planned though delayed till then. The preparations on the part of the Romans to invade, and on that of the Carthaginians to defend Carthage were made on a stupendous scale. The Roman armament consisted of 330 ships of war manned with soldiers and mariners to the amount of 140,000 men. That of the Carthaginians was more numerous still, for they had 350 galleys equipped by 150,000 mariners and troops. The Roman historians have entered minutely into the particulars of the celebrated engagement that ensued upon the meeting of those immense fleets. To the naval and military commanders of our own day the technicalities would doubtless prove interesting, but the general reader only looks to results and not to the tactics that produced them. Hanno and Hamilcar, with the Carthaginian fleets under their command, were met near Ecnomus in Sicily, by the Roman navy, which was conducted by the consuls Regulus and Manlius. This battle was a series of actions between different parts of the fleet, fought with various success on both sides. The Romans appear to have shown the most courage, while the Carthaginians displayed more finesse. Their dread of the corvi seems to have lost them the victory, for these machines were new to them, and proved powerful auxiliaries to Roman valour. Victory followed in the track of Roman boldness, and the flight of the Carthaginian admirals left their country open to invasion. The consuls put into a Sicilian port to refit before making their descent upon the African coast.[167] The Romans lost twenty-four ships, but sank thirty and took sixty-four from the Carthaginians, whose great nautical skill did not avail them against the novel machines and great military talents of their foes. Their late reverses made the Carthaginians desirous of peace. Hanno went himself to the consuls in the hope of gaining those advantages by negociation that he had lost in war. This attempt was unsuccessful, and a legionary tribune even cried out "that he ought to be detained as a prisoner, as Cornelius the former consul had been." But the consuls, who knew that Cornelius had fallen into the hands of the Carthaginians through his own rashness, silenced the man, and turning to Hanno said, "The faith of Rome secures thee from that fear."[168] Hanno departed in safety, but he could not effect the pacification he desired. The consul Regulus embarked for Africa, and landing near the town of Clypea made himself master of that place, which he fortified and garrisoned. An immense number of prisoners and a great deal of plunder fell into the hands of the Romans. Regulus, far from availing himself of this opportunity to enrich himself, was troubled at the accounts he received from Rome, respecting his domestic affairs. The same person who brought the commands of the senate, that he alone was to conduct the war, while his colleague Manlius returned to Italy, probably informed him of the bad state of his farm of seven acres; for in his letter to that august body he complained of the arrangement, alleging, "that B.C. 256. the husbandman who had managed his farm was dead, and that his place was ill-supplied by a day-labourer, who had stolen his implements of agriculture and carried off his stock, and that these misfortunes made his presence absolutely necessary at Rome, that he might provide for the wants of his wife and family."[169] Poverty did not disqualify a Roman from serving his country in the highest offices of state; yet the heart of the statesman and warrior must often have been torn at the reflection, that while his time and energies were devoted to the service of his country abroad, his family were pining for the necessaries of life at home. The poverty of Regulus was the voluntary poverty of integrity. He might have been a rich man if he had not preferred being a great one. The senate ordered his farm to be cultivated, and his family maintained, at the public expense; a measure that allowed him to pursue his victorious march with a mind at ease. The progress of the Roman commander was indeed followed by the most rapid conquests, town after town was taken before the Carthaginians could march to their relief. On the banks of the river Bagrada, not far from the capital, the daring Roman encountered a new and terrific enemy, for an enormous serpent opposed the passage of the army, like the genius of the country, ready to maintain the land against the invaders.[170] Not a man dared cross the guarded stream, and the legions regarded their singular opponent with superstitious dread, considering it as an omen fatal to the success of the African expedition. With the presence of mind that marks the great man in every age, Regulus commanded his war engines, such as he commonly used in the siege of fortified towns, to be brought out against the monster. These balistæ threw great stones at the reptile till its hard impenetrable scales, which were proof against the showers of darts hurled against them, yielded to the immense stones slung by the engines, and the death of the creature left the passage of the Bagrada free to the Roman soldiers.[171] Regulus sent the skin of this serpent to Rome, where it was long preserved in a temple; it measured one hundred and fifty feet, and was very bulky.[172] The consul, who had taken eighty towns on his march, laid siege to the city of Actis, a place of great importance. Hitherto the Carthaginians had given themselves little concern about the progress of the Romans, but as they approached nearer to the capital they became alarmed, and appointed Bostar and Hasdrubal, the son of Hanno, to command their armies, and raise the siege of Adis. They also sent for Hamilcar from Heraclea, in Sicily, for the same purpose. The dilatoriness of the Carthaginians seems very extraordinary; it probably arose from their contempt of the scanty force left under the command of Regulus by his colleague Manlius, which consisted of only forty ships, fifteen thousand five hundred foot soldiers, and five hundred horse. The Carthaginian generals resolved to give the Romans battle without delay, but they posted themselves on the high ground, where their cavalry and elephants, in which their strength mostly lay, could not act to any advantage. Regulus, perceiving their error, led his foot soldiers up the hill and gave the enemy a complete overthrow. The mercenaries, hired by the

Carthaginians, fought with great bravery, but the want of skill displayed by their generals was not even atoned for by personal courage. They fled, and left their camp to the victorious Romans. Regulus, following his advantages, entered Tunis, and encamped within its walls,[173] where he wintered.

The senate of Carthage received the tidings of the lost battle and the fall of Tunis, with despair. The capital was ill-defended and overstocked with inhabitants, provisions were scarce and dear, and the city wholly incapable of standing a siege. Nor were the Romans the only enemy with whom they had to contend; for the Numidians[174] had invaded the country, and were destroying it with fire and sword. The influx of a mighty multitude of fugitives, "bringing with them fear and famine," completed the picture of national distress; yet there were wealthy merchants in Carthage base enough to take advantage of the calamitous state of their country, to raise the price of grain to such a height as to render it unattainable to the poorer classes of their B.C. 255. fellow-citizens.[175] In this ruinous state of public affairs, the senate received with surprise and joy an intimation from Regulus that he was willing to treat with them. These feelings were changed to grief and indignation when they learned the conditions which, even in their present state of distress, were too degrading for free men to accept. The Roman consul demanded "that they should give up their possessions in Sardinia, Corsica, and Sicily; restore the Roman prisoners, and ransom those the Romans had taken from them; paying an annual tribute to the republic for ever, and that, in future, they should fit out but one ship of war for their own service, and that they should furnish the Romans with fifty triremes whenever Rome required a supply of vessels for extending her foreign conquests."[176] The ambassadors, who were three elders of the Carthaginian senate, tried every argument to induce the haughty Roman to recede from his hard conditions, but received this brief reply, "that those who could not conquer the Romans must learn to obey them."[177]

The Carthaginian senate indignantly rejected the conditions, which roused at once the national spirit. It is always dangerous to drive a people to despair. No commander has ever done so with impunity. Regulus was destined to feel the terrible reaction his insulting terms and haughty reply had created. The people sought to propitiate their gods by offering to Moloch their young children who, from the arms of this idol, were rolled into a burning furnace below. This dreadful sacrifice was followed by the self-immolation, for their country, of many others;[178] perhaps these were the parents of the sacrificed children who voluntarily filled the same burning grave. But the deliverance which these abhorrent and unnatural rites could not procure was finally effected by foreign aid. The pride of the Carthaginians was already roused when, just at this critical period of their history, a body of Greek mercenaries arrived, whose commander Xanthippus the Lacedæmonian, beholding the resources the Carthaginians still possessed, declared "that the rapid success of Regulus might be entirely imputed to the incapacity of their own leaders rather than to the martial spirit of the Romans themselves." The degraded Carthaginians took courage, and felt that they were again a free people. Xanthippus was entrusted with the command of the army, which he diligently instructed in the Greek discipline and method of warfare. The soldiers were convinced at once that they were under a man of courage and ability, and with one voice demanded to be led against the invaders of their native soil.[179] The two rival armies finally encamped upon a great plain near Carthage, the river alone dividing them from each other. This stream the Roman pro-consul had the rashness to cross, leaving the Carthaginians full space and freedom for the action of their cavalry and elephants. Of this fatal blunder the Greek commander took advantage; and though the army of the Romans was more numerous than that of their opponents, the Carthaginians totally defeated it, the invaders, with the exception of two thousand men who saved themselves by flying to Clypea, being slain or taken captive by the victors.[180] Among the prisoners was the pro-consul Regulus himself who, in this calamitous battle, lost the fruit of so many conquests, and his liberty. The Carthaginians, who were cruel by nature, and irritated by the insolence with which the unfortunate Roman consul had treated them in the brief period of his triumph, heaped upon the head of their illustrious captive those insults that base minds are apt to show to fallen greatness. To scanty food, and deep dungeons, the proud Roman was superior, but he had an unconquerable antipathy to an elephant. His enemies kept one of the largest and most savage of the species near their unfortunate captive purposely to aggravate his painful and weary imprisonment.[181]

Conscious that they owed their deliverance to Xanthippus, the Carthaginians were desirous of retaining his services, having practically learned, remarks Polybius, the truth of this maxim of Euripides, "that one wise head is worth many pairs of hands," but the brave and prudent Lacedæmonian refused the honour they designed him of becoming their commander-in-chief, for he was well B.C. 255. acquainted with their fickle and jealous national character, and preferred returning with his riches and renown to his own country.[182]

Appian mentions the prevalent report made by some authors that a Carthaginian commander destroyed Xanthippus and his mercenaries during the homeward voyage, according to the orders he had received from the senate. Polybius mentions these authorities, which he considers unworthy of credit.[183] He speaks of the return of the brave Greek with the certainty of a military author who is relating a fact.[184] The loss of a single battle had deprived the Romans of the fruits of their late victorious expedition to Africa. Clypea, which had received the fugitive legionaries who had had the good fortune to escape the vengeance of the Carthaginians, was soon besieged. The soldiers defended themselves with dauntless resolution, till the report that a Roman fleet had put to sea commanded by the consuls, obliged their enemies to raise the siege and fit out a naval armament to oppose their landing. The Carthaginians lost the battle, which was fought near the promontory of Mercury. The victorious fleet swept on to Clypea and took on board their countrymen, to whom the success of their arms had brought deliverance.[185] Near the coast of Sicily, the triumphant navy was scattered and destroyed by a dreadful storm, only eighty ships remaining uninjured out of four hundred. The whole coast from Camarina to the promontory of Pachynus was encumbered with the dead bodies of the Romans. Nor was this immense destruction of human life and ships of war the only injury done them, for the treasures which Regulus had amassed during his brief career of conquest, and stored in Clypea, foundered with the galleys.[186] This disaster is imputed by Polybius to the rash obstinacy of the pro-consuls Fulvius and Æmilius, who, in defiance of the advice given them by the pilots not to steer at that season for the African side of the island, chose to do so because they hoped to take the towns on that coast which belonged to the Carthaginians, as if (remarks the historian) their indomitable pride could subject even the elements to their dominion.[187]

The senate immediately ordered a new fleet of 220 vessels to be built, and this great undertaking was actually completed and the ships fitted for sea in the short space of three months. The consul Cn. Cornelius Scipio Asina took the command of that part of the Roman fleet which had escaped the storm. He was the same person formerly captured by Carthalo, the Carthaginian admiral. He took Cephalædium, and in conjunction with Atilius besieged Drepanum, but the capture of Agrigentum by Carthalo made him abandon the siege and attack Panormus [Palermo], which with the assistance of his colleague Atilius he took, leaving a large garrison in the place to maintain his new conquest. Cneius Cornelius obtained a triumph for this success.[188]

The new consuls, Cneius Servilius and Caius Sempronius, sailed for the coast of Africa with the Roman fleet, and plundered the towns that lay near the adverse shore. Passing near the Syrtis Minor, the fleet was grounded at ebb-tide, nor could the mariners get the stranded vessels afloat at the flood-tide without the sacrifice of the rich booty that had been acquired during the expedition.[189] The fleet was still more unfortunate upon its return, when it was shipwrecked upon the Sicilian coast, with the loss of 140 vessels. This second destruction of their naval force by storm made the Romans resolve to confine their operations to the land, and to use their remaining ships for transports only. They now centered their attention upon Sicily, of which they already held Panormus and many other important towns. Hasdrubal, the Carthaginian commander, had been sent to defend Lilybæum, a maritime place of great importance in Sicily. He had with his army 140 elephants, and was very desirous of coming to an engagement with the Romans. They, however, who foolishly imputed the defeat and captivity of Regulus and his army to these beasts rather than to the wisdom and bravery of Xanthippus the Lacedæmonian, dared not face the Carthaginians. The proconsul Cæcilius Metellus did not suffer himself to be drawn into an engagement till he had devised some method of rendering his opponent's elephants useless.[190] B.C. 254. He permitted Hasdrubal to ravage the country round Panormus, and even allowed him to cross the river within a mile of the town—near the walls of which he had caused a deep trench to be dug. He gave orders to his light troops to skirmish with the enemy until near the trench into which the dartmen were to leap and gall the elephants with their weapons. The consul's directions were exactly executed. The elephants advanced to the trench, when, being galled by the darts thrown at them, they turned round and carried terror and confusion into the ranks of their own infantry, when Cæcilius charged the Carthaginians, and defeated them. Hasdrubal lost all his elephants[191] and 20,000 men in this battle of Panormus. These captive beasts were cruelly hunted in the circus and put to death.[192]

Metellus had taken at the battle of Panormus thirteen noble Carthaginians,[193] for whose exchange the senate of Carthage were desirous to treat, or rather under that colour to negotiate with the Romans an advantageous peace through the mediation of the unfortunate pro-consul Regulus.[194] The ingratitude of his country had not however obliterated from the heart of the noble Roman that love for Rome which in this and the succeeding century was the ruling passion of her citizens. He was taken from the dungeon in which he had languished five years, and was ordered by his captors to effect the exchange of the prisoners for his own person, or to procure the required peace. If the negotiations were not concluded he was to return to them.[195] Regulus took the oath required from him, and accompanied the ambassadors to that ungrateful city which had lauded his conquests and disregarded his captivity. He refused to enter Rome, remaining without the gates with the embassy, declaring to his former friends, "that though a foreign slave he would not break the laws of the Romans, which denied admittance within her walls to strangers"—words that proved how deeply the iron of captivity had entered the soul of the proud and high-minded Roman. Another and bitterer trial awaited him—an interview between the captive in his degradation and his wife Marcia. She brought with her their children. The gloomy and cruel future suffered no ray of joy to warm the heart of Regulus, whose firm resolution he knew must tear him from these beloved objects, for whose support he had suffered anxiety even while pursuing his career of conquest. With the certainty of life-long captivity or the threatened death of torture—alternatives sufficient to shake the determination of the firmest mind—Regulus took leave of his distressed family to attend the audience given by the senate without the gates to the Carthaginian ambassadors, opening his commission with these brief but affecting words, "Conscript fathers, a Carthaginian slave comes to you commissioned by his masters to treat for peace and an exchange of prisoners."[196] Having thus declared the cause of his return, the captive would have withdrawn from the assembly, but the Carthaginians commanded him to remain with the senate; while they withdrew that the discussions between Regulus and a body, of which he was still a member, might not be restrained by their presence.[197] The senate would not conclude a peace which would have ensured the liberty and saved the life of Regulus. Whether he really opposed the pacification seems doubtful, though mentioned as an historic fact;[198] but all authorities agree that he himself excepted against being exchanged for the noble Carthaginians.[199] Some mystery seems to be concealed, notwithstanding the unity in the statements of ancient writers; and if it be permitted to give any individual opinion against their evidence, it might be urged that the senatorial body, not Regulus, refused the exchange, but that some specious arguments were used to induce him to break his plighted word, a measure to which his noble and upright mind would not consent. Over counsels so disgraceful the Roman historians may have thrown a veil, by imputing to the eloquent patriotism of the victim of the unfeeling policy of Rome, the rejection of the peace and the refusal of the exchange of the prisoners. If we take this view, and it is most likely the true one, how honourable was the conduct of the captive, how unfeeling that of the senate! B.C. 251. Indeed what motive could have induced Regulus to return to Rome, unless he hoped to regain his liberty either by means of the exchange of prisoners, or by the terms of an honourable peace? His refusal to accompany the embassy would have been as truly patriotic as his revisiting Carthage afterwards. "He voluntarily returned to his enemies," are the words used by Florus.[200] His adherence to his oath is mentioned in the Epitome of Livy, by Cicero, Horace, Valerius Maximus, and many others. Upon that honourable fulfilment of his engagement to the Carthaginian senate rests the true glory of Regulus, the pride of Rome and her disgrace, for the life of such a man was worth any sacrifice she could make.

The peace was rejected, and Regulus returned with the embassy to Carthage to die, but whether his glorious existence languished away in the dungeon to which he nobly returned, or the cruel ingenuity of a barbarous people wreaked upon his person the tortures enumerated by Florus and Valerius Maximus, and glanced at in the Epitome of Livy, has been for ages an unsettled question.[201]

The Roman consuls, Atilius and Manlius, besieged Lilybæum, which was the most considerable place the Carthaginians held in Sicily, but the town was gallantly defended by Himilco, who made frequent sallies from the gates, and these were attended with as great loss of life as a succession of pitched battles; but the Carthaginian commander being in want of everything, Hannibal was sent to convey supplies of men and provisions into Lilybæum. This he effected, although the Roman fleet was stationed on each side the harbour; for having manned his deck with ten thousand soldiers, he crowded all his sails and entered the port, taking advantage of the brisk gale, and passing through the midst of their navy, brought the supplies into the town to the surprise and admiration even of the enemy.[202]

Himilco made an unsuccessful attempt to burn the Roman outworks, but was repulsed with great loss.[203] This undertaking however was accomplished some time after by some Greek auxiliaries, who took advantage of a great storm to fire them,[204] a misfortune which obliged the Romans to turn the siege into a blockade. Upon this disaster being known at Rome, ten thousand men offered themselves as volunteers to assist the consuls Claudius Pulcher and L. Junius Pullus in the reduction of Lilybæum. As soon as these gallant Romans entered the camp, Claudius instead of following his instructions chose to make an attempt by sea upon the strong city of Drepanum, of which Adherbal was governor. As Drepanum was a wealthy place, the consul found no difficulty in engaging the volunteers in this service. Adherbal, an experienced commander by land and sea, lost no time in getting out his ships and arming the citizens, for he was obliged to take his soldiers to augment his naval force.[205] He took out his fleet, which he placed behind some rocks, charging his people to keep their eye upon his galley, as he would lead them in person. The greater part of the Roman vessels were suffered to advance, when Adherbal with his fleet appeared from behind the rocks and came suddenly upon them. Claudius gave a sign to his galleys to tack about, but this threw his ships into dreadful confusion; some grounded and others were damaged by running foul, so that he found himself in a fearful predicament. A fight, very disastrous for the Romans, ensued, in which it seems Claudius showed neither courage nor conduct. He was defeated with the loss of ninety-three vessels and twenty thousand men,—eight thousand Romans perished in the engagement.[206]

The quæstors not being strong enough to cope with the Carthaginian fleet, made for the coast, and got among the rocks. At this time, when Junius Pullus, ignorant of their situation, had steered with the fleet for Lilybæum, the sight of Carthalo's vessels compelled this commander to take up a perilous position near the coast. The Carthaginian stationed himself between the two fleets, which lay at his mercy, when the approach of a storm made him weigh his anchors and double Cape Pachynus in great haste, leaving the Romans to contend with the strife of the elements. So destructive was the tempest that not a vessel under the command of the B.C. 249. consul or the quæstors escaped its rage. Junius saved his men, though he lost his ships; but hoping to cover his misfortunes at sea by his successes on shore, stormed and took the city of Eryx, and plundered the temple of Venus Erycina, which was the richest and most beautiful sacred edifice on the island.[207] Certainly idolators have shown little reverence to the shrines of the deities they worshipped, while pursuing foreign conquests. But neither the wealth of this plundered fane nor the value of the city he conquered could console the consul for the loss of the fleet, for he killed himself, rather than live disgraced like his colleague by a public trial for putting to sea without attending to the auspices.[208] A mutiny among the troops under Carthalo, occasioned his recall by the senate of Carthage, and Hamilcar Barca, the father of the great Hannibal,[209] was appointed to take his command in Sicily, in the eighteenth year of the war. This celebrated commander made a descent upon the coast of Italy, plundering the Bruttians and Locrians, after which he landed in Sicily, and encamped upon a wide plain, lying upon the top of a mountain between the cities of Eryx and Panormus, near the sea coast. Thus strongly posted, Hamilcar Barca soon got possession of the city of Eryx, which lay half-way up the mountain; but the Romans had garrisons both above and below, so that each army was, in a manner, besieged by the other for the space of three years, without the Romans being able to retake the city they had lost, or Hamilcar to dislodge them from their position. At Rome a lady was fined for uttering a foolish and unfeeling speech on the following occasion. As Claudia, the sister of Claudius Pulcher, who lost the battle of Drepanum, was returning in her chariot from a public show, she was impeded in the street by a press of people, upon which she lost her temper, and cried out, "Gods! how this city is overcrowded; I wish my brother Claudius was alive again, and had the command of another fleet." For these words the ædiles cited her before the tribes, who made her pay 25,000 asses of brass; so that this odious remark cost Claudia about 80*l.* 14*s.* 8*d.*, reckoning the fine after the rate of British currency.[210] Claudius had been dead three years: he had been brought to trial for his defeat, which was imputed to his contempt for the auspices, and would have been condemned if a thunder-storm had not occurred at the very time, which put an end to the judicial proceedings, his accusation and deliverance originating in the absurd superstition of his fellow-citizens. He was the son of the great censor, and was surnamed Pulcher from the singular beauty of his person. He must not be confounded with Appius Claudius Caudex, the distinguished consul whose expedition to Messina gained him that addendum to his name. He was, most likely, his nephew. In Sicily the occupation of Eryx by the Carthaginians prevented the legions from taking Lilybæum, while their want of a fleet enabled its brave defender to maintain his advantageous position. To build a navy for the express purpose of dislodging Hamilcar from this city was a measure of necessity; but the exhausted state of the Roman exchequer left no funds for the purpose. Some wealthy citizens generously supplied the means, and patriotically built and fitted out two hundred quinqueremes at their own expense, for this important service. The senate and people engaged to repay the loan at some future period.[211] The consuls for the year, A. Postumius and C. Lutatius Catulus, were ordered by the senate to carry on the war in Sicily, but the religious scruples of the pontifex maximus prevented Postumius, who was the high priest of Mars that year, from leaving Rome. This superstitious notion led to the creation of a new officer in the republic, a prætor peregrinus, who took charge of those affairs abroad which the prætor urbanus superintended in the capital. Both these magistrates were chosen by the centuries in comitia; their stations were decided by lot.

Lutatius was a valiant and able plebeian, the first of his family who held the consular dignity. Aware that the continuance of the Carthaginians in Sicily depended upon their keeping possession of Eryx, he resolved to intercept the fleet which was to sail from Carthage with supplies of men and provisions for its defenders. The fate of the war depended upon the capability of the Roman navy to effect this object. To discipline his mariners and instruct B.C. 242-247. them in the art of rowing, and in naval tactics, was not the sole care of Lutatius. He attended to the personal comforts of his men, that they might be in fine condition when called upon to encounter the enemy. Before he left Italy, however, he wished to have his fortune told by the divining lots kept in the temple of Fortune, at Præneste.[212] His intention coming to the ears of the senate, caused a prohibition against the use of any species of divination but those permitted by the laws of Rome.[213] In the month of February the superstitious consul, with his destiny still unread, accompanied by Valerius Falto, the prætor peregrinus, sailed from the Tiber; but discovering that the Carthaginian fleet was not at sea, commenced the siege of Drepanum, where he received such a severe wound in the head that he was actually keeping his bed, when the Carthaginians took advantage of the westerly wind to bear down upon the place. The Roman fleet, with its wounded consul and the prætor peregrinus, Valerius Falto, got out on the morning of the 10th of March, and performed its difficult enterprise so ably and energetically, that fifty Carthaginian ships were sunk and seventy captured. The remnant escaped through the sudden change of wind, which allowed them to hoist a press of sail and escape to Hiera.

The war being now virtually ended by the loss of the Carthaginian fleet, Hamilcar received orders from his government to make the best terms he could for Carthage.[214] To the first demand of Lutatius he returned an indignant refusal. To give up the Roman deserters, appeared to him unjust and derogatory to the national honour; but the idea of surrendering his arms awoke the pride of a warrior who was yet unconquered by the enemy. "Never will I give up those weapons to the Romans which I received from my country to use against them;

rather will I remain here and defend Eryx to the last moment of my life."[215] Lutatius Catulus gave up the humiliating clause, and allowed the brave garrison of Eryx with its intrepid general to march out of the city they had so gallantly and successfully defended, with the honours of war.[216] Hamilcar, who had formed plans respecting Spain which he thought would compensate his country for the loss of the beautiful and fruitful island he was compelled to yield with Eryx, made no objection to the terms imposed upon him by the ten commissioners sent from Rome for that purpose. He ratified the treaty, and quitting the city,[217] marched for Lilybæum, leaving to Gisco, the governor of that city, the important commission of embarking the army for Carthage. As these troops were chiefly composed of mercenaries Gisco prudently embarked them in small divisions, that the Carthaginian government might pay and send them home as they arrived, and thus avoid the danger of having a disbanded foreign army at their gates.[218]

The termination of the first Punic war gave great satisfaction to the Romans, for it had lasted twenty-two years, and had exhausted the means of the republic. The immense loss of human life had diminished the citizens of Rome, for the census exhibited a great decrease of population, occasioned by the long struggle between the two mighty republics. Both had tried their strength and the event had proved that the younger, freer, poorer, and more upright state, would eventually prevail over the older, more despotic, wealthier, and less honourable one. Public virtue opened in this century every office of trust to the Roman however impoverished his condition might be, but riches were the qualification required by Carthage for her rulers, and her merchant city was certain to fall in a contest between national honour and national wealth.

The possession of Sicily consoled the Romans for the calamities of war, for it became the granary of Rome, and the triumphs accorded to Lutatius Catulus the consul, and Valerius Falto the prætor peregrinus, were unusually splendid.[219] A great depreciation of the Roman currency was occasioned by the Punic war, if we may trust Pliny, who states, that the as had sunk from twelve ounces to two.[220] All Sicily received Roman laws with the exception of Syracuse. A prætor was sent B.C. 241. thither to govern the province, and a quæstor to regulate its revenues.[221] This was the first foreign conquest of great importance made by the Roman republic, for we can scarcely call any state within the limits of Italy by that name, since she considered every Italian town and state as a part of her rapidly increasing dominion. The prophecy of Pyrrhus was accomplished; Sicily had been the battle-field of Rome and Carthage, but Rome had gained the victory which he had not foreseen.

<hr size=2 width="10%" align=center>

[1] Fasti Capitolini.

[2] Polybius, ii. 19.

[3] Hooke.

[4] Arnold; Niebuhr; Bunsen; Orelli.

[5] Arnold.

[6] Livy, x. 15.

[7] Arnold.

[8] Hooke.

[9] Livy, x. 20. In this battle the consul vowed a temple to Bellona, which he fulfilled for the gratification of his family pride. His own achievements and those of his ancestors forming the subjects of the bas-relievos that adorned the frieze of the building. He afterwards dedicated the fane, which must have been one of the best finished fabrics of the time. This temple is considered a proof that he had gained his share of the victory.O

O Orelli; Juris Latinar. Collect. No. 539.

[10] Livy, x. 21.

[11] Fasti Capitolini.

[12] Livy, x. 23.

[13] *Ibid.*

[14] Arnold; Livy, x. 20, 21.

[15] Arnold.

[16] Livy, x. 25.

[17] Arnold; Livy, x. 26.

[18] Livy, x. 27.

[19] *Ibid.*, 26; Polybius, ii. 19.

[20] Arnold; Orelli.

[21] Hooke; Livy, x. 27, 28.

[22] *Ibid.*

[23] Livy, ix. 27.

[24] *Ibid.*, x. 29.

[25] Fasti Capitolini.

[26] Livy, x. 29.

[27] *Ibid.*

[28] Livy, x. 29; See Appendix. (p. 233)

[29] Livy, x. 29.

[30] Livy, x. 30.

[31] *Ibid.*

[32] Orosius, iii. 21; Zonaras.

[33] Hooke; Livy.

[34] Hooke; Livy, x. 37.

[35] Livy, x. 38, 39.

[36] Fasti Capitolini.

[37] Val. Max. vii. 2; Livy, x. 40.

[38] Livy.

[39] Livy, x. 40, 41.

[40] *Ibid.*, 46.

[41] Pliny, vii. 60.

[42] Hooke.

[43] Val. Max. iv. 1; Livy, x. 45; Orosius, iii. 22.

[44] Eutropius, ii.; Zonaras.

[45] Livy, Epit. xi.

[46] Orosius, iii. 22.

[47] Orosius, iii. 22; Hooke's Rome.

[48] *Ibid.*

[49] Plutarch; Val. Max. v. 7.

[50] Cicero, Verres, v. 30.

[51] Ovid, Metam.

[52] Ogulnius, who was at the head of this silly deputation,[P] saw with delight the reptile come out of a hole at the foot of the statue of the god, in obedience to the voice of the priest. He affirmed that it followed him through the city to the ship destined to convey it to Italy, and coiling itself up in the cabin, never moved from the corner to which it had retreated till the mariners put into Antium, where there was a temple dedicated to Æsculapius, whereupon it quitted its quarters in the cabin, and swimming on shore, took possession of a palm-tree, where it remained three days, at the end of which period it thought proper to return to the ship.[Q] But its vagaries, it would seem, were not yet over, for when the vessel entered the Tiber along the banks of which altars were erected in honour of the new deity, the serpent left it again, disliking the smoke of the incense, and taking to the water swam up the stream till it reached a little island near the walls of the city,[R] where, perhaps, it hoped to lie concealed out of the reach of noise and intrusion, following its natural

solitary habits. Here a temple was built in the form of a ship, and dedicated to Æsculapius, where the tame serpent was greatly venerated. The story may be true, if the person who had the care of the reptile accompanied Ogulnius to the ship, while its behaviour on the voyage may be referred to instinct. It seems that the priests of Æsculapius reared and sold these serpents to credulous strangers; nor is it unlikely that some remedy for the plague was given with the reptiles. The pestilence, however, had disappeared before the serpent arrived at Rome. This adventure happened in the consulate of Postumius and Junius Brutus Bubulcus.S The travertine which forms the foundations of the temple is found at this day cut into a rude resemblance of the trireme that brought home the reptile.

P Valerius Maximus, i. 8.

Q Ovid, Metam. xv. 622; Val. Max. i. 8.

R *Ibid.*; *Ibid.*

S Hooke.

[53] Livy, Epit. xi.; Eutropius, ii.

[54] *Ibid.*

[55] *Ibid.*

[56] Arnold; Pliny, Nat. Hist. xviii.

[57] Livy, Epit. xi.

[58] Dion. Hal.

[59] Hooke.

[60] Fragmentum Fast. Capit.

[61] Auc. de Viris Illus.

[62] Polybius, ii. 19. Appian.

[63] *Ibid.*

[64] Appian; Polybius, ii. 20.

[65] *Ibid.*, xix.; Florus, ii. 13.

[66] Pliny, xxxiv. 6; Val. Max. i.

[67] Pliny, xxxiv. 6; Val. Max. i.

[68] Dion. Hal., in Legat.

[69] See Appendix. (p. 241)

[70] Plutarch, in Pyrrhus.

[71] Plutarch.

[72] Fasti Cuspiniani.

[73] Zonaras, viii.

[74] Zonaras, viii.

[75] Justin, xviii. 1; Zonaras, viii.; Plutarch, in Pyrrhus.

[76] Val. Max. v. 1.

[77] Zonaras, viii.

[78] Plutarch, in Pyrrhus.

[79] Plutarch, in Pyrrhus.

[80] Zonaras; Plutarch.

[81] Dion. Hal.; Plutarch.

[82] Zonaras, viii.

[83] Dion. Hal., in Legat.; Zonaras, viii.

[84] Plutarch.

[85] Plutarch, in Pyrrhus.

[86] Plutarch, in Pyrrhus.

[87] Appian.

[88] Plutarch; Appian.

[89] Cicero, in Brut. xvi.

[90] Plutarch.

[91] Florus, i. 18; Plutarch.

[92] Zonaras.

[93] Zonaras, viii.

[94] Plutarch.

[95] Justin, xviii. 2; Polybius, iii. 25; Livy, Epit.

[96] Plutarch, in Pyrrhus; Zonaras.

[97] Eutropius, ii. 14; Appian; Plutarch.

[98] Zonaras, viii. 6.

[99] *Ibid.*

[100] Hooke.

[101] Plutarch.

[102] Plutarch, in Pyrrhus; Appian.

[103] Plutarch.

[104] Dion. Hal., xix.; Val. Max. i. 1.

[105] Orosius, iv. 2.

[106] Eutropius, ii. 14.

[107] Plutarch, in Pyrrhus.

[108] Florus, i. 18.

[109] Zonaras, viii.; Livy, Epit. xiv.; Val. Max. iv. 3; Eutropius, ii. 15.

[110] See Appendix. (p. 255)

[111] Florus.

[112] See Appendix. (p. 255)

[113] Livy, Epit. xiv.; Zonaras, viii.

[114] Polybius, i. 7.

[115] Zonaras, viii.

[116] Pliny, xxxiii. 3.

[117] Hooke's Rome.

[118] Eutropius, ii. 16; Val. Max. vi. 5.

[119] Eutropius, ii. 16; Val. Max. vi. 5; Pliny, Nat. Hist. cxi.

[120] Val. Max. vi. 5.

[121] Hooke's Rome.

[122] Livy, Epit. xv.; Val. Max. vi. 6.

[123] *Ibid.*

[124] Cicero; Suetonius.

[125] Orosius, iv. 5.

[126] Hooke's Rome; Val. Max., ix. 1; Zonaras, viii. 7; Orosius, iv. 5.

[127] Zonaras.

[128] *Ibid.*, viii. 7.

[129] Arnold's Rome, ii. 532.

[130] Zonaras, viii. 7.

[131] Polybius, i. 7; Strabo; Diodorus Siculus in Eclog. 866.

[132] Hooke.

[133] Zonaras, viii. 8; Polybius, i. 10.

[134] Hooke; Polybius, i. 11.

[135] Arnold.

[136] Arnold; Zonaras, viii. 9; Dion Cassius, Frag. Vatican, lviii.

[137] Zonaras, viii. 8; Polybius, i. 11; Diodorus.

[138] Arnold; Zonaras.

[139] Polybius, i. 11.

[140] Arnold.

[141] Hooke.

[142] Hooke; Zonaras, viii. 9; Polybius, i. 12.

[143] Polybius, i. 11.

[144] Diodorus, in Frag.; Arnold.

[145] Polybius, i. 20.

[146] Polybius; Hooke.

[147] Polybius, i. 19.

[148] Polybius, i. 19.

[149] *Ibid.*

[150] *Ibid.*, 20.

[151] *Ibid.*, 21.

[152] Polybius; Hooke.

[153] Polybius, i. 21.

[154] *Ibid.*, 23.

[155] *Ibid.*

[156] Val. Max., in Extern. vii. 3. Hannibal, though near the coast of Africa, dared not approach it for fear of being crucified, till a friend had made the extent of his misfortune known to the Carthaginian senate, which was done by him in the following ingenious manner:—"Your admiral desires to learn of you whether, in case the Romans appear at sea with a great fleet, he is to give them battle?" "Doubtless, he ought to fight," was the unanimous rejoinder. "He has fought, and is vanquished," was the brief reply. This adroit method of telling bad news saved Hannibal from the crucifixion he feared, for it was the barbarous practice of the Carthaginian government to inflict this punishment upon their commanders, in most cases where unexpected defeat occurred, whether they were in fault or only unfortunate. Polybius, i. 24.

[157] Cicero, De Senectute.

[158] Hooke's Rome.

[159] Hooke; Cicero.

[160] This Scipio's tomb and epitaph are extant; he was the son of that Scipio who styled himself the conqueror of Lucania.

[161] Zonaras, viii. 11.

[162] Diodorus.

[163] Florus; Orosius; Zonaras, viii.; Livy, xxii. 60.

[164] Pliny, xxii. 6.

[165] Polybius, i. 24.

[166] *Ibid.*, 25.

[167] Polybius, i. 26, 28.

[168] *Ibid.*, 29.

[169] Auctor. De Viris Illustris. in Regulus; Val. Max., vi. 6.

[170] Florus, ii.; Zonaras, viii.

[171] *Ibid.*

[172] Pliny, viii.

[173] Polybius, i. 30.

[174] *Ibid.*, 31; Diodorus, Frag. Vat. xxiii. 4.

[175] Hooke's Rome.

[176] Polybius, i. 31; Dion Cassius, Fragm. Ursin. 148.

[177] *Ibid.*

[178] Arnold; Polybius; Diodorus, xx. 14; Frag. Vat. xxiii.

[179] Polybius, i. 32.

[180] *Ibid.*, i. 34.

[181] Hooke.

[182] Hooke; Polybius.

[183] Hooke; Appian.

[184] Polybius, i. 34.

[185] Hooke.

[186] Polybius, i. 37; Florus, xi.

[187] Polybius.

[188] Fasti Capit.

[189] Zonaras, viii. 14; Orosius, iv. 9; Polybius, i. 35.

[190] Polybius, i. 40.

[191] Florus, ii.

[192] Pliny.

[193] Florus, ii.; Livy, Epit.

[194] Florus, ii.; Livy, Epit.

[195] Florus, ii.; Livy, Epit. xviii.; Appian Zonaras, vi.

[196] Hooke.

[197] *Ibid.*

[198] Livy, Epit. xviii.; Florus, ii.; Cicero, Off.

[199] Livy, Epit.; Zonaras, viii. 15; A. Gellius, v. 14.

[200] Florus, ii.; Epit. xviii.

[201] Florus, ii.; Val. Max. i. 7; Quintus Curtius. See Appendix. (p. 279)

[202] Polybius, i. 44.

[203] *Ibid.*, 98.

[204] *Ibid.*, 98.

[205] Orosius, ix. 10; Polybius, i. 5; Diodorus, Frag.

[206] See Appendix. (p. 280)

[207] Polybius, i. 55.

[208] Cicero; Val. Max.; Arnold.

[209] Polybius, i. 56.

[210] Livy, Epit.; Suetonius, in Tiberius, § 1.

[211] Polybius, i. 59.

[212] Cicero, De Divinat. ii. 41.

[213] *Ibid.*

[214] Polybius, i. 2; Diodorus, Frag. Vatican, xxiv.; Cornelius Nepos, in Hamilcar, i.

[215] Cor. Nepos, in Hamilcar.

[216] Cor. Nepos, in Hamilcar. See Appendix. (p. 284)

[217] Livy, Epit.; Polybius, i. 66.

[218] See Appendix. (p. 284)

[219] Livy, Epit.

[220] Pliny, Nat. Hist. xxxiii. 44.

[221] Hooke.

CHAPTER VII.

A.U.C. 513-539. B.C. 241-215.

Revolt of the Faliscans.—Noble speech in their favour.—Fraudulent policy of the Senate.—
Secular games.—Fate of Glycias.—Hamilcar's Spanish expedition.—Hannibal's vow.—
Designs of the Romans on Carthage.—Remonstrance of Hanno.—Temple of Janus
closed.—First divorce.—Parental control.—Piracies of Queen Teuta.—Campaigns in
Illyria.—Conclusion of the first Illyrian war.—Human sacrifices.—Roman victory in
Etruria.—Spirited conduct of Flaminius.—His victories.—The Roman champion
Marcellus.—Spolia opima.—Second Illyrian war.—Victories of the consuls Æmilius and
Livius.—Art of surgery.—Destruction of Egyptian oratories by Paulus Æmilius.—State
of Latin literature.—Second Punic war.—Review of Carthaginian conquests in Spain.—
Hannibal's march across the Pyrenees to the Rhone.—The consul Scipio at Marseilles.—
Prepares to defend Italy.—Hannibal's march to Italy.—Arrival in Insubria.—
Consternation at Rome.—Naval victory of Sempronius.—He takes Malta.—Recalled to
Italy.—The consul Manlius defeated.—Battle of Trebia.—Filial piety of young Cornelius
Scipio.—Treason of the Gauls.—Battle of Thrasimenus.—Victory of Hannibal.—Fall of
the consul Flaminius.—Defeat of Centenius.—Brief speech of the Roman prætor
Pomponius.—Fabius Maximus pro-dictator.—Hannibal ravages Campania and
Samnium.—Hannibal's stratagem.—Cold reception of the dictator at Rome.—Rashness
of his colleague Minucius.—Generosity of Fabius.—Scipio's popular government in
Spain.—Varro made consul.—Battle of Cannæ and annihilation of the Roman legions.—
Patriotism of young Cornelius Scipio.—Carthaginian embassy to Rome.—Roman
captives left in slavery.—Conspiracy of Pacuvius.—Capua revolts to Hannibal.—
Patriotism and prudence of Fabius Buteo.—The Gauls defeat the consul Postumius and
his army.—Fabius Maximus made consul.

THE termination of their long contest with the rival republic of Carthage left
the Romans for a few months at peace. This unusual state of repose was
disturbed the following spring by the revolt of the Faliscans,[1] a people who for
more than a hundred and fifty years had been subject to Rome, and who actually
formed a part of the civic tribes. The Romans, therefore, were compelled to send
their consular armies against an enemy within thirty miles of their gates. Quintus
Lutatius and A. Manlius reduced the revolt after a desperate resistance upon the
part of the Faliscans, which lasted six days, a long duration considering the
resources of the people were confined to their own rash personal valour. In this
foolish attempt the unfortunate citizens of Falerii lost their city, all their private
property, and half their territorial B.C. 241. possessions. The Romans, however,
considered the consuls had been far too lenient. Papirius humanely represented
to the people "that the vanquished Faliscans had surrendered themselves to the
faith not to the power of Rome." His noble remark satisfied the Romans, for an
appeal made to the national honour in that age was seldom made in vain.[2]

During three years and a half in which her rival Carthage was engaged in the
mercenary war, Rome gave apparently a fine proof of her faithful adherence to
the peace lately sworn to the Carthaginians, by refusing the gift of Sardinia from
the hired troops of the Punic state, who, following the example of the

mercenaries in Africa, had taken possession of that island. But when the Carthaginians endeavoured to recover it, the Romans pretended that the naval armament was designed to make a descent upon Italy. A declaration of war on the part of Rome followed this misunderstanding, and the Carthaginians were compelled to purchase peace by the surrender of Sardinia, and the payment of 1200 talents.[3] This fraudulent policy was certainly very disgraceful. Hamilcar advised his countrymen to comply with these conditions, but his pacific counsel did not originate from any friendly feeling towards the Romans to whom his hatred had increased tenfold, but from the strong law of necessity. He bequeathed his hatred as a legacy to his son.

The Romans at this time offered their services to Ptolemy Euergetes, king of Egypt, against Antiochus, of Syria, profanely styled the God. Fortunately for Ptolemy he had got rid of his enemy before the arrival of the ambassadors from his dangerous friends, who found they had nothing to do beyond receiving the monarch's thanks.[4] The consular campaigns in Italian Gaul and Liguria were unfortunate. In his first battle the consul Valerius was defeated with great loss, nor did his decisive victory obtain for him a triumph, because he had risked the action before the prætor Genucius Cipus, who had been sent to his assistance, had time to effect a junction with him.

King Hiero came to see the secular games, which were celebrated with great pomp. He made the Romans a munificent present of corn.

The war in Italian Gaul terminated in the quarrel between the Gauls and their allies the people of Transalpine Gaul, with whom they fell out. The consul Lentulus wisely remained a spectator of the contest, which he turned to his own advantage by compelling the nations, who had lost their chiefs, to accept such conditions of peace as he chose to impose.

The other consul, Varus, was ordered to Corsica to reduce that island again to the Roman yoke from which it had revolted. Unable to transport his whole army at once, he sent Claudius Glycias with part of the troops thither, but this officer instead of fighting concluded a disadvantageous peace with the Corsicans. The consul not only annulled the treaty and reduced the island, but gave up Claudius to them. The people, however, who bore no resentment against the man, sent him back to the consul, who despatched him to Rome, where he was put to death in prison by order of the senate. His dead body was dragged by a hook and cast into the Tiber.[5]

Hamilcar sailed for Spain this year, taking with him a young child, the destined scourge of Italy and Rome.[6]

The Romans certainly merited the hatred of the Carthaginians by their renewed attempt to break the peace which had been so dearly purchased by the African republic. They, however, abandoned their design after the spirited remonstrance made by Hanno, the youngest of the ambassadors sent to them by Carthage to complain of their want of faith. "Well then," said he, "if you are resolved to infringe the treaty, put us in the same condition as we were before it was made by giving up Sicily and Sardinia, with which we purchased of you not a short truce but a lasting peace."[7] The senate were ashamed of their double dealing, and the peace was confirmed between the rival republics.[8]

It was upon this occasion that the temple of Janus was shut for the second time since its foundation by Numa. B.C. 236. War however in the dawn of the state was, as we have before noticed, an absolute and fatal necessity, but at this period it had its continuation in ambition. This peace was by no means universal, for the Romans could not maintain their power that very year in Sardinia or Corsica,[9] or even guard their frontiers against the Italian Gauls and Ligurians without the help of arms.[10]

The first instance of a legal divorce took place in the following year by Carvilius Ruga putting away a wife he is said to have loved and esteemed on account of her barrenness, the law allowing this to be a just cause of separation. That it had never been put in force before speaks highly for the morality of the Roman people, conjugal fidelity being the basis of national virtue and honour. The man who destroyed the matrimonial bond for so slight a cause opened a wide door to the corruption of morals and manners which the practice afterwards occasioned.[11]

The Æbutii being tribunes of the people, and perceiving that the jurisprudence of Rome required alteration, proposed abrogating some useless laws of the twelve tables, and founding a new order of magistrates to be called centumvirs. These judges were to be chosen out of every tribe for their general ability and good conduct. They were to assist the prætors, and their decisions were still referable to those magistrates, and related to civil matters only. Though called centumvirs, they amounted to 105, and were afterwards augmented to 180.

In the consulship of M. Æmilius Lepidus and M. Publicius Malleolus, Flaminius, one of the tribunes, occasioned some disturbance in Rome by proposing in comitia that the lands lately taken from the Gauls should be divided among the poorer citizens. Neither the menaces of the consuls, nor the representations of the senate, could silence Flaminius; but what the government could not effect parental authority achieved, for when Flaminius entered the comitia, and mounted the rostrum, to propose the law, his father quietly followed him up, and, taking him by the arm, led him home to the surprise and astonishment of the whole assembly,[12] and the measure fell to the ground.

The subjects of Teuta, regent-queen of Illyria, who governed that country for her young step-son Pinneus, committed a great many acts of piracy upon merchant-vessels belonging to the republic. Whereupon the senate despatched ambassadors demanding redress for this grievance,[13] which was the more annoying on account of the proximity of Illyria to the Roman territories, it being situated upon the shores of the Adriatic directly opposite to Italy. Teuta, whose subjects acted by her authority, gave the ambassadors an insolent reply, importing "that it was never the custom of princes to prevent their subjects from getting what advantage they could from the sea." The Roman ambassadors calmly answered "that they had the excellent custom of punishing private wrongs by public revenge,[14] and that they should find a way to make her change her royal institutions." The queen, incensed at their reply, caused them to be murdered on their homeward journey. A war with Rome necessarily followed this wicked and impolitic action. The senate erected statues to the memory of the murdered ambassadors, and demanded the persons of the assassins, which being refused by Teuta, the consuls Postumius Albinus and Fulvius Centæmalus, were sent with a fleet and an army to invade Illyria.

Teuta insolently sent her fleet to plunder the Grecian coast, which seized upon Corcyra (now Curzola), before Fulvius could relieve that place. But Demetrius, who commanded the garrison, hearing that Teuta was displeased with him, surrendered the city to the Roman consul. Postumius landed his forces, and took the strong city of Apollonia, of which he made Demetrius governor. While he was thus employed Fulvius, his colleague, cleared the seas of the Illyrian pirates, and then, his year being out, returned to Rome. Postumius was continued as pro-consul to the great annoyance of Queen Teuta, who, being afraid of continuing the war, sent to Rome to solicit for peace, which was granted her upon such hard conditions that she gave up the regency B.C. 228. of her son to Demetrius of Pharos, the Roman governor of Corcyra;[15] a measure of absolute necessity, for the Romans insisted upon the surrender of the greater part of Illyria, obliged the Illyrians to pay them annual tribute, and would not permit more than two unarmed ships belonging to the queen to sail beyond Lissos, a seaport on the confines of Macedon and Illyria.

The Greek states, which had suffered greatly from the piracies of this female sovereign, received the ambassadors Postumius sent to explain the cause of the Illyrian war very kindly, and the Corinthians invited them to be present at the Isthmian games. At Athens, that people conferred upon the Romans the privileges of citizenship, and admitted them to the Eleusinian mysteries. Thus honourably and successfully ended the first Illyrian war.[16] Seldom have the annals of Rome recorded a foreign war undertaken on such just grounds.[17]

The insurrection of the Italian Gauls, and the injury done to the capitol by lightning, led to the cruel sacrifice of two Gauls and the same number of Greeks, in the ox-market, to avert an old prediction, found in the Sybilline books, which declared that these nations would possess Rome. The pontifices, by making these persons occupy living graves in Rome, pretended to fulfil the prophecy without injury to the republic.[18]

In Etruria, the Roman prætor and his army fell into a snare laid by the Gauls, and, after his defeat, entrenched himself on a hill at night, expecting every moment to be destroyed by the enemy. The consul Æmilius marched to his relief, but the Gauls retreating from the consular army, fell in with that commanded by Atilius Regulus. In the battle the Roman consul was killed, but the contest was maintained gallantly by his lieutenant, while Æmilius was fighting with the allies of the Gauls in the rear. The victory was won by the Romans, who took ten thousand captives, and one of the Gallic kings, the other destroyed himself. The consul Æmilius was granted a triumph.[19]

The senate having determined to make Italian Gaul a Roman province, sent the consuls Flaminius and Furius Philus with two armies to accomplish the object, but recalled them after they had crossed the Po, and were in sight of the

Insubrian army. The recall of the consuls originated in the superstitious fears of the Roman people. Sights had been seen in the air in Etruria; three moons had appeared at Ariminum; at Picenum the waters of a river were changed as red as blood; and all Italy had been shaken by the earthquake that overturned the Colossus of Rhodes.[20] These wonders no doubt originated in the commotions of the earth, and the electric state of the atmosphere at the time; but the fact of a vulture having chosen to alight in the forum appears to have excited the fears of the superstitious Romans more than the marvels already quoted. Aware that some defect in the augural ceremonies would be discovered to render their election invalid, the consuls did not open the despatches till after they had gained the battle in which they were about to engage.[21] Flaminius, when he had read the letters, quietly remarked to his more timid colleague, "that the victory proved the correctness of the auspices;" adding, "that he should continue the war and teach the Roman people a useful lesson, that they might not be deceived by auguries or anything else."[22] Flaminius continued the campaign with considerable advantage, while the consul Fulvius remained encamped, afraid of the consequences of his disobedience. Upon their return the consuls met with a cold reception, and with difficulty obtained their triumph.

The celebrated Claudius Marcellus and Cornelius Scipio continued the war with the Gauls. The Insubrians demanded peace, but this was refused them; upon which they hired an army of Gæsatæ, who, with their king Viridomarus crossed the Alps to the assistance of their allies, and passing the Po entered Liguria, which formed a part of the Roman territories. Near Clastidium the two armies met, and Viridomarus challenged Marcellus to single combat, when he fell by the hand of the consul. The Gæsatæ discouraged by the death of their B.C. 223. king instantly fled.[23] Mediolanum (now Milan) upon the report of the success of Marcellus, surrendered to Cornelius Scipio. The whole of Insubria and Liguria were united into a Roman province and called Cis-alpine Gaul. Italy became Roman from this time. The triumph of Marcellus was remarkable for being the last in which the spolia opima were carried, for the victorious consul bore upon his shoulders as a trophy the arms and clothing he had won from Viridomarus.[24]

Nothing remarkable took place in the annals of the republic till the second Illyrian war, which was caused by the piracies committed by Demetrius of Pharos, whom the senate had made the guardian of the young king Pinneus. Being sure of the protection of king Philip of Macedon, Demetrius set the Romans at defiance. After the census had been taken, the consuls Livius Salinator and Paulus Æmilius undertook the Illyrian war, and embarking for Illyria quickly reduced the country. The defeat of his army and the storm of Pharos compelled Demetrius to fly to Macedon. The Romans did not deprive the young sovereign of his dominions on account of the misconduct of an officer whom they had appointed for his guardian.[25] The consuls returned to Rome for their triumphs, but they were both called to account respecting the amount of the booty taken in this war. Paulus Æmilius cleared himself, and Livius was condemned by every tribe but one, the Mævian, an affront he never forgave.

The introduction of surgery into Rome by Archagathus of Peloponnesus, was one of the events of this year. This surgeon was built a shop at the public expense, but his method of cure was severe, and his art fell into disuse.[26] Roman colonies were planted at Placentia and Cremona, and the sanctuaries dedicated to the Egyptian deities were commanded to be destroyed, because one of the laws of the twelve tables forbad the worship of strange gods. Paulus Æmilius, throwing off his consular robe, took a hatchet in his hand and levelled them to the ground; no person but himself daring to brave the anger of the foreign deities.[27]

Before entering upon the eventful period of the second Punic war, some account of Rome and the state of her literature may be interesting to the reader. The art of painting was introduced by Fabius Pictor before the existence of Latin literature was known in any other form than the ancient traditionary lays, of which Livy is supposed to have made considerable use in his Decades.

Rome owed her first drama to Livius Andronicus, a foreigner, who was the freedman of Livius Salinator, and the preceptor of his patron's children: he was probably a Greek captive, but whether taken in the Illyrian war, or captured from the Greek cities of Italy, may be a question. He acted a part in his own tragedies. The first drama ever performed at Rome took place in the year 514. His tragedy of Ulysses was considered his best work.[28]

Cneius Nævius, a Campanian, who had served in the Roman army, composed his first tragedy five years after Andronicus had given the Romans a Latin drama. He was a soldier by profession, having served in the first Punic war. He composed the history of his campaigns in Saturnian verse, and this poem is supposed to be the first Latin composition deserving of the name of history.[29] It was from him Virgil took the idea of the shield of Æneas.[30] This ancient Latin poet wrote many plays. Some of these productions were composed in his captivity in the house of Metellus, the consul, whom he had offended in a line[31] which has come down to our own times. The proud Metelli were a plebeian family, and though bearing the stamp of nature's nobility upon them, were not sufficiently magnanimous to overlook the satirical allusion to their recent consular rank; nor did they limit their displeasure to confining the satirist, they drove him from Rome. Nævius died at Utica, in Africa. A few fragments alone remain of this father of Latin history and poetry.

Till this time the Sibylline books comprised the written literature of Rome, but being in Greek hexameters could only be read by the learned persons who had their guardianship. We have already noticed the probability that B.C. 228. these mysterious volumes contained some of the scriptural prophecies, interspersed with heathen oracles and other superstitious matters.

Quintus Fabius, the Roman annalist, was about to play his part in the eventful drama of his own times, which he afterwards commemorated in his Greek history of Rome.

Flaminius, in his censorship 534, had made the fine road called after him, the Flaminian way between Rome and Ariminum (Rimini), a noble work of great public utility. He also built a circus in the Campus Martius for the use of the Roman people, whose fondness for the national games was an increasing taste, though it had not in this age become a passion. The peaceful works of several illustrious censors long outlasted the conquests of the mighty republic,[32] and indeed are still extant and useful.

The habits and customs of the Roman people were still frugal and simple. Luxury had not yet given to the citizen of Rome any covering for the head. The people seldom partook of more than two daily meals. This frugality at first originated in necessity, which use strengthened into habit. Much of the greatness of the ancient Roman arose out of his temperate use of all animal enjoyments.

Ancient Rome has been raised from the dust and ashes of centuries by the Chevalier Bunsen and its historian Arnold, whose researches have brought the early republican city before the modern reader's eyes just as she existed in the fifth and sixth centuries.[33]

With chariot races and horse races the Roman people had been familiar since the institution of the great games, and the charioteers were already distinguished by their colours. The Roman people were still simple, austere, and virtuous. Poverty did not debar the patriot from serving his country, and it had its pride as well as wealth. The republic was uncorrupted by foreign customs or foreign gold, for the period of national virtue had not yet passed away. In the science of war the Romans had already acquired some knowledge and experience from Pyrrhus, but it was to their great master, Hannibal, that they owed that pre-eminence which gave the greater part of the known world to their dominion. The record of the second Punic war, therefore, comprises the most momentous and interesting portion of the history of the Roman republic, one too no longer obscured by the mist of mythic gloom, but transmitted to us by Polybius the friend and contemporary of Scipio Africanus, the conqueror of him who conquered Italy but did not conquer Rome. We are now arrived at the period when the great struggle for mastery took place between the republics of Rome and Carthage. The great Carthaginian, Hamilcar, carried with him to Africa an undying hatred to the Roman name, that hatred he transmitted to his young son Hannibal. Having terminated the tremendous Mercenary or Inexpiable war, the exigencies of Carthage made Hamilcar turn his arms against Spain, a country inhabited by a race of brave, bold, but uncivilised men, from whom he hoped to raise an army after he had succeeded in conquering and civilising them. Nor were the hopes of the Carthaginian limited to the defence of his own country, for, being one of a city of merchants, he considered the commerce of Spain as the most valuable fruit of his intended conquest. The expedition of this truly great man was eminently successful; during the nine years he passed in Spain, he both conquered and civilised the Spaniards. His assassination in Lusitania[34] deprived his son of the benefit of his experience, though Hannibal, then about eighteen, found in his brother-in-law, Hasdrubal, a faithful guardian. This commander built New Carthage,[35] the Carthagena of modern history. His wisdom and moderation won the affections of the native princes, to whom the invaders brought with commerce the arts of peace. The conquests and dominion of Hasdrubal reached the ears and excited the jealousy of the rival republic, who sent ambassadors to induce him to sign a treaty by which the Carthaginians were restrained from carrying their arms beyond the river Iberus. Hasdrubal did not scruple to subscribe to the agreement because he knew many years must elapse before the

Carthaginians could infringe it. After he had governed in Spain eight years with great success he was murdered by a slave, and his young relative Hannibal B.C. 228. was elected by the army in his room, and their choice was ratified immediately by the senate of Carthage.[36]

Hannibal was not a man very likely to observe the treaty Hasdrubal had made with the Romans. He quickly subdued the nations between him and the river Iberus, till nothing but Saguntum lay within its prescribed boundary. An embassy from Rome warned the young commander that this city was under the protection of the Romans, and Hannibal was also reminded of the treaty made between them and Hasdrubal. Hannibal, who had inherited from his father a deep hatred to the Romans, received the embassy with great haughtiness; remarking, "that the Romans had treated the Saguntines very ill, for when their arbitration had been requested by that people, in a matter respecting a sedition, they had put several magistrates to death, and otherwise misconducted themselves. He added that the Carthaginians were always the friends of the distressed, and that he did not intend to let this injustice pass unrevenged." The ambassadors departed, and Hannibal laid siege to Saguntum, and in spite of his declaration to the Romans, the oppressed Saguntines, he professed to assist, defended their city with unparalleled bravery. While thus employed, another embassy was despatched to him, but he would not permit the envoys to advance, declaring "that he could not ensure them a safe conduct, nor had he time to give them audience."[37]

The news of the fall of Saguntum was carried by the Roman ambassadors to Carthage, and Hanno, the enemy of Hannibal's family, enforced their complaint to the senate. In a flaming oration he declared, that the ruins of Saguntum would fall upon Carthage, and even advised the senate to give up the conqueror to the Romans, and to renew the treaty. The sight of the wealth sent by Hannibal to Carthage, rendered the oration inspired by hatred useless. The senate gave this unsatisfactory reply to the Roman ambassadors, "That the war was not begun by Hannibal, and that the Roman people would act unjustly towards Carthage if they preferred the recent friendship of the Saguntines to their ancient one with the Carthaginians."[38] The Roman senate understood the answer in its true sense, and made immense preparations for war. Yet the Romans did not come to an open rupture with Carthage, for the senate sent a third embassy thither to demand satisfaction for the destruction of Saguntum. Receiving no reply from the senate, the eldest ambassador, gathering up the skirt of his robe, said, "Here I bring you peace or war; take which you will." "Give us which you please," was the general reply of the Carthaginian senators. "I give you war, then," answered the Roman ambassador, letting his robe fall to the ground. "We accept it, and will maintain it with the same spirit," was the emphatic rejoinder of the Carthaginian senate.[39]

The business of the ambassadors did not terminate with their unsuccessful negotiations at Carthage. They received orders to cross into Spain, to dissuade the nations on the northern side of the Iberus from entering into alliance with Hannibal. The Bargusians alone received them favourably. The rest of the nations bade them seek for friends among those who had never heard of the desolation of Saguntum, for the miserable fate of that city would be a warning to the Spanish nations to put no trust in Roman faith or friendship. The Roman envoys then passed into Gaul with the same object in view.[40] When they solicited that people to refuse Hannibal and his army a passage through their country into Italy, their request was received with rude bursts of laughter: so strange did it seem to them that they should be expected to expose their lands to the risk of being plundered by Hannibal's troops to preserve those of strangers. It was some time before the elder part of the assembly could silence the younger, from whom these expressions of contemptuous derision proceeded. They then replied, "That neither had the Romans deserved so well, nor the Carthaginians so ill at their hands, that they should take up arms in behalf of either; but added, they had heard the Romans had taken from their countrymen B.C. 228. their possessions in Italy, and had constrained them to pay tribute."[41] The ambassadors after this repulse repaired to Marseilles, which place was in alliance with them. The Marsigli informed them that Hannibal had been beforehand with the Gauls, to whom he had given gold and alluring promises. The envoys returned to Rome much mortified by their failure.[42] Hannibal settled himself for the winter at New Carthage, from whence he despatched a great body of Spanish troops for the defence of Africa, in exchange for fifteen thousand Africans; which he put under the command of his brother, Hasdrubal, who was to govern Spain during his command in Italy. In the spring he took the field at the head of ninety thousand men, and commenced his march towards the river Iberus. He had taken care to secure a passage through Gaul before he put his vast army in motion.[43] He quickly subdued the nations between that river and the Pyrenees, leaving an officer named Hanno with an army to keep the conquered country in awe and watch the Bargusians, who were friendly towards the Romans. The difficulty of the passage over the Pyrenees intimidating some of Hannibal's Spanish soldiers he wisely dismissed them, with fair words, to their homes. He passed the mountains into Gaul with fifty-nine thousand men, but found the people on the other side with arms in their hands, ready to give him battle. His gold and conciliating speeches induced these tribes to give up their hostile intentions, nor did he meet with any opposition till he reached the banks of the Rhone, where he found the Gauls upon the eastern shore bent upon barring his passage. He hired, however, a great many boats from those tribes inhabiting the western side, who being a commercial people were extremely desirous of his absence. Here Hannibal felled timber and constructed numerous floats.[44] Hanno by his directions crossed the river higher up, and fired the camp of the hostile Gauls, on the east side of the river, which he did very successfully. As soon as Hannibal saw the smoke he commenced the embarkation of his army in the face of the Gauls, who uttered dreadful howls, brandishing their weapons in defiance. The shouts of Hanno's solders behind them occasioned them, however, to turn round, when perceiving their camp in flames they fled in confusion to their native villages.[45]

The Roman consul Cornelius hoping to prevent Hannibal from leaving Spain, embarked with his army at Pisa,[46] and arrived safely after a voyage of five days at Marseilles, where he heard that the Carthaginian general had already crossed the Rhone. The news appeared incredible to him therefore he sent three hundred horsemen, under the care of some Gauls belonging to his allies, to ascertain the truth of the report. These scouts encountered near the camp of Hannibal five hundred Numidian cavalry, whereupon a sharp skirmish took place on the spot, in which the Romans gained the victory.[47] Upon the return of the detachment Cornelius Scipio landed all his troops and marched in search of Hannibal, but that great commander had passed the river three days before the Roman consul had reached its banks. He then embarked his army, and sending the greater part into Spain with his brother Cneius, sailed for Italy, hoping to reach the Alps before Hannibal could cross them.

Hannibal continued to advance with great celerity towards the Alps, through that part of the country called the island that lay between the Rhone and another river. The name of that nameless stream has occasioned a great many disputes among learned men, it is sufficient for us that Hannibal passed through the country it watered, and arrived in time to prevent a battle between two brother princes who were contending for its possession; Hannibal decided the matter by espousing the cause of Blancas, the eldest prince, who out of gratitude clothed his troops, gave them provisions and arms, and undertook to guide them with his army to the passage of the Alps.[48] Nothing could be more fortunate for Hannibal than the assistance of his new ally at such a critical moment as this.[49]

The natural difficulties of the passage[50] were augmented B.C. 228. by the attacks of the fierce mountain tribes who, posting themselves in the heights above, hurled stones and darts upon the ascending army. Their howls frightened the horses, who ran back upon the beasts of burden, whom they rolled with their leaders down the precipices. Hannibal, knowing that the loss of his baggage would involve that of his army, and noticing that his assailants retired to their homes at night to some town, sent detachments at dusk to seize the heights from whence his march had been interrupted, and to make themselves master of the place. When the town was taken he found corn for his army, and recovered his missing men and baggage.[51] For three days he pursued his march without interruption, when he was met by other Gauls, who brought olive branches and garlands in testimony of good-will, and offered to guide the Carthaginian army across the mountains.[52] Hannibal accepted their offer, but he took hostages for their good faith, and arranged his march in such a manner that his baggage and beasts of burden were secure from attack or depredation. It was well he did so, for his new friends conducted his army into a close defile overhung by rocks, where they suddenly deserted him, joining their ambushed countrymen on the crags above. His loss in this attack was great, and he was obliged to encamp upon a flat rock all night to defend his baggage.[53] Fortunately when his enemies saw the elephants they ran away in great fear and confusion. The next day was like the former passed in a series of skirmishes and disasters, but the great Carthaginian and his army, upon the ninth day of his difficult enterprise, gained the summit and looked down upon the fruitful plains of Italy. Here he halted, that his troops might have a few hours' repose and the stragglers and wounded come up. The lost horses, mules, and elephants, arrived safely at the camp, without any guide but their own sagacity, having followed the line of march.[54] The sight of the new fallen snow, the autumnal season, and the hardships they had encountered and must still encounter, struck every man but the intrepid leader with dismay, who pointing to the fertile plains of Italy cheered their drooping courage with these animated words: "There, cast your eyes upon those fruitful fields; the Gauls who inhabit them are our friends, and wait impatiently for our coming. You have scaled not only the walls of Italy but those of Rome. What remains to be done is all smoothness and descent; one battle, or at most two, and the capital of Italy must be ours."[55]

After two days' rest the camp was broken up and the dangerous march commenced. Henceforward the Carthaginian army had to contend not with the mountain people but with the savage grandeur of nature, who opposing her icy ramparts to the ambition of man seemed to stand guard over the fair plains below. The descent appeared as dangerous as the ascent had been difficult, the slippery nature of the ground, the steep precipices, and the cold occasioned many miserable disasters attended with great loss of life. At length the army reached a place which they could not pass. Hannibal himself ran to learn the cause of the delay, and saw at once that if to proceed was impossible, to go back was equally so. In this emergency his great mind devised a remedy, for his coolness in time of danger was never surpassed by any thing but his activity. He found a place in which he might encamp, cleared away the snow, and ordered steps to be cut in the solid rock, by the means of which his army might continue their march.[56] As soon as the passage would allow his horses and cattle to descend he sent them to feed in the green valleys beneath. But the elephants required more room and it was four days before the Numidians, to whom the task was assigned, could get them through. At length the wonder was accomplished, and Hannibal and his army stood upon the plains below.[57]

Hannibal's celebrated march took fifteen days in its accomplishment.[58] It was accomplished exactly five months and a half from the time he left New Carthage, in which period he had traversed more than a thousand miles.[59] The men who composed his army bore evident B.C. 228. marks of the toils and hardships they had endured. Famine and fatigue were written upon their countenances, so that they rather resembled a horde of savages than what they were, a brave and well-disciplined army.[60] The startling fact that Hannibal was in Italy filled Rome with consternation; but he was besieging its towns before the Romans were aware of his presence in that country.

Sempronius was recalled when about to invade Africa to assist his colleague. This consul had gained a naval victory over the Carthaginians, besides taking the island of Malta. He was about to drive the Carthaginian fleet from the coast of Calabria, when he received the commands of the senate. He entrusted his fleet to his lieutenant Pomponius, and Æmilius, the prætor of Sicily, and set sail with the rest of the squadron for Ariminum.[61]

The discontented Gauls, near the Roman colonies of Placentia and Cremona, were in open revolt at the time of Hannibal's expedition into Italy. They rose and drove the Roman population to Mutina (Modena), which place they immediately besieged.[62] The prætor Manlius hastened to its relief, but fell into the ambush laid for him by the Gauls, and lost a great part of his army. The enemy followed him to Tanetum and besieged him there. Notwithstanding their late victory the

Gauls, upon the approach of the other prætor Atilius,[63] who marched from Rome to succour Manlius, broke up the siege and fled. The Roman legion effected a junction with Scipio at Placentia, and the army, with the consul at their head, threw a bridge over the Ticinus, and advanced to meet Hannibal. Both generals encouraged their soldiers by orations. Scipio appealed to the feelings of men who loved their families and worshipped their country; Hannibal to warriors for whom there could be no retreat, no middle path between death and victory.[64] The absolute necessity of victory, on which the preservation of the invaders depended, caused the defeat of the consular army. The gallantry and filial piety of his young son, Publius Scipio, the same who in after years acquired the surname of Africanus, preserved the life of the wounded consul, who fled with his routed army across the plains of the Po, pursued by Hannibal, who found the bridge destroyed by the Romans, only reaching the spot in time to take prisoners six hundred men who had just completed the work of its destruction. Two days after he passed the Po by a bridge of boats,[65] when finding the Romans in sight he offered them battle, but, being unable to bring them to an engagement, encamped some miles from them.

When a country is entered by a foreign enemy the chances are in favour of the invaded, if they make a prudent use of their means of defence. Thus the annals of the world will show more routed invading armies than victorious ones. The Romans displayed more rash courage than prudence in meeting their enemies in the field, instead of availing themselves of their better knowledge of the localities and climate of Italy. To consummate bravery and consummate military talent, the Carthaginian general added consummate forecast, a quality in which the Romans were deficient. They took no precautions, like men ignorant of their skilful and wary foe whose youth was prematurely endowed with the wisdom of maturer years. Scipio in attempting to stop the advance of Hannibal had only displayed proper activity and spirit, but his defeat had given him some experience by which he resolved to profit. The treacherous massacre of some Romans in the night by those Gauls who were serving in his army,[66] might perhaps induce him to cross the Trebia and encamp in a strong position on a height above that river; but the advice he gave Sempronius to abstain from fighting with Hannibal, and to leave the Carthaginian to strive with the cold and stormy season as his worst opponent,[67] was the wisdom of a general who had measured swords with the greatest commander of the age, and knew that Rome could not yet produce his match. He did not then foresee that in his son he was educating the military rival and conqueror of that man whom he considered the elements alone were able to subdue. Modern defensive warfare has acted upon the counsel given by Scipio to Sempronius. It was this wise policy that drove Napoleon, the Hannibal B.C. 228. of our times, from Russia, and gave his invading legions icy tombs in a distant region. Sempronius rashly disregarded the prudence of his wounded colleague, whose defeat he probably imputed to want of skill. His recent conquest of the island of Malta and the arduous march he had accomplished, traversing the whole length of Italy in forty days, inspired him with too much self-confidence to attend to the defeated consul. From Ariminum (Rimini) he marched through a level country undisturbed by Hannibal, who was stationed between the Romans and Placentia, and reached the left bank of the Trebia, where Scipio was strongly posted. Hannibal, who was aware of the condition of Scipio, must have wished the junction to take place between the consular armies or he would have prevented it. His military genius was too transcendent to have made such an oversight, and the pains he took to draw Sempronius over the river proves that the consul owed his uninterrupted march rather to design than accident. Sempronius sent assistance to the neighbouring Gauls, whom the Numidian cavalry were plundering, but his success did not prevent a body of these light horsemen from crossing the river and showing themselves in the vicinity of the Roman camp.[68] Their giving way before the Roman cavalry and crossing the river seems to have been the signal of battle, for the consul issued orders to the whole army to cross the Trebia for immediate action. Cold, wet, hungry, and weary as they were, these brave and dauntless Romans did not hesitate to meet a well-fed and well-appointed army, having their own camp in their rear for retreat, should the fortune of the day go against them.[69] Hannibal, who had posted his youngest brother Mago, with two thousand men in a dry water-course, saw with pleasure the Romans pass the ambush, without perceiving the snare. After which he marched out to meet them, being only a mile in advance of his camp. In the early part of the battle of Trebia the elephants and cavalry of Hannibal easily defeated the cavalry of the consular armies; but the conflict between the infantry was so sternly maintained that the loss of the battle of Trebia was mainly owing to the sudden attack of Mago on the Roman rear.[70] The wings already routed fled towards the river, whereupon the legions, surrounded as they were, cut their way through the enemy, and made for Placentia. The Roman cavalry suffered dreadfully, being mostly slaughtered before they reached the river. The Carthaginians made no attempt to pursue their victory through the cold and rapid Trebia, for the weather was very inclement, and many men and most of the elephants perished on that victorious plain.[71] It was owing to this diversion made by the elements in his favour that Scipio was able to gather together the wreck of the combined army into the asylum of his camp. He recrossed the river in the night, passed the quarters of the victorious Carthaginians, if not undiscovered, at least unmolested, and gained Placentia without any untoward accident.[72] The battle of Trebia, with which Hannibal's first Italian campaign ended, was fought in mid-winter; and he had won his quarters in Cis-alpine Gaul by his victorious sword. He did not place any faith in the people with whom the inclemency of the season had made him a sojourner. When the Gauls, who had risen upon the Romans in their own camp, brought to him the heads of their officers and proffered their services, Hannibal gave them a courteous reception, but he declined their services, veiling his disgust at their treachery under an assurance that they would do him more good by persuading their countrymen to join him than by entering his army themselves. He felt he could place no confidence in such faithless men.[73] If the Cis-alpine Gauls had wished well to the Carthaginians they speedily changed their regard into hatred. A great army in quarters, even in a country friendly to them, soon becomes an intolerable nuisance. The Gauls were weary of supporting the troops of Hannibal, and gave sufficient proof of their discontent to make him desirous of removing his camp to Etruria, by crossing the Apennines. His attempt was rendered abortive by the dreadful wintry storms which compelled him to return.[74] Though Hannibal had endeavoured to conciliate the Gauls by dismissing without ransom those he had taken prisoners in the towns he had captured, or in the armies he had defeated; yet he certainly distrusted them, seldom wearing B.C. 217. the same dress while he remained in their country, assuming also false hair of different colours. He even frequently concealed his youthful features beneath the grizzly locks of old age.[75]

In Spain the Romans were more fortunate than in Italy, for Cneius Scipio had defeated Hanno, and subdued the nations between the Iberus and the Pyrenees.[76]

The Romans raised new levies, garrisoned their towns, and solicited the aid of Hiero, of Syracuse, which that generous prince and firm ally immediately accorded them. They equipped a fleet to guard the coast, and took every precaution that prudence suggested to prevent the farther advance of Hannibal. They elected Flaminius and Servilius Geminus to the consulship. The first was a man of talent, and in choosing him a second time for the chief magistracy, the people hoped to provide a leader fitted for such a crisis; but the high rank of Servilius must have been the cause of his election, since his name was undistinguished.

Hannibal, who was tired of his winter quarters, forced a passage over the Apennines into Etruria, an undertaking attended with great difficulty and loss, owing to the marshy nature of the ground lying below these mountains. The cold and damp affected him so severely, that he lost the sight of one of his eyes. The consul Servilius marched to Ariminum (Rimini) from whence Scipio departed to Spain, of which country he was made pro-consul. Flaminius superseded Sempronius in Etruria, but being encamped near Aretrium,[77] and suffering Hannibal to pass near him on his way to central Italy, the Carthaginian wasted the country he traversed on every side, making his march resemble a predatory descent upon a wealthy and defenceless people, rather than an expedition whose object was the destruction of Rome and the conquest of Italy. Flaminius, though brave, was no match for the able Hannibal. His mistake regarding the object of his opponent, prevented him from summoning his colleague, to whom he communicated nothing respecting the march of the enemy, beyond the fact that he had crossed the Apennines and was in Etruria.[78] He followed closely the steps of Hannibal till his opponent had made choice of a proper spot for the grave of the Roman army. He found it in a defile near the lake Thrasimenus, now called Lago di Perugia, and then bent his great military genius to draw his rash enemy into the snare laid for him. Aware of the defect of Flaminius, whom he had heard was a rash hot-headed man, he began to burn and waste the lands of Cortona, which he did to enrage the consul and induce him to fight.[79] Flaminius needed not any exciting cause to do what he had already determined upon doing, so, slighting the advice of his officers, he followed the army of Hannibal, who was on his way to Rome, between the lake Thrasimenus and the town of Cortona.[80] The Carthaginian perceiving that the ground was favourable for him, took up his post upon a hill above a narrow valley leading from the lake. On the eminences upon the right he posted his slingers and light-armed troops; on the left his cavalry and the Gauls. But the advancing consul had not only to contend against the skill of one of the greatest generals the world ever produced, since even the powers of nature warred against him; for he encamped at night by the lake shore, and in the morning found himself encompassed by a dense fog, (the precursor of the coming earthquake,) which veiled Hannibal and his army from his sight. He, supposing the vapoury curtain was nothing beyond the mists common to vales in the vicinity of lakes and hills, set forward in search of Hannibal, under the impression that the fog was in his favour by concealing his movements from the Carthaginians. He commenced ascending the hills, when the consular army was suddenly beset by an unseen foe. The Romans did not give way under circumstances so disastrous and unforeseen. They fought not only with resolution but with fury, like men resolved to defend Italy and Rome to their last breath. The earthquake that overthrew many of the Italian cities, and levelled mountains, and displaced rivers, was unheeded by the combatants.[81] "None felt stern nature rocking at his feet" while engaged in this sanguinary battle, in which the brave despair of the Romans, and the courage of the Carthaginians, long strove for mastery in B.C. 217. that fatal valley. But Hannibal's generalship prevailed, and Flaminius found, with fifteen thousand Romans, an honourable grave at Thrasimenus; claiming for his unfortunate gallantry the tears of the country he loved, and in whose defence he died. Of the remains of the consular army, six thousand men cleft their way through the Carthaginian host with their swords, while fifteen thousand more, who had taken up their quarters in a village, were compelled to surrender to Maharbal,[82] being completely surrounded, without food or water. Hannibal showed little magnanimity on this occasion to the Romans. He denied Maharbal's right to give quarter to his vanquished enemies, leaving the shadow of death to impend over valiant men, whose only crime was the rash boldness of their fallen leader. His reproaches were in as bad taste as his threats—both were unworthy of him. To the Italians and Gauls found in the hostile ranks he shewed a generous policy. To them he announced himself as the deliverer of Italy, giving them freedom and courteous words.[83] He caused a search to be made for the slain consul, who owed his death to a Gallic horseman, who, it was said, singled him out, crying out to his countrymen as he speared him, "So perish the man who slaughtered our brethren, and robbed us of the fields of our forefathers."[84] It was no difficult matter to discover the person of a Roman consul, whose purple or scarlet[85] dress distinguished him on the field of battle. Probably Flaminius, after his fall, was despoiled of his robe, for his body was not found, though his victor wished to give his remains an honourable burial.[86] Hannibal only lost fifteen hundred men at the battle of Thrasimenus. To thirty of his own dead he gave a solemn funeral; the Gauls, who comprised the greater part of his slain, were either interred by their own people or left to the wolf and vulture. At Rome, where confused accounts were received of the defeat, the people ran in crowds into the forum to hear the fatal truth. The prætor Pomponius announced it from the rostra in these brief but emphatic words, "We are vanquished in a great battle." The tidings of the victory of Hannibal over Centenius, whom the other consul, Servilius, had despatched to join his colleague with four thousand cavalry, completed the disastrous news of the day. In this emergency the Roman senate created a pro-dictator, and in choosing Fabius Maximus Cunctator they showed great judgment; for Fabius was a man who combined prudence and foresight with the courage of a Roman commander. As the army of Servilius was allotted to him he only raised two legions; but learning that the Carthaginian fleet had intercepted some vessels carrying out provisions to Cneius Scipio's army in Spain, he ordered Servilius to arm the ships at Rome and Ostia for the protection of the coast of Etruria. He then commenced his march to meet Hannibal, not, however, with the intention of fighting him, but to save his country by keeping that great captain in check. Hannibal was allowed to waste the country from the Tiber to Spoletum unchecked by a Roman army. Spoletum closed its gates against the terrible Numidian horsemen, unawed by the dreadful renown of the Carthaginian leader.[87] Polybius and Livy have described the foreign races which the march of Hannibal's army brought together on the left bank of the Tiber, as "fierce guests, whose wild war cry and dark forms, armed with long lances and mounted on fiery steeds, carried death and dismay in their fleet course throughout the undefended country."[88]

Hannibal clothed and armed his people with the Roman spoils won from them in the fatal defiles of Thrasimenus.[89] The victor being near the coast of the Adriatic, availed himself of the opportunity his proximity afforded to send despatches to Carthage with the intelligence of his success. How proud must the conqueror of Italy have felt while recording his triumphant march from the Alps, and triple victories over the armies of the rival republic to Carthage B.C. 217. whose drooping fortunes his valiant arm and powerful intellect had raised from the dust to such a proud position. After relating his exploits to the Carthaginian senate, he marched into Apulia, which he ravaged, when, finding that Fabius was encamped near Æcæ, a town of that country, he drew near the trench that surrounded the camp and offered him battle. Of this challenge Fabius took no notice, to the astonishment and indignation both of Hannibal and the Roman soldiers themselves.[90] Minucius, his master of the horse, spirited up his men to demand to be led against the Carthaginians. But nothing could induce Fabius to risk the chance of a battle. He contented himself with cutting off the enemy in small parties. Hannibal marched into Samnium, which he pillaged, and then entered Campania near the pass of Mount Callicula, contrary to his intentions, for he ordered his guides to lead him by that of Casinum. His imperfect pronunciation of the word which they mistook occasioned them to bring him to Casilinum, a town situated on Mount Vulturnus at the foot of Mount Callicula. Enraged at the mistake, he ordered the principal guide to be crucified, to make the others more careful for the future. A tremendous instance of severity for an error originating from himself.[91] While the Carthaginians were plundering Campania, Fabius pitched his camp upon Mount Massichus, from whence he witnessed the spoliation of this rich and beautiful country. His soldiers enraged called him the pedagogue of Hannibal, and Minucius ridiculed him openly, asking "if Fabius chose the situation of his camp that he might hide himself in heaven and cover himself with clouds?" To these taunts Fabius calmly replied, "that he was not a man likely to change his resolution through dread of sarcasm or reproach," adding "that it was no inglorious thing for him to fear for the safety of his country." He never altered his conduct this summer, "declaring that the man who suffered himself to be influenced by the calumnies of others, was not fit to command."[92]

Hannibal, like a prudent general, began to think of his winter quarters, for Campania was a wine country, and did not grow sufficient corn to provide for the wants of a great army. He resolved to return by the same mountain pass that had admitted him. This Fabius took every possible precaution to prevent by posting four thousand men to guard the outlet, and encamping with his army upon Mount Callicula, which commanded it, taking care to garrison the town of Casilinum on the other side the pass.

Finding himself thus barred in by the Roman army, Hannibal delivered himself by the following singular stratagem. At night he ordered Hasdrubal to select two thousand of the strongest oxen, and to direct his men to fasten to the horns of these creatures faggots of dry wood and to bring them to the foot of a hill not far from the mountain pass. Then the herdsmen were to fire the wood and endeavour to drive the cattle to the top of the height. The light-armed infantry were to follow them as quickly as possible. The cruel device was promptly executed, and Hannibal marched his army to the pass. The Romans seeing the fires, and supposing that the Carthaginians intended to escape over the heights, quitted the pass in haste to prevent their design, and hurried to the hills above in search of the enemy, while Hannibal and his army cleared the gorge. The oxen, mad with pain, ran about firing the brushwood, which prevented the Romans from engaging with the light infantry.[93]

Before daylight Hannibal sent a large body of Spaniards to the relief of his troops. These brought them off successfully, to the great mortification of the Romans. This stratagem was a standing jest against Fabius,[94] who, notwithstanding the ridicule it occasioned, never deviated from the line of defensive warfare he had first adopted.

Hannibal, after ravaging Samnium, returned to Apulia and seized Geronium, where he took up his head-quarters. Fabius, who had followed his march, stationed himself at Larinum, from whence he was summoned to Rome to assist at a solemn sacrifice. Before quitting the camp in obedience to these absurd commands, he strictly forbade Minucius, his master of horse, to venture an engagement with the enemy. At Rome the pro-dictator found himself an object of suspicion, for Hannibal, either through courtesy or policy, had forbidden his foraging troops to pillage the lands of B.C. 217. Fabius. This circumstance naturally excited doubts, and the senate refused to grant money for the ransom of 247 prisoners of war, although the terms of their redemption were agreed upon with Hannibal. Fabius ordered his son to sell the family estates to redeem the family honour. He purchased the liberty of the Roman captives with the money thus raised, nor would he receive back from them the price of their ransom. This noble disinterestedness was a sufficient refutation to the suspicions some weak-minded men entertained respecting his faith.[95] Notwithstanding the orders of the pro-dictator, Minucius led his army up to the very intrenchments of the enemy, as if to dare the great Carthaginian captain to come out. Hannibal did not accept the challenge, for the greater part of his army were foraging at a distance. The return of Hasdrubal with four thousand men extricated him from his enemies, when the Romans retreated, and Hannibal took more care of his camp for the future.[96]

The success of Minucius lowered Fabius still more in the eyes of the senate and people. The tribune Metilius proposed that Minucius should be invested with equal authority, but no person spoke for the measure but Terentius Varro, a butcher's son, who from being a shopkeeper had become a pleader, and was at this time a favourite with the people. He now harangued them so effectually that Minucius was declared a pro-dictator the same day. Fabius on his return induced his new colleague to divide the army, still keeping upon the hills, from whence he could observe the movements of Hannibal and Minucius. Hannibal, who of the whole Roman army feared no man but Fabius, easily drew Minucius into an engagement near Geronium, and having laid an ambush round about a hill which Minucius attempted to seize, would have annihilated his army but for the timely aid of Fabius, who, upon beholding his peril, cried out, "Let us hasten to the rescue of Minucius, who is a brave man and loves his country," adding, "and if he has been too hasty, we will tell him of it some other day."[97] Hannibal, seeing the admirable order in which Fabius marched to the relief of Minucius, remarked to one of his friends, "Have I not often told you that that cloud hovering upon the mountains would one day break upon us in a storm?"[98] He stopped the pursuit by sounding a retreat. Minucius, grateful for his deliverance, resigned his new dignity and marched to the camp of Fabius,[99] expressing his wish to serve under his command for the future. Fabius embraced his late contumacious master of horse, and the example of the leaders was followed by the soldiers. As his office was nearly expired, Fabius sent for the consuls from Rome to take the command of the army. Atilius and Servilius acting by his advice, did not venture to attack Hannibal.

Notwithstanding the successes gained by Hannibal in Italy, the senate sent to ask the annual tribute of the young Illyrian king. Nor did they forget to demand Demetrius of Pharos from his protector the king of Macedon. National pride made them refuse at this time forty golden vases which the city of Parthenope (Naples) offered to bestow upon them, lest the neighbouring nations should think that the commonwealth had become poor. In Spain the affairs of the republic prospered, for when Publius Cornelius Scipio came thither in the quality of pro-consul, he found that twenty cities had surrendered to his brother Cneius, who was universally respected in that country.[100] The pro-consul increased the good-will of the Spaniards towards Rome on the following occasion.

Hannibal, before he left Spain, had rebuilt and fortified Saguntum, and placed there the noble children he had received from various Spanish nations as hostages for their parents' good behaviour.[101] Abelox, a Spaniard of illustrious birth, and a personal friend of Bostar, the Carthaginian commander, was desirous of conciliating the Romans, from whom he hoped to derive great advantages. He persuaded Bostar to send the hostages back to their several countries under his guidance, which measure he declared would bind their parents to the

Carthaginian interest for ever. Bostar fell into the snare with easy simplicity, whereupon the treacherous Abelox sent information of his march to the proconsul, who intercepted him and seized upon the hostages. Their crafty leader B.C. 216. advised Scipio to send them back to their parents, which he did immediately under the care of Abelox, who represented the character of the proconsul in such a favourable light that the parents, not knowing the trick, yielded to the feelings of gratitude the action inspired, and became the allies of the Roman republic.[102] Such was the flourishing condition of Scipio in Spain, while Hannibal gathered, on his way to his winter quarters in Apulia, the wealth of the Italian plains. Corn, oil, and wine were so plentiful in his camp that the toil-worn horses were bathed in wine, as a medicament, or, possibly, a charm to improve their jaded condition. But the Romans found no mercy at the hands of men so merciful to their steeds. Yet neither the lenity of Hannibal to the Italian prisoners nor his severity to the Romans could seduce the first, nor intimidate the other. The Roman colonies stood firm, and Rome, defeated in every battle, and shorn of her power, retained her indomitable spirit, and true to herself, did not deign to solicit peace from Hannibal. The Roman people, though united in their determination of continuing the war, were discontented with those who had hitherto conducted it, for they imputed the national disasters, not to the remarkable genius of the great Carthaginian leader in the science of war, but to the incapacity of their own generals. A man either risen from the ærarian class, or descended from a plebeian family who had been degraded to it, possessed himself at this period of the confidence and suffrages of the people. Terentius Varro, whom the plebeian party, to their own disgrace and the misfortune of their country, elevated to the consulship, was the son of a butcher, and had been a butcher himself, a trade he had quitted for the wealthier calling of a shopkeeper. His wealth or eloquence had successively obtained for him the magistracies of Rome; all of which, with the exception of the popular tribuneship, he had filled before arriving at the consulship. This favourite of fortune, notwithstanding the opposition of the aristocracy, obtained the suffrages of the Roman tribes,[103] and actually held the comitia for the election of his colleague, Paulus Æmilius, an able soldier, but a very unpopular person. As no mention of any military exploit performed by Varro has been recorded in history, we may be certain that his popularity with the people was not founded on his personal services in the field. His only claim rested upon the liberal use he made of his wealth and his talents for oratory.[104] More judgment was displayed by the people or their rulers in their choice of pro-consuls and prætors: Publius Cornelius Scipio retained his proconsular government in Spain, and the late consuls remained in the field with the rank of pro-consuls. Claudius Marcellus, a name already distinguished in the records of his country, was made prætor of Sicily, Postumius Albinus of Cisalpine Gaul.

Hannibal maintained his post at Geronium, paying the most scrupulous attention to the wants of his army, composed of men accustomed, when not in action, to plentiful meals and luxurious repose.[105] Half of his troops were Gauls, Spaniards, or Africans, bound by no ties to the Carthaginian conqueror beyond interest or fear. The newly-raised Roman legions, eight in number, were required by the senate to take a solemn oath of obedience to the consuls before commencing their march.[106] At this time Hiero presented the republic with a statue of Victory, of solid gold, 75,000 bushels of wheat, and 50,000 bushels of barley. He also offered the services of a thousand slingers and dartmen to the senate, in order to carry the war into Africa. The senate accepted the costly present, and placed at the disposal of T. Otacilius the pro-prætor of Sicily, twenty-five quinqueremes to put Hiero's suggestion into practice, if he thought it expedient to do so.[107] Of the soundness of Hiero's advice Scipio's campaigns in Africa at a later period forms the best commentary. The history of Syracuse in the daring expedition of Agathocles offered him a fortunate precedent. According to the old and very imperfect Roman calendar, it was in the commencement of harvest that Hannibal opened his third brilliant campaign, by seizing upon the castle of Cannæ, a strong fortress containing the supplies of the two pro-consular armies.[108] It is supposed that in B.C. 216. Apulia, where the corn is early ripe, the period denoted by harvest took place some weeks earlier than was assigned by the ancient uncorrected almanack then in use. Hannibal, by this master-stroke, placed his well-fed and well-appointed army, between the Romans and the ripe corn-fields of Apulia, while he was possessed, by the capture of their great magazine, of their garnered supplies. Involved in this dilemma, the pro-consuls had no means of obtaining provisions for their armies, as Hannibal commanded the neighbouring country, and possessed the means of cutting off all their supplies. To fight or retreat were the only alternatives then left in their power. In reply to their despatches to the senate, respecting the difficulties of their situation, they were advised to risk a battle as soon as the consular armies should effect a junction with those under their command. Paulus Æmilius and his inexperienced colleague found their mighty opponent busily engaged in securing the grain then ripe, being stationed upon the left bank of the river Aufidus. In pitching the Roman camp within six miles' distance of Hannibal, Varro chose an open plain, better suited for the evolutions of the admirable cavalry of the enemy than for his own infantry, in which the strength of Rome mainly lay.[109] His experienced colleague pointed out his error, entreating him with great earnestness not to give their skilful adversary such an advantage, advising him to take up his position on the rising ground, near the sea, at a greater distance from the Carthaginian camp.[110] Varro, who, on each alternate day, held the supreme command of both consular armies, rejected with indomitable ignorance the counsel of Æmilius, and rendered his military blunder irrevocable by taking up a position between Hannibal and the sea.[111] Æmilius, the following day, displayed more science, by crossing the Aufidus, and forming a camp for a part of his own army upon the high bank, in order to secure corn on the southern side, and to intercept the enemy's foraging parties should he send them forth in that direction. Hannibal approached nearer to the Romans, but if he designed this as a challenge to Paulus Æmilius that prudent consul did not accept it,[112] having been strongly advised by Fabius not to come to a battle with Hannibal.[113] Notwithstanding his wise precaution, a sharp skirmish took place between the Roman and the Numidian cavalry, while the former were getting their supplies of water, in which the Romans had the disadvantage, for they did not obtain their object, and were forced to take shelter in their camp, being followed to its very gates by these formidable horsemen.[114]

Varro, upon the fatal first of August, announced his intention of giving battle to Hannibal by exhibiting the consular robe by way of ensign,[115] a rude practice common in all ages of the republic. This signal appeared at daybreak, flying above his pavilion, for it was his turn to command the combined armies of Rome, though the daring courage of the man was unaccompanied by any military skill on the part of the general. At sunrise Varro crossed the river Aufidus with the army of the great camp, uniting his forces with those which Paulus Æmilius had placed on the right bank of the river, and drew them out in battle-array. Hannibal, notwithstanding the superior numbers of the enemy, did not hesitate to cross the river, leaving his own camp behind, for generally prudent, in almost every instance, he had waited for the Romans to attack him, but the dispositions made by Varro assured him that a fortunate boldness was alone requisite to ensure him victory. While reconnoitering this immense consular force, Hannibal made a brilliant reply to Gisco's timid remark, "that the number of the enemy was very surprising;" "There is something still more surprising, which has escaped your attention, that in all that vast host there is not one man named Gisco." This repartee made those about Hannibal laugh heartily, and the jest being circulated through his army, not only excited general mirth, but inspired universal confidence, a confidence fatal to the Romans. Nor did his brief address to his soldiers, "Your fate is on your swords," give them less encouragement.[116]

To soldiers the description of this ancient battle might prove very interesting, as related by the great military B.C. 216. historian Polybius, or copied by Livy from the earliest Roman annalist, Fabius, whose personal experience of a war in which he served, must have rendered his details interesting. To the general reader it will be sufficient to state that the Roman army was badly posted, and the arrangements for the battle made without skill or judgment by Varro, and that the consular soldiers had the sun in their faces, while to the glare was added the heat of the south wind, with its clouds of dust.[117] Instead of forming the infantry in line, Varro adopted the unusual plan of marshalling them in columns, which deprived them of the advantage of their superiority in numbers, and gave room for the evolutions of Hannibal's cavalry.[118] The Roman front, charged by Hasdrubal, was galled by the Balearic slingers, whose weapons were stones, which they hurled against soldiers unaccustomed to that barbaric mode of warfare. The Gauls and Spaniards, well mounted and armed, were an overmatch for men of feebler mould of body, and less defended by art. The consul Æmilius, who commanded the cavalry, was wounded early by the slingers, and unhorsed,[119] but his being on foot caused his cavalry to dismount, a mistake of which Hannibal took advantage;[120] but though surrounded by the horsemen of the enemy, the consul supported his reputation as a soldier on this disastrous day till he fell covered with wounds. When the rout became general, Lentulus, a legionary tribune, saw the consul sitting on a stone, wounded and bleeding; whereupon he alighted from his horse, and offering him the animal, besought him to save himself by flight, but Æmilius refused to accept it, bidding him shift for himself, since he neither wished to accuse his colleague, nor be accused himself, for the loss of that day's battle. He told Lentulus to charge the senate to fortify Rome, and bade him remind Fabius that he had remembered his counsel to the last; he then besought him to lose no time. Lentulus saved himself by the swiftness of his horse; but the wounded consul Æmilius fell by the Carthaginian dartmen, who were ignorant of his name and rank.[121] The Roman army fought desperately, but no efforts on their part could redeem the misfortunes of the day. Hasdrubal, following up his victory, had no sooner achieved the destruction of the greater part of the Roman cavalry, when he rode to the assistance of the Numidians against the Italian horse, whose flight only gave them to surer slaughter. From that work of death, the fierce and able cavalry general turned to carry destruction into the cumbrous columns of the Roman legions. It appears that the ardent courage of these legionaries had carried them into the heart of the Carthaginian army, their victorious course occasioning them to be exposed on all sides to their foes, unable to advance or retreat, and wedged too closely by their own density, even to defend their lives. Such was their helpless situation when the approach of Hasdrubal devoted them to the slaughtering sword, these brave Romans disdaining to ask quarter.[122] Nearly seventy thousand men fell in this fatal battle, and all the cavalry, with the exception of two hundred and seventy, with which the consul Varro fled to Venusia,[123] and two thousand captured by the Carthaginians. Besides the gallant consul Paulus Æmilius, the pro-consuls Atilius and Servilius, Minucius Fabius, master of the horse, two military quæstors, twenty-nine legionary tribunes, and eighty persons of senatorial rank or descent, were left dead upon the field.[124] This dreadful defeat at Cannæ was always considered one of the greatest national calamities that ever befel the Romans, and the poet Lucan has frequently alluded to it in his fine historic epic.[125] Varro, though brave, had not the courage to die, like his colleague, on the fatal plain; but it certainly required some boldness to present himself to the senate, and enter a city his rashness had filled with disappointment, humiliation, mourning, and woe. He was, however, received with kindness and commiseration at Rome, and the senate even returned him thanks "for not despairing of the commonwealth."[126] The people crowded to meet and pay him respect in his misfortunes; "very different conduct from that of the Carthaginians," remarks Livy, "who generally ordered, on such unfortunate occasions, their generals to B.C. 216. be put to a cruel death."[127] Varro had certainly acted upon the instructions given him by the senate, and had shown courage in both engagements. The people, in electing him to lead an army destined to encounter Hannibal, were more in fault than he.

Hannibal hurried from his victory on the plain, and hastily crossed the river to succour his own camp, besieged at this very time by a strong body of Romans left on the other side of the river for this difficult service by the consuls. The Romans, who had been unable to force it, retreated to the great camp which they were compelled to surrender. Their example was followed by their comrades in the little camp on the opposite side of the river, with the exception of some brave fellows who cut their way through the victorious enemy and retired to Canusium.[128] The destruction of the consular and pro-consular armies cost Hannibal six thousand men; that he had lost so many proves that the Romans had not been deficient in courage but in skill. The officers of his staff gathered round the great Carthaginian to congratulate him on his victory, mixing with their compliments their individual opinions upon the use to be made of his unexampled success.[129] Most of these recommended their victorious leader to rest his troops for a day or two before he undertook any fresh enterprise. Maharbal alone pressed him to lose no time. "Follow me," cried he, "that you may learn the importance of this victory. I will instantly march away with the cavalry, and be at Rome before they have notice of my coming. In five days we shall sup in the capitol." Hannibal replied, "that what he proposed was so momentous that he must take time to consider it." "Nay, then," cried Maharbal, "I find that no one man is endued by the gods with all talents. Hannibal knows how to conquer, but he does not know how to make use of his victories."[130] "This day's delay," remarks Livy, "saved the commonwealth and city of Rome."[131]

At Rome great preparations were made to insure the public safety. The women were forbidden to appear in the streets because their lamentations would excite a general mourning, since there was not a family in Rome that had not lost a relative or friend at Cannæ. Marcus Junius Pera was chosen dictator, and Sempronius Gracchus was appointed his master of horse.[132] Four legions and a thousand horse were raised among the citizens, and eight thousand slaves were bought of their masters, and enrolled as soldiers. These were called volones,[133] from the word by which they signified that they would serve in the war. The nobles and the Roman tribes brought their gold and silver ornaments into the public treasury. These contributions were voluntary. It was the unanimous act of a patriotic people. The Roman silver coin issued at this time was alloyed with copper, which debasement had never taken place before.[134]

Hannibal was willing to receive the ransom of his prisoners. These unfortunate persons had been left to guard the Roman camps, which office they had faithfully fulfilled, nor had they capitulated before they had gallantly resisted the victor, and even then surrendered upon honourable terms.[135] He sent ten of these captives to Rome with Carthalo to treat for their own redemption with the senate.[136] The word of these Romans was considered sufficient security for their return, for the example of Regulus had not been lost upon the Carthaginians. Marcus Junius pleaded the cause of these unfortunate men with great feeling and eloquence, but either through want of money or policy the senate refused to pay the ransom demanded for them, alleging that the Roman soldiers must henceforth conquer or die. Some of the prisoners chose to remain, but the greater part returned with Carthalo to their chains, and it is surprising that none of them offered to serve with Hannibal after they had been deserted by their country.[137] The victorious Carthaginian left to his brother Mago the charge of reducing the towns of Samnium and Bruttium, and led his army to Capua, which place was disaffected to the B.C. 216. Roman government, although it was not only a municipium or free town, but had a senate and was even allowed the rare privilege of intermarrying with the Romans. After the battle of Thrasimenus, Pacuvius Calavius, the governor of the town, and the son-in-law of Appius Claudius, had resolved to deliver up the place to Hannibal, but being an ambitious man he paused and considered that it would be better to make the Capuans independent both of Rome and the Carthaginians.[138] The Capuans agreed to admit Hannibal upon his promise of treating them as a free and independent state.[139] They also stipulated that three hundred Roman knights, the prisoners of Hannibal, should be given to them that they might exchange them for some noble Capuans then serving in the Roman army. Hannibal granted their demands, and the people gathered together all the Romans in the place and suffocated them in the public baths, a measure as impolitic as it was cruel and cowardly.

Only two persons remonstrated against delivering Capua to the Carthaginians. Perolla, the son of Pacuvius, who was with difficulty prevented from stabbing Hannibal, by the tears and persuasions of his father, and Decius Magius, who was a friend to the Romans. Hannibal induced the Capuans to deliver Magius to him, and sent him in chains on board a ship bound for Carthage. Fortune favoured the captive, for a tempest drove the vessel into the harbour of an Egyptian town called Cyrene, where the prisoner saw and clasped the statue of Ptolemy Philopator for protection. The Carthaginians did not dare to take him away from that asylum of the unfortunate, and the Cyrenians sent him to Alexandria to the prince whose clemency he had implored, who gave him a kind reception.[140]

Hannibal despatched his brother Mago to Carthage to relate his victories to the senate, and to ask for supplies of money, corn, arms, and troops.[141] These demands were joyfully granted by the whole body of senators, with the solitary exception of Hanno, who influenced by his old hatred to the family of Hannibal, or faithful to his ancient opinion, declared "that all success in the field that did not produce the fruits of a lasting and advantageous peace was worse than useless."[142] A wise maxim, though emanating less from the judgment than from the private animosity of the individual.

Junius Pera, the dictator, enlisted eight thousand prisoners confined for debt: their services being the stipulated price of their freedom. These he armed out of the spoils Flaminius had formerly taken from the Gauls, and with these two legions and eight thousand volones marched from Rome. Hannibal made a second fruitless attack upon Naples, and besieged Nola, but not succeeding at that time, took and burned Nuceria, and once more laid siege to Nola. Marcellus drove him from that place by a successful sally.[143] The Carthaginian general next appeared before Casilinum, as he had heard that the inhabitants were favourably disposed towards him. They were so, but a body of men from Præneste passing near the town and learning their disaffection to the Romans, cut the throats of all those who were suspected of disloyalty, and took possession of the town. The approach of the cold season made Hannibal break up the siege, and retire to Capua for the winter. The voluptuous manners of the Capuans were more fatal to the Carthaginians, if we may trust Livy, than Roman valour had been. The life of ease the soldiers of Hannibal led here, unfitted them for scenes of strife and labour in the following spring.[144] As soon as the winter was over Hannibal renewed the siege of Casilinum, where he met with the most obstinate resistance. The garrison, reduced by famine to the necessity of eating the leather coverings of their shields boiled in water, astonished Hannibal by giving him a strange proof of their determination. He had ploughed up the ground round the city to prevent the besieged from obtaining roots, upon this fresh mould they thought proper to cast some turnip-seed from the walls. Upon this fact being told to Hannibal, he cried "What, am I to sit here till their turnips are grown?" and he offered them terms of capitulation. They were suffered to march out of the place, upon condition that each freeman should pay for his ransom seven ounces of gold.[145] B.C. 215. At Rome the vacancies in the senate left by the loss of Roman life at Cannæ were filled up by the prudence of the new dictator, Fabius Buteo, who put upon the list all those who had filled the offices of curule magistrates, tribunes of the people, plebeian ædiles, quæstors, and even such of the people who had spoils won by their own hands from the enemy to show, or soldiers who had received the civic crown as the reward of their valour.[146] Thus Fabius Buteo chose from all ranks one hundred and seventy-seven senators, their public worth being his only criterion for their fitness for legislature. This wise and patriotic measure pleased the people, because it tended to promote the interests of every individual who bore the proud name of Roman. Nothing but national union could hope to subdue an enemy brave and subtle like Hannibal. Sempronius Gracchus and Postumius Albinus were elected consuls for the ensuing year; but this had scarcely been done before intelligence arrived at Rome with the disastrous news that Postumius and his army had been totally destroyed by the Gauls.[147] This was the last misfortune of an unfortunate year. Marcellus was elected in the room of the slain consul, but it thundered at the time, and this circumstance rendered his election illegal, as displeasing to the gods, and Fabius Cunctator was chosen in his place.[148]

<hr size=2 width="10%" align=center>

[1] Livy, Epit. xix.; Zonaras, viii. 18; Polybius, i. 45; Orosius, iv. 11; Eutropius, ii. 28.

[2] Valerius Maximus, vi. 5.

[3] Polybius, i. 88; Appian, De Reb. Punic. c. 5.

[4] Eutropius, iii. 1.

[5] Val. Max., vi. 3. But if the victim was the viator of Claudius Pulcher, whom that proud patrician had named dictator, that circumstance sufficiently accounts for the cruelty and contempt of the Roman people.

[6] See Appendix. (p. 288)

[7] Dion Cassius, Fragm. Ursin, cl.

[8] *Ibid.*

[9] Livy, Epit.; Zonaras; Arnold.

[110] *Ibid.*; Dion Cassius, in Fragm.

[111] See Appendix. (p. 289)

[112] Val. Max., v. 4.

[113] Polybius, ii. 2; Appian, in Illyri.

[114] Pliny, xxxiv. 6.

[115] Polybius, in Illyri, ii. 12.

[116] Polybius, ii. 12; Zonaras, viii.

[117] See Appendix. (p. 291)

[118] Such abhorrent sacrifices were seldom resorted to by the Romans, but the practice was dreadfully common in Greece, where whole hecatombs of virgins were immolated for the supposed benefit of the state. Zonaras, viii.; Orosius, iv. 13.

[119] Polybius, ii. 24, 31.

[120] Zonaras, viii; Orosius, iv. 13.; Plutarch, in Marcellus.

[121] Polybius, ii. 32, 33.

[122] Zonaras, viii.

[123] Plutarch, in Marcellus; Polybius, ii. 34.

[124] Plutarch, in Marcellus.

[125] Polybius, iii. 16-18, 19.

[126] Pliny, xxix. 1.

[127] Val. Max., i. 3.

[128] Clusius.

[129] Niebuhr, Introductory Lecture.

[130] Niebuhr, Introductory Lecture.

[131] "Fato Metelli Romæ fiunt consules."—Orelli.

[132] Niebuhr, Introd. Lecture, p. 24.

[133] See Appendix. (p. 295)

[134] Polybius, ii. 36; Appian, Hispan. 8; Livy, xxii. 10.

[135] *Ibid.*, xxi. 2.

[136] Polybius, ii. 13. "There is some dispute about the age of this celebrated commander, but if the dates of Polybius respecting his years at the time of his father's embarkation for Spain, and the length of Hamilcar's and Hasdrubal's government are correct, he must have been six-and-twenty at the time of Hasdrubal's murder."

[37] Appian, Hist. xi.; Polybius, xxi. 9.

[38] Polybius, iii. 17.

[39] Livy, xxi. 18; Polybius, iii. 33; Zonaras, viii. 22.

[40] Livy, xxi. 19.

[41] Livy, xxi. 20; Polybius, iii. 33.

[42] Polybius, iii. 34.

[43] *Ibid.*

[44] Polybius, iii. 42.

[45] *Ibid.*, 43.

[46] *Ibid.*, 41, 42.

[47] Livy, xxi. 29; Polybius, iii. 49.

[48] Polybius, iii. 49; Livy, xxi. 21.

[49] See Appendix. (p. 300)

[50] The reader will recall the march of Suwarrow with the allied army, and its ruinous consequences, in the last century, when the Russians, though accustomed to a rigorous climate, sank under the hardships they encountered in attempting to force the passage of the Alps. The ambition and the genius of Napoleon formed the noble road of the Simplon in another part of these mountains—a work that will survive the memory of his conquests, since, though the motive may be questioned, the utility is enduring, and the Romans themselves have been surpassed in this monument of modern skill and industry.

[51] Polybius, iii. 51.

[52] *Ibid.*, 52.

[53] Polybius, iii. 53.

[54] *Ibid.*, 54.

[55] Polybius, iii. 54; Livy, xxi. 35.

[56] Polybius, iii. 55.

[57] See Appendix. (p. 302)

[58] Polybius, iii. 60.

[59] *Ibid.*

[60] See Appendix. (p. 303)

[61] Polybius, iii. 41; Livy, xxi. 49.

[62] Polybius, iii. 40.

[63] Livy, xxi. 39, 40.

[64] Livy, xxi. 46; Polybius, iii. 56.

[65] Polybius, iii.

[66] *Ibid.*, 47.

[67] Polybius, iii. 72.

[68] Livy, xxi. 49; Polybius, iii. 71.

[69] Polybius, iii. 72.

[70] *Ibid.*, 73.

[71] Livy, xxi. 56.

[72] Polybius, iii. 74.

[73] Polybius, iii. 67.

[74] Livy, xxi. 58.

[75] Polybius, iii. 75.

[76] *Ibid.*, 76.

[77] Livy, xxii. 2.

[78] See Appendix. (p. 307)

[79] Livy, xxii. 4.

[80] Polybius, iii. 82.

[81] Livy, xx. 5; Plutarch, in Fabius Maximus.

[82] Livy, xx. 5; Plutarch, in Fabius Maximus.

[83] Polybius, iii. 62.

[84] Livy, xxii. 6.

[85] This colour is still disputed by the learned; some suppose it to have been a crimson doubly dyed, till nearly as dark as purple. The translators of the New Testament have not agreed in rendering the colour of the robe in which our Lord was arrayed in mockery by Herod, one calling it a scarlet, the others a purple robe.

[86] Livy, xxii. 7; Val. Max., v. 1.

[87] Livy, xxii. 9; See Appendix. (p. 310)

[88] Livy, xxii. 46; Polybius, iii. 114.

[89] It is peculiarly difficult to determine the spot where the valiant legions found their grave, but in a country subject, like Italy, to convulsions of the earth, the face of the ground may have materially changed during the long lapse of so many centuries.

[90] Livy, xxii. 12; Plutarch, in Fabius Maximus.

[91] Livy, xxii. 13.

[92] Plutarch, in Fabius Maximus.

[93] Polybius, iii. 93; Plutarch, in Fabius.

[94] Plutarch; Livy, xxii. 18.

[95] Plutarch, in Fabius Maximus.

[96] Polybius, iii. 94.

[97] Plutarch, in Fabius.

[98] Polybius, iii. 105; Plutarch, in Fabius.

[99] Livy, xxii. 30.

[100] *Ibid.*, 22.

[101] Polybius, iii. 98.

[102] Polybius.

[103] Valerius Maximus, iii. 4; Livy, xxii. 35.

[104] See Appendix. (p. 316)

[105] Arnold; Strabo.

[106] The vow which they had been accustomed to make, that they would not abandon their ensigns through fear, nor quit their ranks unless to recover a weapon, strike an enemy, or save a citizen, was no longer a voluntary act; it was exacted from every Roman henceforth, as a part of his duty.

[107] Livy, xxii. 37.

[108] Polybius, iii. 107.

[109] Polybius, iii. 110.

[110] *Ibid.*

[111] Livy, xxii. 45; Polybius, iii. 3.

[112] Plutarch, in Fabius.

[113] See Appendix. (p. 318)

[114] Plutarch, in Fabius.

[115] Plutarch, in Fabius; Florus.

[116] *Ibid.*

[117] Florus; Plutarch, in Fabius.

[118] Polybius, iii. 113.

[1119] Plutarch, in Fabius.

[1120] *Ibid.*

[1121] Livy; Plutarch, in Fabius.

[1122] Plutarch, in Fabius.

[1123] Polybius; Florus, ii.

[1124] Livy, xxii. 44.

[1125] Pharsalia.

[1126] Florus; Plutarch, in Fabius.

[1127] Plutarch, in Fabius; Livy, xii. 44.

[1128] Polybius, iii. 116; Livy, xxii. 49.

[1129] Plutarch, in Fabius.

[1130] Livy, xxii. 51; Plutarch, in Fabius.

[1131] *Ibid.*; *Ibid.*; See Appendix. (p. 321)

[1132] Livy, xxii. 57.

[1133] "Volo," I will.

[1134] Florus, ii. 6.

[1135] Livy, xxii. 56-58.

[1136] The price demanded by the Carthaginian general was by no means exorbitant. The horsemen were each valued at five hundred denarii (16*l.* 2*s.* 11*d.*), the soldiers were rated at three hundred (9*l.* 3*s.* 9*d.*), and the slaves at one hundred (3*l.* 4*s.* 7*d.*)

[1137] Livy, xxii. 57; Polybius, vi. 58; Appian, vii. 28.

[1138] Livy, xxiii. 2, et seq.; See Appendix. (p. 323)

[1139] Livy, xxiii. 5.

[1140] Livy, xxiii. 10.

[1141] *Ibid.*, 2, 13.

[1142] Livy, xxiii. 14.

[1143] Plutarch, in Marcellus.

[1144] Livy, xxiii. 18; Florus.

[1145] Livy, xxiii. 20.

[1146] Livy, xxiii. 23.

[1147] *Ibid.*, xxiii. 24; Polybius, ii. 118.

[148] Livy, xxiii. 31.

THE Roman senators took admirable measures for the defence of Rome against the invader who had carried a foreign war into the heart of her finest provinces. Fabius Maximus received the command of the army of Junius Pera, and Marcellus that of the two legions raised for the defence of the capital. The latter formed his camp at Suessula, a city near Nola. The prætor, Lævinus, was ordered to protect Apulia, and twenty-five ships were placed at his command to defend the coasts of Brundusium and Tarentum, while the other prætor, Flaccus, with the same number of vessels, guarded those near Rome.[1]

Terentius Varro, still a favourite with the people, was B.C. 215.again entrusted with the charge of an army in Apulia.[2] While Lævinus was at Luceria his scouts captured a party of Macedonians, whose splendid national costume, being peculiar to that people, proclaimed their country.[3] Although these Macedonians were really ambassadors from king Philip, their master, to the camp of Hannibal, to join him in a league offensive and defensive against the Romans, Xenophanes, an artful Athenian diplomatist, persuaded the prætor that they were ambassadors to Rome, who gave them guides and safe conduct thither. They got safe to Hannibal, ratified a treaty with the Carthaginians, which is still extant, having been preserved in Polybius, and embarked again for their own country with Mago, Gisco, and Bostar, three ambassadors sent by Hannibal. The ship was taken by the other prætor, Flaccus, to whom the wily Athenian told the same story as to Lævinus, but the presence of the Carthaginians on board the vessel invalidated his account, and Flaccus sent them to Rome. The sight of the treaty moved the indignation of the senate, who determined to repel the threatened invasion of Philip, by carrying the war into Macedon.[4]

The Roman armies gained some advantage over Hannibal in various parts of Italy.[5] Marcellus being apprised of the disaffection of the citizens of Nola, encamped near that place, and Livy relates that he defeated Hannibal, but this is considered doubtful, as Polybius has not recorded it. He, however, certainly ravaged the lands of the Samnites and Hirpinians, since those nations sent a complaint to Hannibal, respecting their mutual sufferings, couched in simple but forcible language, in which they told him, "That they had been so much distressed by the Romans since the battle of Cannæ, that it seemed to them that it was not the Carthaginians but their enemies who had gained that great victory." Hannibal recounted his past exploits, and promised them redress as soon as he had gained another victory. He then dismissed the complainants.[6] It is not known why twelve hundred and seventy-seven Spanish and Numidian horsemen deserted to the Romans, to whom they remained faithful, and by whom they were rewarded some years afterwards with lands in their own countries.[7] In Sardinia, Manlius Torquatus gained a great victory over the rebels and Carthaginians. The Scipios in Spain maintained the honour of the Roman arms, though they complained that they were in want of money, clothing, and provisions, without which necessaries they could not keep a standing army. As the Roman treasury was in an exhausted state, the rich citizens were urged by the senate to advance money for that purpose, upon the promise of being paid as soon as the state should be in a condition to do so.[8] The sum was raised without difficulty. This is one of the earliest instances on record of a national debt, but the creditors of the Roman republic received no interest for the loan; it was lent upon the national faith, the only recompence the patriotic lenders required being the success of the Roman arms against Hannibal.[9]

In Sicily, the death of king Hiero, at the advanced age of ninety, occasioned changes in the politics of Syracuse which led to unexpected results; involving that war with Rome which ended in its final reduction. The grandson and successor of king Hiero was also the grandson of the famous Pyrrhus, king of Epirus, whose daughter, Nereis, was the wife of Gelon and mother of this Hieronymus, who, for his own misfortune and that of his country, was a sovereign at fifteen, though under the legal guardianship of his uncle, Andranodorus, and fourteen other persons.[10] The boy-king was ambitious, for the blood of Pyrrhus was in his veins, and demanded the island of Sicily of the Carthaginians as the purchase of his secession from the Romans. The Carthaginians did not hesitate to allow his claims, for the island with the exception of Syracuse being in the possession of the Romans, the concession they made to the aspiring young prince appeared of little moment[11] to a people not very scrupulous in regard to public faith.

Appius Claudius Pulcher, prætor of Sicily, upon B.C. 215.learning the intentions of the boy-king, sent ambassadors to the court of Syracuse, reminding him of the long friendship and alliance between the Roman republic and his grandfather, which he entreated him to renew in his own person. Some attempt at intimidation was couched in the remonstrance of the Roman magistrate, which inflamed the pride of the haughty and high-spirited youth.[12] Hieronymus before summoning his council to determine upon the answer to be given to the Roman embassy, had previously insulted those who composed it, by asking them, "Whether they had come off well at Cannæ, for Hannibal's envoys had told wonderful things of his success in that battle. However, as soon as he could get at the truth he should know how to act."[13] The Roman ambassadors treated him like what he really was, an ill-mannered child requiring reproof, assuring him, in return for his rude speech, "that when he knew how to give a proper answer to persons of their character they would revisit his court."[14] Among those who met the king in council, were Hippocrates and Epicydes, the Carthaginian envoys, who being Syracusans by descent, and citizens of Carthage by birth, were selected by Hannibal for the express purpose of prejudicing the young prince against the Romans, to induce him to break the league Hiero had made with them. The silence of the Syracusans, who feared him, probably confirmed Hieronymus in his intentions; three ancient Greeks, however, advised him by no means to renounce the alliance of Rome. Andranodorus by urging his ward to seize the present crisis, which would render him the master of Sicily, proved that his nephew was only acting under his direction. The young king heard him with deep attention, and then asked Hippocrates and Epicydes for their opinion. "We agree with Andranodorus," was their brief reply. "The question is settled," returned the prince, "we are no longer the allies of Rome." In speaking thus, Hieronymus appeared like a dignified young man; but nothing could be more absurdly childish than his final answer to the Roman ambassadors, who were recalled to hear his decision. "He was willing," he said, "to renew his alliance with Rome, provided the Romans would restore to him all the money, corn, and presents king Hiero, his grandfather, had bestowed upon them." Among the last he particularised, "the golden statue of Victory, the last gift of the generous king of Syracuse." Then, in order to ask enough, he added to these ridiculous demands, "the cession of half the island of Sicily, which was to be given up to him as far as the east of the river Himera."[15] The ambassadors retired in disgust without making him any reply.[16]

The party in favour of the Romans was still strong in Syracuse; but whether the conspiracy of which its ambitious king soon became the victim emanated from the Romans themselves, or those who wished well to them, is uncertain, but that it originated from Roman influence is rather supported by circumstantial evidence,[17] since Hieronymus had not only sent back Hippocrates and Epicydes to confirm the treaty with Carthage, but had begun to make active preparations for war. His assassination in passing through the streets of Leontini by the conspirators, assembled in an empty house, took place at the very time when the unfortunate prince was marching with his army to attack the Roman province.[18] The signal for his slaughter was given by one of his own attendants, while the sudden rush of many armed men upon their youthful and unsuspecting sovereign was too unexpected to allow his guards to interpose between the assassins and the person of the king.[19] The dispersion of the army was followed by the attempt of one part of the conspirators to excite the inhabitants of Leontini to join them in the republican war-cry of liberty, while the other hurried to Syracuse to keep possession of the city for themselves and their allies.[20] The report of the murder of the king had, however, reached Andranodorus, who took possession of the island of Ortygia, in which the royal citadel, the palace of the sovereign, was situated.[21] The murderers entered Syracuse in the evening with the robe and diadem of the unfortunate prince. The cry of liberty was again B.C. 215. raised by these wretches, a cry to which Syracuse responded. Even those who had taken possession of the public granary on the island for Andranodorus yielded it to the republican party.[22] Andranodorus, alarmed at the progress of the popular movement, surrendered to the revolutionists the citadel and treasury, for which he received, with Themistus, the brother-in-law of the murdered king, a share in the new government. The connection between the late royal family and the guardian and brother-in-law of Hieronymus naturally excited the jealousy of his murderers. Nor is it improbable that Andranodorus and Themistus were endeavouring to restore the government to its legitimate form. According to some accounts these newly elected captains-general, who had married Demarata the daughter of Hiero, and Harmonia his grand-daughter, were plotting for the sovereignty, which they claimed in right of their wives; but confiding their secret to Aristo the tragedian, he betrayed it to the prætors, whereupon the aspirants to sovereignty were slain by their command in the senate-house;[23] after which Sopater, one of the Syracusan prætors, harangued the people so effectually against the female descendants of the royal family, that not only Demarata and Harmonia were put to death at their desire, but also Heraclea, the other daughter of Hiero, with her family. As Heraclea had never conspired against the newly-instituted republic, and the royal blood of these females constituted their sole crime, the versatile populace repented of these barbarous murders, and, incensed against their authors, declared the prætorship vacant, and demanded new magistrates. In the election every person was allowed to vote, to the subversion of all legal authority, and the intriguing brothers, Hippocrates and Epicydes, were chosen prætors. As deputies had been sent, upon the death of Hieronymus, to Appius Claudius to renew the friendly feeling formerly existing between Rome and Syracuse, the new Syracusan prætors did not openly espouse the cause of Hannibal, because a strong party in the town favoured the Romans, for many persons believed that the pro-consul Appius was concerned in the conspiracy of which the unfortunate boy-king had become the victim. While the affairs of Syracuse were in this state of confusion, the Roman fleet, commanded by Appius Claudius, came into the bay; this movement alarmed the Carthaginian faction, who incited the people to oppose their landing should they dare to attempt it. Appius, who knew that the Carthaginian fleet was then lying off Cape Pachynus, made no movement of this kind, his object being merely to encourage the friends of Rome to declare themselves in her favour.[24]

The Roman deputies, sent to ratify the treaty by the consul Marcellus, were very coldly received, and it was hotly debated whether the republic of Syracuse should not break off the treaty, and declare war against Rome. Apollonides, an aged citizen, at length prevailed upon them to make peace with the Roman republic, by assuring them that though this act would compel them to a war with Carthage, yet that might not happen for years, while one with Rome would follow instantly upon their breaking off the treaty. His wise counsel was taken, greatly to the displeasure of the Syracusan prætors, and the negotiations with Rome were concluded. A few days after the pacification had been ratified, the township of Leontini sent to Syracuse to demand troops to defend the frontier. This was readily accorded, and Hippocrates, with four thousand men, marched to that place. This general, who was resolved to break with the Romans, invaded the territories of the republic, and slew the men sent by Appius to defend them. This hostile act was followed by a formal complaint from the consul Marcellus, who demanded satisfaction for the infraction of the peace by the dismissal and exile of the Syracusan prætors Hippocrates and Epicydes. Expecting that this demand would be made, Epicydes hastened to join his brother at Leontini, for he knew the mutability of popular favour at Syracuse too well to trust himself to it in the absence of Hippocrates and the army.[25] Arrived at that place, he represented to the inhabitants that they ought to become a free state as well as Syracuse, upon which city they were at present dependent. The Leontinians were easily persuaded to assert their rights, and when Marcellus sent to them to banish the factious Syracusan prætors, they haughtily replied, "that B.C. 214. they had not signed the treaty of peace with Rome, nor were they bound by an act to which they had not been a party."[26] The Syracusans, equally incensed with the Romans at this bold avowal upon the part of the Leontinians, resolved to reduce the refractory city into obedience. The Roman soldiers, who had fled formerly from the battle of Cannæ, entreated the consul Marcellus to give them an opportunity to retrieve their character by serving in this war. He wrote to the senate in their behalf, but his request was denied. He was grieved at this refusal, and afterwards complained in the senate "that for all his services they would not allow him to rescue from infamy those unfortunate citizens."[27] There is no doubt that the policy of Marcellus was better than that of the Roman senate. All governments ought to be paternal, and a father would be justly considered cruel who would not allow erring children to retrieve their past misconduct. These men would, most likely, have become exemplary citizens instead of despised and disaffected exiles. Leontini was quickly taken by Marcellus, but the authors of the misfortune, the factious Hippocrates and Epicydes, fled to Herbessus. Marcellus spared the inhabitants of the conquered city, with the exception of two thousand deserters, whom he ordered to be put to the sword.[28] The Syracusan generals with their army, ignorant that Marcellus was master of Leontini, were marching to aid him in the reduction of that place, when they heard the report that the Roman consul had utterly destroyed the town and its inhabitants; an exaggeration of what had really befallen it. The Syracusan army, incensed at this false statement would not join Marcellus; and Sosis and Deinomenes, were forced to yield to the general remonstrance and stop at Megara, after which concession they prevailed upon the soldiers to march to Herbessus in pursuit of Hippocrates and Epicydes.[29] The brothers, who were aware that they possessed some influence with an army chiefly composed of mercenaries, many of whom had formerly served under them, resolved to yield themselves up to them, entertaining a certain hope that, from their prisoners, they should soon become their leaders. Bearing olive branches in their hands, they went forth as suppliants to meet the troops of Sosis and Deinomenes, when they were met by Cretan mercenaries, who had been taken by Hannibal when in the service of Rome, but had borne arms for him, and had been formerly commanded by those who now implored their mercy. The wily brethren easily induced them to promise not to yield them up to the Romans or Syracusans.[30] As soon as the Syracusan prætors heard of their coming, they demanded their wardship, which was refused by the whole army, who were ready to revolt. Then Hippocrates and Epicydes forged a letter in the name of the Syracusan prætors to the consul Marcellus, "complimenting him upon the pretended destruction of Leontini, and advising him to come and massacre the mercenaries at Megara, as Syracuse would never know peace while foreign soldiers were in her service." The sight of this false document kindled a mutiny among the mercenary soldiers, who were far more numerous than those of Syracuse. Sosis and Deinomenes, the prætors, fled to Syracuse; and Hippocrates and Epicydes with difficulty prevented the mercenary troops from slaying those from Syracuse.[31] They sent before them the report of what they pretended had been done by Marcellus, at Leontini. This put all Syracuse in a state of commotion. Yielding to their first feelings they refused admittance to the Romans; and the authors and contrivers of this confusion took advantage of it to enter a gate broken down for that purpose by the popular party within the city. By general acclamation they were declared magistrates; and having stormed and taken that part of the town called Achradina, whither the ex-magistrates and the Syracusan soldiers had retired, they took the place the same day massacring all they found there.[32] Marcellus hearing the tidings of this new revolution, and the manner in which it was brought about, sent deputies to explain his conduct at Leontini, demanding the traitors Hippocrates and Epicydes to be given up, and offering, upon that condition, to renew the treaty with Rome, but if this was refused he should declare war against the place. The deputies were not allowed to enter the city; Epicydes B.C. 214. spoke to them from the walls to this effect: "If you had brought us any message we should have given you an answer. When the government of Syracuse is in the hands of those to whom you address yourselves you may come again. If your consul is for war he will find the siege of Syracuse a different affair to that of Leontini."[33]

Marcellus did find it so, for though he immediately invested it by sea and land, he found it defended by a mightier power than arms. The genius of the philosopher Archimedes was engaged in the defence of his native city. Of royal descent, this great man brought his favourite pursuits of geometry and mathematics to bear upon the art of mechanics, ennobling a pursuit hitherto practised by persons without education or mind.[34] The friend and relative of

Hiero, the good Archimedes was above party, his defence of Syracuse against the Romans was an act of pure patriotism. Plutarch affirms that it was king Hiero who first persuaded the philosopher to apply the theories of science to the arts of peace and war, "turning his abstracted notions to matters of sense by adapting them to the uses of common life." When he made the celebrated remark which is so well known to every reader,[35] the monarch to whom he addressed it demanded a proof of his power. Archimedes ordered one of the king's galleys to be manned and laded, and then placing himself at a distance, only moved a machine composed of ropes and pullies with his hand, and drew her to him as gently and easily as if she were under sail. Hiero, astonished at the mechanical genius of Archimedes, entreated him to make him some war engines for attack and defence; during the long and peaceful reign of Hiero their services had not been required, but the glory of defending his native city was reserved for the old age of the Syracusan sage.[36]

Ignorant of the powerful resource the enemy possessed in this peaceful philosopher, the Romans, whose grappling machines had insured their victories over the experienced Carthaginians by sea, while their own nautical skill was yet in its infancy, considered Syracuse as already won, when directed by Marcellus, their great battering machine, borne upon eight galleys, approached the walls. Nor were the Syracusans at all easy at the sight of this monstrous piece of mechanism, till those invented by Archimedes rendered it useless.[37] He placed upon the walls war engines, armed with huge beams, that struck and sank the Roman galleys at a single blow. Some ships of this devoted fleet were hoisted in the air, by means of iron grapples and hooks, and were plunged to the bottom of the sea. Others were drawn by ropes and pullies to the shore and dashed against the rocks. It was a fearful spectacle to see a ship suspended in the air till all the hapless crew were shaken out, then split against the walls of the city or sunk in the sea. As for the Roman engine called sambuca, upon which the consul relied so much, it was crushed and annihilated by one of the balistæ of Archimedes: as the weight of the stones cast by this engine is supposed to be fabulous it is better not to name the amount, but only to cite the fact.[38] But of all these machines, that called the crow was the most formidable to the besiegers, for it dropped upon the decks of their galleys and sank them in the sea. This was a crow with two claws, with a long chain let down by a lever. The weight of the iron made it fall with violence, and drove it into the planks. Then the besieged, by a great weight of lead at the upper end of the lever, weighed it down, and consequently raised up the iron of the crow in proportion, and with it the iron to which it was fastened, sinking the poop at the same time into the water. After this the crow, letting go its hold all of a sudden, the prow of the galley fell with such force into the sea that the vessel filled and sank. Nor was Appius Claudius by land less exposed to unknown perils than his superior in command at sea, for the balistæ of Archimedes not only hurled stones but darts and bolts from the walls, and as these implements of destruction were concealed from the sight,[39] B.C. 214. the soldiers believed the darts came from the gods, which superstitious notion added to the distress caused by the missiles.[40] Marcellus, whose military talents were equal to the emergency of his present situation, remarking that the machines that destroyed his ships required room, drew nearer to the walls to prevent their action. Archimedes instantly brought out against him engines with shorter beams, which became equally annoying. He also placed some called scorpions in the holes of the walls, which were unseen, but did great injury to the consul's soldiers. Marcellus could not refrain from laughing at his engineers and mechanists. "Why do we continue," said he, "to contend with this mathematical Briareus, who has shamefully baffled us by land and sea, hurling his hundred bolts like the many-handed giant of the fable?"[41] and he turned the siege into a blockade, for even the genius of an Archimedes could not withstand famine.

Leaving the Roman consul before Syracuse, we must return to the early part of this remarkable year, whose events are left untold, to record the revolutions that followed the murder of the boy-king Hieronymus, which were so complicated that they required an uninterrupted narrative.[42]

The Roman war with Macedon commenced rather earlier than the horrors we have been describing, and continued during the siege of Syracuse. King Philip of Macedon was a prince of considerable talent, uniting to personal valour the hereditary beauty of his remarkable race. His character singularly resembles that of his great namesake and ancestor Philip of Macedon, and if he had been placed in the same historical era he would have done perhaps as much for Macedon as that able and unscrupulous prince. No talent, however, could raise again the doomed dynasty of the Macedonian kings. The third monarchy had received its prophetic sentence with its foretold aggrandisement, and the eyes of Alexander the Great must have looked upon the prophetic roll explained to him by Jaddua, the high priest of the Jews. Philip, the Theban hostage, was the primary cause of the political grandeur of Macedon, which Alexander the Great raised to its immense height by his twelve years of tragic conquests, but to concentrate it again required what Philip the younger could not effect, the reversal of the divine decree.

Philip opened his campaign against the Romans by the siege of Apollonia, from which place he was repulsed. The seizure of Oricus consoled him for his failure, for he won the place before the prætor Lævinus could relieve it. He re-invested Apollonia[43] which was re-enforced by Nævius Crista, who succeeded in getting into the city, and soon after stormed the Macedonian camp in the night. King Philip, brave as he was, fled to his ships, which refuge he gained with difficulty.[44]

Several features of this year rendered it at Rome a remarkable one. The consular elections were rendered invalid by Fabius Cunctator, who declared that the nomination of Æmilius Regillus was illegal because he was the high priest of Quirinus, and that T. Otacilius was unfit for that important office. "Remember," said the old man to the people, "you are going to fight Hannibal," and he called upon them "to elect men of talent fit for war and council, who were capable of contending with the renowned Carthaginian invader."[45] The people understood his allusion and re-elected him, with Marcellus for his colleague. Otacilius, whose wife was the niece of Fabius, was deeply hurt by his uncle's manner of excluding him from the consulship.[46]

The censorship of M. Atilius Regulus and P. Furius Philus was remarkable for putting in force the law called the Oppian, because framed by Oppius, to restrain the women from too great love of finery in dress and gold ornaments. The censors also undertook to punish the men who had given any cause of offence to the state. B.C. 214. Among these were included Cæcilius Metellus, who with his companions had formerly determined to leave Italy. Metellus was degraded from his rank, but in the following year, when tribune, he endeavoured to prosecute the censors, but was silenced by the veto of the whole tribunitial college.[47]

Some Romans who had broken their plighted faith to Hannibal, by remaining at Rome, whither they had come with Carthalo, to the injury of the national honour, instead of returning to him, according to their promise, were degraded by the censors for that breach of their word. Two thousand young men of full age, who had refused to defend their country against the invaders, came under the same censure, being sent to Sicily to serve on foot in company with those men who had been charged with misconduct at the battle of Cannæ, nor were they to be released from their degradation till the war should be concluded.[48] Certainly the censors were to be commended for their conduct upon this occasion, since want of faith and patriotism are unpardonable faults in men born in a free country, such being the vices of slavery, though even the slave may by a natural greatness of mind sometimes rise above such selfishness. The punishment inflicted upon these persons was followed by very happy results. The citizens, the soldiers, the people, all united in acts of generosity and patriotism. The soldiers refused to receive pay from the military quæstors,[49] and every senator furnished and maintained eight sailors at his own expense. Masters of families provided mariners or rowers according to the censorial assessment for the expedition of Otacilius to Sicily.[50] Never was Rome really greater in moral dignity than during the war of Hannibal, and one of the main causes of her lofty standard lay in the manner in which the censors exercised their mighty power over the whole Roman people, a power to which vice was compelled to bow, and from which neither wealth nor rank nor even popular influence could claim exemption.[51]

Hannibal passed the winter at Salapia in the society of a lady whom he loved, and whose influence retained him by her side in unwonted inactivity.[52] This renowned warrior was the husband of a Spaniard, the daughter of the proprietor of one of those mines for which Spain was anciently celebrated, the treasures of which have been long exhausted.[53] The republic wisely retained her old and experienced officers in their several stations of Spain, Sardinia, and Syracuse. Where in fact could she find abler men or more devoted to her service than Marcellus, the Scipios, Lævinus, and Scævola? Quintus Fabius being a consul this year ensured to the army the wisdom and experience of his father, who chose to serve under him, as his great-grandfather, Fabius Maximus, had formerly done in the consulship of Fabius Gurges.

While the Fabii commanded at Suessula, in Italy, Dasius Altinius, who had induced the people of Arpi to revolt to Hannibal, offered at this time to restore it again to the Romans.[54] Some officers in the consul's army recommended him to give up this double-dealing traitor to the vengeance of his own countrymen, but the elder Fabius thought otherwise, remarking, "that however despicable in character such men might be and unworthy of trust, yet in the present state of affairs no discouragement should be given to those who took steps to return to their former obedience." Altinius was allowed his liberty with certain restrictions in the day-time, but at night-fall he was regularly put in ward. If this want of confidence did not touch the feelings of the traitor, a more fearful lesson was given him by the Carthaginian leader, who was informed of his absence from Arpi and guessed its cause. The wealth and the family of the traitor were at Arpi, upon both Hannibal laid his unsparing hand. The unfortunate wife and children of Altinius at his command were put to the torture, and afterwards burned alive. This revenge wreaked upon the innocent and helpless blighted the laurels of the great Hannibal, and exhibited him to the world as the barbarous murderer of women and children.[55]

The consul stormed and took Arpi. The Fabii permitted the garrison to march out with the honours of war to join the army of Hannibal. Some of the citizens of Capua B.C. 213. returned to their allegiance and went to the camp of the prætor Fulvius, who promised that their lands should be restored after the reduction of Capua. The prætor Sempronius stormed the town of Aternum, in which he found much money, and took many prisoners. Some advantage was gained by the consul Sempronius, which was followed by the return of several of the Bruttian nations, but these were counterbalanced by a victory gained by Hanno, the Carthaginian general, over the army of the Roman prætor stationed in Bruttium.[56]

One of the most remarkable events of the year was the alliance made by Scipio in Spain with Syphax, king of the Massæsyllians (the people of western Numidia) who promised to make war with the Carthaginians,[57] for the Scipios had conceived the bold project of transferring the war to Africa as the surest way of ridding Italy of Hannibal, a design afterwards carried into effect. The Carthaginians perceiving that this alliance of the African king with Rome boded no good to Carthage, engaged Gala, sovereign of the Massylians (the people of eastern Numidia) on their side. He sent Masinissa, his son, a youth of seventeen, against Syphax, who defeated that prince with great loss, and obliged him to retire to Mauritania.

Marcellus left Appius Claudius before Syracuse with the greater part of the army, while he marched to retake some towns in Sicily that had revolted to the Carthaginians. He also defeated Hippocrates when on his way to join Himilco, the Carthaginian, who had landed with an army and numerous elephants to reinforce Hannibal. Hippocrates lost his infantry, but escaped with his cavalry to Himilco.[58] The Carthaginian did not venture to attack Marcellus, he turned his arms against those Sicilian cities that remained faithful to the Romans. Murgantia betrayed the Roman garrison and admitted the enemy. Enna was suspected of the same intention by Pinarius, the governor of that city, who cruelly massacred all the inhabitants, to prevent a supposed treason. Marcellus, if he did not counsel, approved of this barbarous action, for he granted the plunder of the unfortunate town to the soldiers who had depopulated it. This cruelty proved as impolitic as wicked, for superstition had consecrated the spot from which Pluto carried off Proserpine, and its destruction was considered impious as well as barbarous. Many Sicilian cities deserted on this account to Hannibal. While the heathens of Sicily were mourning over the city and temple of Proserpine, those of Rome were alarmed at the multitude of strange gods that crowded her temples. "Prone it should seem to idolatry," the conquests of this people introduced new objects of worship from the lands they had vanquished: even those idols that had proved so useless to defend their own votaries. At length the government interposed, and the prætor, ascending the rostrum, read to the multitude the edict of the senate, that restrained these innovations, and commanded all books of prayer, divination, or sacrifice, to be brought to him by the first of April, that from henceforth the old ritual might be used.[59] It was not only from new deities, but from the ancient worship of Mammon to whom no temples were erected, although he was still the sovereign of sordid hearts, that Rome required to be purged. In the consulship of Claudius Pulcher and Fulvius Flaccus, Postumius and some other base wretches, took advantage of the state of affairs to enrich themselves by a cruel practice, unheard of till they planned it. The publicans, or farmers of the revenue, had engaged to supply the government with arms and provisions for Spain, and the senate promised to pay for these stores, even if any accident by sea prevented their delivery. Postumius and his companions in iniquity, sent stores to sea in old leaky vessels, containing a few goods, and those of bad quality. The frequency of these shipwrecks excited, after a time, the suspicions of the public, and the criminals were convicted, fined, and imprisoned. Postumius broke his bail and fled, and Rome was freed from the extortion of a bad citizen.[60]

Tarentum was betrayed into the hands of Hannibal by some of the chief citizens, who took advantage of the fondness of Livius, the Roman governor, for the pleasures of the table, to open the gates of the city to the Carthaginians. Nicon and Philemenus, undertaking to furnish the governor's table with game, of which he was exceedingly B.C. 213. fond, he gave them permission to leave the town to hunt, and as they always brought him the supplies they promised, he never expressed the least surprise at their continued absence of a night. When the time was come Nicon admitted Hannibal at one of the gates, while Philemenus, with a thousand Africans, appeared at that where the sentinel was accustomed to admit him.[61] As Philemenus was attended by two huntsmen, bearing between them an enormous wild boar, upon whose size they commented, the unsuspecting sentinel, who did not notice the foreigners behind them, stooped to examine the animal, when he was slain by a thrust from the spear Philemenus carried. The treacherous huntsmen then joined Hannibal in the forum. All the Romans residing in the place were slain; for Hannibal caused his trumpeters to sound a charge after the Roman manner in the theatre, which attracted them to the spot, were they were immediately massacred.[62] The governor Livius escaped, but the Roman garrison within the citadel held out bravely, and made several attempts to drive Hannibal from the place. To repel these attacks he strongly fortified the town on the side facing the citadel, though not without being repeatedly harassed by the besieged, who, when he was ready to assault their stronghold sallied out and burned his machines. This accident made him turn the siege into a blockade.[63] To secure the Tarentines from famine, and to famish at the same time the Roman garrison in the citadel, which commanded the entrance of the fort, he, by one of those strokes of genius that mark the great man, transported the shipping from the haven by land, by this means supplying the Tarentines with provisions and excluding the garrison from their supplies, the citadel being then commanded by the ships of the Tarentines.[64]

The indolent Capuans, who were threatened with a siege for which they were unprovided, applied to Hanno for provisions.[65] This demand he readily granted, but was surprised at his allies sending a few carts for the great stock of corn he had collected for them. He reproved their want of forecast, and appointed another day on which they were to fetch the provisions away. They carted what they could convey to Capua, and got ready a number of wains for the rest. The citizens of Beneventum, where Hanno was encamped, informed the Roman consul Fulvius, of this, who immediately marched thither and finding Hanno in the field providing for his allies, stormed and destroyed his camp.[66] Hanno retired to Bruttium,[67] but soon after defeated the prætor Atinius, and took Thurii. He was urged by the Capuans, who had lost their corn, to come and defend them in person, this he declined, although he sent them two thousand men. Near Capua the brave and patriotic pro-consul, Sempronius Gracchus, was betrayed into an ambush, by Flavius, a Lucanian traitor, who, till then, had always appeared the friend of the Romans. He pretended to have something of a private and important nature to communicate to the pro-consul respecting the citizens of Lucania, who, he affirmed were waiting for him near a certain spot.[68] Attended by his lictors and a troop of horse, the unsuspecting Sempronius followed him, and found himself encompassed by a large body of Carthaginians. Wrapping his cloak round his left arm the betrayed warrior rushed upon the traitor, but was slain before he could avenge his death upon Flavius. Hannibal, who honoured the fallen brave, bestowed a funeral pile upon his remains, and spoke with respect of his memory.[69] The garrison in the city of Tarentum having obtained supplies, gallantly held out; but disappointed in his hope of reducing the citadel by means of Hanno, Hannibal defeated the army of Centenius Penula in Lucania,[70] and gained a complete victory over that of the prætor Fulvius, in Apulia.[71] Notwithstanding these reverses to the Roman army, the consuls, Appius and Fulvius, in conjunction with the prætor Claudius Nero, commenced the siege of Capua. About this time Marcellus stormed and took Syracuse, which he found no easy matter to effect, notwithstanding the treason of Sosis, the brazier, who let him into the city; but this did not prevent the B.C. 213. besieged from fighting for their liberty with obstinate courage.[72] Plutarch says in his life of Marcellus, that he surprised the city while the inhabitants were celebrating the festival of Diana, and were in a state of inebriety. However, Achradina still held out, which was the finest quarter of Syracuse, and with Ortygia, hoped for relief from Bomilcar, the Carthaginian admiral, who was upon the coast with a great fleet. A dreadful plague ravaged Syracuse, which destroyed a vast number of people, particularly those Carthaginians who were within reach of the tainted air.[73] Hippocrates, one of the factious Syracusan prætors, with Himilco, the

Carthaginian general, and the African troops under their command, perished during the pestilence, which did not affect the health of the Romans, who during the long blockade were acclimated to the bad air.[74] Epicydes, after the death of his brother, went to ask the assistance of Bomilcar, whom he wished to engage the Roman fleet. The Carthaginian, who had no such intention, sailed back to Africa, upon which Epicydes retired to Agrigentum; upon which the Syracusans in Achradina massacred the generals he had appointed, chose new magistrates, and demanded peace of Marcellus. The deserters, who expected to be delivered up to the vengeance of the Romans, persuaded the mercenary troops that they would undergo the same punishment if the treaty were concluded. The soldiers upon this rose upon their commanders, whom they murdered, together with such of the Syracusans who were inclined for peace. Marcellus is said to have wept over the disasters of this magnificent city, which, surrounded by armies, and already half taken, was torn with factions within.[75] Still he gave it up to the rage of his barbarous soldiery, although he spoke of mercy to the inhabitants. The treaty for capitulation was in hand at the very time when Mericus, a Spaniard, and one of the six generals chosen by the soldiers to defend what remained unconquered of Syracuse, admitted him into the gate of Ortygia, near the fountain of Arethusa.[76]

Marcellus suffered the deserters to escape, but he gave up both Achradina and Ortygia to his soldiers, who committed every excess that passion could suggest or cruelty perform. Among the victims of war perished Archimedes, the philosopher, who, intent upon a demonstration in geometry, had taken no precaution for his safety. Even the entrance of a strange soldier, sword in hand to slay him, did not disturb his mind. "Hold one instant, and spare my life till I have finished my demonstration," quietly remarked the philosopher; but the soldier, who knew as little of mercy as of geometry, killed him immediately.[77] Marcellus is said to have lamented his death, but he certainly took no pains to preserve his life. Cicero, when quæstor in Sicily, one hundred and thirty-six years afterwards, discovered the tomb of Archimedes by the sphere and cylinder inscribed upon it. The conduct of Marcellus, at the fall of this city, leads us to conclude that he would have felt more if he had wept less.

During the next consulate, that of P. Sulpicius Galba and Cn. Fulvius Centumalus, the inhabitants of Capua, straitly besieged by the Roman armies, implored Hannibal to deliver them from the calamity impending over them. He marched to their relief, but found it impossible to drive the Romans from the field, nor yet to bring them to battle. Then he formed the bold design of appearing before the walls of Rome, hoping to seize the capital while unprepared for a siege and ignorant of his approach. If he had done this after his victory of Cannæ, the attempt might, perhaps, have been crowned with success, unless the great event in the history of mankind, in due time to be accomplished, was inseparably connected with the rise of the Roman power.[78] The time for surprising Rome was gone by for ever, and when Hannibal crossed the Anio, and encamped within five miles of the capital, he found the alarm experienced by the Romans only induced them to take the wisest and best means that prudence could suggest for the preservation and defence of the city. It happened fortunately for them, that one of the newly raised legions was within the walls of the city; and that the citizens were B.C. 211. engaged in choosing from among themselves another legionary body, when the tidings of Hannibal's approach reached them.[79] Sulpicius and Fulvius, the consuls, marched out with the army, and encamped before its walls, ready to deliver it or die in its defence. The spirit of the Romans appeared to rise with the exigences of the moment, and so little was the public confidence abated by the presence of the renowned Carthaginian, that, if we may trust Livy, the ground upon which his camp then stood, was put up to auction and realised its full value. This induced Hannibal to play the practical joke of selling the bankers' shops round the forum, an act imputed to rage; but that probably emanated from the same humorous spirit that had formerly given rise to the brilliant repartee, made by him to Gisco, upon the morning of the battle of Cannæ. He is said to have rode slowly under the walls of Rome, actually hurling his spear at the Colline gate, in proud defiance; but seeing that Rome was too strong in her internal resources,[80] as well as in the courage of her sons, the bold Carthaginian abandoned his attempt, and commenced pillaging the adjacent country.[81] The consuls followed his line of march, and encamped within ten furlongs of the invader. Hannibal, anxious to preserve the spoils he had taken, forded the Anio, but being attacked by the Romans, lost a part of his booty, and three hundred of his men, who were taken by his pursuers. Finding no enemy before him, he faced about, and turning upon the consuls, stormed their camp that night; but was unable to destroy the fugitives who had taken a strong position upon a steep hill.[82] Not stopping to dislodge them, he hurried forward, hoping to surprise Rhegium; this he failed to effect, although he actually captured many persons belonging to the city, who were taking their pleasure in the country beyond the walls.[83]

Capua, in want of provisions, and abandoned by Hannibal, sent letters by some Numidians, to implore him to save them. Their messengers were betrayed to the Romans, who barbarously scourged and maimed them, and having cut off their hands, sent them back to Capua in that miserable condition.[84] This sight filled the wretched inhabitants of the revolted city with despair. In the senate, Vibius Virrius, when he found the senators inclined to capitulate, bade them abandon the useless idea, and free themselves from the tortures preparing for them by an act of self-destruction. "Death," said he, "is our only refuge. I have prepared an entertainment at my house, where, when we have finished our repast, a cup shall go round which will end our days and misfortunes together." He rose and twenty-seven senators followed him to his dark festival; the rest remained to endure the tortures of the conquerors, from which the others had emancipated themselves by a voluntary death.[85] The Capuans made terms with the pro-consuls, but whatever the agreement may have been it certainly was not adhered to, since the garrison was seized as well as the senators, their treasures were torn from them, and themselves detained in doleful captivity. Appius Claudius, who was disposed to be more merciful to this unhappy people than his colleague, was dead of his wounds; but Fulvius went with a body of horse to the cities whither they had been sent prisoners, and ordered them to be scourged with rods and beheaded by his lictors. Jubellius Taurea, a native of Capua, upon beholding this dreadful execution, reproached the pro-consul with his cruelty, and demanded to be slain with his countrymen. This Fulvius refused affirming that he was mad with rage and despair. Jubellius told him that he had slain his wife and children to save them from dishonour, and was come hither not to witness the deaths of the senators, but to die with them; and that since Fulvius would not slay him, after having caused him so much misery, he would slay himself. These words were followed by his stabbing himself to the heart, and falling dead upon the steps of the tribunal.[86]

The Romans refused Fulvius a triumph, alleging that he had only recovered, not added to, the territorial possessions of the Commonwealth.[87] In fact they were disgusted with the ferocity of the stern old man. The recovery of Capua was followed by the acquisition of several important places in Acarnania, which were won from the king of Macedon. Indeed, the pro-prætor, Lævinus, B.C. 211. with great address and profound policy, had managed to embroil king Philip of Macedon with the Grecian states, some of which he also induced to seek the alliance of Rome. The Ætolians, from whom Acarnania had been torn by king Philip, were the first to make a treaty with the Romans, and their example was followed by the Eleans and Lacedæmonians, and by the kings of Pergamus, Thrace, and Illyricum.[88] The Lacedæmonians, it is true, long debated the propriety of a measure that would make Philip of Macedon their enemy, and Lyciscus, the orator boldly declared that the new friends of the Ætolians, the warlike and politic Romans, would soon become their conquerors, and, in time, the sovereigns of Greece.[89] That people nevertheless joined the league, because they wanted the wisdom and forethought of Lyciscus. Lævinus took from the Macedonians the island of Zacynthus and two cities of Acarnania, which he bestowed upon the Ætolians. Having thus prevented Philip of Macedon's descent into Italy, by involving him in a war with most of the Grecian states, he made Corcyra his head-quarters during the winter season.

Marcellus, upon his return to Rome from Sicily, claimed the honour of a triumph. This was denied him through the rigid etiquette that ordained that no commander, however valiant or fortunate, should make a triumphal entry without his army, that of Marcellus being absent in Sicily. He chose to decree himself one upon the hill of Alba, and the following day enjoyed an ovation, one, indeed, of the most magnificent upon record. The Syracusans had always excelled in the fine arts, and the noble statuary and masterly paintings exhibited to the admiring eyes of the Roman people awakened a feeling that Rome never lost.[90]

At the elections for the consulship a singular instance of moderation and prudence occurred. The first century that voted named Torquatus Manlius and T. Otacilius as fitting persons for that honour, and the others seemed quite willing to follow their example, and Manlius was congratulated upon his nomination to a dignity that he had not sought, but he declined it on account of a weakness in his eyes, declaring "that that man whose infirmities compelled him to look through the eyes of others was unfit to be either a general or pilot."[91] This did not satisfy his constituents who, with repeated cries, named him again, but with no better success than before. "No!" cried he, "I can neither bear your manners, nor you my government. Return to your voting-place, and consider that

Carthage is making war in Italy, and that Hannibal is her general."[92] His constituents perceiving that Manlius spoke with honest sincerity, named Marcellus for the fourth, and Lævinus for the second time, to the consular dignity. If every man nominated to high command in a state were to act with the patriotic moderation and self-denial of Torquatus Manlius, fewer public disasters would occur in every country.

Lævinus was dangerously ill at Corcyra when he was elected with Marcellus to the consulship. Upon his return to Rome his kind and benevolent character made him much desired both by the Sicilians and Campanians, for Marcellus was accused to the senate of cruelty to the Syracusans, a charge from which he had not then legally cleared himself. Lævinus was beset on his route by crowds of Campanians who conjured him to protect them from the cruelty of the pro-consul Fulvius Flaccus. Lævinus requested his unfortunate clients to follow him to Rome. Near the gates of the city he encountered the Sicilians who were the accusers of Marcellus, and all the complainants chose to enter it in his train. After Lævinus had given an account to the conscript fathers of his transactions in Greece, they proceeded to assign to each consul his province. Lævinus was nominated to Italy, and Marcellus to Sicily; upon which the Sicilians uttered a loud cry, and besought the senate to kill them all rather than subject them to the government of their bitterest enemy. This incident did not speak much for the mercy of Marcellus, though he is praised for that quality by his biographer.[93] The senate desired him to exchange provinces with his colleague. Lævinus consented to the arrangement, which was made to the great delight of the Sicilians. Nevertheless they, the Syracusans, desired to place their city under the patronage B.C. 210. and protection of Marcellus; and Syracuse, from that time, was protected by the family of the Marcelli.[94]

The fate of Capua and Campania was now pronounced by the senate. Capua was no longer a Roman city, it was deprived of all its privileges, and its inhabitants were carried away and replaced by Roman colonies; Campania was degraded and robbed of its ancient monuments.

The Roman navy was equipped by the voluntary contributions of the rich and noble without the government being compelled to levy an oppressive tax. Two traitors in Salapia, a considerable town in Apulia, delivered it up to Marcellus, but five hundred Numidian horsemen defended themselves with such bravery that only fifty were left alive, these surrendered themselves prisoners to the consul. This was considered a great loss to Hannibal, and Livy affirms that from henceforth he had no reason to boast of his superiority in cavalry. The city of Tarentum still held out, though the Roman fleet sent to relieve it had been totally defeated at sea and the admiral slain.[95] Marcellus made himself master of several towns in Samnium, and took three thousand Carthaginians prisoners,[96] but these successes were more than balanced by the victory gained by Hannibal near Herdonea over Fulvius Centumalus, who was slain, together with eleven legionary tribunes, and his camp destroyed.[97] A drawn battle was fought between Marcellus and Hannibal, near Numistro, in Bruttium; night parted the combatants, but Marcellus at dawn offered to renew the combat which had been very sanguinary though undecided. This Hannibal declined, and commenced his retreat, followed by Marcellus, and the rest of the campaign was spent in pursuit and retreat on the part of these celebrated men.

Fulvius Flaccus found means to convey corn and troops to the Roman garrison in the citadel at Tarentum, and the possession of Agrigentum, which was betrayed to the consul Lævinus by an act of private revenge on the part of Mutines, a brave Numidian officer, whom Hanno had degraded from his rank, gave the Roman arms in Sicily a superiority that they ever after maintained. Six towns were stormed by the Romans, twenty were betrayed, and forty surrendered. Lævinus thus became master of Sicily.[98] Valerius Messala, the admiral of the Sicilian fleet, brought back from the coasts of Africa, which he had been ravaging, the important news that the Carthaginians were fitting out an armament to re-conquer Sicily. The dictator Fulvius managed to have Maximus Cunctator and himself elected to the consulship. There was some opposition made to the re-election of Maximus, it being a violation of the old law to allow any individual to hold this distinguished office two successive years. Fulvius cited in his colleague's favour a recent edict, which permitted this innovation, while Hannibal should remain in Italy, by which means the able Fabius Maximus was declared duly elected.[99]

Twelve Roman colonies planted by Rome refused to furnish their quota of men, arms, and money. The republic was compelled to overlook their disobedience, not being in a state to enforce her claims.[100] The exchequer still contained a treasure which had been accumulating there since A.U.C. 396, B.C. 358, being the twentieth part of every slave's purchased freedom. This had been preserved against a time of public difficulty and danger, and was devoted to meet the present crisis. The fruitful lands of Campania were farmed for the good of the state, as the unfortunate inhabitants had been destroyed or driven out by the Romans in the course of the war. Fabius Maximus laid siege to Tarentum, while Fulvius and Marcellus made war upon Hannibal.[101]

Tarentum was betrayed to the Romans through the agency of a young Tarentine female, whose brother was serving in the Roman army.[102] The brother, who was sent into the city as a deserter, easily swayed her to serve the interest of his general, and she seduced her lover, the commander of the Bruttian troops, from his allegiance, and induced him to open the gate to the besieging army. Fabius Maximus behaved with great cruelty upon this occasion, for he spared none he found in arms. Thirty thousand of the inhabitants were made slaves, their effects were sold, and the money brought into the public treasury. Fabius looked with a cold eye upon the noble statues and fine paintings of the Tarentines, and when the officer who B.C 209. was taking an inventory of the precious furniture belonging to the unfortunate citizens asked him, "What he should do with the gods" (the statues and paintings), he replied, "Let us leave to the Tarentines their angry deities," in allusion to the fighting attitude in which these were represented. An immense quantity of gold and silver was found in this commercial city, but Fabius paid it all into the exchequer, reserving nothing for himself but a colossal statue of Hercules. Fabius Maximus is accused of having stained his laurels with the barbarous massacre at Tarentum.[103] Marcus Livius, the governor of the citadel, proud of its defence and envious of the success of

Maximus, said to him at Rome in a boasting manner, "I, not Fabius, was the cause of recovering Tarentum." "True," replied Fabius laughing, "for if you had not lost the town I had never recovered it."[104] Upon the news of the fall of this city reaching Hannibal, as he was on his way to relieve it, he made this remark, "The Romans have their Hannibal. We have lost Tarentum by the same arts by which we won it."[105] He marched to Metapontum and laid a snare for Fabius, by sending persons to treat with him about betraying that city to the Romans. The consul was in danger of falling into the snare laid for him if the augurs who suspected it had not declared the auspices were unlucky. New emissaries were sent again, and these being threatened with the torture confessed the truth.[106]

Marcellus and Quinctius Crispinus were chosen for the consulate this year, but the dignity was fatal to them both. They wished to possess themselves of the city of Locri in the south of Italy, but finding Hannibal near them, they sent a detachment to besiege the place by land, while the admiral of the fleet stationed to guard the coast was to invest it by sea; but Hannibal surprised these troops, killed two thousand of them, and made twelve hundred prisoners. Marcellus and his colleague then encamped between Bantia and Venusia. The desire of Marcellus had long been that he might fight a last decisive battle with Hannibal, it was his hope, we are told, by day, and his dream by night, but the wily Carthaginian did not choose to put his hitherto invincible fortune to this test. He chose to rid himself of his illustrious rival in a less honourable manner. He purposely left a hill between his camp and that of the two consuls apparently unoccupied, while he secretly laid an ambush among the thickets with which it was covered, conjecturing that Marcellus would endeavour to possess himself of the ground.[107] The two consuls, the younger Marcellus, and a guard of 270 Tuscans and Fregellans went to view the hill, and fell into the snare laid for them by Hannibal. At the first discharge of darts and spears the Tuscans fled, but the Fregellans closed firmly round the consuls, till Marcellus received a thrust from a spear and fell dead from his horse. His colleague Crispinus, though mortally wounded, spurred his fleet steed and fled to the camp. Then these gallant men finding resistance hopeless, took up the young tribune Marcellus, who was lying wounded on the ground, and bore him to the camp, leaving the remains of his great father on the fatal hill. In this skirmish only forty Roman soldiers were slain, but eighteen were taken prisoners, and five lictors. Hannibal, as soon as he learned the fruits of the stratagem, repaired to the spot, and regarded the remains of his great rival with some admiration, but no exultation. His acute perception of his own interest did not, however, fail him upon this occasion, for he drew the seal-ring from the finger of the illustrious dead, intending to make use of it as a key to open many important towns in the vicinity.[108] He ordered a magnificent funeral for the slain consul, and enclosing the ashes in a costly funeral urn, sent them to his son as a proof of his esteem for the brave Roman who had so long defended his country. Plutarch and some others declare that the Numidians quarrelled for the silver urn and scattered the ashes, but Livy says they were delivered to his son.[109] Crispinus, though his wounds were mortal, survived long enough to circumvent Hannibal's designs. He wrote to all the cities in the Roman interest to warn them against acting upon commands or suggestions contained in letters signed with the name or sealed with the ring of Marcellus, who, unfortunately for his country, had fallen. No city paid attention B.C. 208. to the forged letters sent by Hannibal but Salapia, in Apulia, the citizens of which pretended to believe what the epistle affirmed, that Marcellus and a Roman detachment would be at the gates of their city the following night. Hannibal, who had caused six hundred men to be clothed and armed after the Roman fashion, sent them thither, not doubting that he should be master of Salapia by the following morning. The Salapians, as soon as they had admitted as many as they could manage, dropped the portcullis, and slew them, while a shower of darts from the ramparts drove back the rest, to the great mortification of Hannibal.[110] However, as nothing discouraged him long, he hastened to the relief of Locri, then besieged by land and sea. The Roman admiral Cincius behaved very ill upon this occasion, for he took on board the land forces and fled with his fleet for Rome, abandoning in his haste all the engines used in the siege.[111]

The consul Quinctius Crispinus, who had broken up his camp after the death of his colleague and occupied one hastily formed in the mountains, withdrew with his army to Capua, when finding his end approaching, he wrote to the senate to send some members to him, who might receive his last instructions for the benefit of the republic. This was the first intelligence that had reached the Romans of the death of Marcellus. Three senators were despatched to the dying Crispinus, who still devoted his fleeting moments to the service of his country. They asked him to nominate a person of worth and integrity as dictator, to hold the comitia for the election of consuls to replace himself and Marcellus. He named Torquatus Manlius before he expired.[112]

Upon the coast of Africa the Roman arms were very successful: Valerius Lævinus ravaged the shore with a fleet of a hundred ships, and defeated that of the Carthaginians at Clypea. In Greece the Ætolians kept king Philip in full employment, and prevented him effectually from making a descent upon Italy. He won several victories over them, and even attacked the Roman army while they were ravaging the lands about Corinth, and obliged them to embark in disorder.[113] Sulpicius, the pro-consul, gained some advantage in his turn at Elis, but this did not prevent Philip from tearing from the country-people twenty thousand head of cattle which they were conveying to the fortress of Pyrgus for security.[114] Fortunately for the Ætolians, and Romans, a false report of this sovereign's death occasioned the Dardanians to invade Macedon, and forced him to return to look after the affairs of his own kingdom.

During the contest with Hannibal the two Scipios in Spain waged a continual war with the Carthaginians for the possession of that country. The victory of Munda gained the brave Roman brothers the city of Saguntum, and prevented Hasdrubal, the brother of Hannibal, from immediately joining that great commander in Italy, according to the instructions he had received from the Carthaginian senate. When Hasdrubal joined Hannibal his departure was as fortunate for the Romans in Spain, as impolitic for the Carthaginian interest in that country.[115] The Scipios acquired an immense influence over the native Spaniards, employing in their armies twenty thousand Celtiberians, while in order to detach their countrymen in Italy from Hannibal's service, the Roman pro-consuls employed three hundred Spanish noblemen who were sent by them on this difficult and delicate mission to Italy.[116] The return of Hasdrubal to Spain occasioned the desertion of the Celtiberians from the Scipios, who returned to their own homes,[117] a practice common to all Celtic warriors when they have amassed sufficient plunder. If we may trust Appian the Scipios had advanced the Roman eagles as far south as the valley of the Guadalquiver, anciently called the Baetis, where they had taken up their winter quarters.[118] These advantages were lost by the deaths of these brave brethren in two separate engagements with Hasdrubal, for that able commander, who possessed much of the military talent of his brother Hannibal, vanquished Publius Scipio, who was slain in the action. Another victory, won twenty-seven days after the first, ended in the defeat and death of Cneius Scipio.[119] Marcius, a young Roman centurion of great bravery, assumed the title of pro-prætor, and headed the B.C. 208. army in Spain in preference to Fonteius, the lieutenant of the Scipios.[120] The senate did not acknowledge Marcius for pro-prætor, but sent Claudius Nero to Spain with a considerable army and the authority of pro-consul.[121]

Publius Scipio presented himself to the Roman people as a candidate for the pro-consular government of Spain. He was only in the twenty-seventh year of his age, which disqualified him for the high office for which he solicited. He had been curule ædile, but had not been a prætor, nor even a pro-prætor,—in fact the services of his father and uncle, his own early acquaintance with war, patriotism, and noble filial love, were his sole recommendations to his constituents. Fortunately for Rome these found him favour with the people.[122] His eloquence, full of nervous boldness, proved to them his intimate knowledge of the affairs of that country in which his dearest and nearest relations had found graves, and inspired his auditors with confidence, and his conduct fully justified their choice. As for the statements of some early writers respecting the dissoluteness of the young pro-consul's morals before his elevation to the government of Spain, his very appointment gives a sufficient refutation to the groundless charge, for virtue was an essential qualification for any public office in that age when the censors or masters of public morals possessed an absolute power over all classes of the people. Lucius, his elder brother, at a later period of life, was called to account for immoral conduct, and it is possible that his youth was no better than his manhood. Publius gave sufficient reason in his whole public life to justify the conclusion that his active youth was as stainless as his riper manhood. He described himself to Masinissa "as one who had always been the master of his own passions," and his history has fully borne out the noble assertion. The first two years of his government were employed in making treaties with the Spanish nations, and conciliating the affections of his allies. The capture of New Carthage, or Carthagena, was an exploit that gained him much fame as a general, while his conduct to the inhabitants won the esteem even of his enemies. Following the examples of his father and uncle, he dismissed all the Spanish hostages to their own people and homes, and this generosity emboldened the wife of Mandonius, the brother of Indibilis, king of the Ilergetes, to throw herself at his feet, with her daughters and nieces, and implore him to treat his captives with more respect than the Carthaginians were accustomed to do.[123] The tears and blushes of the young females easily betrayed the nature of their fears, which the modesty of the noble matron would not permit her to express. Scipio assured her "that they should be treated with as much respect in his camp as if they had been his own mother and sisters;" and the young Roman honourably kept his word. A few days after this a beautiful princess, who was contracted to Allucius one of the princes of Celtiberia, was taken captive and brought into his camp. Though very young and susceptible, Scipio mastered the admiration he felt at the sight of the lovely Spaniard, and sending for her affianced lord, presented her to him, "assuring him that if his bride had been in the home of her parents she could not have been treated with greater respect and delicacy."[124] Allucius received his wife with gratitude and emotion, and readily promised to become the friend and ally of Rome. Scipio, as generous as he was continent, presented to the young couple, as a marriage-portion, the rich ransom sent to him by the parents of the lady. This conduct was not only virtuous but politic, for Allucius gained over many neighbouring nations to aid the Romans by relating to them this proof of the young Roman commander's continence. This instance of forbearance in the young victor has been doubted; two ancient authors have pronounced it a fabrication,[125] and a great modern historian[126] has adopted their views. In the face of ancient scandal, and more recent incredulity, a remarkable witness to the fact remained in the cabinet of the late king of France in the votive shield presented to Publius Scipio by a grateful people. This, if it have escaped the crucible of the revolutionists, may still be in existence, but however this may be, its identity has been clearly made out, and recorded by the antiquarian Spon, in whose learned work an engraving of this interesting B.C. 207. relic may be seen.[127] Time and oblivion, which had long kept this memorial of the continence of Scipio Africanus, at length yielded it up in order to render justice to the virtue of a slandered hero of antiquity. The resemblance between his conduct to the Spanish ladies to that of Alexander in regard to the family of Darius, gave rise to these unfounded doubts. But even if Scipio had fixed his eyes upon that brightest page of Alexander's history, and admired and imitated it, that imitation ought neither to have detracted from the merit of a fine action, nor tended to disprove it. How valuable, indeed, is the study of history, which furnished in Alexander's life an example worthy even of the imitation of a Scipio!

Leaving Scipio in his province, it is time to return to the Roman metropolis, where the consular elections were about to be held to replace the two brave men who had fallen in the consular purple, an honourable pall for Romans at such a crisis—

"For those in Glory's bed who sleep
Weep fondly, but exulting weep.
The fairest wreath that Fame can bind
Is ever with the cypress twined."

The report that Hasdrubal, the brother of Hannibal, was crossing the Alps, on his way to join the Carthaginian army, with sixty thousand men, obliged the senate to look out for citizens of eminent wisdom and bravery to fill the consulate, which had been left vacant by the deaths of the great Marcellus, and the patriotic Crispinus. They thought that these qualities were to be found united in the persons of Claudius Nero and Livius Salinator, though not in each individual, for the first was bold and daring, the last cool and calculating, though he had formerly shown much spirit in the Illyrian war.[128] He, however, opposed his own election on account of the false accusation formerly brought against him, which had occasioned him to quit public life in disgust, for his farm in the country; till Marcellus and Lævinus, who had a high opinion of his wisdom and probity, compelled him to return to Rome and his senatorial duties. A long beard, neglected dress, and silence, marked his keen sense of the injustice of the commons. He gave his vote for or against a measure, by an affirmative or negative alone, till M. Livius Macatus, his friend and kinsman, was falsely accused, when the occasion awoke his oratory once more to the surprise and admiration of his hearers. "Here is the very man we want," remarked the senators, "for a consul," and the comitia of the people approved their choice and confirmed it by vote.[129] Livius exerted his indignant eloquence to oppose his re-election to this dignity: "If I am considered worthy to be chosen to the consulate a second time, why was I condemned? If that condemnation was just, why am I placed at the helm again?" His passionate resentment was mollified, however, by the entreaties of the senate and the people. He was elected in conjunction with Claudius Nero. Their several provinces were decided by lot. He was directed to oppose Hasdrubal, while Claudius Nero was ordered to face Hannibal in Bruttium. As Livius Salinator and Claudius Nero were at variance, old Fabius wished to make them friends before quitting Rome. "For what purpose," replied Livius, "we shall both serve our country better if we feel that a rival's eye is upon all our actions?"[130] The senate interposed, and these foes were publicly reconciled. To the temporising advice of Fabius respecting Hannibal, he bluntly replied, "that he meant to fight for glory and victory, or revenge on his own countrymen, whose injustice still rankled in his breast," a sentiment worthy of Diogenes.[131] Hasdrubal, who had not yet been able to cross the Pyrenees, was compelled to that measure by a great victory gained by Scipio, which made his retreat into Gaul absolutely necessary.[132]

Hasdrubal marched from Spain to Gaul, and then into Italy, without experiencing any of those attacks from the mountain tribes, that had impeded his brother's progress; for he had the forecast to send messengers before him to assure them, that his object in crossing the Pyrenees and the Alps, was to find a way into a distant country with B.C. 207. which he was at war. As soon as he had passed the Alps, he laid siege to Placentia, and sent a letter to Hannibal, to "inform him of his coming, and that he was on the route to Umbria, where he desired his brother to meet him,[133] when they would march upon Rome by the Flaminian way." The prætor, Hostilius, who had gained some advantage over Hannibal, captured the messenger on his way, and intercepted the important communication. He did not open the letter, but sent it with a strong guard to the consul Nero, at Canusium.[134] That general, with the promptitude that marked the great commander, resolved to leave his province, though contrary to law, in order to effect a junction with Livius, the other consul, and give battle to Hasdrubal, before his brother could come up with him. He wrote letters to the senate informing them of his intention, and marched immediately for Umbria.[135]

This crisis was the most momentous period of the struggle between Hannibal and the Roman republic. Upon the energy and expedition of the consul Claudius Nero, as well as his military skill, the existence of Rome depended. The fate of his country was in his hands; he knew and felt his mighty responsibility, and prepared to meet the trial with the valour and forecast of Hannibal himself. So careful was he in keeping his expedition a profound secret, that not one among the seven thousand chosen soldiers, who followed their intrepid leader, was aware of his design till the proper time was come, and their forced march had placed them at a distance from Hannibal.[136] In fact Nero, in this glorious epoch of his life, had omitted nothing that a prudent general ought to remember, and no impediment opposed his rapid march to the maritime colony of Sena, where his colleague, Livius, was stationed. His progress was greeted with joy by the people of Italy, who aided him with free hearts and willing hands. His chosen few were full of patriotic feeling, proud to share the toils and dangers of their general. The prayers and tears of the country people, whose blessings and vows seemed to call in the aid of religion to the assistance of these gallant soldiers, stimulated them to still greater exertions;[137] and in little more than six days since Nero quitted Apulia with his little army, Livius Salinator received from his colleague due warning of his approach, and in return had advised him to enter his camp in the silence and secresy of night.[138] By the regulations of Salinator, the troops of Nero were to share the quarters of the encamped consular army, as any attempt upon their part to increase their means of accommodation might have made the enemy acquainted with his coming with reinforcements. We are assured that his little army had been increased by veterans past the age of service, and youthful patriots not yet legally qualified by their years to serve their country, whom the patriotic consul had permitted to join the gallant enterprise. Nero must have received this general enthusiasm as his best and holiest auspices; and though, upon the following morning, he was urged by Livius, the consul, and Porcius, the prætor, to give his wearied soldiers more repose, Nero wisely allowed not a moment to escape, for these glowing feelings to cool, or Hasdrubal to advance one step nearer towards his brother. The consular robe was hoisted, and the Roman soldiers quitting their camp, came forth and formed for battle.[139]

Their challenge was immediately met by Hasdrubal, whose camp lay within half a mile of his opponent's; but the cautious Carthaginian, in reconnoitring the enemy, perceived that some increase of their numbers had taken place; he, therefore, retreated to his camp, and sent forth some horsemen to observe that of the Romans more closely. A trivial circumstance gave the necessary information to Hasdrubal, for the daily routine of the Roman camp was marked by the sound of the trumpet, which was heard as usual once in the camp of Porcius; but the double flourish in that of Livius, marked the presence of his colleague within his lines. How heavily must these martial notes have fallen upon the ears of the brave Carthaginian; how unaccountable must have appeared to him the presence of Nero at Sena! Did he fear for the safety of Hannibal, or for himself, in that moment when doubt was changed to fateful certainty? History has not told what Hasdrubal thought or suffered; she only relates the result of his bitter conviction. Hasdrubal extinguished B.C. 207. all his fires, and in the shadow of night commenced his retreat,[140] and had fallen back fourteen miles upon the Metaurus, when the desertion of his guides left him to contend with his difficult and intricate route alone and unassisted. Unable to find any ford, he traversed the winding steeps that enclosed the river, whose ascent was toilsome and seriously impeded his march.[141] He encamped, and the Gauls, according to their usual custom, drank so deeply that by dawn, when the Romans overtook the Carthaginians, they could not be roused from their oblivious slumbers.[142] Retreat was rendered impossible, and Hasdrubal was compelled to venture upon the chances of a battle;[143] which, though long and obstinately contested between himself and the consul, Livius, on the left Roman wing, was won by an able manœuvre, boldly conceived and skilfully executed by Nero, who, finding he could make no impression on the Carthaginian front, where Hasdrubal had posted his elephants, passed behind the troops of Livius and Porcius, to attack the right flank and rear of the enemy. The fortune of the day was then decided— though the enemy stood firm to the last; till Hasdrubal, riding into the midst of a Roman cohort, sought and found there a soldier's grave,[144] shared with ten thousand Carthaginians and two thousand Romans.[145]

The victors stormed and won the camp, slaughtering the inebriated Gauls,[146] whose condition deprived them of the power of self-defence. Besides the rich plunder and the capture of four living elephants, it was the happiness of the Romans to restore to freedom three thousand of their countrymen, whom their valour gave back to their delivered country; for every man in the Roman army must have felt, that that day's success had struck to the cause of Hannibal a fatal blow. Not an enemy would have escaped from the slaughter of the battle of Metaurus, if the great fatigue the Roman soldiers had endured, would have permitted them to pursue the fugitives. For when advice was sent to Livius the next day, that a body of Ligurians might be overtaken and put to the sword, as they had neither commanders nor ensigns, he replied, "No matter; let some live to carry the news of our victory and their defeat."[147] Nero left the camp of Livius the following evening, and was entrenched in his own in the short period of six days. The first intimation of his brother's defeat and death received by Hannibal, was given him by the sight of his head, flung, by the order of the consul, before his advanced guards.[148] "It is like the fortune of Carthage," remarked the great Carthaginian, overlooking his own family loss in that of his country, to whom Hasdrubal had been a loyal and devoted servant; for if any man ever lived exclusively for his country, that man was Hannibal. Much of his success was owing to the military skill and devoted attachment of his brothers; and the tragic communication of the defeat and slaughter of Hasdrubal, was full of unmitigated horror. Nero stained his laurels by this barbarous outrage on the feelings of Hannibal, though it, perhaps, originated more from policy than triumph.

At Rome the immense anxiety of the people was excited not relieved by the report of a great battle having been fought and won on the Metaurus by the consular army. None dared to believe what had not been officially announced, for the news had been brought to the camp at Narnia by two horsemen, natives of the place, Nero having stationed two legions there to guard that part of the Flaminian way. Men could not conceive how in the brief space of two days such intelligence could reach Narnia, and all was doubt and wild conjecture.[149] Modern times can show a parallel state of public dread and doubtful expectation. Many persons living on the eastern coast of England can remember seamen hearing at sea the far-distant thunders of Waterloo borne on the strong wings of the east wind, yet deemed impossible to be heard by human ears at such a distance, and how contrabandists forgot the caution so necessary in their mysterious trade to spread abroad the glorious tidings that the mighty arm of Wellington had smitten down the colossal power of Napoleon, and stretched his eagles in the dust. Few dared to give their statement credence till confirmed some hours later by the despatches of the victor. Rome like our own London awaited in trembling hope the official confirmation of the victory. B.C. 207. But it came at last, that laurel-crowned letter, to meet which the mighty living stream of human population poured forth over the Milvian bridge, in eager and joyful anticipation. Brief was the answer the consular officers gave the Roman people, but it told of safety, victory, and freedom. "The consuls were alive; Hasdrubal, the brother of Hannibal, was dead; and the victorious legions had sustained little loss." Attended by the crowd L. Veturius Philo, P. Licinius Varus, and Q. Metellus, entered Rome, and with difficulty gained the sanctuary of the senate-house, to which the Roman people sought in their patriotic curiosity to gain access. But when Veturius, after reading the consular letter to the senate, came into the forum and read from the rostrum the despatch, he was heard in silence till the mighty emotions of the public mind swelled from whispered murmurs into one mighty plaudit, terminating in a long loud hurrah, in which they vented their deep heartfelt joy.[150] The devout gratitude of a people is always interesting, even when their adoration is ignorantly misplaced, for the feeling that filled the temples of Rome with worshippers only wanted purer light to elevate it into the sublimer worship of the Supreme Being. But denser darkness must overshadow the Roman people before the dayspring from on high could dawn upon them, for they were a moral people, and the age was still virtuous, two centuries of guilty greatness must pass away before the promised advent, of which some traditionary traces lingered in Italy.[151]

The consuls returned at the close of the year and their public entry was greeted by a delivered people, with the most flattering testimonials of gratitude. Livius Salinator alone appeared in the triumphal chariot, while by his side Claudius Nero rode on horseback without his army or the gorgeous pomp that glittered round his colleague. Livius had commanded the army at Metaurus, and military etiquette denied the consul Nero his full honours, unless his soldiers then left in his province could share them with him. Every eye, however, was admiringly fixed upon the true hero of that glorious day,[152] for success had given to the noble rashness of the energetic consul the names of valour and wisdom. His career in Spain had not afforded any proof of the consummate military talent he had displayed in this campaign, yet it could not have been the growth of a day. He had never before been invested with the consular purple, nor had acted upon his sole responsibility, therefore his eminent abilities had had no theatre for display. Why he never was thus honoured again probably originated in the jealousy of the senate, but he was afterwards chosen for the censorship, being one of the seven censors enumerated by Suetonius in the pedigree of the Emperor Tiberius.[153]

The news of the naval victory gained over the Carthaginians by Lævinus added to the national joy, which was increased by the information communicated by the pro-consul Sulpicius, that Attalus, king of Pergamus, and his allies, had found employment for the restless genius of Philip of Macedon, by providing him with too many wars and commotions at home to allow him troops or time for his projected invasion of Italy. "The loss of his valiant brother Hasdrubal, and the preoccupation of king Philip, convinced Hannibal that the conquest of Italy was no longer practicable. This conviction did not depress his firm and vigorous mind, which remained as invincible as when he first commenced his unrivalled career of conquest." Success never carried him beyond the bounds of prudence and moderation, nor had adversity power to abase him, for he always rose superior to fortune. The son of Hamilcar did not arise in the zenith of his country's greatness, he was born when her ruin was rushing forward to a climax—a ruin his transcendant talents and devoted patriotism delayed, but could not avert. The new consuls, Cæcilius Metellus and Veturius Philo, men of distinguished valour, were sent to Bruttium to act in concert against Hannibal. At Consentia they felt the superiority of his genius, and foiled in the field durst not force his camp.

In Spain for the last two years Scipio had maintained an obstinate war with Mago, the brother of Hannibal, Hasdrubal, the son of Gisco, and Masinissa, the Numidian prince. To these generals, who were all persons of ability, was added another named Hanno, sent to replace Hasdrubal, Hannibal's brother. Silanus, the pro-prætor, B.C. 207. defeated Hanno and Mago, taking the former prisoner during the battle. The following spring Mago, Hasdrubal, the son of Gisco, and Masinissa, combined their armies and made great preparations for war against the Romans, but Scipio marched to meet them near the town of Silpa, and gave them such a terrible overthrow that he broke in a great measure the Carthaginian power in Spain. Hasdrubal fled to the coast and got on board a Carthaginian vessel. Mago escaped to Gaul, and Masinissa was persuaded to make alliance with the Romans through the able negotiations of Silanus.[154] These reverses of the Carthaginians in Spain inclined Syphax, the former ally of the Romans, to break the treaty he had made with his new friends and return to his old ones. He was easily induced to do this by Lælius, the lieutenant and personal friend of Scipio. Still the wary Syphax would not conclude the treaty unless the pro-consul would come to Africa and ratify it in his presence. Scipio, who had formed the bold design of concluding the war begun in Italy at Carthage, embarked with Lælius for Africa, leaving the government and the army in Spain to the able command of Marcius.[155]

Here by accident or design he met Hasdrubal, the son of Gisco, whom he had lately vanquished in Spain, and this general, struck with his talents and captivated by his manners, appears to have foreseen the object of his coming to the court of Syphax, for he, through the instrumentality of the Numidian king, wished to come to terms with the illustrious Roman. Scipio replied to these overtures, "that he held no power from his government to treat with

Carthage."[156] Upon his return to New Carthage Scipio entertained his army with a show of gladiators, in honour of his father's and uncle's memory. At these games two Spanish princes fought for a principality,[157] and these barbarous diversions formed a suitable prelude to the severity he was about to display to those cities which had revolted from the Romans after the defeat and death of those in whose names the shows were given. Castulo was sacked and burned by Marcius, its ashes forming the grave of its inhabitants, who were all put to the sword.[158] This terrible example reduced the people of Astapa to despair, who finding resistance no longer possible threw themselves upon one funeral pile.[159] These horrors stain the government of Scipio in Spain and tarnish the verdure of his laurels. The dangerous illness of the pro-consul occasioned, soon after, the revolt of Indibilis and his brother Mandonius;[160] nor was this the only disturbance which occurred during his malady, for eight thousand legionaries who had received a report of the pro-consul's death on the banks of the Suero, where they were stationed, suddenly rose against their officers, whom they drove away from their camp, and elected five-and-thirty of their own body for their leaders, choosing Atrius and Albius for their generals with the titles of consuls.[161] These magistrates assumed the dress and state pertaining to the dignity they had usurped, being attended by lictors carrying the fasces, and an honorary guard.[162] Mago sent the revolted troops a considerable donative, in the hope of engaging them in the Carthaginian service. They accepted the gift but did not add to this meanness the deeper guilt of enlisting themselves against their countrymen.[163] The recovery of their general awakened the loyalty of his soldiers, nor did the arrival of seven tribunes in the camp on the Suero increase their fidelity to their new consuls. These officers, whom they had expelled from their body with contempt, brought them not only the intelligence of Scipio's recovery but the promise that upon their repairing to Carthagena in a few days the arrears due to each soldier should be paid.[164] These arrears Scipio well knew were the true cause of the revolt. The Spaniards dispersed, for the name of Scipio was sufficient to quell men who though brave were not a united people.

The seven tribunes, during their interview with the mutineers, had obtained the names of all the leaders of the revolt, and it is probable even induced them to put themselves *en route* for New Carthage, where a proclamation had been issued by Scipio for the payment of the army.[165] It is certain that their old tribunes met them on the road, and communicated to them that M. Silanus was to march from New Carthage with all the soldiers quartered there B.C. 206. against the disaffected Spaniards. The unsuspecting rebels withdrew to their barracks for the night, little dreaming what scene the morning was preparing for them. The ringleaders, including the mock-consuls, supped with the tribunes, by whom their persons were quietly secured.[166] In the meantime the loyal troops in the city marched to the gates, which they manned, waiting there for orders to enter the market-place to surround the rebels from the Suero as soon as those, in obedience to the military order, had entered it. The sight of Scipio seated in state on his military tribunal, pale from the severe fever that had nearly brought him to the grave, but sternly still, surprised them, and in mute amazement and terror they beheld the columns marching down upon them from every street.

The sight of the five-and-thirty ringleaders brought to the tribunal of their general for judgment, the rash confidence that had led them unarmed into his awful presence, must have made that moment an age of misery to these guilty soldiers. If they gave vent in words to their feelings, the silence imposed by the sonorous voice of the crier made them await in awe-struck wonder their condemnation by their judge.[167] His stern reproof they supposed would conclude with their sentence. It did so, but not in the manner they expected, for Scipio declared his justice would be satisfied with the punishment of the few while his mercy should be extended to the many. His reply was answered by the clash of arms, and again the voice of the crier was heard calling over the list of those doomed names, whereupon the five-and-thirty prisoners were bound, scourged, and beheaded in the sight of their comrades. This terrible scene concluded by the pro-consul pronouncing a general amnesty for the past. The military oath was then retaken by each mutineer, after which every soldier received with gratitude and surprise the full amount of his arrears.[168] The disaffection of these men ended with this extraordinary military drama, for Scipio, as soon as he was recovered put himself at their head. After reminding them that he could not bear to punish soldiers who had served with his father and uncle, as the sight of them moved him to tears, he said he should feel no compunction in chastising the rebels against whom he was then leading them.[169] His address conciliated them so entirely that Indibilis and Mandonius were defeated in a pitched battle, and came as suppliants to implore his mercy.[170] He granted them their lives, after reproaching them with their ingratitude and breach of faith. Notwithstanding his clemency and their promises, these princes revolted as soon as Scipio left Spain, being not at all scrupulous respecting their word. The defection of the Numidian prince Masinissa from the Carthaginians was a great acquisition to Scipio at this time, for he was a person of talent, and enjoyed a brilliant reputation as a cavalry general. He concluded his alliance with the Romans at a private interview granted by the pro-consul. We are indebted to the surprise expressed by the new ally of Rome at the youthful appearance of the Roman commander, for the personal description of Scipio left us by Livy, by whom we are told, "that this hero wore his long hair flowing down his back in ringlets, that his complexion was blooming, his beautiful countenance full of majesty and sweetness, his manners courteous and graceful, his dress neat but not fine, being simple and unostentatious, as became a soldier whose time was too valuable to allow of much study in regard to costume." We must conclude either that Scipio did not wear at this interview the superb official dress denoting his pro-consular rank, or that the absence of jewels and those elaborate ornaments which usually adorned the princes of Africa and Asia made his habit appear plain to the eyes of Masinissa. Scipio, on his part, was struck with the personal advantages of his guest, whose countenance full of fire and spirit promised in him a valuable ally to the Roman republic.[171] The cruelty and rapacity of Mago, the brother of Hannibal, completed the ruin of the Carthaginian cause in Spain. He was at Gades, when he received a summons for Italy, and commenced upon a Carthaginian colony his B.C. 206. work of sacrilege and extortion by plundering the temples and robbing the rich citizens, which caused the populace to shut their gates upon him after his return from his unsuccessful attack upon Carthagena. As the Gadetans were a Punic colony he sent deputies to complain of their conduct, upon which the chief magistrate and treasurer of the city went out to apologise for the affront, which they assured him did not originate with themselves but the people. Mago, like a cruel and unreasonable man, would not listen to their defence, but had them barbarously scourged and crucified. This wicked and impolitic action made the Gadetans submit themselves to the Romans as soon as Mago had left Spain.[172]

Scipio having completed the temporary conquest of the country, was summoned to Rome, and two pro-consuls, Cornelius Lentulus and Manlius Acidinus, were sent to govern Hither and Farther Spain, as the new provinces were denominated. He was scarcely gone before Indibilis and Mandonius revolted again, but were defeated by the pro-consuls with great slaughter. In this battle Indibilis was slain, and the Spaniards, to procure peace, sent Mandonius in bonds to the Roman camp.[173] After this war Spain remained for some years in a state of perfect obedience to the Roman government. L. Marcius concluded a treaty with Spain which formed for two centuries the model for all future agreements with that warlike and turbulent people.[174] Scipio, who aspired to the consulship, and to wage war with Hannibal, was permitted to return. Before his public entrance into Rome, he gave the senate, assembled in the suburban temple of Bellona, an animated narrative of his conquest of Spain. He was not allowed a triumph, on account of the absence of his army, and his want of rank. Besides these objections, a more stringent one was urged, neither he nor his army had been consecrated by the greater auspices. The youthful conqueror of Spain submitted to these regulations, for which he consoled himself by making his entry remarkable by an immense quantity of gold and silver ostentatiously borne before him;[175] a pleasant sight to those creditors who had advanced large sums upon the national faith—a debt only to be valid in the event of the expulsion of Hannibal. He gained his consulship in conjunction with Licinius Crassus, and was nominated to the province of Sicily, which allowed him to carry the war of Hannibal into Africa, for which his appointment in that island offered great facilities. In the senate he proposed the plan with all the fiery eloquence of youth and genius, but he found himself opposed by the wary prudence of the aged Fabius Maximus, who ridiculed the design and gave a critical analysis of the exploits of the young consul and his own, not quite so favourable to Scipio as to himself.[176] Scipio replied to this in a strain of satire, but being unable to conceal his determination to appeal to the people upon an affair that must tend to the glory of the country, had nearly lost his cause by his imprudence. However, upon his reminding them of the success of Agathocles and Atilius Regulus, and that the reverses of the last had not originated with himself, he wrung a reluctant consent from the senate that, if necessity required it, he might cross the sea to Africa, and, with this concession, the young consul was forced to be content.[177] Scipio obtained leave of the senate to ask the allies of Rome to contribute men and ships for his projected expedition to Africa, but owing to the opposition of old Fabius Maximus, no supplies of the kind were allowed him from his own government beyond the bare permission of raising volunteers from Rome.

Young, popular, and eloquent, the idol of the day found no difficulty in persuading the warlike youth of Rome to follow him in an expedition where glory was sure to be the reward of valour. The chilling influence of Fabius was, however, exerted to damp the rising flame in Rome, but in the provinces many cities voluntarily taxed themselves to contribute a quota of ships and soldiers.[178] Nor were the allies less generous; and, at the end of five-and-forty days, the enterprising Roman set sail with thirty new galleys and seven thousand volunteers.

Mago, the brother of Hannibal, at this time took Genoa, his army being greatly increased by the Gaulish nations flocking to his standard. The senate, alarmed B.C. 205. at his progress in Liguria, sent Marcus Livius with his Volones to Ariminum, and Lævinus, with the legions that had been stationed for the defence of the metropolis, to Arretium.[179] These reverses in Liguria were counterbalanced by the brilliant success of Octavius, the prætor of Sardinia, at sea over the Carthaginians. The plague raging among the warring armies of Rome and Carthage occasioned for a time a cessation of hostilities in those parts where Hannibal and Licinius commanded.

Scipio carefully repaired the shipping he found in Sicily, and manned them with the veteran soldiers of Marcellus. He gave the command of these galleys to his friend Lælius, and sent him to ravage the coasts of Africa. The descent of Lælius filled the Carthaginians with terror, and they hastily despatched embassies to Philip of Macedon, to Syphax, and many other princes, to induce them to unite with them against Rome. Hannibal and Mago received at this time commands to prevent Scipio from leaving Sicily for Africa. Lælius not only amassed a quantity of booty,[180] but he saw and conferred with king Masinissa, who, though stripped of his dominions, had still some troops at his command with which he offered to aid the consul's landing, of whose success he seemed confident. He also cautioned Lælius to depart before the Carthaginian fleet could intercept him, as it was already under way for that purpose. Lælius returned to Sicily without any delay and landed in safety with his booty.

Some exiled Locrians[181] kept up a correspondence at Locri, a city of Bruttium, then garrisoned by Carthaginians, and these exiles informed Scipio that the inhabitants were so well affected towards the Romans that they might easily surprise the city. He despatched Pleminius, with two tribunes and three thousand men, thither. Pleminius soon made himself master of one citadel, while the Carthaginians still maintained possession of the other, waiting for the coming of Hannibal to raise the siege in person. As the city lay between these citadels, and Hannibal found that the inhabitants were determined to admit the Romans, he gave up the enterprise, and advised the Carthaginians to fire the citadel, and quit Locri altogether. They did so and Locri was yielded to the Romans. Scipio gave the government of the city to Pleminius, being ignorant of the avaricious and cruel character of the man, who treated Locri with as much severity as if it had been a conquered city, rifling the inhabitants, and plundering the sacred edifices. Nor were the tribunes less extortionate, and the rapacious trio were employed in stripping the Temple of Proserpine when their soldiers fell out, and several of those of Pleminius were wounded. Pleminius in a rage ordered the tribunes to be whipped. Their soldiers rescued them from the lictors, whom they beat severely, and, seizing upon Pleminius, cut off his nose and ears, and left him bleeding in the temple.[182] The report of this outrage done to a Roman pro-prætor brought Scipio to Locri, who ordered the guilty tribunes to be sent to Rome in chains, and reproved Pleminius for his misconduct in the affair, charging him to behave leniently to the inhabitants, who made great complaints of his extortion and cruelty. He did not deprive him of his government, as he ought to have done, being moved by the sight of his suffering and disfigured person. Scarcely had Scipio departed before Pleminius tortured the tribunes to death, and fined and slew many of those Locrians who had dared to complain of his oppression. The Locrians despatched deputies to Rome the following year to plead their cause before the senate, and obtained the redress they sought. Pleminius was sent to Rome in chains, but died in prison before his trial came on. The commissioners who had been sent to Locri for the arrest of Pleminius, had orders to convey Scipio to Rome, in case they could prove that the young consul had been a party in the cruelty of Pleminius, or was wasting his time at the theatre, of which folly Marcus Cato thought proper to accuse him to the senate. The austere Cato was no admirer of the generous Scipio, whose quæstor in Sicily, he had been, where his close attention to his general's accounts had displeased Scipio, who had intimated to him that he did not require such an exact quæstor, and Cato had quitted his office and the island in disgust. He became from that time Scipio's adversary upon this and every other occasion through life.[183] The deputies executed their B.C. 205. delicate commission with honest impartiality. They found the young consul employed daily and hourly in preparing for his African expedition, and full of zeal for the deliverance of Italy from Hannibal, which he confidently expected would be the result of his invasion of the Carthaginian territories. As the Locrians themselves acquitted the consul of all blame beyond misplaced confidence in his officers,[184] they bade him go and fulfil the great expectations the Roman people had formed of his worth and valour. They prayed the gods to grant him success and added, "that if such a general and such an army could not conquer Carthage she must be invincible."[185] After the favourable report made by the commissioners to the senate respecting Scipio's conduct, the consul was permitted to embark for Africa, and allowed to take with him all the Roman soldiers then in Sicily. Scipio Nasica was chosen this year to receive the image of Cybele brought from Pessinus in Phrygia to Rome, to stop the ravages of the plague.[186] The Sibylline books in prescribing this remedy had added, that this venerated image, which was a shapeless stone without beauty or proportions, "must be placed in the hands of the wisest and most virtuous man in Rome, or the remedy would prove useless." Publius Cornelius Scipio Nasica was the citizen thus honoured.[187]

The Roman republic found itself able to punish the twelve colonies who had refused to pay their annual levies. They were obliged to submit to the imposition of a new yearly tax, and the ancient quota was nearly doubled. The refractory colonies, considering the magnitude of their offence, thought themselves happy that their punishment was so light. The senate also gave orders for the repayment of monies lent by private individuals to the state, which were to be made in three instalments to the creditors of the republic.

Scipio only bore the rank of pro-consul when he embarked for his celebrated expedition to Africa from Lilybæum, an enterprise so long projected and delayed. Lælius commanded the fleet, and the pro-consul stood upon the poop of his galley to take leave of the immense multitude who came to the shore from distant parts to wish him health and success.[188] After the herald had commanded silence,[189] Scipio invoked all the gods and the goddesses of earth and sea to bless his enterprise, and make it prosperous for the benefit of Rome and her allies. He prayed "that he might return with his troops uninjured, triumphant, and loaded with spoil, and that they might execute on Carthage all that that haughty republic designed to do against Rome." The heathen prayer ended, Scipio commanded a victim to be slain and its entrails cast into the sea, after which he weighed anchor with a fair wind, to the sound of martial music. Upon nearing the hostile coast he asked of the pilot the name of the nearest point of land in sight. He was answered "The Fair Promontory," and hailing the appellation as a lucky omen, resolved to disembark there.[190] He had scarcely effected his landing when he was joined by Masinissa with two hundred horsemen. He ordered the fleet to proceed to Utica, and encamped upon some heights near the sea, where the next day his advanced guard fell in with a body of five hundred Carthaginian horse, commanded by a young officer named Hanno, totally routing them and slaying their leader.[191] Emboldened by this success, Scipio marched to Locha, a wealthy city where he expected to find a rich booty; but his scaling ladders were scarcely raised before the timid inhabitants capitulated by sending a herald to request their lives, offering at the same time to leave the city. Scipio accepted the prayer of the citizens and commanded a retreat to be sounded; but the ferocious soldiery refused obedience to the voice of mercy, and left no living creature to carry the disastrous tale to Carthage. Scipio found the offenders too numerous to punish, but he put to death three centurions who had encouraged the troops in their work of universal carnage and rapine.[192] B.C. 205. This terrible instance of insubordination has been but too often repeated in modern times and Christian lands to excite surprise here, although it awakens horror. The same event that had given the Romans a firm ally in Masinissa had also procured them a foe in Syphax. The patriotism of Sophonisba, the daughter of Hasdrubal, and the grand-daughter of Gisco, had made her a willing bribe in the hands of the senate of Carthage, and her hand was the reward of Syphax's defection from Rome,[193] as the landless prince Masinissa seemed a less valuable ally than the powerful African monarch.[194] In this decision the astute Carthaginians displayed more world-craft than judgment, for the talents of Masinissa made him at least a very dangerous foe.[195] Scipio laid siege to Utica without success, for Hasdrubal with a numerous body of troops, aided by Syphax in person, with fifty thousand horse, obliged the Roman general to abandon the enterprise. He entrenched himself upon a promontory at whose base his fleet lay at anchor, having the camps of Hasdrubal and Syphax in sight, resolving to occupy this strong position till the return of the vernal quarter.

We must now return to Rome, where the quarrels of the two censors, Livius Salinator and Claudius Nero, occupied the public mind more than the military movements of Scipio. The old grudge between these eminent men broke out during their exercise of this honourable office. It was the business of the censors to examine into the morals and conduct of the tribes and even of the senators; but before giving up the censorship they chose to censure themselves, by affixing a mark of infamy upon each other's names—names hitherto respected by their fellow-citizens. Nero and his colleague were both of the equestrian or knightly order, and certainly Nero began the quarrel by attacking the honourable character of his enemy, nor could he assign any better reason than the former condemnation of his enemy by the people, though Livius had effaced that unjust sentence by his conduct during his second consulship, which was fresh in the memory of the people, who, nevertheless, favoured the rival censor.[196] When Nero's name was called over, Livius, in his turn, ordered it to be struck off the list, alleging that "he had borne false witness against him, and that his reconciliation with him was insincere." Nero numbered his colleague among those persons who were deprived of the rights of Roman citizenship, though obliged by law to pay taxes. Livius treated his enemy in a similar manner;[197] and actually disenfranchised all those tribes which had voted against him, leaving only the Mæcian, which had stood by him on his trial.[198] He laid a tax on salt, as a mark of resentment against the people, which gained him the name of Salinator, which cleaves to him to this day. At the census, made memorable by these ridiculous quarrels, the number of Roman citizens capable of bearing arms, amounted to two hundred and fourteen thousand persons. It may be observed, that the private resentment of the censors did not prevent them from paying proper attention to their accounts, for no census had ever been more minutely taken. How intensely absurd was this contest between the men whose united talents had saved Italy; but nothing, indeed, ever appears so foolish as the follies of the wise. The union of these irascible persons had, during their consulship, been productive of such immense public benefit, that could they have laid aside their hatred during their censorship, their exercise of that office might have been an equal blessing to their native city.

In Africa Scipio retained the rank of pro-consul, and was continued in his command. He made some attempt to regain Syphax, but the ascendancy a beautiful and talented Carthaginian wife held over the mind of the Numidian king, rendered them abortive. Finding in his sword a fairer chance of success with

Syphax than his arguments, the Roman pro-consul attacked the camps of the Numidian king and Carthaginian general, which he stormed and burned, defeating the troops of both with great slaughter.[199] Syphax, after this repulse would have come to Scipio's terms, but the tears and prayers of Sophonisba were sufficient to change his resolution. Leaving the siege of Utica in haste to encounter the Carthaginian forces on the Great Plain, a second splendid B.C. 204. victory attested the military genius of Scipio.[200] Hasdrubal fled to Carthage, Syphax retreated to his own country, and Tunis opened her gates to receive the conqueror. Here he beheld Carthage from the spot whence the gallant and unfortunate Regulus had formerly in the full pride and flush of victory, refused to hearken to any terms short of absolute conquest. But a wiser general than the rash Regulus was here, and prudence was combined in Scipio with the courage of the Roman and the skill of the general. The Carthaginian senate, alarmed for the safety of the capital, sent messengers with orders to command the return of Hannibal and his troops to Africa for the defence of his native land. That great general, finding his game of war at an end in Italy, employed himself in commemorating his campaigns on "the temple of the Lacinian Juno," near Crotona.[201] No fruit remains of all his splendid victories but these records. How differently might his career have terminated if the national assembly of Carthage had supplied the patriotic and hitherto invincible Hannibal with arms and troops sufficient to complete his rapid conquest of Italy by that of Rome, but this jealous and short-sighted body considered their own private gains before the good of their country. The Carthaginian senate despatched Hamilcar with a hundred galleys with directions to burn the Roman fleet. Scipio descried the approach of Hamilcar in time to preserve his shipping, although, if the Carthaginians had been prompt and courageous, the fleet must have been lost. Six galleys alone fell into his hands, with which he hastily returned to Carthage. Masinissa and Lælius in the meanwhile followed the rapid flight of the defeated Syphax. In the short space of fifteen days the young Numidian prince had recovered his own kingdom, and aided by the Roman legions had not only fought and vanquished his enemy, but carried him captive to the gates of his own capital city Cirta, where the sight of the royal prisoner created so much terror and surprise that its inhabitants threw them open to the conqueror.[202]

The victor had scarcely alighted at the gate of the palace, when he was met in the portico by the queen, who had formerly been affianced to him, and was the fatal cause of Syphax's enmity to the Romans, and of his own fortunate alliance with that victorious people. Sophonisba fell at the feet of the conqueror, and with tears and sighs entreated him not to give her, a free-born Carthaginian, into the hands of the Romans, but rather to kill her that moment than reserve her to adorn a barbarous triumph. The fair Carthaginian accompanied her words by clasping the king's knees, regarding him with tearful eyes, full of seducing tenderness. He gave her his right hand in token that his honour was pledged to grant her request, and becoming instantly enamoured resolved to marry her that day as the only means of performing his oath. The wife of Masinissa he thought would not be demanded from her husband to play a part in the public pageant of the conqueror.[203] They were immediately married, a circumstance that must have aggravated the misfortunes of the captive spouse of the faithless Sophonisba. The arrival of Lælius disquieted the royal lover, who, blinded by his passion, had not contemplated the chances of his displeasure. Lælius claimed the queen from her newly-wedded lord, but yielded to the entreaties of Masinissa, who besought him to allow her to remain with him till the arrival of the pro-consul, and this concession was granted by Lælius. Syphax in the meantime was sent in chains to the Roman camp, where he excited much commiseration. Upon Scipio asking him the reason of his broken faith with the Roman republic, he laid the whole blame upon his wife, whom he denounced as the fatal cause and equally fatal reward of his disobedience.[204] He spoke with just resentment of Sophonisba's indelicate marriage with Masinissa, and, animated by the force of jealousy and outraged love, remarked, "That she would be the ruin of the other Numidian king, as she had been of him by the aid of her genius and beauty, for that Masinissa being a young man, her power would be still greater over his heart than it had even been over him, a man of maturer years;" and he artfully added, "that Sophonisba could never be brought to favour the Roman cause, so deep, so immovable was her love to her country." The complaint of Syphax fully convinced B.C. 203. Scipio of the necessity of separating his brave ally from the fair captive he had dared to espouse. Master of his own passions, Scipio could not sympathise with the enamoured Numidian, whom he sent for in haste to oblige him to give up his newly-wedded wife. History has preserved the reprimand given by the young pro-consul to the youthful king on the virtue of overcoming the passions in a commander, and the advice would have been admirable if it had not involved either a breach of faith or the guilt of murder. He finally claimed the captive in the name of the Roman people, assuring Masinissa that his whole future career depended upon his obedience. Masinissa retired to his tent in tears, and gave way to loud lamentations, his groans and sighs being heard by the soldiers who kept watch around the pavilion. At length ambition won the victory over love, and the warlike ally of Rome, drawing from beneath the folds of his vest the deadly poison always carried by the sovereigns of Numidia about their persons, gave it to a trusty slave with this message for his queen: "Masinissa, unable to fulfil the duties of a husband to his wife, by affording her his protection according to his marriage engagements and his own wishes, performs his other promise, that she should not be delivered up alive to the Romans. Sophonisba, mindful of her father, her country, and the two kings whose wife she has been, will consult her own honour."

The sight of the deadly draught fully explained to Sophonisba the ambiguous message: "I accept," said she, "my husband's marriage gift, since he can do nothing kinder for his wife; but I should have died with more honour if my marriage had not been the precursor of my funeral." The beautiful Carthaginian then took the fatal cup, drank its contents without any perceptible change of countenance, and died with the reckless courage of heathenism. Scipio censured the precipitation of Masinissa, which had led to such a tragedy; but whether he blamed the act that deprived Rome of a captive and himself of the brightest gem of his anticipated triumph, or the suicide, admits at least of a doubt.

The following day he solemnly invested Masinissa with the robes, the crown, and sceptre of a king, and a curule chair, holding out to his ambitious ally the hope of possessing all Numidia, foreseeing that these honours would be the surest method he could devise to console the dispirited prince for the loss of his lately wedded wife. Scipio sent Lælius with Syphax and the Numidians to Rome, but the captive king did not live to grace a Roman triumph, for he died at Alba before the return of his victor to Italy.[205] The pro-consul took up his head-quarters at Tunis once more, where he received a deputation from the abject Carthaginians, praying for peace, and throwing the whole blame of the war upon Hannibal, but the terms proposed by the young Roman were so exorbitant and degrading, that even they could not accept them. To their remonstrances Scipio haughtily replied, "that he came to conquer the Carthaginians not to make peace with them." Then the senate of Carthage resolved to send for Hannibal, as the only measure they thought likely to ensure the salvation of the republic.[206]

In Italy several battles had been fought between the Carthaginians and the Romans, the success of which on either side was doubtful, till Mago, the brother of Hannibal, encountered in Insubria Cornelius Cethegus, the pro-consul, where he was given a mortal wound, and was forced to yield the hard-fought honours of the day to the Roman commander. He had scarcely retreated into Liguria before he received the orders for his immediate recall from his government. He obeyed them instantly by embarking with all his army, but died off the island of Sardinia of his wound. A storm dispersed the Carthaginian fleet, and many of the scattered ships fell into the hands of the Romans.

Hannibal received the commands of the Carthaginian senate with tears of indignation. He traced his own ruin to the envy and jealousy of Hanno, whom he affirmed would rejoice in his enforced banishment from the theatre of his glory—Italy. He concluded by declaring that the Carthaginians, not the Romans, had vanquished Hannibal. Even after his embarkation the great captain of the age was seen to turn his head and look long and regretfully upon the shores he was quitting, till increasing distance hid them from his sight. The joy was great at Rome when the departure of Hannibal was known there, though some B.C. 203. of the senatorial body thought it disgraceful to the Roman name that the invader should have been permitted to depart unpunished with his laurels green and unsullied. Old Fabius Maximus declared that Rome was never in a worse condition, for his cold cautious prudence despised the bold genius of Scipio.[207] Whatever the private feelings might be of those individuals who composed the government, they ordered a solemn thanksgiving to the gods for the departure of the national foe, as a testimony to the people that they sympathised in their rejoicings.

The death of Fabius Maximus put a stop to his forebodings. He was greatly lamented by his countrymen, who, finding he had not left wherewithal to bury him, voluntarily taxed themselves to give his remains a magnificent funeral.[208] The consul Cæpio fought a battle with Hannibal in Bruttium, but nothing is related of its success. The only memorable action recorded of Geminus, the other consul, in Gaul, was his recovery of his father and uncle from the captivity in which they had languished for sixteen years among the Boii, having long been supposed dead. He entered Rome with these dear and long lost relatives on either hand, a proud triumph for the son and nephew, although it might not add to the laurels of the general.[209]

Hannibal, so eagerly expected by his dastardly countrymen, was greeted by an omen emblematical of the fallen fortunes of his country. As he drew near the coast a sailor posted upon the mainmast was asked by the great captain, "Whether he could discover any object upon the shore." "I see," replied the mariner, "the ruins of a tomb upon an eminence." Even the mighty mind of Hannibal was shaken by a presage so ominous of the fate of Carthage, and he ordered the fleet to pass the place. It possibly occurred to him that all states in turn resemble this ruined sepulchre, placed on a height, making their fall appear more remarkable from the proud pre-eminence they had once held. Flying from this dreary emblem of the fortunes of his country, Hannibal finally disembarked his troops at Little Leptis, a city between Susa and Hadrumetum.[210]

It was resolved at Rome to prosecute the war in Africa with vigour, and Tiberius Claudius Nero was ordered to command the fleet on the coast of Africa, under the direction of Scipio, the pro-consul, whose orders he was to obey, an unusual circumstance.[211] The great military talents of Scipio, and his brilliant success in the conduct of this war, occasioned the reversal of the general custom. Servilius Pulex, the other consul, was to direct the movements of the army stationed in Etruria. As Scipio wasted their territories with fire and sword, and gave no quarter to the towns he stormed, the Carthaginian senate commanded Hannibal to put a stop to his universal devastations, by bringing him to an engagement as speedily as possible.[212] Hannibal marched to meet his opponent in the direction of Zama, a town in Numidia Proper, about five days' journey south-west of Carthage. The spies he had despatched to reconnoitre the camp of Scipio fell into the pro-consul's hands; and expected nothing less than that death which, by the established laws of nations, has always been accorded to persons detected on this perilous service. Scipio magnanimously caused them to be sent back to Hannibal, but not before they had been conducted throughout his camp, and had been fully informed respecting its strength and numbers.

This noble boldness won the admiration of the great Carthaginian, and he demanded an interview with a foe, whom he thought worthy of being his private friend. Scipio granted his request, and the two great captains of the age met at Naragara to speak of peace. Upon an open plain between the rival camps, the Roman and Carthaginian generals came on horseback, followed by an equal number of their guards. These fell back at a given signal from their leaders, who advanced to meet each other, attended by their interpreters. They looked long and earnestly upon one another before either spoke; Hannibal was the first to break silence.[213] "He lamented the ambition of the rival republics, which had been the cause of so much misery and bloodshed on both sides, when nature had evidently bounded their dominions to the shores of Italy and Africa; while the Roman and Carthaginian had, in consequence of their aggressions, seen each other at the B.C. 202. gates of their respective capitals. He avowed his wish for peace; and his fears that the youth of Scipio, and his consequent inexperience of the chances of fortune, would make him averse to pacific arrangements. That, for his part, he never wished to leave to fortune what reason might decide." Then delicately glancing at his splendid career in Italy, he proposed himself, as an example of the inconstancy of human affairs; who, after conquering in Italy, came to treat in Africa with a Roman, for the preservation of himself and his country. He alluded with much feeling to the faithlessness of his citizens, respecting their infraction of the late treaty; and concluded his oration with these remarkable words, "It is I, Hannibal, who now ask for peace;—I ask it, because I think it expedient for my country—and thinking it expedient, I will inviolably maintain it."[214]

Scipio, less eloquent, but as determined upon war as Hannibal was inclined for peace, would not recede from the conditions he had lately offered the Carthaginian senate. He remarked, "That if Hannibal had appeared as desirous of peace before quitting Italy, it would have been granted him upon more honourable terms; but that the advantages of war were seemingly inclined to the side of Rome;" and in conclusion said, "The Carthaginians must submit to us unconditionally, or vanquish us in battle." They parted with feelings of mutual esteem, to make preparations for the decisive contest. Upon the plains near Zama, Hannibal experienced his first and last defeat, for there Scipio pitched the Roman standard for the future conquest of the world. This victory, won by the Roman pro-consul, annihilated for ever the power, the political importance of Carthage; whose senate, humbled to the dust, received more humiliating terms than those they had previously rejected.[215] Polybius, the military historian, who has given a minute account of this memorable battle, affirms that nothing could be more admirable than the dispositions and arrangements of Hannibal, who took every precaution to ensure success becoming a great general; and imputes Scipio's victory to some deity who favoured Rome, rather than to the superior talents of the younger general. That light that gleamed on the darkness of the heathen writer, upon the decrees of Providence, "who gives not the race to the swift, nor the battle to the strong," might even then be seen in the inspired pages of Daniel, where the power of the fourth monarchy may still be traced from its rise to its fall. True, Carthage is not named nor pre-figured there; but in the seventh chapter and twenty-third verse of that prophecy, it is recorded, that the fourth monarchy "should devour the whole earth;" and the Bible reader will find, that no power was able to stand against that which the Lord had raised up, to bring His mighty purposes to pass.

Hannibal fled to Hadrumetum, but not before the defeat was total, and the rout general. Summoned to preside in a council at Carthage, he declared that the republic had no alternative but peace, and his voice decided the question at once.[216] Scipio, who had given orders to Cneius Octavius to lead his troops to Carthage, went on board the fleet as if he intended to besiege the devoted city by land and sea. Such in reality was not his purpose; for he had received intelligence of the embarkation of the consul, Nero, for Africa, and had determined to finish the war before another should share the glory of the expedition with him. He was met by a galley filled with deputies, with olive branches in their hands; but he did not choose to listen to their prayers, coolly dismissing them with the intimation that he would be found at Tunis.[217] In that city, in the view of the capital, he proposed to the embassy of nobles who came to meet him, terms that left to Carthage little beyond the territories she possessed in Africa before the war that deprived her of her fleets, her wealth, her independence, and her noblest born; not leaving her even the power of protecting the unfortunate, for all Roman deserters, fugitives, and slaves were demanded by the proud victor. So hard appeared the conditions to many in the senate that Gisco rose to persuade his countrymen to reject them, but Hannibal obliged him to quit the rostrum, and speedily convinced the assembly that the terms must of necessity be accepted, and Scipio was informed of their decision the same day.[218] Ambassadors were accordingly despatched to Rome to induce the victorious republic to ratify the B.C. 202. peace. The destruction of Carthage was long debated, but Scipio's declaration that to raze this great city would draw down upon the Romans the hatred of the whole world, inclined the majority of the assembly to the side of mercy.[219] Hasdrubal Hædus, who had been chosen chief ambassador on account of his known hatred to the family of Hannibal, threw the whole blame of the war upon that patriotic Carthaginian. He was asked—"What gods his countrymen could invoke to witness their oaths?" A sarcastic reflection upon the proverbial want of faith of the Punic nation. To which interrogatory of the senate Hædus promptly replied, "The same who have so severely punished us for the breach of them."[220] The victorious Scipio was then fully empowered to conclude the treaty of peace, and the deputies returned to Africa. Scipio, by the terms of the treaty, received four thousand deserters who had taken refuge at Carthage. These he put to death. The foreigners and slaves were beheaded, but the Romans, whom he considered more culpable, were crucified, as an example to others.[221] No commander could be more tremendously severe than the youthful conqueror of Hannibal. The national disgrace of the Carthaginians was felt less severely than the enormous tribute, which amounted to nearly two millions of our currency, which was to be paid in annual divisions for fifty years. The covetous citizens and rich senators burst into tears when the propositions respecting the first instalment were made in the senate, though they had seen with dry eyes their fleet of war just consigned to the flames, in compliance with the treaty. Hannibal laughed as these mercenary hearts unveiled themselves in his presence. Hasdrubal Hædus indignantly reproved him for his ill-timed merriment, charging him at the same time with being the cause of the calamities they were bewailing. Hannibal declared that his laughter arose from the bitterness of his soul: They should have wept, he said, for the misfortunes and degradation of their country, not for the loss of their wealth. They had seen Carthage disarmed and defenceless amidst armed nations without a tear, but when money was required they wept as if they were at their country's funeral. "Oh, Carthaginians! believe me, you have bewailed the least of your misfortunes." With these ominous words the great Carthaginian captain quitted the venal assembly.[222]

Scipio returned to Rome to enjoy his well-merited triumph, which surpassed all that had yet been seen at Rome in splendour and interest.[223] The appellation of Africanus was added to his name, not by any decree of the senate, but by general adoption.[224] His victory over the hitherto unconquered Hannibal added the proudest laurel to his wreath of military glory. Thus ended the second Punic war, to the humiliation of Carthage and aggrandisement of Rome. How little could the victor of Thrasimenus and Cannæ have foreseen the fatal result of his unparalleled course of military glory. Hannibal was born a century too late for the restoration of his country, for even his genius could not retard her fall.

After the close of the second Punic war, some men of talent recorded its eventful history. Quintus Fabius Maximus Pictor, the earliest Roman historian, did not, compose his work in Latin, but in Greek, an early instance of pedantry, unless we suppose that he dared not commit to the familiar custody of the Latin language the whole substance of what he wrote in Greek. He was followed, in his preference of the Grecian tongue, by Cincius Alimentus, a person of prætorian rank, who also made use of it for his history of Rome. "He was prætor in the second Punic war, and was taken prisoner by the Carthaginians, and wrote what he knew. He also composed works on 'Chronology,' 'Roman Antiquities,' and on 'The Consular Power.' His Roman history was translated by Claudius Acilius, but neither his translation in Latin, nor the original, are extant."[225] The history of Fabius is also lost to the moderns as a whole, but a great part of it is thought to exist in the "Decades" of Livy, who drew his materials, for the early part of his history, from him. By many authors he has been confounded with Fabius Pictor, the first Roman painter, whose son or nephew he may have been, since he also bore the cognomen of Pictor. He had been a prætor, and is supposed B.C. 202. to have derived his documents from his own illustrious and ancient house, for whose use he probably composed the annals of those wars in which he had been personally engaged.[226] Thus he gave a brief outline of Roman history till he had reached that point where he could avail himself of existing records, when his narrative became more minute,[227] and was no longer dependent upon ancient Latin lays and mythic traditions.[228] "His real subject was indeed the second Punic war,[229] with which he was contemporary, but he had likewise given a complete account of the first war with the Carthaginians. He shewed great partiality to his countrymen, and endeavoured to justify them in everything.[230] Great use has been made of this work, now lost to modern research, by Appian and others, and it is also referred to by Polybius, Livy, and Dionysius."[231]

The Scipios were a learned race, and the conqueror of Hannibal was an early Latin poet, though only two lines are extant of his composition, which are quoted by Cicero, who contrasts the activity of the great Roman with the luxury of Sardanapalus, with this eulogium: "How much more sincere the happiness of Africanus, while he addresses his countrymen in these incomparable lines—

Desine, Roma tuos hostes
Namque tibi monumenta mei peperea labores."[232]

These lines, however, contain more self-praise than good Latin or poetry, notwithstanding the encomium of Cicero.

Ennius, a native of Tarentum, was born in the same year and day as the great Scipio, whose actions furnished the subject of his epic poem. His works were considered fine in his own age, but are not extant; the poet being only now remembered for his generous attachment to his illustrious friend and patron, whom he followed into exile. It is related that when Æmilia, the widow of Africanus, removed the ashes of her husband to Rome, she placed the statue of the poet by the side of him whose misfortunes he had shared, and whose actions he had celebrated. Time has revealed the sepulchre of the Scipios in which a bust, supposed to be that of Ennius, was discovered.[233] Ennius, besides this epic, was the author of tragedies, satires, and annals, all of which are lost.

Plautus, the son of an Umbrian slave who had received his liberty, flourished in this era. His real name was Marcius Accius, but his splay-feet obtained for him that of Plautus, which he still retains. His dramatic pieces, twenty in number, survive. The date of his birth is uncertain, but he certainly died in the first year of Cato's celebrated censorship. Ennius and Nævius were his predecessors in writing for the stage, but Plautus is still considered as the father of the Latin drama.

Portius Licinius Tegula was a comic writer of this era. Statius, an Insubrian Gaul by birth, was a slave at Rome, who had his liberty and the name of Cæcilius given him by a generous master. He was the friend of Ennius, whom he only survived a few months. If Celtic were the tongue spoken in Milan, his native city, and Insubria his country, Statius wrote in a foreign language in clothing his ideas in Latin. Cicero considers his style harsh, so does the learned Varro; Velleius Paterculus places him in the same rank as Terence and Afranius.

<hr size=2 width="10%" align=center>

[1] Livy, xxiii. 31, 32.

[2] The penitence of Varro appears to have mollified the public mind. He let his hair and beard grow, never took his meals upon a couch according to the prevailing fashion of the times, and became modest and diffident in his manners. This humility was the means of placing him again at the head of an army.—Hooke. Val. Max., iv., 5.

[3] Livy, xxiii. 33.

[4] *Ibid.*, 38; Polybius, vii. 2.

[5] Polybius, xxiii. 37.

[6] *Ibid.*, 40.

[7] Livy, xxiii. 46.

[8] Livy, xxiii. 48.

[9] *Ibid.*

[10] Livy, xxiv. 5, 6; Zonaras.

[11] Livy, xxiv. 6; Polybius, vii. 4.

[12] Livy, xxiv. 6; Polybius, vii. 4.

[13] Livy, xxiv. 5, 6.

[14] *Ibid.*

[15] Polybius, vii. 5; Livy, xxii. 37.

[16] Polybius, vii. 5; Livy, xxii. 37.

[17] Polybius, vii. 2; Livy, xxiv. 5.

[18] *Ibid.*, 7.

[19] Polybius, vii. 6.

[20] Livy, xxiv. 7.

[21] *Ibid.*, 21.

[22] Livy, xxiv. 21.

[23] *Ibid.*, 25.

[24] Livy, xxiv. 27, et seq.

[25] *Ibid.*, 28, 29.

[26] Livy.

[27] Plutarch, in Marcellus.

[28] Livy, xxiv. 30, et seq.; Plutarch, in Marcellus.

[29] *Ibid.*; *Ibid.*

[30] Livy, xxiv. 30.

[31] *Ibid.*, 30, 31.

[32] *Ibid.*, 31, 32.

[33] Livy, 33.

[34] Polybius, viii. 5; Livy, xxiv. 34; Plutarch, in Marcellus.

[35] Confident of his own vast resources, he had formerly told king Hiero, "that he could move the earth if he had another earth to stand upon;" a saying that may be forgiven the heathen mechanist and philosopher, though it would have been impious and daring in the lips of a Christian Newton.

[36] Langhorne's Plutarch, Life of Marcellus.

[37] Plutarch, in Marcellus; Polybius; Livy.

[38] Plutarch, in Marcellus.

[39] Plutarch, in Marcellus; Polybius, viii. 6, 9; Livy, xxiv. 34.

[40] Plutarch, in Marcellus; Livy; Polybius.

[41] Langhorne's Plutarch, Life of Marcellus.

[42] It is still uncertain whether Hippocrates and Epicydes were the occasion of the murder of the royal family; some accounts making them the exciters of that horrid tragedy, while others represent them as not entering Syracuse till it had been acted. The deed itself and the series of commotions following it resemble those acted in France in the first revolution, for history is really full of parallelisms, of which the commotions in this Sicilian city furnish some of the innumerable instances. Of the character of the grandson of Hiero we know nothing, but his youthful ambition and activity so early developed might possibly have ripened into the military talents of his valiant and ambitious grandfather, the destructive Pyrrhus. If it were so, Hieronymus was cut off for the good of mankind, although nothing can exonerate his murderers from such a cruel and cowardly crime.

[43] Livy, xxiv. 40.

[44] Ibid.

[45] Ibid., 8.

[46] Ibid., 9.

[47] Ibid.

[48] Livy, xxiv. 18.

[49] Ibid., xxiv. 18.

[50] Ibid.

[51] Montesquieu, Spirit of the Laws.

[52] Appian, vii. 43; Pliny, iii. 16; Lucian.

[53] Arnold.

[54] Livy, xxiv. 45.

[55] Ibid.

[56] Livy, xxiv. 47.

[57] Livy, 48.

[58] Ibid.; Plutarch.

[59] Livy, xv. 1.

[60] Ibid., 3.

[61] Polybius, viii. 19; Livy, xxv. 8.

[62] Polybius, viii. 31.

[63] Ibid., 32; Livy, xxv. 10.

[64] Polybius; Livy.

[65] Polybius, viii. 34, 36; Livy, xxv. 11. This manœuvre has been much admired, and at the siege of Constantinople was imitated by Mahomet II., who was a learned man, as well as a great warrior, and turned his historical reading on that occasion to good account.—Knolles.

[66] Polybius; Livy, xxv. 11.

[67] *Ibid.*, 14.

[68] *Ibid.*, 16.

[69] *Ibid.*

[70] *Ibid.*, 19.

[71] *Ibid.*, 20, 21.

[72] Plutarch, in Marcellus.

[73] Livy, xxv. 23, et seq.

[74] *Ibid.*, 26.

[75] *Ibid.*, 24; Plutarch, in Marcellus.

[76] Livy, xxv. 30.

[77] Livy, xxv. 31; Plutarch, in Marcellus; Val. Max., viii. 7.

[78] This appears to be the case, and the reader is entreated to compare historical events in sacred history with that of Rome; for unless Rome had held dominion, not only over Judea, but the world in general, the prophecies respecting Christ could not have been fulfilled to the very letter.

[79] Appian, vii. 38; Polybius, ix. 3, et seq.; Livy, xxvi. 7, et seq.

[80] Livy, xxvi. 10.

[81] Polybius, ix. 6.

[82] *Ibid.*, 7; Appian, vii. 40.

[83] Polybius, ix. 7.

[84] Livy, xxvi. 12.

[85] *Ibid.*

[86] *Ibid.*, 15.

[87] Val. Max., xi. 84.

[88] Livy, xxv. 24.

[89] Polybius, ix. 22.

[90] Plutarch, in Marcellus.

[91] Livy, xxvi. 22.

[92] *Ibid.*

[93] Plutarch, in Marcellus.

[94] Livy, xxvi. 38; Plutarch, in Marcellus.

[95] Livy, xxvi. 39.

[96] Plutarch, in Marcellus.

[97] *Ibid.*

[98] Livy, xxvii. 4.

[99] Livy, xxvii. 6.

[100] *Ibid.*, 9.

[101] Plutarch, Life of Marcellus; Livy.

[102] Plutarch, Life of Fabius.

[103] Plutarch, in Fabius.

[104] *Ibid.*

[105] *Ibid.*

[106] Livy, xxvii. 16.

[107] Plutarch, Life of Marcellus; Livy, xvii. 27, 28.

[108] Plutarch, in Marcellus.

[109] Livy; Augustus Cæsar.

[110] Livy, xxvii. 28.

[111] *Ibid.*, 29.

[112] *Ibid.*

[113] *Ibid.*, 30.

[114] Livy, xxvii. 32.

[115] *Ibid.*, xxiv. 48; Appian, vi. 15.

[116] Livy, xxv. 32.

[117] *Ibid.*, 33.

[118] Appian, vi. 16.

[119] Livy, xxv. 34, 36; Appian, vi. 16.

[120] Livy, xxv. 36, 39.

[121] *Ibid.*, xxvi. 17.

[1122] *Ibid.*, 18; Polybius, x. 6.

[1123] Polybius, x. 18; Livy, xxvi. 49.

[1124] *Ibid.*

[1125] See C. Nævius Valerius Antias, as quoted by A. Gellius, vi. 6; Arnold.

[1126] Niebuhr.

[1127] <u>See Appendix. (p. 359)</u>

[1128] Livy, xxvii. 33.

[1129] Livy, xxvii. 34.

[1130] *Ibid.*, 35; Val. Max., iv. 2.

[1131] Livy, xxvii. 40.

[1132] *Ibid.* 2; Polybius, x. 35, 36. Sir Walter Raleigh and Hooke doubt the fact as being very impolitic on the part of Scipio, but Scipio was young, and at that time perhaps rash, and might not weigh the ill consequences that might have followed Hasdrubal's irruption into Italy; and it seems more consistent to follow these ancient historians than the critical remarks of modern authors upon them.

[1133] Livy, xxvii. 43.

[1134] *Ibid.*, 40, 41.

[1135] *Ibid.*, 43.

[1136] Livy.

[1137] *Ibid.*, xxvii. 45.

[1138] Livy, xxvii. 46.

[1139] *Ibid.*

[1140] Livy, xxvii. 47.

[1141] *Ibid.*

[1142] Polybius, xi. 3.

[1143] Livy, xxvii. 48.

[1144] *Ibid.*, 49; Polybius, xi. 2.

[1145] Polybius, xi. 3.

[1146] *Ibid.*

[1147] Orosius, iv.; Livy, xxvii. 50; Polybius, xi. 3.

[1148] Livy, xxvii. 50.

[1149] *Ibid.*, 50.

[150] Arnold; Livy, xxvii. 51.

[151] Virgil; Æneid.

[152] Livy, xxix. 37.

[153] Suetonius, in lib. ii.

[154] Polybius, xi. 20; Appian, in Iberia.

[155] Livy, xxviii. 17.

[156] *Ibid.*, 18.

[157] *Ibid.*, 30.

[158] Appian, vi. 33; Livy, xxviii. 20.

[159] Livy, xxviii. 22.

[160] *Ibid.*, 24.

[161] *Ibid.*, 34.

[162] *Ibid.*, 25.

[163] Appian, vi. 34.

[164] Livy, xxviii. 25.

[165] *Ibid.*

[166] *Ibid.*, 26.

[167] *Ibid.*

[168] Polybius, xi. 30; Livy, xxviii. 29; Appian, vi. 36.

[169] Livy, xxviii. 32.

[170] Polybius, xi. 31, 33; Livy, xxviii. 33, 34.

[171] The reverses of the Carthaginians, according to Appian, were not the real cause of Masinissa's defection from them. His affianced wife, the beautiful and captivating Sophonisba, the daughter of Hasdrubal, had been just promised to king Syphax, as a bribe to induce him to break his league with Rome; and the revengeful Numidian resented the affront with the deep hatred of his country. He, however, concealed his anger from the Carthaginians, and concluded the treaty with Scipio with such secresy that Mago quitted Gades without being aware of his defection.—Livy, xxviii. 33.

[172] Livy, xxviii. 36, 37.

[173] *Ibid.*, xxix. 1.

[174] *Ibid.*, xxviii. 37; Appian, vi. 37; Cicero.

[175] Livy, xxviii. 38.

[176] Plutarch, in Fabius.

[177] Livy, xxviii. 45.

[178] *Ibid.*

[179] Livy, xxviii. 46.

[180] *Ibid.*, xxix. 4.

[181] *Ibid.*, 5.

[182] Livy, xxix. 5.

[183] Plutarch.

[184] Livy, xxix. 22.

[185] *Ibid.*

[186] *Ibid.*, 14.

[187] It was upon this occasion that the vestal Quinta Claudia vindicated her chastity by drawing the vessel that contained the image by attaching her girdle to it, after several yoke of oxen had in vain laboured to extricate the ship from the sand-bank upon which it had struck. As Quinta Claudia belonged to a powerful and wealthy family, her extrication of the stranded vessel was doubtless an ingenious contrivance, for it cannot be supposed that the people who ascribed divine virtues to a stone said to have fallen from Jupiter upon Mount Ida, were likely to inquire too closely into the supposed miracle. From that day Quinta Claudia was considered the chastest woman in Rome.— Appian; Suetonius, in Tiberius.

[188] Livy, xxix. 25.

[189] *Ibid.*, 27.

[190] *Ibid.*, 29.

[191] *Ibid.*, 34.

[192] Appian, in Punic.

[193] Val. Max.

[194] Livy.

[195] For this account of Masinissa see Livy, xxix. 29-33.

[196] Livy, xxix. 36.

[197] Livy, xxix. 36.

[198] Suetonius, in Tiberius.

[199] Polybius, xvi. 1; Livy, xxx. 3; Val. Max.; Florus.

[200] Polybius, xiv. 7; Livy, xxx. 8.

[201] Polybius, iii. 33, 56.

[202] Appian, in Punic.; Livy, xxx. 11, et seq.

[203] Appian, in Punic.; Livy, xxx. 11, et seq.

[204] *Ibid.*

[205] Livy, xxx. 16.

[206] *Ibid.*

[207] Plutarch, in Fabius.

[208] Plutarch.

[209] Livy, xxx. 18, 19.

[210] Polybius, xv. 1; Livy, xxx. 25.

[211] Livy, xxx. 27.

[212] Appian, in Punic.; Polybius, xxv. 3, 4.

[213] Livy, xxx. 30; Polybius, xv. 6.

[214] Livy, xxx. 30; Polybius, xv. 6.

[215] *Ibid.*

[216] Livy, xxx. 30; Polybius, xv. 6.

[217] Livy, xxx. 35.

[218] *Ibid.*, 38.

[219] Appian, in Punic., pp. 31, 32.

[220] Livy, xxx. 42.

[221] *Ibid.*, 43.

[222] Livy, xxx. 43.

[223] Polybius says, "that Syphax in chains formed a part of the show," but Livy asserts that his death took place some time before.

[224] Livy, xxx. 45.

[225] Niebuhr, Introductory Lecture.

[226] Niebuhr, Introductory Lecture.

[227] Dionysius, i. 6.

[228] No family in Rome had produced more eminent men than the Fabii, and it may fairly be inferred that a race of such historical importance would preserve the record of their remarkable actions. The history of Fabius is said to have been written in very beautiful Greek. His proficiency in that language was doubtless the reason he was chosen to consult the oracle of Apollo at Delphi in this century; for though Grecian learning was even then cultivated

in Rome, it had not become so generally known as in the following age. Fabius brought his history down from the time of Romulus to the year of Rome 536.

[229] Niebuhr, Hist. Rome.

[230] Polybius, cited by Niebuhr.

[231] Niebuhr.

[232] Thus translated:—

"No more, Imperial Rome, thy rivals dread,
With trophies have my toils thy towers adorned."

[233] A curious plate of this ancient sepulchre will be found in "Venuti's Antichità di Roma," which will remind the reader of the English tombs in the Elizabethan era, which were mostly the works of Italian artists.

CHAPTER IX.

A.U.C. 553-568. B.C. 201-186.

Political intrigues of king Philip.—Arrogance of king Philip.—The Romans threaten him.—The Roman senate made king Ptolemy's guardian.—Marcus Lepidus sent to Egypt.—Hamilcar storms Placentia.—Battle of Cremona.—Successes of king Philip.—Despair of the inhabitants of Abydos.—Interview between king Philip and Sulpicius.—The Macedonians follow the Romans to Athens.—King Philip's dauntless speech; his bravery; his sacrilege; his defeat at Octolophus.—The Romans joined by the Ætolians.—Maledictions of the Athenians.—Roman reverses in Gaul.—Interview between king Philip and Flamininus.—Successes of the Romans.—A Macedonian governor in Argos; his noble behaviour.—Consular success in Italy.—Conferences between king Philip and Flamininus.—The Roman senate refuse him peace.—Thebes and Bœotia won by stratagem.—Battle of Cynocephalæ.—Arrogance of the Ætolians.—Philip sues for peace.—Flamininus at the Isthmian games.—Liberty proclaimed to Greece.—Gift of Roman slaves to Flamininus; his triumph.—King Antiochus offends the Romans.—Oppian law repealed.—Escape of Hannibal.—Roman war in Greece.—Hannibal and king Antiochus.—Roman injustice to the Carthaginians.—The Ætolians conspire against the Romans.—Marriage of Cleopatra to king Ptolemy foretold in Scripture.—Scipio and Hannibal.—Philopœmen, his defeat at sea and victory on land.—Assassination of Nabis.—Antiochus lands in Greece; his jealousy of Hannibal.—King Philip joins the Romans.—Acilius in Thessaly.—Battle of Thermopylæ.—Antiochus at Ephesus.—Insolence of Acilius.—Flamininus intercedes for the Ætolians.—King Philip's present; restoration of his son.—Naval victory of Livius.—Conquest and colonization of Boian Gaul, by Scipio Nasica.—War in Asia conducted by the Scipios.—Antiochus offers to treat with the Romans.—Opposition of king Eumenes.—King Antiochus fulfils a scriptural prophecy; sends an embassy to Scipio Africanus; offers to restore his son.—Noble reply of Scipio; he falls sick with grief.—Antiochus generously restores his son.—Scipio's gratitude.—Battle of Magnesia.—Antiochus sues for peace.—Escape of Hannibal.—Embassies to the senate.—The Ætolians ask for peace.—Conduct of Manlius in Galatia.—Ten commissioners sent to Greece.—Curious Sibylline prophecy.—Manlius plundered in Thrace; his reproof; his triumph.—Cato and the Petillii accuse the Scipios.—Imprudence of Africanus.—His noble reply to Nævius.—Retires to Liternum.—Lucius Scipio condemned; his poverty.—Fine conduct of Sempronius Gracchus to the Scipios.—His marriage to Cornelia the daughter of Africanus.—Her general historic appellation.

THE Roman republic had never forgotten that king Philip of Macedon had been her enemy at a time when his hostility was causeless and annoying. She had compelled him to abandon his projected descent upon Italy, and had even forced him to become her reluctant ally, yet she was not satisfied; the debt was still unpaid, the old feeling of animosity was not extinguished, and her victories over Carthage had paved the way, not only for the subjugation of that rival state but also for the conquest of Macedonia. As Philip was in alliance with Rome at this time the Romans wanted some pretence for an open rupture with him. This was by no means difficult to find in a prince of an ambitious and intriguing character like Philip, who sowed dissensions continually among his neighbours, for the

309

extension of his own dominions and political importance.[1] The allies sent ambassadors to Rome to inform the senate of their victory at Chios, and to state their grievances. Philip, at the same time, made his complaints to Rome, alleging that Aurelius, the Roman ambassador in Greece, had raised levies of troops in that country and commenced hostilities against his officers. He also demanded the restitution of Sopater, who, with four thousand Macedonian mercenaries, had been taken prisoners at the battle of Zama by Scipio. This demand was certainly very arrogant, as an ally of Rome had no right to permit his people to enter the service of a power with which that republic was at war. The consul Aurelius Cotta declared that Philip had provided Sopater with arms and money at his own expense to assist the Carthaginians. He also justified his conduct towards Philip's officers, whom he had merely restrained from pillaging the allies of the republic. The senate refused, as a matter of course, to deliver up Sopater and his mercenaries, and threatened king Philip with war unless he quitted his present line of conduct. They assured the deputies from Greece of the protection of the republic in these emphatic words, "That the senate would take care of the affairs of Asia." Ambassadors from Egypt arrived at this time at Rome, claiming the protection of the republic for her ancient allies against the kings of Macedon and Syria. This was instantly granted, and Marcus Lepidus was appointed the guardian of the young king.[2] It must be owned that if the Romans wanted a decent excuse for making war with and punishing their old enemy a great number of most unexceptionable ones presented themselves in a very short space of time, but of king Philip of Macedon it might be said as of Ishmael in holy writ, "His hand was against every man and every man's hand was against him." Sulpicius was detained in Italy by the breaking out B.C. 201. of a war in Gaul. This insurrection had Hamilcar, the Carthaginian, for its origin and leader. He had been left in Italy by Mago, as a thorn in the sides of the Romans. The storm of Placentia and the siege of Cremona showed the republic that they had no feeble foe to cope with, but a brave and experienced officer of Hannibal's army. They sent a complaint to Carthage of the misconduct of Hamilcar by ambassadors, who were engaged also to ask Masinissa for some squadrons of Numidian horse for the better prosecution of the Macedonian war.[3] The prætor Furius had the honour of concluding the war in Gaul by gaining a victory near Cremona. The Carthaginians punished Hamilcar by confiscating his estates and effects, and sent large presents of wheat to conciliate the Roman government, which was justly offended at the conduct of Hamilcar. The ambassadors obtained from Masinissa a thousand Numidian horse and a present of corn for the Macedonian expedition. They had instructions to see king Philip upon their return, and remonstrate with him upon his conduct towards the allies of Rome. While Sulpicius had been detained in Italy the king of Macedon had not been idle. He had ravaged the lands of Athens, taken the towns of Maroneia and Ænus, marched through Chersonesus, destroying and wasting it; and passing the straits besieged Abydos,[4] which was forced to yield, but not until the king had opened a formidable breach in the walls. At first Philip refused the besieged life and liberty, and they determined to kill their wives and children, and die themselves rather than fall into his hands. The desperate valour they displayed made the besieger more clement, and he granted better terms to this brave and unfortunate people. After they had surrendered their city they remembered their solemn oath, and determined to put themselves and their families to death according to the fearful tenor of their vow. They had commenced their frantic design when the bitter irony of the conqueror put an effectual stop to it, for he caused a proclamation to be made by a herald, "That all those persons who wished to cut their throats or hang themselves should have three days allowed them for that express purpose."[5] Marcus Æmilius, the young Roman ambassador, obtained an audience of king Philip and demanded of him, "Why he had treated the Athenians and Abydenens with such severity, who had never done anything to injure him?" "You are arrogant," replied the king in answer to the spirited interrogatories of the Roman, "but I forgive and excuse it for three reasons. You are a Roman—a young inexperienced person—and are besides a very handsome man. I hope Rome will not violate the treaty between us, but if she does, with the help of the gods, I know how to defend myself."[6] Æmilius was then dismissed.

Sulpicius, being too late for action when he arrived in Greece, wintered at Apollonia, from whence he sent Claudius Centho to protect the Athenian territory from Philocles and the Macedonians. Centho acquitted himself admirably of his commission, and also planned a naval expedition to Chalcis, which he stormed and took, burned king Philip's magazines and stores, levelled his statues, and returned loaded with the wealth of the piratical city to Athens.[7] Philip was not a prince likely to remain inactive at such a crisis, he marched to Chalcis, hoping to revenge himself upon the Romans. They were at Athens, whither he followed them. The Athenians were drawn up before their town to defend it, a measure Philip thought the celerity of his march had left them no time to adopt. "Do you wish to seek me? you will find me in the heat of the battle; fix your eyes upon me there," cried the royal warrior to his soldiers, "and remember that where the king is there his people ought to be."[8] A speech worthy of a sovereign. With these words, he fell upon the Athenians and drove them within their walls. The appearance of the Romans and Pergamenians near the city, ready to give him battle, made the king give up the projected siege; but at Eleusis, whither he retired, he committed unheard of excesses; neither the mausoleums of the dead, nor the temples of the gods, nor the images of the deities themselves, being spared by him. He hastened to Argos to induce the Achæans to accept his assistance against Nabis, the tyrant of Lacedæmon, which they prudently declined, upon which he returned to Attica B.C. 200. to renew his work of destruction. He was compelled to leave Bœotia, which he had also invaded, to defend Macedon from Apustius and the Romans, who had been commissioned by Sulpicius to lay it waste.

Scipio Africanus was chosen censor, and promoted to the presidency of the senate. Sulpicius was continued in Macedon as pro-consul, and was scarcely come out of his winter quarters before several petty sovereigns whose dominions bordered upon Macedon came to court the Roman alliance. Philip, fearing that the Ætolians would also join the league against him, sent ambassadors to the diet that people were holding at Naupactus, where his embassy found Furius Purpureo upon the part of the Romans, and the envoy from Athens, who came to complain of the sacrilegious conduct of their master. The Macedonians had the privilege allowed them of speaking first, no small advantage in a war of words. They made the grasping ambition of the Romans the theme of their orations, and assured the Ætolians that in assisting that unprincipled people to conquer Philip, they were affixing the yoke of those barbarians upon themselves. The Athenians in their turn expatiated upon the cruelty and impiety of Philip, who had violated the sepulchres of the dead, and defaced not only the sacred temples but the divine images themselves. This charge greatly moved the assembly, whom the Athenians entreated "to join the *two most formidable powers, those of Heaven and Rome.*" Furius Purpureo spoke in justification of his people, retorting upon king Philip the charge of ambition and cruelty, while inviting the Ætolians "to unite with the Romans in conquering the Macedonian, if they did not wish to perish with him." The Ætolians would have done so if their prætor Damocritus had not reminded them that no question relative to peace or war could be decided in an assembly like that, but in a general diet. This he said to gain time, intending that the Ætolians should not declare themselves till one or other of the great powers desirous of their assistance had gained some signal advantage.

Near Demetrias, in Thessaly, several skirmishes took place between the Macedonian and Roman squadrons. Philip, anxious to redeem his character from the charge of impiety towards the dead, was very attentive in honouring the remains of his own soldiers. The unfortunate result of the battle at Octolophus, fought between king Philip and Sulpicius, dispirited the Macedonians. Two several actions had preceded this engagement upon the same spot within two days, but on the third king Philip lost his expected victory by his own rashness, and with difficulty preserved his life. The Ætolians espoused the cause of the Romans after Philip's defeat, to the great displeasure of that able prince, who had made his retreat good.[9] The consul Sulpicius followed him through the mountain passes into Eordæa, but went no further, ultimately resuming his old station at Apollonia. His reverses did not prevent Philip from punishing the Ætolians, and Amynander, king of the Amathians, whom he defeated and drove out of Macedonia, which he had invaded. Anaxagoras, his general, beat the Dardanians, and forced them to retire.[10]

Apustius, with the Roman fleet and that of king Attalus, sailed for Athens, where he was received by the Athenians with great joy, as his presence secured them from king Philip. They ventured to denounce the most solemn curses against the Macedonian monarch and his family, and even his ancestors. They destroyed his images and those of his predecessors, threw down the temples in which divine honours had been lately paid to their statues, abolished their festivals, and commanded the priests when they prayed for the Athenians and their allies to utter the extremest maledictions upon king Philip, his children, servants, sea and land forces, race, and kingdom. They also adjudged the punishment of death to any individual who should dare to defend his character or praise his person.[11] This absurd decree excited the mirth and contempt of the Romans, and doubtless afforded the witty subject of the Athenian maledictions with food for his sharp irony, in which no man of his day surpassed him.

Unable to take Thaumacia in Thrace, Philip returned to Macedonia, leaving his opponent the consul Villius to winter at Apollonia. After a sharp contest, Quinctius Flamininus and Ælius Paetus were elected to the consulship, and Macedon fell to the lot of the former. Flamininus, B.C. 199. though thirty years of age, had never filled any public office of consequence before assuming the consular purple, yet he possessed great courage and ability, though his talents had not till then found a fitting sphere of action. From the celerity used by the new consul in his preparations for the Macedonian war, king Philip entertained an idea that he should find in him a more formidable adversary than he had met in the cautious Sulpicius, or slothful Villius. In the hope of defeating the ex-consul before the arrival of his successor in office, he marched to Apollonia and encamped near that city, having taken up a very strong position upon the sides of two mountains, parted by the river Aous. Villius, learning the arrival of king Philip, went out to examine his encampment, but being a timid person, when near enough to view the manner in which the king had entrenched himself, returned to his head-quarters at Apollonia, where the new consul Flamininus found him upon his arrival. Philip obtained through the agency of an Epirot leader, a personal interview with his opponent, and from that moment dropped the absurd notion he had previously entertained of the barbarism of the Roman people. Flamininus spoke Greek fluently, and his mild and pleasing countenance presented to the king nothing barbaric in manner or appearance, for even the prejudices of the royal Macedonian could not call the noble disinterestedness, that asked nothing for the Roman republic beyond justice for her allies into anything resembling savage rudeness.[12] His demands, nevertheless, appeared extravagant, for Flamininus not only required the restitution of the Greek cities conquered by Philip but those his ancestors had formerly won. "What cities would you have me restore?" asked the monarch. "All Thessaly," was the laconic reply. "What more, consul, could you have demanded if you had conquered me?"[13] was the indignant rejoinder of the warlike and ambitious monarch as he quitted the presence of Flamininus. The breaking up of the conference was the signal for the immediate commencement of hostilities between the Romans and Macedonians. Four days from that date Flamininus had driven the king from his strong entrenchments, and made himself master of his camp. Philip gathered together his troops and retired to the vale of Tempe, from whence he despatched reinforcements to the Greek cities in his interest.

Flamininus was not a man likely to lose the fruits of his late victory by delay. He marched through Epirus, following the retreat of Philip and entered Thessaly, which unfortunate country was likewise invaded by the Ætolians and Athamanians in opposite directions. Several fortresses were stormed and taken by the consul, but at Atrax the bravery of the Macedonian garrison compelled him to retire, even after he had effected a breach in the walls, for they formed themselves in a phalanx to defend the broken rampart, which they covered and maintained in spite of the efforts of Flamininus and his victorious legions.[14] By sea the Roman arms prospered under Lucius Quinctius, to whom his brother Flamininus had given the command of the allied fleet, which combined those of Rhodes and king Attalus with the Roman naval force. After taking Erotina and

Carystus, cities on the sea-coast of Eubœa, he appeared before Cenchrea, a port of Corinth. He resolved to winter in Phocis, which was conveniently near Anticyra, a city on the gulf of Corinth, for his supplies to come in. The city had to be taken, but this he effected in the course of a few days, as well as the capture of several other important places.[15] Nor was he less fortunate in his negotiations with king Philip's allies, for learning that the Achæans had exiled their prætor Cycliadas, who was in the Macedonian interest, and chosen Aristænus, who favoured that of Rome, he sent to them, offering to place Corinth under their government, as it had formerly been. Still the Macedonian faction was so powerful with some, and the jealousy of the Romans and Macedonians so great with others, that it was long before the Achæans could resolve to join the allies against king Philip. As it was, the deputies from three cities, Argos, Megalopolis, and Dymæ, quitted the assembly without giving any decision. The rest of the Achæans joined the Romans in the siege of Corinth, which was fully invested by land and sea. This place, strong by nature, and admirably defended by Philocles, one of king Philip's best generals, aided by those Roman deserters who had B.C. 198. served under Hannibal in Italy, withstood successfully the siege, which the allies reluctantly raised. Argos was then besieged by Philocles, when the new governor, who was commanded by the diet to hold the cities for the allies, finding himself abandoned by the inhabitants, who favoured king Philip, was forced to capitulate. Although he sent off the garrison, for whom he had made honourable terms, Ænesidemus preferred remaining there with a few chosen friends. Philocles sent to ask the reason of his stay and what his intentions were. "To die in the place committed to my care," was the magnanimous reply of the Achæan. Philocles, who could not appreciate the greatness of mind displayed by the governor, commanded some Thracian archers to discharge their arrows at him and his devoted company.[16] The senate and people of Rome were so well pleased with Flamininus, that they granted him large reinforcements of men, ships, and arms, and continued him in his command in Greece as pro-consul. His brother remained admiral of the fleet. They appointed him Sulpicius and Villius for lieutenants. At this time two new prætors were appointed to take charge of Hither and Further Spain, as the extension of the Roman dominions required more officers of this kind, which were now six in number. Unconscious of the decision of the Roman senate and people in his favour, Flamininus resolved to conclude the war before the arrival of one or both of the consuls should tear his laurels from him by reaping the fruits of his victories, and as the time appeared too short to accomplish this by the sword he was willing to effect a peace by negotiation. Philip, who was extremely desirous of coming to terms with the Romans, agreed to meet the pro-consul on the sea-coast, near the city of Nicæa. Philip did not choose to trust himself on shore. He remained in a ship of war, while Flamininus stood on the land.[17] "Why do you not come on shore?" bluntly asked the Roman; "we should hear each other better. Which of us do you fear?" "I fear the gods alone," replied the king, "but there are some men with you that I cannot trust, and least of all the Ætolians." "The danger is equal on both sides," was the rejoinder of the Roman. "There is always some risk in conferences with enemies." "No," said Philip, "the danger is not equal; were Phæneas dead, the

Ætolians might easily choose another prætor, but were I killed, the Macedonians could not so readily find another king."[18] After this sally an awkward silence ensued, till Philip reminded Flamininus "that he who was to prescribe the terms of the peace was to be the first speaker, not he who was to accept them." Then Flamininus demanded that the towns taken in Illyria since the peace, should be restored to the Romans, that their deserters should be given up to them, that he should evacuate the Egyptian cities taken from king Ptolemy, that he should immediately leave Greece, and satisfy the just claims of the Roman allies.[19] This last clause occasioned such a volley of complaints and invectives upon the part of the allies, as must have daunted any man who had possessed less courage or less levity than king Philip. He ordered his ship to be brought nearer the shore, and affected to pay the deepest attention to the orations of Alexander and Phæneas, who spoke on the part of the Ætolians, occasionally criticising the style of the oratory, or interrupting the speakers with some bitter jest, or one of those brilliant repartees for which he was celebrated throughout Greece. He finally requested the substance of the demands of the Greeks in writing, remarking, "that he was alone, and had none to assist him with counsel." The pro-consul, who probably thought that in a war of words this monarch required no assistance, replied, "You deserve to be alone, for you have deprived yourself of all your friends." The king, though he felt the bitterness of the retort, only smiled in return.[20] The conference broke up, with the promise of being renewed upon the following day. To avoid the repetition of the contentions that had disturbed this meeting, Flamininus and king Philip alone were to be the contracting parties on the morrow. To convince the Roman pro-consul that he had no distrust of him, Philip landed with his two secretaries, and privately offered to restore to the Romans what he had taken from them in Illyria—Pharsalus and Larissa to the Ætolians—Parca to the Rhodians—Argos and Corinth to the Achæans, and promised to give up the ships and prisoners that he had B.C. 197. taken from king Attalus. Flamininus submitted those conditions to the allies, who received them with noisy disapprobation; upon which Philip proposed another conference at Nicæa. At this last meeting he agreed to refer the dispute to the decision of the Roman senate, to which the allies and Flamininus consented, and deputies were sent from each party to Rome.[21] The allies impressed upon the senate the necessity of obliging the Macedonian to give up the cities of Demetrias in Thessaly, Corinth in Achaia, and Chalcis in Eubœa, which places they denominated the fetters of Greece. The senators interrupted the Macedonian ambassador, in the commencement of his oration, by demanding "If his master intended to give up those important places," and, upon his replying that he had received no instruction upon that head, dismissed him without giving him a hearing. Philip, who found all hope of peace was gone, began to prepare for war by making a present of Argos to Nabis, the tyrant of Lacedæmon,[22] for as he could not keep that city he thought to secure it from the Romans by this method. Nabis, after plundering it, and treating the inhabitants with great cruelty, went over to the Romans, as his best chance of retaining possession of it, and furnished his new allies with six hundred Cretans to assist them in the war with Macedon. Philip was deeply mortified at seeing himself outwitted by Nabis, but it is a remarkable fact that deceitful persons are often ensnared by each other in matters where honester men would have escaped. Flamininus got possession of Thebes in Bœotia, in a way quite worthy of king Philip himself, for hearing that a diet was to be held there, he left his quarters, attended by king Attalus and his guard, and advanced towards the city. He had, however, placed two thousand Hastati among the hills, ready to enter the place as soon as the gates should be opened to receive him.[23] The Theban prætor and the inhabitants seeing the pro-consul so poorly attended, came out unarmed to receive him. The Hastati then appeared and the Bœotians, betrayed into an alliance with Rome, were only permitted to hold their assembly that they might appear to do that willingly which was no longer in their own choice. At this diet king Attalus was seized with a fit of apoplexy, from which he never recovered. He was carried on board his own galley where he died. He was succeeded by his eldest son Eumenes. Flamininus marched into Thessaly to carry on the war against king Philip.[24] At Cynocephalæ a decisive but sanguinary battle decided the fate of the Macedonian war. Once the Roman legions gave way but were promptly succoured by a body of Ætolian horsemen.[25] A military tribune then charged the Macedonian phalanx in the rear, and as a body of men in this order cannot face round, they were compelled to fly or perish without the power of self-defence.[26] The broken phalanx fled, and the fortunes of the royal Macedonian fled with it. The defeat of one of his generals in Achaia, added to the train of disasters consequent upon his overthrow, and, under the pious pretext of giving the rites of sepulture to his unburied dead, king Philip solicited peace of the victorious pro-consul. Flamininus was not at all averse to any pacification that would be honourable to the Roman republic; but he did not inform the Ætolians of the overture made by king Philip, because they claimed the victory of Cynocephalæ, and allowed Flamininus a very small share in the glory of that day, which occasioned a rising hatred between him and his boastful allies. He found Philip perfectly willing to accede to the terms which he had refused when unconquered. The Roman senate was to arbitrate between him and the Grecian states. To these articles many were added, but these of course emanated from existing circumstances. He gave his heir apparent Demetrius as a hostage for his good behaviour, together with some other Macedonians of rank, and paid two hundred talents in advance of the tribute, according to the conditions of peace imposed upon him. The young prince and the money were to be given back in case the senate refused to ratify the treaty. The articles of the peace that gave liberty to Greece, and restored to her all of which the ambitious king Philip had deprived her, pleased every one but the Ætolians, who were dissatisfied because that monarch was neither killed nor dethroned.[27] Flamininus coldly remarked, "that the destruction of the Macedonian kingdom was not for the B.C. 196. interest of Greece, who would lie exposed to the irruptions of the barbarous nations beyond it, from which the existence of that monarchy defended her." This was good policy, doubtless, and if Flamininus had added, "defended Greece from Rome," he would also have spoken the truth, as the Ætolians, in common with the other free states, at no distant date had cause to remember. The senate granted a peace which deprived Macedonia of the greater part of her army and navy, imposed a ten years' tribute upon her, and robbed her king of the pleasure of making war without the consent of the Romans. The senate demanded the cession of the three important cities already named as the fetters of Greece, but Flamininus, who did not wish to yield up his proud title of liberator of Greece, prevailed upon his government to hold these cities for a limited period only.

The conclusion of the Macedonian war was preceded by the defeat and captivity of Hamilcar, and the re-conquest of Cis-alpine Gaul by Cethegus, while Minucius committed great devastations in the territory of the Boians and Liguria.[28] Flamininus, at the Isthmian games, commanded a herald to proclaim liberty to Greece.[29] It was a proud day for the victorious Roman general, and a happy one for his Grecian allies, when the voice of the sacred officer was raised to utter the blessed sounds of peace and freedom, upon which the momentary silence of the hushed assembly was broken by a long loud shout of joy that was heard as far as the sea-shore. Flamininus, the idol of the hour, was obliged to avoid the pressure of the adoring crowd by retreating to a place of safety, as he was in danger of suffocation from the grateful multitude. Among the many honours heaped upon the great Roman, none could have interested him more than the gift of twelve hundred Roman slaves, who had been taken in Italy by Hannibal and sold in Greece.[30] These persons the Achæans redeemed and presented to the conqueror, a noble present, worthy of them who gave and him who received it. These captives afterwards adorned the triumph of the victor at Rome, following his chariot on foot, and, at their own request, wearing the cap of liberty, the sign of their manumission, on their closely-shaven heads, as a proof that they considered themselves indebted to Flamininus for their freedom.[31] The conclusion of the Macedonian war has always been considered a glorious era in the annals of the Roman republic. The moderation and wisdom of Flamininus had ensured the respect and esteem of all Greece, and Rome appeared more truly great while giving liberty to those states, than in seeking her own aggrandisement by endeavouring to annex them to her already wide dominions.

The Macedonian war was scarcely brought to an honourable conclusion, before Antiochus the Great, invaded Thrace, which his ancestor, Seleucus Nicator, one of Alexander the Great's captains, had formerly taken from Lysimachus.[32] He intended to recover this country, rebuild Lysimachia, and bestow the kingdom upon one of his sons. As the ambitious Romans did not desire the presence of this monarch in Europe, some of the council of ten, who were then in Greece, endeavoured to persuade him to give up his project. Antiochus, as ambitious as the proud republicans, refused to withdraw his armies; asserting that he had as much right to be out of Asia, as the Romans had to be out of Italy,[33] an incontrovertible truth from the mouth of an unconquered prince. A false report of the death of Ptolemy Epiphanes, occasioned his departure, for he sailed immediately for Egypt, with the intention of taking possession of that kingdom. He was quickly undeceived; but having narrowly escaped shipwreck, wintered at Antioch, his capital. His son, Seleucus, remained at Lysimachia, superintending the rebuilding of that city with a numerous army.

The consulship of Marcus Porcius Cato and L. Valerius Flaccus, was memorable for the repeal of a law, whose continuance in the jurisprudence of the republic, was considered peculiarly vexatious by the Roman ladies of this period. Indeed, neither the glorious conclusion of the Macedonian war, the rebellion in Spain, nor the ambitious designs of Antiochus at this time engaged the public attention at Rome, which was engrossed entirely by the endeavours of the feminine part of the state to get B.C. 195. the Oppian law repealed, which forbad them the use of sumptuous furniture, carriages, or apparel.[34] This female faction proved invulnerable to reason, conjugal authority, or the invectives of the austere Cato, whose consulship they had chosen for the assertion of what they considered their just rights. Never since the world began had a body of people been so urgent and so united in their claims. Every female of high or low degree, joined in the petition to the comitia for the repeal of the law, which they induced Valerius and Fundanius, tribunes of the people, to present in their general name. Nor were they satisfied with the promises of these magistrates, whom they had seduced into pleading their cause, for they crowded into the forum to hear the arguments of their champions; having also provided themselves with some pieces of eloquence in their own behalf. For what man could be properly qualified to speak upon the fashion of women's apparel, at that or any other period of time? and so the ladies thought, for they stood undauntedly before the tribunal of the austere Cato, and put their petitions into the hands of every man who came to listen to the important debate.[35] These petitions were, doubtless, their own compositions; and, if they had been preserved, would have given us the most correct notions of female costume in those days, and of their talents in asserting their feminine privilege of being fashionably dressed.

Cato, horror-stricken at their pertinacity and boldness, complained "That the women, not contented with braving their husbands at home, even carried their audacity into the forum. That this was a conspiracy of women;" ungallantly asserting, "that there was no mischief of which that sex would not be capable, if they were suffered to meet and cabal together, either in private parties, or public assemblies." He even proceeded to invectives, and said some unhandsome things about "curbs for untameable animals," exceedingly provoking for Roman ladies to hear; dwelling sarcastically upon the impropriety of their speaking to strange men in the streets, to engage them in their foolish cause, instead of persuading their husbands at home. But the more he inveighed against their love of finery, and perseverance in endeavouring to obtain a legal right to appear in it, the more obstinately bent they appeared to enforce their claims. Two tribunes, named Brutus, of the Junian family, voted against the repeal, of which they afterwards must have repented, as the "untamed animals," as Cato denominated the female petitioners, besieged them in public and private from that moment, giving them no quarter from their tongues till they had carried their point. Their advocate, Valerius, made an eloquent oration in favour of his fair clients;[36] declaring, "that their appearance in public far from being mischievous to the counsels of men, had always been productive of good. That they had deprived themselves of their ornaments, sumptuous apparel, and chariots when the state was in danger, and by this generous self-sacrifice had provided for its exigencies; but that now the war of Hannibal was over, they naturally desired to resume their feminine rights. He could not see why the women of Rome should be kept in mourning; for what was the mourning of women, but the laying aside of their ornaments and gaiety of apparel. Shall men wear purple, shall the dead be wrapped in it, shall our horses be adorned in it, and our wives be forbidden the use of a purple cloak? As for their gold ornaments, may they not be as serviceable to us in some future time of calamity, as they have lately proved?" He expressed his opinion "of the injustice done to the Roman ladies by the continuance of sumptuary laws, that did not affect the Latin females, who were allowed to wear the purple and jewels that these were forbidden to use. How mortifying this must be to female minds, which small matters easily disturb," added the gallant tribune; "they have no magistracies, no triumphs, no sacerdotal dignities, no spoils nor trophies of war; ornaments and dress are the triumphs of women, in these they delight. We are told that if we repeal the Oppian law, you will not be able to restrain them by your private authority. While fathers and husbands are alive, the subjection of women can never cease. They would rather have their dress regulated by you, than by the law; and it ought to be your choice rather to be styled B.C. 195. fathers and husbands than masters.[37] The consul makes use of some invidious expressions—a sedition, a conspiracy of women, as if they were going to seize the Sacred Mount or Aventine Hill. No, Romans, their weakness must submit to whatever you are pleased to determine; but the greater your power, the more moderate you ought to be in the use of it."[38]

The eloquent and gallant appeal of Valerius made a great impression upon the comitia; but it was too late to determine the question that day, and the decision of the assembly was put off to the next. The women made such good use of the intervening hours, by besieging the houses of the refractory tribunes, whom Cato had induced to oppose the repeal; that wearied out by their reproaches, tears, and entreaties, the two Brutuses yielded up the point to get rid of their importunities, and voted for the abolition of the obnoxious law the following day, which was accordingly repealed; and the female conspirators retired to their houses to enjoy the privilege of adorning themselves, which had just been secured to them by the legislature, after their own pleasure and discretion.

Cato embarked for Spain, exchanging his wordy war with women for sterner ones with free-born men, who abhorred the Roman yoke, and had united to shake it off. As he was an admirable disciplinarian, and accustomed himself to the temperance he enforced, he quickly formed his newly raised levies of troops into a well-appointed army, and a decisive victory ensured the preservation of the Roman possessions in Spain.

The wisdom and excellent government of Hannibal, who was prætor of Carthage at this time, excited the jealousy of the Roman senate, and the fatal envy of the Barcine faction.[39] Great in the council-chamber as in the field, the illustrious Carthaginian had reformed many abuses in public offices, and had caused the quæstors to be reduced from perpetual into annual magistrates. He had prevented a new and oppressive tax from being raised to pay the Roman tribute, by examining and inspecting the public accounts, and obliging those persons who had embezzled the revenue to restore it to the treasury, the tribute being paid without an additional tax. These acts which justly endeared him to the people excited the hatred of the aristocracy, by whom he was denounced to the Roman senate, and accused of plotting with Antiochus, king of Syria, against the republic.

Scipio, generous as he was brave, spoke in the senate in favour of the man he had vanquished in battle, and declared that in his opinion it would be unworthy of the Roman government to take any notice of the quarrels of the Carthaginian nobles with Hannibal. But the name of Hannibal still sounded harshly in Roman ears, and the conscript fathers despatched commissioners to Carthage to accuse their old enemy of the facts that his base countrymen had laid to his charge, and which whether true or false came badly enough from them.[40] The Roman deputation concealed their designs under colour of settling some disputes between their old ally Masinissa and Carthage, but Hannibal was not deceived by this pretence, but departed that evening without assuming any disguise or appearing to be aware of the designs the Romans had in view. He rode all that night till he arrived at a tower of his own on the sea-shore, where he had a ship ready provisioned and manned against a time of danger long foreseen by his acute and penetrating mind. His regret was for his country, "whose misfortunes he regarded far more than his own," remarks the Roman historian Livy.[41] The fugitive reached the island of Cercina and secured his personal safety by one of those bold strokes that distinguished him from all other men. Finding the haven crowded with shipping from Carthage, and having reason to dread his own countrymen as much as the Romans, he took advantage of their ignorance of his flight to secure their fidelity by a singular stratagem. He invited all the masters and seamen belonging to the Carthaginian vessels to a feast and sacrifice upon the sea-shore, and requested them to erect tents with their yards and sails. Proud to be the guests of Hannibal the Carthaginian seamen immediately accepted his invitation, and converted their canvass into tents and feasted with him till late that night, when overcome with weariness and wine they sank into a deep sleep. Then Hannibal, secure from treason or pursuit, sailed for Tyre, where he B.C. 195. was honourably received, and from whence he repaired to Antioch, but finding Antiochus was then at Ephesus he followed him thither, and was welcomed with much pleasure by that prince, who was upon the point of a rupture with the Romans.[42]

Flamininus was still continued as pro-consul in Greece, where his arms and negotiations had been productive of so much advantage and glory to the republic. As the senate had great reason to distrust the character of Nabis, their new ally, whom they suspected of being in league with Antiochus against Rome, he was directed to punish that tyrant without further delay. Flamininus called a general diet at Corinth and made a proposition to the assembly respecting Argos, which he was desirous of taking out of the hands of Nabis and restoring to the Achæans, provided the deputies from the Grecian states were agreeable to that measure.[43] All expressed their approbation of this design of Flamininus but the Ætolians, who accused the Romans of ambition, and declared that Greece could not be called free while their legions remained there; that they themselves would recover Argos, and restore it to the Argives as soon as Flamininus and his soldiers had departed for Italy. The intemperance of Alexander, the prætor of Ætolia, who spoke in the name of his countrymen, excited the indignation of all the Grecian deputies, and they were unanimous in their votes for the war against Nabis, upon which the Ætolians withdrew.

After dismissing the ambassadors sent to him by Antiochus to treat for peace, on the grounds that the senate alone were qualified to receive them, Flamininus marched to Argos, expecting some movement on the part of the Argives would open the city gates to his legions. Being foiled in these expectations he marched along the banks of the Eurotas, destroying the country as far as Lacedæmon, while his brother, Lucius, besieged the important city of Gythium by sea, which was valiantly defended till the approach of the Rhodian and Pergamenian fleets compelled the garrison to capitulate. As this city was called the port of Lacedæmon, the terrified Nabis offered to make peace, but the terms offered by Flamininus did not please the Lacedæmonians, who when asked by Nabis respecting the answer he ought to give, replied, "Give him no answer at all, pursue the war." The Romans with a well-disciplined army made their way into the city at the breaches they had opened, upon which the cowardly Nabis was about to run away and leave the capital to its fate, when Pythagoras his son-in-law fired the adjacent houses, which measure obliged the Romans to withdraw. Nabis, however, who possessed the abject nature of the slave as well as that of the tyrant, sent Pythagoras to entreat Flamininus to grant him peace upon the terms he had lately offered him. The haughty Roman, disgusted with his pusillanimity, ordered his messenger to be expelled with scorn from his tent, but Pythagoras at length obtained a hearing, when it was agreed that Nabis should restore Argos, yield up the towns he held in Crete, retain only two galleys, pay tribute to the Romans, and give up his son and five other hostages to them as pledges for his future good conduct.[44] Argos had driven out the Lacedæmonian garrison while Flamininus was besieging Nabis, but the fate of Lacedæmon excited the pity of all Greece and the indignation of the Ætolians, as that renowned city lay in slavery at the mercy of Nabis, while her lawful king Agesipolis was in the Roman camp. Flamininus about to return to Rome convened a diet at Corinth, and entered upon a recapitulation of his own actions and those of his predecessors since the first moment the Romans entered Greece. He was greeted with rapturous applause till he mentioned Lacedæmon, which he declared he could not restore to liberty without totally destroying the city, when a dead silence ensued. He announced his departure for Italy, and recommended them to preserve a strict union among themselves as the surest means of securing their liberty, as the weakest party in cases of disunion is apt to appeal to foreigners, and then all become slaves to the power called in as arbiter between them. The assembly, touched even to tears by the affectionate counsel of Flamininus, received his farewell address with promises to abide by it, and he returned to Rome, where he was honoured with a splendid triumph of three days' duration.[45]

The long-expected embassy from Antiochus at length B.C. 194.arrived at Rome. After much fruitless negotiation Menippus, on the part of the king, entreated the Roman senate would defer war, and send an embassy to his master's court. The ambassadors had scarcely quitted

Rome before the Carthaginians informed the Roman senate that Antiochus was preparing for war, by the counsel of Hannibal, who was endeavouring to bring him to an open rupture with the Romans. Of the truth of this report there could be no doubt, as Hannibal had sent a Tyrian to persuade his degenerate countrymen to join him and Antiochus against the Romans in a descent on Italy,[46] the only part of the dominions of the warlike republic which could be assailed with success. Ariston was ill received, and was forced to escape, but not before he had affixed a writing over the president's seat, purporting "that he had no commission to treat with private persons but with the senate of Carthage only," an ingenious method of securing the friends of Hannibal from punishment.

Masinissa had made great encroachments upon the Carthaginian territory lately, being certain that his allies the Romans, would justify him in anything he undertook against that people, and so it proved, for though the senate sent commissioners from Rome (of which Scipio Africanus was one), far from obliging Masinissa to restore the city and lands of Emporia, they obliged the complainants to pay five hundred talents for the profits of these possessions since they had been claimed by the king of Numidia. This was a bitter thing to the selfish and avaricious Carthaginians, who only felt the national degradation through the medium of their pecuniary losses.[47]

The Ætolians who for some time past had distrusted the Romans, whose presence in Greece militated against the liberty of the free states, were extremely desirous of forming a league against the republic. They despatched messengers to king Philip, Nabis, and Antiochus, to induce them to join the confederacy against Rome. The Macedonian and Syrian monarchs were too wary to come to an instant decision, but Nabis, wishing to regain what had been taken from him in the last war, instantly declared his intentions by laying siege to Gythium. Antiochus, being desirous of strengthening his power by allying himself to several influential princes prior to engaging in the Roman war, and having intentions against Egypt, gave his daughter Cleopatra to Ptolemy Epiphanes in the hope of making her subservient to his designs upon the dominions of her husband. An account of this celebrated marriage will be found in Josephus, which was foretold in the book of Daniel.[48] Antiochus then turned his arms against the Pisidians, which occasioned his absence from Ephesus when the embassy from Rome arrived in that city. Scipio Africanus, who accompanied the ambassadors, contracted here an intimacy with Hannibal, and these rivals, who had hitherto met as the champions of their several countries in the field, conversed as friends at Ephesus. It was said that Scipio once asked Hannibal "whom he considered the greatest general in the world?"[49] The Carthaginian named "Alexander the Great." "And the next?" demanded Scipio. "Pyrrhus," was the ready reply. "And whom do you place next?" asked the Roman. "Myself," replied the great Hannibal, who probably did not consider that Scipio's single victory over him entitled the Roman to be ranked above him. "And if you had conquered me?" demanded Scipio. "Then," replied Hannibal, with equal readiness and courtesy,

"I should have given myself the first place."[50] At Ephesus, Hannibal attended a lecture upon the military art given by the philosopher Phormio, and listened for four hours to the duties to be practised by a general, with edifying attention. The audience, delighted at the eloquence of the theorist, asked the celebrated practitioner in the art of war, "What he thought of it?" who replied, "that he had met with many a silly old fellow, but never with so great a fool as this."[51] A useful hint to all public speakers never to venture on subjects upon which they are not qualified to speak.

Villius, the other Roman ambassador, went to Apamea, where he obtained an audience with Antiochus, but the conference was abruptly broken off by the king of Syria's B.C. 194. receiving intelligence of his son's death, upon which he gave way to the most passionate grief. He has been accused of the murder of the prince, but this is very unlikely as he was a young man of great promise, and bore his own name.[52] When Antiochus returned to Ephesus, he shut himself up in his palace, and though he sent for Villius to this city it was long before he would see him or his colleague Sulpicius. The Romans could obtain no direct answer, but "that he had as much business in Greece as they had in Sicily or any part of colonial Greece in Italy," upon which they returned home. Antiochus immediately held a consultation with the general officers of his army respecting the expediency of the war with the Romans. From this council Hannibal was sedulously excluded, for his intimacy with the Romans had excited the suspicions of Antiochus, who did not choose to consult him upon his project of invading Italy.[53] Informed of the reason of this exclusion by some of his friends, Hannibal solicited an audience of the king, and, in an eloquent speech, avowed his mortal hatred to the Romans, which had never altered since the hour in which his father Hamilcar had caused him to take a solemn oath to that effect upon the altars of his country's gods. He spoke of the wars he had waged against them as a proof of his sincerity, and declared that he was only there seeking enemies to Rome.[54] Antiochus appeared convinced of his sincerity, and the war with Rome was determined upon. Aware of the preparations Antiochus was making, the Roman republic took the prudent precaution of guarding the eastern coast of Italy. Fleets were stationed in Sicily and Greece, and Flamininus himself was despatched to the latter country as ambassador from Rome, assisted by three others.[55] As soon as he arrived the Achæans asked his permission to punish Nabis, who had ravaged some part of their territories. He granted it, but advised them to delay hostilities till the Roman fleet should arrive. They debated the matter in full diet, and determined to attack Nabis without delay. They chose Philopœmen for their general, and gathering together a few galleys attempted to raise the siege of Gythium, but were repulsed by the Lacedæmonian fleet. Shortly after this he landed and burnt the camp of Nabis, and recovered his reputation by giving the tyrant another overthrow by land, for naval warfare was an art in which the valiant Greek was unskilled.[56] Flamininus and the ambassadors passed from state to state, to induce them to unite against Antiochus, but a spirit of disunion and disaffection had spread amongst them. The inhabitants of Demetrias in Thessaly, had heard a rumour that their city would be bestowed upon Demetrius, the heir apparent of king Philip, who was then a hostage at Rome.[57] The Ætolians openly declared their intention of calling in the king of Syria to restore liberty to Greece, and passed a decree to that purpose before Flamininus' face. He calmly asked for a copy of the decree, upon which the prætor, Damocritus, the old enemy of Rome, told him—"They had no time then, but that he should be informed of its meaning upon the banks of the Tiber." This idle boast was followed up by some bold measures to get possession of Demetrias, Chalcis, and Lacedæmon. The first the Ætolians gained by treachery, but the second, though won by the same detestable means, was lost as soon as gained. The Ætolians sent thither Alexamenus with a thousand foot soldiers and some horsemen, under the pretence of assisting Nabis against the Achæans. Nabis, without the slightest suspicion, accepted the offer of the new comer to discipline the Lacedæmonian troops against the coming of his royal Syrian ally, and Alexamenus assassinated him during one of those reviews, which were held on a plain without the city walls. Philopœmen soon after appeared before the town in the character of her deliverer, and Lacedæmon was no longer a kingdom but a republic, forming a part of the Achæan league.[58] Chalcis remained unshaken in its fidelity to Rome. Thoas repaired to the court of Antiochus, whom he persuaded that all the states of Greece were in eager expectation of his coming to abjure the Roman interest.[59] He also besought him to abandon the invasion of Italy, or at least to give the chief command to one of his own generals, rather than to Hannibal, B.C. 193. who would claim the whole glory of the expedition as his own. Antiochus, who had before entertained suspicions of the illustrious exile, was easily induced by Thoas to give up the advantage he would have gained in having the first soldier in the world for his lieutenant. He promised to embark for Greece, which, he was falsely assured by Thoas, was wholly in the Ætolian interest. He landed at Demetrias with a numerous army, and was immediately recognised by the Ætolians for their general. Antiochus vainly endeavoured to induce the Achæans to preserve a neutrality during the approaching war. They declared openly and at once for the Romans. The Athamanians were persuaded to join the Syrian interest, through Philip the brother-in-law of their prince, Amynander, who, deducing his descent from Alexander the Great, hoped to induce Antiochus to advance his claims to Macedon. Hannibal, whose wisdom in council was as great as his military talents, had advised the king of Syria to gain over king Philip, whose interest it must be to forsake the Romans; but Antiochus, who had determined upon favouring the claims of his new ally, applauded the counsel, but did not choose to follow it.[60] This was at Chalcis, which had recently opened her gates to Antiochus, upon the report of the defeat of five hundred Romans who were hastening to relieve her, and the king made the city his head-quarters, having fallen in love with a beautiful girl, whom he married soon after, and, forgetful of the war, passed his time there with her in pleasure and festivity.[61]

The Romans, bent upon carrying the war into Asia Minor, made active preparations for that purpose. The newly-elected consuls, Scipio Nasica, and Acilius Glabrio, drew lots for the command in Greece, but Acilius obtained it, and departed with the consular army, which amounted to ten thousand foot, two thousand horse, and fifteen elephants. He had Lucius Flamininus for his lieutenant; and Cato, so celebrated under the surname of the Censor, was his legionary tribune.[62] The kings of Macedonia, Egypt, and Numidia, offered to assist the Romans in this war; Philip, whose interests inclined him to aid his old enemies, proved a most useful partisan. The progress of the consul was rapid, and, with the assistance of his Macedonian ally, he subdued all Thessaly. At a town called Pellinæum, Philip the pretender to the crown of Macedonia was taken, to the great joy of king Philip, who, in a sarcastic tone, addressed his rival by the name of Brother and King; this insulting speech was characteristic of the Macedonian monarch. Antiochus made himself master of the celebrated pass of Thermopylæ, to prevent Ætolia from being invaded through Locris. He had posted men upon the cliffs above, to secure him from the fate of Leonidas, who, with his patriot band, after maintaining the pass for three days against the millions of Xerxes, was overpowered from the heights above. Cato, however, whose historical recollections were as vivid as those of Antiochus, had been beforehand with him, and taken possession of Mount Œta. In the night he drove down the Ætolians, whom the king had sent to guard the pass, after which he fell upon the Syrians below, while Acilius forced the king from his strong position and gained a complete victory. Antiochus, with five hundred horsemen, the remains of his fine army, fled to Elateia, and from thence to Chalcis, whence he sailed to Ephesus with his newly-married queen. The Ætolians alarmed at the successes of Acilius, came, as they said, to submit themselves to the faith of Rome. Acilius took advantage of some ambiguity in the expression,[63] to impose hard terms upon the deputies, whom he even threatened with chains, and a truce of ten days was all the favour they could obtain of him. They changed their intentions, however, as soon as Antiochus sent them word that he was coming back to Ephesus with an army, accompanying these tidings with a sum of money. Whereupon they retired into Naupactus, which city they resolved to defend against the Romans. Heracleia was taken a few days afterwards, when Damocritus, notwithstanding his arrogant boast, surrendered the citadel at discretion. Flamininus saved Chalcis from being plundered, and compelled Messene to join the Achæan league. Amynander of Athamania, finding himself driven out of his dominions by Philip of Macedon, sold the island of Zacynthus, which had formerly been given him by that prince, to the B.C. 192. Achæans. This was claimed from them by the Romans, and ill consequences might have followed, if Flamininus had not convinced the Achæans that its possession would be injurious to their interests. He compared the Achæan confederacy to a tortoise covered with its shell, which is secure from all attack till it stretches any part of its body beyond that shield. "Such," he said, "was the Peloponnesus to the league, and to get beyond that natural boundary was to weaken the whole." Zacynthus was immediately given up.[64]

King Philip found his alliance with the warlike republic highly profitable to him. He was winning back all the cities formerly taken from him by Flamininus, when that great commander thought it time to look after this zealous friend of Rome.[65] As soon as he arrived at Naupactus, the distressed Ætolians, who were then straitly besieged by Acilius and the consular army, besought his good offices; and Flamininus, who never made war when an advantageous peace could be made, induced Acilius to grant them a truce, till they could send ambassadors to

Rome to treat for pacification.[66] The success of the Roman arms occasioned many embassies to the senate, for those states that had taken no part in the war, were eager to prove their neutrality. Among these, Epirus and Bœotia were foremost. Philip of Macedon sent a splendid golden crown to adorn the capitol, in memory of the Roman victory over Antiochus. This present pleased the senators so much, that they thanked the ambassadors for the good service done by their master to the republic, and sent him back his son.[67] They also promised to excuse Philip from paying the remainder of the tribute, if he adhered faithfully to their interests during the war.

Livius, the Roman admiral, received orders to attack Antiochus, in Asia, a project never suspected by that monarch, till Hannibal made him aware of the necessity of defending the Chersonesus, by garrisoning its towns and fitting out his fleet.[68] Polyxenidas, who commanded it, fell in with Livius off the Ionian coast, and was defeated with great loss. Then the senate of Rome determined to carry the war by land and sea into Asia, and made preparations to that effect. Scipio Nasica completed, at this time, the reduction of Boian Gaul, and colonies were sent from Rome to take possession of half the lands of the conquered people.

Lucius, the elder brother, and Lælius, the bosom friend of Scipio Africanus, were chosen to fill the consulship this year. Lælius, who was an experienced commander, naturally desired to undertake the war in Greece; and he advised Lucius, instead of deciding their several provinces by lot, to refer the choice to the senate, not doubting that he would be given the preference. Africanus recommended his brother to accept the proposal; and then, when the matter was debated, offered to serve under him as his lieutenant,[69] a strong proof of his fraternal love. The senate instantly assigned the coveted province to Lucius Scipio, whose inexperience would be assisted by the transcendant military talents of the great Africanus.

The Scipios, with an army composed of thirteen thousand foot and five hundred horse, landed at Apollonia, and marched through Thessaly and Epirus to Amphissa, which town had just been won by Acilius, although the citadel still held out. Here the Athenians interceded for the Ætolians, who were blockaded in Naupactus, and desired a truce for the purpose of treating with the senate. Lucius Scipio was with difficulty persuaded to grant them this favour, and that only at the intercession of his brother.[70] Acilius resigned his command and returned to Rome. The Scipios marched through Macedonia and Thrace, conducted by king Philip in person, of whose good intentions towards them they took care to be informed, before entering his dominions. Nothing, however, could exceed his courtesy, nor did he leave them till they had arrived on the shores of the Hellespont. Livius, the Roman admiral, had taken Sestos, but had been forced to raise the siege of Abydos. The prætor, Æmilius, at this juncture arrived to take the command of the fleet, which sailed for Pergamus, which was then besieged by Antiochus and his son Seleucus in person. King Eumenes hastened to defend his own B.C. 190. country, aided by the Rhodians, who, being a great naval power, easily equipped a new fleet. The intelligence that the consul was on his way to relieve Pergamus, alarmed Antiochus; who, dreading the combination against him, offered to treat with Æmilius, who was willing to give him peace. The determined opposition of king Eumenes prevented this, and Antiochus continued his ravages in the territories of that prince, and after taking Berea and many towns, fell back on Sardis.[71] Diophanes, the Megalopolitan, relieved Pergamus, and drove Seleucus out of that country. By sea, Antiochus sustained several severe defeats. Hannibal, who encountered the Rhodian admiral at Side, lost the battle by that part of the fleet which he did not command in person being dispersed, and leaving him to sustain unaided the whole force of the enemy.[72] He was then driven into a port of Pamphylia, and blockaded by twenty ships under the command of an experienced officer, appointed by the victorious Rhodian admiral. Antiochus, becoming apprehensive respecting the result of the war, endeavoured to gain over the princes and free estates of Greece then in alliance with Rome, but to no purpose. He was finally obliged to determine the matter by the sword, and ordered Polyxenidas to bring the Roman fleet to a second engagement. This the Syrian admiral effected off Myonnesus, in Ionia, but was defeated with the loss of more than half the naval force possessed by his sovereign.[73] Upon the receipt of the disastrous intelligence Antiochus cried out, "that some god disconcerted his measures. Everything fell out contrary to his expectation. His enemies were masters of the sea; Hannibal was shut up in a port of Pamphylia; and Philip assisted the Romans to pass into Asia."[74]

No attempt had been made by the Syrian monarch to dispute with the Romans the important passage of the Hellespont. He had even rendered the city of Lysimachia incapable of defending itself, or opposing the march of the consular army, by withdrawing the garrison from that place. The Scipios had scarcely effected their landing in Asia[75] before the panic-stricken Syrian sent to propose terms of peace apparently to the advantage of the Romans, backed by a private message to the renowned Africanus, which he considered must effect the pacification he desired. He offered to quit Europe, to give up his claims to all the cities in Asia in alliance with the republic, and to defray half the expenses the Romans had incurred in carrying on the war. The consul refused to accept the terms unless the king would bind himself to remain within the boundary of Mount Taurus. Then the ambassador, taking Scipio Africanus aside, offered him, in the name of his master, the second place in his empire, and the restitution of his son, who had fallen into the hands of the Syrians.[76] The Roman calmly replied, "If Antiochus restores me my son I shall esteem it as the noblest present his munificence can make me, and if he will be contented with my private acknowledgments for a personal favour he shall ever find me grateful. In my public capacity I can neither give nor receive anything from him, but the best advice I can offer him is that he will desist from war, and refuse no conditions of peace." Upon hearing this reply to his private offer to Africanus, Antiochus considered that he could but submit to the Romans after he had been vanquished, and determined on war. Scipio Africanus, though he had behaved upon this trying occasion like an intrepid and patriotic Roman, felt like a man and a father. He fell sick with grief at Elæa, and was considered in great danger. Antiochus, who was encamped with his troops near Thyatira, touched with the sickness and sorrow of his rival, sent him back his son, an act of kingly generosity which instantly restored his suffering enemy to health. Scipio Africanus bade the Syrians thank the king in his name, and advise him by no means to risk a battle till he had joined his brother in the Roman camp. The meaning of this message is unknown, but probably Africanus wished to avoid the necessity of a battle by a lasting and honourable peace.[77] That Antiochus regarded it in this light may be presumed by his conduct, for he retreated to Magnesia, whither he was followed by the consul, Lucius Scipio, who had resolved upon concluding the war without his illustrious brother, B.C. 190. to whom his success he was aware would otherwise be imputed. The consular army numbered with the allies barely thirty thousand men; that of Antiochus consisted of seventy thousand foot, and twelve thousand horse. This huge body suffered total defeat. The loss of the Syrian monarch, reckoning the prisoners taken by the Romans, amounted to fifty-five thousand men. The victory was, comparatively speaking, a bloodless one to the Romans, on whose side not more than three hundred foot and twenty-five horsemen were slain. Lucius Scipio obtained the name of Asiaticus by this victory. He had been nobly supported by Eumenes, king of Pergamus, and his brother Attalus, throughout the day, and to the valour of these princes might be attributed, in a great measure, the signal success of the Roman army over Antiochus. Antiochus sent ambassadors to the consular camp at Sardis to solicit peace,[78] which was granted by the conqueror, upon the following terms: "The Syrian monarch was to evacuate Europe, confine himself within the limits of Mount Taurus, and was to pay fifteen thousand talents of Eubœa for the expenses of the war. He was required to give up Hannibal and five Greeks who were enemies to Rome, and to make amends to king Eumenes, by paying him four hundred talents,[79] and the corn he owed his father." Though the conditions were hard the ambassadors, who had instructions to close with any terms the Romans chose to demand, immediately accepted them, promising to send twenty hostages as security for the fulfilment of the treaty.[80] The great Hannibal had not waited for the chains of Rome. He fled into Crete as soon as he heard of the victory gained by the Romans in Magnesia.

The Ætolians had quickly dispossessed king Philip of the territories of Amynander, king of Athamania, which they restored to the rightful owner. Amynander, however, sent an embassy to Rome, being desirous of holding them by the consent of the senate.[81] Eumenes, king of Pergamus, and the ambassadors from the Rhodians to the republic, appeared at Rome with Aurelius Cotta, who brought the news of the victory of Magnesia, and the ambassadors from Antiochus for the ratification of the peace. Eumenes, who had performed great services for the republic, wished for a grant of the country lying between Mount Athos and the sea, which the Romans had just forced Antiochus to cede to them. Of his assistance and great achievements he spoke modestly, referring them to the consul and his lieutenant, from whom said he, "I would rather you should hear them than from me." Yet he took care to speak of his assistance and that of his family in such a manner as to show clearly that he thought they deserved a rich reward, though it was no easy matter for the senate to bring him to name his expectations.[82] He had no sooner done so when the Rhodian ambassadors opposed his request, affirming that though they had a high respect for the king, yet their love of liberty and desire of preserving it must render them averse to seeing him made such a powerful monarch. They reminded the senate that the Romans had generally fought for the liberties of the Greeks. "Let, then," said they, "those who desire to have a king possess one, but let the Asiatic Greeks, who have the same love of liberty as the Romans, experience from you that regard for freedom which constitutes you the deliverers of Greece." The senate was pleased with the speech of the Rhodian ambassadors, and promised to send ten commissioners into Greece to settle the claims of the allies of Rome in a satisfactory manner.[83] At present it adjudged Lycaonia, the two Phrygias, and the two Mysias, to king Eumenes. Lycia, a part of Caria, and the country near Pisidia was allotted to the Rhodians. Those cities of Asiatic Greece, which had aided the Romans against their lawful lord Antiochus, were pronounced free.

The return of the Scipios to Rome left the conduct of the Ætolian war to the consul Fulvius, who besieged Ambracia, a city on the borders of Epirus, which the Ætolians were obliged to surrender, but not before it had made a vigorous defence.[84] This fickle and proud people saw the absolute necessity of obtaining peace from the Romans, which through the intercession of the Athenians they procured upon worse terms than any other Grecian state, though they had formerly materially aided Flamininus against Philip of Macedon, for the senate chose to B.C. 189. consider the Ætolians not as old friends but as new enemies.

Manlius the other consul had been sent into Asia to punish the Gallo-Greeks or Galatians for aiding Antiochus in the late war.[85] The son of Antiochus, prince Seleucus, attended the march of the Roman consul, who quickly subdued the country, and obliged the various tribes into which the Galatians were divided to sue for peace.[86] Manlius behaved with great rapacity during this war, for which he was afterwards called to account.

A census was taken this year, when it appeared that the number of Roman citizens capable of bearing arms amounted to two hundred and fifty-eight thousand, three hundred and eighteen. The Roman admiral Labeo, while lying off the island of Crete, demanded that four thousand Roman slaves should be given up to him, which was immediately granted by the Cretans. Labeo for this service was honoured with a triumph. The ten commissioners settled the affairs of Asia and Greece at this time. They obliged king Antiochus to surrender all his elephants, his long ships, and to give his son and namesake as a hostage to Rome. The republic claimed none of the conquered countries, but power, fame, increase of political importance and immense wealth, flowed to her from the war that had given liberty to Greece.

An old oracle found in the Sibylline books charged the Romans not to pass the limits of Mount Taurus under the penalty of slaughter and destruction. Livy, the historian, gravely relates that one of the charges exhibited against Manlius upon his return related to a design of his to pass what was then called the fatal boundary.[87] The mighty energy of mind and personal bravery of the Romans was alloyed with weakness, for no nation was ever more deeply tinctured with superstition than that which conquered and overawed the world. Manlius, on his march to Italy through Thrace, was set upon in a wood by a body of ten thousand Thracians, who took from him a great part of the plunder he had amassed in

Asia, for the army were passing through a defile and could not form in order of battle. They escaped with difficulty from the ambush laid by this wild and predatory people, and got to Apollonia where they wintered.[88]

The two great Scipios were accused this year of having taken bribes from king Antiochus,[89] and embezzled the public money. Two tribunes, both of the name of Petillius, at the instigation of Cato, moved that Africanus should be asked to give an account of the spoils taken in the Asiatic war, and of the gold paid by Antiochus. Upon which the accused rose indignantly; and taking a book out of his bosom, replied; "This contains an exact account of all you wish to know, both of the money and the spoil." "Read it then," returned one of the accusers, "and let it be deposited in the public treasury." "No," replied Scipio Africanus, "I shall not put such an affront upon myself." He immediately destroyed the book, unread, before the assembly; a rash action, if he were innocent of the charge, to which he gave some validity, by the destruction of documents which ought to have cleared his character. His enemies took advantage of his proud self-reliance to ruin him. Marcus Nævius, another tribune, cited him to appear before the people to answer the charges already preferred against him in the senate.[90]

This man could bring no proof to substantiate his accusations against the great Roman, but the generosity of the king of Syria in restoring his captive son; for the narrow-minded tribune was incapable of appreciating the compassion Antiochus had felt for the parental sufferings of a foe. He decried the fraternal love that had induced Africanus to serve under his brother Lucius as his lieutenant, declaring that on that occasion he had played the part of a dictator to the consul, instead of rendering to him the obedience of an officer. Fortunately for Scipio, Nævius did not confine himself to that point alone; he displayed at once the envious passions that impelled him to make his public accusation, by asserting[91] that Publius B.C. 189. Scipio Africanus had gone into Asia to persuade both the Greeks and Asiatics, as he had done the natives of Spain, Gaul, and Africa, that one man was the pillar and support of the Roman republic, that Rome was sheltered under the shadow of Scipio, and that his single voice had superseded the decrees of the senate and the people of Rome. He did not stop here, but revived the old clamour respecting the luxury Scipio had been charged with at Syracuse, and his unfortunate appointment of Pleminius, from which accusations made against him in his youth he had formerly been honourably exonerated.

It was upon the anniversary of the battle of Zama that Nævius, through envy or inadvertence, preferred these charges against the conqueror of Hannibal. With the proud consciousness of pure and stainless patriotism Scipio Africanus addressed the assembly in these words:[92] "On this day, Romans, I conquered Hannibal and the Carthaginians. It will ill become us to spend it in wrangling and contention. Let us not be ungrateful to the gods, but leave this fellow here and go to the Capitol, to return thanks to the great Jupiter for that victory and peace which beyond all expectation I procured for the republic."[93] A movement was seen among the tribes, a simultaneous movement, the result of deep and concentrated feeling, and they followed Scipio Africanus to the Capitol. The envious tribune, Nævius, alone remained in the comitium with the town-crier, whose office, perhaps, obliged him to stay behind. This signal triumph, though it silenced Nævius, did not prevent the Petillii from citing Scipio Africanus a second time to answer the charges of embezzlement they had brought against him in the senate, for they were of that order "who hunt the steps of glory to the grave."

The accused withdrew to Liternum, but his brother Lucius appeared in his behalf and pleaded illness in excuse for his illustrious relative's absence. This plea did not satisfy his enemies, who were about to condemn him by default, when Lucius entreated them to name another day for the trial. T. Sempronius Gracchus, a tribune of the people, alone negatived the decree against Africanus. He declared "that if the accused would return to Rome and ask his assistance, he would speedily put an end to the disgraceful process," for that to make such a man stand before the rostra as a criminal exposed in his age to the insults of young men, would be more disgraceful to Rome than to him. "Will no merit, no dignities," continued the generous and self-appointed plebeian champion, "ever procure for great men a sanctuary where their old age, if not revered, may at least be inviolate?" This defence of an absent enemy by a man of known worth and probity, had a powerful effect upon the people, even the accuser felt ashamed, and the single veto of Sempronius Gracchus legally ended the prosecution. The senate thanked the magnanimous tribune in full assembly for having made his private feelings give way to the public good. Lucius Scipio was involved in the same charge of embezzlement of public money, and with his quæstor and lieutenant was tried and condemned, being adjudged to pay the enormous sum of four millions of sesterces.[94] Scipio Asiaticus refused to give bail for the payment of the fine, asserting his innocence with great earnestness and indignation. He was seized and was about to be dragged to the common prison, when Sempronius Gracchus again interposed his veto. He said; "That he never would suffer a Roman general to be thrown into a prison in which captives taken by him in battle had been confined,[95] though he would not prevent the proper officer from entering the house of the condemned and raising the sum upon his effects." This was accordingly done, but the goods of Scipio Asiaticus did not reach the value of the fine, and no article of Asiatic origin was found among them. The whole charge emanated, most probably, from envy and party spirit. The family and friends of Asiaticus would have assisted him in the payment of the fine, as well as relieved him from the pecuniary distress it occasioned him; but he refused their aid, preferring poverty to a measure that might lead to a tacit admission of his guilt; his conduct looks like innocence.[96] The Scipios, out of gratitude to Sempronius Gracchus, bestowed Cornelia, the daughter of Africanus and niece of Asiaticus, upon the generous tribune. This illustrious lady was B.C. 189. afterwards celebrated in history as the mother of the Gracchi. Scipio Africanus never returned from his voluntary exile: he died at Liternum,[97] and marked his resentment to his ungrateful country by forbidding his ashes to be carried to Rome. The words "Ingrata Patria ne ossa quidem mea habes"[98] were inscribed, by his command, upon his tomb.

<hr size=2 width="10%" align=center>

[1] See Appendix. (p. 392)

[2] Justin, xxx. 2; Valerius Maximus; Livy.

[3] See Appendix. (p. 393)

[4] Livy, xxxi. 26.

[5] Polybius, xvi. 15.

[6] *Ibid.*

[7] Livy, xxxi. 22.

[8] *Ibid.*

[9] Livy, xxxi. 38, 39.

[10] *Ibid.*, 40.

[11] *Ibid.*, 44.

[12] Plutarch, in Flamininus.

[13] *Ibid.*

[14] Livy, xxxii. 13.

[15] *Ibid.*, 18.

[16] Livy, xxxii. 25.

[17] Polybius, xvii. 1; Livy, xxxii. 32.

[18] Polybius; Livy.

[19] *Ibid.*

[20] Polybius, xvii. 7.

[21] Polybius, xvii. 7.

[22] Livy, xxxii. 38.

[23] *Ibid.*, xxxiii. 1; Plutarch, in Flamininus.

[24] Plutarch, in Flamininus.

[25] Polybius, xvii. 15.

[26] Plutarch, in Flamininus.

[27] Livy, xxxiii. 12.

[28] Livy, xxxii. 30.

[29] Plutarch, in Flamininus.

[30] *Ibid.*

[31] Plutarch, in Flamininus.

[32] Appian; Justin, xxvii. 1.

[33] Polybius, xvii. 31; Livy, xxxiii. 39.

[34] Livy, xxxiv. 1.

[35] *Ibid.*

[36] Livy, xxxiv. 1.

[37] Livy, xxxiv. 1.

[38] *Ibid.*

[39] *Ibid.*, xxxiii. 45, et seq.

[40] Livy, xxxiii. 45, et seq.

[41] *Ibid.*

[42] Livy, xxxiii. 45, et seq.

[43] *Ibid.*, xxxiv. 22.

[44] Plutarch, in Flamininus.

[45] *Ibid.*

[46] Appian, in Syr., 90; Justin, xxxi. 4, 5; Livy, xxxiv. 60.

[47] Polybius, Legat., 108.

[48] Appian, in Syr., 88; Josephus, xii. 3; Daniel, xi. 17. <u>See Appendix. (p. 412)</u>

[49] Plutarch, in Flamininus; C. Acilius, Ap.; Livy, xxxiii. 14.

[50] *Ibid.*

[51] Cicero's Orations.

[52] Livy, xxxv. 15.

[53] *Ibid.*, xxxv. 19.

[54] Polybius, iii. 11.

[55] Livy, xxxv. 21.

[56] Plutarch, in Philop.

[57] Livy, xxxv. 31.

[58] Plutarch, in Philop.

[59] Livy, xxxv. 43.

[60] Livy, xxxv. 50.

[61] Plutarch, in Philopœmen.

[62] Livy, xxxvi. 4.

[63] "Fidei se permittere."—Polybius, Legat., 14.

[64] Plutarch, in Flamininus; Livy, xxxvi. 31.

[65] *Ibid.*, 34.

[66] Livy, xxxvi. 22-25.

[67] Polybius, Legat., 15.

[68] Livy, xxxvi. 41.

[69] Livy, xxxvii. 1.

[70] Polybius, Legat., 17; Livy, xxxvii. 7.

[71] Polybius, Legat., 21.

[72] Cornelius Nepos, in Hannibal; Livy, xxxvii. 25.

[73] Livy, xxxvii. 30, 31, 33.

[74] Appian, in Syr., 105. See Appendix. (p. 419)

[75] Livy, xxxvii. 1, 7.

[76] Livy, xxxvii. 36.

[77] *Ibid.*

[78] Polybius, xxi. 13.

[79] 2,900,000*l.*—Arbuthnot.

[80] Polybius, xxii. 7.

[81] Polybius, Legat., 26; Livy, xxxviii. 1, et seq.

[82] Livy, xxxvii. 52, et seq.; Polybius, Legat., 25.

[83] Polybius, xxii. 7.

[84] Livy, xxxviii. 3.

[85] This people, according to Livy, were a Gallic colony who, in the time of Brennus, had wandered through Thrace, and settled in Asia beyond Caria and Phrygia, in an inland part of the country. In after days a Christian church was founded here by St. Paul, who addressed to his converts the fine epistle that bears their name.

[86] Livy, xxxviii. 19; Polybius, xxii. 16-24.

[87] Livy.

[88] The pro-consul Manlius, accused of rapacity towards the Galatians, and disregard for the Sibylline books, by the ten commissioners who had just returned from Asia and Greece, was censured by the senate, but obtained the triumph he demanded.

[89] Aulus Gellius, iv. 18.

[90] Livy, xxxviii. 50, et seq.

[91] Livy.

[92] Aulus Gellius, iv. 18.

[93] *Ibid.*

[94] Livy; about 32,229*l.* 13*s.* 4*d.*, Arbuthnot.

[95] Aulus Gellius, vii. 19.

[96] See Appendix. (p. 426)

[97] Near Naples.

[98] My ungrateful country shall not contain my remains.

CHAPTER X.

A.U.C. 568-587. B.C. 186-167.

King Philip and the Roman commissioners.—His cruelty.—His embassy.—Complaint of the Lacedæmonians.—Lycortas defends his countrymen.—Appius Claudius intimidates the assembly.—Cato's censorship.—Choice of a wife.—Opinions.—Accusation of king Philip.—Mistake of his son.—The arbitration of Flamininus rejected by the Achæans.—Philopœmen marches to Messene.—His captivity and death.—His death revenged by Lycortas.—His funeral.—Death of Scipio and of Hannibal.—The Roman senate and Achæan league.—King Philip puts his son to death.—King Philip's dejection.—His death.—Succeeded by Perseus.—Murder of Antigonus.—The Roman consuls die in office.—The son of Africanus prætor peregrinus.—His seal ring.—Struck off the senatorial list.—Rome paved by the censors.—Politic conduct of Perseus.—Revolt of the Dolopians.—Embassy to Perseus.—Cruelty of Popillius Lænas.—King Eumenes accuses Perseus at Rome.—Speech of the Macedonian ambassadors.—King Perseus tries to kill Eumenes.—Recovery of that prince.—His reproof to his brother.—Incivility of Perseus to the Roman ambassadors reported to the senate.—Macedonian war.—New privileges granted to Licinius.—Speech of a centurion.—Artful conduct of Marcius Philippus.—Victory of Perseus.—His timidity.—His proposal.—His retreat.—Victories of the Roman Admiral.—Licinius defeats Perseus.—Victories of Perseus.—Revolt of the Epirots.—Appius Claudius repulsed.—Success of Perseus.—Haughty behaviour of the Roman ambassadors in Greece.—Deification of Rome.—Absurd behaviour of Perseus.—Recovers from his panic.—Marcius Philippus loses his military reputation.—His mean behaviour to Appius Claudius.—Perseus relieves his towns.—Æmilius Paulus made consul.—His little daughter and her dog Perseus.—King Perseus in want of allies.—His offers to king Eumenes.—Bad conduct to Gentius.—Double dealing with the Gauls.—Clondicus and his questions.—Equivocal reply by Antigonus.—Return of the Gauls.—Avarice of Perseus.—Fine remark of Livy upon this prince.—Æmilius Paulus goes to Macedonia.—Success of Anicius.—Gentius surrenders Scodra and gives up his family.—Paulus joins his army at Phila.—Sends his son and Scipio Nasica to seize the pass.—Æmilius Paulus and Perseus meet in fight.—Flight of Perseus.—Eclipse of the moon.—Battle of Pydna.—Cowardice of Perseus.—Alarm of Paulus for his son.—Return of Scipio Æmilianus to the camp.—Macedon submits to the Romans.—Perseus takes sanctuary at Samo-Thrace.—His misconduct.—His misery.—Loss of his treasures.—Wretched situation.—Betrayal of his family to the Romans.—His surrender.—His abject behaviour.—Cruel comment of Æmilius Paulus.

THE suppression of a licentious society called the Bacchanalian, indicated a change in the manners of the Roman people. It was, probably, a sort of club, an institution considered "injurious to the morals of the Roman youth," such being, in fact, the terms used respecting its prohibition.

A defeat in Liguria formed an unusual feature in the annals of this year. In the next, commissioners were sent to Greece to settle the disputes between king B.C. 186. Philip of Macedonia, and king Eumenes of Pergamus. Philip, whose perception was remarkably acute, discerned in the slights he had received from the Romans in return for his services, their designs on Macedonia. He realised at once the exigences of his situation, and decided upon his means of defence. He

336

knew the natural strength of Macedonia, and that her inhabitants were not only hardy, but constitutionally brave. His ambition had, however, diminished both the population and revenues of his kingdom. To improve its internal resources and re-people it, were the only measures that could successfully preserve it from the growing power of the Roman republic, which, having conquered Italy, and established herself in Greece, was preparing for the conquest of Macedonia. Philip brought colonies of warlike tribes from Odrysia, who had not heard of the Romans, which he planted along the sea-coast from Thrace to Macedon, removing to Emathia the former inhabitants of those parts. He took some towns in Thrace, the possession of which, in case of a second war with Rome, he considered would be important to him. He next turned his attention to the increase of his revenues, by encouraging commerce and working the mines, by which he opened a new source of wealth.[1] It would have been well for Philip and for Macedonia if, instead of his continual wars, he had earlier sought the good of his country in the blessed arts of peace, while he only retarded the fall of his kingdom by his wiser policy for a few years. These proceedings of Philip, though justified by necessity, were watched with jealousy by the Roman senate, and they decided that he should not only withdraw his garrisons from the towns he had conquered while acting as a partisan in the wars of Rome, but should also give up Ænus and Maroneia, two cities, to king Eumenes, whose proximity to Lysimachia and the Chersonesus made that monarch beg them of the Romans as desirable acquisitions. Philip made spirited remonstrances against this decree, but in vain; his Roman allies had not forgotten his former designs upon Italy. He could obtain no redress, though he despatched an embassy to Rome to procure it if possible. The following year Appius Claudius was sent to Greece, to see whether king Philip had complied with the decision of the senate, and had withdrawn his garrisons from Ænus and Maroneia, for it should seem Maroneia had entreated Rome to constitute her a free city. Claudius following his instructions, compelled the Macedonian monarch to withdraw his garrisons from both places. Philip, equally incensed with the Romans and the people of Maroneia, gave orders to Onomastus his lieutenant, to let the fierce Thracians into the town the moment he withdrew the garrison. Onomastus, nothing loth, directed Cassander, a Macedonian officer, to open the gate by night to these barbarians, who slaughtered the greater part of the inhabitants and sacked the town.[2] The Roman commissioner charged this outrage upon king Philip, who denied it, but as Appius Claudius insisted that the authors of it should be given up to the senate, Philip agreed to send Cassander, the meaner agent in the treacherous massacre, but refused to give up Onomastus, a useful officer, who, being in his confidence, knew more of his political intrigues than he wished the Romans to be acquainted with. Cassander died on his way to Italy, being, it is said, poisoned by his orders. He sent his son, Demetrius, to Rome with an embassy, charged to lay his complaints and produce his justification before the senate.[3]

Some exiled Lacedæmonians accused the Achæans of murder, and also of breaking down the walls of Lacedæmon, and many other things contrary to the laws of Lycurgus.[4] The Achæan prætor Lycortas, who was the father of Polybius, the celebrated historian, justified the conduct of the League with regard to Lacedæmon. The murders committed in that place, he declared had been perpetrated by the exiles themselves: that the walls had been broken down in compliance with the laws of Lycurgus, but that finding the city in a state of anarchy, the Achæans had united it to the League, and given it equal privileges and laws. He then asked Appius "why the Romans obliged the Achæans, their friends and firm allies, to give an account of their conduct to them, as if they were indeed their vassals and slaves: was the voice of Flamininus's herald, that had proclaimed liberty to Greece, but an B.C. 186. empty sound? The vanquished," continued Lycortas, "would have us violate compacts that have been confirmed by the most solemn oaths. No, Romans, we honour you, and we fear you too, but we reverence more, we dread more, the immortal gods." Appius Claudius briefly recommended the assembly to merit the favour of the Romans by a ready compliance while they might, and not to wait till their obedience was a matter of compulsion. The assembly heard him with mingled feelings of fear and rage, but they dared not express their resentment, so they left the affairs of Lacedæmon in the hands of the Romans.

The election of Cato to the censorship in conjunction with his friend and patron, Valerius Flaccus, gave rise to many reforms very offensive to the aristocracy.[5] Like a wise legislator, Cato laid heavy taxes upon those articles of luxury that ought only to be used by wealthy persons, who can afford to pay highly for the indulgence. This measure ought not to have displeased the higher ranks, as it prevented their state from being imitated by those beneath them, and restrained imprudent extravagance in all. Yet it did offend them, and they murmured continually at the price he made them pay for sumptuous dress and furniture, chariots, slaves, and women's toilettes, which were all taxed within three per cent. of the real value. Nor did this celebrated censor confine his attention to mere matters of finance; he instituted a rigorous scrutiny into the character of the senators, and struck off the roll seven whose conduct would not bear investigation, considering that the legislators of a great country ought to be freer from vices and crimes, than persons in less exalted stations. Lucius, the brother of the great Flamininus, was expelled for murdering a Boian Gaul; his brother, Titus Quinctius Flamininus, who believed him to be innocent, insisted that he should have a trial, but the investigation covered Lucius with merited infamy. Cato won the respect of all, and the affection of some, during this censorship; though he had his faults, and was close in money-matters, never losing sight of his own interest for a moment,[6] nor was he free from envy; but Plutarch has made his readers so familiar with the domestic character and employments of this celebrated man, that they seem intimately acquainted with him; and it must be acknowledged that his stern integrity in public life was not the fruit of a harsh temper, as he was the most tender and judicious of fathers. We are told, "that in making choice of a wife he preferred birth before wealth or beauty, considering that though women of family may have pride, yet it made them avoid low dishonourable actions, and inclined them to be virtuous and obedient to their husbands." He was frequently heard to say, "that men who beat their wives and children laid their sacrilegious hands upon the holiest things in the world; and that he would rather be considered a good husband than a great senator."[7] The people loved him, and erected a statue to his honour in the Temple of Health, with an inscription denoting that he had saved the morals of the commonwealth; which luxury, before his censorship, was fast undermining.

The enemies of king Philip of Macedonia were not slow in discovering that complaints against him would not be ill-taken at Rome. In a short time the senate received many accusations levelled at this object of general distrust. At the head of his accusers was found as usual the ambitious ally of Rome, Eumenes, king of Pergamus. Demetrius, who had accompanied the Macedonian embassy and was then in the metropolis, fulfilling the difficult mission of defending his father, found it no easy matter to answer the charges laid against his ambitious parent.[8] He had been provided with a private book of instructions, which contained some reflections upon the conduct of the Romans, never intended for exhibition in the senate, which the prince had in his bosom at the time when the affairs of Macedonia were under examination there. Demetrius, who was unfit for the perplexing part assigned him by king Philip, had scarcely commenced his oration, before the senators interrupted him by asking, "If he had no private instructions from his father respecting the matters which he wished to be explained to them." Demetrius, who was young and inexperienced, fell into the snare, and read aloud a record of Philip's bitter and indignant feelings, without reservation, B.C. 183. from beginning to end; excusing, however, whatever was likely to give offence; submitting, at the same time, the affairs of Macedonia to the senate,[9] whom he held in almost Roman veneration. The senators, who had obtained from the unwary prince his father's real opinions concerning the hard dealings of the republic towards him, betrayed no resentment, but declared that for his sake they would overlook his father's faults; and not only send an embassy to arrange the affairs of Macedonia in a satisfactory manner, but would let king Philip know that they did this for the sake of his son, Demetrius.[10] The young prince returned to Macedonia with his heart full of this fatal flattery to meet the irritated father and sovereign, whose secret thoughts he had unwarily betrayed. Quintus Marcius was appointed ambassador to settle the affairs of Macedonia and Greece. Those of Lacedæmon were now decided by the senate, who pronounced the sentence of death recorded against the exiles to be unjust, and commanded them to be recalled. The city, however, was still to remain a part of the Achæan league.[11] The Messenians, at this time, asserted their independence, by breaking from the Achæans. They solicited the good offices of Titus Flamininus, who was the enemy of the great Philopœmen, from what cause is not generally known; unless that valiant Greek lifted the veil of moderation, beneath which the powerful republic covered her ambitious designs on Greece. Flamininus endeavoured to arbitrate between the Messenians and the Achæans; but as he had no authority for that purpose from the senate, the Achæans asked him, "To give his reasons in writing." But he did not consider it prudent to do so, and Philopœmen, in the quality of prætor of the Achæan league, proceeded against the revolted city. He was now seventy years old, and scarcely recovered from a dangerous fever; nevertheless he mounted his horse and gallantly headed the expedition. Close to the city near Evander's hill, he fell in with Deinocrates, whom he quickly routed;

when a reinforcement of five hundred horsemen galloped up to the assistance of the Messenians, who rallied and attacked the victorious Achæans. In the fight that ensued, Philopœmen was wounded and fell from his horse. Upon which a panic seized the army, who fled, leaving their general in the hands of the enemy.[12] The wounded and illustrious Greek "received such treatment as he never supposed he could have suffered even from Deinocrates."[13] By his base command, his hands were bound behind his back, and he was grossly insulted. He was finally consigned to a dungeon called the treasury. This place was nearly without air, and totally without light, being closed by an immense stone, drawn to its place with a pulley. The Messenians left the captive in this prison without food or water, alone with his greatness and misfortunes. When the Achæans learned that their leader was alive and the prisoner of Deinocrates they were seized with generous shame, and hastily choosing Lycortas for their leader marched to his rescue,[14] but Deinocrates who expected this movement sent the executioner to the captive with a cup of poison. Philopœmen calmly took the fatal draught in his hand, his last words being marked by the same noble disregard of self and love for Greece that had characterised his life. He asked, "If there were tidings of Lycortas and the cavalry" and when the executioner told him that they had all escaped, he said, "Thou bringest me good tidings; we are not in all respects unhappy." Then he smiled upon the minister of death, nodded to him, and drinking off the poison died instantaneously.[15]

The report of his murder filled the Achæans with such grief and indignation, that all the young men were eager to revenge their general. Lycortas laid Messene waste on every side till the Messenians, many of whom had opposed the barbarous conduct of Deinocrates towards his captive, opened their gates to the Achæan general and offered to deliver up those persons who had voted for the death of Philopœmen.[16] Deinocrates killed himself, but those who had wished to add torture to the calamities of the illustrious captive were reserved by an act of barbarous justice to meet the doom they would have accorded him. The remains of Philopœmen were burned B.C. 183. with great pomp, his ashes being gathered up and enclosed in a silver urn. To Polybius the future historian, a brave and beautiful youth of twenty years of age, who had fought in the unfortunate action in which his general had been captured, was accorded the distinguished honour of bearing the relics of Philopœmen. He owed this distinction to his being the son of Lycortas the victorious avenger of the dead. This urn, half hidden by garlands and ribbons, was the object of general reverence and affection. The soldiers betrayed no elation at a victory whose insignia were blended with the emblems of mourning. The superbly armed and mounted cavalry closed the march, taking the way to Megalopolis, the native city of the deceased hero. Crowds of aged people and young children awaited the coming up of the army to touch the funereal urn and bewail the dead. These mourners followed the ashes of their great countryman and entered Megalopolis with his remains. As the procession came in sight a cry was heard along the streets of the city, raised by the inhabitants who lamented their worthiest son and with him their lost political importance.[17]

To this deep grief succeeded a sterner scene, one rendered familiar to the English reader by the bas-reliefs on Grecian and Syrian tombs in the British Museum, the slaughter of the prisoners, an act of cruel revenge considered glorious in lands where even a high degree of civilisation had not yet rendered the people merciful to fallen foes, whose execution always took place at the interment of slain heroes. Nor was this barbarous custom confined to men; women and children were immolated—Greek women, whose retired habits and amiable manners left them free from political intrigues or cruel counsels. These were torn from the sacred asylum of home to share the doom of fathers, husbands, and brothers—the virgin daughter and sister, the wife and mother with her babes. Such was the inhumanity of the polished states of Greece till the preaching of St. Paul gave them Christianity in the place of the cold philosophy of the schools. The interment of Philopœmen and the immolations to the manes of the dead hero were followed by the erection of statues to his memory in his native city and throughout Achaia.

This year was remarkable for the death of the three greatest men of the age, Hannibal, Scipio, and Philopœmen.[18] The Romans had long regarded Hannibal's residence at the court of Prusias, king of Bithynia, with jealousy. They knew that the great Carthaginian was the implacable enemy of Rome, and the embassy of Flamininus, though it openly concerned the disagreements between the king of Pergamus and Prusias had as its private object the surrender of the person of Hannibal.[19] Prusias, pressed by Flamininus to give up the exile, who was his guest and had served him in his wars, suffered his fears to betray him into a base and dishonourable action. Hannibal, who had long expected this demand upon the part of the Romans, had had some subterraneous passages hollowed under the castle of Libyssa, where he dwelt, to provide for his escape if his liberty should be endangered; but his secret had been betrayed, for the egress was barred by his enemies, and nothing remained for him but to fall alive into the power of the Romans or to die by his own hand. The great Carthaginian quickly made his decision, taking from his finger a ring,[20] which contained a deadly poison, he said, "Let us deliver Rome from her perpetual fears and disquiets, since she has not patience to wait for the death of an old man. Flamininus's victory over an enemy unarmed and betrayed will not do him much honour with posterity." Then having invoked the vengeance of the gods upon Prusias for his ingratitude and violation of the claims of hospitality, he pressed the poisoned ring to his lips and expired. His last words were prophetic, for the dark stain of infamy tarnished the fame of Flamininus for ever, who is remembered as the destroyer of Hannibal rather than B.C. 182. as the liberator of Greece.[21] The news of his death gave displeasure to the senate, who charged Flamininus with having been too precipitate in occasioning the destruction of a vanquished enemy incapable of injuring the republic by reason of his exile and advanced age. If Flamininus really committed this base action upon his own authority, and to increase his fame, as Plutarch thinks he did,[22] he certainly gained by it a very infamous celebrity.

Marcius, the ambassador sent to adjust the affairs of Macedonia and Greece, had found the Achæans by no means inclined to permit the interference of Rome respecting those cities that had either revolted or were inclined to revolt from the league. In return the Romans would not grant the Achæans any assistance against Messene, neither would they prohibit the subjects of the republic from sending arms or supplies from Italy thither. The success of Lycortas at Messene made the senate commit the strange inconsistency of assuring the Achæan league that no aid should be sent from Italy to the Messenians when this conquered people were no longer in a situation to require it.[23]

The murder of Demetrius, the son of king Philip, of Macedonia, by the command of his father, was the leading event of the year,[24] as it occasioned the elevation of his illegitimate brother Perseus, with whom the Macedonian dynasty was doomed to close. Demetrius was the favourite not only of the Macedonians but of the king-making republic of Rome. He had given constant offence to his father Philip by praising the Romans and disparaging the Greeks, even the rude architecture of Rome being preferred by him to that of Greece, which had never been surpassed then, nor equalled now. This preference for Rome, and his imprudence respecting the secret instructions of his father, made king Philip jealous and afraid of his son. Perseus, aggravated the misunderstanding between them by declaring that Demetrius was conspiring with the Roman senate to deprive the king of his life and crown. Aware of the hatred and rivalry existing between his sons, Philip sent a private embassy to Rome to learn from Titus Flamininus whether the young prince was guilty of the charge. Apelles and Philocles, the ambassadors, were considered unprejudiced men by the king, but they secretly favoured Perseus. They brought a letter from Flamininus,[25] which Livy considers a forgery, in which the writer owned "that Demetrius had been faulty, but that if he had been ambitiously desiring the throne of Macedonia, he had never conspired against his father's life." He added a few words in his own justification, declaring "that he was not the man who was likely to become the adviser of any impious undertaking."[26]

Ten years passed over the Roman republic of little historical interest, but in all countries the barrenness of events marks a period of prosperity. The peaceful state of Rome during this period was not a cessation from war but a freedom from domestic broils. For the Romans had continual struggles to maintain their conquests, so that the temple of Janus always remained open, even in years considered tranquil. Some indication of the increasing luxury of the Romans is to be found in a sumptuary law limiting the number of guests a host might receive at his table. Orchius, a tribune of the people, passed this law during the consulship of Cornelius Cethegus and Marcus Bæbius.[27]

The following year the Villian law, which restricted the exercise of the magistracies to men who had attained to a certain number of years, was passed.[28]

The death of Philip, king of Macedon, was one of the few foreign events of interest during the internal rest enjoyed by the Roman people.[29] Able, politic, warlike, and B.C. 176. insatiably ambitious, this later Philip was less fortunate than the great Macedonian monarch whose name and dignity he shared, and to whom in valour and policy he bore a strong resemblance. The father of Alexander the Great was, however, more tender in his parental and domestic ties. But if the younger Philip had disregarded the voice of nature he had been the most miserable man in his dominions since the fatal hour in which he had caused the death of his son.[30]

An unsuccessful expedition against Istria by the consul Manlius Vulso, and its conquest by Claudius Pulcher during the following year, are among the few leading events of the time.

Cornelius Scipio Hispallus and Q. Petillius Spurinus, both died in office. The first of apoplexy in the act of descending the Alban-hill, the second was slain in battle in Liguria.[31]

Two years later the son of the great Scipio stood for the prætorship, and was elected; for his opponent, who had been his father's secretary, gave up the contest out of respect for the memory of Africanus. It happened that the office of prætor peregrinus fell to his lot, upon which his friends advised him to resign it, considering him unfit for a post requiring much ability, which Scipio accordingly did. Yet Cicero commends his parts, while mentioning the delicacy of his constitution. The censors struck his name this year from the list of senators. It is said that his relations prevailed upon him to discontinue wearing a seal ring with his father's head upon it, considering that his incapacity disgraced the great Scipio.[32] Rome was paved this year, for the first time, by the censors, since it was rebuilt by Camillus, so slow was the advance of the warlike Romans in works of public utility and convenience, even in the sixth century.

The successor of king Philip was regarded by the Romans with mistrust and jealousy, on account of the death of Demetrius, which his machinations had caused, for the murdered prince had preferred the favour of the senate to his duty. Perseus, well aware that the Romans only waited for a pretence to invade his dominions, endeavoured to gain the affections of his people by a kind and affable behaviour. He recalled those exiles who had fled from Macedonia on account of debt, restoring to them their estates, and satisfying their creditors out of the public treasury. He gave a general amnesty to those who had been convicted or suspected of treason.[33] To obtain the friendship of the Greeks, he sent back to the Achæans the fugitive slaves who had taken asylum in Macedonia. As his father had been considered a very sacrilegious man, he undertook a pilgrimage to Delphi, attended, however, by his army. The Greeks at first were greatly alarmed at this pious expedition, till he expressed his desire to live upon amicable terms with his neighbours, adding, that he hoped the remembrance of past animosities between the Greeks and Macedonians would be buried in his father's sepulchre. The Romans were very sorry for this moderation on the part of Perseus, as they secretly hoped he would have done some mischief on his way to the Grecian cities. As for the Greeks, they conceived a very high opinion of this prince, who certainly did not possess the ardent passions of his father. Perseus possessed a natural talent for eloquence and did not want parts. He was very temperate in his diet and was of a strong constitution, but he had many vices and few virtues, and whatever his capacity might be, his temper was cruel and avaricious, and his dignity confined to personal appearance alone.

The Dolopians at this time revolted from Perseus and appealed to Rome. Perseus quickly reduced them to B.C. 172. obedience, not admitting the Romans as judges between him and his own subjects. An embassy had been sent to Macedonia to complain of the presence of the Bastarnians in Dardania, for the Dardanians had besought the protection of the Romans against Perseus as well as their aid to drive out these barbarians. The real business of these ambassadors was to play the part of spies, but the king of Macedonia did not choose to see them always pleading illness or business by way of excuse.[34] These envoys informed the senate that Perseus was preparing for war. The senate, nevertheless, sent a new embassy to his court.

C. Popillius, the consul, a man of a harsh and cruel character, attacked the Statiellians, a peaceful people of Liguria, before the gate of Caristum, their chief city, slew ten thousand of them in battle, and took seven hundred prisoners.[35] He then assaulted the town, which was surrendered to him. Popillius, contrary to the usages in such cases, plundered and demolished it, and sold the inhabitants for slaves.[36]

The presence in Rome of that old enemy to the Macedonian dynasty, Eumenes, king of Pergamus, hastened the rupture between Perseus and the Romans. He came, he said, to give the senate warning of the machinations of the Macedonian king, to whom Seleucus, the son and successor of Antiochus the Great, had given his daughter Laodice, in marriage, adding, that Prusias, king of Bithynia, had married the sister of Perseus. Eumenes, after denouncing the Ætolians and Achæans, as the secret allies of the Macedonian prince, assured his hearers, that if he had been their spy he could not have given them more information respecting the affairs of Macedon.[37] The communication of the royal spy caused the ill-reception of the Macedonian embassy which had lately been despatched by king Perseus to the senate, who paid no attention to the defence made by Harpalus, the ambassador, for his master's conduct; Harpalus perceiving this, spoke thus: "The king earnestly wishes you to believe that he has given you no cause to look upon him as your enemy, but if he finds that you are seeking a quarrel with him, he will not want courage to defend himself. The chance of war is equal, and the event uncertain."

At this time several deputations from Asiatic and Grecian cities, anxious to know which part to take in the approaching crisis, came to Rome. That from Rhodes accused king Eumenes of ambition and misconduct in Asia, but this did not prevent the Romans from loading that prince with presents. Apprised of Eumenes' object in coming to Rome by Harpalus, who easily divined it, Perseus resolved to assassinate the king of Pergamus on his return from Delphi, where it was the intention of Eumenes to sacrifice. He employed for this purpose Evander, the general of his auxiliaries, and three Macedonians, who, hiding themselves behind a ruined wall in a hollow way, let his companion Pantaleon, an Ætolian chief, pass on without injury, but they rolled great stones upon the head and shoulders of the king of Pergamus, and left him for dead on the spot. The assassins ran away, supposing that they had accomplished their object, but upon Pantaleon raising the king up and calling to his attendants to take charge of him, he soon revived, and the next day embarked on board his own ship for Corinth, and from thence to the island of Ægina, where he was cured.[38]

The Carthaginians sent an embassy to Rome to ask redress from the injuries and aggressions done to their territories by Masinissa, who had seized upon lands given by Syphax, at the intercession of his wife Sophonisba, to the Carthaginians. These lands had been won from the Carthaginians by Gala, the father of Masinissa, from whom they had been taken by Syphax. Gulussa, the son of Masinissa, came to Rome as his father's ambassador to justify his conduct. The senate promised to see the Carthaginians righted, and while they assured the Numidian prince of the friendship and regard they felt for his father, declared that they could not countenance him B.C. 171. in making aggressions upon the lands of Carthage. They advised Masinissa to send another embassy to Rome, that the affairs of Numidia might receive all possible attention.[39]

The report of the attempted assassination of king Eumenes excited great indignation against Perseus, and the return of the ambassadors from Macedonia, who had been insulted by that monarch and ordered to quit his dominions in three days, was received as a declaration of war, and due preparations for the long-talked-of expedition against Macedonia were immediately commenced, though the war was not formally declared till the ensuing consulship. To the Romans were committed the fulfilment of most of the historical prophecies of the Book of Daniel, where, under the similitude of the fourth monarchy, the universal dominion of the mighty republic, and her annihilation of the empire of the third monarchy established by Alexander the Great and his successors, is plainly revealed.

To P. Licinius Crassus the war in Macedonia fell by lot, but C. Cassius Longinus was entrusted with the military care of Italy. As it was the intention of the republic to reduce Macedonia into a Roman province, two legions of six thousand foot and six hundred horse were granted for the war. To these legions were added sixteen thousand foot and eight hundred horsemen, provided by the Italian confederates. The Romans received proffers of assistance at this time from the kings of Syria, Egypt, and Cappadocia. The Greeks were compelled by the power Rome had acquired over them to give them aid. The kings of Bithynia and Illyricum took no part in the struggle. Cotys, king of the Odrysians in Thrace, was the only ostensible ally of Perseus. "If Perseus, however, had been liberal of his gold, the whole body of Roman allies would have become his own."[40] "For at the commencement of the Macedonian war the republic had few open enemies, and no real friends."[41] Besides the forces granted to Licinius, he had the privilege of selecting from the veteran soldiers and centurions under fifty years of age, any number he chose. This was contrary to the law, which allowed the veteran of forty-five years to withdraw himself from the military profession, and pass his days in the bosom of his own family.[42] Before the Roman consul departed from Italy, the senate despatched ambassadors throughout Greece to confirm the Greeks in their fealty. Perseus had again sent an embassy to Rome to demand the occasion of the presence of Roman armies in his neighbourhood, and to offer satisfaction for any injury done by him to the republic or her allies. This message did not apply to the consular army, but to that of the prætor, Licinius, which lay at Apollonia. The ambassadors were dismissed, and referred to the consul for an answer who would shortly be in Macedonia with an army.

Notwithstanding this treatment, Perseus lost time, through the able diplomacy of Marcius Philippus, one of the Roman ambassadors sent to Greece. That artful politician persuaded the king to meet him, whom he deceived into granting him a truce, and sending an embassy to the senate. The folly of Perseus was inexcusable, because when he asked the ambassadors, of whom Marcius Philippus was one, the reason of Roman armies being near his frontiers, they had replied with effrontery as well as falsehood, "For the protection of the Greek cities." Marcius Philippus left Epirus to effect another stroke. He did not choose to treat with the Thebans and Bœotian states as one general league or united state, but severally; by this means breaking, not only their political union, but their political importance.[43] At Rome, some of the senators blamed the deceit of the ambassador, although they did not scruple to profit by it.

Perseus' embassy was received and admitted to an audience, and dismissed the city that day, but it was permitted to remain thirty days in Italy. Licinius, the consul, was at Apollonia before the ambassadors of Perseus reached Pella. Upon the majority of his council declaring for war, Perseus said with some spirit, "Then let us have war, and the gods grant us success." If the moral and political conduct of this prince had been equal to his resources, he might have been successful; for he was at the head of a fine army of three and forty thousand men, and was well provided for this long anticipated war. Greece and the neighbouring states had conceived a high opinion of his courage and ability; and, at this time, he B.C. 171. possessed the affections of his subjects. He was an able speaker, and his oration to his army was received with great applause, and had the effect of kindling general indignation against the Romans. Perseus did not allow these feelings of animosity and patriotism to die away; he marched boldly into Thessaly to meet the Roman army, took Elateia and Gonnus, towns situated in the entrance of the celebrated vale of Tempe, and after fortifying that pass, encamped at the foot of Mount Ossa, where he awaited the arrival of the consular army. Licinius marched from Apollonia to Larissa, and fixed his encampment by the river Peneius. The arrival of Eumenes, of Pergamus, and his brother Attalus, strengthened the Roman army by five thousand men. The king had left his brother, Athenæus, to garrison Chalcis on his way hither. Other auxiliaries came in to augment the consular army.[44] Perseus endeavoured for several successive days to draw the Romans from their entrenchments. He at length led his army within half a mile of the camp, probably imputing the supineness of Licinius rather to want of courage than over-caution. The consul well knew that the king of Macedonia was destitute of the means of carrying the trenches, which required a different body of troops; he did not give him battle in person, but despatched his light-armed infantry, cavalry, and auxiliaries to meet him, holding himself prepared to join them in case of their requiring assistance. The king's army was victorious, for the Romans lost two thousand men and two hundred horse; the Macedonians forty foot and twenty horse. The captains of the phalanx wished the king to head it and storm the camp; but the project was too bold, and involved too much personal risk, to suit the character of Perseus, who appears to have been rather incapable of continued effort than to have wanted talent.[45] Courage, certainly, was a quality in which he was deficient. Evander, the Cretan, who was aware of his cowardice, advised him to return to the camp, and by no means to hazard Macedonia upon the chance of one enterprise. "His present victory," the adroit courtier added, "would gain him an honourable peace, or many new allies for the war." Perseus easily adopted counsel that suited the timidity of his character; he led his reluctant army back to his camp. King Eumenes, who gave the royal Macedonian no credit for courage and promptitude, recommended the consul to pass the river without delay. Licinius did so in the night; and when the king of Macedonia, ashamed of his weakness, led his army the following morning to the river, he found his enemy safely encamped upon its banks.

The military movement of Perseus between Tempe and Larissa and his choice of the rising ground at Mopsium for his camp, induced the Romans to take up a stronger position upon another part of the bank of the Peneius. Here they were reinforced by Misagenes the son of Masinissa, who brought them three thousand horse and foot and twenty-two elephants. Perseus, who was desirous of obtaining peace sent to the consul, and offered to submit to the terms formerly imposed upon his father. Philip had been defeated—Perseus was victorious. The Romans drew their own conclusion from this absurd proposal, and in general council decided to give this answer to the man whose mean spirit could not be elevated even by success. "That Perseus must surrender himself and his kingdom to the Romans, or expect no peace."[46] His friends entreated the king to win the pacification by arms, but Perseus hearkened to the suggestions of his timid mind and once more offered the Romans terms. "He was willing to pay a heavier tribute than his father Philip had done." This was an attempt to purchase the absence of the Romans. It was peremptorily rejected. The king of Macedonia retreated to Sycurium, leaving his reasons for the retreat, if he had any besides timidity, unknown.

The Roman admiral, C. Lucretius, was besieging Haliartus in Bœotia, when his brother Marcus meeting at Dyrrachium a great many vessels belonging to Gentius, king of Illyricum, seized upon them, pretending to take Gentius for an ally of Perseus, though this prince had observed a strict neutrality during the war.[47] He also took the ships belonging to the Issæans and Dyrrachians. Haliartus was seized and sacked, but Thebes opened her gates. The prætor sold that part of the population which favoured Macedonia, for slaves, but entrusted the B.C. 171. government of the city to the friends of Rome, and then returned to the fleet. He was afterwards fined for oppressing the Roman allies.

Perseus while at Sycurium marched towards the Roman camp, with the intention of setting it on fire, but being foiled in his attempt retreated to Mopsium, where he fell in with some parties of the Roman reapers, and took a thousand carts and six hundred prisoners. He also attacked a body of eight hundred soldiers, who were stationed to guard the reapers. The consul with his legions hastened to their relief and repulsed the king, who retreated with the loss of three hundred and twenty-four men. He retired to Macedonia and took up his winter quarters, but not before he had gained a naval victory at Oreus.[48] Licinius laid siege to Gonnus, hoping to gain an entrance into Tempe, but failing in this enterprise marched into Perrhæbia and captured some towns there, and made himself master of Larissa in Thessaly. He took up his winter quarters in Bœotia, leaving a part of his army in Thessaly. In Illyricum one of the lieutenants of Licinius behaved very ill; having spared two rich towns in that country, in the hope of inducing others to surrender unconditionally, but being disappointed in his expectations, plundered those upon his return he had before treated with clemency,[49] a truly detestable transaction. Cassius, the other consul, then stationed in Gaul, who was exceedingly desirous of sharing in the Macedonian war, attempted to enter that country through Illyricum without waiting for the commands of the senate. He was hastily recalled and severely reprimanded, not only for acting without orders but for attempting a dangerous experiment calculated to show the barbarous nations an easy road to Italy.

Perseus, on finding his only ostensible ally, Cotys, king of the Odrysians, was invaded by the Pergamenians and Thracians, marched to his relief—delivered him and resumed his winter quarters. He was at this time strengthened by the revolt of the Epirots, who deserted the Romans and made an alliance with him. The consul Hostilius Maximus, to whom the war in Macedon and the charge of the fleet was committed, behaved very ill to the Greek allies, and proved himself unfitted for the commander of an army. Twice he attempted to enter Macedonia, and twice he was totally defeated.

Perseus defeated the Dardanians at this time, and destroyed their army of ten thousand men; while his garrison at Uscana repulsed Appius Claudius, with immense loss; for Perseus had taken Uscana and the neighbouring towns from the invaders, in which he captured four thousand Romans. He was at Aperantia, in Ætolia, when he heard of the victory gained by Clevas, his lieutenant, over Appius Claudius.

The Roman commissioners, sent to secure the assistance of the Greek allies, used threats and persuasions to ensure their object. They ventured to accuse Lycortas, and his son Polybius, of disaffection to Rome; but as they could not substantiate the charge they let it drop. The ill-success of the Macedonian war occasioned much discontent at Rome; for Perseus was generally victorious, and if he had known how to make use of victory, the Romans must have been driven from the frontier.

An embassy from the town of Alabanda, in Asia Minor, bringing costly presents and a crown of gold, as an offering to the temple of Jupiter Capitolinus, was gratifying to the national pride. The people of Alabanda had just built a temple and dedicated it to the goddess Rome: an impious piece of flattery that soon ceased to be singular.

The victories of Perseus, when compelled into war by the Romans, prove that he was not altogether what they have represented him. He possessed the skill of a general, without the courage of a man; a singular want in the son of such a brave prince as king Philip. To face him, a bold, enterprising consul was required, but the people of Rome preferred a crafty politician. Their choice, therefore, fell upon Marcius Philippus who had proved himself an able and unscrupulous diplomatist, and to him, at this crisis, was entrusted the conduct of the Macedonian war. But this consul, though a man of talent, was no warrior, and the glory of the republic was not advanced by him.[50] Marcius and the troops

348

from Italy arrived at Pharsalus, where he found the consular army. He resolved to enter Macedonia B.C. 170. without delay, and took the road by the lake Ascuris. Macedonia was defended by nature, and Marcius met with great obstacles in his invasion of that country. He had taken the precaution of sending a detachment of four thousand men to occupy the most advantageous positions that presented themselves. The difficulty of the march was so great that it took the detachment two days to traverse fifteen miles. On the third the troops occupied a hill overlooking the mountain pass, which they found guarded by Hippias and twelve thousand men. Marcius and his army marched to the relief of his detachment, and fought a battle with Hippias for three successive days. The scene of conflict being upon the ascent of a steep mountain, necessarily limited the number of the combatants. To proceed was hazardous; to return, seemed to compromise the honour of the consul. He left a part of his army with his lieutenant, Popillius, and with the rest of his legions marched through dangerous ways, never before traversed by the steps of a great host.[51] After seven miles of toilsome labour, the army reached the open plain, where the consul was joined by Popillius. Here they halted, but resumed their march, which they accomplished in four days, arriving, unmolested, in the fields near Heracleium, between Tempe and Dium, where the king of Macedonia and the greater part of his army were encamped.

Perseus did not defend his country, though he ought to have annihilated the invaders, for which the imprudent position of the consul afforded him a fine opportunity, for he was master of the heights above the plains the Romans had entered, whose exposed situation admitted of no extrication. The fate of the consul and his army depended upon the energy and promptitude of the King of Macedon, who, instead of availing himself of the important crisis, cried out, "that he was conquered, and without striking a blow," fled with his army from Dium to Pydna. He had, in the extremity of his fear, ordered his naval stores to be burned at Thessalonica, and his treasures at Pella to be cast into the sea. Nicias fulfilled the last command; but Andronicus, who probably considered the order for the destruction of the naval stores as the mandate of a madman, forbore to execute it. Perseus, when out of the reach of the Roman legions, was ashamed of his folly. He punished Nicias with death for his obedience, and Andronicus for his prudence; or rather for the fatal knowledge these men possessed of their sovereign's weakness and incapacity. He compelled Hippias and Asclepiodorus to leave the Macedonian passes unguarded by recalling them, though he reviled these officers for having permitted the Romans to enter Macedonia. His withdrawal of the garrisons from the towns about Tempe was followed by the reduction of Dium by the consul, who continued advancing for three days, when he was compelled to retreat, being destitute of supplies.[52] The fleet came to assist him at this critical juncture; but, unfortunately, the store-ships were left at Magnesia.

The prætor, Lucretius, found plenty of corn in the towns of Tempe. He sent Marcius Philippus word that a convoy of provisions was on its way to Dium. The consul, who was sorely distressed, marched to Phila, a town between Tempe and

Dium; and, if he saved his army from the danger of starvation, lost his military reputation for ever by this mistimed retreat.

Perseus, during this crisis, had employed himself in recovering the treasures Nicias, by his command, had thrown into the sea. His fright was over, and he had ceased to consider the Romans invincible. He recovered Dium and the other towns he had lost, fortifying them with all haste. Marcius took Heracleium, and made roads, and constructed magazines; but he had lost the favourable time for pushing forward, when Perseus was panic-stricken, and the garrisons about Dium and Tempe withdrawn. Winter was coming on, and the nature of the country precluded the possibility of his doing anything to retrieve his lost reputation during the remainder of his consulship. Nor B.C. 169. did his jealousy of Appius Claudius redound to his honour; for when that commander required the aid of five thousand Achæans in Epirus, Lycortas having sent his son to the consul, to offer assistance to the Romans on behalf of the League, his proffer was rejected with courteous words by Marcius, who forbade the League to furnish troops.[53] This meanness, unworthy of a Roman and a brother soldier, gave Perseus' affairs a favourable turn; but unfortunately he had neither courage nor ability to profit by this crisis.

At Rome the Voconian law, forbidding any woman from becoming an heiress, was enacted; a measure that while it invaded the rights of female property, prevented those scenes of domestic misery that have ensued too often from interested marriages.[54] Voconius also added to this law a clause, forbidding any person rated in the censor's books from leaving above a fourth part of his personal property to a female.[55] A new law was also passed respecting the rights of freedmen to votes. They were incorporated with one of the city tribes, that called the Esquiline, and thus obtained their suffrages, which they were in danger of losing through the attempt made by Sempronius Gracchus, one of the censors; but Appius Claudius, his colleague, secured to this body their franchise.

The Roman senate and people saw plainly that the war of Macedonia required a man of bravery, ability, and prudence. They recognised in Æmilius Paulus all these qualifications, for though sixty years old, he was as enterprising as in youth.[56] Upon his return to his own house after his province was assigned him, Æmilius Paulus met with an omen that appeared to him prophetical of good fortune. He found his little daughter Tertia in tears, and being a fond father took her in his arms and tenderly caressing the child, enquired the cause of her grief. The little girl replied, sobbing, that her dog Perseus was dead; and this accident, so important to her and so trifling to the world at large, seemed a certain presage of victory to the veteran statesman and warrior: for even strong minds are sometimes affected by superstition. The Roman affairs in Macedonia were in a bad condition. The army wanted provisions, the navy men, arms, and clothing. King Eumenes, who had not received the attention he expected from Marcius Philippus, had sailed away in great displeasure, taking with him his Gallo-Greek horsemen, although the consul had solicited their services.[57] Perseus learning this, thought it a favourable crisis to send ambassadors to the court of this prince, as well as to those of Antiochus the Great (then at war with Ptolemy of Egypt) and Prusias, king of Bithynia, representing to them "that the fall of the

Macedonian dynasty would be followed by the ruin of their own.[58] That the Roman government being free must ever be hostile to nations ruled by despotic kings. That they ought for the preservation of their mutual interest to negotiate a peace between Macedonia and Rome; or if that was refused to their intercessions, to unite in arms against the haughty republic, the general enemy of sovereigns." This was sound reasoning, for Perseus was an eloquent prince, and probably might be wiser on paper than he was in action.[59] Eumenes offered to remain neutral if the king of Macedonia would give him hostages and a thousand talents, or he would assist him in the war upon the payment of fifteen hundred. Perseus made no scruple about the hostages, but he could not resolve to part with his money. However, he promised to deposit it in the sanctuary of Samothrace till the peace was concluded. But as the temple and island of Samothrace belonged to the Macedonian sovereign, Eumenes had no security for the sum if Perseus chose to withhold it after the war was concluded. "Thus," remarks Livy, "these two kings acquired nothing but infamy by their negotiations."[60]

Perseus behaved in a base and dishonourable manner to Gentius, king of Illyricum, whom he involved with the Romans in a manner that ended in the ruin of the Illyrian prince. The price of Gentius' friendship being 300 talents, Perseus paid 200 in advance, and sent the rest sealed up under the care of some Macedonians, who had orders to travel in as dilatory a manner as they could. B.C. 169. Gentius in the meanwhile arrested the Roman ambassadors and treated them as spies, thus irrevocably incurring the displeasure of the formidable republic, with whom Perseus was at war. He had no sooner done this than the king recalled the money, as the conduct of the Illyrian prince must oblige him to become his ally without the gold.[61] Nor did Perseus behave any better to the Bastarnians,[62] a nation of Gauls lying beyond the Danube,[63] from whom he demanded assistance, promising to pay them very liberally, and to give them money in advance. Twenty thousand of these savage warriors obeyed the summons. Perseus, however, only sent a few fair speeches and trifling presents. Clondicus, one of their chiefs, demanded of Antigonus, "If the king of Macedonia had sent by him the promised advance to the soldiers."[64] Antigonus replied in the negative. "Then tell thy master that the Gauls will march no farther till they have received both money and hostages." Antigonus carried this peremptory message to the king, who declared in council that he only required the services of five thousand horsemen. Antigonus was deputed to inform the Gauls of the royal determination. Clondicus bluntly demanded, "if he had brought the money to pay the five thousand?" Upon which Antigonus, not having the cash nor even the promise of it, began to make some apologies and evasions, which the Gauls received with contempt, and immediately commenced their homeward march.[65] They permitted Antigonus to return uninjured, which was certainly more honourable conduct than could have been expected of barbarians. "Thus Perseus," remarks Livy, "acted like a careful treasurer for the Romans, as if he wished to preserve his money for them undiminished."[66]

The amount of the army raised for Æmilius Paulus's expedition to Macedonia has been variously stated by ancient historians, some representing it as not exceeding 26,000. It appears that Octavius, the admiral, and Anicius, the prætor, set out for Macedonia at the same time as the consul. Anicius was ordered into Illyricum, and in thirty days had wholly reduced the kingdom of Gentius. The tidings of his arrival and his conquests reached Rome at the same moment. Gentius had retired with his family to Scodra, his capital, a place rendered almost impregnable by nature.[67]

Gentius had a garrison of fifteen thousand men, and was well provisioned, but his ill-treatment by Perseus had dispirited him, and when the besieged imprudently made a sally upon the Romans, which was followed by defeat and great loss of life, he surrendered himself and his family to the prætor, falling at his feet with tears and imploring his mercy.[68] Æmilius had a rapid passage from Brundusium to Corcyra, and in five days we find him sacrificing to Apollo at Delphi, and joining his army in as short a period of time at Phila not far from the Enipeus. Perseus had fortified that bank of the river which guarded Macedonia, so that it seemed inexpedient to Æmilius to force a passage that way.[69] There was another route over Mount Olympus by Pythium, and the road was better than mountain passes generally are, but it was carefully guarded by a fine body of troops. To force this passage appeared to the consul by no means impossible. He entrusted this important commission to his son Quintus Fabius, his son-in-law Scipio Nasica, and a body of five thousand men, who marched towards the sea and encamped at Heracleium. After the army had been refreshed it arrived at Pythium, where they passed the night. But though the Romans left with Æmilius at Phila knew not the destination of their comrades, Perseus received information of it from a Cretan deserter who stole away from Nasica and brought the important tidings to the Macedonian monarch. Perseus sent Milo, with two thousand men, to take up a position upon the heights. With regard to the manner in which Nasica forced the road, historians differ;[70] but he effected his important object.

Perseus, with his usual timidity, broke up his encampment, B.C. 168.the fine situation and fortifications of which had excited the admiration of the Roman consul, and retreated to Pydna, leaving the passage into Macedonia by this river open and undefended. Perseus chose a good position at Pydna, on a plain with rising ground on either side and covered with a river in front. His army, which was courageous and loyal, assured him "that he might rely upon men who were about to fight for their wives and children, their country, and their liberty." Nothing but a commander of bravery and resolution was required by the Macedonians. Æmilius, who had passed the river and joined Nasica, was now in front of Perseus, the shallow river alone dividing him from the enemy. Both armies were eager to engage, and Nasica, flushed with his late triumph, entreated his general to pass the boundary stream and commence the contest.[71] "If I were of your age I should certainly do so, my friend," replied Æmilius, smiling, "but the many victories I have gained have made me observe the errors of the vanquished, and forbid me to give battle immediately after a march, to an army well drawn up and regularly appointed." Perseus offered the Romans battle, and Æmilius drew up his men as if he intended to accept the challenge, but this movement was only to form his encampment without molestation.[72] A reason beyond fatigue probably made him decline the engagement; he knew that the moon would be totally eclipsed that night, a fact which Sulpicius Gallus, a learned legionary tribune, had communicated to him, and with his leave to the army. This was on the evening of the third of September, if we follow the imperfect Roman calendar, but the eclipse really took place on the twenty-first of June. Though the consul understood the cause of the coming obscuration, yet he was not without some feeling of superstition upon the occasion, and was anxious to propitiate the planet by a sacrifice.[73] He offered eleven heifers, while the Roman soldiers clashed brazen vessels and held up lighted torches and faggots to help the moon as soon as she began to lose her lustre. Uninstructed in the mysteries of nature, the Macedonians on the opposite side of the river looked upon the eclipse as a portent foreboding the ruin of the kingdom they were to defend. They uttered dismal howlings, and whispered to each other that the king would certainly fall, yet the superstitious fears of these brave men did not lower their courage nor prevent them from defending his person and realm. At daybreak the consul offered twenty-one oxen to Hercules, and vowed a hecatomb to the god if he should be successful. He had observed upon the preceding day how greatly the noontide heat and glare had inconvenienced his men, and he did not marshal his army till near sunset. It is doubtful how the battle was begun,[74] but it is certain that the king took no part in it, for after he had made an oration to his soldiers and had issued his orders he retired to Pydna in order to sacrifice to Hercules. "As if Hercules," remarks Plutarch, "would accept the sacrifice of a coward, or grant victory to him who would not fight."[75] The battle was gallantly fought on both sides, although it lasted but a short time.[76] The appearance of the celebrated Macedonian phalanx made a powerful impression upon the mind of the consul, who often recalled it as the most formidable spectacle he had ever seen. It required the greatest efforts upon the part of the Romans to break this formidable body, and more than once Æmilius despaired of effecting it. He, however, at length discovered some openings between the Macedonian shields, caused by the nature of the ground, and there he directed his charge.[77] Once broken, the phalanx was no longer terrible, as the short swords of the Macedonians were not B.C. 168. fitted to cope with the Roman weapons which were more effective, in fact the long shields of the Macedonians secured the Romans from their attacks.

Marcus, the son of Cato, having lost his sword, considered this misfortune so disgraceful that he called to his friends on every side to assist him to recover it. A brave band of young men followed him and drove the enemy back. Others seeing their success flocked to that part of the field where the fight was the hottest. Three thousand Macedonians fell upon the spot, and those who fled were slaughtered without mercy.[78] Twenty-five thousand Macedonians died that day, while the loss of the conquerors amounted to little more than one hundred. This victory decided the fate of Macedonia. The whole Roman army joined in pursuit of the fugitives, from which they did not return till night. The victorious consul found the camp illuminated, while his own tent and those of his officers were adorned with boughs of laurel and ivy by the servants. These demonstrations of joy, however, gave no pleasure to the victor, who was a tender father. His youngest, best loved son, Emilianus, was missing,[79] and the pride of the Roman commander was lost in paternal anguish. As this youth, afterwards so celebrated under the name of Scipio the younger, was very young, rash, and brave, and moreover was greatly esteemed by the army, the soldiers gathered round their general's tent with torches in their hands to ask tidings of their favourite, having left their suppers in haste as soon as they were apprised of his loss. Some were seeking him in the trenches and among the slain in silence, while the name of Scipio was uttered by others in tones indicative of sorrow, when at that instant the youth appeared in person attended by a few friends, "having followed the pursuit like a generous young hound carried too far by the heat of the chase."[80] His father welcomed him with joy equal to his past anxiety.

Perseus, as soon as he received intelligence of the defeat, fled from Pydna with a few friends and his cavalry. Some foot soldiers flying from the slaughtering swords of the enemy reproached these horsemen, whom they overtook, and began to pull from their horses as cowards and traitors to their country. Perseus, always thoughtful for his own safety, left them to fight it out, and with a few followers pursued his flight towards his capital. He took off his crown, which he carried in his hand, and divesting himself of his purple robe alighted from his horse, which he led.[81] Gradually his friends, under one pretence or other, deserted the fallen monarch, so that when he arrived by midnight at Pella he was almost wholly unattended.[82] Before morning, conscious that he neither deserved nor possessed a friend, Perseus withdrew from Pella in company with Evander, the assassin, and two other persons; he was guarded by five hundred Cretan mercenaries, and thus attended came three days after his defeat to Amphipolis. Here he endeavoured to speak to the citizens, holding his young son Philip in his arms, but as his tears and emotion would not allow him to proceed in his oration, Evander spoke for him; he was, however, interrupted by the people, who cried out, "Hence, depart; must we be ruined for you?"

Perseus took the warning implied by these unfriendly words, and embarked with his treasures and five hundred Cretan mercenaries (who knew he had money and followed him for the sake of that and not from love to his person), on board some vessels that lay in the river Strymon. He had a considerable number of gold and silver vessels with him, some of which he flung down among the Cretans upon the shore for a largess, as a means of ensuring their fidelity, before he trusted himself with them on the river.[83] When he arrived at Galepsos he repented of his liberality, for the plate he had bestowed upon them was worth fifty talents; and he was now near the sacred island of Samothrace, whose privileges even the conquerors he knew would not dare to violate. He discovered at this juncture that some of the urns and vases had been used by Alexander the Great, and persuaded B.C. 168. the Cretans, with tears, to give up a part of them, upon the promise of paying thirty talents for those he had selected.[84] He broke his word as soon as he was received into the sanctuary.[85]

The sanctuary in which Perseus and his unfortunate family took refuge, was esteemed the holiest place in the heathen world. It was dedicated to Cybele, and the mysteries connected with the polytheism of Greece were said to be derived from thence.[86] This oldest repository of superstition contained records of the various changes that had taken place in the earth from the earliest period of time. The convulsions that had rent Italy from Greece, and Gibraltar from Africa, were there chronicled and described.[87] Could these records have come down to us, we should have known many important facts respecting our own island, and the period when it was separated from France. The disappearance of the island celebrated in ancient geography by the name of Atalantis, was perhaps noted in these lost chronicles of Samothrace, of which only a fragment remains.

In this sanctuary, whose precincts even the mighty republic dared not violate, the last Macedonian monarch took refuge. He made choice of the altar dedicated to Castor and Pollux, as his peculiar asylum. Here it is probable that his wife, with his other children and their attendants, joined him; for no mention is made of their leaving Pydna with him. He took up his abode in a house within the bounds of the temple with his family, and bestowed therein his treasures, whose possession consoled him for the loss of Macedonia.

The flight of the king, and the loss of the army, so dispirited the Macedonian people, that no captain attempted to unite the scattered forces that yet remained, for the general defence of the country.[88] Hippias, who still guarded the pass of Ascuris, Pantauchus, and Milo, yielded themselves and the troops under their command, with the town of Beræa, wherein they had taken refuge. Pydna, and six thousand foreign mercenaries in the service of Perseus, surrendered to the Romans. These fugitives followed the advice given them by the Macedonian generals, who, upon being abandoned by their sovereign, discontinued the war. Leaving the city to be plundered by the victorious army, Æmilius Paulus marched to Pella, expecting to find the treasures of Perseus in that place. He only discovered the three hundred talents of which the king had defrauded Gentius. Macedonia submitted entirely to the Romans; it ceased to be a nation from the moment the Romans gained the victory of Pydna.

Octavius, the admiral, arrived at Samothrace a few hours after it had given the privileges of sanctuary to Perseus and his ruined fortunes. For that abject prince had written to Æmilius Paulus, informing him of his abode, and imploring his compassion. Compassion was a virtue in which the proud Roman was deficient; and as the fallen monarch had superscribed the letter "King Perseus to the Consul Paulus," he did not choose to give either a written or verbal answer to the supplication.[89] Perseus, who had a great sum of money at command, thought it possible that he might make a bargain for the security of himself and family, or hoped to effect his escape during his negotiation with the Romans. He sent another letter to Æmilius, omitting the style proper to his rank, though he demanded its restoration, and made his recognition as king of Macedonia one of his conditions of surrender. The consul and the Roman admiral remained inflexible. "He must yield himself, his family, his treasures, and his shadow of a title unconditionally to the Roman people," was the only reply they gave the defeated prince.

A young Roman named Atilius asked the Samothracians, "How they dared pollute their holy island by receiving into their sanctuary a man stained with the B.C. 168. blood of king Eumenes, whose assassination had been attempted by a fugitive claiming protection from them, within the precincts of the temple of Delphi." Though this question was evidently pointed at the monarch who had taken hold of the altar of Castor and Pollux, the priests referred it to Evander, the Cretan general, the agent who had been formerly employed by Perseus to destroy the king of Pergamus. They signified to the Macedonian prince, "that Evander must clear himself from this accusation by a fair trial; or if, conscious of guilt, he durst not abide the enquiry, he must no longer profane by his presence the holy place in which he had taken sanctuary." Nothing could be more honourable and honest than this proposition.

To an innocent man falsely accused, such an opportunity of clearing his character, would have been deemed fortunate, but Evander, the guilty tool of Perseus, trembled to meet such an ordeal. His feelings, however, must have been calm to the tumultuous fears of the degraded monarch of that kingdom, which Alexander had made the greatest in the world.—of that, which Philip, his own father, had gallantly defended against the king-making republic, a kingdom which, though doomed to fall, ought to have seen its fate shared by its last sovereign. The trial of Evander then, was not more terrible to his mind than to that of Perseus, for it alarmed the guilty principal as much as his instrument. If Evander denounced him as the author of the assassination, his sanctuary privilege was lost. His criminal emissary was a Cretan too, a nation proverbial for want of faith. In this emergency he besought Evander to kill himself, as he would certainly be put to death if proved guilty on his trial. Evander, who had no greater liking to a violent death than the king himself, promised to do so; but said that he preferred taking poison to falling upon his sword. But Perseus, who divined his intentions, caused him to be murdered, to prevent his meditated escape. He bribed the magistrate to countenance the report, that Evander had committed suicide. The knowledge of this fact alarmed those persons who still clung to the fortunes of the fallen monarch: they quitted his service abruptly, none remaining with him but his pages and his own family. In despair, he resolved to escape to his ally and friend, Cotys, king of Thrace; for he thought his treasures would secure him an asylum at his court. A Cretan, named Oroandes, or Oramates, the master of a vessel lying in the harbour, agreed to take the king, his family, and possessions, on board at night.[90] Without entertaining the slightest suspicions, Perseus trusted the treasure on board the ship, preparing to follow it at night, with his wife and children. He wandered along the shore, but no ship appeared, and when daylight came some persons told him that the vessel of Oroandes had stood out to sea some hours before. Bitter groans burst from the heart of the miserable prince, he uttered piercing cries as he looked at his wife and young children, and found himself robbed, not only of the treasures he had trusted to the treacherous Cretan, but of the hope of liberty and life. Perseus and his wretched family had climbed over a wall that bounded a garden, passing through a narrow window, to reach the sea-shore. His Queen and her royal infants, who were unaccustomed to hardship, and were now taking their first bitter lessons in adversity,[91] had found their escape a work of time and difficulty; yet they must return by the way they came, if they wished to recover their sanctuary. With much toil and difficulty they effected this without being discovered; though the asylum thus regained could not preserve them long from the fate they dreaded. Octavius, the admiral, issued a proclamation, offering those Macedonians who had taken sanctuary with Perseus their lives, effects, and lands in Macedonia, provided they gave themselves up to the Romans. The pages came immediately forth and surrendered themselves without delay. Their example was followed by Ion, the Thessalonian, the favourite of the king, to whose care he had entrusted his queen and children. This man treacherously betrayed his important charge, by delivering up the family of his master to the Romans.[92] Perseus appears to have been a tender husband and father, and the loss of his family filled up his cup of bitterness, which the triumph for which he was destined made overflow. Plutarch says, "The strong necessity of nature compelled him to yield himself to those who B.C. 168. had his children in their keeping, and he surrendered himself to Octavius." The Roman fleet, which had only remained at Samothrace to obtain possession of the king of Macedonia and his family, stood out to sea. At Amphipolis Æmilius, apprised by express of his coming, sent his son-in-law, Tubero, and some persons of rank to meet his captive.[93] Perseus, covered with a mourning-cloak, was conducted to the consul, at whose feet he threw himself, imploring his pity in the most moving manner. The consul, who had prepared, not only a speech, but some tears, for this important scene, in which he intended to perform his part with great dignity, found his intention frustrated by the mental and bodily prostration of the captive. The conquest of a kingdom and army governed and led by such a faint-hearted person as Perseus appeared to rob Æmilius of his brightest laurels. The proud Roman, who unreasonably expected to find constancy and courage in a prince who, if he had possessed either, would not have been his prisoner, forgot a famous oration he had composed upon the mutability of fortune, and reproached his fallen foe for his pusillanimity, concluding his barbarous attack by assuring him "that cowardice was held in great contempt by the Romans." After these insolent remarks, the Roman conqueror raised up the wretched suppliant, crushed down with the weight of his great misfortunes, and gave him into the hands of his son-in-law, Tubero.[94] The oration with which Æmilius had designed to greet or console Perseus, he appears to have delivered to his own sons and sons-in-law with some alterations, which doubtless met with more attention from the learned family group than it could have received from the miserable and heart-wrung captive for whose benefit it had been expressly composed. Thus set in dishonour and darkness the mighty third monarchy of the prophet Daniel, whose power had risen suddenly with Alexander, and was divided not destroyed,

> "When, midst a thousand and a thousand dreams,
> Death placed his hand upon the conqueror's cup,
> And stayed him banqueting at Babylon,"[95]

but found the consummation of its ruin at this time, when the Romans, according to the prophecy, destroyed "the residue" and entirely subjected it to their iron rule.[96] How much useless trouble has been taken by unbelievers to invalidate certain plain passages of scripture referring to historical events, when an impartial examination would have proved their authenticity, and not only have established the faith of the reader, but ended the ceaseless prevarications and contentions of unbelief.

<hr size=2 width="10%" align=center>

[1] Polybius, de Virt.; Livy, xl. 3.

[2] Polybius, Legat., xliv.; Livy, xxxix. 34.

[3] Polybius, xxiii. 14.

[4] Livy, xxxix. 36.

[5] Plutarch, in Cato Major.

[6] *Ibid.*

[7] Plutarch, in Cato the Censor.

[8] Polybius, Legat., 46; Livy, xxxix. 46.

[9] Polybius, Legat., 46; Livy, xxxix. 46.

[10] Polybius, xxiv. 2-6.

[11] Polybius.

[12] Plutarch, in Philopœmen; Livy, xxxix. 49.

[13] Plutarch, in Philopœmen.

[14] *Ibid.*; Livy, xxxix. 49, 50.

[15] *Ibid.*

[16] Plutarch, in Philopœmen; to the end.

[17] Plutarch, in Philopœmen.

[18] Livy affirms that Scipio was dead when Cato entered upon the office of censor the year before, as his first act was to choose his friend and colleague Valerius Flaccus president or prince of the senate, which he would not have done had Scipio been living, as the presidency was for life. Cato, however, was not a very likely person to suffer a voluntary exile to retain a dignity whose duties rendered his presence necessary at Rome; the general opinion of ancient historians, therefore, which assigns the year preceding as the date of the great Scipio's death is the most correct.—Hooke's Roman History.

[19] Justin, xxxii. 4; Plutarch, in Flamininus.

[20] Juvenal, Sat., 10; Livy, xxxix. 51.

[21] Plutarch, in Flamininus.

[22] *Ibid.*

[23] Polybius, Legat., 51.

[24] Philip had only two sons, Perseus and this Demetrius. The Romans say that the elder was born of a concubine and Demetrius of a legitimate wife, but this has been doubted. A bitter hatred and jealousy had grown up between the brothers, greater perhaps than would have existed had they been the children of one mother.—Polybius, Legat., 50; Livy, xxxix. 53.

[25] Livy, xl. 23.

[26] This epistle, whether a true document or atrocious forgery, proved the death warrant of the weak Demetrius, who was poisoned by his father's orders, Philip believing that he was punishing a traitor. This murder covered king Philip with horror and remorse, when he became aware of the machinations Perseus had practised against his victim, of whose innocence he was at last convinced. Demetrius, however, certainly accelerated his fate by his own imprudent conduct.

[27] Macrobius, Saturnal., ii. 13.

[28] See Appendix. (p. 438)

[29] Livy, xl. 54.

[30] See Appendix. (p. 439)

[31] Ridiculous portents had preceded the decease of these consuls. The liver of the ox Cornelius was sacrificing could not be found in the boiler, from which it had no doubt been extracted; and in four beasts sacrificed in succession to Jupiter by his colleague, that important organ was wholly wanting. Petillius was followed to Liguria, where he found a grave, by these portents, for on the morning of the engagement the keeper of the sacred

chickens was heard to say, "That something had gone wrong with them, and the consul knew it well enough." In his address to his soldiers Petillius said, "I shall this day take Letum," meaning the mountain upon which the enemy were posted. This name signifying also death, seemed to them indicative of his doom. The consul was slain upon the hill, thus verifying the evil omens that had preceded the morning's march. Valerius Lævinus, his successor, shared his fate, for he too was killed in Liguria. The consul Æmilius Lepidus redeemed the honour of the consular purple, by obtaining a triumph for his victories in Liguria.

[32] The reader will remember that the exquisite art of engraving upon precious stones, and even upon diamonds, was not then lost, but was in perfection.—Hooke, v.

[33] Polybius, Excerpt., 20.

[34] Livy, xlii. 2.

[35] Livy, xlii. 7.

[36] He would have been punished for his cruelty and injustice in the next consulship, if his brother had not been made consul.

[37] Livy, xlii. 5; Polybius, Legat., 74.

[38] As it was everywhere reported that he was dead, his brother Attalus, who was in love with his sister-in-law, began to court her and to take steps for putting himself in possession of his brother's kingdom. Eumenes did not resent this conduct upon his return to Pergamus; he contented himself with whispering to Attalus, "Another time be certain of the king's death before you think of marrying the queen." A mild and suitable reproof.

[39] Livy, xlii. 23.

[40] Polybius.

[41] Hooke's Rome.

[42] See Appendix. (p. 443)

[43] Polybius, Legat., 43; Livy, xlii. 43.

[44] Livy, xlii. 57.

[45] Plutarch's Life of P. Æmilius.

[46] Polybius, Legat., 69.

[47] Livy, xlii. 48.

[48] Plutarch, Life of P. Æmilius.

[49] Livy, xliii. 1.

[50] Livy, xliv. 2, et seq.

[51] Livy gives rather a marvellous history of the manner in which the consul accomplished his march. He says that the descent was so steep that for nearly four miles the men rolled themselves down the declivities, fearing to take an erect position. The elephants were let down by bridges laid from cliff to cliff covered with turf. These were placed one below another, and when one of the huge beasts was got upon a bridge, the posts were cut that supported it, and he slid down to the next till he reached the bottom of the mountain. He declares this method was pursued by Hannibal in his march over the Alps.

[52] Livy, xliv. 7.

[53] Polybius, Legat., 78.

[54] See Appendix. (p. 451)

[55] Livy, xlv. 15.

[56] Plutarch declares that he was chosen for the leader in this war; Livy, that Macedonia fell to him by lot.

[57] Plutarch, in Paulus Æmilius.

[58] Valerius Antias; Livy.

[59] Polybius, Legat., 85; Livy, xliv. 24.

[60] *Ibid.*

[61] Plutarch, in Paulus Æmilius; Appian, in Frag.

[62] Supposed to be Germans or Goths of Celtic origin.—Dr. Latham.

[63] Plutarch, in Paulus Æmilius.

[64] Livy, xliv. 26.

[65] Dion Cassius.

[66] Livy.

[67] In after ages it was this city that drew from her besieger, Mahomet the second, a remark expressive of his admiration at her rock-founded walls. "Oh what a fair and stately place hath the eagle chosen to build her nest and rear her young ones in," and his cannon vainly played against a stronghold defended by Scanderbeg in person and fortified by nature and art.—Knolles, History of Turks, Mahomet II.

[68] Appian in Illyricum; Livy, xliv. 31.

[69] Plutarch, in Paulus Æmilius; Appian, in Fragment.; Livy, xliv. 32.

[70] See Appendix. (p. 454)

[71] Plutarch, in Paulus Æmilius.

[72] Livy, xliv. 36.

[73] Which Hooke has described with amusing quaintness as doing his duty to the moon.

[74] Livy tells us, "that about three in the afternoon a Roman horse got away from his rider and made for the river, into which he plunged, that a contest arose between some Romans and Macedonians for the possession of the animal, and that this trivial incident brought on the decisive engagement that followed. The Macedonians fought bravely, fulfilling the promise they had given to their recreant sovereign."—Livy, xliv. 40; Plutarch, in Paulus Æmilius.

[75] One writer, whom Plutarch describes as an eyewitness and styles Posidonius, "affirms that Perseus, though he had received a hurt the day before by a kick from a horse, was in the battle heading his phalanx, when he received a severe wound, which obliged him to retire to Pydna." It must be confessed that this account does not at all agree with the conduct of Perseus during the whole course of the war.

[76] Plutarch, in Paulus Æmilius.

[77] *Ibid.*

[78] Plutarch, in Paulus Æmilius.

[79] *Ibid.*

[80] *Ibid.*

[81] Plutarch, in Paulus Æmilius.

[82] Plutarch ascribes this universal desertion to his reproaching his friends with the loss of the battle, and adds "that he slew his treasurers as soon as he got to Pella; these unfortunate men having come forward to receive him." Some authorities state that he killed the governor, and as none of his great officers chose to obey the summons that commanded their attendance, it looks as if this account were true, and that they feared to face the fallen tyrant.—Livy, xliv. 43.

[83] Plutarch, in Paulus Æmilius.

[84] Plutarch, in Paulus Æmilius.

[85] "Thus playing the Cretan with the Cretans," remarks Plutarch, for the national want of faith in these islanders had passed into a proverb. In later times the great apostle St. Paul justified the national character given of them by Callimachus from whom he quoted, when in his epistle to Titus he says, "The Cretans are always liars, even as one of their own poets has said, which witness is true."

[86] Plutarch, in Paulus Æmilius.

[87] Humboldt, Aspects of Nature.

[88] Livy, xliv. 45, 46.

[89] It is stated on the authority of Livy that the persons sent by the king were men of such mean birth and condition that Paulus wept that a mighty sovereign should have no better messengers to send to him on such an important occasion. The tears of the conqueror, though recorded by an historian of credit, if genuine, had a different source; the reader, however, will hardly think the incident credible at all.—Livy, xlv.

[90] Plutarch, in Paulus Æmilius.

[91] *Ibid.*

[92] *Ibid.*

[93] Some authors affirm that the consul reproved Perseus for having so unjustly waged war with the Romans, though Perseus had vainly sued for peace to the senate, but bade him take courage, as the clemency of the Roman people, which so many kings and nations had experienced, afforded him not only a hope but an assurance of life. If Æmilius really made this speech it must have been in irony, for the Romans were celebrated for their cruelty to their royal captives, who were generally put to death at the moment when the chariot of the victor was turned to the capitol.—Plutarch.

[94] Plutarch, in Paulus Æmilius.

[95] "Heads of Ancient History" by Hudson Gurney.

[96] Daniel vii. 7.

CHAPTER XI.

A.U.C. 586-608. B.C. 168-146.

Miraculous report of the battle of Pydna at Rome.—Dilemma of the Rhodian ambassadors.—Remarkable prophecy fulfilled by the Romans.—Epiphanes resigns his Egyptian conquests.—Congratulatory embassies to Rome.—Adulation of Masinissa.—Roman tyranny in Greece.—Long exile of the Achæans in Italy.—Polybius the historian.—Friendship of Æmilius Paulus and his sons.—Cruelty and treachery of the Romans to the Epirots and Illyrians.—Triumph of Æmilius Paulus opposed by his army.—His domestic calamities.—His triumph.—Perseus and his captive family.—Death of Perseus in captivity.—Pathetic speech of his conqueror.—Roman literature.—Harsh conduct of the senate to Rhodes.—Ambition of Attalus.—Impious flattery of king Prusias agreeable to the senate.—Cato defends the Rhodians.—King Eumenes contemptuously treated.—Judas Maccabeus claims the protection of Rome.—First treaty between Rome and Judea.—Murder of the Roman ambassador at Laodicea.—Spirited advice of Polybius to prince Demetrius.—The prince recovers Syria.—Kills the young king.—Retains Syria.—Cato sent to Carthage.—Desires the destruction of that city.—Answer of Scipio Nasica.—Contempt of Cato for philosophers and philosophy.—Civil war in Egypt.—The senate favour Physcon.—Generous behaviour of Philometor.—The senate favour the impostor Alexander Balas.—His victory and reign.—Third Punic war.—Battle between the Numidians and Carthaginians.—Delight of Scipio at the spectacle.—Rome acts basely to Carthage.—Despair of the ambassadors.—Their cowardice and treachery.—Resolution of the Carthaginian people.—Censorinus repulsed.—Bravery of Scipio.—Death of Masinissa.—Polybius and Scipio.—Scipio chosen to conduct the war.—Scipio's terms rejected by Hasdrubal.—Storm of Carthage.—Meanness of Hasdrubal.—Despair of his wife.—Carthage pillaged and destroyed.—Sale of the captives.—Corruption of Roman manners.—Dissensions between the Achæan league and the Lacedæmonians.—Success of the League.—Roman interference.—Corinthian mob insult Aurelius Orestes.—Mild character of Metellus.—His terms rejected by the League.—Battle of Scarpheia.—Metellus takes Thebes, invests Corinth and Chalcis.—Escape of the Achæans.—Mummius carries on the siege of Corinth.—Diæus repulses the Romans.—Roman victory.—Flight and suicide of Diæus.—Barbarity of Mummius.—Desolation of Corinth.—Greece a Roman province.—Ignorance of Mummius.—Polybius and the Greek cities.—Masterpiece of Aristides.—Bargain made by Mummius.—His valuation of gems of art.—Lucullus defrauds him of some paintings.—His poverty and integrity.—His surname.—Metellus called Macedonicus.—Roman government in Spain, from A.U.C. 558 to 607.—People of Certima.—Courtesy of Gracchus.—Numantine war.—Victory of Carus.—Clemency of Marcellus.—Cruelty of Sergius Galba.—Escape of Viriathus.—His stratagem.—His victories.—Cuts off the allies.—Twice defeats the prætor.—Opens a brilliant campaign.—The Roman senate resolves to send a consular army against the brave Viriathus.

WE are gravely assured by Plutarch, that on the fourth day after the battle of Pydna had decided the fate of Macedonia, it was rumoured in the upper seats of the theatre, where the Roman people were assembled to witness the equestrian games, "that a great victory had been gained by Æmilius, which had overthrown the kingdom of Macedonia; whereupon the people clapped their hands, and repeated it everywhere as truth."[1] This ingenious falsehood, probably invented to please the spectators of the games, is treated by the great heathen philosopher and biographer as a miraculous fact.[2]

The ambassadors sent from Rhodes to mediate a peace between Perseus and the Roman senate, did not arrive till after the battle of Pydna.[3] They were treated rather as the enemies than the allies of Rome. Modern diplomatists would not have delivered their letters, when they found how matters had gone with Perseus. The Roman senate received their awkward congratulations upon the conquest of Macedonia with evident distrust. The political importance of Rome was so much increased by the fall of a warlike kingdom that had, in some measure, set limits to its power; that the republic decided all matters of dispute between rival states, and even curbed the ambition of Syria and Egypt. As the object of Popillius Lænas' embassy to Antiochus Epiphanes (then employed in besieging Alexandria), is connected with prophetical Scripture history, it may be necessary to give a slight review of the successors of Antiochus the Great, to understand the reason of the interference of Rome between him and Egypt. Antiochus the Great had been killed while plundering the temple of Jupiter Belus, by the people of Elymais, whose religious feelings he was violating in this sacrilege.[4] Seleucus Philopater, his successor, demanded of the Romans the person of his younger brother, Antiochus, then a hostage at Rome, offering to replace him with his own son, Demetrius. Heliodorus, the treasurer of Seleucus, poisoned his master and usurped the Syrian throne, before B.C. 168. Antiochus arrived in Syria; but Eumenes, king of Pergamus, assisted to expel the intruder, and gain the kingdom for himself.[5] Antiochus took the name of Epiphanes, or illustrious; and being a bad bold man, resolved to extend his dominions without the slightest regard to justice, or respect for the ties of consanguinity. He cast his eyes upon Egypt, and made war upon his nephew, Ptolemy Philometor, whom he vanquished in two battles, and finally took prisoner. The Alexandrians declared Physcon king, under the name of Ptolemy Euergetes; upon which Antiochus renewed the war, took Pelusium, and laid siege to Alexandria, in which city Physcon and his sister, Cleopatra, then were.[6] These royal personages sent to the senate demanding assistance; upon which Popillius Lænas was commissioned to order Antiochus and Ptolemy Philometor, in whose name that monarch was now carrying on the war, to desist, unless they wished to make Rome their enemy.[7] Antiochus, fearful of provoking the ambitious republic, by whom his father had formerly been defeated, obeyed the commands of the senate; but being a crafty person, restored to Ptolemy Philometor, Memphis and all that he had taken from him, with the exception of Pelusium, by which place he could enter Egypt, in case the royal brothers should make war upon one another, as he hoped and expected they would. Philometor, as amiable and honourable as Physcon was wicked and base, was easily persuaded by his sister, Cleopatra, to enter into an agreement with his brother, by virtue of which they were to reign conjointly. Antiochus, enraged at the seeds of discord he had sown between the brothers not producing the fruit he expected, made war upon them, notwithstanding the entreaties of his nephew, that he would suffer him to enjoy in peace that part of Egypt which he had restored to him. He was on the way to Alexandria, when the Roman ambassadors met him, within four miles of the city, and stopped his march. The former hostage of Rome had known and esteemed Popillius, and he now advanced and offered him his hand in remembrance of their former friendship. Popillius, instead of taking that pledge of amity, put into the extended hand of the Syrian monarch the decree of the senate, commanding him to withdraw his fleet and armies and return to his own country. Antiochus read the document, but gave no direct reply to the ambassadors, merely telling Popillius "that he would consult his friends." Popillius immediately traced a circle round the king with the vine-branch which he held in his hand, and said in a peremptory tone, "Your answer before you leave this circle." For a moment the proud monarch regarded the prouder ambassador in silence, astonished at the boldness of the demand, and then replied in a tone more humble, but in a style no less laconic, "The senate shall be obeyed."[8] The senate was obeyed, for the Syrian monarch quitted Egypt and returned to his own land.[9] Antiochus Epiphanes is the same prince who plundered Jerusalem, profaned the temple, and filled Jerusalem with slaughter.[10] It is probable that his compliance with the commands of the senate, arose from his having just received tidings of the conquest of Macedonia.

Popillius had scarcely returned to Rome before a splendid embassy arrived from the kingly Egyptian brothers, to thank the senate for their deliverance from the tyranny of Antiochus. The terms were singularly impious in which the Egyptian ambassadors expressed the feelings of their masters—"The two kings and Cleopatra, thought themselves more indebted to the senate and people of Rome than to their own parents, or even to the immortal gods."[11] Masgaba, the son of Masinissa, came to Rome to congratulate the Roman senate and people upon their victory over Perseus. He enumerated all the supplies his father had sent to the Romans in Macedonia during the four years of the war, lamenting, with African adroitness, that these had been requested as a favour instead of being claimed as a right—that they had been B.C. 168. paid for, not accepted. Masgaba did not, however, restore the money, which would have been a better proof of his sincerity. He told the senators that his father considered them as the lords and sovereigns of Numidia, declaring that it was the intention of Masinissa to come to Rome to thank Jupiter for the success of the Roman arms in Macedonia. The fathers in return were equally flattering, for they styled Masinissa "an honest man, who was grateful for, and deserved their favours, and graciously intimated (having, it should seem, no wish for his company,) that he could thank the gods in Numidia, at home, as well as in Italy, or his son could now do it for him."

Ten commissioners were appointed to regulate the affairs of Macedonia, and five to arrange those of Illyricum. Epirus had been reduced by Anicius, the prætor, before they arrived, but the heavy hand of Æmilius Paulus had not then been laid on that unhappy nation. The conqueror of Macedonia travelled through Greece to view, at his leisure, a country so celebrated for arts and arms, where, indeed, civilisation had flourished while the rest of the world, with the exception of one favoured spot, was plunged in darkness and barbarism.[12] At Amphipolis he proclaimed the liberty, or rather the subjection of Macedonia, in Latin, to the deputies he had summoned from every city belonging to the conquered people.[13]

This decree was explained to the assembly by the prætor Octavius, in the Greek language. Macedonia was divided into four cantons, of which Amphipolis, Pella, Thessalonica and Pelagonia were declared the chief cities. No person was permitted to marry, or purchase lands or houses, out of his own district; but each canton was to have the right of electing its own magistrate. This policy annihilated for ever the independence of the people, by an act that destroyed their union, while the clause that prohibited any native of Macedonia from working in the gold and silver mines ruined the national wealth. The conquered people were, however, permitted to labour for their own profit in those of copper and iron. Only half the annual tribute levied by their kings was to be paid to the victorious republic. Macedonia was thus constituted a Roman province.

Æmilius was met by a body of Ætolians attired in deep mourning, as he was returning from his travels. They came to complain of two of their countrymen, Lyciscus and Tisippus, who had surrounded the place where the diet was held, and had put to the sword five hundred and fifty principal men and exiled others of their nation. This outrage had been sanctioned by the Roman commander, Bæbius, who had not only furnished the murderers with men and arms, but had given the property of the slain and exiled to their destroyers and accusers.[14] In making enquiry into this massacre the political not the moral conduct of the accused was taken into consideration by the pro-consul and the commissioners. Bæbius was the person upon whom justice was executed, because he had employed Roman soldiers in this detestable massacre; but the exiles were formally banished because they were patriot Greeks, not Roman sycophants. Æmilius summoned for trial from Ætolia, Acarnania, Epirus, and Bœotia to Rome all those who had been denounced to him as unfriendly to the Roman interest.[15] Callicrates, the traitor, had given in a list of those Achæans whom he hated, and this list, as a matter of course, contained the names of those who best loved their country. The commissioners sent two of their number, C. Claudius and Cn. Domitius, to the Achæan diet, to accuse those named by Callicrates[16] of having assisted Perseus with money, and to take possession of their persons. One of the deputies made the accusation, and demanded that those should be pre-sentenced to death whom he was about to name. The palpable injustice of the demand, and the audacity with which it was made, moved the general indignation of the assembly. "Pre-sentenced!" was the angry rejoinder. "What justice is this? Name them first, and let them answer for themselves, and if they cannot be cleared, we will instantly condemn them." "All your generals, as many as have led your armies, are guilty of this crime," haughtily replied the Roman. "If this be true," answered Xeno, "then I have also been a friend to Perseus, for I have commanded the Achæan army. But, if any one accuse me, I am ready to answer him, either here immediately, or at Rome before the senate." This declaration from the lips of a man B.C. 167. of worth and integrity was the very pretext the subtle deputy required. "You are right," he replied, "that will be the best way." He then by an edict ordered more than a thousand of the principal Achæans to be carried to Rome, to clear themselves from charges of which he was well aware they were entirely innocent.[17] Only three hundred of these lived to return, for seventeen years elapsed before they obtained a decree for their liberation.

Amongst these was the celebrated historian Polybius, and he owed his preservation to the friendship the sons of Æmilius Paulus had conceived for him, as through their instrumentality he remained at Rome, instead of sharing the fortunes of his countrymen in Etruria.[18] It was probably at Rome that he wrote his histories, and acquired the necessary information respecting the wars of Hannibal. This admirable military historian was minutely studied and even epitomised by Julius Cæsar, and the study of his works have formed a prominent part of military education ever since. It was the happy fortune of Polybius "to die at home at last," beloved and respected by all his countrymen.

At Amphipolis, Æmilius had the bad taste to exhibit sumptuous games to the conquered people, in which the spoils of their country formed the proudest part of the show.[19] From these diversions he hurried to execute the sentence of the senate against Illyria and Epirus, to which countries the prætor Anicius, their brave and clement conqueror, had granted merciful conditions. The cruelty of the senate did not originate in revenge but from cupidity. It was their intention to retain the whole of the Macedonian spoil, and to grant in lieu of it the plunder of Illyria and Epirus to the Roman army. Æmilius does not appear to have been averse to a measure that blighted the laurels he had gained in Macedonia. He despatched his son Fabius and his son-in-law Scipio Nasica into Illyria to ravage that unfortunate province, whilst he marched in person into Epirus to execute the commands of the senate.[20] He first communicated to Anicius what was about to be done, and then sent to every town orders to withdraw the garrisons, under colour of bestowing upon them the same freedom lately granted to the Macedonians.[21] He also summoned ten of the principal inhabitants from these devoted towns to repair to his quarters. He ordered these persons to collect all the gold and silver that could be found in the temples and houses, and to bring these treasures into the market-places without delay, promising the people liberty as the price of their wealth.[22] The command ought to have excited suspicion, but the Epirots then, as in our own times, prized their freedom beyond silver or gold, they had found honour in their Roman conqueror Anicius, and they did not doubt the pro-consul's word. Upon the appointed day they brought their effects to the appointed places, and delivered them to the Roman officers. This was the signal for pillage and universal slavery; seventy towns were plundered in one day, and one hundred and fifty thousand persons were sold as slaves, a sentence worse than death to a people who valued liberty as their first earthly blessing. Plutarch remarks in his brief narration of the fact, "each soldier received eleven drachmas for his share of the booty. How shocking was such a destruction for the sake of such an advantage."[23] He does not, however, give the transaction the condemnation it merited, out of regard to his hero, of whom he seems to be remarkably fond. The particulars are more minutely related by the great Roman historian Livy. Æmilius Paulus did not enrich himself with the spoils he had torn from the Epirots, neither did he appropriate the wealth of Perseus to his own use, the library of the king was the only thing he took from Macedonia, which he presented to his sons, who were learned men.[24] He passed from Greece to Rome to demand the triumph his military prowess had merited, and found himself opposed by his own army, that very army by which he had achieved the conquest of Macedonia. The severity of his discipline, and his withholding from them the spoils of the conquered country, were the reasons they assigned in the assembly of the people. Strange to say they found men eager to aid them in this slight put upon their general. Sergius Galba, a tribune of the second B.C. 167. legion, spoke for four hours against the triumph with such effect that the first tribes actually voted for its being withheld, till Marcus Servilius turned the tide of popular favour towards Æmilius by a speech full of cutting irony levelled at his accusers, and the triumph already decreed by the senate was confirmed by the people.[25]

Perseus, reserved for this last indignity, vainly implored the conqueror to spare him the humiliation of walking in the procession. Æmilius sarcastically remarked, "That it had been in his own power to prevent it, and was so still if he chose." But the suicidal act at which the haughty conqueror indirectly glanced, required more courage or less reflection than the vanquished possessed. Some traditionary notion of a future state might linger in the mind of the last king of Macedonia, and forbid him to send his sin-laden soul to its final tribunal. For the light of inspiration had flashed upon Alexander the Great, though, as a divine of the Church of England remarks, "All those grand things spoken of him by the prophet Daniel had been drowned in the cup of inebriety."[26] Whether his constitutional timidity or some dread of future judgment influenced Perseus is uncertain, but he did not prevent the degradation by adopting the criminal method pointed out to him by his victor.

History has given an ample record of this triumph from her tragic roll, and has related the interesting fact that the cup of the victor and the vanquished overflowed at the same moment with woe. A son of Æmilius Paulus died five days before the triumph of his father, and the stern Roman was a tender parent. Another fell a victim to the same disease three days after its consummation, as if God were displeased at the young and innocent children of Perseus being made a part of the spectacle, and thus reminded the conqueror "not to be high-minded but to fear." The triumph lasted three days. It was the most splendid Rome had then witnessed.[27] Upon the first day were exhibited the statuary, paintings and colossi brought from Macedonia, where the arts had flourished under the fostering care of Philip and his son Alexander the Great. These were drawn upon two hundred and fifty chariots. The second day's spectacle was probably more agreeable to the feelings of a martial people too little acquainted with peace to prize the master pieces of sculpture and painting, which require an educated eye to perceive their beauties. Costly armour, and weapons of war formed its attraction; even the clangor of the javelins had charms for those whose youth and middle life had been passed in strife. The money, the hoards of Perseus, the gold and silver vessels of the royal house of Macedonia, the plate used by Alexander the Great, were now displayed to the admiring eyes of the Roman citizens,[28] for the third monarchy of scripture was overthrown, and the power of the fourth was rising on its eagle pinions to overshadow the earth. The third day presented, however, the most interesting sight, for the victor and the vanquished appeared together. The victor with his private grief sternly imprisoned in his heart, and the vanquished with his public woe. The children of Perseus, too young to feel their degradation, had been taught by their nurses and governors to clasp their little hands and stretch them towards the spectators as if to ask their pity.[29] These infantine gestures, proceeding from unconscious babes innocent of crime, touched the hearts of those to whom they made their mute appeal. Their attendants followed them weeping, and directed the attention of the crowd to the royal children, as if they felt rather for their hard fortune than their own. Perseus came next, clothed in black and wearing slippers, after the fashion of his country. He looked like a man altogether astonished and bereft of reason through the greatness of his misfortunes. He preceded his friends, whose countenances expressed the depth of their compassion for him, whom they still rather looked upon as their king than as the author of their calamities. The golden crowns of the conqueror were carried before his chariot. "He came clothed in gold and purple, bearing a laurel branch in his right hand, a man," remarks Plutarch, "worthy to be beheld without these ensigns of power."[30] Contrary to the general custom the captive monarch was not put to death when the chariot of the victor was turned towards the capitol. He was lodged in the common gaol at Alba in the country of the Marsians, and Livy B.C. 167. speaks of the decent lodging and food he enjoyed at the public charge.[31] No mention is made of the wife of Perseus, she was probably dead before he came into Italy. The daughter of the fallen king of Macedonia and one of his sons died soon, the historian adds, "it is uncertain how." But the loss of maternal care and the change from delicate nurture to neglect, sufficiently accounts for the deaths of the royal infants. The youngest son grew up in slavery, and being ingenious in carving ivory earned his living by making toys, till he became sufficiently versed in Latin and accounts to fill the place of a clerk in one of the public offices in Rome, and afterwards to the senate. Perseus, either cruelly deprived of sleep by his Roman guards or unable to endure the noisy disturbance of his felon companions, died for want of the repose to which he had been accustomed.[32] His misfortunes and separation from his family would probably have caused a sleepless pillow, even if that pillow had not been haunted by the remembrances of guilt. "In such poverty ended the royal house of Macedonia, about 160 years after the death of that monarch, to whose ambition the world seemed too narrow."[33]

The triumphs of Anicius, the prætor, and Octavius, the admiral of the fleet, followed that of Æmilius. King Gentius and his family adorned the spectacle of Anicius, who had taken many captives in the Illyrian war; but these triumphs did not excite the same interest as that last act in the Macedonian tragedy, in which Perseus and his children had been the performers. Among the Macedonian prisoners was found a son of Cotys, king of the Odrysians in Thrace. His father had sent ambassadors to Rome to obtain the clemency of the senate for this prince, whom he assured them had been forced from him as a hostage by Perseus, together with some others.[34] The senate humanely delivered up the son of Cotys and his companions without ransom, desiring nothing but the friendship of his father in return.[35] Polybius seems to think this action was more politic than magnanimous, but if it were policy it was at least founded on consummate wisdom.

The triumph lately enjoyed by Æmilius Paulus was concluded as it began, with domestic sorrow, for he followed to the grave another hopeful young son.[36]

His two eldest had been adopted into the families of Scipio and Fabius, so that none were left to carry down his own illustrious name to posterity. "For the songs of victory and triumph were mingled with the mournful dirges of death."[37] It was upon this occasion that Paulus Æmilius, though he commenced an oration upon the instability of fortune, concluded it in a more natural and parental manner with these pathetic words, "The man who led the triumph is as great an instance of the weakness of human power as he who was led captive, but with this difference, that the sons of Perseus who was conquered are alive, and that those of Æmilius who conquered him are no more." "Perhaps there is some superior being,"[38] remarks the biographer of the illustrious Roman, "whose office it is to cast a shade upon any great and eminent prosperity, and so to mingle human life that it may not be perfectly free from calamity; 'but those,' says Homer, 'may think themselves most happy to whom fortune has given an equal share of good and evil.'" Such is the dim shadowy glance the heathen philosopher caught of the Sublime Being, whom he might have better known had he sought Him in the light of the Gospel, which was then shedding around pure rays from the uncorrupted source of Truth. It is sufficient, however, to prove "that God has never at any time left man wholly without an internal witness of himself arising from the outward view of the things he has created," as well as from the exercise of his reasoning faculties upon the accidents and vicissitudes of human life.

Roman literature was in its dawn when the conquest of Macedonia brought to Rome with the captives some knowledge to enlighten the conqueror. The extension of the Roman power in Greece had already had a civilising influence upon the stern republicans, whose swords were destined to give laws to Athens. Polybius wrote his histories during his enforced sojourn at Rome, his prison being the house of Paulus Æmilius, whose learned sons B.C. 167. loved and cherished the victim of Roman tyranny, to whom they were delighted to give a home. Ennius, the friend and companion of Scipio Africanus, was dead, but his mantle had fallen upon Pacuvius, his nephew, who gained great fame in this age as a tragic writer. He was also well skilled in painting. "Orestes," one of his tragedies, was admired by Cicero, and praised by Pliny the naturalist, yet Cicero was not an admirer of his style. Nothing now is extant of Pacuvius but those two lines that moved the populace to madness at the obsequies of Julius Cæsar. Cato, the censor, wrote some moral verses or distichs that still bear his name, and are suited to the capacity of children. Some doubts exist, however, whether the book was really written by him. But when we remember the careful manner in which he educated his son, it is probable that he composed it for his instruction. Of his "Origines," only fragments are extant, comprising the history of Rome from the kings to the prætorship of Sergius Galba,—a loss much to be lamented. This work was written in Latin prose. This noble old Roman spoke well, and the specimens of his oratory which are left us, though tinctured with the peculiarities of the speaker, are yet strong, and always to the point. His most unsuccessful one was that against the repeal of the Oppian law, but Demosthenes or Cicero would have come off no better with such opponents and in such a cause. The Roman ladies we remember exerted their talents in some literary compositions, which they arranged in the form of petitions, and put into the hands of every man who came into the forum to hear their cause. The genius of woman was awakened by the bold attempt of man to retrench from her apparel the various colours, trimmings, and graceful superfluities which, in her ideas, are calculated to add to her charms and ensure their success. These feminine pieces of eloquence are lost, but the caustic railings of their adversary and the successful oratory of their champion Valerius still survive. Cato also wrote a work on agriculture, which has come down to us, and some beautiful remarks on family government, preserved by Plutarch in his life, which exhibit him under the amiable character of a kind husband, admirable father, and just master. Cato despised Greek, which began to be studied in his time, and soon became an essential in the education of young men of family, and his invectives were levelled against what he considered a worthless acquisition. He changed his opinion before the close of his life, and learned to read that beautiful language in his old age.

Terence was an African or Carthaginian slave, born in A.U.C. 559, B.C. 195, eleven years before the death of Plautus. His master, Terentius Lucanus, discovered the genius of the young captive, and gave him his liberty and a fine education. He assumed the name of his generous patron, a general practice with manumitted slaves of that period. The Scipios were men of learning, and the comic muse of Terence was fostered under their patronage. Lælius, the son of the bosom friend of the great Africanus, was one of his patrons. Envy ascribed the works of Terence to his illustrious friends. No doubt their suggestions enabled him to bring them to greater perfection. They are extant, and, though gross, are prized as pictures of the times by learned men. Terence died poor, but his daughter was married to a Roman knight. Besides the productions of Plautus and Terence, both writers of foreign extraction, the Latin language did not possess a regular drama. It had no Æschylus, Euripides, nor Sophocles. Accius succeeded Pacuvius as a tragic writer, he was the son of a freedman. His plays were first acted at the ædile shows of the celebrated Licinius Crassus. He was a favourite with D. Junius Brutus, who erected a temple from his Gallæcian spoils which was afterwards adorned with this poet's verses.

"Soon after Cato's 'Origines,' the History of Rome appeared, by Cassius Hemina, a work derived from ancient authorities and existing documents according to Pliny. He mentioned the secular games of the year 607."[39]

Fabius Maximus, also wrote a History of Rome from the earliest times. This author is supposed to have been the same erroneously called Fabius Pictor by Cicero.[40] Cneius Gellius, a prolix and credulous writer, was an historian of this period.[41] Before Rome boasted a native poet or historian she had orators, for every young Roman, even if he had not been bred to the bar, possessed a natural B.C. 167. flow of eloquence peculiar to himself. It is in republics that this talent has been carried to the highest perfection; thus Athens had her Demosthenes, and in later times Rome her Cicero.

Considerable alteration must have taken place in the Latin language since the reign of Numa, whose writings were obsolete, and could not be read without much study, like the works of our early English chroniclers and poets at this day. The compositions of Numa were written on the inner bark of the linden tree, from whence a book was called *linus*; our word leaf applied to a page of a book, and the French name *livre* for a book, are both derived from the ancient material which served the Latins for paper. These books of Numa had been buried with him, but were said to have been discovered by a husbandman while cultivating the field of Terentius in Janiculum, in the year of Rome 573, but were burned by D. Petillius, Livy says, in consequence of their containing many things contrary to the national religion of Rome at that time. Numa was of opinion that the First Cause was not an object of sense, but "invisible, incorruptible, and discerned only by the mind." This was a remnant of the old Patriarchal faith derived by Numa from his Sabine forefathers, an ancient Lacedæmonian colony. Josephus has preserved a curious document in his Antiquities of the Jews, in which the Spartans lay claim to a Hebrew descent from Abraham and Keturah, from whom the belief that the Eternal Being "was without parts or passions," must have descended to the Sabines from their ancestors. We have seen how Numa corrupted this pure idea of God, in order to rule his people by the aid of superstition.

Such are the scanty records of Latin authors and their names during the first six centuries of Rome. The arts if cultivated at all in Rome were the work of foreign artists. The Greek colonies in Italy furnished Rome with statuary, and the Etruscans gave their conquerors architecture, painting, and funereal urns. We find Rome without commerce of her own, that is she exported no native produce in exchange for what was imported to her great mart. She obtained all her supplies by the sword, or at least by its influence. Her luxuries were of foreign growth, though in this era her wants of this kind were few. Her hardy sons, except in battle, when they wore a helmet, had not yet adopted any covering for the head. The sons and daughters of the republic were more distinguished for nobility of mind than for dress, or state; and the deification of the virtues of fortitude, chastity, and piety tended to increase them in a proud and ambitious people.

Very little change had been made in the original constitution of Rome, which had been restored since the introduction of the college of tribunes, that had wrung from the senate concessions in favour of the people by making the plebeians capable of holding the chief magistracies; and it must be observed that the noblest era of the republic—that era in which she was the most valiant and the most virtuous—dawned at that period, and originated in that measure. With the conclusion of the war of Hannibal the influence of national honour began to decline, that of wealth increased. Patriotism gradually vanished with public faith, and the corrupting and debasing stimulus of gold replaced that lofty impulse. We have seen in the conduct of the Roman senate towards the states of Greece and in the cruel commands she issued to Paulus Æmilius respecting Epirus, the commencement of the decay of that national virtue and justice that had previously been her glory. Rome had not yet reached the zenith of her power, but she had already passed the limits of her true glory, for the real greatness of a people is to be found in their morality, truth, and virtue.

The splendid victories of Rome, her great territorial possessions, her triumph over the remains of the Macedonian empire, her domination over the free states of Greece, already gave her the pre-eminence over the nations of the earth, who were foredoomed to be engulfed within the vortex of her irresistible power. The star of the mighty fourth monarchy was steadily and rapidly rising, and kingdoms and republics despatched their ambassadors from afar to worship its beams. King Eumenes, aware that his intrigues with the unfortunate and guilty Perseus were known to the senate, sent his brother Attalus to congratulate that august body upon the victories of the republic[42] and to solicit their B.C. 167. assistance against the Gallo-Greeks, whom he found troublesome neighbours. Attalus, as able and ambitious as his brother, had either formed the iniquitous design of petitioning the senate to endow him with half that prince's kingdom, or had listened to the seductive suggestions of some of the senators on its possibility.[43]

Eumenes, aware of the senators' intention, and of his brother's willingness to be made their tool, sent Stratius, a physician and confidant of his own, as a spy upon his conduct as well as an adviser. Stratius recommended Attalus by no means to ask for the investiture, as the king of Pergamus was infirm and had no acknowledged heir but himself, adding that in a short space of time he would possess the whole of the kingdom, without being indebted to the Romans. Attalus took the advice, but being determined to profit by the good intentions of the senators towards him, asked for two Thracian cities, Ænus and Maroneia, formerly conquered by king Philip. These were readily granted, but only to induce the royal ambassador to demand a part of Pergamus, thereby meaning to give an occasion for a civil war, and for the dangerous mediation of the Romans. Attalus did not fulfil their intentions, which displeased them so much that they made Ænus and Maroneia free cities, by this act depriving the Pergamenian prince of the gift they had just bestowed upon him, a piece of chicanery very disgraceful to the Romans. The Gallo-Greeks were restrained in their aggressions upon Pergamus, out of motives of policy, or perhaps because their Gaulish origin was displeasing in the eyes of the Roman people.

The Rhodians, had made the most humble and even guilty concessions to Popillius, the Roman ambassador, even to the shameful one of allowing him to condemn those citizens to death who had favoured Perseus.[44] This act, which filled Rhodes with suicides and executions, and expatriated many of her people, could not pacify the haughty and revengeful republic.[45] The Rhodian embassy was uncourteously received at Rome, and Juventius Thalna, the prætor peregrinus, excited the commons against them by raising the cry of war, a cry re-echoed by the consul and all the great military officers who had been lately engaged in that of Macedonia. Cato, the censor, and two tribunes of the people, alone ventured to plead for the Rhodians. Cato the favourite of the plebeian party obliged the prætor to quit the rostra that the ambassadors, Philophron and Astymedes, might be heard in the defence of their country. Nothing could be more humbly submissive than their language; they pleaded their former great services in extenuation of their fault, and avowed the determination of their republic, in the event of a war with Rome, not to defend herself against a power so invincible. This deep humiliation and the sight of the olive branches they extended, moved the senate and people less than the speech of Cato, some fragments of which are still extant, for that worthy, more compassionate towards this people than he afterwards showed himself to that of Carthage, undertook their cause in the following able manner.[46] "I am very apprehensive, conscript fathers, lest intoxicated with our present great prosperity, we should be hurried into some resolutions that will in the end overthrow it. Let us not be too hasty, but take time to come to ourselves. I believe, indeed, that the Rhodians did wish that we had not conquered Perseus, and I believe also that many other states and nations wished the same. Some of them perhaps not out of ill will to us, but fear for themselves, lest there should be no power remaining left to check us, and keep us in awe, and we should become their absolute lords and masters.[47] Yet the Rhodians never openly assisted Perseus. Do but consider with how much more precaution we act with regard to our private affairs. There is not one of us who does not set himself to oppose, with all his might, whatever he thinks is against his own interest. Yet the Rhodians in like case were quiet and passive. Their bitterest accusers have not charged them with anything worse than an inclination to be our enemies. And is there any law that makes inclinations penal? Is there any one of us that would care to be subject to such a law? For my part I would not. Who has not wished to have more land than the laws allow? Yet nobody is punished for this. Does B.C. 167. any man think of rewarding another for having had an inclination to perform a good action which he did not perform. And shall we think of punishing the Rhodians because they are said to have had an inclination to do us some injury, which however they did not do? But it is said the Rhodians are proud. Be it so. What is that to us? Are we angry because there is in the world a people prouder than we are?"[48]

The sound reasoning of Cato delivered the Rhodians from the impending danger of a war with Rome, but not from spoliation. The senate declared, "That they would neither treat them as friends nor as enemies," yet they pronounced Lycia and Caria, provinces they had given to the Rhodians as a reward for their services in the Syrian war, free, and moreover obliged them to evacuate the cities of Caunus and Stratonicia, which they had bought of king Ptolemy's generals, and which produced a considerable revenue.[49] The dispirited Rhodians sent a magnificent golden crown as a present to the mighty republic, whose rapacious robberies they dared not resent, accompanied by an earnest petition for the honour of an alliance with Rome. The senate gave no definite answer to the embassy for two years, but they accepted the crown as a matter of course. This treatment was the more galling to the Rhodians as their policy had never before led them to seek alliance with the Romans, for their own maritime power had made their friendship courted by the neighbouring nations and their hatred dreaded by all.

Prusias, king of Bithynia, came to Rome in person to congratulate or rather to adore the senate, for he greeted them with the prostrations of a slave and the language of the most servile adulation. This was no more than might have been expected from a man who always met the ambassadors of the republic with the closely-shaven head and cap of a manumitted slave with this address, "You see one of your freedmen ready to obey all your commands and to conform himself to all your customs." The kisses he bestowed upon the threshold of the senate-house and the blasphemous salutation, "Hail senators my gods and saviours," from the lips of such a man might shock but could not surprise those to whom it was addressed. Polybius, the historian, asserts that the rest of the speech was answerable to the beginning, such indeed as the free-born Greek was ashamed to repeat, but it pleased the senate, and the low-minded and grasping prince obtained all he required. Scipio Nasica was deputed to attend him to Brundusium, where a fleet, the gift of the senate, was lying to conduct him home, even his expenses were paid to the coast. How the brave Roman must have loathed his mission and its object.[50]

The report that king Eumenes was come to Italy to pay a visit to Rome, displeased the senate who hated this prince, and yet did not wish to come to an open rupture with him. He was met by a quæstor with a decree, passed expressly for his benefit, forbidding all kings to enter Rome. This official was commissioned to enquire of the sovereign, "Whether he had anything to ask of the senate and people of Rome." Eumenes replied, "that he had not," whereupon the quæstor desired him, "to leave Italy immediately." Eumenes sailed for his own country that very night.[51] Innumerable complaints were made to the senate against king Eumenes. That monarch despatched his brothers Attalus and Athenæus to justify his conduct at Rome, where the royal ambassadors were favourably and even honourably received, though commissioners were sent to Asia and Pergamus to examine into the conduct of the king.

During the consulate of Tiberius Gracchus and M. Juventius Thalna, the death of Antiochus Epiphanes occurred. This prince was succeeded by his son Antiochus Eupator, a child of nine years of age, who was left under the care and guardianship of Lysias, a general who had carried on the war with Judea against the patriotic and heroic Judas Maccabeus, but having been defeated by him many times, was forced to grant the Jews a peace with the rights of civil and religious liberty for which they had so bravely contested.[52] This treaty was made in the year B.C. 163: and to secure its fulfilment, Maccabeus applied to the Roman ambassadors, Manlius and Memmius, who were upon their way to Antioch, who promised B.C. 163. him the protection of the mighty Roman republic.[53] This must have occurred A.U.C., 591, but made no figure in the annals of Rome, though it was the beginning of those events in Judea for which indeed this mighty empire alone was raised up, "that they might have their fulfilment in due season."

Demetrius, the son of Seleucus, the elder brother of Antiochus Epiphanes, entreated the senate to restore the Syrian monarchy to him, who was its rightful heir. They refused, intending to take advantage of the minority of the young prince to direct his affairs, and prevent Syria from being troublesome in future to Rome. They despatched Cneius Octavius and two others to assume the government, disable the elephants, and burn the decked ships, a commission the Roman officer found a fatal one, for he was murdered in the gymnasium of Laodicea by Leptines, who was supposed to be an emissary employed by Lysias, if indeed the act did not emanate from the outraged feelings of the people, who saw themselves deprived of the power of resisting the Romans.[54] Lysias sent an embassy to Rome to exonerate the king, but the senate took no notice of the justification; of course the sovereign, scarcely beyond the years of infancy, was innocent of the murder of the ambassador.

Demetrius, the rightful heir of Syria, judging the present crisis favourable for an attempt to recover the kingdom of which he had been unjustly deprived, sent for Polybius, the historian, with whom he had formed a friendship, and asked him, "Whether he had not better ask permission of the senate to return to his own country." The high-spirited and intrepid Greek counselled him by no means to strike his foot twice against the same stone, but to place his hope in himself and to dare something worthy of a king, for which the state of the Syrian affairs offered a suitable opportunity.[55] Demetrius did not at that time follow the wise and manly advice of Polybius. He embraced the course pointed out by a less eminent person. Apollonius another friend recommended him to solicit leave of the senate, for his Syrian expedition, and Demetrius received a second refusal. Still he was undecided how to act till Diodorus came from Syria and induced him to escape from Rome and return to his country. Polybius, through the agency of the Egyptian ambassador, procured him a passage in a Carthaginian vessel bound for Tyre. As Demetrius was supposed to be engaged in hunting, it was five days before his flight from Italy was known to the senate. That body took no steps to recover the fugitive, but despatched Sempronius Gracchus and two others to watch the prince's proceedings.

M. Valerius Messalla and C. Fannius Strabo, the consuls for this year, passed two remarkable laws. That called the Fannian was in favour of temperance, and limited the expenses of every man in his daily food and drink to ten asses, (or seven-pence three farthings). This is the earliest temperance movement upon record, but it was not a voluntary one, since the consul Fannius obtained his object by an act of legislature. It is possible that the sum, small as it appears to us, might have been a liberal allowance in that age.

Demetrius, whom we left on his Syrian voyage, landed in Lycia, from which place he wrote to the senate in a very deferential manner, declaring that he had no ill design against his young cousin Eupator, but that his object in going to Syria was the punishment of Lysias for the murder of Cneius Octavius.[56] The Syrian prince must have had either a poor opinion of the penetration of the august body he addressed or a great one of his own dissimulation, if he supposed credence could be given to the motives he assigned for his escape from Italy. He went by sea from Lycia to Tripolis in Syria, and boldly proclaimed to his countrymen that he came armed with the authority of the Roman senate to claim his birthright. The people already disaffected to the government of Lysias forsook their infant sovereign, Eupator, to gather round the standard of Demetrius. The soldiers delivered up the unfortunate child and his guardian to their rightful B.C. 161. lord, who ordered them both to be put to death.[57] Although Demetrius Soter had possessed himself of Syria by the general consent of the people,[58] he was well aware that without that of the Roman senate his chance of retaining the kingdom was small, he therefore entreated Tiberius Gracchus to mediate a peace for him with the senators, to whom he presented a magnificent golden crown by his ambassadors; he also delivered up the assassin of Octavius, and an orator who had praised his guilty act, to the vengeance of the Roman people. Leptines, the assassin, had offered himself a voluntary victim to save the Laodiceans from danger and punishment. It is probable that he had been actuated by mistaken motives of patriotism in his assassination of Octavius.[59] His behaviour was cheerful during the voyage, and he even declared that the mighty Roman republic would not stoop so low as to take the life of a man of low birth and station. The poor orator and grammarian had neither the firmness nor the foresight of his companion, whose guilty daring he had eulogised, his fear rendered him a maniac.[60] Leptines boldly avowed the deed and his confidence in the mercy of the senate. He was right, it did not suit the Roman government to receive such mean victims and the lives of both were spared. The senate accepted the golden crown sent by the Syrian monarch and promised him protection.

During the consulate of M. Cornelius Cethegus and L. Anicius Gallus the celebrated treaty between Judas Maccabeus on the part of the Jews and the Roman senate was made, whereby the land of Judea was declared free.[61] The fact is recorded in one of the sacred historical books that connects the broken links of the ecclesiastical chain, from the return of the captivity to the alliance between the Romans and the Jews. "Wherefore hast thou made thy yoke heavy upon our friends and confederates, the Jews. If therefore they complain any more against thee we will do them justice, and fight with thee by sea and by land."[62] Such is the epistle sent to Demetrius Soter by the senate of Rome in favour of the inconsiderable people, who had claimed the powerful protection of the republic. The revolted Syrian province, within whose narrow bounds were confined the knowledge of the one true God and the records of his revelation to man, was despised and scorned by the nations, "who sat in darkness and the shadow of death," and nearly two centuries elapsed before the light sprang up destined to bring salvation to the Gentiles, whose aid Maccabeus had sought.

Ariarathes, a prince of Cappadocia, came to Rome to solicit the senate to replace him upon the throne from whence he had been driven by Demetrius Soter, whose sister he had declined espousing. The king of Syria, as much out of avarice as revenge, had placed Holophernes, a supposititious son of the late Cappadocian monarch upon the throne, Holophernes having, it seemed, engaged to pay him one hundred talents for his assistance.[63] Ariarathes pleaded his own cause before the senate. The ambassadors of Holophernes defended their master. The Cappadocians affirmed that their sovereign and his brother were the genuine offspring of the king and queen of Cappadocia; but that the partiality of the mother for her youngest son, had induced her to discard both the elder princes. If the statement of the queen were true, it was natural that the supposititious children, who had been treated as her own for many years, should disbelieve her story, and consider themselves the victims of her excessive tenderness for their younger brother. In this curious case the senate fashioned their judgment according to their policy, by a pre-adoption of a well-known maxim of Machiavelli, "Divide and rule," by which they parted Cappadocia between the rival competitors, not doubting to find their advantage in the division before long.

Cato, the censor, was sent into Africa at the head of a deputation to decide upon the rival claims of Carthage and Masinissa to Emporia, and to a tract of country on the river Tusca. It seems that the wily Numidian, certain by past experience of the good-will of the Romans, was very desirous of the arbitration of their commissioners.[64] Not so the Carthaginians; who, knowing the national antipathy between them and their arbitrators, civilly declined their mediation, declaring "That the B.C. 160. treaty concluded with Scipio Africanus did not want amending; and that nothing more was requisite than that each party should strictly observe the articles of that convention."

Cato brought back from Africa a burning hatred to the African republic. Its political importance was gone for ever; its only power was in its riches; a power that tempted its enemies, and exposed it to the attacks of those who wielded a stronger sword. That wealth appeared to the stern Roman inexhaustible; and he concluded an oration to the senate of Rome, in which he counselled the destruction of Carthage by displaying some fine figs he had brought from Africa, with this brief remark, "The country where this fine fruit grows is but three days' voyage from Rome."[65] From that time Cato never made a speech in the senate-house without concluding it with this uncharitable sentence, whatever the subject might be, "I am also of opinion that Carthage should be destroyed."[66] Scipio Nasica, on the contrary, finished his orations with the same words, accompanied by a negative, "I am of opinion that Carthage ought not to be destroyed."[67] Doubtless the senators must have been highly amused at the contest between these two great men, though Scipio's sentiment emanated from better feelings and more merciful policy than that of Cato.

Two curious laws, the Ælian and Fufian were passed, which indirectly set some limitation to the power of the people. The first forbad the transaction of any business with them upon days or at hours when the augurs and magistrates were observing the heavens, or taking the auspices. The second prohibited this upon dies fasti, or days on which the prætors sat to hear causes, and the courts were open. Cicero styled "these laws the walls of peace and tranquillity."[68]

The Romans extended their foreign conquests to Dalmatia. The Dalmatians had invaded Illyricum, and insulted the Roman ambassadors; but Polybius believes that the Romans made a pretext for the Dalmatian war, to enlarge their territory and afford their soldiers martial exercise.[69]

The sophistry of the Athenian ambassadors, who were all philosophers of different schools, excited the indignation of Cato, who hated philosophy, and called Socrates a babbler. He considered the Roman youth undone if these strangers were suffered to remain; and entreated the senate to settle the dispute between the Athenians and Sicyonians as quickly as possible, lest the manners of the Roman youth should be corrupted from the stern simplicity of their forefathers.[70] Of Carneades, the Academic philosopher, one of these envoys, Cicero spoke in praise, affirming of him, "That he never advanced anything that he did not prove, nor ever opposed an argument that he did not overthrow."[71] No wonder the young Romans of that day were anxious to study eloquence under such a master, and flocked daily to hear him and his gifted brethren. The senate remitted a part of the fine that the Sicyonians had imposed upon the Athenians, in order to hasten the departure of the illustrious strangers.

King Eumenes was dead and his young son Attalus was under the guardianship and regency of his uncle Attalus, when Prusias, king of Bithynia, invaded the dominions of the minor, notwithstanding the remonstrances of the ambassadors despatched from "his gods and saviours," the Roman senate, to put a stop to his aggressions upon the territories of their youthful ally. The threat of a war with Rome and all the nations in league with her, obliged Prusias not only to desist, but to give Attalus twenty ships. He also engaged to pay him five hundred talents in twenty years by way of compensation for the injury he had done him.[72] The Roman armies passed the Alps to recover the towns of Nicæa (Nice) and Antipolis (Antibes) for the people of Marseilles or Massilia, which the Oxybians and Deciatans, originally Ligurians, had taken from them. The invaded people entreated the Roman consul to aid them, who defeated their enemies and restored their towns.[73]

Ptolemy Philometor came to Rome to complain of his brother Physcon, by whom he had been driven from his throne.[74] The senate settled the quarrel in their usual manner, by dividing the Egyptian dominions between the disputants. B.C. 155. To Philometor they adjudged Egypt, to Physcon Cyrenaica. The younger prince came to Rome to petition for the island of Cyprus in addition to what had been already granted to him.[75] The senate, gave the petitioner the investiture of the island, of which commissioners from Rome were to put him in possession. The decree was not only opposed by Philometor but by the people of Cyrenaica themselves, who took arms against their new lord, whom they defeated in battle. Soon after this defeat an attempt was made by the Cyrenians to assassinate Physcon, upon which this prince came to Rome to display his wounds and charge the crime upon Philometor, whose fraternal feelings had led him often to pardon his wicked and unnatural brother. The senate, to their disgrace, took the part of this monster, whose atrocities have placed him at the head of all the tyrants of antiquity, and ordered their Asiatic and Grecian allies to assist him against his virtuous brother, and to put him in possession of Cyprus.[76] Notwithstanding their favour Philometor defeated and took his brother prisoner, but with his usual generosity, gave him a compensation in lieu of Cyprus, set him at liberty, and promised him his daughter in marriage. The Romans did not interfere in this arrangement. It is probable that they were weary or ashamed of their ally.

A tribune of the people, L. Cotta, this year endeavoured to evade the payment of his debts, because his office rendered his person sacred. The fraudulent attempt disgusted the whole tribunitial college, who announced their intention to him of buying up his debts and becoming his creditors, which obliged Cotta to abandon his dishonest design.

The young king of Pergamus and the son of Demetrius Soter chose to visit Rome. The Syrian prince was displeased with his reception and returned home in haste. It is probable that the presence of Heracleides with Alexander Balas in the metropolis might be the cause of his abrupt departure. This Balas was an impostor set up by Heracleides as a son of Antiochus Epiphanes, out of revenge for his expulsion by Demetrius Soter. His claim was supported by Laodice, the daughter of Epiphanes, and by all the Asiatic princes, who were jealous of

Demetrius. The Romans also acknowledged him for the son of Epiphanes, and issued a decree in his favour. The Syrian monarch was slain in battle while defending his dominions which were invaded by Alexander Balas with troops furnished by the allies of Rome from Egypt, Pergamus, Cappadocia, and Judea.[77] The impostor ascended the throne of Syria, and his medals are still to be found in the cabinet of the curious collector in attestation of his successful fraud, which had been supported by the senate, for Rome had already become the arbitress of the destinies of the world, the mighty power that, kingless, made and unmade kings.

Rome, though still at peace with Carthage, had no intention of permitting her fallen rival to remain in existence; either as a dependent state or even as a province like Macedonia, she aimed to crush, annihilate, and destroy the people who had invaded Italy and carried a desolating war to her very gates. To assist them in their meditated work of destruction king Masinissa was always at hand. This prince, an able warrior and unscrupulous politician, had many partisans, even in Carthage, who advised their fellow citizens to submit to all his extortions and aggressions rather than come to an open rupture with this formidable warrior. These persons, amounting to forty in number, were banished with some justice by the Carthaginian senate who distrusted them.[78] The exiles repaired to the court of Masinissa, who sent them under the care of his sons, Micipsa and Gulussa, to Carthage, in order to demand their recall. This was not only refused but Gulussa was waylaid on his return, and some of his attendants were slain. Masinissa immediately laid siege to Oroscapa, a town belonging to the Carthaginians, with a great army. Hasdrubal was sent against the king with a large force when the battle took place, of which Scipio was the delighted spectator,[79] he having lately come from Spain to procure elephants for the consul Lucullus for the Roman war in that country. The B.C. 154. warlike Numidian soon afterwards invested the Carthaginian camp, and obliged his enemies to pass under the yoke unarmed, the only alternative allowed them by the conqueror. Nor was this the worst, for the exiled traitors were restored, and a heavy fine was laid upon the Carthaginian state. Gulussa, mindful of the attempt made upon him by the Carthaginians, despatched a troop of horse after the unarmed military multitude, and took such a cruel revenge that few returned to Carthage to publish there the tale of their disgrace. The Romans took advantage of this dreadful reverse, to commence the exterminating war they had long meditated against Carthage. A pretence was wanting, but as the Romans were determined upon the destruction of Carthage, they found several unexceptionable ones. According to their account, the death-doomed Carthaginian people had attacked their ally, Masinissa, in a most unjust and causeless manner; they had refused Gulussa admittance within their gates, although he had Roman ambassadors with him; they had also equipped a fleet, and raised troops, contrary to the purport of their last treaty with Rome, and that to injure a faithful ally of Rome.[80] Before these reasons for war with Carthage had been published by the senate, the astute Carthaginians, who had divined them, ordered a herald to declare Hasdrubal and his officers traitors to the state for having opposed king Masinissa. After this farce they sent an embassy to Rome to extenuate their conduct, and to implore the clemency of the senate. The Delphic oracle was not more enigmatical, nor more unwilling to give a direct answer to a plain question, than the national council of Rome. All that the puzzled ambassadors could learn was, that "Rome must be satisfied." Another embassy was despatched from Carthage to ask the "means by which Rome was to be satisfied." To which the senate replied, "That the Carthaginians knew very well." The people of Utica, better skilled it should seem in this diplomatic language than the Carthaginian senate, made an absolute surrender of themselves and their city to the Romans; thus providing them with a useful port for their ships. Their submission was graciously accepted.[81] An immense armament was prepared for the Carthaginian war, under the command of the consuls, L. Marcius Censorinus and M. Manilius Nepos. The former was to direct the operations of the fleet; the latter of the army, which consisted of 80,000 foot and 4000 horse.[82] The fleet sailed for Sicily, but remained at Lilybæum waiting for final orders from the senate. These preparations alarmed the Carthaginians, and a third embassy was sent to Rome with offers of unconditional submission on the part of that unfortunate people. The Roman senate accepted them; but demanded three hundred of their noblest youth as hostages for their performance of the unknown conditions about to be imposed upon them.[83] When those who brought the hostages to Lilybæum, desired to hear the terms of the peace between Rome and Carthage, the consuls replied, "That the pleasure of the senate would be told the Carthaginians at Utica," for which port the fleet was ready to sail. The arrival of the fleet and armament at Utica astounded the Carthaginians, and the senate of Carthage despatched ambassadors to the consuls' camp to enquire, "Why they were invaded after they had sent the hostages, and expressed their willingness to submit to the conditions proposed by the Roman republic."[84] Censorinus might have said, "By the right of the strongest;" but he merely replied, "We told you in Sicily that you should know our pleasure at Utica. You must give up all your arms, for if you sincerely desire peace what occasion can you have for them?" The ambassadors reminded the consuls that Hasdrubal, whom they had banished, was at the head of an army of 20,000 men, and that Carthage would be wholly at his mercy if he chose to revenge upon her, when unarmed, the sentence of death the senate had passed upon him. "Against that danger the senate and people of Rome will B.C. 149. provide," replied Censorinus.[85] The Carthaginian people had the weakness to comply with a command, that left them without national honour or defence.[86] They delivered up their arms and war engines, which were sent to the Roman camp without delay. A train of priests and senators followed the waggons that consigned to implacable enemies the weapons they ought to have wielded to repel their invasion.

Censorinus received the deputation seated upon his tribunal.[87] He praised their obedience, but entreated them to bear with fortitude the recital of the decree of the Roman senate. "Yield up your city to us, and transplant yourselves to any part of your own country that may suit you; provided it be ten miles distance from the sea, for we are determined to demolish Carthage."[88]

This announcement filled the ambassadors with astonishment, rage and despair. They uttered loud cries, rent their garments, and tore their own flesh, reviled the Roman senate, consuls, and people, and finally, overcome by their own feelings, fell prostrate upon the earth half-dead. To these unbridled passions the Roman consul opposed an iron calmness that no distress could move, nor did his colleague display more feeling. "They waited," remarks Appian, "till the storm was over, knowing that mighty calamities at first create in those who are struck by them a boldness which necessity subdues, and thus it happened to these Carthaginians, who soon condescended to use arguments and entreaties." Hanno Gillas besought humbly "that the Carthaginian nation might be permitted to send an embassy to Rome before the sentence was executed upon their city." This was haughtily and peremptorily refused. "Begone," replied the consuls, "hitherto we have considered you as ambassadors." Upon the lictors approaching to expel them from the camp, these men suddenly displayed the baseness of their minds. They dared not carry the decision of the Roman senate to Carthage unless shielded by the mighty power of Rome. They entreated the consul to send a fleet thither, that their fellow citizens might receive the fiat of the senate from the Romans, and not from themselves alone.[89] Where was the lofty spirit of Hannibal, where was the pride of the people who had conquered Italy and advanced their standard to the gates of Rome? There was nothing in these senators but that base love of money and engrossing selfishness for which Hannibal had formerly reproached them. Censorinus complied with their entreaties; twenty ships drew near the coast while the Carthaginians returned to spread dismay and indignation through the betrayed city. In silence they reached the senate-house, returning no answer to the anxious crowds who thronged about the doors. One at length announced the decree of the Roman senate to the rest of the Carthaginian senators. He was answered by a loud cry which was echoed by those without, from whence it was borne along and prolonged throughout the city in one deep wail of national woe. But the spirit of the people awoke. They reproached their pusillanimous rulers for having left them without arms. Parents bewailed their children, torn from them to purchase a delusive peace, and execrated Roman treachery. "War, war!" was the general cry, and preparations for resistance were instantly made. Stones were gathered up in heaps for defence, till new arms could be made. Men, women, and children laboured night and day in the workshops, and the women cut off their long hair to serve as ropes for the war engines.[90] These labours, that national spirit, if exerted before the invaders had set a step upon the shores of Africa, would have saved the people who, more patriotic than their rulers, were prepared to defend their hearths and altars to the last.[91] The banished Hasdrubal was recalled with his army to defend his country without, while another Hasdrubal, the son of a daughter of Masinissa by a Carthaginian, was to command the forces within the city.[92] The Roman consuls who considered the place already won made no haste to invest it. Masinissa, having no intention of conquering Carthage for the Romans, answered their request for aid by remarking "that he should send it when it was needed." When this prince offered his assistance, the consuls haughtily replied, "That when they wanted his help they would ask for it."[93]

Censorinus, who had commenced the siege, was driven back when he attempted to enter the breach he had B.C. 149. opened in the walls; and but for the bravery of the legionary tribune, Scipio Æmilianus, who covered his retreat, would have been defeated with loss. The Carthaginians destroyed a great part of the Roman fleet by firing their old ships, and letting them drive with the wind among those of the enemy. Nor was Manilius more fortunate against Hasdrubal in the field; for this consul was compelled to retreat, and owed his own safety, and that of the Roman legions, to the courage and forecast of Scipio Æmilianus, who with three hundred horsemen covered his retreat. Censorinus returned to Rome to hold the election for the new consuls, without having performed any service to the republic, except the treacherous part allotted to him by the senate, whose willing agent he had been. The choice of the Romans fell upon Sp. Posthumius Magnus and L. Calpurnius Piso Cæsonius. To this last the conduct of the African war fell by lot. Manilius remained in that country with the title of pro-consul. The death of Masinissa deprived the Romans of an ally and the Carthaginians of an enemy.[94] He was ninety years old at the time of his decease, and had experienced more bad and good fortune than any prince of his time.[95] Himilco Phamæas, the general of Hasdrubal's cavalry, basely deserted to the Romans with two thousand two hundred horse. He pretended that his treason to his country arose from his esteem for Scipio Æmilianus.[96] Neither the consul Calpurnius, nor the pro-consul, Manilius, did anything remarkable in Africa. Their military operations were confined to unsuccessful attacks upon Clypea and Hypogreta, cities on the coast; and they took up their winter quarters at Utica, without effecting a single object they had undertaken. The Carthaginians requested aid of many nations, and even sent to demand it from Macedonia, where an impostor, calling himself Philip, the son of Perseus, had usurped the authority of a king.[97] Disappointed in her commanders in Africa, Rome turned her eyes upon Scipio Æmilianus, whose bravery and good conduct had drawn praise even from Cato the censor, who had applied to him and the consuls, a line from Homer's Odyssey, "He alone has understanding, the rest are shadows." From his seventeenth year, when he made his first campaign in Macedonia under his father, the life of the younger son of Æmilius Paulus had been passed in war. His love of glory once led to a curious conversation between himself and the historian, Polybius, who, being a friend of his family, was often in his father's house at Rome. On one of these occasions, when they were alone together, Scipio said to the illustrious Greek, "What is the reason, Polybius, that in conversation you always address your discourse to my brother Fabius, without taking any notice of me? I am afraid that you have the same opinion of me as the citizens have, who think me slow and indolent, and averse to Roman customs, because I do not apply myself to pleading causes. They say that the family from which I am descended requires a different sort of representative to what I am, and this gives me great uneasiness." Polybius, surprised at this discourse from a youth of seventeen, assured him that he addressed Fabius as the elder, not out of any disrespect for him; and begged him, by all the gods, not to entertain such a suspicion, as he was certain both the sons of Æmilius Paulus had sentiments and opinions in common. The historian then promised to aid him in his search after fame, remarking "that it was highly commendable in a young man descended from such a family to consider indolence as a crime. As for the studies you and your brother are engaged in, you can never want preceptors while Greece sends so many to Rome. But in regard to the object you have most at heart, you will not find a more fitting companion or instructor than myself."[98] At these words of Polybius, Scipio took him by the hand, which he pressed affectionately, saying "I wish I might see the day when, neglecting all other things, you would come and live with me, and make me your principal care. Then I should think myself not unworthy of my ancestors."[99] From that day Polybius never quitted him, and a friendship, close as that between a father and son, subsisted between them. Scipio's affection for his mother, Papiria, the divorced wife of Æmilius Paulus, and great liberality to her, gained him the esteem of his fellow B.C. 148. citizens; for he bestowed upon her the splendid wardrobe, jewels, and equipages of his deceased aunt Æmilia, the widow of the great Scipio, whose heir he was.[100] Filial love was still a Roman virtue, and those who had seen the deserted wife, poor and despised, admired the generosity of her affectionate son. Nor was he less bountiful to his female cousins, the daughters of Scipio Africanus, half of whose portions were still unpaid. This duty devolved upon Æmilius' heir, and he augmented it from twenty to five-and-twenty talents each; paying the money two years before it was legally due, to the surprise of their husbands Scipio Nasica and Tiberius Gracchus. He relinquished to his brother, Fabius, the whole of the inheritance of Æmilius Paulus, that he might be as rich as himself.

The people at this juncture remembered these things, and not only made him consul but assigned him Africa for his province; to the displeasure of his colleague, Livius Drusus, and of the senate. For he was not of the age required by law, nor had he held any of the higher magistracies, which were necessary steps. Cato, upon his death-bed, had earnestly recommended Scipio Æmilianus to his countrymen, as the only man capable of that work of destruction he had so long advocated. He did not live to see the success of his advice; but the people, who loved this popular censor, proved that they remembered it by their adoption of his counsel. From Utica the young consul hurried with his levies to save Mancinus, whom he found posted upon a rock, from whence he could not retreat after his unsuccessful attack upon the city. He was destitute of food when the skill and bravery of Scipio was exerted successfully to deliver him.[101] Scipio's first care was to restore the discipline of the Roman army before he ventured to attack the doomed city, for heretofore pillage not the siege of Carthage had been the object of the soldiers, who dividing themselves into predatory bands roamed through the country in search of plunder. The Carthaginians, always cruel and suspicious, put to death their governor, that Hasdrubal whose descent from king Masinissa formed his only crime. He was accused of treasonable practices by his namesake, the commander-in-chief. The assassination of this unfortunate man in the senate-house proves the weakness and treachery of that degraded assembly. Scipio made himself master of the Isthmus and built a wall twelve feet in height, which crossing it from sea to sea cut off the supplies of Carthage in that direction. He also raised a vast mole at the mouth of the port. A new passage to the sea was however opened by the besieged, who were in danger of starvation. They built and equipped a fleet of fifty galleys, which they sent against the Romans. As the particulars of this battle are not distinctly known it could not have led to any remarkable results on either side, but a great victory gained by Scipio before he took up his winter quarters left Carthage nothing but her walls and her famishing population.[102] Hasdrubal tried to engage king Gulussa as a mediator between the Romans and the Carthaginians at this dangerous crisis. "He was willing," he told that monarch, "to submit to any conditions provided the city was spared." "You talk childishly," replied Gulussa, "when you demand the same terms that the Roman senate refused before the city was invested." Hasdrubal declared, "that the situation of Carthage was not yet desperate, that he confided in the assistance of the immortal gods, for whose sake and for the sake of piety to them," he added, "I entreat by you the consul to spare the city."[103] Scipio, we are told by Polybius, smiled at this appeal to his piety and pity, from a man stained with the blood of the Roman prisoners, whom he had put to death by torture. He, however, sent the king with an offer of life and liberty to the Carthaginian general to be extended to any ten families of friends he might choose to name, together with six slaves and ten talents for himself, provided he would submit.[104] Hasdrubal replied, "The day will never come when the sun shall see Carthage destroyed and Hasdrubal alive." Unfortunately for the patriotism of Hasdrubal this noble reply was but an empty boast. Carthage did not fall till the consulship of C. Cornelius Lentulus and L. B.C. 147. Mummius, when Scipio, who was continued in the command of the consular army in Africa, prosecuted the siege with vigour.[105] He carried the wall on the side of the port and forced his way into the great square of the city, where he remained till the following night. He could not invest the citadel till the streets were destroyed which led to it. The houses being manned and fortified allowed no approach to the Romans.[106] By the command of Scipio they were fired, and the last catastrophe of this mighty city presents a harrowing picture, the description of which could only give pain to the reader. During six days of toil and slaughter,[107] Scipio never closed his eyes, but towards the consummation of the tragedy he seated himself upon an eminence that overlooked the fallen city and with tears in his eyes recited those lines from Homer where Hector foretells the destruction of Troy. The tears said to be shed by conquerors must certainly flow from some feelings unconnected with pity. When Scipio fired the city he knew the excess of human misery that mandate must cause. He spoke to Polybius, who was near him, of the rise and fall of empires, and his fears lest Rome should one day "suffer the same fate."[108] He feared, perhaps even in that hour of triumph, that a retributive and avenging power existed to destroy the queen of the earth, the scourge and ruler of all nations. The citadel submitted and obtained mercy; fifty thousand men and women, miserable in attire and woeful in mien, came forth to slavery. The Roman deserters, to whom this doubtful clemency could not be extended, defended themselves in the temple of Æsculapius. They were headed by Hasdrubal, whose wife and children were sheltered in this last stronghold of their country. Famine was within and war without, yet the rock-based fane was still capable of resistance. Hasdrubal stole out with an olive branch in his hand and cast himself upon the conqueror's mercy. The sun shone upon the flames of Carthage, and he was living a fugitive and a slave. The pro-consul seated the Carthaginian general at his feet and drew the attention of the deserters to him, but they only cursed and derided the man who had given himself up to the destroyer of Carthage. Firm to the last they fired the temple, resolving to perish rather than fall alive into the hands of Scipio. The wife of Hasdrubal, adorned with the splendour suited to her former station, appeared on the roof of the temple with her children in her arms, from whence she addressed the pro-consul, whom she entreated to punish her degenerate husband for preferring a life of slavery to an honourable death. Then turning to Hasdrubal she vehemently and passionately reproached him, who was destined to adorn the triumph of the conqueror, telling him that the flames which were then about to destroy her and his children were better than the shame and ignominy of the fate he had chosen. After cutting the throats of her children to save them from a more painful death, she cast herself and these unfortunate infants into the flames. This suicidal action, fierce and unfeminine as it was, sprang from a stern patriotism, that claimed and won the admiration of the Romans. The last act was worthy of the tragedy of Carthage. It was characteristic of the ardent temperament of the people, which civilisation had never softened and that ruin could not tame.[109] Scipio gave the plunder of this great commercial city to his soldiers, reserving the gold and silver and the offerings found in the temples for the use of the state. The senate, to whom he announced his conquest, ordered him to conclude the demolition of the city.[110] He obeyed the mandate and publicly thanked the gods for his success. Such of the deserters as fell into his hands were exhibited in the games he gave in honour of the deities. They were torn to pieces by wild beasts, a terrible pastime that soon became prevalent throughout the vast Roman empire.[111] A magnificent triumph was awarded to the conqueror at Rome. He also received the name of Africanus, but Scipio the younger is the appellation by which he is distinguished in history. Ninety-seven thousand Carthaginians were sold for slaves, and Carthage was no more. The corruption of the morals and manners of the republic of Rome take their date from this period. B.C. 146. "The elder Scipio," says Velleius Paterculus, "opened a way to the power of the Romans, the younger a road to their luxury. For when the fear of Carthage, that rival of Rome, was totally removed, the Romans did not gradually depart from virtue but ran precipitately into vice." The destruction of Carthage did not satisfy the ambition of Rome. Greece was destined to swell the conquests of the invincible republic; Greece that had tamed the pride of the Persian—Greece from which Rome had received a code of laws—Greece the mother of arts and civilisation. Intestine divisions, the bane of all states, but the ruin of small independent ones, brought the Romans and Greeks into a contest, which ended in the subversion of the weaker people.

The Lacedæmonians, never firm members of the Achæan league, fell out with the states composing it about rights and privileges; who, in their turn, were not backward in enforcing their own, at a moment when a close union of interests ought to have bound them together, if they wished to retain their nationality, and avoid the degradation of becoming a province of Rome. They could scarcely hope to cope with the gigantic power that had over-shadowed them with her doubtful protection. Their safety consisted in a steady adherence to each other. This was abandoned for petty views and trifling self-interested questions; and

Greece, like a broken phalanx, lost her strength and capability of defence. Both parties applied to Rome to settle their disputes. Aurelius Orestes was commissioned by the senate for this purpose; but before he could arrive, Damocritus, the general of Achaia and the league, had settled the affair with the sword, and beaten the Lacedæmonians in the field.[112] Metellus, the pro-consul in Macedonia, had vainly endeavoured to dissuade the Achæans from this rash enterprise, for Damocritus would not receive his advice. His successor in the prætorship of Achaia, Diæus, less headstrong, concluded a truce before the arrival of the arbiter, Orestes, and his colleagues at Corinth. These commissioners immediately convened the Achæan assembly, and declared the will of the senate of Rome; which announced that Sparta, Corinth, Argos, Heracleia, near Mount Œta, and Orchomenus in Arcadia, not being anciently of the Achæan body, should now be separated from it, and become free and independent states. The Achæans saw in this declaration the death-blow of their liberty. The multitude, always swayed by feeling rather than reason, did not wait for the decision of their representatives; they insulted the commissioners, and took from beneath the asylum of their own roofs those persons who were supposed to be averse to the league. Sextus Julius was immediately sent from Rome (where Aurelius Orestes had duly reported the insulting behaviour of the Corinthians) to complain of their misconduct, and declare the willingness of the senate to pardon it, if their decree were respected and obeyed. As Carthage was not then taken and the Roman republic had a war in Spain to maintain, Diæus and Critolaus both considered this moderation to be caused by fear. That it arose from policy there can be little doubt, when we consider the position in which Rome was placed at this time. Critolaus, who was again prætor of Achaia, promised, on the part of the Achæans, to send ambassadors to Rome to apologise for the misconduct of the multitude. He also appointed a meeting to be held at Tegea, for the final adjustment of the Lacedæmonian affairs. Julius Sextus agreed to meet the states composing the league at that place, and quitted Ægium, where the assembly was held, without suspecting that Critolaus was imposing upon him. Upon the day appointed he attended the assembly at Tegea, where he only found Critolaus, who stated that he could conclude no business without the concurrence of his nation, as this was not a general meeting; but that the great assembly would be held six months from that time, when the matter might be reported and considered. Sextus Julius in disgust returned to Rome.[113] Critolaus, under false pretences, passed from city to city to inflame the Greeks against the Romans, and to engage them in the war against Sparta. He induced the magistrates to suspend all prosecutions for debt during that period, a measure that rendered the war very popular.

Metellus, the pro-consul of Macedonia, sent four B.C. 146. Romans of rank to the general meeting at Corinth, to effect a peace if possible; "but," says Polybius, "the Achæans were at this time out of their senses, especially the Corinthians." The deputies sent by Metellus were insulted and expelled from the assembly with great rudeness, and the war against Sparta was openly declared. Thebes and Chalcis joined the league, "for if Critolaus and the Achæans were mad, they found other states as mad as themselves." Metellus not wishing at this juncture to push matters to extremity, sent again to the Achæans to assure them of forgiveness, if they would consent to the dismemberment of Sparta and the other states formerly named by the Romans. This proposal was rashly rejected by the assembly.[114]

By Thessaly, Metellus marched to Scarpheia, in Locris, at which place he gave the Achæans an overthrow and took many prisoners. Critolaus was either drowned by accident, or committed suicide after the lost battle. Diæus succeeded to his command, and enrolled the slaves (whom he manumitted on this occasion) in his army.[115] Metellus marched to Thebes, which was nearly deserted, its inhabitants having fled at his approach. Here he behaved with lenity, and restrained his soldiers from rifling the temples, robbing the houses, or slaying the people. He put Pythias, the chief magistrate, to death as the author of the revolt, the only instance of severity given by him in Thebes. The Roman pro-consul then marched to Corinth, and still disposed to treat with the Greeks, sent three principal persons of Achaia to persuade them to accept his terms of peace, which did not vary from those originally proposed by him. The sight of a Roman army under their walls inclined the Corinthians to listen to them, till Diæus and his powerful faction over-ruled them. He brought matters at once to a crisis by imprisoning the deputies. The bribe of a talent, however, effected their liberation; for Diæus' patriotism was not of a genuine character, it could stoop to corruption.

The consul Mummius, a man of a different order from the brave and clement Metellus, marched to Corinth to take the conduct of the Achæan war. "Metellus fought," remarks Florus, "and Mummius came to the victory."[116] The pro-consul returned to Macedonia, and left the imprudent Corinthians to their fate. The Romans of the advanced guard were repulsed by the besieged headed by Diæus with great loss, but this advantage only accelerated their ruin; for their leader, rendered rash by this success, gave the legions of Mummius battle just at the entrance of the isthmus, and was totally defeated.[117] He made no attempt to retreat into Corinth, a city strong by nature and possessing a citadel, that, with an able commander, would have defied for years even the arms of Rome; but fled precipitately to his native city, Megalopolis, where he killed his wife that she might not adorn a Roman triumph, poisoned himself, and setting fire to his house mingled the ashes of his family with those of his hearth.[118] This domestic tragedy was followed by that of Corinth. The consul Mummius marched through its gates, which he found open and undefended, for the city was nearly deserted by its inhabitants; women, children, and feeble old men, incapable of offering resistance, alone met the consul's sight. The first he preserved for the woes of slavery, the men were indiscriminately put to the sword. The place was then plundered of its gold, silver, paintings and statues; after which spoliation it was fired by the order of Mummius and reduced to ashes.[119] The walls of Corinth were beaten down, and the lands of the Corinthians given to the Sicyonians. Achaia was declared a Roman province, and had a prætor assigned it from Rome. Mummius got into his own possession those inhabitants who had abandoned the city undefended to his rage, as well as those soldiers who had fled from his victorious legions. These he sold for slaves.[120] The cities of Thebes and Chalcis, which had been spared by Metellus, a braver and more merciful commander, were plundered B.C. 146. and ravaged by the order of the consul, and popular governments were abolished throughout the Grecian cities. Greece was a province of the Roman empire. This severity of Mummius has always been considered odious. His name was execrated in Greece then, and it is detested still by those who read it in her annals.

To Polybius, the historian, was assigned the humiliating office of making the enslaved Grecian cities acquainted with the laws imposed upon them by the conquerors. We are told that the uprightness of his character, and the benevolence of his disposition rendered him a fitting person for this employment. The selection suited the subtle policy of the senate, as a Greek agent would be more acceptable to the vanquished people than a foreigner and a Roman. The event justified their choice. A pure and disinterested motive alone influenced Polybius. Statues were erected to their brave and wise countryman in every city, by the grateful Greeks, with this inscription: "Greece would not have erred if from the beginning she had followed the counsels of Polybius, and when through error she came to need assistance, she found it in him."

Nothing surprised the accomplished historian who possessed that refined taste and critical judgment in the fine arts for which his countrymen were distinguished beyond all the nations of the earth, more than the ignorance of Mummius as to the value of Grecian painting and sculpture. He saw rude soldiers throwing dice upon the famous Bacchus of Aristides, supposed to have been one of the finest paintings in the world.[121]

The plunderer of Corinth did not enrich his family, he was unable to portion his daughter, and gained little beyond a triumph, the execration of Greece, and the surname of Achaicus. He seems to have been actuated by pure destructiveness, which he considered a duty. Metellus had the name of Macedonicus, and a triumph awarded him for quelling the revolt in Macedon.

It has been necessary to omit the history of the Roman government in Spain, in order to present unbroken narratives of the third Punic war, and of that between the Romans and the Achæan League. We must therefore return to that period when Cato, the censor, left Hither and Further Spain in perfect tranquillity in the beginning of the sixth century. His successor, Scipio Nasica, took many towns in Further Spain, as the Roman province which lay between the mouth of the Iberus to Gades (Gibraltar) was called, while that lying between the Iberus and the Pyrenees was denominated Hither Spain. The restless nature of the haughty natives made the Romans unable to maintain their dominion over them without incessant war. Scipio Nasica defended the Further Province with success against the Lusitanians, who had invaded and plundered it, taking from them their booty near Silpa. His successors, Fulvius Nobilior and Æmilius Paulus, for several years kept advancing north of the Tagus, and Postumius Albinus, A.U.C. 574, A.D. 180, effected the conquest of Lusitania. Continual wars, nevertheless, were carried on in Spain, for the allies of the Romans were converted often into enemies, and even their feuds with each other frequently ended in a war with their nominal conquerors.[122] Before the subjugation of Lusitania, when C. Flaminius Nepos, in the Hither Province, took some cities on the borders of Celtiberia, that nation immediately declared war with the Romans, and being

390

joined by the Lusitanians, defeated the prætors of both provinces on the banks of the Tagus, but two years afterwards were routed by the same Roman commanders, who for a short time restored the province to tranquillity. Celtiberian Spain was, however, in open revolt, till reduced into obedience by the pro-prætor Flaccus. The prætor Tiberius Sempronius Gracchus was forced to take the field against the Celtiberians the following year. A curious anecdote is related of his war with this people. He surprised Munda, after which he invested Certima, when he received a message from the besieged assuring him they would come out and fight with the Romans if they were sufficiently numerous, but that some of their countrymen were encamped in the neighbourhood, with whose help they could face him, if he would give them permission to pass his lines. Gracchus gave the safe-conduct they required, to this single-hearted people.[123] After a time they returned to the Roman camp with ten deputies from their allies. These strangers asked for drink. It was in the heat of the day, and they were B.C. 146. thirsty. We are not told what beverage was brought forward upon this occasion, but as they demanded more it probably was something more to their taste than water. "We are sent by our nation," remarked the eldest deputy, "to ask upon what you depend since you carry war into this country." The simplicity of the question amused the Roman general, who replied with equal plainness, "Upon a good army, which if you please you shall see." The sight of the legions satisfied the deputies of the impolicy of assisting the beleaguered town of Certima, which surrendered to the Romans the same day.[124]

These Celtiberians were determined to fight Gracchus and defend their own liberty, though they had resolved to run no risk for their neighbours of Certima. Gracchus defeated them in the field, and took Alce, their capital city, as well as one hundred and three towns (or castles according to some authors) in a few days. Things after this remained quiet in Hither Spain till the Lusitanian war. In Further Spain the prætor Calpurnius Piso was defeated by the Lusitanians, and the following year L. Mummius also lost a battle, but covered his misfortune by several victories over the same people. This Mummius was the same who afterwards, when consul, destroyed Corinth. The same year the Celtiberian war commenced, which arose from a dispute with the city of Segeda, on the part of the Romans, who ordered the inhabitants to discontinue some enlargements and improvements to their town, which they were walling round preparatory to receiving an increase of inhabitants from another district. The Romans considered this an infraction of a treaty they had formerly made with Gracchus. This the people of Segeda denied, declaring that the agreement forbade them to build new towns, not to repair old ones.[125] As to the demand made by the Romans for auxiliary soldiers and tribute money, they proved that they had been long exempted from such levies, which it seems was true. They went on with their wall in defiance of the Roman prætor till the coming of the consul, T. Fulvius Nobilior, obliged them to leave it unfinished and take refuge with the Arevacians, a Celtiberian nation, whose capital city was called Numantia, at the head of the Durius. Carus, a brave man of Segeda, laid an ambush for the Roman consul, whom he defeated, but being carried too far by the heat of the pursuit lost his life, and with it four thousand men, who were charged and slain by the

Roman cavalry having the care of the baggage.[126] Near Numantia, the Celtiberians made head again, and were upon the point of defeat, being unused to the elephants in the Roman army, when one of these huge beasts being wounded, faced about, and attacked in his frantic rage the Roman legions, all the other elephants joined him in this work of blind destruction, and the consular army was defeated with great loss. The revolt of Ocilis, a town containing the Roman magazines, followed fast upon this misfortune; and the consular army, unable to take up their winter quarters, suffered greatly from cold and famine, many soldiers dying from these causes. M. Claudius Marcellus succeeded Fulvius Nobilior in the command of the consular army in the Hither Province. He compelled Ocilis to submit, fining the inhabitants thirty talents. This mildness induced the brave Numantines to treat with them, and he would have granted them peace but for the clamour raised by the Spanish nations in alliance with Rome. These declared that the Arevacians ought to be so severely dealt with as to ensure their obedience when the Roman legions were withdrawn. The consul, willing to spare the Numantines, whose total destruction was glanced at by these outcries, sent deputies from the Arevacians to the senate that they might plead their own cause before that august body. He permitted their enemies to do the same, and both parties obtained an audience of the conscript fathers.[127]

The Arevacians spoke bravely yet with modesty; glancing slightly at their success, yet expressing their desire of a lasting peace. To both the same answer was given; "The consul Marcellus would inform them of the pleasure of the senate;" that general had orders to continue the war. Licinius Lucullus, one of the new consuls for the next year, was ordered into Hither Spain, but he could not raise the levies. The report of Fulvius Nobilior, and the sufferings of his army, chilled the ardour of the Roman youth. Scipio Æmilianus alone volunteered for a service considered so dangerous. His speech to the companions B.C. 154. of his own age re-animated them, and the levies were speedily enrolled, for he was beloved in Rome, and his example was followed by great numbers of his fellow citizens. Marcellus, before the coming of Lucullus, had made peace with the Arevacians and their allies having fined them six hundred talents. Lucullus, who was covetous both of fame and money, invaded the Vaccœans, a people bordering upon the Arevacians, and at peace with Rome;[128] crossing the Tagus he besieged one of their towns called Cauca, but consented to receive six hundred talents, and to spare the town if it opened its gates. His demand was complied with, but Lucullus was cruel and treacherous as well as avaricious, he requested the inhabitants of Cauca to admit a garrison of two thousand soldiers. The request assumed the nature of a command, it was complied with, the Romans as soon as they entered the place opened the gates to the consular army, an indiscriminate massacre followed in which few of the inhabitants escaped.[129] The slaughter of 20,000 innocent men did not satisfy Lucullus, he hoped to gain money and fame at Intercatia, but the inhabitants possessed no treasures beyond their liberties and perhaps their native manufactures. They defended their town with a large army of horse and foot, and even when the consul made a breach in their walls he gained no advantage over them, being repulsed when he attempted to enter the town. Famine, however, wasted both besieged and besiegers. The

Intercatians were willing to treat, the Roman consul to be treated with, but the remembrance of Cauca, deprived them of all faith in him. Scipio became the guarantee of his general, and the Intercatians purchased the departure of the Romans by six thousand coats, some cattle, and fifty hostages. From Intercatia, Lucullus marched to Pallantia, whither the report of his treachery and avarice had gone before him. Here he was repulsed by the valour of the inhabitants, who pursued the consular army to the banks of the Durius. The consul took no steps to cover his disgrace, but retired to his winter quarters with more wealth than honour.

In Further Spain, during the preceding year, the prætor Atilius Serranus gained some advantages, but a general revolt in his own province followed his successes.[130] Sergius Galba when he took the prætorship suffered a dreadful reverse, but gathering together his scattered forces and raising 20,000 men from among his allies, he took up his winter quarters with a care for his own safety, that by no means increased his military reputation.[131] His avarice brought him into the field again, for the success of Lucullus in Lusitania inspired him with the hope of gain. He entered that country and began to pillage it on every side. The Lusitanians alarmed at his progress wished to make peace. The prætor expressed his willingness to come to terms, and proposed a change of province to them, offering to place them in a fairer and more fruitful part of the country than their own, provided they laid down their arms and permitted him to divide them into three companies. It is difficult to imagine how these credulous Lusitanians could be persuaded to a measure like this, for the unrivalled eloquence of Sergius Galba could hardly have had any effect upon them. Their compliance was the signal for massacre, few escaped, but among the few, Viriathus, to become the leader of the living, the avenger of the dead. The soldiers reaped little pecuniary advantage from the slaughter, the spoil filled the heavy coffers of Sergius Galba. At Rome, Cato, the censor, excited the public indignation against the man who had covered the Roman name with infamy, but the great eloquence of the accused saved him with the people, who listened to his fine oratory and acquitted him.[132] The consequences of his wickedness produced very fatal results to his countrymen in Spain. A brave and exasperated nation with a love of freedom, deep hatred to the invaders, and deprived of all reliance in the boasted Roman faith by fatal experience, only required a patriotic leader. They found one in Viriathus, who from a shepherd and a hunter became a soldier and their general.

The successor of Sergius Galba, C. Vetilius, attacked the Lusitanians near Turdetania and defeated them. The fugitives took refuge in a situation which exposed them to the horrors of starvation. The Roman prætor offered to treat with them, but Viriathus reminded them of the treachery of the Romans and the folly of trusting to a B.C. 151. powerful people, renowned for their want of faith. He bade the fugitives rely upon him for their deliverance.[133] They confided in his promise and Viriathus commenced his brilliant military career by extricating his countrymen from their perilous position, which he effected in the following manner. He drew up his army as if with the intention of giving battle to the Roman legions. At a given signal the troops, all but a thousand horse, were to disperse on every side, but their rendezvous was to be the city of Tribola, when

Viriathus, with his cavalry, alternately advanced and retreated till his troops were in safety, the prætor not daring to attack him or pursue the fugitives, through dread of falling into an ambush, which he apprehended was designed by Viriathus.[134] In the night Viriathus joined his army at the place he had named. The prætor marched thither to give the Lusitanian army battle but fell into the snare laid for him by the Lusitanian commander, whose army was greatly augmented by the fame his late stratagem had gained him among his own countrymen.[135] Surrounded on every side the prætor was taken prisoner by a Lusitanian, but his captor ignorant of his quality, and considering him only as a fat old man who would be unsaleable as a slave, slew him on the spot. The quæstor shut himself up in Carpessus with six thousand men who had escaped with him thither. He ordered five thousand of his allies to face the victorious enemy, who cut them off to a man. The Roman commander remained in Carpessus till the arrival of the new prætor, C. Plautius Hypsæus. This officer after suffering two dreadful defeats went into his winter quarters in the middle of summer; according to the account of Appian, who makes this satirical remark upon the early close of Plautius' unfortunate campaign. Viriathus[136] reaped fresh laurels the two succeeding years in the prætorships of C. Caudius Unimanus and Nigidius Figulus. His success and great military talents demanded more able generals than had yet been opposed to him. The Carthaginians were no longer a people, Corinth was in ashes, and the Roman senate insatiate of dominion resolved to send once more a consular army into Spain[137] to crush a brave and patriotic nation, whose sole motive for waging war was the preservation of that liberty which is the sacred birthright of all men. The man upon whom the defence of his country had fallen, from a shepherd had become a leader, before whom even the Romans had learned to tremble; the Höfer of an earlier day, as intrepid, gallant, patriotic, and in the end as unfortunate.[138]

<hr size=2 width="10%" align=center>

[1] Plutarch, in Paulus Æmilius.

[2] Plutarch lived in Christian times and was not a Christian, yet he believed in miracles—it must have been the doctrines not the supernatural events recorded in the scriptures that left him a priest of Apollo. The pure humble self-denial enjoined by the Christian code, and, above all, the atonement was opposed in all things to the proud philosophy of the schools. Idolatrous rites in honour of deities "whose attributes were rage, revenge, and lust," partook of the character of the beings to whom they were offered. Philosophers who participated in such religious ceremonies as these were unlikely to receive the faith "as it is in Jesus."

[3] Livy, xlv. 3; Polybius, Legat., 88.

[4] Strabo, xvi. 744; Appian, in Syr. 116; Polybius, Legat., 72 and 82.

[5] Polybius.

[6] Hieronymus, in Daniel; Prideaux; Livy, xliv. 19.

[7] Livy, xlv. 11.

[8] Polybius, Legat., 92.

[9] In the eleventh chapter of Daniel the whole history of the war between Syria and Egypt is prophetically described, and in the thirtieth verse the interference of Popillius, which put an end to the war, is spoken of in these words; "For the ships of Chittim shall come against him, whereat he shall be grieved and return," Daniel, xi. 30. Italy is the Chittim of the Bible.

[10] See also Dan. xi., from end of verse 30.

[11] Livy, xlv. 12.

[12] See Appendix. (p. 469)

[13] Livy, xlv. 19.

[14] Livy, xlv. 28.

[15] *Ibid.*, 32.

[16] Pausanias, in Achaia, 10.

[17] Pausanias.

[18] Polybius, Excerpt. xxxi.

[19] Plutarch, in Æmilius.

[20] Upon this dark passage in the life of Paulus Æmilius, Sir Walter Raleigh makes the following remark:—"This was a barbarous and horrible cruelty; as also it was performed by Æmilius with mischievous subtilty."

[21] Livy, xlv. 34.

[22] Plutarch, in Æmilius.

[23] *Ibid.*

[24] *Ibid.*

[25] Plutarch, in Æmilius.

[26] Jeremy Taylor.

[27] Plutarch, in Æmilius.

[28] Plutarch, in Æmilius.

[29] *Ibid.*

[30] *Ibid.*

[31] Livy.

[32] Diodorus Siculus, in Frag.; Sallust, Frag., iv. 6.

[33] Hooke's Roman Republic.

[34] Livy, xlv. 42.

[35] Polybius, Legat., 9.

[36] Livy, xlv. 40; Plutarch, in Æmilius.

[37] Plutarch, in Æmilius.

[38] Plutarch.

[39] Niebuhr, Int. Lecture, v.: Pliny, Hist. Nat., xiii. 13.

[40] Niebuhr.

[41] *Ibid.*

[42] Livy, xlv. 19; Polybius, Legat., 93.

[43] Livy; Polybius.

[44] Livy, xlv. 10.

[45] *Ibid.*

[46] Aulus Gellius.

[47] Aulus Gellius; Hooke's Rome.

[48] Aulus Gellius; Hooke's Rome.

[49] Polybius, Legat., 99 and 114.

[50] Livy, xlv. 44; Polybius, Legat., 97.

[51] Polybius, Legat.

[52] Livy, Epitome, 46.

[53] 2 Maccabees, xi.

[54] Polybius, Legat., 108; Appian in Syri., 117.

[55] Polybius, Legat.

[56] From the people of Babylon (whom Demetrius delivered from the exactions of two creatures of Antiochus Epiphanes, named Timarchus and Heraclides) this prince obtained the appellation of Soter or Saviour, which he ever after retained. Heraclides saved his life by flight to be the agent of the King of Syria's destruction in after years.—1 Maccabees, vii.; Justin, xxxiv. 3.

[57] Polybius, Legat., 120.

[58] *Ibid.*, 122.

[59] *Ibid.*

[60] Justin, xxxvi. 3.

[61] 1 Maccabees, viii.

[62] See Appendix. (p. 488)

[63] Polybius, Legat., 126.

[64] Appian, in Punic., 37.

[65] Plutarch, in Cato Major.

[66] *Ibid.*

[67] *Ibid.*

[68] Hooke's Rome, vi. 23.

[69] Appian, in Illyricum; Polybius, Legat., 125; Livy, Epit., 47.

[70] Plutarch, in Cato Major.

[71] Cicero, de Oratore., ii. 38.

[72] Polybius, Legat., 136.

[73] *Ibid.*, 134.

[74] Livy, Epit., 46.

[75] Polybius, Legat., 113.

[76] *Ibid.*, 132.

[77] 1 Maccabees, x.; Josephus, xiii. 5.

[78] Appian, in Punic., 38.

[79] Here he beheld, without danger to himself, one hundred thousand men engaged in the work of destruction, a sight he thought no person had ever enjoyed before him, except Jupiter and Neptune in the Trojan war. "The spectacle," he frequently declared, "gave him more exquisite delight than any battle he had ever witnessed," though he had been a man of war from his earliest youth. He endeavoured to mediate a peace between the belligerent powers after the battle, which could scarcely be called a Numidian victory, but returned to Spain without composing their differences.

[80] Livy, Epit. xlix.

[81] Appian, in Punic., 68, 69.

[82] Appian, in Punic, 42; Polybius, Legat., 142.

[83] Appian, 44.

[84] *Ibid.*

[85] Appian, 44.

[86] *Ibid.*

[87] *Ibid.*, 80.

[88] *Ibid.*

[89] *Ibid.*

[90] Strabo, xvii. 832.

[91] See Appendix. (p. 496)

[92] See Appendix. (p. 496)

[93] Appian, in Punic., 57, et seq.

[94] Appian.

[95] See Appendix. (p. 497)

[96] Appian, in Punic., 65.

[97] See Appendix. (p. 497)

[98] Polybius, Excerpt., 31.

[99] *Ibid.*

[100] Diodorus Siculus.

[101] The epitome of Livy states that Mancinus had actually taken and held part of the city. A manifest mistake.—Livy, Epit., 51.

[102] Appian, in Punic.

[103] Polybius, Excerpt. de Virt. et Vit.

[104] Hooke's Rome, vi. 57.

[105] Polybius; Appian.

[106] Appian, 79.

[107] *Ibid.*

[108] Polybius.

[109] This dreadful incident is from Appian; Hooke doubts its truth, but it agrees with the manners of the Carthaginians, whose very religion was stained with infanticide, attended with the direst horrors that a cruel and unnatural superstition ever devised.

[110] Livy, Epit., 51.

[111] Appian, in Punic., 185; Livy, Epit., 51.

[112] Pausanias, in Achaia, 18, et seq.; Hooke's Rome, vi. 66.

[113] Pausanias, in Achaia; Hooke's Rome, vi. 69.

[114] Pausanias, in Achaia, 14.

[115] *Ibid.*, 14.

[116] Polybius.

[117] Florus.

[118] Pausanias, in Achaia, 14.

[119] *Ibid.*

[120] It was during this mighty conflagration that the celebrated amalgam called Corinthian brass is said to have been formed; gold, copper, and silver having melted and flowed together into one precious mass, which was considered, in future ages, as a more valuable metal than pure gold. This account, though given by Florus and others, seems hardly consistent with the previous one of the sacking of the city before it was fired. It is more likely that it was a recent discovery of the Corinthian people, and that the Romans plundered the foundry of its contents.—Florus; Livy, Epit., lii.; Pausanias, loc. cit.

[121] Polybius as quoted by Strabo. See also Appendix. (p. 507)

[122] Florus, xi. 18; affairs of the Hither Province.

[123] Livy, xl. 30.

[124] Livy, xl. 30.

[125] Appian, in Iber., 279.

[126] Appian, in Iber., 280.

[127] Polybius, Legat., 141.

[128] Posidonius, ap. Strabo, iii. 162.

[129] Appian, in Iber., 283.

[130] Appian, in Iber., 287.

[131] Hooke's Rome, vi. 88.

[132] Livy, Epitome, xlix.

[133] Livy, Epitome, lii.

[134] Appian, in Iber., 289.

[135] *Ibid.*

[136] *Ibid.*, 292.

[137] Viriathus, the champion of Lusitania, had always shown a contempt for pleasure and festivity, and even upon one of those occasions, on which the sternest minds might have bent to a custom so long established, did not yield. He did not join in his own bridal festivities, but bore behind him on his horse, his newly-wedded wife to his mountain home.—Liberty of Rome; Diodorus Siculus, xxxiii.

[138] Florus, ii. 7.

CHAPTER XII.

A.U.C. 609-633. B.C. 145-121.

The Romans defeated in Spain.—Appius Claudius and his daughter.—Defeat of Metellus Calvus.—Humanity of Macedonicus.—Amusing anecdote of Tremellius Scrofa.—Pompeius repulsed at Numantia.—Desperation of the slaves.—Consular army surrounded by Viriathus.—Cæpio accessory to the murder of Viriathus.—Siege of Numantia.—Vote by ballot.—Manlius condemns his son.—Consular imprisonment.—Misfortunes of Mancinus.—Tiberius Gracchus and the Numantines.—The senate refuses to ratify the peace.—Mancinus given up.—The Numantines reject the victim.—Conquest of Northern Portugal by Brutus.—Bad results of the war in Spain.—Siege of Numantia.—Courageous despair of the Numantines.—Tribuneship of Tiberius Gracchus.—Some account of his early life.—Internal misery of Italy.—Licinian law.—Rupture between Tiberius and Octavius.—Choice of Mummius for the tribuneship.—Tiberius Gracchus deposes Octavius.—Loses a friend.—Entrusts his family to the people.—His political designs.—Legacy of king Attalus.—Tiberius charged with ambitious views.—Teasing questions.—Waning popularity of Tiberius.—His defence.—Offers himself for a second tribuneship.—Opposed by the tribunes.—His timidity.—Watched by his friends.—Omens.—Blossius induces him to go to the Capitol.—Tumults.—Senatorial proceedings reported by Fulvius Flaccus.—The people attack the tribunes.—Scipio Nasica's appeal to the consul.—His refusal.—Nasica leads the senators against Tiberius Gracchus.—His death.—Indignity offered to his remains.—Fate of his friends.—Reply of Blossius.—Unpopularity of Nasica.—His exile.—Opinion of Scipio Æmilianus.—Crassus and Caius Gracchus associated in the commission by the senate.—End of the Servile war in Sicily.—Contested election.—Scipio's speech.—Bad compliment to Roman ladies.—Defeat and death of Crassus.—The Agrarian law.—Sudden death of Scipio Æmilianus.—Aliens excluded.—Quæstorship of Caius Gracchus.—His vision.—His popularity in Sardinia.—His return to Rome.—Elected to the tribuneship.—His oratory.—Its wonderful effects.—Prosecutes his brother's murderers.—His mother, Cornelia, intercedes for Octavius.—His laws.—Meanness of Calpurnius Piso.—Great national works of Caius Gracchus.—Just division of time.—Roman successes.—Caius Gracchus' second tribuneship.—Fannius made consul.—Drusus becomes more popular than Gracchus.—Gladiatorial show.—New law of C. Gracchus.—He refounds Carthage.—Portents.—Return to Rome of Gracchus.—Deserted by his friends.—Alien act illegally enforced.—Impeachment of Fannius.—Opimius a consul.—C. Gracchus a private citizen.—Attempt made to repeal his laws.—Insulted in the capitol by the lictor Antyllius.—Affray.—The lictor killed.—Commission of Opimius.—His decree.—Caius Gracchus and his father's statue.—Guard kept by his friends.—Carouse of Fulvius Flaccus.—His defensive measures.—Parting between Licinia and Caius Gracchus.—Caius goes to the Aventine Mount.—The consul Opimius rejects the terms.—Storm of the Aventine.—Death of the Fulvii.—Temple of Diana.—Escape of Caius Gracchus.—Self-devotion of his friends.—His death.—Comparison between the two Gracchi.—Proud affection of Cornelia for their memory.—Descendants of Caius Gracchus become Christians.—St. Paula and St. Eustochium his lineal descendants.—His line does not end with her dedicated celibacy.

QUINTUS FABIUS ÆMILIANUS, to whom the conduct of the war in Further Spain had been assigned, performed nothing worthy of record in that province.

His army was defeated by Viriathus during his absence at Gades for the purposes of devotion, for the Fabii ascribed their origin to Hercules, to whose temple the consul paid his unseasonable pilgrimage.[1] The election to the consulate of the cruel and avaricious Sergius Galba, in conjunction with L. Aurelius Cotta, the tribune who had formerly endeavoured to defraud his creditors, reflected no honour upon the Roman republic. Both were desirous of being sent to Spain, where Galba had reaped a golden harvest. The matter was referred to Scipio, who said, "I think they both ought to be sent thither; because one has nothing—and the other nothing can satisfy."[2] This sarcastic remark was the reason why Fabius was continued in the command of the consular army in Spain.

A new regulation was made in regard to the exercise of the prætorian office. All civil causes were to be judged by the prætors urbanus and peregrinus. The other four prætors were to try criminal causes at Rome for the first year;[3] and in the second, they must go to their foreign provinces, with the rank of pro-prætor. This union of two distinct offices, that of judge and military governor, seems incompatible; the sacred character of the first, if exercised with impartiality and benevolence, accorded ill with the fierce unrelenting spirit of the latter. The Romans were better soldiers than dispensers of justice.

The choice of the senate and people for the consulate fell upon Quinctius Cæcilius Metellus Macedonicus and Appius Claudius Pulcher. The former is said to have been successful in the Hither province; but Quinctius, the prætor in Further Spain, was defeated by Viriathus. The consul, Appius Claudius, who had Cis-Alpine Gaul assigned him, made war with the Salassians, in the hope of obtaining a triumph. He was defeated in the first battle, but was more fortunate in the second, for he slew five thousand men, the legal number for entitlement to that barbarous show. His demand was resisted, upon the grounds that the Roman loss in the first battle was as great as that of the enemy in the second; and the quæstor was restrained from paying any B.C. 145. money out of the public treasury for that purpose. As Appius was wealthy and powerful, he resolved to triumph at his own expense;[4] a measure that offended the people so much that one of their tribunes attempted to pull him out of his chariot, but was prevented by the address of his daughter, Claudia, a Vestal virgin. Passing through the crowd, she threw herself between the tribune and her father, opposing to his sacred power one deemed yet more sacred by the Roman people, and rendered still more holy by her courageous filial love. She ascended the chariot, and the triumph of the consul was no longer obstructed by the resistance and clamours of the crowd.[5] This was the first and last time a woman ever entered a triumphal chariot at Rome; but Claudia's was a feminine triumph, when she covered her father with the shield of her sacerdotal office. Her filial piety on this occasion was admired and commended even by his enemies.

Q. Fabius Servilianus took Further Spain for his province, and Viriathus for his opponent. He brought with him 16,000 foot, and 1600 horse from Italy. Micipsa, king of Numidia, furnished him with three hundred cavalry and ten elephants. With this host he encountered Viriathus, and was totally defeated on the open plain by an army not amounting to half his own. The routed Roman legions retreated to Ituca, a town in Bætica. Viriathus, being straitened for provisions, fell back on Lusitania, with his victorious troops.[6]

The pro-consul, Metellus Macedonicus, who was as remarkable for his clemency as for the severity of his military discipline, showed on one occasion great compassion.[7] He was besieging Nertobriga, when the young children of Rhetogenes, a deserter from that city, were exposed by the inhabitants to the strokes of the battering ram. The father, nothing daunted, desired the pro-consul to continue the siege against his fellow-citizens; but Metellus resolved not to outrage humanity by slaying these innocent victims of war; he broke up the siege, though certain of gaining the place. His forbearance restored the confidence of the Celtiberians, and several cities immediately submitted to him unconditionally.[8] This good action of Metellus was also an admirable political stroke.

A revolt in Macedonia, occasioned by an impostor calling himself Philip, the elder son of Perseus, was quelled by the quæstor, L. Tremellius, who defended the Roman camp in the absence of Licinius Nerva, against 17,000 men headed by the counterfeit prince. Tremellius gained a complete victory and finished the war. This valiant quæstor obtained the surname of Scrofa from a circumstance that did not redound so much to his honour as to his ingenuity. His slaves had captured a stray sow upon their master's estate, who ordered the beast to be killed for family consumption. The owner, a neighbour, came to the quæstor's house to demand his property. Upon which he hid the dead sow under his wife's bedclothes and obliged her to lie down upon it, assuring the owner, who demanded a search and entered the apartment for that purpose, that there was no sow in the house but what was in that bed. The man, who probably considered the speech as an ill-compliment to the lady, was satisfied and departed.[9]

There was a great contest for the censorship this year, but Scipio gained it; his opponent was Appius Claudius. The number of Roman citizens, capable of bearing arms when this census was taken, amounted to 428,342. The war in Spain was successfully carried on, most of the cities of Celtiberia having been reduced by the pro-consul.[10] Numantia and Termantia still asserted their independence, though desirous of obtaining peace. The consul Pompeius offered terms to the deputies, the rejection of which rendered war inevitable. The clause requiring the surrender of their arms filled them with astonishment. "Is it thus you treat brave men? They never quit their arms but with their lives,"[11] was their indignant reply. Pompeius was repulsed from both these cities. Malia surrendered to him, and he vanquished the Edetanians, B.C. 141. whom he sold for slaves. A frantic love of liberty drove these men to acts of violence and despair; some killed themselves, others destroyed their masters, and those bound for Italy bored holes in the bottoms of the vessels that were carrying them to a more distant slavery, and so perished. The people of Lanci, though garrisoned by four hundred Numantines, agreed to deliver the town provided their lives were spared. The Numantines, aware of their intentions, attacked their new enemies; and during the fight the Romans entered the town and slew the inhabitants, but spared, at the consul's command, the garrison. This was a disgraceful affair.

In Further Spain, the pro-consul, Fabius Servilianus, more cruel than able, laid siege to Erisane. Viriathus repulsed Fabius from Erisane, and obliged him to take up a dangerous position among the rocks, whence there was no outlet by which the pro-consular army could escape. In defending the land of his birth, the brave man's knowledge of his own country must always give him a great advantage over the invader. A solid and lasting peace with Rome, and the independence of his country, was all Viriathus fought for. He neither wished to starve the pro-consular army into a surrender, nor yet to charge it in its present dreadful situation. He asked and obtained a peace, which was confirmed by the senate. By it, "Viriathus was declared the friend and ally of the Roman people, and the lands possessed by the Lusitanians were secured to them."[12] The treaty with the Lusitanians and Romans was not lasting, it was dissolved the following year, for the consul, Cæpio, who succeeded Fabius Servilianus in the further province, urged the senate to renew hostilities. Having obtained consent, he marched to Arsa, the residence of Viriathus, hoping to make himself master of the place. Viriathus, who was wholly unprepared for war, retreated to Carpetania, whither he was pursued by the consul. He saved himself by stratagem, and despatched three friends to treat with Cæpio for peace, a dangerous expedient for one whose only safety lay in war. The consul found the fidelity of these deputies assailable; for the sake of large bribes they agreed to murder their friend and general. They accomplished their treacherous purpose undiscovered; and, stained with the blood of their noble countryman, whose throat they had cut in his sleep, hastened to the Roman camp, where they gained nothing by their treason but contempt, for the consul assured them "that the Romans never favoured men who slew their generals; referring them to the senate for their reward."[13] Thus perished the patriotic Viriathus, who always sought the good of his country, uninfluenced by ambitious hopes or private views. From a shepherd he became a warrior and leader of armies, but the power he attained neither corrupted his heart nor destroyed the purity of his intentions. His murder gave the death-blow to the liberty of his country, while it left a stain on the annals of Rome. He was honoured by a magnificent funeral, and after the performance of his obsequies the Lusitanians elected a general in his room to lead their army, but Tantalus wanted the eminent talents of his illustrious predecessor, and the army was soon after surrounded and compelled to surrender to the consul. As Pompeius was always unfortunate in the Numantine war, he concluded a peace with that brave people without reference to the senate, the besieged agreeing to pay the Romans thirty talents, to restore the prisoners of war, and give up the Roman deserters. The consul Popillius Lænas was indignant at the manner in which his predecessor had concluded the war, and his anger alarming Pompeius, he denied the fact. Popillius Lænas referred the matter to the senate, who refused to ratify the treaty, though the Numantine deputies at Rome fully proved that it had been made.

The preceding year the prætor, Hostilius Tubulus, was accused of taking bribes in his capacity of judge. He fled from Rome, and perished by his own hand to avoid the ignominy of a public execution. Several laws were passed this year at Rome for the benefit of the commons; that of Gabinius, by which the votes of the citizens were taken by ballot, to prevent corruption on one side and undue influence on the other, appears to have been a wise and salutary one. It was performed in this manner. Every citizen wrote the name B.C. 140. of the candidate he favoured upon a tablet, which was put in a box prepared to receive the votes. It was afterwards proved that even the vote by ballot could be bought, since the right to vote was not restricted to men of blameless integrity, which alone could have secured the privilege from being sold. C. Memmius Gallus also framed a law that condemned any informer convicted of bearing false witness to be marked in the forehead with the first letter of the word calumniator. The word it seems was then spelled with a k, as that was the initial by which the criminal was ever after distinguished.

A severe instance of Roman justice was given in this consulship by T. Manlius Torquatus, who demanded of the senate to be constituted judge on the trial of his own son, D. Junius Silanus Manlianus, who, while prætor of Macedonia two years before, had been guilty of great oppression, and had taken bribes of the Roman allies. After two days of patient investigation he gave sentence against the criminal in these words: "Since it has been proved that Silanus, my son, has unjustly taken money of the allies, I judge him unworthy of my family or to serve the republic, and forbid him to appear in my sight for ever."[14] This condemnation from the lips of his father affected the mind of Silanus so much that he destroyed himself that night. The stern Roman made no lamentation for him nor concerned himself with the obsequies of a son who had disgraced him. The office he took upon himself was voluntary, he was compelled to it by no imperative duty, and his country did not require this total sacrifice of natural affection. The public virtue of the Manlian family would have shone brighter if they had been as much distinguished for paternal affection as for rigid impartiality and justice.

A new feature in Roman warfare appeared this year in the servile war in Sicily, which it is said first originated in the cupidity of the Roman knights, who held large estates in that island. These proprietors employed slaves in preference to free labourers, and thus filled Sicily with half-starved captives, who pillaged the natives to satisfy their own hunger. Eunus, a Syrian slave, a diviner by profession, whose juggling tricks had gained him the reputation of being a prophet, was consulted by the slaves of Damophilus of Enna, "if the time they had appointed for the murder of their cruel master and his wicked wife, Megallis, was the proper one; he assured them that the gods would be propitious if they were expeditious." Upon which four hundred slaves rose against their tyrants, whom they brought to a trial among themselves. Damophilus they condemned and slew, but Megallis was delivered by them to her female slaves, by whom she was scourged to death. To the daughter of this wretched pair, a mild and compassionate young woman, who had often pleaded for the captives, they all united in showing mercy, their gratitude inducing them to convey her to Catana, where she had relations, in whose protection they left her. Eunus was chosen by the insurgents for their king and leader; after which the servile revolt became general throughout Sicily, and lasted several years.

Scipio Nasica and D. Junius Brutus held the consular fasces this year. Brutus was appointed to Spain. He built Valentia for a refuge for the soldiers of Viriathus, who by a former agreement were to be removed to a new settlement. Nothing is related of Nasica but the manner in which he silenced the people, who attempted to drown his voice while speaking against a measure proposed by the tribunes respecting purchasing corn in the distant provinces in a time of scarcity: "Be silent," cried he, "I know better than you what is expedient for the good of the republic." In this instance, at least, it appears he was wrong. The marking feature of the year was the imprisonment of both the consuls, while raising the levies for Spain by the tribunes of the people, who demanded the exemption of ten citizens from the list. Upon their resisting this innovation they were both consigned to durance for a few days, a measure without any precedent. The tribunes of the people sat in judgment on a military deserter, who had left Spain without a legal discharge from the service. This man, who was named C. Mateius, was sentenced to be severely whipped in the sight of the new recruits, and to be sold. The sum fixed upon the unfortunate deserter was only seven farthings, a price which degraded him below the value of the meanest slave. It ought to be remembered that the military scourgings still unfortunately B.C. 139. in use in our army are derived from heathen examples, which ought not to have furnished either precedents or models for a Christian people.

The consul Hostilius Mancinus was sent to Spain to reduce Numantia. Being repulsed, he retreated from the city in the night, but was overtaken and defeated with great slaughter. He withdrew with the shattered remnant of the consular army to some place which afforded no egress for his troops. Surrounded by the Numantines, Mancinus was willing to accept terms from his enemies, who did not refuse his overtures, only requiring that his quæstor, Tiberius Gracchus, should be empowered to frame the treaty, and engage for its fulfilment by his countrymen. It was the remembrance of his father's honourable conduct in Spain that led the Numantines to place this confidence in the son.[15] They courteously restored to Gracchus his book of accounts, which had fallen into their hands when they sacked the Roman camp. This and a box of incense was all he would receive at their hands, though they offered him many presents. The terms of the treaty are unknown, we only know that it was signed by the consul, the quæstor, and all the Roman officers, and that it saved twenty thousand Romans from certain destruction.[16] The Roman senate, not choosing to ratify the treaty made by Mancinus, dismissed the Numantine ambassadors, and finally delivered up the late consul to their vengeance, for which the surrender of Postumius in the matter of the Caudine forks afforded a precedent. Mancinus, like that unfortunate general, was willing to atone for his military failure by a voluntary submission to slavery or death. Naked to the waist, and disarmed, he was led by the chief herald to the gates of Numantia, with his hands bound behind his back, and in that miserable state was presented to the generous Numantine people. They, however, indignantly rejected the offered victim, declaring "that the blood of one man could not atone for the breach of faith of a whole nation."[17] Mancinus remained in this condition till night, for the consul Furius would not receive him into the camp till the chickens were consulted, who happening to eat their supper with a good appetite,[18] procured his admission.[19] The augurs, perhaps compassionating their unfortunate countryman, pronounced the auguries to be favourable.

The Lusitanians maintained a guerilla warfare with the pro-consul Brutus, rushing down from lurking places in the fastnesses of their native mountains, to surprise the Roman detachments, and after the capture returning home to divide the spoil. Brutus resolved to attack them in their native villages, where he met with as many women in arms as men.[20] He succeeded in subduing the Lusitanians on the south side of the Durius, which he crossed, and reached the fabled Lethe, or river of oblivion. Although this was not the same stream that the poets of Greece and Rome had described, its name had such terrors for the superstitious Roman soldiers that nothing but the boldness of their general could overcome them. Brutus himself taking a standard from the bearer advanced to the fatal river, and by this action alone induced his troops to follow him. He marched against the fierce Bracarians of northern Portugal, where he again found female warriors ready to die in defence of their families. Some of these Amazons killed themselves and their children rather than submit to slavery.[21] After the reduction of the Bracarians, he subdued the country of the Gallæcians, quite to the ocean on the west. For these exploits he obtained the surname of Gallæcus.

The consul Æmilius engaged in an unjust war with the Vaccæans, and induced his father-in-law, the pro-consul, to join him in the same disastrous enterprise, though he received letters from the senate forbidding him to continue hostilities with a people at peace with Rome. He chose to besiege Pallantia, assisted by Brutus. Both generals were compelled to retreat with loss and disgrace; Brutus losing before that place the hard-earned laurels he had gained in Portugal. The brave Pallantines pursued the united B.C. 137. consular armies and slew six thousand men, without sustaining much injury themselves.[22] Fulvius Flaccus advanced the arms of the republic in a different direction by gaining a victory over the Ardyæans, a seafaring people of Illyricum, who, after their defeat, were transported into an inland part of the country, and it is supposed that Illyricum itself was this year made a prætorian province of the great Roman empire.[23]

The bad success of the Roman arms in Hither Spain determined the people to choose an officer of great talents and experience for that province. They elected Scipio Æmilianus a second time to the consular dignity, and though it had been rendered illegal for any individual in the republic to hold that rank a second time, the law was waived in favour of the great merit of the man of their choice. Scipio, who imputed the failure of the Roman armies in Spain to their want of discipline, commenced an active reform in the manners and morals of his troops directly he arrived in his province. Everything that induced sloth or luxury was banished from the Roman camp. Two thousand disorderly women were expelled, no utensils for the kitchen but pots and spits were allowed, and no beds unless stuffed with straw or leaves were permitted to the soldiers. The sudden deprivation of all the indulgences to which they had been accustomed might have occasioned a mutiny but for the example given by the general himself, who endured the same hardships and inconveniences as his troops, which silenced

406

their murmurs.[24] He spent several months in disciplining the consular army, till he considered them capable of meeting the brave Spaniards, by whom they had hitherto been vanquished. While foraging in the country of the Vaccæans, a party of his horse fell into an ambush laid by the Pallantines, but they were extricated from their danger by the consul, whose vigilance and activity were more than a match for the enemy. He encamped in the neighbourhood of Numantia, and passed the winter in tents, contrary to the established practice of his predecessors. He received a reinforcement about this time from Micipsa, king of Numidia, of slingers, archers and elephants, sent to him under the command of his nephew Jugurtha, of whom mention is now made for the first time in Roman history. Though his year was out before he commenced the siege of Numantia, Scipio remained with the army in Hither Spain, with the rank of pro-consul. The Numantines could no longer cut off the Roman foraging parties, such attempts ending in their defeat, a new feature in the war, for till then "no one ever expected to see a Numantine turn his back on a Roman." Upon the Numantines being reproached on their return by their fellow citizens, and reminded "that they had fled from an enemy they had often vanquished in the field;" they replied, "The Romans are indeed the same sheep, but they have got a different shepherd."[25] Numantia being situated on the side of a hill, at the foot of which flowed the river Durius, Scipio caused a deep trench to be drawn in a circuit of six miles about the town.[26] In those places where the river interrupted the works, he secured it with strong chains and beams, so that no communication by means of boats could be carried on between the besieged and their friends without. The Numantines seeing from their walls these preparations for blockading the city, came out of their gates and offered the pro-consul battle. This was declined by Scipio, whose method of warfare in this instance was to starve his enemies, not to encounter them. Beyond the trench he built a wall eight feet in height, and flanked by towers one hundred and twenty feet from each other. The Numantines made vigorous sallies to destroy the stupendous works raised for the ruin of their city, but the vigilance of the pro-consul prevented all chance of their success. Rhetogenes, a brave Numantine, with five of his friends and some servants, passed the Roman lines by means of portable bridges, and having slain the guards who watched them, went to various cities to implore aid against the common foe. But a dread of the Romans had fallen upon the Spaniards, and the young men of Lutia, amounting to four hundred, were the only persons who would volunteer in their behalf. The patriotic design of these B.C. 134. gallant youths was made known to Scipio by the elder citizens of the place. He appeared before Lutia at sunrise with an army and demanded them. His summons was obeyed, upon which he ordered their right hands to be cut off, returning to his camp after he had inflicted this outrage on brave men. No commander was ever more unscrupulously severe than the younger Scipio, whose refined education had not softened his unrelenting temper. For six months the valiant Numantines endured the miseries of famine, at last they despatched a deputation to their able enemy, entreating him to grant them honourable terms or to change the blockade into open warfare, "We are guilty of no crime," said the chief of the embassy, "in fighting for our wives and children, our liberty and country. Justice requires that you, Scipio, who are a brave man, should spare the brave. We are ready to surrender if you will grant us terms befitting men to accept. If you will not treat with us give us at least an opportunity of fighting that we may die like men."[27] To this manly eloquence, so truthful and so brave, the pro-consul coldly replied, "that they must yield up their city and their arms and surrender at discretion." They refused compliance and returned to the city in despair.[28] The besieged drank deeply of a beer called Celia,[29] before they made one last furious attack upon the Roman lines, and when they failed in that impracticable attempt returned to perpetrate the last act of their despair. They slew their wives and children, set fire to their city, "and left nothing of Numantia[30] but the name, and the blackened walls."[31]

For nearly a century the public mind in Rome had been too much occupied with offensive and defensive war to maintain that struggle between the two orders of which the state was composed, upon which the liberty of all free constitutions really depends. The distinguished plebeian families in Rome were too much blended by their alliances with the patricians to look to the interests of their own order, the rich and unprincipled among them united with the nobility to oppress and keep down the middle class, of which they only nominally formed a part. Some of the aristocracy were still patriotic and well-meaning; probably quite as much so as the richer and more influential portion of the plebeians, who could hardly be considered in the beginning of the seventh century of Rome to form a true plebiscum. According to a natural principle, if any government acknowledged such a one, we should suppose that men belonging by birth to the plebeian, and allied by blood and marriage to the patrician race, would have been admirably qualified to support the interests of one without encroaching upon the privileges of the other. Such had been the case during that glorious period of the republic, when public virtue not wealth had been the qualification for the chief magistracies, but that period had gone by, the democracy of Rome was expiring with the decay of national honour. Public faith was indeed wholly dead, a fact sufficiently attested by the destruction of Carthage, the violation of the peace made by Mancinus with the Numantines, and the appropriation of Greece in defiance of treaties, to which the Roman senate or Roman consuls had solemnly sworn. The very necessity for votes being taken by ballot shows that corruption was sapping the democracy through the people themselves, in whom the desire of gain was overpowering the principle of national integrity. Whenever such declension is found in a free state, that state, whether republican or monarchical, is rushing forward to final ruin, the republic falls to the strongest sword and receives a military despot for her sovereign, while the monarchy sinks into political insignificancy like Spain, or is engulphed like Poland. To attempt to stay the coming ruin in such crises is the duty of wise and enlightened men, and such are generally found in the highest order of the middle class, standing in the breach alone, and unaided by those of their own rank, exposed on every side to the rage of an incensed aristocracy and the malice of a corrupt democracy. Such men are charged with sedition, yet they are not engaged in subverting the political institutions of their country, B.C. 134. but are endeavouring to restore them. These patriots are born too late for their own age, a fact which ensures them a political martyrdom without permitting them to achieve their glorious object. While Scipio the younger was employed in the reduction of Numantia the return of a young man, who had served with credit, as quæstor, under the consul Mancinus to Rome, occasioned that struggle between the oppressed portion of the commons and the senate, which has been very improperly styled by the Roman historians a conspiracy.[32] But though the evidence of such authors as Florus and Tacitus, has been generally considered high authority, those persons who have adopted their views have forgotten the era of despotism in which they wrote, nor considered that different ideas respecting the glorious brother reformers who bore the name of Gracchus, would have involved them in personal peril. Facts are the only true foundation upon which we can ground any just opinion of the characters of two illustrious men, whose bright names have been too often vilified, because stolen to sanctify the unholy cause of faction. Tiberius and Caius Gracchus would have scorned the modern demagogues whose base ends were concealed beneath the shadow of their true and disinterested patriotism. Some honourable mention of Tiberius has already been made in relating the unfortunate campaign of the consul Mancinus. He had previously served with his brother-in-law Scipio the younger in Africa with great credit. His admirable conduct in Spain had not only prevented him from sharing the fate of Mancinus but had induced the Roman people to exempt all the officers of that ill-treated consul from the same penalty. By birth and marriage Tiberius Gracchus was connected with the most distinguished plebeian and patrician families in Rome, and was therefore well suited to become, upon a natural principle founded on mutual advantages, the advocate of his own order and a mediator for them with that whose alliance and blood he shared. In following this principle he acted like a true Roman, in whom its abandonment would have involved a national crime. This distinguished patriot was the son of Tiberius Sempronius Gracchus, a man of consular rank, who had served his country with credit, and of Cornelia, the daughter of Scipio Africanus. His grandfather Sempronius had fallen in the defence of Italy at the battle of Cannæ, and his family had always been remarkable for their firm adherence to their own order. Left an orphan at an early age, the care of his education had devolved entirely upon his mother Cornelia, whose maternal care he shared with Caius, his youngest brother, and Sempronia his sister.[33] The noble matron had inspired her sons with a spirit of public virtue from their earliest years. She wished, she told them, "to be known to posterity as the mother of the Gracchi rather than as the daughter of the great Scipio." History has assigned Cornelia that proud distinction, of which she was ambitious. Even at this distant day she is recognised by no other name. She had in the meridian of her beauty refused the hand of king Ptolemy Physcon, of Egypt, that she might devote herself to her children,[34] and the stainless morals and exalted patriotism of the brothers speak still to the fact that virtuous maternal guidance is the surest way of forming great and distinguished men. Cornelia was a very learned and accomplished woman, who had imbibed the taste of her father for literature. She did not confine herself to the education of her own children but superintended that of several other families, as we are informed by Tacitus,[35] who states this to have been a common practice in the middle ages of the republic. Unfortunately for Rome, themselves, and her, the difference between the ages of her sons prevented them from acting in concert. Could these stars have moved in the same orbit their course would have been irresistible. Tiberius as he grew towards manhood gained such an extraordinary reputation that he was admitted into the college of Augurs rather on account of his virtue than his great connections.[36] Appius Claudius, then president of the senate, offered him at a public entertainment his daughter in marriage, which being joyfully accepted, his intended father-in-law announced the engagement upon his return home in a loud voice to B.C. 134. his wife in these words, "Antistia, I have betrothed our daughter Claudia." Upon which Antistia replied, "What need of such haste unless Tiberius Gracchus be the man you have chosen for our son-in-law."[37] This hasty union between Tiberius and Claudia being productive of much happiness, proved how wisely Appius had acted in his choice of a husband for his daughter. In his passage from Spain to Italy, to give an account of his quæstorship, the miserable condition of the people had painfully attracted the attention of the future reformer. He found the land filled with slave-cultivators,[38] whose unpaid tillage had superseded the hired work of the free labourer. He saw that even the wretched state of these slaves was less pitiable than that of the Italian peasant, whose labour-market their forced taskwork had forestalled.[39] He saw at this period the cause that actually annihilated Rome some centuries later, a cause that threatens every country with ruin in which slavery still exists. The servile war then raging in Sicily,[40] and historical recollections of the inexpiable war of Carthage furnished Tiberius Gracchus with dreadful examples of the consequences of slavery. The remedy for these would have been best found in emancipating the slaves and forming them into distant colonies for their final settlement, and in abolishing the practice of slavery. This plan does not appear to have struck his mind, he sought a temporary remedy that might have checked the disorder but could not effect a permanent cure. He hoped to bring this mighty change to pass by the revival of the Licinian law, which forbade any Roman citizen to possess more than five hundred acres of land,[41] a law unrepealed but which had fallen into disuse. The disputes respecting the former enactment of this edict must be fresh in the mind of the reader, who doubtless remembers that the Agrarian, of which the Licinian was a branch, provided by the sale of the conquered lands for the wants of the poor citizens, but these lands had been gradually occupied by the wealthy members of both orders in defiance of that law, which had limited the possession of the conquered lands to five hundred acres, a law constantly evaded by the great landed proprietors. If however they had employed free labour in cultivation the mischief would not have been very great, but they compelled their slaves to work on their farms contrary to a clause in the same law, which required them to hire a certain proportion of free-labourers in their tillage. Neither the restoration of the conquered lands to the poor, nor the limitation which restricted the number of acres each man might occupy of these lands could really stop the evil, for land does not increase with population, and the more conquests Rome made the more slaves would be sent into Italy to deprive its free people of the means of gaining their bread by the honest labours of their own hands. We remember

410

that in the earlier period of the republic the poor plebeian would have scorned to let himself out for hire, but the increase of population must have long subdued his pride and compelled him to work or starve. If he could get no employment his condition was pitiable, indeed so pitiable that even in the early part of his tribuneship Tiberius Gracchus sought a remedy for this evil state of things by the revival of these obsolete laws.[42] In his patriotic attempt the young tribune of the people did not stand alone, for many of the great and good of that day united with him. Among these we find his own father-in-law Appius Claudius, the prince or president of the senate. Crassus, the chief pontiff, and Mucius Scævola, one of the consuls, all of whom warmly seconded his views, men well versed in jurisprudence, for they considered that putting the Licinian law in force was the only measure that could preserve the commonwealth from ruin. Tiberius it must be remembered did not want to make new laws but to restore old ones, he was not seeking to change the constitution by adding to it, but to reform it by bringing it back to its ancient form. He commenced his brief political career in the consulship of Mucius Scævola and Calpurnius Piso, and concluded it before his tribuneship was ended, to describe which is the painful but interesting task of the historian. In bringing forward his bill Tiberius at first acted with prudence and moderation. He did not intend to enforce the heavy fines which the infringement of the Licinian B.C. 133. law involved, nor yet to tear from the present possessors the lands they had usurped without compensation, on the contrary they were to receive their full value out of the public treasury. "There never was a milder law made against so much injustice and oppression. For they who deserved to have been punished for their infringement of the rights of the community and fined for holding the lands contrary to law, were to have a consideration for giving up their groundless claims and restoring the estates to such as were to be relieved. But though the reformation was conducted with so much tenderness the people were satisfied, they were willing to overlook what was past, on condition that they might guard against future usurpations. In this just and glorious cause," continues the same author,[43] "Tiberius exerted an eloquence that would have adorned a worse and which nothing could resist. How great was he when the people were gathered about the rostrum, and he pleaded for the poor in language like this. 'The wild beasts of Italy have their caves to retire to, but the brave men who spill their blood in her cause have nothing but air and light. Without houses, without any settled habitation, they wander from place to place with their wives and children, and their generals at the head of their armies do but mock them when they exhort their men to fight for their sepulchres and domestic gods, for among such numbers, perhaps, there is not a Roman who has an altar that belonged to his ancestors, nor a sepulchre in which their ashes rest. The soldiers fight and die to advance the wealth and luxury of the great while they have not a foot of ground in their own possession.[44] A warlike people has been subdued, in our eyes, to give way to a crowd of slaves.[45]'" These truths coming from a man of wealth, connection, and influence, who had no base interest to advance, and whose character was high and stainless, had their weight with his colleagues in office as well as with the people. For "he was a man of the finest parts, the greatest innocence of life, the purest intentions; in a word, adorned with all the virtues of which human nature, improved by industry, is capable."[46] This encomium is confirmed by the reluctant testimony of Cicero, who owns "that Tiberius Gracchus in nothing fell short of the virtue of his father, Sempronius, or his grandfather, Africanus, but in this, that he forsook the party of the senate."[47] Such was the young tribune who brought from its obscurity the obsolete Licinian law, with purer motives and cleaner hands than he who had framed it. The avarice of the rich, and the pride of the noble, were equally exerted to throw out a bill so fatal to their supposed interests. At the head of the party was Scipio Nasica, the patrician relative of Tiberius, but his deadly enemy. The opposition of the senatorial party could not, however, affect the passing of the law; and they knew it well; that depended upon the tribunitial college, to which the people had delegated their power. If the ten tribunes agreed upon the measure, it would pass into a law; but if there was one dissentient vote among them, the matter would fall to the ground. They found in the person of Octavius Cæcina, a tribune whose veto would prevent the measure; but it is uncertain how they gained him over, for he was a particular friend of Tiberius, and was eminent for virtue and integrity.[48] Whether the patricians and wealthy plebeians won him by persuasions or appeals to his individual interest, for Octavius possessed more public land than the Licinian law allowed, is uncertain. It might be that the intimate friend of Gracchus was aware that he was projecting other reforms beside the revival of this bill; and designed to manumit the slaves and form them into distant colonies, and perhaps put a bar to future slavery altogether. The reflections made by Tiberius while travelling through Italy, upon the miseries endured by the poor free labourer and wretched slave, makes such a conclusion not unwarrantable.

The first intimation of his change of politics, given by Octavius to his friend, was his public veto against the bill when Tiberius attempted to read it from the rostra.[49] The astonishment and indignation of the patriotic tribune excited him beyond those bounds of prudence and B.C. 133. propriety, within which he had hitherto confined himself. He no sooner found the bill lost through the defection of Octavius, than he proposed it in a new and more objectionable form, in which the compensation offered to the usurpers of the conquered lands was withdrawn.[50]

Marcus Octavius Cæcina from that moment was recognised as the head of the party which opposed the measures of Tiberius, and from that time the former friends never met without dissension; yet mutual respect, founded upon their former friendship, restrained either from the use of personal invective, though each champion maintained his own opinion with obstinacy and vehemence.[51] Octavius, however, acted with more moderation than his opponent, for he limited the exercise of his tribunitial authority to his resolution of negativing the new bill; while Tiberius was determined to put in force the vast powers his office legally conferred upon him, and even to go beyond them. He, therefore, issued an edict forbidding all magistrates to exercise their authority till the bill was accepted or rejected by the people, under the penalty of heavy fines. He affixed his own seal to the door of the temple of Saturn, to prevent the quæstors having access to the public treasury which was there. In doing so he did not, however, pass the legal bounds of his own office. These measures exasperated the rich so much, that they were resolved to keep no terms with him, and even suborned assassins to attempt the life of the man they feared and hated. Tiberius, aware of his danger, no longer appeared unarmed. He wore a dagger under his robe for his personal defence.[52] In his determination to carry his law into effect, he appears to have imputed the opposition of Octavius to interested motives, since he offered to indemnify him for the loss he would sustain by its coming into operation out of his own ample fortune. His proposition was peremptorily and indignantly rejected.[53]

The popular excitement was not confined to Rome; the people of Italy felt themselves deeply interested in the fate of the bill, and flocked to the metropolis to be present at the approaching crisis.[54] When the day of decision came and the people were called upon to give their votes, it was discovered that the urns in which the balloting tablets were to be cast were missing, having been abstracted by some wealthy persons who were determined to put a stop to the business.[55] Tiberius finding that the tide of popular feeling was in his favour, resolved to oppose fraud by open force. Two of his friends, men of birth and consular dignity, dissuaded him from a measure that might lead to civil war; they even fell at his feet and entreated him by no means to put his design into execution, but to refer the matter to the senate.[56] That body had too many wealthy members to allow the revival of laws that aimed at depriving them of lands which they had unjustly and unlawfully appropriated. In the senate-house Tiberius, as might have been expected, found no favourers of his law, though he exerted his eloquence in the vain hope of convincing its members that, in carrying the obnoxious measure into effect, he was about to make himself a great pecuniary sacrifice.[57] Their rejection of the bill induced him to take a step, which none of his friends then, nor his admirers now, can justify. He determined to depose his opponent from the tribuneship, unless he would withdraw his opposition to the law.[58] He had no precedent in the political history of Rome for such an expedient; nor had he any right to break one law in order to restore another. If the Licinian law were a part of the jurisprudence of the country, that which rendered the person and office of a tribune of the people sacred during his period of magistracy, was equally so. From the B.C. 133. senate-house Gracchus returned to the forum, and commenced his design by taking Octavius by the hand and entreating him to gratify the Roman people by voting in favour of their rights; since he must be aware that it was nothing unjust nor unlawful they required of him.[59] This was constitutionally true, although Tiberius was about to carry a lawful measure by illegal means. Octavius as inflexible as himself, was determined upon giving his veto against the bill, and refused to give his former friend the assurance for which he was pleading.[60] Then he avowed his intention of appealing to the people, unless Octavius would tender his own resignation, or accept of his, urging him to put one or other of these measures to the vote in the following manner, "Will Octavius propose to the people that Tiberius shall resign?" Octavius refused to risk a proposition that was not only illegal, but which would expose him to the fury of the mob; from which, perhaps, in the hour of popular excitement, even his sacred office would not have shielded him. "Then," replied his opponent, "since Octavius will not demand the resignation of Tiberius—Tiberius will demand the resignation of Octavius." He dismissed the tribes, convening them for the following day, when this new and unconstitutional question was to be tried.[61] Upon this measure the life and death of Tiberius Gracchus really hung. In his eloquent appeal to the people, he was pronouncing his own funeral oration. Young, rash, and enthusiastic, yet seeking the good of his country, he was about to cast away the shield afforded by the inviolability of his office, by depriving his rival of its privileges and protection. The fateful morning came, and showed Tiberius that his illegal proceedings had alienated some of his friends and made him many new enemies. He was, however, rashly resolute, and after once more vainly urging his colleague to withdraw his opposition to the law, he called upon the people to depose Octavius for having deserted their cause by his declared intention of negativing the bill. The tribes proceeded to vote, and when seventeen had already given their voice for the degradation of Octavius, and the eighteenth, which would give the majority for that measure, was about to follow their example, Tiberius Gracchus bade them pause. He then turned to his opponent, whom he passionately embraced, entreating him by their former friendship not to compel him to proceed with the business, but to save himself from degradation by withdrawing his veto.[62]

Octavius betrayed considerable emotion, for his eyes were full of tears. If he did really waver in his resolution, he mastered the feeling, and bade Tiberius "do what he would."[63] The time, indeed, for retracting his veto was gone by, to have yielded before might have been public virtue, to have done so now would have been a want of moral courage. It was perhaps the quiet dignity displayed by him upon this trying occasion, that made Plutarch style him "a grave and wise young man."[64] The decision of Octavius Cæcina was followed by the eighteenth tribe giving their votes for his deposition, when Tiberius, having gained the majority, ordered an official, one of his own freedmen, to compel the deposed tribune to come down from his seat on the rostra. The resistance of Octavius to this unlawful proceeding was followed by a scene of riot and confusion, which required the personal interference of Tiberius, himself in his public capacity, with the assistance of the party whose cause he had sustained, to preserve the degraded tribune from being torn to pieces by the populace. In this struggle the faithful servant of Octavius lost an eye, so brutal and furious was the excited mob.[65] Nothing could be more injurious to the cause of which Tiberius was at once the hero and the destined victim, than this popular outbreak, which he vainly exerted his influence to check, but the words of the greatest poet of our own times may be applied to him with great propriety, "The hand that kindles cannot quench the flame." The law, and with it those enactments, which formed a branch of it, objects legal in themselves, were illegally and even violently carried;[66] for Tiberius replaced the deposed tribune with Mummius, one of his own clients.[67] It should seem that the other members of the tribunitial college were either on the side of Tiberius or had left to Octavius the dangerous distinction of giving the dissenting veto. If the B.C. 133. latter were indeed the case, it shows that the tribunitial authority was a remedy ill-calculated to preserve the true balance between the people and the senate. The bill was no sooner passed than it was requisite to nominate three commissioners for carrying the Agrarian into effect, the Licinian law being only an amendment of that great legislative act, which had cost Spurius Cassius his life. Tiberius, according to the custom on such occasions, nominated himself, his father-in-law, Appius Claudius, and his own brother, Caius Gracchus, then absent before Numantia with Scipio, for commissioners;[68] for the struggle between the senate and Roman people took place before the fall of Numantia. The commission would only remain in force for one year, and the power of choosing his coadjutors was vested in him who had effected the measure. The fact that Tiberius Gracchus could find no persons out of his own family to carry out the commission proves that his late arbitrary and unconstitutional act had disgusted his friends the consul Mucius Scævola, and Crassus the supreme pontiff. If, indeed, his two nearest relations were joined with him in commission, Octavius and Scipio Nasica were also nearly related to him who were his deadly foes. Scipio Nasica, his cousin, openly declared his hostility by allowing Tiberius the paltry sum of nine oboli a day from the public treasury to defray the expenses of the commission, and by denying him the use of a tent.[69] Could we obtain sufficient insight into the customs of these times, we should probably find that Nasica went by the strict letter of some obsolete law at a period when nine oboli per diem was considered a fair remuneration, and the hardy habits of the earlier republicans made a tent a superfluous luxury, else Nasica, unless a precedent for his parsimony was actually in existence, would hardly have put such an affront upon a man of high rank and eminent dignity in the person of Appius Claudius, the prince or president of the senate. At a crisis when his friends were fast falling from him, the sudden death of one of his warmest supporters alarmed Tiberius Gracchus, who, from the appearance of some spots on the person of the deceased, perhaps erroneously, attributed his fate to poison. His fears were not confined to himself, he trembled for his infant family, whom he brought into the forum, pathetically confiding them with their mother to the protection of the people.[70] The popular champion had, indeed, his moments of weakness, and this appears to have been one of them, for the action does not look like a political ruse. His younger brother Caius, then only twenty years of age, possessed more firmness, being neither so rashly bold nor unseasonably timid, and his return to Italy occasioned the new law to work vigorously. The measure, however, was a weak remedy for a powerful disease, the poor citizens expected more beneficial results, and perhaps had dreamed of riches rather than the mere alleviation of their poverty. He had promised, if we may credit Velleius Paterculus, the right of franchise to the Italians in case of his re-election to the tribuneship, a measure considered factious and unwise even by a great historian of our own day;[71] though the fearful record of the social war at a much later period may perhaps lead some readers to consider that it might have been well for Rome and Italy if Tiberius had been permitted to redeem his pledge to the Italians. He promised to shorten the term of military service, and to divide the judicial power in ordinary criminal cases between the equestrian order and the senate;[72] the last measure was effected some years later during the tribuneship of his brother Caius.[73] Tiberius resolved to offer himself to the people as a candidate for a second tribuneship, for which some precedents existed, as his only means of defence against the prosecution which he was fully aware was awaiting him at the close of his office. To secure his re-election and satisfy his constituents, he proposed in the senate a distribution of the treasures lately bequeathed by Attalus, the deceased king of Pergamus, to the Roman people,[74] among the poorer B.C. 133. citizens, to provide them with tools and cattle for the cultivation of their new allotments of land. As these allotments were not even apportioned, the senate refused to sanction the measure, nor did they pay more regard to the claim he advanced respecting the disposal of some cities.[75] He must have expected this, but some indications of a change of feeling in his own college and in the people he championised, gave him warning that his popularity was on the wane. The scornful rejection of the proposal to appropriate the treasures of king Attalus emboldened Pompey, one of the tribunes, to charge Tiberius Gracchus with having received from Eudemus, the bearer of the last testament of Attalus, a royal robe and diadem, a charge really intended to ruin him with the people.[76] This ridiculous accusation was followed by several irritating and perplexing questions from various members of the national council, calculated to put him out of temper or off his guard, a severe trial to a young and inexperienced man, whose rash disregard for a sacred institution had alienated some friends and created a host of enemies.[77] Quintus Metellus reproached him for taking state upon himself, when he supped in public, by being attended by the rabble with lighted torches, a thing never allowed by his father, Sempronius Gracchus. Annius, a subtle disputant, asked him a puzzling question, to which Tiberius made no reply. "Would you fix a mark of infamy upon my name if I should appeal to one of your colleagues? And if he came to my assistance would you in your anger deprive him of the tribuneship?"[78] These accusations and sharp questions must have clearly indicated to Tiberius the dark storm that was gathering round him. By an illegal act of his own exerted against a colleague, he had deprived himself of the shield of defence afforded him by the nature of an office deemed sacred and inviolate. In deposing Octavius he had disarmed himself, and armed the opposing party against his own life and liberty. He must have been aware, from the examples of Marcus Manlius Capitolinus and Spurius Cassius, that the bare suspicion of aspiring to the regal dignity was likely to ruin him with the people, whose love to those patriotic individuals had not survived those imputed acts of ambition. He made his defence in the forum with eloquence and ability, though every word he uttered was numbering the hours of the speaker.[79] "The person of a tribune I acknowledge is sacred and inviolate, because he is consecrated to the people and takes their interests under his protection. But when he deserts those interests and becomes an oppressor of the people; when he retrenches their privileges and takes away their liberty of voting, by those acts he deprives himself, for he no longer keeps to the intention of his office. Otherwise, if a tribune should demolish the Capitol, and burn the docks and naval stores, his person could not be touched. A man who should do such things as those might still be a tribune, though a vile one; but he who diminishes the privileges of the people, ceases to be a tribune of the people. Does it not shock you to think that a tribune should be able to imprison a consul, and the people not have it in their power to deprive a tribune of his authority, when he uses it against those who gave it? For the tribunes, as well as the consuls, are elected by the people. Kingly government seems to comprehend all authority in itself, and kings are consecrated with the most awful ceremonies; yet the citizens expelled Tarquin when his administration became iniquitous, and for the offence of one man the ancient government, under whose auspices Rome was erected, was entirely abolished.[80] What is there in Rome so sacred and venerable as the Vestal virgins, who keep the perpetual fire? Yet if one of them transgresses the rules of her order she is buried alive. For they who are guilty of impiety against the gods, lose that sacred character which they held only for the sake of the gods.[81] So a tribune who injures the people, can be no longer sacred and inviolable on the people's account.[82] He destroys that power in which his strength lay. If it be just for him to be invested with the tribunitial authority, by a majority of tribes, is it not more just for him to be deposed by the suffrages of them all. What is more sacred and inviolable than the offerings in the temples of the gods? Yet no one pretends to hinder the people from making use of them, or removing them whenever they please. And, indeed, that the tribune's office is not inviolable and unremoveable appears from hence, that several have voluntarily laid it down, or been discharged at their own request."[83]

B.C. 133.

Many, doubtless, who heard his speech, wished to prove to Tiberius that neither his person nor office were sacred in their eyes. They only wanted a fitting opportunity, which already was near at hand. The aristocracy of power represented by the senate, united to that represented by plebeian wealth against the champion of the people, were ready to oppose the re-election of Tiberius Gracchus, and their influence extended to the tribunitial college, since the presiding tribune at the comitia raised a doubt respecting the propriety of re-electing a tribune for the ensuing year.[84] He was requested to withdraw, and permit Mucius or Mummius, the personal friends of the candidate, to collect and scrutinise the votes. This the whole college refused to allow, whereupon the friends and partisans of Tiberius Gracchus contrived to protract the business to be done till it was requisite to adjourn the meeting to another day.[85] Some, however, affirm that Gracchus himself, upon beholding more enemies than friends in that assembly, was alarmed and himself appointed another. He passed the evening in the forum, where he appeared in deep mourning, and once more confided his wife and children to the protection of the people.[86] He had received some information, after he had dismissed the assembly, calculated to awaken his anxiety for himself and them. His partisans pitched their tents about his house, and for that night, at least, guarded their leader well. Appian charges him with concerting some designs with his own friends, who occupied the Capitol, ready, upon a given signal, to repel any attack upon him by force.[87] Several unfavourable omens alarmed Tiberius Gracchus the following morning. He who had been a member of the augural college was naturally affected by a circumstance that appears extremely childish to a Christian reader. "At break of day, the chickens had given him warning that some danger threatened his person; one only chose to come out of its coop, and then not to feed, merely stretching out one leg and raising its left wing, after which actions it returned to its pen."[88] Against this foolish superstition few members of the augural college would have been proof in that credulous age; the fine mind of the Roman reformer was not, and he became silent and dejected.[89] "The eggs of a serpent were said to have been found in his magnificent battle helmet," a fable credited by his biographer, who speaks of its alarming him.[90] He stumbled in the act of crossing the threshold of his house, and paused as if afraid; but when about to proceed, the unexpected sight of two ravens again shook his nerves, and once more inclined him to go back. Blossius, of Cumæ, one of his friends, remarking his hesitation, reminded him "that it ill became the son of Sempronius Gracchus, the grandson of Scipio Africanus, and the protector of the Roman people, to disappoint his friends, and expose himself to the contempt of his enemies, for the sake of a false step or the sight of a raven."[91] The admonition was not made in vain. The doomed tribune, with the shadow of his coming fate depressing his soul, quitted his home never to repass its threshold, and took the way to the Capitol with his followers.[92]

The city, even at that early hour, was thronged by excited crowds resembling "an armed camp"[93] rather than a peaceful metropolis. The reception of Tiberius at the Capitol was enthusiastic and sufficiently encouraging to reassure him, for he was greeted with loud shouts and lengthened plaudits. He took his seat during this burst of popular feeling. The commencement of the business of the day was interrupted by the mob, as soon as they discovered that the tribunes opposed the re-election of their favourite, upon the old ground that a tribune of the people was disqualified for serving that office two successive years.[94] At that moment, Fulvius B.C. 133. Flaccus hurried from the senate, and by his signs and gestures, induced the crowd to make way for him. This senator, as soon as he reached Tiberius Gracchus, told him that the armed patricians, with their slaves and clients, were coming down, not only to take his life but to fall upon the comitia, who were without any means of defence.[95] Tiberius Gracchus, upon receiving this astounding intelligence, being unable to make himself distinctly heard, raised his hand to his head, thereby intimating to the people that his life was in danger. This action was misconstrued[96] into a preconcerted signal to his followers, who immediately tucked up their gowns, seized the staves of the officials which they divided among themselves, and commenced a violent attack upon the opposing tribunes.[97] The priests, during the contest, shut the gates of the temple of Jupiter; while those partisans of the senate, who had been driven from the popular assembly, rushed into the temple of Faith, where the senators were sitting, with exaggerated statements respecting what had passed in the comitium. They even affirmed that Tiberius Gracchus had been seen to raise his hand to his head, in order to obtain from the people a kingly crown.[98] Scipio Nasica, at that time chief pontiff, demanded of the consul, Mucius Scævola, "Why he did not take immediate measures for the salvation of the state and the destruction of the tyrant."[99] To this stern relative and bitter foe of Tiberius the consul replied with the spirit and dignity becoming a virtuous man and just magistrate. "That if Gracchus seduced the people into passing illegal measures he should consider them as invalid and treat them accordingly, but that he would not become the author of a civil war, nor yet put a Roman citizen to death untried and uncondemned."[100] This noble declaration drew from Scipio Nasica this fierce and unwarrantable rejoinder, "Since the consul betrays and abandons the republic let those who would save Rome follow me." As he uttered the words he threw a fold of his robe over his head, while the senators wrapping their gowns round their left arms to form a shield for their personal defence, ran with their leader to the Capitol, followed by their attendants carrying clubs. They had armed themselves with the feet of the benches from which they had hastily risen at the appeal of their stern commander, believing that they were hastening to the defence of their country, instead of hurrying to commit a murder. Forcing their way through the people by dealing their blows right and left upon the crowd, who fled in all directions before them, they made up directly to their victim, slaying those friends of the devoted tribune who attempted to defend his person. Tiberius Gracchus made an effort to save himself by flight, leaving his gown in the hand of his foremost enemy, but stumbling over the bodies of his fallen adherents was struck on the head by Publius Satureius, a member of the tribunitial college, with the foot of a bench. This dreadful blow was seconded by L. Rufus, who afterwards boasted of a deed which robbed Rome of one of her noblest citizens.[101] Three hundred of his friends and clients died with Tiberius Gracchus in this civic tumult, which cruel as it was, appears to have been at least unpremeditated on the part of those by whom it was perpetrated. The remains of these victims were flung indiscriminately into the Tiber that night,[102] nor could the prayers and remonstrances of Caius Gracchus rescue the mangled form of the patriot he revered and the brother he loved from this great indignity. It has been said that young Caius had been proposed as a candidate for the tribuneship by his unfortunate brother,[103] but his age must have disqualified him for that important office, or else Tiberius might have safely committed his great reforms to him, who was afterwards described by Cicero "as one displaying brilliant parts and a manly mind even in boyhood, and being deeply learned and studious while still a child in years,"[104] and who was described by Livy, "as more eloquent than his brother."[105] Caius certainly was not present at this fatal election, the reason of his absence is unknown, but perhaps Tiberius, B.C. 133. whose thoughts and energies were centered on the cause for which he died, chose to face the danger alone that his brother might in some more auspicious time conclude what he had begun. His appearing boldly on that disastrous day to claim from the slayers of Tiberius the remains of the martyred tribune, which he proposed to bury by night in a manner unsuitable to his family and magisterial office in order to avoid any fresh cause of excitement,[106] proves that the younger brother of Tiberius was as courageous in his fraternal affection as he was bold and wise. Besides the three hundred whose glory it was that they died and were cast into the Tiber with Tiberius, the senate put to death many of his friends and clients, not sparing the use of the torture.[107] These were probably Greeks and Italians not possessed of the full civic franchise, for among these unfortunate persons we find the names of Diophanes, the rhetorician, and Caius Billius, who were put to death without trial.[108] Blossius of Cumæ during his examination before the consular magistrates respecting the share he had taken in what the senate styled the sedition of Tiberius Gracchus, boldly acknowledged his complete devotion in all things to the commands of his unhappy friend. "What if he had bid thee burn the Capitol," sternly demanded Scipio Nasica, whose pontifical hands were deeply stained with his cousin's blood. "That Tiberius Gracchus would not have done," was the calm reply. "But if he had," retorted Nasica repeating the ensnaring question. "Then it would have been right for me to have obeyed him, since Tiberius Gracchus would not have commanded anything but what was beneficial to the commonwealth."[109] Such was the noble testimony given by the confidential friend and adviser of Tiberius Gracchus when confronted by his powerful and vindictive enemies in the face of torture and death. His witness ought to be considered a sufficient attestation to the public integrity of this illustrious Roman. Blossius escaped from the vengeance of the senate to Pergamus, where Aristonicus, the natural son of king Attalus, opposed with open force the transfer of his father's kingdom to the Romans.[110] The love of the poor plebeians clave to the memory of their martyred tribune,[111] while their unmeasured hatred to Scipio Nasica made it necessary for him to leave Rome and Italy, the commission with which he was charged by the senate being an expedient for removing him to Asia, far from the scene of his triumph and disgrace.[112] But the weight of the national odium was too heavy for a proud man like Scipio Nasica to bear. He could not, even in that distant clime, escape from the reproaches of his own conscience, which told him "that he had been too wrathful and too rash," though his crime had not been premeditated, but had been "a sudden isolated fact,"[113] originating in circumstances erroneously reported and greatly exaggerated. Scipio the younger during these terrible scenes was in Spain before the death-doomed city of Numantia. Upon his receiving information of the struggle between the senate and popular party, which had ended so fatally for the people and their leader, he showed no sympathy for his cousin's fate, but expressed his opinion of its justice and necessity by quoting this line from Homer,

"So perish all who in such crimes engage."[114]

The political career of Tiberius Gracchus only lasted six months, Cicero styles his tribuneship a reign,[115] and speaks of his slaughter in terms of approbation.

This was the first time since the expulsion of the Tarquins that Roman blood had been shed in civic strife, for Spurius Cassius and Manlius Capitolinus were the victims of unfair trials, in whose unjust sentences the people participated. Spurius Mælius was the victim of an assassination, pronounced legal by the dictator, then the supreme magistrate, by whom the whole power of the republic was represented; but the tumult in which Tiberius fell was a struggle between the opulent and noble and the poor, in which the champion of B.C. 133. the impoverished plebeians became the victim of a sudden but fierce onslaught. The scene itself must have resembled some of the contested elections in England before the wisdom of the legislature provided an effectual remedy to check the violence of party spirit, by limiting the period of the contest to one day.

Tiberius Gracchus had, by destroying the sanctity of his office, aimed the first blow at his own life. Even his warmest friends and admirers must blame his conduct in the deposition of Octavius Cæcina as unconstitutional, violent and illegal. He perished in his twenty-ninth year and bequeathed his reputation and example to his greater younger brother. Some fuller notice of Tiberius Gracchus will be given at the close of his successor's career, which like his own ended too soon for his country. To conciliate the people the senate continued young Caius Gracchus in the commission for dividing the conquered lands, associating with him his own father-in-law, Licinius Crassus, and retaining Appius Claudius, who had stood in the same relation to his brother Tiberius.[116] Both these eminent persons died in the following year,[117] whereupon the charge devolved upon C. Papirius Carbo and M. Fulvius Flaccus. Caius Gracchus took little part in the commission, withdrawing himself from that public career which had commenced so inauspiciously and was destined to end as disastrously.

The dreadful servile war in Sicily was brought to a conclusion by the consul P. Rupilius, which had desolated that island during six years. The slaves, generally victorious over the Roman prætors, gradually increased in numbers, till two hundred thousand men thirsting for revenge strove to win for themselves a name and country. Eunus, their king and leader, with his own hand had slain his master's guests; men who, while they had diverted themselves with his buffoonery, in their convivial hours had not even dreamed of the talents for war and revenge that lurked beneath the character of the jester, the object of their gibes and perhaps contemptuous pity. Cleon, the leader of the revolt at Agrigentum, joined Eunus and became his general,[118] a measure that surprised the Romans, who had expected that these rival chiefs would have made war upon each other, but they wisely united together, considering that in unanimity lay their only chance of success. Calpurnius Piso, the preceding year, put a stop to their victories by defeating the slaves at Messana, he crucified all his prisoners, and left to the survivors no hope of mercy. The war was then renewed with greater fury by men urged forward by despair.[119]

The consul Rupilius came into Sicily to terminate the dreadful contest. He laid siege to Enna and Tauromenium, both of which places were betrayed into his hands. Twenty thousand slaves perished in these towns. Eunus, with six hundred followers, escaped from Enna and took refuge among rocks and precipices, whither they hoped the Roman army could not pursue them. Their stronghold was, however, fully invested, when the adherents of Eunus killed themselves that they might not fall alive into the hands of the Romans. Their leader, with two others, hid himself in a cave, from whence he was dragged forth and sent in chains to Morgantia, where he died of neglect in great misery[120] of the same disease which afterwards consumed Sylla and Herod the Great.

The consuls, L. Valerius Flaccus and P. Licinius Crassus, had a warm contest for the command of the expedition against Pergamus, where a natural brother of Attalus disputed the validity of the testament of the last sovereign in favour of the Roman republic. They were opposed by Scipio Æmilianus, whose talents and success in war would have decided the matter in dispute but for his extreme unpopularity. C. Papirius Carbo, one of the tribunes, crushed his hopes at once by asking him in full assembly "what he thought of the death of Tiberius?" Upon which Scipio boldly replied, "that in his opinion he was justly slain." The groans and cries of the people betrayed their vehement indignation. "Cease your noise," rejoined the candidate for their favour. "Do you think by your clamour to frighten me, who am used unterrified to hear the shouts of embattled enemies,"[121] words that closed the military and political career of Scipio the younger.

A censorial edict this year put forth by Metellus Macedonicus B.C. 132. in recommendation of marriage, was by no means complimentary to the softer sex, as he declared, "there was no living comfortably with them, nor living at all without them, yet he strongly advised wives to be taken for the good of the republic."[122] How these necessary evils received his commendations we are not told, but probably not very graciously.

The consul Crassus, who had the charge of the war in Pergamus, thought more of riches than of fame. He was attacked on the march by the Pergamenians, his fine army totally defeated, and himself taken prisoner. To avoid slavery he wounded a Thracian soldier in the eye, who slew him in return.[123] Perperna concluded the war in Pergamus by taking the king prisoner, whom he designed to exhibit to the Romans in his triumph. The victorious consul died, however, before his return.

This year the tribune Atinius Labeo made a furious attack upon the person of the censor Metellus Macedonicus, whom he seized and was hurrying to the Tarpeian rock with murderous intentions, when the victim was rescued from him by another tribune, who came with the sons of Metellus just in time to save him.[124] This outrage was in consequence of his expulsion from the senate by Metellus, the preceding year. Foiled in taking the life of the censor, the malicious tribune consecrated the whole estate of his enemy to Ceres, a measure which obliged him to live upon the bounty of his friends, a galling expedient to the valiant and virtuous plebeian, who had filled the highest offices of the state with honour to himself and profit to the republic. Atinius Labeo passed a law that from henceforth the tribunes of the people should be senators. They possessed before the power of convening the senate at their pleasure.

The consul Aquillius concluded the conquest of Pergamus by poisoning the springs of water which supplied the besieged town,[125] he is also accused of selling the greater Phrygia to Mithridates for money, and otherwise misconducting himself in his province. Pergamus, with the Roman acquisitions in the East, received the general appellation of the province of Asia.

Papirius Carbo and Fulvius Flaccus had succeeded the deceased commissioners, Appius Claudius and Licinius Crassus, in the division of the conquered lands. They were not men of cool heads and tranquil tempers, and the division which since the death of Tiberius Gracchus had proceeded amicably, was now prosecuted with animosity and party spirit.[126] The partisans of the senate looked upon Scipio Æmilianus as their head, and it was determined upon their part to elect him to the dictatorial office for the settlement of these disputes,[127] from which it had pleased them to dismiss the triumvirate. The consul Tuditanus had already refused the office of umpire. Scipio, dauntless by nature, never suffered fear to stand in the way of his ambition, he was prepared to overcome every obstacle, and to him the senate looked up as to their constituted head in the approaching crisis. The whole body accompanied him to his house, a mark of respect in which the Latins and Italians joined to do honour to the rich and great in the person of the illustrious champion of the patrician order. The following morning Scipio, their idol of the preceding day, was found dead in his bed.[128] No appearance of bodily injury was discernible on the lifeless remains, though some livid spots were perceived on the features which were attributed by his friends to poison, who openly charged the Sempronian family with the crime of destroying the man who was an opponent of those principles for which Tiberius had died. Scipio it was argued did not love his wife Sempronia, the sister of the Gracchi, who, in conjunction with her mother Cornelia, and her brother Caius, was suspected of a murder that deprived the senatorial party of an able leader at a critical juncture.[129] The high character of these persons, and their near relationship to the dead ought to have shielded their names from suspicion. The slaves belonging to the household of the deceased were put to the torture, and these unhappy creatures confessed "that certain people unknown to them were admitted by a back B.C. 129. door into the house, and had strangled their master, adding that they dared not discover the murderer through fear of the people with whom Scipio Æmilianus was so unpopular."[130] That a man at the age of fifty-six, who had retired to his bed in the apparent enjoyment of health, should die suddenly is a common occurrence; the momentous period of time in which Scipio's death happened, was the only remarkable circumstance connected with it. As for the confession drawn by agonising inflictions from miserable slaves, it probably had no foundation but in their desire to escape from pain. Humanity recoils at the ordeal, and forgives the device by which they obtained their release. Carbo was suspected of the supposed murder by some, Fulvius Flaccus by others, while even Caius Gracchus was glanced at, but no enquiry out of the tortured household of the deceased was made.[131] A post-mortem examination would have saved a number of innocent persons, and ascertained whether the great Roman had died a natural death. But the noble medical science was at that time wholly unknown at Rome. Scipio Æmilianus, the younger Scipio of history, was a brave and successful, but cruel commander; learned himself, and a patron of learned men. The friend and protector of Polybius, was fond of music and an admirer of poetry. The son of Æmilius Paulus, however, resembled in nothing, but in his military reputation, the great Scipio Africanus whose name he bore. He lived on unhappy terms with Sempronia, the sister of the Gracchi, to whom his frequently expressed public opinion respecting the expediency of her brother's death, must have given extreme pain. No popular commotions followed the death of the head of the senatorial party, for that party still kept its ascendancy, and the state remained internally tranquil. Two years afterwards, the pardon granted to the citizens of Phocæa, who had joined Aristonicus in the succession war of Pergamus, was honourable to the senate. This city, which had been condemned to be razed, was spared at the intercession of the inhabitants of Marseilles, a Phocæan colony, still retaining with its language and customs, their old attachment to the parent state. The Romans listened to the prayers of their firm allies, and pardoned Phocæa for the sake of Marseilles.[132]

The tribune, Junius Pennus, this year carried a law into effect for excluding aliens from Rome.[133] This measure related to the Italians, whom the Agrarian commissioners hoped to propitiate by the promise of the Roman franchise being extended to them. Many of the Italians who were rich, and held larger portions of the conquered lands than the law allowed, withdrew their opposition, it is thought, upon this hope being held out to them, and came to Rome to keep the popular party in mind of their gage. The law of Pennus was to them a sentence of banishment. Caius Gracchus quitted Rome soon after the law had been passed, which virtually exiled so many of his own and his deceased brother's friends. He sought to banish in the stirring scenes of a military life, his disappointment at the ascendancy of the aristocracy, and the bitter remembrance of the fate of Tiberius. Like that lamented brother, he entered on his public course as military quæstor,[134] for he accompanied the consul, Aurelius Orestes, to Sardinia, where an insurrection had broken out.[135] Hitherto this virtuous and talented young man had led a comparatively private life, for one flung so prematurely into the vortex that had engulphed Tiberius. He had already seen service in Spain, having served with credit in several campaigns under his kinsman, Scipio the younger.[136] His canvass for the quæstorship met with no opposition from the party in power, who were anxious to be rid of a young man holding the same political opinions as the great tribune they had slain; but possessing more energy, power, and firmness, mightier eloquence, and more universal genius. In the suspicions entertained by the aristocratic party respecting the sudden death of his cousin, Scipio, the name of Caius Gracchus had been implicated without any just grounds for the aspersion.[137] His association with Fulvius Flaccus and Papirius Carbo, in the triumviral commission for some time, was not only hurtful to his reputation, but must of B.C. 129. necessity have involved him in much intricate and perplexing public business; for these violent party men went all lengths, and committed much injustice, under the colour of legal right and lawful restitution, for they deprived many landed proprietors of their estates without any cause but their own caprice. We do not know what part Caius Gracchus took in these disputes, although his name has been associated with them; but whether on account of his being a commissioner, or from any decisive attempt of his own to carry the matter through, seems doubtful. The remembrance of his brother's fate checked his impetuous temper, and even restrained him from displaying in the forum his natural gift of impassioned eloquence. On one occasion his splendid genius burst from its cloud, for he threw off his reserve to plead the cause of a friend, and was listened to with deep attention, admiration, and pleasure.[138] He appears, in a fragment still extant of another oration, to have given the real cause of his silence in reciting the close of his brother's brief career, as if he dared not rely upon the people's fidelity to their leaders.[139] He had formerly supported Carbo against his own brother-in-law, Scipio, in endeavouring to carry a law into effect making it legal for a tribune to be re-elected for the following year.[140] He had also spoken in favour of the Italians, for the design of Tiberius, in respect to the extension of the Roman franchise, was warmly supported by his brother. Young as Caius Gracchus then was, he must have studied the condition of his country well, to have discovered the fact, "that the commonwealth contained not

424

two classes alone but many." When once a country has reached such a pitch of civilisation as to contain numerous grades, an extension of her franchise seems an absolute necessity. England has lately done this, and Caius Gracchus, when he stated in the forum, "that a republic must be composed of many classes,"[141] was developing a great political problem, upon the right understanding of which depends the existence of national liberty. Such a principle is really opposed to anarchy, and few who attentively consider the social war which desolated Italy when the franchise was denied, but will allow there was at least much wisdom in the measure.

In seeking the office of quæstor in a distant province Caius Gracchus had resolved to give up his political career from motives connected with personal safety; that such was the case appears from the dream or vision, in which his slaughtered brother seemed to reveal to him his future fate. "You may linger, Caius, you may recoil from my doom as you will, but you cannot avoid your destiny; your death will be the same as mine." The canvass of Caius was not concluded when he believed that he had received this supernatural warning, respecting his future political career and its dreary close.[142] The incident proves how much the mind of Caius dwelt upon the brief public life of his brother, which his inclinations strongly prompted him to follow, while prudence restrained a dictate that would ensure him that brother's fate. In sleep, when the guard he kept over his feelings was withdrawn, it was natural that his busy imagination should represent Tiberius Gracchus as speaking to him thus. Plutarch, who believed in apparitions, imputes the after political course of Caius, "to an unavoidable and over-ruling destiny, an influence he could not escape."[143] But the principles of Caius Gracchus, being the same as those of his brother, led him finally to adopt the very measures which must lead to the same results. The age was superstitious, and the dream or vision had its influence even upon the powerful intellect of one of the firmest men of that era. In Sardinia the young quæstor obtained a brilliant reputation for his conduct in the field and in the camp.[144] To his general, we are told, he was always respectful, mild, and obliging; while in temperance, simplicity of diet, and love of labour, he excelled even the veterans.[145] It has been truly said, "that he is unfit to command who has never learned to obey." Caius had practised obedience as a necessary qualification in a general; the consulship being open to the laudable ambition of every Roman citizen. A hard winter in Sardinia obliged the B.C. 129. consul to send to the neighbouring towns for a supply of warm clothing for his troops. The towns appealed against the levies to the Roman senate,[146] who desired Aurelius to find some other expedient. Caius Gracchus relieved the perplexed consul from this difficulty, by making a progress through the island, and requesting as a personal favour, the supplies which had been denied to the consular authorities; and they were immediately accorded to him, through respect to his stainless character.[147] The matter being reported at Rome excited much jealousy there, and the animosity of the senate was increased soon after by the ambassadors sent by Micipsa, king of Numidia, "assuring them that his master was sending a large supply of corn, as a present to the Roman consul in Sardinia, out of regard to Caius Gracchus;" which intimation displeased the senators so much, that they drove the ambassadors out of the assembly, adding opprobrious words to that uncourteous action.[148]

The elevation of Fulvius Flaccus to the consulship occasioned great mortification to the senate, for Fulvius, though a man of immoral life was a great reformer. His proposal "that the rights of Roman citizenship should be granted to the Italian allies,"[149] alarmed the senators, who condescended to use entreaties with the consul that a measure which would place the subjects of the republic on a footing with her citizens should be withdrawn.[150] He made no reply, but the law was not carried owing to the military expedition of Fulvius against the Saluvians, a people of Gaul, who had invaded their neighbours of Marsilia, the faithful allies of Rome.[151] There can be little doubt that it would have been sound policy if the republic had granted the rights and privileges of citizens to all her subjects; the revolt of Fregellæ soon afterwards and the spirit of disaffection manifested by other Italian towns, showing the expediency of the measure.[152] Numitorius Pullus, the chief of the rebellion, basely betrayed Fregellæ to the Roman prætor, Opimius, who razed it to the ground.[153] The consular army was recalled from Sardinia, though Aurelius was continued in the command of that island by the senate, that his young quæstor might be prevented from displaying his talents in the forum, for they did not suppose that he would leave Aurelius to whom he was attached.[154] They were greatly mistaken, for Caius, who perfectly understood their policy, appeared suddenly at Rome, a measure that displeased his friends as well as his enemies, for it was contrary to military etiquette for a quæstor to leave his general. The censors summoned him to answer for his conduct, before whom he clearly proved that he had acted in obedience to the laws and not in defiance of them. He had already served twelve campaigns instead of ten and had remained with his general two full years, though legally he could not have been compelled to serve but one in his province.[155] Foiled in this attempt, his enemies accused him of having excited the revolt in Fregellæ and disaffection in other Italian towns, but from these charges he completely cleared himself.[156] In vindication of his conduct in Sardinia we find him speaking with the pride of integrity, nor does it appear that his high moral character was ever impugned. Aulus Gellius has preserved a fragment of his oration to the people, which proves that the impetuous Caius Gracchus held the passions of his youth in absolute subjection, that though incorruptible he surrounded himself and others with an atmosphere of purity even in his most festive hours.[157] "In the discharge of my office I have always pursued what I thought your interest required, not any ambitious views of my own; I gave no splendid entertainments, but your children were as sober and decent at my table as when in the presence of their officers in the camp. If any courtesan has entered my house or any man's slave has been enticed by me let me be esteemed the most profligate and most contemptible of mankind. I have been above two years in the province, yet no man can say with truth that I ever received even the smallest present from him, or that he was at any expense on my account. When I returned to Rome my purse which I had carried out full I brought back empty, B.C. 123. whereas others having carried into the province vessels full of wine have brought them back full of money."[158]

It was this upright character that in the following consulship of Cæcilius Metellus and T. Quinctius Flamininus gained Caius Gracchus the tribuneship, an office that had proved fatal to his noble-minded brother. His mother Cornelia forgot her patriotic spirit while with maternal solicitude she urged him to decline the dangerous distinction that had already deprived her of a son.[159] But if the doom of Tiberius was before the eyes of Caius his brief but bright career flashed across them too, and he was determined to pursue the same principles, even if they led to the like end. He had no sooner offered himself as a candidate for the tribuneship when his voters flocked into the forum from every part of Italy till it could not contain them, and many gave Caius their suffrages from the tops of the nearest houses.[160] Yet the senatorial party was still so powerful that the popular candidate only obtained the fourth place on the list. He entered his political career at the same age his brother had attained when elected to the tribuneship. But Caius beside the patriotic purposes of Tiberius had another in view which however unlawful in Christian eyes in our own better day, in that heathen land of which he was a native, and in every country where the light of the gospel has not shone was and is still considered a sacred duty; he desired to revenge his brother's death. This purpose was apparent from the moment he entered upon the momentous business of his office. All his orations from the rostrum dwelt upon the absorbing feeling of his soul—the fate of Tiberius Gracchus. His impassioned eloquence originated in his deep idolatrous love for his noble-minded and unfortunate brother. To his talent for oratory, at least, the Greek and Latin historians have done ample justice, for it was felt, appreciated, and admired, even by his enemies. "It is a well attested fact," remarks a great modern historian, "that in point of talent Tiberius Gracchus was excelled by his brother Caius. We have properly speaking no specimens of the oratory of Tiberius, but of the speeches of Caius there are several fragments extant, which perfectly justify the praise bestowed upon them by Cicero,[161] who could not be mistaken on that point. It is likewise highly probable that Caius was more of a statesman than his brother, he displayed at any rate more political talent."[162] The punishment of his brother's slayers, for murderers we can hardly call them, since the slaughter of Tiberius appears to have been an unpremeditated crime, engrossed the first energies of Caius Gracchus, who spoke of that action in a strain of rapid, concise, and passionate eloquence, whose force our own language cannot adequately convey, though it presented a complete series of historical paintings to the minds of the excited audience. "The murder of Tiberius—his body dragged through the streets and flung into the Tiber—his friends condemned to death without trial"—was his constant theme, one too calculated to excite popular indignation and rage, but it was while describing his own forlorn and distressful state that the eloquence of Caius reached the hearts of his hearers, "Ah miserable man, whither shall I seek for refuge and consolation. To the Capitol? no, the blood of Tiberius, a brother's blood, flows there. To my own home? no, for there a mother sits weeping and lamenting for her son in dejection and misery."[163] This oration, delivered with the force and feeling of one who had seen and personally experienced and suffered what he described, combined with something in the tone and gesture of the speaker, so powerfully affected the audience—that friend and foe, patrician and plebeian, simultaneously burst into tears, unable to resist the words, the look, the pathetic eloquence of the speaker.[164] It was the magic of feeling by which his hearers were thus spell-bound, for what Caius Gracchus spoke he had felt in his bereaved and affectionate heart.

His appeals to the sympathy of the people were followed by the introduction of two bills, both of which were aimed at the enemies of Tiberius. One to disqualify any magistrate who had been deposed from his magistracy from holding any public office in the state, was aimed at Marcus Octavius Cæcina;[165] the other, rendering it a capital crime to banish a Roman citizen without trial, B.C. 123. was levelled at Popillius Lænas, who had exiled many of the friends of Tiberius. This law, founded on a solid principle of public right, terrified that guilty citizen, who, flying to escape its sentence, was condemned by Caius Gracchus to perpetual banishment by the old form of being interdicted the use of fire and water in Italy.[166] Popillius was of a plebeian family of some eminence in history, a fact which proves that the bitterest enemies of Tiberius were found in his own order. The first law was not carried into effect,[167] for Cornelia interceded for Octavius; in regard to him she did not share those indignant feelings that had made Caius Gracchus exclaim at the sight of Popillius Lænas and Octavius Cæcina, "those men are the murderers of Tiberius."[168] She exonerated Octavius from the charge of murder, and her near relationship to him[169] urged her to plead for an intrepid man who had perhaps opposed her son from a principle of duty. This champion of wealth and rank, has been represented by some as an old rival and foe of Tiberius,[170] whose bitterest adversaries were numbered among his near relations, but others consider his political rupture with that unfortunate tribune as the sudden wrenching away of the ties of a long tried friendship.[171] In respect to Octavius, the champion of the people was more to blame than he; but if in error, that error was bitterly atoned by a violent death and ignominious sepulchre. Cornelia pleaded, and pleaded not in vain with her distinguished son, for maturer years had sobered down her maternal ambition, and the loss of Tiberius had rendered her more feminine and wise.[172] The next public act of Caius Gracchus' tribuneship was enforcing the Agrarian law of Tiberius, annexing to it, however, a new clause by which the recovered lands were adjudged to pay an annual tribute into the public treasury, in fact a land-tax.[173] As it is impossible to state whether the laws ascribed to Caius Gracchus were passed in his first or second tribuneship, it will be best to enumerate them together. He limited the term for the commencement of military service to seventeen years, by forbidding any Roman citizen to be enrolled before his attainment of that age.[174] This law it was said was framed to check an abuse practised by the senatorial party in putting down the names of their infant sons to shorten the time of their legal service. But from whatever cause it originated, the law was a wise one, which allowed time for growth, bodily strength, and education, before the recruit was compelled to make his first campaign. His second military regulation obliged the state to furnish the soldier with his arms and clothing, these necessaries hitherto having been deducted from his pay.[175] To Caius Gracchus is ascribed the manner in which the centuries voted, the precedence, by his regulation, being given by lot, and not by reference to the censor's books as in former times. He also applied the treasures of king Attalus to a fund for the purchase of corn at the price of five sixths of an *as*[176] for the modius or peck, which would make the value of a quarter of wheat about one shilling and eight-pence of our currency.[177] Having thus provided the people with cheap bread, the patriotic tribune next furnished them with the means of purchasing corn at this easy rate. He provided for this, like the great and enlightened man he certainly was, by a number of useful public works, which survived their author for many ages, associating his name with the Roman people as a general benefactor.[178] The granaries called the Sempronian were built by him for the reception of the corn. The corn-law had been violently opposed by the aristocracy, and especially by Calpurnius Piso,[179] a man of rank, who had been consul during the fatal tribuneship of Tiberius Gracchus, and was his personal enemy. The corn was only sold at the cheap rate once a month,[180] and was designed for the relief of the poorest citizens alone, but as no such limitation had been made by the law, one of its staunchest opposers presented himself, in the person of Calpurnius B.C. 123. Piso, as a monthly purchaser of the grain stored for the poor. Gracchus indignantly charged this wealthy pauper with inconsistency, in taking the benefit of a measure to which he had offered so much opposition; to his remonstrance Piso tauntingly replied, "I should certainly endeavour to prevent my property being awarded to the people by you; but if you were to do so, I would try to get my full share of it."[181] This provoking conduct was rather to be imputed to malice than to avarice, being probably designed to throw ridicule upon a law that had not provided for such a contingency. The honourable mind of Caius Gracchus had not imagined that any class but the poorest could apply for the cheap corn; but it is to be feared that the example of Piso was not without followers. The law passed by Caius Gracchus which removed from the senatorial to the equestrian order the right of judicature, was designed, not only for the prevention of partiality, but also to lessen the influence of the senate. It worked admirably for fifty years, till the general corruption extended to the class upon which those lofty privileges had been conferred. Cicero speaks highly of this change,[182] while a very great writer of the last century considered it subversive of the Roman constitution, by destroying the balance of power subsisting between the several orders, and inclining it too much to the people.[183] In bestowing the rights of Roman judicature upon the equestrian order, Caius hoped to secure greater impartiality in the dispensation of justice; but the remedy was insufficient to cure the disease. The sacred character of the judge ought not to have been limited to any order in the state, since knowledge, ability, and integrity are its sole requisites. In England, many shining ornaments of the bench have been men of inferior birth and station. In proposing this bill, Caius Gracchus was observed to change his position in the rostrum, and to turn his face towards the forum; as if he acknowledged by that action the power and majesty of the Roman people.[184] Was not the question one that regarded them more closely than the aristocracy, since the labouring classes were more likely to suffer from partial judgment than the more powerful orders of the state? In the laws and measures enacted by Caius we shall find nothing unjust, nothing injurious to any class of the republic; and though of a more impetuous character than Tiberius, he was far less rash in the exercise of his public functions. The law of Caius, prohibiting the trials of Roman citizens for capital offences,[185] without the consent of the people, resembles one of our own code, which suffers not any person to be tried on a criminal charge, before a bill has been found by the grand jury for authorising that measure; it not being considered lawful to submit any individual to the indignity of a trial, without a just and proper cause for doing so. The varied talents of Caius Gracchus were not confined to the important reforms and changes already enumerated. He was deeply versed in a science then little studied and less known, that of political economy. Hitherto the magnificent works of the republic had been mainly performed by captive or servile hands; but he wished to find work for honest poor men, and in order to effect an object so wise and laudable, made his tribuneship rival in utility some of the celebrated censorships whose vast labours it successfully imitated. His laws for beautifying and improving the roads of Italy remained a lasting benefit to that country and Rome for centuries; water-courses were cut, bridges were built, the distances were accurately determined by mile-stones,[186] measured from that celebrated one in Rome called Aureamiglia, at the foot of which Otho afterwards planned the revolution that raised him to the empire.[187] The great tribune Caius Gracchus gave his personal attention to these useful objects, displaying surprising energy and practical knowledge in every department he inspected,[188] even carrying his improvements to providing travellers with stones, that they might mount their horses with more ease.[189] Of the value of time no man was more fully aware than Caius Gracchus, and that he made the most use of a blessing so B.C. 123. commonly wasted, is apparent from the vast improvements he effected in the short space of two years, an immense work alone for the lives of most individuals. If we knew nothing more of him than these fruits of his tribuneship, it would be unjust not to consider him a great man. His biographer has not, however, left us to our own conclusions respecting the economy Caius used in respect to time, "for he assures us that though his occupations were so multifarious and various, he was never at all embarrassed by them; so justly did he apportion his time to business, conversing with ambassadors, officers, soldiers, architects, and workmen with equal propriety and ability, yet always preserving his dignity of station and character, while courteously suiting himself to those of the persons to whom he was speaking, so that the superiority of his attainments and charm of his manners, won the reluctant admiration even of his enemies."[190] What a fine picture is this of a great statesman and accomplished gentleman, one suitable to every age, although such men are rare ornaments, even to an age.[191] In affirming, that Caius was a greater man than his brother, Tiberius, Niebuhr is fully borne out by fact.

While Caius Gracchus was legislating, building, and constructing highways, the consuls were advancing the conquests of the republic.[192] Metellus took the islands called Baleares, now known by the more familiar names of Majorca and Minorca,[193] and built several towns, in which he established Spanish colonies. Sextius Calvinus, the pro-consul, concluded the war in Gaul with the Salluvians, which nation with their king he entirely subdued. He built a town in Provence, in a place abounding with hot and cold springs, which he named Aquæ Sextiæ, or Water of Sextius. This city is now called Aix, having lost in this softer sound its original Latin appellation; it is still celebrated for its baths. This was the first Roman colony founded in Transalpine Gaul.[194]

The re-election of Caius Gracchus to the tribuneship took place without any opposition on the part of the college, and by the universal suffrage of the people, who possessed this liberty of choice in case fewer than ten candidates presented themselves as aspirants to this office.[195] His great public works being then unfinished, would have justified such a proceeding, even if it had not been legal as it was. At this time Caius Gracchus was in the zenith of his power and popularity, a power he had not misused, a popularity he fully deserved. But if none dared to oppose his return to office,[196] there was one who tried her most earnest persuasions to induce him to give up the dangerous distinction. The maternal heart of Cornelia trembled for her son, but her anxious tenderness was less regarded by him than the welfare of the people. The letter is still extant in which her reasons are given with force and clearness.[197] Caius Gracchus next turned his attention to the important work of colonisation, by which he hoped to provide effectually for the wants of the poorer citizens by planting several colonies in Italy, while he proposed for the impoverished Italians the more distant country of Africa,[198] measures calculated to relieve the state as well as to benefit the colonisers, tending also to increase his popularity, although he did not make use of his great influence over the people for a worse purpose than to entreat their suffrages for Fannius Strabo, a candidate for the consulship. His request surprised the aristocracy, who suspected him of aspiring to that dignity himself.[199] The people immediately returned the man Caius Gracchus was pleased to prefer, in conjunction with Domitius Ænobarbus, a measure that by excluding Opimius, an oppressive oligarch, rendered him the deadly foe of the influential tribune.[200] In his second tribuneship Caius gave an instance of public justice which merited both commendation and imitation. Fabius, the pro-prætor of Spain, had sent a great deal of corn to Rome, which he had taken from the Spaniards without paying for it. Caius inveighed against the injustice of an action that must prejudice the allies against Rome, and finally sold the grain and remitted B.C. 122. the money to the persons from whom it had been taken.[201] The uprightness of the great tribune, his pure morality and stainless character, rendered his enemies unable to attack him on points in which so many public men are vulnerable. They found, however, a way to shake his popularity by making a tool of one of his own colleagues. This tribune, whose name was Livius Drusus, fell into the views of the aristocratic party,[202] but whether through envy of his distinguished colleague or from interested views, is uncertain. The senate used this man as a counterpoise to the ascendancy of Gracchus.[203] Under the direction of that body he proposed a number of laws calculated to attract their favour from Caius to himself. He removed the land-tax, which formed a clause in the Agrarian law, a measure of course very acceptable to the poor plebeians.[204] The champion of the Commons had planted two colonies at Capua and Tarentum, but not without experiencing much opposition from the senate, who readily accorded to his rival the power of forming twelve in various parts of Italy, which should be exempt from all taxation.[205] The popularity of Drusus was increased by these measures, while that of Caius Gracchus was on the wane. The serpent cunning of Drusus won more upon the populace than the manly and uncompromising integrity of their late idol. A trivial matter of dispute raised up in his own colleagues a new and formidable set of enemies to Caius Gracchus, the occasion was this. A show of gladiators was to be given the people in the forum, but the tribunitial magistrates, wishing to gain something by letting out seats for hire, surrounded the arena with high scaffoldings furnished with benches, which would prevent those for whom the spectacle was intended from beholding it at all.[206] He made a remonstrance to the tribunes respecting this arrangement, threatening to remove the seats from which they expected much emolument, but finding his representations disregarded, ordered the scaffolding to be levelled during the night.[207] Caius Gracchus had no respect of persons in matters of right and wrong, and his energy, promptitude, and firmness, enabled him to carry any resolution he formed into instant execution. His colleagues did not expect he would have enforced his objections by the removal of the impediment, and they hated him for this instance of impartiality.[208] In regard to the amusement itself there can now be but one opinion, but even this wise and virtuous heathen in giving his countenance to a cruel diversion had not risen beyond the spirit of his age and country. He experienced from this time much opposition from his colleagues, and found his laws outvoted on every occasion. His plans respecting the extension of the Latin and Italian franchise were thrown out,[209] and he already felt the approach of the storm that was about to overwhelm him. His law respecting the assignment of the provinces to the prætorian and pro-consular magistrates before the elections came on, was framed in order to prevent those who held the office from using their influence to procure that which offered the best field for exaction and spoliation. It was usual for the consul to be sent abroad with the rank of pro-consul, and the prætors also in their second year had a foreign jurisdiction appointed them. The law of Caius Gracchus limited the term of these magistracies to one year only, for the better protection of the provinces.[210] To his benevolent and enlightened views Pergamus was indebted for its existence as a people.[211] The eventful political career of Caius Gracchus was drawing to a close, and his last public act was the colonisation of Carthage,[212] in which he was deeply interested, as it offered an asylum to the Italians, for whose benefit it was expressly planned. This law, though proposed and carried by Rubrius, is usually ascribed to him, indeed his nomination as the presiding commissioner seems to put the matter out of doubt. The senate, in awarding to him the settlement of six thousand persons in this colony, got rid for two months of the man they dreaded, whose engagement in so unpopular a measure tended to lower him in the eyes of a fickle and ungrateful crowd. The curse of Scipio the younger upon those who should impiously B.C. 122. endeavour to raise again from the dust of desolation the fallen rival city, seemed to stamp the enterprise with a gloomy character. Even Caius Gracchus, while devoting himself to the formation of the colony, with his mighty energy of mind and purpose, was not proof against the superstitious opinions respecting this measure. In tracing the bounds of Junonia, the name assigned by him to the new city, the wolves carried away in the night the strips of hide by which the measurement of the circumference was ascertained. As the raw hides of the animals sacrificed on such occasions were used for the purpose there was nothing remarkable in the portent, yet it troubled his mind.[213] The sacrifices were hurled from the altar by a furious whirlwind, which flung them far beyond the inaugurated bounds of the colonial city, and the staff of the first standard was broken by its force.[214] With depressed spirits and sad forebodings Caius Gracchus laid the foundations of a city which rose from its dust and ashes in another age at the despotic command of the uncrowned sovereign of Rome, Julius Cæsar. It was destined to become, not only a great commercial city, but a glorious Christian church.

The absence of Gracchus on this inauspicious commission, had greatly lessened his already waning influence with the people. He removed his residence from the Palatine to a quarter nearer the forum, but whether to conciliate the people or from motives of prudent economy is uncertain, though his enemies imputed it to the desire of gaining popularity.[215] The first decisive blow struck against the political power of the patriotic tribune came from Fannius, a false friend for whom he had solicited and obtained the consulship from the people, for this magistrate issued an edict forbidding all the allies or inhabitants of Roman cities from coming within five miles of Rome to give their votes for any measures proposed by Gracchus. In virtue of this order, the Italians and foreigners, incorporated with the tribes, were commanded to leave Rome.[216] Caius Gracchus requested the ejected to remain, promising them his support and protection.[217] He found, then, how evanescent and uncertain was the nature of popular applause, for the people themselves seconded Fannius by authorising a measure that struck at the rights of Roman franchise.[218] So averse, however, was Gracchus to anything resembling tumult, that he beheld one of his country voters led away to prison by a lictor in attendance upon the consul Fannius without the slightest attempt to rescue a man whose friend and guest he had been.[219] He took no factious means for doing justice to the wronged individual, though he exhibited articles of impeachment against Fannius, which, in his quality of tribunitial magistrate, was not only legal but his bounden duty to do.[220] The political career and life of Caius Gracchus depended upon his re-election to the tribuneship; that useful, patriotic, and honourable public career was ended for ever; that virtuous life was drawing to its close. In presenting himself a third time before the people who had deserted him, Caius Gracchus could have felt little confidence in their support. One account ascribes his exclusion to a false return of the votes, which, though given in his favour, were not fairly summed up;[221] but the close of the elections saw him a private man, and Opimius, his deadly enemy, a consul. In regard to his having been passed over by the people, some just reasons might be alleged in favour of his exclusion. A full number of candidates presented themselves for the tribunitial magistracies, and it is uncertain whether a distinct precedent existed for a third re-election. But the centuries, by voting Opimius into the consulship, virtually deserted Caius Gracchus, abandoning their champion and benefactor to his implacable and ungenerous enemies. A bill to prevent the unpopular colonisation of Carthage was introduced in the assembly of the people; a measure by which the rising party tested its growing strength. The failure of that act would involve that of the laws instituted by Caius Gracchus during his tribuneships.[222] That the law would be abolished he must have felt assured, while traversing, with rapid steps, the portico commanding a view of the proceedings, as a private spectator; no longer screened from party fury by that influential office he had exercised during his brief period B.C. 121. of popular favour. Unfortunately for him and his lost cause, Caius Gracchus was not alone; his dreary promenade was shared by men less patient of insult, and more sensitive respecting the loss of their own popularity and the triumph of the senatorial party. Fulvius Flaccus, his colleague in the triumviral commission for the division and recovery of the conquered lands, a man of intemperate habits and dissolute life, was with him that morning, having led a band of clients and followers to the Capitol, with the express intention of defending the colonization of Carthage, and the laws of Caius Gracchus should they also be attacked. Papirius Carbo had forsaken the ex-tribune, and was in the ranks of his enemies. The customary sacrifices were offered by the consul, before commencing the important business of the day,[223] when Antyllius, one of the lictors of Opimius, as he was carrying away the entrails of the victim, rudely jostled Caius Gracchus and his friends, accompanying his uncivil action with these insulting words, "Make way there, ye bad citizens, for honest men," stretching forth his naked arm towards them with a gesture indicative of contempt.[224] This opprobrious language was addressed to Roman gentlemen of birth and education; one of whom, Fulvius, had lately held the consular magistracy. Caius Gracchus, for whom the insult was more particularly designed, vainly strove to save the wretch who offered it from the consequences of his brutal folly, for Antyllius perished by the hands of those whose anger he had so wantonly provoked; for they fell upon him with the long styles[225] they used for their writing tablets, and which served the Roman citizens, not only for pens, but for those daggers they were forbidden to wear in the city. The slaughter of Antyllius, though provoked by his own misconduct, not only exasperated the senate, but offended and alienated the people, for the man was one of their own class, whom they regarded as a victim unjustly immolated, while engaged in the performance of a religious rite. No one lamented the rash revenge his friends and partisans had taken on the lictor more than Caius Gracchus, who saw in it the downfall of his party, and anticipated already the fate of his brother.[226] The assembly, however, was abruptly broken off by the very heavy rain, which, being unusual in that climate, compelled the people to retire to their homes.[227] The following morning the consul Opimius convened the senate in haste, announcing to its members, "that the republic was in danger." His exaggerated statement[228] received full credence; the Capitol was occupied by an armed force; while in order to move the feelings of the people, the body of the slain lictor was exposed at the door of the temple in which the debates were made. Upon Opimius was then conferred that kind of dictatorial power, which the Roman consul might exercise with the permission of the senate upon extraordinary occasions, that body giving it in these ambiguous words, "Let the consul provide for the safety of the commonwealth," such being the form in which the investment of that authority was always made. Opimius no sooner received power to destroy the best and greatest Roman of the age, than he opened his commission by citing Caius Gracchus and Fulvius Flaccus before the senate, to answer for what his decree styled "the murder of the lictor, Antyllius." He had taken extraordinary pains to ensure the success of his designs, by convening the patrician and equestrian orders; directing, moreover, that each knight should be attended by two armed servants,[229] while the decree was being proclaimed to the people in the forum, in the hearing of those it so nearly concerned. Caius Gracchus, upon leaving a spot which had witnessed so often his triumphs, was observed to look long and fixedly upon his father's statue, and was even seen to shed tears.[230] The contrast between the glorious past and the cheerless future, was too much in that sad hour even for him. The effigy of Sempronius Gracchus, with his double consular honours, stood serenely before him, unconscious of the desertion and danger of his distinguished and unhappy son. Nature, during that survey, gushed to the eyes of the doomed Roman, whose sensibility excited for a few hours the better feelings of the fickle populace, who united B.C. 121. to defend the threatened home of their late idol; for his deep dejection had moved them, and they could not resolve to abandon such a man to his enemies in his despondency and woe. In solemn silence many kept guard about him that night,[231] which was destined to be his last. While Caius passed his sad hours with his family in the company of an affectionate and noble-minded wife, Fulvius Flaccus, a man of haughty temper and factious spirit, one who had been not only a man of war from his youth, but the consular general who had subdued a brave people of Gaul,[232] was preparing to meet the consul, Opimius, with open force, and to seize the Aventine, the stronghold of the plebeian order, with a band of armed friends and clients. In order to drown the anxious thoughts the prospect of engaging in a civil war might have excited in his followers, and perhaps to stifle his own, Fulvius spent the night with his adherents in a deep carouse, from the effects of which he had not recovered, when his guards with difficulty awoke him at dawn, so much was he overpowered by the wine he had taken.[233] Hastily arming himself and his clients with the spoils won by him from the Gauls during his consulship, Fulvius marched at their head to the Aventine Mount, of which important post he intended to make himself master.[234] Caius Gracchus, to whom the idea of civil war was dreadful, prepared to quit his home in his gown, his only arms a short dagger for personal defence, when his wife Licinia, perceiving his intention, threw herself at his feet, and holding her little son in one hand detained him with the other, while she sought to change his purpose by these moving words:—"You do not now leave me, my dear Caius, as formerly to go to the rostra in the capacity of tribune or lawgiver, nor do I send you out to a glorious war where, if the common lot befel you, my distress might at least have the consolation of honour. You are going to expose yourself to the murderers of Tiberius without arms indeed, and this is noble rather to suffer than to do an injury. But it is throwing your life away without any advantage to the community. Faction now reigns, outrage and the sword are the only measures of justice. Had your brother fallen before Numantia, a truce would have restored to us his body. Now, perhaps, I also must become a suppliant to some river or the sea to discover where your body lies concealed. For after the murder of Tiberius what confidence can we have either in the laws or the Gods."[235] In her affecting appeal to her unfortunate husband the Roman wife had not forgotten to plead for her country, but indirectly, as one not qualified by conjugal subjection to dictate to him; yet she, by commending him for going forth unarmed as one rather about to suffer innocently than to strive unlawfully seemed to suggest to his mind that in civil war there must be guilt. Licinia, even in her devoted love to her Caius, had not forgotten that she was a Roman, and though he disengaged himself gently from her detaining arms, the line of conduct adopted by him proved that in his last hours of active life Caius Gracchus remembered the wise counsel given him by his wife in her eloquent and touching tenderness. The parting with a husband she felt she was losing for ever was too much for Licinia, who sank fainting at his feet, wholly overpowered by her over-wrought and agonised conjugal feelings. Her husband took advantage of her swoon to leave her, for the Aventine Mount, where Fulvius and his party expected him. The domestics, aware that his own house was no longer a safe asylum for the wife and son of the denounced patriot, carried the fainting mother and unconscious child to the house of her brother Licinius Crassus.[236] Seldom has the tragic pen of history described a more affecting scene than this parting between Caius Gracchus and Licinia, one that the painter might embody and the poet celebrate in song. A few faithful friends and clients accompanied Caius in his dreary march to the Aventine Mount, where he did not appear under the character of an insurgent warrior, but of a man whom unfortunate circumstances had involved with a party who had adopted means for their personal defence he could not cordially approve.[237] We therefore find him employed in checking not fomenting the anger of Fulvius, who was burning to kindle the torch of civil war, by persuading him to send his youngest son, a beautiful and ingenuous youth, with the sacred caduceus B.C. 121. of the herald in his hand, to the senatorial party in the forum, with proposals of peace. The boy executed his difficult commission with so much modesty and good feeling, that many persons about the consul, moved by his tears, besought Opimius to come to terms of accommodation with the insurgent party.[238] He haughtily refused to do so, bidding the youthful messenger assure those who sent him, "that it was not by messages of peace, but by unconditional surrender of themselves as criminals that they could hope to appease the senate." With these words, he "ordered the youth to depart, nor presume to return unless he were the bearer of the only conditions on which he would condescend to treat with the insurgents on the Aventine hill."[239] Upon learning the result of the youthful envoy's mission, Caius Gracchus resolved at first to go alone to the senate and plead his cause and that of Fulvius before them, but in this wise and virtuous determination he was overborne by the remonstrances of Fulvius, and their mutual friends.[240] In an evil hour for his own fame, he gave up his purpose, for his surrender of himself would for ever have exonerated him from the imputed guilt of civic strife. He would have come before that vindictive assembly with no other arms than his unrivalled eloquence, and with hands unstained with the blood of the worthless lictor, and a heart pure as his hands. He once more prevailed upon Fulvius to send his youngest son to negotiate a peace, but this time Opimius seized the person of the youthful ambassador, whom he threw into a prison destined to become his early grave.[241] The consul, bent on revenge, marched to the Aventine Mount with the armed patrician force, backed by a strong body of Cretan archers.[242] Arrived before the place, he proclaimed a full pardon to such of the insurgent party who would immediately lay down their arms, but he offered for the heads of their leaders their full weight in gold. The greater part of the adherents of the proscribed chiefs instantly accepted the terms, and the first flight of the Cretan arrows dispersed the rest.[243] Fulvius Flaccus and his eldest son took refuge in an old bath, from whence they were dragged forth by the soldiers and put to the sword.[244] Caius Gracchus, who had taken no personal part in the short conflict, retired to the temple of Diana, on the Aventine,[245] attended by three faithful friends, Pomponius, Licinius, and another unnamed person, but this devoted triumvirate certainly included Philocrates, his own freedman. In this asylum Caius Gracchus meditated self-destruction, he was deterred from this act of despair by Pomponius and Licinius, who took his dagger from him and urged him to escape, and their arguments prevailed.[246] These attached adherents vainly attempted to procure for the deserted idol of the people the loan of a horse from some who called upon him to escape with loud cries. Fear, however, had fallen upon them, and none would venture to aid the design they recommended.[247] Then Caius Gracchus, in the bitterness of his soul, proved how self-interested their attachment to him had been since it would not stand such a trial as this. From the base, unstable, and ungenerous crowd he turned in that dark hour to those who were ready not only to help but to die for him. By their advice "he leaped down from the steep wall of the temple of Luna, now the church of St. Alessio, in order to reach the Sublician bridge,"[248] whither he was hotly pursued by enemies stimulated by fierce revenge and grasping avarice, two of the worst and most powerful passions of the human breast, in its state of unregenerate corruption. Unarmed, but not alone, Caius Gracchus crossed the bridge, his friends Pomponius and Licinius nobly securing his free passage with their lives.[249] Entering a wood consecrated to the Furies,[250] his path still tracked by relentless foes, nothing remained to Caius Gracchus but to die either by his own hand or by those of his pursuers. The accounts vary respecting the manner of his death, some affirming that he fell by the sword of Philocrates, who instantly despatched himself,[251] while others describe that faithful servant clinging so closely to the person of his master that the weapons of his enemies slew them both at once.[252] Thus in the prime of early manhood died B.C. 121. Caius Gracchus, and with him perished the democracy of Rome, of which he was virtually the last representative.[253] His own order certainly contained his bitterest foes, his enemies in the tribunitial college were of it, so was Opimius the consul, while the mass of the people he protected were poor, and degraded, without courage or loyalty to him whom they only idolised as long as he could provide for their personal wants. He was as much the victim of the wealthy corrupt men of the plebeian order as he was of the senators.

The death of this illustrious champion of an ungrateful people closed the last act of that day's dreary tragedy, in which three thousand citizens were unjustly butchered.[254] Opimius paid the enormous price he had set on the head of his fallen foe. The base wretch who brought it is said to have increased the weight of the skull by removing the brain and filling up the ample space with lead, an act worthy of such a mercenary monster. The remains of Caius Gracchus were flung into the Tiber, as those of Tiberius had been eleven years before, his followers also sharing the same dishonoured grave. Some pious hands rescued the mangled form of the great tribune from the river and bore them to Misenum, the home of Cornelia, of her who was the daughter of Scipio Africanus, and the mother of the Gracchi. The murder of the beautiful and dutiful youngest son of Fulvius Flaccus by Opimius was the worst act of the guilty day. That innocent victim of filial love was strangled in prison by command of the ruthless consul.[255] Licinia, the woeful widow of Caius Gracchus, was not only stripped of her dowry, but forbidden to mourn for her illustrious consort.[256] The prohibition could only have extended to her dress, or to those outward manifestations of sorrow that might have excited the compassion of the people; to whom the sight of the bereaved matron in the garb of widowhood, might have recalled too vividly the remembrance of the illustrious dead; but to stop the tears of a woman must have been too difficult an achievement, even for a consul to effect. The property of the slaughtered Romans was confiscated to the state, and the infant son of Caius Gracchus was robbed of his inheritance, nothing being left him but the mighty name of his distinguished father.[257] Lucius Opimius, having completed his work of murder and pillage, built and dedicated a temple to Concord, as if he gloried in the destruction of his fellow-citizens. The morning after the consecration of the building, this sarcastic line appeared under the inscription,

"Madness and Discord rear a fane to Concord."[258]

The characters of Tiberius and Caius Gracchus appear to have been essentially different, although their political opinions were alike: those of the younger having been formed by his elder brother, for whom his veneration was extreme. In giving the palm to Tiberius, Plutarch, their biographer, has rather asserted his own opinion than substantiated his judgment by facts; but his comparison is too poetical and elegant to be omitted here, though well known to many readers.[259] "As in the statues and pictures of Castor and Pollux, there is a resemblance between the brothers, yet there is still a difference in the make of him who delighted in the cestus, and in the other whose province was horsemanship: so while these young men strongly resembled each other in point of valour, temperance, liberality, eloquence, and greatness of mind, there appeared, nevertheless, in their actions and political conduct no small dissimilarity. In the first place, Tiberius had a mildness in his look and a composure in his whole behaviour; Caius as much vehemence and fire; so that when they spoke in public, Tiberius had a great modesty in action, and shifted not his place; whereas Caius was the first of the Romans that in addressing himself to the people moved from one end of the rostra to the other, and threw his gown off his shoulders. The oratory of Caius was strongly impassioned and calculated to inspire terror; that of Tiberius was of a more gentle kind, and pity was the emotion it raised.[260]

"The language of Tiberius was chaste and elaborate, that of Caius splendid and persuasive. So in their manner of living, Tiberius was plain and frugal; Caius, B.C. 121. when compared to other young Romans temperate and sober, but in comparison to his brother a friend to luxury. Hence Drusus objected to him that he had bought Delphic tables, not only of silver but of very exquisite workmanship, at the rate of twelve hundred and fifty drachmas a pound." From this passage we may infer, that Caius possessed more taste for the fine arts than his brother. "Their tempers were no less dissimilar than their language. Tiberius was mild and gentle, Caius high-spirited and uncontrolled. Such was the difference between the two brothers; but in the valour they exerted against their enemies, in the justice they did their fellow-citizens, in attention to their duty as magistrates, and in self-government in respect to pleasure, they were perfectly alike."[261]

Tiberius was nine years older than his brother, consequently their political career took place at different periods. This was a great disadvantage to both, and was indeed the chief thing that prevented their success; for had they flourished together, and acted in concert, such an union would have added greatly to their force, and might have rendered their strength irresistible.[262] Caius Gracchus was perfectly aware of the impetuosity of his temper, and was anxious to restrain it within due bounds. His voice was loud and clear by nature, and on any sudden emotion the speaker was apt to raise it to a height beyond that assigned to graceful oratory by the rules of art.[263] To warn him against this error he was accustomed to be attended in public by one of his servants, a musician, who used, by a note on the flageolet, to give notice to his master to modulate his tones and lower them to the proper pitch.[264] From a fragment extant in Aulus Gellius of one of his orations to the people, we shall find that this gifted man possessed an intimate acquaintance with the selfish motives of orators in general. "If you wish," he said, "to make use of the wisdom and the valour of those among you, and if ye enquire after them, ye will find that none of us come up to this place to address you without reward. All of us who speak here seek something for ourselves, nor does a single man present himself on the rostra, for any other reason than that he may take something away with him when he has done. I, myself, now speaking to you, do not appear without a design; yet it is not money, but good report and honour that I seek at your hands."[265] But if the disposition of Caius Gracchus was more impetuous, and his oratory of a more stormy character than the softer style of his brother, he was less rash in his actions, never in his legislative acts over-stepping the strict letter of the law. No illegal assumption of power marked his tribuneship; and while Tiberius owed his death to his unlawful deposition of Octavius, that of Caius was caused by the rash revenge taken by his friends—a revenge he endeavoured to prevent. The mischance which befell Antyllius would, in a Christian land and free country like our own, have been pronounced by the verdict of a British jury, manslaughter. Party spirit in the consul and senate of Rome, gave the name of murder to a sudden and unpremeditated act.[266] It is said that Caius Gracchus, in the temple of Diana, invoked a solemn curse upon the poor plebeians, whom he pronounced to be men unworthy of their privileges, birthright, and civic liberty.[267] The assertion scarcely agrees with his character, though he might, with the prophetic spirit so often traced in the last words and acts of the dying, have spoken of that ruin their abandonment of him involved. The history of the tribuneships of these illustrious brothers is the history of Rome, during the short period of their public and political career. We are too apt to try these great Romans by the rules of a free monarchical government like our own, instead of those of the Roman commonwealth—a form based on very different principles. No republic nor free government can subsist without a democracy, and for the restoration and maintenance of the democracy, the Gracchi lived and died. The historians of the corrupt later commonwealth would not, and those of the despotic empire dared not, praise them, thus they have come down to us B.C. 121. under a cloud of disadvantageous circumstances. Their glorious names have been profaned by interested men, to advance and adorn the unhallowed cause of faction; till many have confounded the characters of these virtuous and truly patriotic tribunes with the immoral and venal demagogues of France, who dared in the last century to quote their example to cover their own illegal inroads upon the constitution of their country. In upholding the democracy of Rome, in advocating the rights of the poor and oppressed, no men ever displayed more disinterested zeal and self-devotion than Tiberius and Caius Gracchus. "The Roman people repenting when too late of their ungrateful desertion of their champions consecrated the places where they perished. They reared altars and erected statues to their memory where incense was burned and prayers daily said, as to the gods themselves," remarks Plutarch, who also mentions, "that their effigies standing in the most conspicuous part of the city received the same marks of idolatrous veneration."[268] Cornelia passed the rest of her virtuous life at Misenum, where she lived long in the enjoyment of the society of her friends, employing her time in literary pursuits.[269] She often spoke of the exploits of her father Scipio Africanus but more frequently of her own sons, relating their actions, sufferings, and deaths, in the cause of liberty, without a tear, as if she were recounting to her friends the history of two ancient heroes. Her patriotism appeared in the reply she made to some person who alluded to her misfortunes, when she said, "I can never be called unfortunate for I have given birth to the Gracchi."[270] Few could comprehend the feelings of Cornelia or understand her proud maternity. "Some therefore imagined," remarks Plutarch, "that age and the greatness of her misfortunes had deprived her both of sensibility and understanding, but they rather wanted understanding themselves who could not discover how a noble mind can support itself against distress. Fortune may often defeat the purposes of virtue, yet virtue in bearing affliction can never lose her prerogative."[271] Both the Gracchi left posterity, but the children of Tiberius died young. To the son of Caius remained the sole distinction of transmitting to succeeding ages the illustrious Sempronian line. It never lost its hereditary reputation for eloquence, even when it had become corrupt, immoral, and tarnished with the vices of the times of Augustus and Tiberius.[272] One of the name was banished by the first, and put to death by the second, for an intrigue with Julia, the daughter of Augustus and the wife of Tiberius.[273] Another Gracchus was satirised by Juvenal.[274] In a later period all the descendants of the

Gracchi and Scipios became Christians,[275] when the line recovered its ancient virtue and morality, united to that charity and forgiveness of injuries it till then had never known, adorning the Christian church in the persons of Saint Paula, and her daughter, St. Eustochium.[276] It was from Blæsilla, her mother, that St. Paula derived her illustrious Roman descent.[277] The conversion of the Sempronian house seems to cast a glow of immortal glory over a time-honoured race so often associated with the conflicts of war, the contests for civic liberty, and the advance of civilisation in the historic records of ancient Rome. Those who revere the interesting and patriotic Gracchi will rejoice that their descendants became members of the Christian church.

---

[1] Appian, in Iber., 291.

[2] Val. Max., vi. 4.

[3] Hooke's Rome, vi 96.

[4] Val. Max., v. 4.

[5] Suetonius, in Tiberius.

[6] Appian, in Iber., 292.

[7] Florus, ii. 17; Val Max., v. 1.

[8] Florus; Val Max.

[9] Macrobius; Hooke's Rome, vi. 101.

[10] Valerius Maximus charges Metellus, the pro-consul, with having disbanded many soldiers, starved the elephants, and destroyed the arms of the Cretan soldiers, out of pique at being superseded by a man who was his enemy. His evidence is unsupported by any other author, and does not agree with the generous character of Metellus.—In Iber., ix. 3.

[11] Diodorus Siculus, Excerpt., 34.

[12] Diod. Sic. in Eclog., 32; Livy, Epit., 54.

[13] Livy, Epit., 54; Florus, ii. 17; Vel. Pat., 2.

[14] Val. Max., v. 8; Cicero; Livy, Epit., 54.

[15] Plutarch, in T. Gracchus.

[16] At Rome some dreadful misfortune was predicted of Mancinus, from the first moment of his assuming the consular purple. A mare had produced that day a foal with five legs; and the sacred chickens, when consulted by the

augurs, instead of taking their food greedily had made use of their wings, flying away into a neighbouring wood and returning no more. Such were the foolish notions entertained by the mightiest heathen people in the world.—Jul. Obsequi a Prodig., 83.

[17] Appian, in Iber., 302; Cic. de Orat., ii. 41; Plutarch, in T. Gracchus.

[18] *Ibid.*

[19] Appian, in Iber., 295.

[20] *Ibid.*

[21] Orosius, v. 5; Appian, 300.

[22] Orosius, v. 5; Livy, Epit., lvi.

[23] Pighius.

[24] Val Max., ii. 7; Livy, Epit., lvii.

[25] Florus, ii. 18; Plutarch, in Apotheg.; Hooke's Rome, vi. 127.

[26] Hooke's Rome, vi. 127.

[27] Florus, ii. 18; Orosius, v. 6; Appian, in Iber., 309.

[28] Appian relates that the ambassadors were slain upon their return by their own countrymen, but as this is recorded by no other historian, Hooke thinks there is reason to disbelieve his statement, particularly as it does not agree with the generous character of the Numantines.

[29] Beer, we find from Tacitus, was a drink peculiar to all the Celtic nations.

[30] Florus, loc. cit.; Orosius, loc. cit.

[31] See Appendix. (p. 527)

[32] Florus; Tacitus.

[33] Plutarch, in Tib. Grac.

[34] *Ibid.*

[35] Dialogue on Oratory.

[36] Plutarch, in Tib. Grac.

[37] Plutarch, in Tib. Grac.

[38] *Ibid.*

[39] *Ibid.*

[40] Florus, iii.

[41] Plutarch, in Tib. Gracchus; Appian, in Bell. Civ., i. 9, 10.

[42] Plutarch; Appian.

[43] Plutarch, in Tib. Gracchus.

[44] *Ibid.*

[45] *Ibid.*

[46] Vell. Pater., ii.

[47] Cicero; Or. de Harusp., 19.

[48] Plutarch, in Tib. Gracchus.

[49] *Ibid.*

[50] Plutarch, in Tib. Gracchus. The reader, by referring to the original law of Licinius, will find that the limitation of landed property, which might appear to the natives of a free country like our own, an aggression on national liberty, only related to the occupation of the conquered territorial acquisitions of the republic, for which neither rent nor money had been paid. A Roman citizen might buy or hire of the state to any amount. These occupations had been probably made during the magistracies of the parties, since the wealthy plebeian was equally concerned with the patrician in this work of spoliation on the domain land. The presentation of the bill divested of the compensation clause was therefore peculiarly rash and unwise, since it arrayed the whole body of dishonest proprietors against the patriotic tribune.

[51] Plutarch, in Tib. Gracchus.

[52] *Ibid.*

[53] Appian, de Bell. Civ., i. 10.

[54] Plutarch, in Tib. Grac.

[55] *Ibid.*

[56] Appian, de Bell. Civ., i. 11.

[57] *Ibid.*

[58] Plutarch, in Tib. Gracchus; Appian, de Bell. Civ., 12.

[59] Plutarch, in Tib. Gracchus.

[60] *Ibid.*

[61] *Ibid.*

[62] Plutarch, in Tib. Gracchus.

[63] *Ibid.*

[64] *Ibid.*

[65] *Ibid.*

[66] Appian, de Bell. Civ., i. 13; Plutarch, in Tib. Gracchus.

[67] *Ibid.*

[68] Livy, Epit., viii.; Appian; Plutarch; Velleius Paterculus, ii, 2.

[69] Plutarch, in Tib. Gracchus.

[70] Plutarch, in Tib. Gracchus.

[71] Velleius Paterculus, ubi supra; Arnold's Rome; Hist. Later Roman Commonwealth, 81.

[72] Velleius Paterculus.

[73] Plutarch, in C. Gracchus.

[74] In respect of the legacy left by Attalus of his dominions and treasures, there were many opinions, some imputing his bequest to his desire of preserving his people from the miseries of a disputed succession, he having no legitimate son, while others considered his will the act of an insane man. Foreigners did not scruple to call the testament itself an impudent forgery, concocted between Eudemus, the Pergamenian minister, and the Roman senate. In fact, if the king had really bequeathed his goods to the Romans, both senate and people had chosen to construe his legacy into the bequest of his whole dominions.—Sallust, Frag., iv.; Plutarch, in Tib. Gracchus.

[75] Plutarch, in Tib. Gracchus.

[76] Plutarch.

[77] Plutarch, in Tib. Gracchus.

[78] *Ibid.*

[79] Plutarch, in Tib. Gracchus.

[80] *Ibid.*

[81] *Ibid.*

[82] *Ibid.*

[83] Plutarch, in Tib. Gracchus.

[84] *Ibid.*

[85] *Ibid.*

[86] *Ibid.*

[87] Appian, 15.

[88] Plutarch, in Tib. Gracchus.

[89] *Ibid.*

[90] *Ibid.*

[91] *Ibid.*

[92] Velleius Paterculus, ii. 3; Cf. Aulus Gellius, ii. 13.

[93] Dion Cassius, Fragm., lxxxviii.

[94] Appian; Plutarch, in Tib. Gracchus.

[95] Plutarch, in Tib. Gracchus.

[96] *Ibid.*

[97] Appian, 15.

[98] Plutarch, in Tib. Gracchus.

[99] Cicero de Officiis, i. 30; de Claris Orator., 28; Plutarch, in Tib. Gracchus.

[100] Plutarch, in Tib. Gracchus.

[101] Cicero de Officiis, i. 22-30; Velleius Paterculus, ii. 3; Plutarch, in Tib. Gracchus.

[102] Appian, de Bell. Civ., i. 14; Plutarch, in Tib. Gracchus.

[103] Dion Cassius, Fragm. lxxxviii.

[104] Cic. Brut., 33.

[105] Livy, Epit., lx.; Aulus Gellius, x.

[106] Plutarch, in Tib. Gracchus.

[107] *Ibid.*

[108] *Ibid.*

[109] *Ibid.*

[110] *Ibid.*

[111] Appian, de Bell. Civ., i. 17.

[112] Plutarch, in Tib. Gracchus.

[113] Arnold, Hist. Later Roman Commonwealth.

[114] That great poet appears to have supplied his admirer with a verse on all occasions, whether the subject was the massacre of the inhabitants of a great city or the slaughter of a near kinsman.—Plutarch, in Tiberius Gracchus. Appian, the historian, with more feeling, concludes his account of the tragedy, in which Tiberius was an actor, with these words:—"Thus, Gracchus, pursuing with too much violence the best designs for his country's good, was, while a tribune, slain in the Capitol."—Appian, de Bell. Civ.

[115] De Officiis, i. 22-30.

[116] Plutarch, in Tib. Gracchus.

[117] Livy, Epit., lix.; Appian, de Bel. Civil., i. 18.

[118] Diod. Siculus, Eclog. xxxiv.

[119] Orosius, v. 9.

[120] Diod. Siculus, Eclog. xxxv.; Orosius, v. 9.

[121] Cicero pro Milon.; Vell. Pat., ii.; Val. Max., vi. 2.

[122] Aulus Gellius, i. 66; Livy, Epit., lix.

[123] Val. Max., iii., 2; Florus, ii., 20.—Strabo differs from the ancient historians, who have related his end in the manner just quoted. He says "that the consul Crassus died in battle."

[124] Cicero, pro Dam., 47; Pliny, Nat. Hist., vii. 45.

[125] Florus; Appian.

[126] Appian, de Bell. Civ.

[127] Cicero, in Somm. Scipion.

[128] Velleius Paterculus, ii. 4; Appian, 20; Livy, Epit., lxix.

[129] Plutarch, in C. Gracchus; Appian.

[130] Plutarch, in C. Gracchus.

[131] *Ibid.*

[132] Justin, xxxvii. 1.

[133] Cic. de Off., iii. 11.

[134] Cicero, Div., i., 26; Plutarch, in C. Gracchus.

[135] *Ibid.*

[136] Plutarch, in C. Gracchus.

[137] *Ibid.*

[138] Plutarch, in C. Gracchus.

[139] Liberty of Rome; Scholia di Angelo Mai; Cicero, pro Sull.

[140] Livy, Epit., lix.; Cicero de Amicit.

[141] Liberty of Rome; Festus, iii. v.; Respublicus.

[142] Plutarch, in C. Gracchus; Cicero, de Divin., i., 26.

[143] Plutarch, in C. Gracchus.

[144] *Ibid.*

[145] *Ibid.*

[146] Plutarch in C. Gracchus.

[147] *Ibid.*

[148] *Ibid.*

[149] Appian, de Bell. Civ., i. 362.

[150] Val. Maximus, ix., 5.

[151] Appian, de Bell. Civil., ii., 34; Livy, Epit., lx.

[152] Livy, Epit. lx.

[153] Cicero, de Finibus, v. 22.

[154] Plutarch, in C. Gracchus.

[155] *Ibid.*

[156] *Ibid.*

[157] Aulus Gellius, xv. 12.

[158] Aulus Gellius, xv. 12.

[159] Frag. Cornelius Nepos.

[160] Plutarch, in C. Gracchus.

[161] Cicero, Epit.; Brutus, 32.

[162] Niebuhr, Lecture xxviii.

[163] The sense of the Latin, cannot be rendered without an amplification fatal to its noble and pathetic brevity.

[164] Cicero, de Orat., iii., 36.

[165] Aulus Gellius, xi. 13; Plutarch, in C. Gracchus.

[166] Cicero, pro Domo suâ, xxxi.

[167] Diod. Siculus, Reliq., xxxiv., xxxv. 25; Cornelius Nepos.

[168] Plutarch, in C. Gracchus.

[169] Dion Cassius, Frag. xxxvii.

[170] *Ibid.*

[171] Plutarch, in C. Gracchus.

[172] Diod. Siculus, Reliq., xxxiv., xxxv.

[173] Livy, Epit., lx.

[174] Plutarch, in C. Gracchus.

[175] *Ibid.*

[176] Livy, Epit.; Appian, de Bell. Civ.

[177] See Appendix. (p. 562)

[178] Plutarch, in C. Gracchus.

[179] Cicero, Tusculan Disputat., iii., 20.

[180] Livy, Epit., lx.; Appian, de Bell. Civ., i. 21.

[181] Arnold, Later Commonwealth.

[182] Cicero, in Verrem.

[183] Montesquieu, Spirit of the Laws, i. 20; and see Appendix (p. 563).

[184] Plutarch, in C. Gracchus.

[185] Plutarch, in C. Gracchus.

[186] *Ibid.*

[187] *Ibid.*

[188] Hist. Tacitus.

[189] Plutarch, in C. Gracchus.

[190] Plutarch, in C. Gracchus.

[191] *Ibid.*

[192] *Ibid.*

[193] Strabo, iii.; Florus, iii. 8.

[194] Livy, Epit.

[195] Arnold, Later Commonwealth; Appian, i., 21.

[196] Plutarch, in C. Gracchus.

[197] Epistolæ Corneliæ, apud Fragmenta Cornelii Nepotis.

[198] Plutarch, in C. Gracchus.

[199] Plutarch, in C. Gracchus; Appian, de Bell. Civ., iv., 32.

[200] *Ibid.*

[201] Plutarch, in C. Gracchus.

[202] Plutarch, in C. Gracchus; Tac. Ann., iii., 27.

[203] Suetonius, in Tiberius.

[204] Appian, de Bell. Civil.

[205] Plutarch, in C. Gracchus; Appian, de Bell. Civil., i. 23.

[206] Plutarch, in C. Gracchus.

[207] *Ibid.*

[208] Plutarch, in C. Gracchus.

[209] Plutarch, in C. Gracchus; Velleius Paterculus, ii. 6; Appian, Bell Civil., i. 3.

[210] Cicero, pro Dom., 9.

[211] Liberty of Rome; Cic., in Verr., act ii. lib. iii. 6.

[212] Plutarch, in C. Gracchus; Appian, Bell. Civil.

[213] Plutarch, in C. Gracchus.

[214] *Ibid.*

[215] Liberty of Rome.

[216] Plutarch, in C. Gracchus.

[217] *Ibid.*

[218] Cicero, Brut., xxvi.

[219] Plutarch, in C. Gracchus.

[220] *Ibid.*

[221] *Ibid.*

[222] Appian, i. 24.

[223] Florus, iii. 15.

[224] Plutarch, in C. Gracchus.

[225] *Ibid.*

[226] *Ibid.*

[227] Plutarch, in C. Gracchus.

[228] Appian, 25; Plutarch, in C. Gracchus.

[229] Plutarch, in C. Gracchus.

[230] *Ibid.*

[231] Plutarch, in C. Gracchus.

[232] Florus.

[233] Plutarch, in C. Gracchus.

[234] *Ibid.*

[235] Plutarch, in C. Gracchus.

[236] *Ibid.*

[237] *Ibid.*

[238] Plutarch, in C. Gracchus.

[239] *Ibid.*

[240] *Ibid.*

[241] Vell. Pat. ii. 6; Plutarch, in C. Gracchus.

[242] Plutarch, in C. Gracchus.

[243] *Ibid.*

[244] Plutarch, in C. Gracchus.

[245] *Ibid.*

[246] *Ibid.*

[247] *Ibid.*

[248] Vell. Pat., ii. 6; Niebuhr, Lecture xxix.

[249] Vell. Pater., ii. 6; Plutarch, in C. Gracchus.

[250] Val. Maximus, vi. 8.

[251] Val. Maximus, vi. 8; Vell. Pater., ii. 6.

[252] Hooke's Roman Republic.

[253] See Appendix. (p. 577)

[254] Plutarch.

[255] Plutarch, in C. Gracchus; Velleius Paterculus, ii. 6.

[256] Plutarch, in C. Gracchus.

[257] Plutarch, in C. Gracchus; Appian, Bell. Civ., i. 26; Vell. Paterculus, ii. 7.

[258] Plutarch, in C. Gracchus.

[259] Plutarch, in T. Gracchus.

[260] *Ibid.*

[261] Plutarch, in T. Gracchus.

[262] *Ibid.*

[263] Dion Cassius, Frag., xc.

[264] Cicero, de Orat., iii., 60; Plutarch, in C. Gracchus.

[265] Liberty of Rome; Aulus Gellius, xi., 10.

[266] See Appendix. (p.)580

[267] Plutarch, in C. Gracchus.

[268] Plutarch, in C. Gracchus.—The mother of these illustrious men during their infancy was shown by a Roman lady a casket of jewels, who after gratifying her vanity by the display requested to see those of Cornelia. The Roman matron sent for her children, and presenting them to her friend said, "Here are my jewels, my best and only ones." An elegant reproof borrowed from the wife of a celebrated Greek, who had called in like manner her "good man Phocion, her only jewel."

[269] *Ibid.*

[270] Seneca ad Marc. Consol., xvi.

[271] Plutarch.

[272] Tacitus, Annal.

[273] *Ibid.*

[274] Juvenal's Satires.

[275] Prudentius.

[276] St. Jerome, i., 169-70.

[277] St. Jerome, i., 169-70; Gibbon's Decline and Fall.

APPENDIX.

=========

NOTES TO ROME REGAL.

————◆————

CHAPTER I.

Page 2.—The Roman historians and poets deduce the genealogy of Romulus and Remus from Æneas, a Trojan chief, and Lavinia, the daughter of Latinus, king of the Latins; Silvius, their son, becoming the progenitor of thirteen Latin kings, whose united reigns are computed by Sir Isaac Newton to have comprised a longer period of time than the limited extent of human life seems to warrant. The Roman calculation was, however, neither lunar nor solar, the year being completed in ten months, or 304 days, which, in some measure, obviates the objection. The Latin dynasty ended with two princes, Numitor and Amulius. The younger, Amulius, dethroned his brother, putting his nephew to death, and consecrating his niece, Rhea Silvia, or Ilia, to Vesta. Ilia broke her vow of perpetual virginity, and being delivered of male twins in the temple of Vesta, assigned the paternity of her offspring to the God Mars. Amulius ordered his niece to be drowned in the Anio, and directed her children to be thrown into the Tiber, which at that time overflowed its banks. The rude cradle or trough, in which the exposed infants had been placed, was carried by the current to the foot of a wild fig-tree, where it was stranded, and left by the retreating waters; but was found by Faustulus, the principal shepherd of Amulius, who, wondering at the accident which had preserved the foundlings, and admiring their size and beauty, carried them home to his wife Acca Laurentia, a woman whose former dissolute life had obtained for her the name of Lupa, a circumstance that gave rise to the fable that Romulus and Remus, her foster-children, had been suckled by a wolf. In the quarrels between the herdsmen of Amulius and those of Numitor, the dethroned king of Alba, the adopted sons of Faustulus took active parts; which finally led to the capture of Remus, who was carried before Numitor, his grandfather, to whom he related the story of his birth, and who owned him for his grandson. With the assistance of Romulus, Remus effected a counter-revolution, slew Amulius, and replaced Numitor upon the throne. It seems unnecessary to comment upon the improbabilities of this romantic legend, since the bare fact that Numitor was not succeeded by his supposed grandsons, is a complete refutation of the royal origin of Romulus and Remus. The king of Alba merely rewarded the counter-revolutionists with some waste lands about the Tiber, of small value, to which he added the gift of slaves, cattle, and agricultural instruments. Some local landmarks remained for several ages, to attest the fact that the founder of Rome had been a twin foundling, exposed with his brother by some mother desirous of concealing her shame, or by some unnatural father who chose to relieve himself of the task of providing for the wants of his family.

The barbarous custom of exposing infants was as common in Italy and Rome, for centuries, as it now is in all heathen countries. It ceased when Christianity became the religion of the state; but during the period of idolatry and pagan darkness, the Christian deacons employed persons to take up these outcasts, who became the nurslings and children of the Church. Illegitimate children were never recognised by Roman legislation. They are rarely noticed in the Imperial records, and never in those of the Republic.

P. 4.—Hooke and Niebuhr have given us all the variations of the story; while the last, disbelieving it altogether, has made the foundling brothers impersonal nouns, and converted them into brick and mortar, in the shapes of rival towns, Roma and Remuria, and has actually discovered a place which seems to be called by the latter name. He has also imagined a town called Quirium, whose inhabitants were Quirites; but, setting on one side the miraculous part of the ancient story, the geographical flight of Niebuhr's imagination is quite as difficult to receive as the poetical romances of Plutarch and Livy. Unfortunately we cannot replace the legend of Romulus and Remus with anything more probable. Micheli has ascribed the foundation of Rome to a band of Teutonic robbers, upon very slender grounds, that of some Teutonic words occurring in the Latin language; but, as that language was in existence before Romulus, the discovery rather applies to the tongue than to the man who spoke it. A great linguist has, with greater appearance of probability, conjectured that Italy was colonised by Greeks and Celts, and that Latium, lying between those colonies, spoke a mixed language, and that that language was Latin.

P. 9.—"The remembrance of Tarpeia's guilt still lives in a popular legend," remarks Niebuhr; "real oral tradition has kept her name for five-and-twenty-hundred years in the mouths of the common people."

P. 9.—The names of the Sabine wives were bestowed upon the Curies. All married women were to be exempted from servile labours in the household, with the exception of the feminine ones of spinning and weaving. Men were to make way for them in the street, or wheresoever they might meet a Roman matron; to offend her delicacy by word or look, was to be considered and punished as a capital offence. If the wife desired it, the husband must place her on the same footing in regard to his inheritance as his child.[1] He could not sell his wife after he had become possessed of this paternal power (a right to the last hour of Rome's heathen existence he claimed over his offspring), under the penalty of being devoted to the infernal gods.[2] The Roman husband might divorce his wife for adultery, poisoning his children, drinking, or counterfeiting his keys. If he put her away for any other grounds, half his property was consecrated to his injured spouse, the other to the temple of Ceres.

P. 11.—It is thought by a modern historian, that "the clients were not anciently plebeians, but freedmen."[3] They might, perhaps, have been foreigners, whose poverty compelled them to find employment in Rome, and whose unprotected state obliged them to seek a powerful protector out of the patrician order. Clients and freedmen formed chiefly the trading class in Rome; and if a plebeian gave up husbandry, he sank into this lower order of persons, and was no longer a free citizen of Rome.[4] "The Roman plebeians, therefore, in the earlier ages, consisted exclusively of small landholders and free-labourers, and even if many persons of this order lost their estates and were reduced to poverty, it never contained any member engaged in trade, or any kind of manufacture."[5] This contempt for commerce and the industrial arts, formed a leading feature in the Roman character, and marked a people destined to maintain themselves by war rather than by native industry. The devotion of the plebeians to agriculture originated in necessity, for the lands belonging to the growing city were scanty in extent and poor in quality, and any negligence on the part of the cultivators must have led to want and starvation.

P. 14.—Those persons who reject the history of Romulus altogether, remark that Alba Longa vanishes from the scene as remarkably as Romulus himself. "But the existence of the ancient city is still attested by its site being distinctly marked where it stretched in a long street between the mountain and the lake. Along this whole extent the rock is cut away under it right down to the lake. These traces of man's ordering hand are more ancient than Rome. The surface of the lake, as it has been determined by the tunnel, now lies far below the ancient city, and before the lake swelled to a ruinous height, in consequence of obstructions in clefts of the rock, it must have lain yet lower; for in the age of Dionysius and Diodorus, during extraordinary droughts, the remains of spacious buildings might be seen at the bottom, taken by the common people for the palace of an impious king, which had been swallowed up. Above the steep rock a wall was needless,—the approaches on each side were easily barred. Monte Cavo was the Capitoline Hill of Alba, and there is great probability in the conjecture, that as at Rome the temple and citadel were distinct, so Roma di Papa was the citadel of Alba."[6]

P. 16.—The business of these virgins consisted in the preservation of a sacred fire which was always to be kept burning, for upon its continuance the fate of Rome was supposed to depend. No representation of the goddess, to whom the temple was dedicated, was seen in the fane; but in the most secret parts of the temple they kept concealed some mysterious image, which ancient authors affirm was a sitting figure of Pallas, represented with a distaff and spindle in her left hand, and a lance in her right hand, formerly brought from Troy by Æneas.[7] Others believed the mystery was hidden in two barrels, one full, the other empty. The fire by some was supposed to typify either the vital energy of nature, or purity, since fire purifies all things; but whatever might be represented under the allegory of the sacred and undying fire, the worship of this element, and the state of celibacy enjoined on its female priestesses, were extremely ancient. The sacred flame was found at Athens, where its maintenance was confided to aged widows; and at Delphi and in Persia. From the orbicular form of the temples of Vesta, and the method of rekindling the fire by means of the sun's rays,[8] it is supposed this mode of worship was intended to convey to the mind the sun's course in the heavens, and the manner in which his beams enlightened the earth. The hair of the youthful vestals was shaved, to denote their freedom from the strict rule of Roman paternity, and to prove their right to dispose of their property by will. This ornament, so prized by all females, was afterwards suspended near the temple,[9] and doubtless served to remind the priestess that the power of pleasing was taken from her, and that she was denied the exercise of her feminine influence over the hearts of mankind.

P. 18.—Near the Colline gate a little subterranean chamber was covered and concealed by a mound of earth, where a bed, a lamp, a breadmill, and oil, were prepared against the coming of the unfortunate and guilty priestess, who, being bound and placed in a covered litter, was borne through the Forum. Care upon these occasions was taken to prevent her cries reaching the ears of the populace, who silently made way for her funeral procession, the same prevailing silence marking the sense of her crime entertained by those whose functions obliged them to follow her bier.[10] "When the litter reached the living grave, the cords with which the victim was bound were loosened, when the high priest, lifting his hands to heaven, repeated in a low voice some prayers suitable to the occasion. The prisoner, still covered, was brought forth and led down to her house of darkness. When the priests retired, the stairs were drawn up and the earth thrown in and pressed down till the vault was filled up." Such is the terrific picture drawn by Plutarch of the living interment of the vestal who had broken her vows,[11] and as the punishment of one of these priestesses took place in the reign of Domitian,[12] he had probably taken his account from some aged person who had witnessed her execution. Several festivals were held in June in honour of the goddess Vesta, in which many curious ceremonies were practised.

P. 28.—The Roman historians, from whom Polybius derived his account of Tarquinius Priscus, assign to him a Greek origin. Cypselus, of Corinth, was the offspring of a marriage of disparagement—a union contracted by a nobleman with a woman of mean birth, whose children could only claim the privileges enjoyed by their mother in her maiden state. By uniting with the Commons, he overcame the oligarchy, and commenced a work of vengeance upon those who had despised his origin and sought his life. Many of the Bacchiads fled, and among the rest, Damaratus, who, having formed commercial relations at Tarquinii, settled at the place, to which he brought great wealth. The sculptors Eucheir and Eugrammus, and Cleophantus, the painter, accompanied him, and the Corinthian exile is said to have taught the Etruscans the art of alphabetical writing. Damaratus married an Etruscan woman of rank, by whom he had the Lucumo and Aruns. He is said to have governed Tarquinii, to which place he had brought much prosperity. After his death, his son, the Lucumo, a title derived from the rank, perhaps, of his deceased mother, found his foreign origin a disadvantage, and resolved to seek his fortune in a rising state, where it would place no bar to his ambitious wish of attaining to eminence.[13] Niebuhr disbelieves the origin of this prince, as, perhaps, he would his existence, if he had not left behind him many mighty works to attest this fact. He contests the parentage and Corinthian descent of Tarquinius Priscus, and particularly that his father, Damaratus, had obtained the government of Tarquinii, because he thinks it was a Latin town; but in his scepticism he unconsciously affords a proof that some close affinity or commercial relations at least existed between Tarquinii and Corinth, the vases peculiar to both towns, being painted alike in colour and design, in fact, being fac-similes of each other; those dug up at this day around Corinth being the same kind as those found at Tarquinii.[14] This circumstance, however trifling, is in favour of the Greek descent of Tarquinius Priscus, and of his father, Damaratus, having brought with him the potters, Eucheir and Eugrammus from Corinth.

P. 32.—This great work is thus ably described by Niebuhr:—"The Cloaca Maxima, which carried off the collected waters of the Velabrum, was one of the most wonderful works of antiquity. The innermost vault of this astonishing structure formed a semicircle eighteen Roman palms in width and height, which was enclosed in a second, and this again in a third, all of which are formed of hewn blocks of peperino, seven and a quarter palms long, and four and one-sixth in height; these blocks are all fixed together without cement. This river-like sewer discharges itself into the Tiber through a kind of grate in the quay, which is in the same style of architecture, and must have been raised at the same time, inasmuch as it dams off the river from the Velabrum, which has been rescued from it. It was only for the Velabrum and the Valley of the Circus that this cloaca sufficed; far more extensive structures were requisite to convey into it the waters drained off from the land about the Subura and the Forums. In fact, a vault no less astonishing than the one already described, was discovered in 1742, passing off from the Velabrum under the Comitium and Forum as far as St. Adriano, forty palms below the present surface. The locality shows evidently that it might be traced from thence under the Forum of Augustus up to the Subura. This later-discovered cloaca is built of travertino, the material," continues our author, "proving it to be less ancient than the regal times, for the kings used Alban or Gabine stone." He does not, however, believe "these immense works to be the same repaired by the censors, in the fifth century of the Roman era, at a cost of a thousand talents (two hundred thousand pounds);" for he says:—"These cloacæ have never required a single farthing to be expended upon them. Earthquakes, the pressure of buildings, and the neglect of fifteen hundred years, have not moved a single stone out of its place," and our author thinks these vaults will remain as uninjured as at this present day at the end of ten thousand years.

P. 38.—The laws and constitution given by Servius Tullius entitled him to the gratitude of the people whose moral and civic position he raised. Whether the alteration in the state originated from policy or benevolence, it was a measure of great wisdom.

P. 39.—"Every Roman was bound under a severe penalty to make a just return of his own person, his family, and his taxable property. The laws prevented the possibility of a false one being made without detection. All children, on their birth, were registered in the temple of Lucina; all who entered youth, in that of Juventas; all the dead, in that of Libitina; all sojourners, with their families, at the Paganalia; all changes of abode, or of landed property were to be announced to the magistrates of the district, or the tribunes. In like manner, notice must be given on the alienation of any article liable to tribute. It was by the plebeians that the censorial tax was paid, its name *tributum*, being derived by Varro from the tribes of this order." It is defined with great accuracy by Niebuhr, as "an impost varying with the exigencies of the state, regulated by the thousands of a man's capital in the census, but not according to his actual income; for the debts of the rate-payer were not deducted from it. In fact it was a direct tax upon objects, without any regard to produce." We may imagine how heavy this burden must have been upon the free and impoverished plebeian. If this arrangement could be considered a relief, how dreadfully oppressive the previous method must have been deemed by the commons!

P. 39.—"The festival called Septimontium preserved," remarks Niebuhr, "the memory of the time when the Capitoline, Quirinal, and Viminal Hills were not yet incorporated with Rome, but when the remainder of the city, to the extent afterwards enclosed (with the exception of the Aventine, which was and continued a borough) by the wall of Servius, formed a united civic community. It consisted of seven districts, which had each its own holidays and sacrifices, even in the age of Tiberius. The union of the whole city, in a military point of view, was effected by a wall, which by Livy is ascribed to Servius Tullius, by Dionysius and Pliny to Tarquin the Proud. But," remarks Niebuhr, "with whatever name it is associated, it was scarcely a less wonderful work than the Cloacæ, and worthy to excite the astonishment of Pliny, in whose time, nevertheless, the incalculable riches of the empire had built the Colosseum. This mound extended from the Colline to the Esquiline Gate, seven stadia, or seven-eighths of a mile. Out of a moat, above a hundred feet broad, and thirty deep— for there is no stone here, only pozzolana—was raised a wall fifty feet wide, and, consequently, above sixty feet high, faced towards the moat with a skirting of flag-stones, and flanked with towers. But the Colline Gate was situated where the Quirinal had sunk to a flat level; and a similar wall connects it with the western steeps of that hill, where we may place the boundary of the ancient Sabine town."

P. 47.—The lower summit of the Tarpeian Hill, now called Monte Caprino, which is separated from the Arx, where the Ara Cœli stands, by a hollow almost imperceptible, was the site of the Capitoline Temple. There was not a flat surface large enough here, so it was gained, as on Mount Moriah, by levelling the peaks, and by walling in a certain space, and then filling it up—works, which in the labour they cost, are not inferior even to the building of the temple. On this area a basement of considerable height was erected, eight hundred feet in compass. It was nearly an equilateral quadrangle, the length not exceeding the breadth by so much as fifteen feet. The triple sanctuary of Jupiter, Juno, and Minerva, underneath the same roof, with party walls to separate them, was surrounded by rows of pillars; on the south there was a triple colonnade, a double one on the other side.

---

[1] Niebuhr, History of Rome.

[2] *Ibid.*

[3] *Ibid.*

[4] Décadence de l'Empire Romain.

[5] Niebuhr, Hist. Rome, vol. i.

[6] *Ibid.*

[7] Plutarch; Herodian; Virgil; Ovid.

[8] Plutarch, in Numa; and in Artaxerxes.

[9] Plutarch, in Numa.

[10] *Ibid.*

[11] *Ibid.*

[12] Suetonius, in Domitian.

[13] Polybius.

[14] Niebuhr, History of Rome, i. p. 109; Pliny, Nat. Hist., xxxv. 43.

NOTES TO ROME REPUBLICAN.

———◆———

CHAPTER II.

Page 73.—"Were the Romans incapable of feeling that the chains which we burst by our own strength are an ornament?" asks Niebuhr. "The defeat of the Tuscans before Aricia is historical. The victory of the Cumans, which led Aristodemus to the sovereignty, was related in Grecian annals. Had not those of the Romans through false shame concealed their humiliation they might have told with triumph how their ancestors burst the yoke imposed upon them, though disarmed and threatened in what they held the dearest."[1]

P. 75.—So careful were the Valerii to retain the privilege granted to their great ancestor, that in the latter days of the republic, when the custom of burning their dead became general with the Romans, they kept up their claim to intermural interment, by causing the bier to be placed in their own family burying ground for an hour, in order to prove their ancestral right to that peculiar distinction which they waived, but had not forfeited.[2]

P. 78.—The original legend relates that two young men of lofty stature and great personal beauty, fought for the Romans, that they were mounted on white horses, but disappeared after the victory was won. These heroes were Castor and Pollux, to whom, in gratitude for their aid the Romans erected a temple in the forum. Strong doubts have been entertained respecting the truth of the narrative of the battle of Regillus and the train of events that led to it, the whole having been taken by Livy, it is supposed, from one of those beautiful ancient lays with which that author from time to time adorns his history. We, however, have nothing to substitute in its place but modern scepticism, therefore it is surely better to give the narrative than leave a chasm. One circumstance seems to attest its credibility, the praise rendered to the exiled Tarquin, who is said to have sat on horseback lance in hand, bearing himself in advanced age as bravely as if he were still young.[3]

P. 83.—Great doubts have been thrown upon the chronology ancient historians have assigned to the taking of Corioli. Livy and Plutarch call this town the chief city of the Volscians, which is a mistake, as Corioli appears in the list of the thirty Latin towns which made a league with Rome, the following year, as independent states. The whole heroic achievements of Caius Marcius are supposed by Hooke and Niebuhr to be placed thirty years earlier than the true period;[4] but, if the author may hazard such a conjecture, it seems not improbable that the storming of Corioli might have taken place many years before the exile of the illustrious Roman who gained his well-known appellation of Coriolanus there. We know that the anecdote respecting the civic garland of oak leaves, said to be won by him in his sixteenth year, at the first battle between Tarquin and his former subjects, must be misplaced as far as the time is concerned, though the fact that he saved the life of a Roman citizen at an early age is perfectly credible. It appears therefore that some of the events at least took place many years later than the date assigned to them by Livy and Plutarch. Hooke first noticed the error in the data, though he does not state the precise grounds: Niebuhr and Arnold have given some substantial reasons for the objection started by the author of the Roman Republic.[5]

P. 84.—This treaty with thirty Latin towns was framed for the mutual defence of the Romans and Latins, and contained a clause by which their armies when united in any expedition should be commanded every alternate year by the generals of each people in succession.[6]

P. 85.—A mysterious and half-defaced fragment in Festus, partially obliterated by fire, is supposed to refer to this period, and seems to prove that the nobility carried on a war with each other, of which some evidence is yet in existence. The statement was inserted by Verrius in his collection, and was retained by Festus in the interesting form in which it is still preserved, standing like a ruined tower to commemorate a cruel and relentless deed. The reader will find in Niebuhr's History of Rome, the document with his restoration; both the original and the matter supplied are marked, to assist his research. "The ritual books had preserved for religious purposes the memory of a dreadful event which the histories of Rome had blotted from her annals. In order that a spot in the Circus which was marked with a pavement of white flag-stones might not be profaned by any one, through ignorance or at least without his expiating his offence, they recorded that it had been abandoned to the manes, as being the place where nine illustrious men who had conspired against the Consul Sicinius, and had been burned alive in the Circus for high treason, were buried. Their names were preserved: five of them had been consuls during the years intervening between 252 and 261, nor among the other four was there apparently one who was not of an illustrious house. These victims were named Opiter Verginius Tricostus, Valerius Lævinus Postumus Cominius Auruncus, Alius Florinus, P. Veturius Geminus, Sempronius Atratinus, Verginius Tricostus, Mutius Scævola, Sextus Furius Fusus." Titus is supposed to be the Verginius whose prenomen has been destroyed by the fire that defaced without destroying the parchment on which the manuscript of Fabius was written; he was consul in the year 253. What a fearful story! the interrupted record of the act of a deep tragedy whose catastrophe is known, but not the events that led to such results. Well might the Roman annalists unite to leave it in the deep oblivion from which an old heathen ritual alone has preserved it, wrapped in a dim veil; the muniment, like the shadow on the sun-dial, pointing to it darkly yet casting no light upon the terrible story.

P. 90.—This year of Rome, 278, is the date assigned by the learned Niebuhr to the great dearth in which the quarrel between Coriolanus and the Commons first occurred. The names of the consuls are certainly very different, but we find these always an uncertain guide, they are obliterated on the Fasti Capitolini for this year, and by reference to the lists of Livy, Dionysius, and Diodorus, we find them quite dissimilar in each authority; but if we follow the simple narrative given by Livy, which is supposed to be one of the old heroic Latin lays, we shall not find those discrepancies which abound in the beautiful biography of Plutarch, and the account given by Dionysius of Halicarnassus.

P. 95.—The author has followed the narrative of Livy, but, according to Dionysius of Halicarnassus, no discoloration of the person or marks of violence appeared to justify the suspicion that he had been murdered by the Patricians. "His body," he says, "was exposed in the Forum before the people, and a notion prevailed that his death proceeded from a stroke from the gods, who disapproved of his enterprise."

P. 102.—The return of Coriolanus, in the character of a revengeful Volscian general, took place much later than the period assigned for it in Roman history. Hooke and Niebuhr have proved that the dates assigned by ancient historians are incorrect, and indeed from the state of the calendar then in use this ought not to surprise us. The nature too of the records of which Fabius made use in his early history were national lays, in which, though the narratives of heroic deeds might be strictly true, a regard to unity and concentrativeness often led the poet to crowd into a few verses, martial deeds which were really divided by long years.

P. 103.—It appears that a slave was being cruelly scourged in the street at the time the solemnities commenced, and that this revolting spectacle crossed the procession of the gods, and gave rise to the dream of a plebeian named Titus Latinius, who reported to the senate that Jupiter had ordered him "to direct the consuls to re-celebrate the games, since one danced at their opening whom he liked not, it being a holiday, not a day for punishment and torment."

P. 109.—Hooke, a valuable documentary historian, pointed out the incorrectness of the dates long before Niebuhr rectified them, and gave these events their proper place. The learned German had never seen Hooke's "Roman Republic," or perhaps he would not in the introductory portion of his lectures, have thrown discredit upon facts which he had himself taken such pains in elucidating and restoring to the records of the times to which they certainly belonged. "The features of the story are strongly marked and clearly discernible," remarks Niebuhr in his history, "when transferred to the place to which it clearly belongs, where it will appear that it is not merely a genuine tradition from very ancient times, which nevertheless might be only a bare fiction, but that it conveys a substantially faithful remembrance of a great man and great events, a remembrance kept up for centuries in the nation without the slightest doubt as to the reality of the facts, and connected with the history of the constitution and laws. And this story would be nothing but an untenable tale if its credibility rested on its belonging to that particular epoch to which the traditional history attached it."

---

[1] Niebuhr, Rome, i.

[2] Plutarch.

[3] Livy, i. 19.

[4] Hooke, Roman Republic; Niebuhr, Rome.

[5] Hist. Rome, ii. 93-99.

[6] Arnold, Rome, i. 153; Cincius de Consulum Potestate (Festus).

CHAPTER III.

Page 112.—It is doubtful whether this account of the manner in which the Romans were surprised is not an addition to the story by Dionysius, since the same occurrence would scarcely have happened twice to the same people in the same place; and a late historian has clearly shown that this locality can only belong to Caudium, the spot where the Romans in a later period passed under the yoke.[1] Livy, with more probability, but less poetry, merely relates that the consul was blockaded in his camp.[2]

P. 115.—This concession gave the Commons the legal possession of a stronghold, and bestowed upon them a freehold confirmed to them by augural ceremonies and sacrifices. When we remember that this hill had been formerly assigned to the Latins as a habitation, with the lands adjoining it, we seem to arrive at the conclusion that the plebeian order were of Latin origin, and not a part of the original Roman colony, and that they only recovered their old rights in the Mount and lands of the Aventine. A brazen pillar, fixed in the temple of Diana, on the Aventine, commemorated the triumph of the Commons, which ensured to them its possession, together with the public or demesne land lying about it as a perpetual freehold inheritance for ever. But how strange sounds the word for ever, when the buildings that crowned the Mount, and which then were the home of a free people, are levelled, and their old inhabitants dust!

P. 116.—Dentatus had won by his own great personal prowess, fourteen civic crowns (the garland of oak, the simple but honourable reward conferred on him who preserved the life of a citizen in battle), three mural crowns, for being the first man upon the breach in besieged towns; one obsidional crown; eight other crowns; eighty-three golden collars; sixty golden bracelets; eighteen lances; twenty-five sets of horse furniture, nine of which had been won in single combats. These military trophies, and the surname of the Roman Achilles, were the only fruits Dentatus had gained during a life spent in the service of his country. He now stood forth in the Forum a redoubted champion of the laws which he hoped would secure his order from want and oppression.[3]

P. 117.—Montesquieu has beautifully defined the law of nations to be naturally founded on this grand principle, that different nations ought in time of peace to do one another all the good they can, and in time of war as little harm as possible, without prejudicing their real interests.

P. 117.—Montesquieu has charged this code with cruelty, its punishments being very severe for offences for which restitution would have provided both the penalty and remedy.

P. 117.—The fragment of this Code of Laws still extant, exhibits a mixture of wisdom and absurdity, mingled with excessive superstition, cruelty, and bigotry. Whatever is really good appears to be derived from the laws of Moses—while the prohibition which forbad the wicked to make an offering to the gods, seems borrowed from the Book of Proverbs, "The sacrifice of the wicked is an abomination to the Lord."

P. 120.—Some families from age to age exhibit the same individuality of character, the same talents, and display the same virtues and vices. The Claudian line is remarkable for a general resemblance of mind and disposition. The Decemvir Appius Claudius, the representative of this house, appears to have possessed the subtle ambition, united to the vicious temperament which distinguished in after ages Tiberius, Caligula, and Nero, but that temperament had not then degenerated into madness, its only fruits in the republican ages being crime.

P. 132.—In his celebrated work, "L'Esprit des Loix," Montesquieu has given, in a single page, the political history of the rise and fall of the Decemvirate. Those comments are in his happiest style.

P. 132.—If the people possessed the power of the plebiscitum, their decree could only be passed in the comitia-centuriata, not in the Comitia Curiata; which, in regard to capital offences, had no authority to punish crime, which a law alone could reach.

P. 136.—There is no reason to believe that the moral responsibility of regulating the manners, and inspecting the conduct of the Romans, was then conferred upon the censors: which apparently grew out of the nature of the office, for as they were the registrars of the Romans, they kept each person in the class in which he was born. The Roman plebeian being a person holding lands of the state, could be dismissed from his tribe if he neglected the due cultivation of his little farm.[4] This erasure from the censor's list caused him to sink at once into the trading class, which was considered a great degradation.

P. 147.—This heathen ceremony was thus performed: The statues of six Grecian deities were taken down and placed on beds or couches round a magnificent table, and feasted for seven days in a sumptuous manner. The

Roman hospitality was not, however, confined to the celestials, the entire population was entertained at the expense of those citizens who were able to afford a public table, the inhabitants of Rome uniting together in offering up sacrifices and prayer. The debtor was liberated from his chains to return to them no more; the slave was released from his tasks; the destitute stranger found food and lodging in every house.

P. 147.—Niebuhr, in his History of Rome, has given a curious description of the manner in which this beneficial work was effected. He personally surveyed the spot, and is surprised at the able manner in which it was performed.

---

[1] Arnold, i. p. 203, foot note.

[2] Livy, iii.; Florus, i.

[3] Livy; Dion. Hal.

[4] Niebuhr, Hist. Rome.

CHAPTER IV.

Page 154.—"There is not a man in Rome," remarks Plutarch, "who does not believe that these imprecations of Camillus had their effect, though the punishment of his countrymen for their injustice was by no means agreeable to him, but on the contrary a matter of grief. Yet how great, how remarkable was that punishment, how singularly did vengeance follow the Romans. What danger, destruction, and disgrace did those times bring upon the city; whether it was the work of fortune, or whether it is the office of some deity to see that virtue is not oppressed by the ungrateful with impunity."

P. 155.—The origin of these predatory nations is involved in gloom, the only information the student can obtain respecting a people so numerous and widely dispersed not being through historic record, but from the affinity of language which still subsists, even at this remote day, among the Celtic branches existing in Europe, Asia, and Africa. These languages, in all their sub-divisions, are traced to Hebrew; and it is a fact, that the Syriac is the medium through which this resemblance is derived, and that the researches of the present century have only confirmed the conjectures of the learned Bishop Lowth, who, finding that the Welsh language abounded in Hebrew words, concluded that the inhabitants of the Principality were of Eastern origin. "The Gauls were Celts, who are said to have left their own country which was too small to maintain their vast numbers, to go in search of another. Part of them took their route towards the Northern Ocean, crossed the Riphæan mountains, and settled in the extreme parts of Europe; and part established themselves for a long time between the Pyrenees and the Alps, near the Senones and Celtorii. But happening to taste of wine there for the first time, brought out of Italy, they so much admired the liquor, and were so much enchanted with this new pleasure, that they marched to the Alps to seek the country which produced such excellent fruit. The man who first carried wine amongst them and excited them to invade Italy, is said to have been Aruns, a Tuscan, a man of some distinction, and not naturally disposed to mischief, but led to it by his misfortunes. He was guardian to an orphan, Lucumo (this was the title of the young man who possessed a Lucumony or lordship), the greatest fortune in the country, and celebrated for his beauty. Aruns brought him up from a boy, and when grown up he still continued in his house upon a pretence of enjoying his conversation. Meanwhile he had corrupted his guardian's wife, or she had corrupted him, and for a long time the criminal commerce was carried on undiscovered. At length, their passion becoming so violent that they could neither restrain nor conceal it, the young man carried her off and attempted to keep her openly. The husband endeavoured to find his redress in law, but was disappointed by the superior wealth of the Lucumo. He therefore quitted his own country, and having heard of the enterprising spirit of the Gauls, went to them and conducted their armies into Italy."

P. 156.—If we follow Livy, the Fabian family was included in the government of the year when the demand was made, but no mention on the tables is found of any Fabii for the ensuing one. Diodorus gives very dissimilar ones, nor do those quoted by Livy agree with his assertion. The measure must have been negatived, or if such candidates were named at all, they must have been outvoted. Nor is the conduct ascribed to Brennus more probable.

P. 159.—Modern history presents to our view a parallel to the caution shown by Brennus on entering the city abandoned to his arms, and the self-devotion of the Roman patriots who remained to perish with it. This parallel is found in Napoleon's Russian campaign, at the precise point when he entered Moscow. In fixing the date, however, of the sack of Rome, some difficulties present themselves, and it seems almost rash to state the chronology of facts so remote. If the events are really rightly placed, Plato and Aristotle were living at the time they took place. Rome was known to the Greeks "as a Grecian city, situated somewhere near the great sea (Mediterranean), whose reported fall by an army of Hyperboreans had reached Heracleides of Pontus from the west;" and this curious passage, in that author's "Treatise on the Soul," is the first mention made of Rome by any Greek writer. Aristotle is said to have mentioned the recovery of Rome by Camillus, whom he calls "one Lucius;" and in the Periplus of Scylax Rome is also mentioned about thirty years after the invasion of the Gauls. So brief and unsatisfactory are the accounts left us of the future mistress of the world by the learned people she was destined to conquer.

P. 159.—The wells of ancient Rome are among its oldest relics; that on the Capitoline hill is cut to an immense depth in the tufa, and is considered by Niebuhr to be the one which supplied the Romans in the citadel with water during its siege by the Gauls. It may be approached by the ruins which bear the modern name of Palazzaccio, below the side of the Tarpeian rock, towards the Palatine (from which place those condemned to death were hurled down), by means of passages cut in the tufa, which are very ancient.

P. 163.—A wild story is related by Livy and Florus, that the Romans, warned by Jupiter in dreams, threw loaves of bread to their starving enemies, in order to persuade them that they had plenty of provisions in the citadel. Ovid quotes this tale in his poems; but perhaps it had no other foundation than an act of private charity, that might have been performed by the Roman sentinels, who, it seems, had formed an intimacy with those of the enemy.

P. 164.—Polybius, who lived nearer the time, makes no mention of the victories of Camillus, and says "that the Romans agreed to the terms proposed by the Gauls," thus intimating that the absence of the invaders was purchased by the Romans in the Capitol. Suetonius, in relating the exploits of one of the ancestors of Tiberius, makes the following curious statement: "Drusus, killing the enemy's general, Drausus, hand to hand, gained a new surname for himself and his posterity. When he was pro-prætor he is said to have brought the gold out of France which was given to the Senones by the besieged in the Capitol, and was falsely reported to have been recovered by Camillus."[1] The reader must remember that the office of prætor was not in existence at that time, and that Rome, environed by hostile nations, had not then extended her conquests to a people of France, situated near Paris.

P. 167.—The Etruscans, it is supposed, had once held the supreme dominion of Italy, to them the Volscians had been subject, and they had also possessed the dominion of the sea. The Greek colonists had, however, deprived them of their naval power, and from sovereigns of the sea they sank into pirates. The government of Etruria was composed of united states which numbered twelve cities, each of these cities having twelve cities under its jurisdiction. These confederacies had filled the line of country included within "the Tiber Macra, the Apennines, and the sea," but this commercial people was not confined to these limits. Another strong confederacy existed to the north of the Apennines, possessing the plains of the Po from the sea to the Trebia, while a third cluster of twelve confederate states were seated in Campania, a fact to which tradition and the existence of Etruscan names affords some proof.[2]

P. 171.—If we follow Livy (and if we do so we must remember that Rome was governed by a military despotism at the time in which he wrote, though the mild character of the ruler had cast a golden gleam over the chains of his subjects), we shall conclude that Manlius actually conspired against the constitution of the Republic, and scarcely veiled his intention of assuming the regal dignity.[3] What, indeed, is the difference between the constituted head of a state, if the power be perpetually invested in one person, and a king? The name may be different, but the authority is the same. Camillus has been charged with this crime, and certainly the hatred between the parties was of long standing, if the great Roman had really deposed Manlius, as has been conjectured, from the consulship before his own exile. But we are assured that Manlius was jealous of the high military reputation of his rival,[4] and Camillus was not in office at the time of the first imprisonment or after arraignment of Manlius, but he might be the original cause of the prosecution of an old foe who had detracted from his exploits and opposed his triumphs. But if Marcus Manlius Capitolinus was the victim of Camillus and the aristocracy, the agents of his ruin were the tribunes of the people, and his executioners the Commons themselves; for if his own order considered him an apostate the popular leaders influenced the multitude to destroy their idol of whom the tribunes had become jealous. Arnold considers their persecution of Manlius a proof of his guilt, but the unfairness of his trial is a presumption of his innocence. "Put not your trust in Princes," is the warning voice of inspiration to the subjects of a monarchical government. To those of a Republic it would have been—"Put not your trust in the People."

P. 175.—Under the Jewish theocracy the debtor was compelled to serve seven years, at the end of which period he was to go out free, yet not without reward.[5] The merciful Lord of Israel had provided for the bondman who was to receive gifts at the hand of his master, that the blessing of the Most High might come upon the house from whence he was departing. The remuneration, in regard to actual value, was a matter of conscience and religion.

P. 176.—Niebuhr in his learned history of Rome has arranged the Agrarian law of Licinius not after Livy, but according to the light of his own deep researches. He has already given convincing reasons that an Agrarian law could only relate to the Ager publicus and that it concerned the Domain land of the Republic: in no wise trenching upon the private rights of any individual; while it demanded restoration of the lands which had been usurped from the public.

[1] Suetonius, in Tiberius.

[2] Arnold's Hist. Rome.

[3] Livy, vi. 18.

[4] Plutarch, in Camillus; Livy.

[5] Deuteronomy, xv. 12-14.

CHAPTER V.

Page 184.—This ceremony has been considered absurd by most historians, who have erroneously imagined it was designed as a remedy for the prevailing epidemic, the plague; Niebuhr has, however, by clearing up the mystery, exonerated the Roman people and their rulers from this groundless charge, for, according to him, and he gives solid reasons for the assertion, "the practice of driving a nail into the wall of the Capitoline temple was a sort of rude chronology, which served to denote the manner in which the calendar was kept when the intercalary month of twenty-two days was inserted in the last period of the secle; the close of every lustre was denoted in the same manner. Thus the ignorance of later times considered that custom absurd to which the Romans were really indebted for the true record of time." "Cincius," continues our author, "had seen similar marks in the temple of Nortia at Vulsinii, and supposed them to be the scores of years made at a time when writing was rare. The object was to determine how many lustres had elapsed since the beginning of a secle, and the close of a lustre was beyond doubt denoted in the same manner."

P. 199.—"The Samnites were a Sabine colony, and boasted a Lacedæmonian descent; they were originally planted in the Apennine heights,"[1] from whence, in consequence of a vow, they sent forth their youth to colonise some other land. That the vow was more political than religious we may easily believe, but it is thus related by the old historians:—"The Sabines had for many years waged an unsuccessful war with the Umbrians, when they bethought themselves of propitiating the favour of the gods by the dedication of everything living born in their land one year to them, they engaging to sacrifice or redeem the increase thus given to them. But the years succeeding the dedicatory one proving barren with regard to the fruits of the earth, made them consider whether in all particulars they had fulfilled their promise. They then remembered that the children born to them that year had neither been sacrificed nor redeemed, so they devoted them all to their god Mamers (Mars),[2] and when they were grown up sent them away to seek for themselves a new country.[3] They followed the track of a young bull, who led them to the land of the Opicans, whereupon they drove out the inhabitants and took possession of some scattered villages, after which they sacrificed their brute guide to their god Mamers, and adopted the form of the animal for their distinguishing cognizance, the figure of the bull still being extant upon the coins of this warlike people.[4]" Such is the legend connected with the formation of a colony which being at first few in number adopted the language of the people amongst whom they settled themselves by force of arms; the vow of their fathers being doubtless a pretext for sending away their superfluous population. The Samnites spoke Opican or Oscan, which is found on the inscriptions of their coins.[5] Their habits were pastoral and predatory, but beyond the great bravery they displayed in their wars with the Romans, we know nothing of them, for the issue of these long and sanguinary contests left Samnium a desert, and her people a remnant.

P. 207.—Tradition has placed the scene of the Roman disgrace in a valley between Arienzo and Arpaja, through which the road from Naples to Benevento now passes. A village in the defile still bears the name of Forchia, and in the middle ages actually retained the appellation of La Furcula Caudina.[6] A modern traveller supposes that a narrow gorge on the little stream of the Isclero, above Sant Agata de' Goti was the spot so injurious to the glory of the Romans.[7]

P. 211.—In Rome we find a vast civilising power combined with military courage and skill, her conquests being ultimately beneficial to those she conquered. In the history of other heathen nations we rarely find this to be the case. "If Rome destroyed, she also created," her wars increasing her civilising influence as well as her political power.

P. 211.—In that age, and in many succeeding ones, the father held an absolute authority over the persons of his children, and if his daughter absented herself three nights from her husband's house, he could give her in marriage to another man.[8] As no instance of divorce had yet occurred, or at least was registered in the annals of Rome, the argument of Fabius was strong and convincing to those who heard him.

P. 212.—"The custom," remarks Niebuhr, "of making literal records of judicial and administrative transactions, of which so many examples are extant, as acta, was certainly derived from very ancient times. All the proceedings of the senate were registered, the ordinances were written down in due form, the prætorian transactions were certainly not entrusted to memory. The census alone occasioned an immense deal of writing, the whole management of the finances and quæstorship still more. With all this no son of a free-born Roman had anything to do, it belonged to the calling of the notaries, except so far as slaves educated for the purpose were trained therein; who, however, after their manumission, purchased their admission into one of the close guilds. Besides the public business, the notaries obtained rich profits from making private documents. Thus there was by no means wanting in antiquity, the most essential part of the business which occupies and supports the class of officials who, though subordinates in reality are not always so in appearance, but far from being deemed a preparatory training for public business, it was divided from these honours by an insurmountable barrier."

P. 212.—In admitting these classes to the privileges of the plebeian order, Appius Claudius was benevolent and wise, with the exception of the clause which prevented the new plebeian from following his old callings, which in almost every case required more talent than that of agriculture. But in this restriction Appius Claudius, bold as he was, was compelled to yield to the prejudices of his haughty countrymen. In admitting a large body of influential persons to civic rights, he did his country a real service, but his motive has been always questioned. He wished, it was considered, to check the elevation of the middle class, and keep it down by means of a new class bound to him by the ties of gratitude. Acting in this somewhat after the fashion of despotic sovereigns in our own days, who wish to bridle the aristocracy by the creation of a middle class, only he wished to keep the plebeian families out of the aristocracy. The difference had become indeed slight, for the offices of state when once shared by the plebeian order left it little to attain to, it had won its rights and proved itself worthy of them. Could Appius Claudius have laid aside his prejudices, and exerted himself to open to them the hereditary honours, the quarrel kept up between the two orders would have died a natural death as in England, where they lie open to all. To his desire, then, of keeping the plebeian order down, may be traced his conduct to the libertini.

P. 213.—"The works which immortalize the censorship of Appius were the reason that in defiance of law and custom, and the severe censures of the tribune P. Sempronius, he retained his office after the eighteen months were expired, in order that another might not have the honour of their completion. The greatest of these is the Appian way to Capua, which must certainly be regarded as his work, although it seems impossible that being as it is one hundred and twenty miles to the place, it could have been designed and executed in four or even five years. And although the paving of it with polygons of lava, which constitutes in reality the incomparable magnificence of Roman roads, did not take place till much later, when in 451 the first mile from the Porta Capena to the temple of Mars was paved with hewn stones (peperino) as a way for riding on horseback and walking. A well-known inscription informs us that there was a carriage road near the temple of Mars. In 453-459, the whole road was paved with lava from thence to Bovillæ." The most essential part of the work, however, is the foundation, the sub-struction through deep valleys, the bridges, the cuttings through hills, and in addition to this the canal through the Pontine marshes with the two-fold object of conveying the necessaries for war from Latium and Terracina, this was of advantage to a state which was by no means master of the sea. Appius did not carry his road through the marsh, as the canal formed a portion of it, which connected the two parts of the real road; this, however, was afterwards effected by Trajan.

P. 213.—"Forum Appii, on the canal, was also built, undoubtedly, by Appius Claudius, a market town, which might be very populous in the winter months on account of the constantly increasing intercourse with the capital, but which even then contained only boatmen and innkeepers."[9] It was here the brethren met and encouraged St. Paul, upon his first coming to Rome as a prisoner who had appealed to the tribunal of the Emperor Nero for that justice he could not hope to obtain in Judea. A measure which led to a more extensive dissemination of the Gospel.[10] "The Appian aqueduct supplied to the Roman people pure water instead of the unwholesome and turbid element supplied by the Tiber. It was the first of these stupendous works built in republican Rome. Tusculum shows still the remains of an older water-vault, but Appius Claudius certainly conferred this benefit upon his native city. His aqueduct collected the springs on the left of the Prænestine road, about eight miles[11] from the Esquiline gate, and conducted them underground that the water might not be cut off in time of war, with the exception of sixty paces of archwork near the Porta Capena, and Cælian and Aventine hills to the place where the distribution began, between the Porta Trigemina and the Clivus Publicius. The depth at which the conduits lie (the construction of which is much facilitated by the tufa of the Roman hills) may be inferred from the fact that only sixty paces of architecture were necessary in the valley between the Cælian and Aventine, and as they lay so deep it is evident, from the nature of the case, that they could only conduct water to the lower districts, that is to the Circus, the Velabrum, the Vicus Tuscus, and perhaps also to the Subura besides, though the supply could not have been very abundant. The merit of discovering the springs which fed the aqueduct, belonged to the censor C. Plautius, who derived the name of Venox from the circumstance, but Appius himself completed the work.[12]"

P. 213.—The free-born Briton does not consider himself degraded by work, though his liberty stands on a firmer basis than that of which the Roman plebeian was so proud.

P. 214.—"This able person was at the head of the notaries, a class not enrolled among the nine corporations of ancient Rome, but which it is presumed became a guild towards the end of the Republic,[13] when wealth in moveable property constituted a second and more influential nobility, the notaries formed a third estate when the government and financial companies required a continually increasing number of book-keepers and clerks. Its importance as an instrument as a matter of course increased in ratio with the greatness of the state and wealth of the people requiring its services.[14]"

P. 215.—Some remains of this ancient forest, whose passage led to such important results, "may still be traced along the ridges dividing the valley of the Tiber from the lake of Bolsena, and from the vale which runs from the foot of the lake down to the sea." "Where the road from Viterbo to Rome crosses them, they are still covered with copsewood, and the small crater of the Lake of Vico which lies high up in their bosom, is surrounded by the remains of the old forest. The hills, are a remarkable point in the landscape, because they run up to a crest with little table land on their summits, commanding an extensive view on either side reaching far away to the south-east over the valley of the Tiber even to the Alban hills, whilst on the north and west they look down on the plain of Viterbo, and the Lake of Bolsena is distinctly visible, shut in at the farthest distance by the wild mountains of Radicofani."[15]

P. 221.—Appius Claudius is said to have assisted his clerk in this useful work, indeed Pomponius charges Flavius with having stolen his book from his learned master,[16] while Pliny states that in collecting the Fasti he only followed the advice of the censor.[17] The change of style from the Etruscan calendar had it seems involved the people in the dilemma that compelled them to apply to the pontiffs to avoid the desecration of those portions of time devoted to religious observances, Flavius is supposed to have framed his calendar by preserving the answers obtained from the pontifices. His tables were covered with gypsum upon which the days of every month were painted.[18] Cneius Flavius was one of the earliest authors of the republic, and composed a work of some merit upon civil law.[19]

P. 221.—These brief chronicles of the sacred college were written by the chief pontiff on a whited table, and contained the events or annals of the year, such as prodigies, pestilences, famines, campaigns, triumphs, and the obituaries of illustrious men—a dry and barren chronicle without ornament or beauty of style. The table when completed was set up in the pontiffs house. This custom, derived from extremely ancient times, ended with the pontificate of P. Mucius, when the supreme pontiff either thought the custom too laborious, or the rise of Latin literature made it appear no longer necessary.

———

[1] Dionysius, ii. 49; Strabo, v. 250.

[2] *Ibid.*; Festus, in Mamertini; Arnold.

[3] *Ibid.*

[4] Arnold; Micheli.

[5] *Ibid.*

[6] Niebuhr; Arnold.

[7] *Ibid.*; Keppel Craven, Tour in Southern Italy.

[8] Montesquieu, Spirit of the Laws.

[9] Niebuhr, Rome, iii. 305.

[10] Acts, xxviii. 15.

[11] Niebuhr, Rome, iii.; Appius Claudius, his works; Frontinus de Aquaeduct., i.

[12] Niebuhr, Rome, iii. 306-8.

[13] Niebuhr, Rome, iii. 299.

[14] *Ibid.*

[15] Arnold, Rome, ii. 252.

[16] Niebuhr.

[17] Pliny, Nat. Hist., xxxiii. 6.

[18] Niebuhr; Aul. Gell., vi. 9; Livy, ix. 46.

[19] Cicero, Orat., i. 41.

CHAPTER VI.

P. 233.—Some ancient authors affirm that the slain Gauls amounted to one hundred thousand.[1] The legions of Decius are said to have caught up the lances of the fallen Gauls, which they hurled at the survivors, who were covered with immense wooden shields.[2] A curious but not very probable anecdote is related of this battle. Before the contending armies joined in fight, a hind chased from the mountains by a wolf rushed among the Gaulish ranks, and was immediately transfixed on the spears of the barbarians. The wolf avoided a similar fate by taking shelter with the Romans, who declared that the slaughter of an animal sacred to Diana would bring defeat to their foes, while the wolf, which had nurtured their founder Romulus, afforded them an omen of victory.[3]

P. 241.—The history of the prince to whom the Tarentines had entrusted their cause had been remarkable for its romantic vicissitudes. Tradition linked his descent to the great names of Achilles and Pyrrhus, from whom his line was distinctly traced.[4] This warrior was the son of that Aeacides who reigned over the Molossians before the death of his cousin the king of Epirus, in Italy, had opened to him the succession of that kingdom. Pyrrhus and his father were both nearly related to Alexander the Great, Olympias, the mother of the mighty conqueror, having been an Epirot princess. Aeacides, in defending the family of the deceased Macedonian hero, left his own exposed to the machinations of Cassander, who easily induced the turbulent Epirot chiefs to depose their sovereign. The absence of Aeacides saved him from death, but his infant son

Pyrrhus owed his life to the fidelity of his nurse and those personal attendants who had escaped from the murderous hands of the rebels.[5] These adherents brought the young child to the court of Glaucias, king of Illyricum, whose marriage to a princess descended from Achilles they thought might interest him in the early misfortunes of a prince of her own house.[6] The Illyrian monarch did not intend to embroil himself with the powerful and unprincipled Cassander; he therefore suffered the infant to remain at his feet in the suppliant posture in which his nurse had placed him, without paying any regard to the entreaties of the queen, whose feminine feelings were moved by the misfortunes of her infant relation. While the king was hardening his heart for the cruel political part his fears urged him to take, his unconscious guest stretched forth his little hands towards him as if to implore his protection, and while he wept, touched the altar sacred to the household gods. This appeal, made by an infant still at the breast, surprised and touched the king, who considered the gods themselves had pleaded the cause of injured innocence.[7] The prayer of the wife he loved obtained a hearing, and the young prince was brought up with their own children,[8] and restored to his throne by his benefactor.

P. 255.—He fell at Argos by the hand of a woman with whose son the monarch was fighting. The young Argive, when sinking beneath the sword of his royal antagonist, was saved by his mother, who, perceiving his danger, flung a stone from the top of her house upon the head of his assailant. The blow was mortal, but if it had not been so the enemies of the fallen warrior completed her work by slaying him upon the spot.[9] Thus died, full of ambitious projects, this remarkable man, distinguished for the vicissitudes of his fortune even from his infancy. Nature had endowed him with many noble qualities, which his boundless ambition and immense destructiveness entirely perverted. His death was a blessing to a world which seemed to him too narrow for his projected conquests. Appius Claudius outlived the sovereign whom his wise counsels had been the means of expelling from Italy.

P. 255.—The beautiful waterfall of Velino is not the work of nature but of this illustrious Roman. M. Curius, the conqueror of the Samnites conferred a lasting benefit upon the Reatinians by a work which "has no equal in the world."[10] The waters of the lake Velinus, like those of the Fucinus, covered many miles of country, the hills obstructing its flowing into the Nera. Curius cut a broad and deep canal through the limestone rock for the length of a mile; through this the stream of superfluous water took its way, and acquired the name of the river Velinus; running "rapidly to the edge of the valley, at the bottom of which the Nera flows, and plunges down from a height of one hundred and forty feet. This is the Cascade delle Marmore, or Terni. Nature has produced far mightier and more important waterfalls, but the most beautiful of all is the work of a Roman. Across the canal he cast a bridge of one arch, in the Etruscan style of architecture, of the largest squares without any mortar. None of these blocks have moved a pins point from their original position, although a huge weight of earth has been pressing upon them for more than two thousand years. Its existence is known to few travellers, who are generally shown another bridge below the falls, of a later date when art was declining in the Empire. The course of the water down the canal was regulated by ditches, and thus the Rosea was gained, the Tempe of the Reatinians, the richest soil in Italy."[11]

P. 279.—The cruelty of the Carthaginians makes the horrifying description of his sufferings very probable. Cicero, in his comparison between the true happiness enjoyed by the virtuous and unfortunate Regulus in his dungeon, and Thorius Balbus, the epicure, pronounces Marcus Regulus to be the happier man: "Even at that moment, when of his own accord, without any compulsion but the plighted word he had given to the enemy, he left his country and returned to Carthage, and lay in prison deprived of rest and food; even then," continues our author, "he was a happier man than Thorius with his bottles and beds of roses."[12] Against the general opinion that Regulus died in tortures, this passage has been quoted from Diodorus Siculus: "When the news of his death reached his native city, with all its real or supposed horrors, the senate gave into the hands of the Atilii, the sons of Regulus, two captive Carthaginian generals, Bostar and Hamilcar, and the mother of the young men stirred up her sons to use them cruelly." The author then relates the death by starvation of Bostar, and that Hamilcar, who was the stronger man, remained alive with the dead body of his companion; and that he implored the compassion of Marcia by reminding her "how careful he had been of her husband," but that she remained inexorable. The report of this cruelty coming to the ears of the tribunes of the people, those magistrates took the surviving prisoner out of the hands of the Atilii; and the senate reproved them for their cruelty, and treated Hamilcar with kindness from that time. No doubt the humanity of the tribunes preserved the life of one of these death-doomed men; but the senate, in placing them in the hands of the outraged family of Regulus, must have clearly foreseen the ill-treatment they would receive. Their reproof was as hypocritical as their conduct. In the account given in this fragment, quoted from Diodorus Siculus, there does not seem much ground for the opinion of Palmerius, that the silence of Polybius, and the evidence it affords, are against the fact that Regulus was tortured to death; especially when we remember the cruel character of the Carthaginian people, it seems more probable that they destroyed him by such terrible means, than that they let him die lingeringly in captivity. Horace makes the patriotism of Regulus the subject of a part of his fifth Ode, which, though inscribed to Augustus, might with more propriety have been dedicated to the stern victim of Roman honour. With Arnold, we sincerely wish that both these dreadful narratives were actually untrue, and had no surer grounds than a crooked and dark policy working out its own ends by harrowing appeals to the national feelings of each nation; but alas, the state of the heathen world makes it but too probable that both statements are true.

P. 280.—Some Roman historians blame Claudius Pulcher more for his want of piety than for the deficiency of skill and foresight which lost him the victory. For when the augur informed him that the sacred chickens would not eat, and that he ought not to engage after such a bad omen; he scornfully remarked, "Let them drink," and immediately ordered them to be flung into the sea,[13] for his firm mind and haughty temper had risen superior to the superstition of the age. He was recalled to Rome and deposed from the consulate. His last consular act betrayed the strongest contempt for the senate and people of Rome, whom he outraged by the nomination to the dictatorship of Claudius Glicia, a viator or serjeant, who was one of his own personal attendants.[14] As he was required to name a dictator for his own trial, his arrogance led him to offer this sarcasm in return. The senate did not put up with the insult but named Atilius Calatinus to that dignity, after solemnly deposing Glicia from his office. Junius the other consul was equally unfortunate, for Carthalo entered the harbour of Lilybæum and burned many Roman galleys, after which he sailed away to intercept the convoy in which the quæstors were bringing provisions and troops for the Roman army.

P. 284.—The conditions prescribed by the Roman consul and so reluctantly acceded to by Hamilcar have been preserved by Polybius. "The Carthaginians shall evacuate Sicily, and pay to the Roman Republic 2020 talents of silver (£437,250) within twenty years. They shall deliver up unransomed the Roman prisoners, and shall purchase the redemption of their own. They shall not make war with Hiero, king of Syracuse, nor with any other ally of Rome. Neither of the contracting parties shall erect fortresses nor levy soldiers in the dominions of the other, nor tamper with the fidelity of their allies."[15] The Roman senate chose to increase the sum levied upon the rival republic to 3200 talents, and they also insisted upon Carthage giving up all claim to the islands lying between Sicily and Italy.[16]

P. 284.—This prudent forecast was rendered useless by the refusal of the senate to pay these small detachments till the arrival of the whole body, because the Carthaginian government had determined to give them less than the sum for which their services had been engaged; the exhausted state of the treasury being the excuse for this breach of the public word. This dishonest arrangement was however as ill-planned as it was disgraceful to the national faith, for as they intended to act unjustly it would have been more prudent not to have waited for the whole injured body of armed and well-disciplined men, before putting their bad design into execution. As might have been expected, the mercenary army when assembled together to receive their arrears broke into open mutiny, and taking up their head quarters in Tunis, about twenty miles from Carthage, were joined by Spendius, a Campanian by birth and formerly a Roman slave, and other men of servile condition, and became the authors of one of the most sanguinary wars ever recorded in history. The particulars of the mercenary war, as it is called, have really no place in the history of Rome, it is sufficient to say that it cost the life of Gisco, and employed in its reduction the time and talents of Hamilcar for three years and a half, that in the course of it Sardinia was lost to the Carthaginians, and that it ended in the total destruction of the mercenaries. From the barbarous spirit exhibited by the parties engaged in it, we find it called the "Inexpiable War." This furious contest weakened Carthage more than the victories of the Romans, and the atrocities acted on both sides are unparalleled even in the blood-stained pages of ancient history.

[1] Duris of Samos; Diodorus; Arnold.

[2] *Ibid.*

[3] Livy, x. 23.

[4] Arnold; Plutarch; Pausanias.

[5] Plutarch.

[6] *Ibid.*

[7] Plutarch, in Pyrrhus.

[8] *Ibid.*; Diodorus, xix.

[9] Plutarch, in Pyrrhus.

[10] Niebuhr, Hist. Rome, iii. 413.

[11] *Ibid.*

[12] Cicero, de Finibus.

[13] Suetonius, in Tiberius.

[14] Livy, Epit. xix.; Zonaras, viii. 15.

[15] Polybius, i. 62.

[16] *Ibid.*, 63.

CHAPTER VII.

P. 288.—Before Hamilcar Barca's departure he offered vows and sacrifices for the success of the expedition. The omens promised a favourable result, whereupon he requested the priests and their assistants, and even his own friends to withdraw while he called his son Hannibal, a boy of nine years old, to join him in his devotions before the altar, as those he had dismissed supposed. Hannibal, however, many years afterwards gave to Antiochus, king of Syria, this account of the interview between him and his father. First Hamilcar asked him in an endearing tone whether he would wish to go with him to Spain. Which question the high-spirited child answered by entreating his father to take him. Whereupon Hamilcar leading him to the altar, bade him lay his hand upon the victim and swear eternal enmity to the Romans, if he indeed determined to follow the fortunes of his father. Hannibal swore—and we shall find him in the maturity of manhood keeping religiously that awful vow pronounced in early childhood.[1]

P. 289.—This change in the married state was imputed to the censors, who observing a laxity of morals and a decrease of population, presumed it was occasioned by interested marriages, and obliged the citizens to swear that they would form no union, unless with the view of increasing their families.[2] Carvilius pretended that after he had taken this oath his conscience would not allow him

475

to retain his childless wife. A foolish pretence, that could not have arisen from the new law.[3]

P. 291.—It is remarkable that the high-spirit of several female sovereigns occasioned the Romans at three several periods of their history considerable trouble.

P. 295.—"Rome had not yet overpassed the space included in her walls by Servius Tullius. The Capitoline and Quirinal hills looked down on the open space of the Campus Martius,[4] the generous gift of a vestal virgin to the Roman people—this field of Mars is now the principal site of modern Rome.[5] The hills rocky and wild in that age boasted their unlevelled escarpments and primeval woods, where the ground was yet unoccupied, though temples and proud patrician buildings disputed with savage nature for their possession. In the valleys beneath, the tall houses roofed with wooden shingles were crowded in narrow streets. The Comitium and Roman forum lay in the midst, occupying the space from the Capitoline hill to the Palatine."

P. 300.—It is a standing dispute among the learned men of this day at what precise point of these mountains Hannibal commenced his ascent, but the modern historians, Catrou and Rouillé adduce some reasons that have inclined the accurate Hooke to suppose that his route lay by the Great St. Bernard. The Roman historians have obscured the truth by introducing many impossible circumstances. The particulars themselves are sufficiently striking without calling in the aid of fable.

P. 302.—Livy declared that the great Carthaginian facilitated his march by making large fires and pouring boiling vinegar upon the rocks, but Polybius says, "that there was not a tree in the place, nor even near it," which fact sufficiently points out the falsehood of Livy's account.

P. 303.—Hannibal, before he departed upon his Italian expedition, had a remarkable dream or vision, so remarkable indeed that we might almost imagine that the great Carthaginian left Spain by Divine commission.

P. 307.—His desire to engage Hannibal had induced him to quit Rome before the due performance of the religious rites proper to the occasion. He probably wished to try his own strength against the Carthaginian leader unfettered by his colleague, since he did not urge his co-operation. Nor did he pay the slightest attention to the letters of recall despatched after him by the senate, that body being displeased by his neglect of the inaugurating ceremonies which the people of Rome considered essential to the consular magistracy.

P. 310.—Although the policy adopted by Fabius was prudent when the transcendent talents of his opponent are taken into consideration, yet there seems something selfish in this abandonment of Italy to sword, flame and rapine. In Russia and Persia, Hannibal would have found the country wasted and destroyed before him, and instead of luxuriating in plenty would have had to contend with famine. In leaving Umbria to him Fabius tacitly acknowledged his own inferiority. In fact throughout these campaigns his object was to defend Rome rather than save Italy.

P. 316.—He must in his outset in life have had as much to contend with from the contempt of the plebeians as the plebeians themselves formerly from the dominant aristocracy, since the haughty Roman despised the commercial arts and preferred the labours of the agriculturist to the wealthier calling of trade. Perhaps Varro had shown the people kindness in times of national distress, but to whatever cause he owed his popularity it remained unshaken even by that fatal defeat which gave to his ignoble name a disgraceful immortality.

P. 318.—Some historians make the victory won by Hannibal, at Cannæ, the fruit of two days battle, in both of which Varro was the commander in chief of the Roman armies. Hooke adopts this opinion,[6] but the skirmish already noticed has perhaps been considered in this light, and the measures taken by Varro for the dispersion of the Numidian cavalry may have led to the idea that he engaged with Hannibal, and successfully repelled the attack of his cavalry by charging with his dartmen, supported by some of his legionaries. Night is said to have parted the combatants, leaving the advantage to Varro.[7]

P. 321.—Polybius, however, who was a contemporary writer and a military author, does not condemn Hannibal's inactivity, because his great superiority over the Roman armies consisted in his cavalry, which would be useless in a siege. Livy has been followed by many ancient authors, and yet Hannibal, who was a prudent commander, took no doubt the wisest part in not driving to extremity a brave and patriotic people.

P. 323.—As the senators were attached to the Roman government, he artfully persuaded them "that the people intended to cut their throats, but that if they trusted themselves to him he would preserve their lives." They fell into the snare and Pacuvius shut them up in a temple, after which he told the people that they had better not change the present form of government, which was good, for a worse, but elect fresh senators for those they intended to put to death, replacing each member with a man of strict honour and probity. Such men, if they were to be found in Capua, escaped the search of her citizens, and Pacuvius then proposed keeping those in office who were in prison, assuring them they would be found courteous and submissive for the future. Accordingly the senators were released, and from that time studied to please the people and Pacuvius, who, in all but the name, was the sovereign of Capua. Hannibal's victory at Cannæ, so fatal to the Romans, inclined the volatile Capuans to the Carthaginian interest; but their near relationship to the vanquished, and the fact that most of the high-born sons of Capua were in the Roman armies, made them act with more caution. They sent to the senate at Rome, ambassadors to demand that Rome and Capua should be invested with equal privileges, and that one of the Roman consuls should be chosen from among the citizens of Capua. These proposals were indignantly rejected.

---

[1] Polybius, iii. 11.

[2] Gell., iv. 3.

[3] Dion. Hal., 93.

[4] Arnold; Bunsen.

[5] Arnold; Bunsen.

[6] Roman Republic.

[7] Hooke; Polybius, i. 101.

CHAPTER VIII.

P. 359.—*Votive Shield of Scipio Africanus.*—In 1656, a fisherman on the banks of the Rhone, in the neighbourhood of Avignon, was considerably obstructed in his work by some heavy body which he feared would injure his net; but by proceeding slowly and cautiously he drew it on shore untorn, and found that it contained a round substance in the shape of a large plate or dish, thickly encrusted with a coat of hardened mud; which the dark colour of the metal beneath induced him to consider as iron. A silversmith, accidentally present, encouraged the mistake, and after a few affected difficulties and demurs bought it for a trifling sum, and immediately carried it home; and after carefully cleaning and polishing his purchase, it proved to be of pure silver, perfectly round, more than two feet in diameter, and weighing upwards of twenty pounds. Fearing that so massy and valuable a piece of plate offered for sale at one time and place, might produce suspicion and inquiry, he immediately, without waiting to examine its beauties, divided it into four equal parts, each of which he disposed of at different and distant places. One of the pieces had been sold at Lyons to Mons. Mey, a wealthy merchant of that city and a well educated man, who directly saw its value, and after great pains and expense procured the other three fragments and had them nicely rejoined, and the treasure was finally placed in the cabinet of the King of France. This relic of antiquity, no less remarkable for the beauty of its workmanship than for having been buried in the Rhone more than two thousand years, was the votive shield presented to Scipio as a monument of gratitude and affection by the inhabitants of Carthago Nova, now the city of Carthagena, for his generosity and self-denial in delivering one of his captives, a beautiful virgin betrothed to Allucius, a Spanish prince, to her lover. This act, so honourable to the Roman general, who was then in the prime vigour of manhood, is represented on the shield, and an engraving from it may be seen in the curious and valuable work of Mr. Spon.—*Hone's Table Book.*

CHAPTER IX.

P. 392.—This sovereign was the son of Demetrius and the great grandson of Antigonus, one of Alexander the Great's celebrated captains. During his minority his kingdom was governed by his uncle Antigonus Doson, who assumed

478

the title of King, and having assisted the Achæans against Cleomenes, king of Sparta, constituted himself after the death of that monarch the protector of Achaia and the arbiter of Greece.

P. 393.—Masinissa had received from the republic the full investiture of his own kingdom, as well as that part of the Massæsyllians which he had conquered from Syphax, and was therefore bound to serve them. Masinissa had improved and civilized his people, having taught them to cultivate their lands and sow them with grain. Till his time they combined the character of the shepherd with that of the predatory warrior, as in Asia the Tartar nations do to this day. Vermina, the son of Syphax was permitted to possess the small part of Numidia left him by Masinissa, and was treated in all respects like a vassal by the haughty nation to whom he was indebted for the remnant of his father's kingdom.

P. 412.—The historical reader will do well to compare the prophecies of the whole of this remarkable chapter with the public and private actions of the Seleucidæ, as detailed in Josephus and other ancient authors.

P. 419.—This remarkable passage is from the pen of a heathen historian, a contemporary with the Emperor Adrian, and a procurator of the Roman Empire. He has not cited his authority for the passage, but he doubtless had found it among the records of the times of which he wrote, since there appears no reason for his putting this speech into the mouth of Antiochus. In the eleventh chapter of the prophet Daniel, so much of the personal as well as public history of this monarch is to be found, that it is by no means unlikely that he was acquainted with it, and acknowledged as a humbling fact that God fought against him. As the book of Daniel had been shown to Alexander the Great by Jaddua, the high priest, and the passages relating to himself interpreted and explained, it is by no means improbable that at least some traditional remembrance of the circumstance might have remained in the family of Seleucus and given rise to this remark.

P. 426.—There were, according to Livy, "various opinions respecting the prosecutions against the Scipios. Some thought it a shameful instance of ingratitude, and more ungrateful than those Carthaginians who banished Hannibal." Others said, "That no citizen whatever ought to be considered above the laws, or too worthy to be accountable to them."[1] This is true, but no charges ought to be exhibited against a public character unless they are founded on fact, and documentary evidence can be produced against the accused, or else the prosecution of the individual sinks into persecution at once.

[1] Livy, xxxviii. 50.

CHAPTER X.

P. 438.—In regard to the consular authority this law only revived one which, though occasionally relaxed when the service of the state required it, had never been wholly laid aside. From a passage in Cicero, the several ages appear to have been regulated upon the following scale:—A Roman citizen might serve as Quæstor, at 31; Curule Ædile, at 37; Prætor, at 40; and Consul, at 43. Whether these limitations were founded in wisdom may be doubted, as many young men of great talents for legislature or war might be wasting their energies in inferior stations, while men of maturer years were sometimes filling offices for which they were not fitted. In the case of Scipio Africanus, who was a pro-consul at 27, this limitation would have been a national misfortune.

P. 439.—The undutiful conduct of Perseus made king Philip entertain doubts respecting the guilt of the unfortunate Demetrius. He imparted his apprehensions to his cousin Antigonus, whom he had always found a firm and attached friend. Antigonus made some inquiries in the palace, and found that the secretary of the ambassadors Apelles and Philocles, was suspected of having counterfeited the seal and handwriting of Titus Flamininus. Upon which Antigonus seized the secretary and led him before Philip, who brought him to confess the fraud by threatening him with the torture. Apelles fled to Italy upon learning the arrest of his agent, but Philocles was put to the torture, and some say confessed the fact, while others declare that he bore the infliction and made no avowal of his guilt. Philip in vain demanded the person of Apelles of the Roman senate.

P. 443.—Twenty-three centurions opposed the decree of the senate. One of these undertook to speak for the rest. The account given by this man of himself presents a lively picture of the manners of the times, the nature of the service, and the military prowess that rendered the Romans the masters of the world.[1]

P. 451.—In despotic states some danger may arise from any individual being possessed of a greater proportion of wealth or influence than the rest. In a constitution like that of England there does not appear any reason for precautions of this kind.

P. 454.—Polybius relates that he fell upon the Macedonians at night, while they were asleep; but Plutarch quotes from Nasica himself, who says, "that he maintained a severe contest for the heights, and was himself engaged by a Thracian mercenary, whom he killed with his own hand, but that after the Macedonian guard were routed he pursued Milo, who was unarmed and without his upper garment, and led his party down into the plain." The disarray of Milo certainly confirms the statement of Polybius. According to the history of the last-named author, Æmilius Paulus was engaged at the same time in two days' successive attempts to cross the river without gaining his object; and on the third, while about to renew the combat for that purpose, he heard a confused noise in the Macedonian camp, whither the ill news of the defeat of Milo had just arrived.

CHAPTER XI.

P. 469.—Need the land of Judea be named, as the single exception where the knowledge of the true God was found and from whence the pure doctrines of Christianity, like fertilising and purifying streams were destined to spread their holy influence throughout the gentile world.

P. 488.—This queen of Cappadocia, who after the birth of Ariarathes, accused herself of having imposed two supposititious sons upon her husband, was the daughter of Antiochus the Great, and her statement whether true or false was believed by her lord. The princes considered themselves injured, and declared that the story originated in their mother's unjust partiality for her youngest son. This appeal of Ariarathes to the senate, brought before that august body as difficult a case for their decision as that celebrated one made by the Israelite mother to Solomon.

P. 496.—The treachery of the Roman senate must excite the detestation of every reader, her proud faith was no more, "the national oath by the faith of Rome" was no longer the attestation of her treaties. She had surpassed even Carthage in falsehood and deceit.

P. 496.—Carthage was three and twenty miles in circuit, and contained seven hundred thousand persons,[1] it was situated within a large gulph or bay, on a peninsula forty-five miles in compass. and joined to the continent by an isthmus three miles broad. The city appears to have been divided into three principal parts, Cothon sometimes called the port, Megara and Byrsa. The last contained the citadel, it stood on the isthmus, and on the very spot of ground that Dido purchased of the Africans. Upon the south side towards the continent the city was defended by three walls thirty cubits high and strengthened with towers rising two stories above the walls. Along and between these walls were barracks for twenty thousand foot, four thousand horse, and three hundred elephants. There is, it should seem, some uncertainty respecting the harbour, arising from the contradictory accounts of Polybius and Appian. Hooke inclines to that of the former, who places it upon the east side of the city. "It was divided into two ports, having one and the same entrance into the sea, which was only seventy feet broad, so that it could be shut up with iron chains. The inner port was for ships of war, and in the midst of it was an island, where was the arsenal in which the admiral resided. The outer port belonged to the merchants."[2]

P. 497.—From the time Masinissa recovered his kingdom from Syphax his prosperity had continually increased. His government was wise and beneficent, and the most perfect harmony subsisted among his sons, a circumstance of rare occurrence in the families of African monarchs. He taught his people to cultivate their fields and raise their own corn, and was as great in the arts of civilisation as in those of war. By his dying request the Romans regulated the succession of his dominions, which they did by directing that his three sons should reign together.

481

Micipsa as treasurer, Gulussa as general, and Mastanabal as judge. Strange to say the kingly union did not destroy the fraternal one. They reigned conjointly till death dissolved their triune authority.

P. 497.—The real name of this impostor was Andriscus. He had been driven out of Thessaly by Nasica the year before, but having defeated and slain the prætor, Juventius Thalna, in the passes of Macedon, he recovered a part of Thessaly again.[3] The Carthaginians recommended him to prosecute the war, promising to aid him with money and ships. His answer is unknown, but as he was defeated in two battles by the prætor, Cæcilius Metellus, and put to death by his command, it mattered not what reply he gave. Another pretended son of Perseus appeared and took the name of Alexander, who was, we have seen, at that very time in Rome. He was driven into Dardania by the vigilant prætor, so that the Carthaginians had little chance of any diversion in their favour from the war in Macedon.

P. 507.—King Attalus purchased this celebrated piece afterwards for 600,000 sesterces[4] at the sale of the plunder of Corinth, but Mummius, who supposed the painting possessed some magical powers independent of the mere magic of art, would not let the royal virtuoso have it, but sent it to Rome by sea with many other masterpieces in sculpture and painting. He made an agreement with the master of the vessel that if any of them were lost or injured he should replace them with others at his own expense.[5] A laughable proof both of his ignorance of art and shrewdness in making a bargain. Some of these gems fell to his own share, for Lucullus borrowed them at the dedication of a temple and refused afterwards to take them down from the walls they adorned, saying, "that Mummius might do so if he pleased, but that he would be guilty of sacrilege as they had been consecrated to the gods with the fane." He bore the loss with patience, for which, says Strabo, he was much applauded. His want of taste and ignorance of their value doubtless was the occasion of his meek endurance of the injury.

---

[1] Hooke's Rome, vi.

[2] Polybius, Excerpt.; Appian, in Punic, 63.

[3] Livy, Epit., l.; Zonaras, ii.

[4] £4,843, British currency.—Arbuthnot.

[5] Velleius Paterculus.

CHAPTER XII.

Page 527.—This account is quoted from Florus and Orosius. Appian affirms that the Numantines surrendered at discretion and were sold for slaves by the victor, who reserved fifty to grace his triumph, and that he burned the city and razed its foundations. Whichever of these narratives deserves credit, the inhumanity of Scipio remains equally conspicuous.

P. 562.—Arnold condemns this Roman poor law as he styles it,[1] though its application in our own days, in the form of relief, would probably be wise and useful. He calls it "unjust,"[2] but the impoverished Roman plebeian, reduced to work for hire by that poverty which had humbled his haughty national pride, was cramped in his exertions by the censorial regulations, which did not permit him to follow the more profitable calling of trade without loss of caste, and found himself also forestalled in the free-labour market by slaves, therefore his pitiable state required alleviation. The treasures of king Attalus could be applied to this fund, and the Roman state, could buy from Africa and Sicily, corn cheap, since these countries produced more than they required for their own subsistence, and the tribute could be paid in corn. A necessity therefore existed for a relief bill, and where can we discover a wiser method of meeting this necessity than that adopted by Caius Gracchus.

P. 563.—"Infinite," according to Montesquieu, "were the mischiefs that arose from thence. The constitution was changed at a time when the fire of civil discords had scarcely left any such thing as a constitution. The knights were no longer that middle order which united the people to the senate; the chain of the constitution was broken."[3] Our author, at the conclusion of his chapter upon the "Judiciary power in Rome," passes a sweeping censure upon the avarice and universal corruption of the body[4] to whom the right of assisting the prætors in their civil capacity was entrusted by the Gracchi, for the measure was planned by Tiberius, though carried into effect by his brother. In submitting to the reader the opinions of two of the most celebrated writers of ancient and modern times upon this law—opinions so contrary respecting its expediency, it may be proper to remark that the equestrian order had not then plunged into those depths of luxury and corruption which rendered it unfit to exercise the important functions of judicature. These vices are enumerated by Montesquieu to justify his idea of the inexpediency of the change. A modern historian supposes, from a passage in the Epitome of Livy, that Caius Gracchus did not wholly remove the judicial power from the senators, but added two equites or knights in that capacity to every senator.[5]

P. 577.—The causes that led to the desertion of C. Gracchus are thus graphically described by a great historian lately deceased:[6] "There are two classes of men, the one consisting of those who are sincere and open, and seek and love the beautiful and sublime, who delight in eminent men and see in them the glory of their age and nation; the other comprising those who think only of themselves, are envious, jealous, and sometimes very unhappy creatures; without having a distinct will of their own, they cannot bear to see great men in the enjoyment of the general esteem. It was these latter that rose against Caius Gracchus. He was too spotless, too pure, too glorious not to be an offence to many, for every one was reminded by his example what he ought to be. It was the greatness of Gracchus which determined them to bring him down. It is not surprising to find

483

that this disposition existed among his colleagues, but thousands of others wanted to make him feel that they had no gratitude for him."

P. 580.—Appian in his history of this civil broil, gives a different account of the affair, and represents the partisans of Caius Gracchus and Fulvius as murdering a private citizen peaceably engaged in offering a sacrifice, for some word or gesture considered by them insulting.[7] That given by Plutarch is too minutely concise to have been invented, but we are not referred in any history of Caius Gracchus or his tribuneship, to a single historian of the period, for any of the facts therein detailed. We know that Junius Gracchanus, one of the dear friends of the great tribune, must have included them in his work on the Roman constitution, but of his history only some fragments remain in Gaius. Much of his biography in Plutarch may have been collected from oral traditions preserved by the Roman people, who repented, when too late, of their base desertion of their best and most disinterested citizen.

---

[1] Arnold, Later Roman Commonwealth.

[2] *Ibid.*

[3] Montesquieu, Spirit of the Laws.

[4] *Ibid.*

[5] Arnold, Later Commonwealth, i. 101.

[6] Niebuhr, Lecture xxviii.

[7] Appian, de Bell. Civil, i. 25.

Printed in Great Britain
by Amazon